D0780852

SALES MANAGEMENT

CONCEPTS, PRACTICES, AND CASES

McGraw-Hill Series in Marketing

Anderson, Hair, and Bush: Professional Sales Management
Bennett: Marketing
Bovée and Thill: Marketing
Bowersox and Cooper: Strategic Marketing Channel Management
Buskirk and Buskirk: Selling: Principles and Practices
Dobler, Burt, and Lee: Purchasing and Materials Management: Text and Cases
Guiltinan and Paul: Cases in Marketing Management
Guiltinan and Paul: Marketing Management: Strategies and Programs
Johnson, Kurtz, and Schueing: Sales Management: Concepts, Practices, and Cases
Kinnear and Taylor: Marketing Research: An Applied Approach
Loudon and Della Bitta: Consumer Behavior: Concepts and Applications
Lovelock and Weinberg: Marketing Challenges: Cases and Exercises
Monroe: Pricing: Making Profitable Decisions
Moore and Pessemier: Product Planning and Management: Designing and Delivering Value
Rossiter and Percy: Advertising and Promotion Management
Stanton, Etzel, and Walker: Fundamentals of Marketing

SALES MANAGEMENT

CONCEPTS, PRACTICES, AND CASES

Second Edition

EUGENE M. JOHNSON
University of Rhode Island

DAVID L. KURTZ
University of Arkansas

EBERHARD E. SCHEUING
St. John's University

McGraw-Hill, Inc.

New York   St. Louis   San Francisco   Auckland   Bogotá   Caracas
Lisbon   London   Madrid   Mexico City   Milan   Montreal   New Delhi
San Juan   Singapore   Sydney   Tokyo   Toronto

Sales Management
Concepts, Practices, and Cases

Copyright © 1994, 1986 by McGraw-Hill, Inc. All rights reserved. Printed in the United States of America. Except as permitted under the United States Copyright Act of 1976, no part of this publication may be reproduced or distributed in any form or by any means, or stored in a data base or retrieval system, without the prior written permission of the publisher.

Permissions appear on pages 518–547, and on this page by reference.

 This book is printed on recycled, acid-free paper containing a minimum of 50% total recycled fiber with 10% postconsumer de-inked fiber.

2 3 4 5 6 7 8 9 0   DOC   DOC   9 0 9 8 7 6 5 4

ISBN 0-07-032652-5

This book was set in Century Old Style by Better Graphics, Inc.
The editor was Bonnie K. Binkert;
the designer was Joseph A. Piliero;
the production supervisor was Richard A. Ausburn.
The photo editor was Elyse Rieder.
Project supervision was done by The Total Book.
R. R. Donnelley & Sons Company was printer and binder.

Library of Congress Cataloging-in-Publication Data

Johnson, Eugene M.
    Sales management: concepts, practices, and cases / Eugene M.
Johnson, David L. Kurtz, Eberhard E. Scheuing.
        p.   cm.
    Includes bibliographical references and index.
    ISBN 0-07-032652-5
    1. Sales management.   I. Kurtz, David L.   II. Scheuing, Eberhard
E. (Eberhard Eugen), (date).   III. Title.
HF5438.4.J62   1994
658.8′1—dc20   93-6423

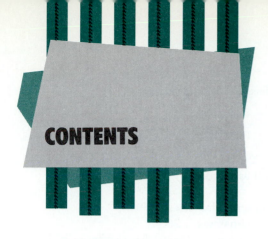

CONTENTS

v

The Personal Selling Function

PART 3   Planning the Sales Effort

PART 4

Developing the Sales Force

PART 5

Directing the Sales Force

PART 6   Evaluating Sales Force Performance

CHAPTER 19 Sales Evaluation   455

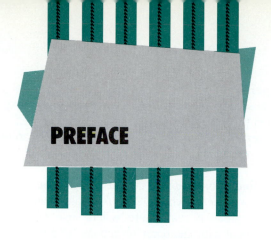

PREFACE

Sales Management has been designed with students' needs in mind and has been thoroughly tested in classrooms throughout North America. This comprehensive text captures the vitality of sales management in an environment that is constantly changing. Noted for its realism in presenting the sales management process, the text incorporates vivid examples of current practices and includes realistic case studies, carefully developed to provide a variety of learning opportunities.

As sales educators, we are primarily concerned with communicating insights into the dynamic real world of sales management. We have tried to present the need for flexibility in sales management by describing the complex environment for the selling process. On the other hand, we have also tried to introduce students to accepted sales management concepts and practices. These principles provide students with a proven body of management knowledge which can be used to cope with the modern selling environment. We hope our readers, students and faculty alike, will agree with us that the book provides a realistic view of contemporary sales management.

This edition of *Sales Management* contains many innovative features designed to make learning easier for students. A test format has been developed which allows each chapter to stand on its own as a complete, systematic learning tool. Each chapter begins with a series of learning goals to direct the student. Then, after a real-world sales management example, the Chapter Perspective provides the student with a preview of the chapter's contents. Figures, exhibits, and examples are used throughout the chapters to illustrate key ideas and to provide supplementary information. Each chapter concludes with a summary of learning goals that relates the chapter material to the specific learning goals established at the beginning of the chapter. The end-of-chapter materials also include both review and discussion questions.

Vivid examples and a lively writing style make for interesting reading. Actual sales management situations begin and end each chapter. In addition, stimulating examples and comments from sales managers and other experts bring the real world of sales management to the classroom. *Sales Management* integrates those examples and comments with key concepts and actual industry practices to provide students with a graphic view of the sales manager's position in industry. Other key elements of the revised edition are:

- **Expanded coverage of the personal selling process** occurs in Chapters 3, 4, and 5 and is intended to provide students—many with no previous selling experience—with a solid foundation in the selling process.
- **A separate chapter on careers** in selling and sales management (Chapter 2) provides an overview of career opportunities and outlines relevant steps in the job search.
- **"Sales Management in Practice" boxes** appear in every chapter and highlight actual company strategies and practices such as Reebok's sales campaign to promote Blacktop sneakers (Chapter 1); real estate sellers' use of *Town & Country's* computer software to deal with customer objections (Chapter 5); and Campbell Soup Company's use of brand sales managers (Chapter 8).
- **Expanded discussion of ethics** in Chapter 2 plus within chapter Ethical Dilemma scenarios challenge students to deal with specific ethical issues often faced by sales managers.
- **Unique, full chapter on international sales strategies** (Chapter 18) which highlights international sales opportunities, examines the differences between domestic and international sales practices, and specifies methods for organizing international sales activities.
- **End-of-chapter cases** offer students opportunities to deal with various sales management functions, such as salesperson selection, training, motivation and evaluation; a variety of other short and long cases are also available in the Instructor's Manual and a case supplement through McGraw-Hill's Primis system.
- **Profiles of successful sales managers,** representing a variety of industries, are interspersed throughout the chapters and provide valuable role models for students. Among those profiled are Chuck Schupp who sells Louisville Slugger baseball hats to professional ball players; Paul Fireman, Reebok's CEO, who has a sales background; James Koch, founder of the Boston Beer Company; and IBM's legendary F.G. ("Buck") Rodgers.

Sales Management is supported by a comprehensive resource package, including:

- **Instructor's Manual**, prepared by the authors, which includes lecture outlines; answers to the text's review and discussion questions; case commentaries; as well as over 90 transparency masters for classroom use.
- **Test Bank** of hundreds of objective questions, also prepared by the authors and tested with a variety of students. The test bank is also available in computerized form.
- **Additional cases** are available through McGraw-Hill's Primis system, an electronic database that allows instructors to custom-tailor a course package of cases, both short and/or long cases, from a variety of sources. Ask your McGraw-Hill representative for more details.
- **Video series** of "Selling Solutions"—four segments professionally produced by the American Management Association and linked to the text—intended to develop students' selling skills.

The authors acknowledge a special debt and thanks to Albert H. Dunn, Professor Emeritus, University of Delaware, who co-authored a previous edition of the text.

The assistance provided by editor Bonnie Binkert and other McGraw-Hill editorial personnel is most appreciated. We also thank the following reviewers of the manuscript; their criticisms, comments, and suggestions played a crucial role in shaping the final product: John C. Crawford, University of North Texas; Dan T. Dunn, Northeastern University; Kevin M. Elliott, Mankato State University; Kenneth R. Evans, University of Missouri-Columbia; Troy A. Festervand, Middle Tennessee State University; Julius Grossman, Mohawk Valley Community College; Jon M. Hawes, University of Akron; Kay L. Keck, University of Georgia; Lynn E. Metcalf, California Polytechnic State University—San Luis Obispo; and David M. Szymanski, Texas A & M University.

Finally, we would like to acknowledge the assistance and support of our research assistants, Ginger Honomichl, Melissa King, Clint Aguiar, and Deepak Jain. They really saved the day on numerous occasions. We sincerely appreciate their efforts.

Eugene M. Johnson
David L. Kurtz
Eberhard E. Scheuing

SALES MANAGEMENT

CONCEPTS, PRACTICES, AND CASES

PART
One

INTRODUCTION TO PERSONAL SELLING AND SALES MANAGEMENT

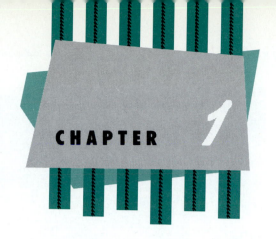

CHAPTER 1

JOB OF SALES MANAGEMENT

LEARNING GOALS

- Describe the nature of personal selling and the changes brought about by business's shift to a customer orientation.
- Outline the role of the sales force in each of the marketing mix variables.
- Trace the process of how sales management has changed.
- Define the critical role, tasks, and activities of field sales managers.
- Assess sales management training and development activities.

THE MODERN SELLING PROFESSIONAL

The competitive environment mandates that sellers not only sell but also serve. All companies have been affected by global competition, but there has been perhaps no industry more heavily impacted than the American automobile industry. Chrysler Corporation, especially, has been through a much-publicized whirlwind of ups and downs for the past two decades. Retired Chrysler Chief Executive Officer (CEO) Lee Iacocca held his position from 1978 to 1992, and as a former salesperson, brought to Chrysler his well-known intuition for knowing what customers want.

When Iacocca took on the job at Chrysler, the company was ailing. Iacocca separated the sales forces for Chrysler-Plymouth and Dodge in order to distinguish the two divisions' marketing approaches. He gave special attention to dealers, providing them with opportunities to attend Chrysler-sponsored week-long grievance sessions. He started huge "tent sales" emphasizing

low prices, offered cash to people who test drove cars, and personally sold large numbers of investors on the value of Chrysler stock. At one crisis point, Iacocca approached the U.S. government for an aid package, which he received.

From a more general management angle, Iacocca's reign was characterized by cost-cutting out of necessity. He established a close relationship with suppliers, influencing them to provide Chrysler with a multitude of money-saving suggestions. Chrysler eliminated 24 percent of its white-collar work force, and product development, marketing, and training budgets were slashed. The number of sales regions was reduced from six to four.

The fact that one out of five minivans sold in the United States are Chrysler's continues to be a company bright spot. The company also recently introduced a new family sedan that looks like a winner. Chrys-

3

ler's bright spots, however, are in the shadow of looming financial problems. Chrysler has a massive debt to finance ($5 billion in a recent year), which the company cannot reduce if it is to spend the money required to improve its products. In one year alone, Chrysler had a negative cash flow of $2 billion.

Chrysler's survival comes down to a question of timing; the company must produce big sales if it is to dig itself out from under its financial burden. Iacocca bought precious time; he sold assets, borrowed from banks, and refinanced debt. In 1991, he went on a month-long international road trip to promote Chrysler stock. The effort, called "Grand Slam," was successful; Iacocca's selling ability moved 35 million shares and brought in $350 million in cash.

Lee Iacocca's selling skills were at times essential for the survival of Chrysler. Iacocca sold the U.S. government, stockholders, suppliers, dealers, and Chrysler employees on his ideas—all of these parties gave him what he wanted when he asked. The confidence in Iacocca, however, may or may not have been transferred to a belief in Chrysler automobiles.

Of all Chrysler's trials and tribulations, perhaps none has been more challenging than Iacocca's retirement. Iacocca's successor, Robert J. Eaton, is a former General Motors executive who, like Iacocca, has a penchant for cost-cutting. With rising stock prices and profits and new Chrysler models

rolling off the line, Eaton has come on board at a time of hopeful opportunity. After months and months of financial losses by Chrysler, however, and coming on board with a stated mission of cutting an additional $750 million in costs his first year, Eaton faces dramatic challenges. In the end, his greatest difficulty may be filling the selling shoes of Lee Iacocca.[1]

In the competitive selling environment that all businesses face, there is no one formula for success, but, if there were, it just might be "find innovative ways to fulfill a deep commitment to customer satisfaction." This was Lee Iacocca's contribution to Chrysler. As you read *Sales Management*, you will learn more about this idea and many others. It is the goal of this text to develop your potential as a sales professional and to arm you with information that is the basis of your own formula for success.

CHAPTER OVERVIEW

Selling. Salesperson. Sales manager. In the past, these terms might have conjured up the image of pushy, fast-talking individuals who preyed on naive customers, selling inferior or overpriced merchandise by getting them to sign purchase orders without first reading the small print. The sales manager was often envisioned as an ill-tempered, cigar-chomping, overweight bully who directed the troops from a cluttered, smoke-filled office by bellowing orders into a phone. Over the years such negative attitudes have proven difficult to erase, leaving people to perceive selling as a "job" (not as a "profession" or a "career") and discouraging students from entering the field.

Although this unflattering image originated with the high-pressure tactics of an earlier, production orientation, its persistence still hides the professionalization that characterizes contemporary personal selling and sales management. Today's salespeople and sales managers are indeed a far cry from the stereotype described above. They are highly trained, skilled, and motivated people who understand that the key to long-term success is customer satisfaction. Instead of overwhelming prospects, modern sellers identify customer needs and develop solutions to problems. Instead of just talking, they make it their business to listen. Instead of forgetting about a customer after an order is obtained, they provide aftersale service. They are professionals, not hucksters.

A strong, dynamic sales force, the backbone of many successful companies, does not just happen; it has to be developed and nurtured. In this book you will learn what a sales manager must do—and do well—to create and maintain a strong sales team. Your learning process begins in this chapter, which reviews changes in marketing and selling, describes the sales manager's role and activities, and highlights the importance of training and development for sales managers.

THE NATURE OF PERSONAL SELLING

personal selling
Aspect of promotion that brings the human element into marketing transactions.

Personal selling is a critical aspect of a firm's promotional strategy. When correctly used and done well, it is a major factor in generating sales volume. It is the part of promotion that brings the human element into marketing transactions. It also increases customer confidence in the supplier, makes it possible for the buyer to act immediately, and simplifies the handling of individual customer problems. This is the role and nature of the business function that sales managers must supervise.

The Human Element Is Critical

Salespeople and customers deal with each other face to face. A partnership is created, one that lasts a long time. For instance, a computer system salesperson will be involved in the installation of the system and subsequent system modifications long after the purchase order has been signed. Familiarity, if not friendship, develops between the salesperson and customer. The salesperson becomes the company for the customer. Buyers do not deal just with an inanimate business organization, but with human beings from that company whom they see personally and know. Since personal contacts are involved, it is more difficult for buyers to ignore or remove the sales influence (in contrast to an advertising message, for instance, which can be easily turned off).

The Customer's Confidence Is Enhanced

Since the customer deals with a supplier through a person, there is great potential for building the customer's confidence in the supplier's products, personnel, and procedures. Of course, the sales representative can muff this opportunity in many ways, such as making delivery promises that cannot be kept or misrepresenting the product. However, if done properly, personal selling offers the opportunity for the salesperson to build a basis of trust and confidence with customers. It is this development and nurturing of long-term relationships based on trust that is essential to sales and marketing success today.

Customers Can Act Immediately

Unlike other means of promotion, personal selling can work for a desired action by customers immediately, here and now. Sales reps can place an order, commit to a purchasing plan for the next quarter, decide on an in-store promotion for the product, and so forth. Personal selling makes it more difficult for the customer to delay or to forget a promised commitment in the future. It provides the opportunity for the salesperson to get the decision that is wanted on the spot.

Customers Are Treated as Individuals

All of the preceding payoffs of personal selling are important, but probably the most valuable is that sales representatives' personal contacts with customers make it possible to customize sales presentations and to handle buyers' problems and complaints on an individual basis. Suggestions and problem solutions that make no sense for one customer may be right on target for another. Only personal selling can deliver such customer-by-customer accommodation. In a broad sense, this is the service aspect of personal selling, to identify each customer's needs and problems and to respond to them individually. This is the "value added" or extra benefit that salespeople can provide. This value added is often the difference between sales success and failure in today's very competitive markets.

CHANGES IN SELLING

The modern view of selling sees salespeople as more than accomplished persuaders and negotiators. They are problem solvers able to meet the needs and conditions of individual customers. They must build and maintain relationships with customers. As a result, modern personal selling is flexible and creative, not simply persuasive. Companies have substantially revised their methods of hiring, training, and supervising salespeople to adapt to new market conditions.

In addition, there is now general recognition that personal selling is more than just making a sale. Salespeople and sales managers are often involved in other important aspects of the total marketing process: distribution, credit, the customer's use or promotion of the product, pricing, and so forth.

With each change in the role of personal selling, sales management has become more important to company success. Sales managers have become the critical link between a firm's marketing strategy and what takes place in the buyer's office.

Marketing Concept

marketing concept
A modern view of marketing based on the propositions of customer orientation, coordination of all customer-related activities, and profit direction.

In large part, selling and sales management have changed because marketing has changed. The modern view of marketing, known as the *marketing concept*, is based on three major propositions: customer orientation, coordination of all customer-related activities, and profit direction.

1. Customer orientation is the focal point of modern marketing. This means that salespeople and their managers must shift from an internal company perspective to the customer's viewpoint. Successful marketing requires a complete understanding of customers—their needs, attitudes, and buying behavior. For example, a car salesperson who knows that a customer is the head of a family, with

SALES MANAGEMENT

REEBOK INTERNATIONAL, LTD.

In extremely competitive and faddish markets such as that of athletic shoes, sellers need every advantage they can get, and adherence to the marketing concept is especially important. Reebok received praise for its marketing of the Reebok Pump, and the company again impressed consumers and critics alike with its marketing campaign for the Blacktop, a rugged sneaker specially designed for use on outdoor courts.

Reebok's marketing research success for the Blacktop was somewhat fortuitous; while involved with a program to build outdoor playgrounds, Reebok executives met outdoor court players and often were told how quickly sneakers wore out. The Blacktop was developed in response to these comments, and stores ordered over two million pairs before the shoes even became available.

A sneaker designed for outdoor use is a great idea, but Reebok's coordinated sales efforts were surely a large factor in the Blacktop success. To promote the Blacktop, Reebok sponsored the Coup de Hoop Blacktop Championship, a nationally televised three-on-three basketball competition. Blacktop advertising does not feature the flying dunkers usually found in basketball shoe ads; instead, the sneaker is promoted by players who say things like "you know you're out of bounds when you hit the trash can."

The Blacktop is a modern-day sales success story, and Reebok, with its response to consumer needs and coordinated promotional efforts, is an example of how a highly competitive seller adhering to the marketing concept can stand out from the crowd.

budget constraints, realizes that a sleek sports model will not fit this customer's needs.

2. Coordination between all of the customer-serving functions of a business is the second fundamental point. For instance, when a salesperson writes a large order, production schedules must be adequate to fill it.

3. Profits are the goal of the business unit. To sell products that do not earn a reasonable profit is unacceptable. In general, satisfying customer needs is the means to achieving sales and profits. However, salespeople and their managers must also control costs as well as generate sales volume in order to maintain acceptable levels of profitability.

Modern Sales Approaches

The evolution of personal selling and the selling process will be discussed in Part 2 and elsewhere in this book. At this point, however, it is useful to introduce some of these ideas of modern selling. In particular, as noted above, many companies are concerned with developing long-term customer relationships. They are demanding more from their salespeople and sales managers. Some of the modern sales approaches include:

partnering Sharing of values between vendors and buyers.

- *Partnering.* Salespeople share the same values with their customers, clearly understand and anticipate their customers' needs and—as partners—have moved from a pure selling to a mutually supporting role in their contacts with customers.

relationship selling Personal selling based on long-term associations with buyers.

- *Relationship selling.* Salespeople are not only expected to sell products, but also to develop associations with customers. These relationships will grow and prosper as the salesperson provides more services, identifies and satisfies new needs, and develops more and stronger contacts with customers.

team selling Sales effort using multiple personnel.

- *Team selling.* Especially for large customers with complex needs, salespeople must work with other company personnel to provide a coordinated approach. Conventional, independent sales approaches and practices simply do not meet the large, complex purchasing requirements of companies that buy multiple product lines and customized products and services.

value-added selling Provision of selling services that exceed the customer's expectations.

- *Value-added selling.* Salespeople are expected to exceed their customers' expectations. The salesperson must go beyond selling products and provide "value-added" services for more demanding customers such as installation, employee training, and product adaptation.

consultative selling Salespeople who act as problem solvers for their customers.

- *Consultative selling.* In their role as consultants, or problem solvers, salespeople must adapt their products or services to the specific needs of customers.

PERSONAL SELLING IN THE MARKETING MIX

Under the marketing concept, marketing research assumes the task of identifying customer needs and problems, while the firm's *marketing mix* is used to deliver solutions. The marketing mix is the set of strategies that a company utilizes to implement its marketing plan and pursue its marketing objectives. It is composed of four major elements: product, price, distribution, and promotion. In line with the changes in markets and marketing strategies, salespeople and sales managers are being asked to play more significant roles in each component of the marketing mix.

marketing mix Strategies that a company utilizes to implement its marketing plan and pursue its marketing objectives.

The Role of Personal Selling in Product Strategy

In the past, salespeople and sales managers had limited input into product development decisions. But under the marketing concept, sales personnel help specify desirable product features and benefits, and provide guidance during the product development phase. They participate in product testing and test marketing. Their input is invaluable when it comes to product mix decisions because of their familiarity with the marketplace. Sales force advice can also be useful with respect to product sourcing. For instance, they may be able to suggest an outside supplier who can provide certain products under a private label arrangement to round out the product mix and make the company a full-line vendor without actually producing every item sold in its own plant.

The Role of Personal Selling in Pricing Strategy

Salespeople and managers can assist in pricing in a number of ways: They can ascertain competitive pricing strategies and gauge market reaction to alternative price levels, they can advise senior management in pricing decisions, or they can be granted some discretion in adjusting prices to market conditions.

cost-plus method Pricing strategy where a markup for profit is added to the product's cost.

Individual product prices are set in accordance with one of two approaches. The most frequently used method is the *cost-plus method*, where a markup for profit is added to the product's cost. Such "cost-based" pricing methods are often employed because of their simplicity. Sales managers are involved not only in setting prices but also in keeping selling costs under control so that the markup does not put the item at a price disadvantage.

"Market-oriented" pricing, by contrast, relies on an assessment of market response to alternative price levels. Market-oriented pricing can be subdivided into

demand-oriented method Pricing strategy where markup for profit is based on what the traffic will bear.

competition-oriented method Pricing strategy where markup for profit is based on the prices that competitors charge.

parity products Items that must be priced at, or below, competitive products.

channel of distribution Route that the title to a product takes from producer to ultimate user.

direct distribution Form of ownership transfer in which the ultimate buyer acquires title directly from the manufacturer of the product.

indirect distribution Form of ownership transfer involving the use of intermediaries who buy and resell the merchandise.

trade Sales jargon for marketing intermediaries (wholesalers and retailers).

promotion The presentation of informative and persuasive messages to a firm's target market in an attempt to stimulate sales.

demand-oriented and competition-oriented methods. The *demand-oriented method* of pricing basically means "charging what the traffic will bear." Sales managers play a major role in this assessment because of their familiarity with customer response patterns, as well as competitive pricing behavior. This latter knowledge is of prime importance if a firm chooses to adopt a *competition-oriented method* of pricing, a strategy where it prices its products at, above, or below competitors' levels. The most frequent of these philosophies is "meeting the competition." Salespeople and managers know from experience whether their buyers view the company's offerings as *parity products* requiring at least equal pricing, as products which can command a premium, or as products which should be priced lower than the competitors'. Effective marketing-oriented firms call on their sales force to assist in determining a pricing approach.

The Role of Personal Selling in Distribution Strategy

The sales force has an even closer connection with the distribution component of the marketing mix. A *channel of distribution* is the route that the title to a product takes from producer to ultimate user. This ownership transfer can take place in two ways: directly or indirectly. In the case of *direct distribution*, the ultimate buyer acquires the title directly from the manufacturer or provider of the product.

Indirect distribution involves the use of intermediaries (wholesalers and retailers) who buy and resell the merchandise. This approach is used for frequently purchased, low-priced items where the expense of going direct would be too high in relation to the product's value. Indirect distribution is used for most maintenance, repair, and operating supply items in organizational markets, as well as most groceries and personal and health care items in the consumer market. Under this option the producer has less control over the marketing process. Even very large manufacturers like Procter & Gamble, Hasbro, Black & Decker, and Mattel have been forced to develop special labels, packages, shipping procedures, inventory management systems, and other modifications to meet the needs of Wal-Mart, Toys 'R' Us, Home Depot, and other giant retailers.

In both instances, direct and indirect distribution, sales management is essential. A product is ultimately meaningless and its advertising wasted if it is not readily available to buyers. The personal selling function has to establish this vital link to the marketplace. In the case of direct distribution, the sales force calls on the ultimate users of a company's products. For those businesses that distribute indirectly, sales management has to secure the support of the *trade*, or intermediaries. Selling to the trade also requires a great deal of work with distributors' customers and prospects.

The Role of Personal Selling in Promotional Strategy

The final element of the marketing mix is *promotion*, the presentation of informative and persuasive messages to the firm's target market in an attempt to stimulate sales. Personal selling is a vital ingredient of this effort, working in conjunction with advertising, sales promotion, and public relations. Advertising is a long-term tool designed to create awareness of a company's products and their major benefits. If it can go one step further and generate a positive attitude or interest on the part of the message recipient, advertising has accomplished the major part of its mission. Sales promotion and public relations techniques support the other aspects of promotional strategy.

While advertising and sales promotion pave the way for personal selling and act in a supportive capacity, the sales force still has its own direct bottom-line orders. As has been said many times, "nothing happens until somebody sells something!"

DIMENSIONS OF SALES MANAGEMENT

The preceding discussion pointed out that the sales force provides an organization with its most vital link to the marketplace. It connects the company with the customers it serves and from which it derives its ability to survive and grow. In a well-conceived and executed sales management program, both customers and company benefit in the long run. The sales force informs the company of the buyers' needs and shows the buyers that the company is able and willing to satisfy them. In this section selected dimensions of sales management are considered, starting with an overview of sales management tasks.

Tasks of Sales Managers

sales management
Management of a firm's personal selling function.

What, specifically, does modern sales management entail? *Sales management* can be defined as the management of a firm's personal selling function. As Fig. 1-1 indicates, sales management's tasks are the analysis, planning, organization, direction, and control of the company's sales activities. These tasks can be described as follows:

- *Analysis.* Review of the firm's internal sales records and salespeople's reports, as well as investigation of market trends and other relevant environmental factors.
- *Planning.* Setting objectives for the firm's sales effort and mapping out strategies and tactics for achieving these objectives.
- *Organization.* Setting up structures and procedures for smooth and effective execution of sales programs and plans.
- *Direction.* Staffing and supervision of the day-to-day implementation of sales policies, programs, and plans.
- *Control.* Performance comparison of actual and planned sales results, examination of the reasons for observed divergences, and evaluation of the need for plan revision.

Sales Management and Change

To accomplish its tasks, sales managers must deal with change. All managers, but especially sales managers, work under constantly changing conditions. New products are introduced, a competitor cuts the price, new government rulings that affect a particular business are issued, new territories are opened—change never stops. A sales manager once said, "The only thing I can be sure about when I get to the office in the morning is that something will be changed from yesterday."

More than anything else, sales management in the coming years will involve coping with a changing, very dynamic selling environment.[2] External factors such as just-in-time production and purchasing, sophisticated computer-based materials plan-

FIGURE 1-1 The Sales Management Cycle.

ning, and changing organizational buying patterns will have a major impact on selling and sales management. In addition, changes in the way goods and services are marketed and sold, including new distribution options, telemarketing, computer-aided targeted marketing, and so forth, must be considered.[3] These and many other changes will be discussed throughout this book.

Andrew Parsons, partner and director of consumer marketing practices for McKinsey & Company, a leading management consultant, has suggested the following:

> Sales management in the 1990s will change from a game of checkers to a game of chess. Previously, sales management was relatively simple, used largely undifferentiated pieces, and chose one of a small number of strategic and organizational approaches. In the new selling environment, the pieces are not standardized, and sales management must choose from a sophisticated body of strategic and organizational alternatives.[4]

Another viewpoint is provided by the authors of a major study of sales force productivity who observed: "One of the most surprising things that turned up in our survey is how many different sales positions, goals, market segments, sales skills, pricing issues, and ROI [return on investment] expectations will have to be managed by top sales executives in the 1990s in contrast to the very simple management challenge of the past."[5] A chart of the changing sales management tasks and other interpersonal relationships is presented in Table 1-1.

Sales Management and Entrepreneurship

Recent research indicates that the attributes associated with successful salespeople and sales managers are also those needed for entrepreneurship. To be specific: Drive, self-confidence, an action orientation, persistence, and risk taking are the prime personal traits desired for sales managers. At the same time, an entrepreneurial organization that is willing to pursue risks is aggressive in the marketplace, has a strong leader with a hands-on management approach, and is close to the customer.[6]

TABLE 1-1   Evolution of Sales Management

1950s–1970s	1990s
% VOLUME SOLD BY TYPE OF SELLER	
100% by direct sales force	75.0% through direct sales
	5.0% through telemarketing
	11.0% through distributors, wholesalers, value added resellers (VARs)
	6.6% through outside sales
	2.4% through others
KINDS OF SALES POSITIONS	
Territory sales reps	Territory sales reps
District managers	Key or major account reps
Regional managers	National account managers
	Customer service reps
	Telemarketing reps
	Administrators
	Sales trainers
	District managers
	Regional managers
	Industry specialists
MARKETING APPROACH	
Mass marketing techniques targeting one type of customer	Market segmentation techniques targeting several "niches"
PERFORMANCE EXPECTATIONS	
Increase overall sales volume	Increase sales volume in strategic markets
Minimize turnover	Increase margin contribution
	Decrease cost of sales
	Attract top sales performers

In the study mentioned above, sales managers identify themselves as the "leading edge" of their companies. They consider sales and marketing to be the most entrepreneurial functions in their firms. Strategy development is the area of sales where entrepreneurial approaches are most important. Sales personnel recruiting, design of sales compensation programs, and finding ways to motivate salespeople are other sales management activities which call for entrepreneurship.[7]

In another study of management trends for the 1990s, the researchers found a similar need for innovative, less conventional managers. It is especially important that managers recognize that change is a way of life in the business world.[8] In assessing what will be needed for management success in the 1990s, the authors concluded that effective managers have the following traits:

- They are change agents, externalists, influencers, developers, and revenue-enhancers.
- They are proactive, not reactive, in thought and action. They are innovators, hustlers, and scramblers.
- They are network builders, team players, boundary-crossers, and resource sharers.[9]

ASSURED ENTERPRISES

SALES MANAGE-MENT

Entrepreneurship is sometimes inspired by negative situations. Say, for example, that a person has a great idea for a very salable new good or service but no available channel of distribution. This situation requires the salesperson to be innovative and energetic if he or she wants to get the ball rolling. The salesperson must be an entrepreneur.

Such was the case with an insurance salesperson named Ted Bernstein in 1982. Bernstein was uncomfortable with the commission-based policies he was selling because he thought that too much money, in the form of hidden costs, went out of client pockets and into salesperson commission checks. With traditional insurance, most of the premiums paid in the early years of a life policy go to commissions or overhead costs. Desiring a more straightforward system, Bernstein developed a type of insurance that included a stated flat sales fee. The overall cost of the Bernstein policy with its associated fee was lower to the customer than standard insurance with the commission hidden in the cost of the policy.

A good, customer-benefitting idea. Right? Bernstein had a problem, however, with developing his own credibility and finding a distribution channel. Life insurance agents did not want to sell Bernstein's insurance because it gave them less income per policy. Lacking the cooperation of the agents, Bernstein proceeded to target lawyers, accountants, and bankers in trust departments; these people would have significant influence over people who came to them for insurance advice. This group of professionals, however, indicated to Bernstein that they were not in the business of selling insurance.

Who would tell the world about Bernstein's new idea? Finally, Bernstein enlisted the attention of journalists by appealing to their role as defenders of the public interest. This group initially saw his request as an attempt to gain free advertising, and they too refused until Bernstein said that he would give them the story without the reporters even using his name or the name of his company. At least that way, Bernstein hoped, the news about a new type of insurance policy would be spread, and then, if all went well, people in the market for insurance would begin to ask their financial advisors about this type of policy.

The strategy worked; insurance of the type Bernstein developed and marketed became the subject of stories in many major publications. Bernstein sent copies of the stories to the lawyers, bankers, and accountants he had talked to earlier. Gradually, Bernstein built his newfound credibility and insurance policy into what is now Assured Enterprises, a company that brought in just under $1 million in revenues in a recent year. Sometimes, it seems, sheer perseverance pays off.

Rewards of Sales Management

Salespersons who show a knack for dealing with change and achieving results through others can advance all the way to the top of an organization. From first-level supervisory positions as district sales managers, they may go on to become regional sales managers, then zone or divisional managers, and maybe even national or general sales managers. Some move even higher into the marketing vice president's spot, or ultimately to the CEO's office. In many organizations, sales managers are given explicit responsibility for developing their people along designated career paths and are themselves evaluated according to their achievements on this score.

A sales manager's job has a number of other rewards and benefits. Most often cited are the following:

1. It is varied and ever-changing, not routine and repetitive. No two customers' or salespersons' problems are ever quite alike. Sales managers get to know and work with a variety of people, inside and outside the company. More than most other managers, their jobs are affected by the challenges of changing market conditions, competitors' activities, and economic factors.

2. It is personally rewarding, and recognized by others. Sales managers and their performance are not hidden away somewhere in the organization. They are challenged to develop people who produce results, and when they do, these results can be a source of great recognition and personal satisfaction to the managers themselves and to their subordinate salespeople.

3. It is financially rewarding. In many companies, sales managers earn substantial salaries and bonuses, and there is good potential for increases. These rewards of sales management and other aspects of a sales career will be discussed in more detail in Chap. 2.

THE FIELD SALES MANAGER

Much of the burden for managing the selling process rests with the first level of management in the sales organization. These managers—with titles such as district sales manager, branch manager, or field sales manager—represent the most critical level of leadership and supervision in the entire sales organization. They have direct control over the field sales force and have ultimate responsibility in given areas. Their effectiveness determines the overall performance of the sales effort. Table 1-2 outlines the titles used to describe field sales managers in a variety of industries.

Field selling organizations are quite varied. Some may have elaborate district offices with a full complement of support personnel. Others may consist of an at-

TABLE 1-2   Common Titles for the Field Sales Manager

Industries	Titles used to describe the field sales manager
Petroleum marketing	Territory Sales Representative Account Representative Retail Representative Merchandising Representative Territory Manager Area Manager
Pharmaceuticals	District Manager Sales Representative
Publishing	Division Manager Regional Manager Sales Supervisor
Transportation services	Account Supervisor Zone Manager Area Sales Manager Senior Sales Manager Northern Sales Vice President
Office equipment	Office Manager Sales Representative General Manager
Corporations	Marketing Representatives Unit Manager Marketing Manager

home office staffed only by an answering service. As a result, the field sales manager's job can range over a wide spectrum. At one extreme, the manager may be a desk-bound executive; at the other, the manager may be a territorial sales representative who happens to have been assigned some administrative duties.

With the vast range of possibilities, it is little wonder that the field sales manager is often in a confusing position. The manager has to interact with people external to the organization (like customers and trade groups) and internally with other departments of the firm. This unique situation has been referred to as a sales management's "boundary spanning role." It is illustrated in Fig. 1-2. It is the field sales manager who is the person "in the middle."

house accounts
Sales accounts serviced by management.

In addition to their administrative duties, field sales managers are sometimes required to handle some accounts personally. Accounts serviced by management are often called *house accounts*. The percentage of a sales manager's time spent in personal selling varies according to the size of the sales force. Larger sales forces dictate that the manager spend less time selling and more time in administrative efforts.

Most authorities in the selling field view the first-level sales manager as a vital link with the marketplace and the field sales force. In fact, it is often said that "no sales force is better than its first line of supervision." Further, as noted in an earlier section of the chapter, this level of sales leadership often provides the training ground for executives destined for higher positions in all areas of the organization.

FIGURE 1-2 The Sales Manager's Boundary-Spanning Role.

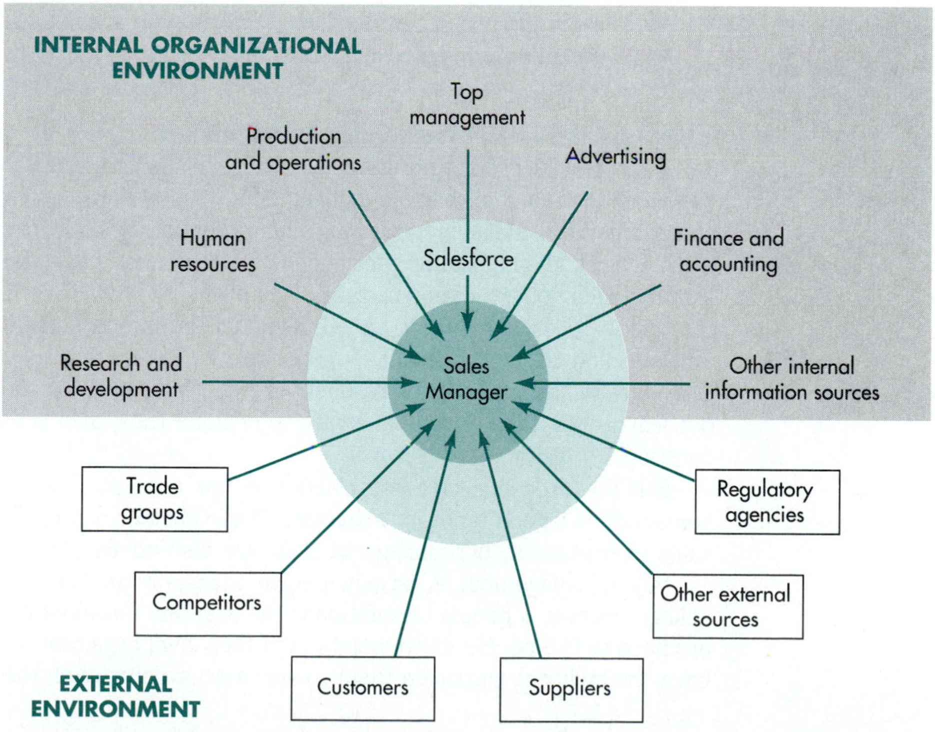

Field Sales Manager's Activities

The major tasks of sales management were identified in an earlier section. As carried out by the field sales manager, these tasks involve the following activities:

1. *Analyze* the conditions of the selling situation.
   - Review individual sales records and performance of salespersons.
   - Assess specific market trends and conditions.
   - Note relevant environmental factors and trends.
2. *Plan* for the immediate situation and the long run.
   - Establish specific sales objectives and develop strategies and procedures to attain these objectives.
   - Transmit objectives, strategies, and procedures to sales representatives.
3. *Organize* the sales team to achieve the objectives.
   - Break the selling tasks and supporting activities into operational parts (jobs).
   - Create specific job descriptions for these tasks and activities.
   - Recruit and select personnel for these jobs.
4. *Oversee* the operations of the sales team to *improve* its performance.
   - Issue the necessary directions and guidelines.
   - Provide the conditions of motivation (incentives) for high sales performance.
   - Train and coach sales team members for better sales performance.
   - Assure the attainment of acceptable levels of sales conduct and ethical behavior.
5. *Evaluate* sales performance.
   - Create and/or administer performance standards and measurements.
   - Collect and analyze performance information against standards.
   - Take indicated remedial actions.

Qualifications for Field Sales Management

To be considered for a first-line supervisory position, sales representatives must have demonstrated an ability to manage their own territories. They must have shown sharp analytical skills in reviewing the potential of their territories, identifying prospects, and pinpointing their needs. They must have demonstrated care in planning their routes, calling patterns, and presentations. They must have evidenced the ability to organize their varied responsibilities and activities in a systematic, efficient, and effective manner. It goes without saying that they would not even be considered unless their sales results were consistently at or above quota. Last, but not least, they should have an ability to critique their own achievements, examine contributing factors, and learn.

But the presence of these abilities is not enough. They merely indicate that somebody is a good territory manager. These abilities act as partial prerequisites to sales management, but managerial skills are also needed.[10]

Sales management is largely people management. In managing the personal selling function, a people orientation is the first and foremost concern. Sales managers have to like people (both members of their own organization and customers) and have the ability to persuade them to act in accordance with the firm's objectives.

Sales management consultant Jack Falvey puts it this way:

> Field sales representatives do not manage themselves well. They cannot be managed by systems no matter how sophisticated or automated. Sales management is a face-to-face discipline that requires that you walk the ground.[11]

Management of a field sales team is both an art and a science, requiring a delicate balance between subjective creativity and objective detachment. Field sales managers need product and technical knowledge and the capacity to conceptualize. Decisiveness will also be necessary in handling the conflicts, problems, and demands that are brought before them, and this decisiveness will need to be tempered with patience and a dedication to listening. Sales managers must also demonstrate, by their actions as well as their statements, a high level of ethical behavior.

In a recent study, a list of desired traits for successful sales management performance was developed. This list, which is shown in Table 1-3, can be used as a guide to select, train, and develop first-level sales managers. As the previous discussion and this list of factors suggest, effective field sales managers lead and develop people. They do not sell. Therefore, the best sales management candidate is not always the best salesperson. A salesperson who is not a superstar may be the candidate who possesses the best managerial skills.[12]

From Selling to Managing

Since most sales managers are former salespeople, they must make the transition from selling to managing. There is an old myth that top sales performers will be outstanding managers. Time and again, this axiom has been proven wrong when firms promoted their best salespeople into managerial capacities and saw them fail.[13] Consider the following situation.

Less than two years ago Marty Roberts was a happy, productive salesperson. Marty had been selling office equipment and supplies for six years. She had always exceeded her quota and had been in the top third of the company's sales force. For three of these six years she had also been the top salesperson in the district. Marty was the ideal salesperson—preferred by customers, respected by competitors, always prompt and complete with sales plans and reports. Last month, a frustrated

TABLE 1-3   Crucial Traits for First-Level Sales Managers

1. Motivation—enthusiasm toward all major tasks with no strong aversion to any required tasks
2. Human relations skills
3. Higher than average energy
4. Ambition—strong personal desire to achieve and advance
5. Human interaction—appropriate level of enjoyment from dealing with people
6. Persuasiveness—interest in "persuasive involvement" rather than tendency to "bully"
7. Behavior flexibility
8. Perception of threshold social cues—sensitivity
9. Intellectual ability
10. Personal impact—i.e., charisma

Marty resigned from the company in order to accept a sales position with a competitor.

What happened? After six years as a successful salesperson, Marty was promoted to field sales manager.

On the surface, Marty's promotion to field sales management was an obvious choice. She had proven herself in the field and was ready to move up. Her promotion was popular with her peers; even her chief rival for the promotion realized that Marty was the logical choice. Why, then, did Marty fail?

As so often happens, Marty made the transition from successful salesperson to unsuccessful manager because her company assumed that a good salesperson would become a good manager. The company failed in its obligation to help Marty make the difficult transition from selling to managing. Although her company had an extensive sales training program and would never put a new salesperson in the field without adequate sales training, the company expected Marty to assume her new responsibilities as a sales manager without providing her with management training and assistance.

The first challenge for any newly promoted sales manager is to make the transition from selling to managing. As a salesperson, Marty was a "doer." She was successful because she was able to meet individual goals by performing various sales tasks. Marty, the successful salesperson, depended upon herself to get things done.

In contrast, as a sales manager Marty was no longer strictly a "doer." She had become a manager of "doers," and was expected to get things done through others (see Table 1-4). Her new situation was similar to the former star basketball player who becomes a coach and must sit on the bench while an inexperienced player misses a foul shot. Sure, Marty could show her salespeople how to call on an account, but she could not make every sale herself. Like the basketball coach, Marty had to recruit and select her people, provide training, motivate them, and then monitor whether or not they were getting the job done. Understanding this fundamental change is crucial if a new sales manager like Marty is to make the transition successfully from "doer" to manager.

Although sales managers must still be "doers," they must learn how to do different things. To be specific, new sales managers must learn how to reorder their

TABLE 1-4   Critical Differences between Selling and Managing

Activity	Sales representative	Sales manager
Primary responsibility	Develop accounts	Develop people
Working relationships	Alone	Through others
Role	Player	Coach
Part of management?	No	Yes, must sell the company plan to reps
Diversity of responsibility	Make calls, sell, and service	Develop people, recruit, select, train, motivate, compensate, run branch office, see key accounts, correspond, work with departments such as advertising, engineering, and credit

priorities. They must understand that their primary function is no longer personal selling. They must resist the temptation to return to the comfortable world of selling when they encounter the frustrations of management.

This is what happened to Marty Roberts. She continued to put the most emphasis on selling because that is what she did best. By doing this, she neglected the important functions of sales management: planning, organizing, recruiting, selecting, training, motivating, and controlling. She simply could not wear the hats of both salesperson and sales manager at the same time. Trying to do too much, she worked longer and longer. Finally, when she could take the pressure no longer, Marty quit.[14]

SALES MANAGEMENT TRAINING AND DEVELOPMENT

As the discussion of the field sales manager's job has indicated, first-level sales managers are crucial to the success of a sales organization. Further, today's salespeople are quite different from the salespeople of yesterday. It is essential that sales managers learn how to manage these better-educated, achievement-oriented salespeople.[15] Therefore, in addition to training and development programs for salespeople, companies must provide adequate training for sales managers.

A survey of human resource specialists identified increased training for first-level managers and supervisors as one of industry's most pressing needs. The most important reason for this is that companies realize that training is necessary to keep them competitive. Also, management training is viewed as a way to retain good people.[16] For first-level managers, communications, team building, and performance management skills were rated as the three most important training needs. Developing subordinates replaced performance management as the third most important training need for middle managers, while introducing and managing change was considered the primary training need for senior managers.[17]

A survey of sales training carried out by Princeton Research and Consulting Center concluded that there is a "great need" for sales management training. The areas of training considered most important were learning how to motivate salespeople, how to manage time effectively, how to coach and train salespeople, how to listen for understanding, how to make the transition to sales manager, how to be effective in the role of sales manager, how to give a presentation, and how to manage the negotiation process.[18]

There is also a growing need for sales management training in those industries such as banking that are trying to develop a sales culture. In particular, some banks are beginning to recognize the need for ongoing sales management training for branch managers.[19] Banks are attempting to develop coaching and other skills needed to stimulate and reward selling in their branches. In addition, upper management also needs training to gain an understanding of the role of selling and sales management in banking.

The most important reason for sales management training is to enhance career development. In particular, training is the key to helping a salesperson make the difficult transition from selling to managing. As the situation involving Marty Roberts revealed, new sales managers must learn how to reorder their priorities to concentrate on managing people who sell, rather than on doing the selling themselves. The best way to prepare salespeople to become managers is to have a total career development program.

Unfortunately, many companies fail to provide formal training when they promote a salesperson to a first-level sales management position.[20] They tend to focus on developing only the skills a person needs for the current job, not for future positions. A sales management training and development program must also go beyond the technical skill level and seek to increase human and conceptual skills as well.[21]

Beyond the transition from selling to first-level sales management, there are other career changes that call for sales management training. Bruce Bastoky, president of the January Management Group, calls the various levels of advancement in a person's career "changes of seasons." He identifies three levels of transition in management: (1) from individual contributor to functional manager, (2) from functional manager to general manager, and (3) from general manager to institutional manager. Bastoky recommends that companies place greater emphasis on fundamental, institutional skills that will make the organization capable of executing a strategy.[22]

GLOBAL PERSPECTIVE

Today, more and more sales managers find themselves dealing with salespeople and customers in foreign markets. Important and sometimes baffling differences in culture, social customs, business practices, political policies, and legal restrictions make international sales managers' jobs quite different from those of their domestic counterparts. Some of the key problems involved in international sales include the following:

- Selling is viewed as a low-status occupation in many foreign countries. As a result, it may be more difficult to attract and retain qualified foreign sales recruits.
- The costs of maintaining a foreign sales force are higher than the costs of a domestic sales force. Included in these higher costs are travel, living expenses, use of interpreters, and less efficient use of time.
- Language and cultural differences can slow down training abroad, and cultural and economic conditions may limit the impact of many forms of sales incentives.
- Different value systems and ethics may affect sales practices. For example, in some foreign countries what Americans consider to be bribes to secure business are considered to be standard business practice.
- Countries vary widely in their degree of sales and marketing sophistication.

A sales manager dealing with international salespeople and customers must be keenly aware of these and other problems and conditions. In the domestic market, top sales supervisors and salespeople sell by creatively adapting their products to the specific needs and conditions of customers. It is the same in managing an overseas sales force. However, sales management techniques and procedures must be adapted to the specific needs, procedures, and conditions of global markets. Most importantly, sales managers must be sensitive to the cultural differences between countries.

ABOUT THIS BOOK

This introductory chapter has described the sales manager's job and identified the ways it differs from other management jobs. A sales manager, or one who aspires to become a sales manager, cannot expect that the skills and knowledge which make one a successful salesperson are needed to be an effective manager. The remaining chapters of this book identify and explain the concepts, activities, and skills which today's sales managers must learn and master.

In Chap. 2, career opportunities in selling and sales management will be identified and discussed. Ethics and professionalism in selling and sales management will also be discussed.

Part 2 of the book will cover the personal selling function. This will involve a review of the evolution of personal selling (Chap. 3), preliminary (Chap. 4) and advanced (Chap. 5) steps in the selling process, and time and territory management (Chap. 6).

Planning the sales effort is the focus of Part 3. First, the personal selling environment will be described in Chap. 7. Then Chap. 8 will present an overview of sales management planning. The last two chapters in this section deal with the important sales forecasting (Chap. 9) and budgeting (Chap. 10) activities of sales management.

Part 4, "Developing the Sales Force," begins with a consideration of sales organization in Chap. 11. Recruiting (Chap. 12) and selecting (Chap. 13) the sales force are the next two topics covered. Part 4 concludes with sales training and development in Chap. 14.

Sales leadership and supervision (Chap. 15) begins the coverage of directing the sales force in Part 5. Next, sales incentives (Chap 16) and compensation (Chap. 17) are discussed. Finally, Chap. 18 in Part 5 takes a look at the emerging issues involved in managing an international sales force.

The last section of the book, Part 6, discusses sales management's role in evaluating sales performance. Developing a sales evaluation program and establishing standards are covered in Chap. 19, along with managing the evaluation program. Part 6, and the book itself, conclude with sales and cost analysis (Chap. 20).

As described above, the chapters that follow will cover the individual subelements of the sales manager's job. Two important observations about these subelements are that: (1) each is interrelated with, and dependent upon, the others and affects their workings, efficiency, and success, and (2) each must contribute to the attainment of sales success.

What the successful sales manager is managing, and what one must learn, is a total, integrated, interactive management system, each part contributing to the common goals of the sales group. This is a critically important aspect of the conditions under which sales managers work.

1. **Describe the Nature of Personal Selling and the Changes Brought about by Business's Shift to a Customer Orientation.**

   Personal selling is a form of promotion that brings the human element into marketing transactions. It increases customer confidence, encourages the buyer to act immediately, and facilitates the handling of individual customer's problems and concerns. The shift of business to a customer orientation is embodied in the marketing concept. Partnering, relationship selling, team selling, value added selling, and consultative selling have all become important in the modern, customer-oriented business environment.

2. **Outline the Role of the Sales Force in Each of the Marketing Mix Variables.**

   The sales force's role might be described as follows:

   Product. The sales force assists in product development, product sourcing, and test marketing.
   Price. Salespeople help decide which pricing strategies to use and evaluate environmental situations relevant to particular pricing strategies.
   Distribution. Personal selling provides the link to either the consumer (in direct distribution) or the trade (in indirect distribution).
   Promotion. Salespeople are responsible for generating the orders upon which companies depend for income.

3. **Trace the Process of How Sales Management Has Changed.**

   As personal selling has changed, the role of sales managers has changed. Selling is no longer a pushy, aggressive enterprise, but rather a cooperative, mutually beneficial effort. In a parallel manner, the sales manager has had to evolve from the stereotypical "ill-tempered bully" to a polished and creative problem solver.

4. **Define the Critical Role, Tasks, and Activities of Field Sales Managers.**

   The role of sales managers is one of coach instead of player. Sales managers must be able to manage those who "do" in addition to "doing" certain tasks themselves. Sales managers have the following tasks:

   Analyzing. This involves the activities of reviewing sales records and salesperson performance, assessing specific market trends and conditions, and noting relevant environmental factors and trends.
   Planning. This involves the activities of establishing and transmitting to salespeople objectives, strategies, and procedures.
   Organizing. This involves the activities of breaking the selling tasks into jobs, creating job descriptions, and recruiting salespeople.
   Overseeing. This involves the activities of issuing directions, providing motivation, and training.
   Evaluating. This involves the activities of creating performance standards, collecting and analyzing performance information, and taking remedial actions.

5. **Assess Sales Management Training and Development Activities.**

The most important characteristic of a sales training program is a career orientation. The program should not only teach new salespeople how to perform their immediate entry-level positions but also prepare them for potential long-term advancement. Training is the best way to help a salesperson make the transition from selling to management.

REVIEW QUESTIONS

1. It is generally desirable for salespeople to have input into marketing mix decisions because salespeople have a unique knowledge or perspective about certain external groups important to the company. Name at least three of these groups. How is salesperson input into marketing mix decisions beneficial?
2. Modern selling involves not merely persuasion but also cooperation. How does the seller help the buyer? How does the buyer help the seller?
3. What are the three major propositions of the marketing concept? Briefly describe what each of these propositions implies for sales management.
4. Define the marketing mix. What are the four major elements of the marketing mix?
5. Sales managers exist in a very dynamic environment. What are the likely changes that sales managers must be prepared to handle? What new methods exist for responding to change?
6. What personality traits seem to be related to success in both sales management and entrepreneurship? What particular sales management activities call for entrepreneurship?
7. What is the field sales manager "in the middle of"? How is the amount of field sales manager selling time related to the size of the sales force?
8. What is the first concern in managing the personal selling function? Why is it unwise to pick managers based only on their sales performance?
9. Why is it so difficult for salespeople to make the transition to management? Discuss how this situation affects the sales organization.
10. What are some of the problems involved in international selling? What is most important for a sales manager operating in a global environment?

DISCUSSION QUESTIONS

1. Describe the best salesperson you ever encountered. What made this person stand out in your mind?
2. Interview a salesperson or a sales manager. (Perhaps this individual will allow you to travel with him or her for a day.) What have you learned from this interview? How would you describe the individual's job?
3. Outline a recent purchase situation involving a salesperson. As a consumer, what did you want from this salesperson? How would you rate the salesperson's actual performance? Give reasons.
4. What rewards would you seek from a sales management career? Why are these rewards important to you? Can you foresee any disadvantages to a sales management career?
5. Throughout this chapter, the sales effort was compared to a sports team, the managers being "coaches," the salespeople, "players." Do you see this as a fitting analogy? In what ways is a sales department like or unlike a sports team?

ETHICAL DILEMMA

As Chap. 1 described, field sales managers often also have some direct selling responsibilities, and these duties sometimes conflict with managing. Suppose a sales manager receives an urgent message from an important customer while working with a sales trainee in the field. How should the manager respond?

SALES MANAGEMENT CASE

Death of a (Type of) Salesman

In the Woody Allen movie *Take the Money and Run*, personal selling is taken to its comic extremes when Allen, guilty of robbery, is forced to endure the inhumane punishment of being locked alone in a prison cell with an insurance salesperson. As was indicated in this chapter, salespeople are often characterized as being pushy and aggressive; however, in the modern selling environment—where techniques such as partnering, relationship selling, team selling, value-added selling, and consultative selling prevail—there is no place for abrasive selling tactics. Salespeople must be concerned about the welfare of their customers.

How many parents gaze into the crib of their newborn and say, "I hope my child grows up to be a used car salesperson?" Probably not many. But while some car sellers' reputations may be warranted, the automobile world has, in reality, changed to keep up with the times. Ford officials say that their best salespeople get to the top through a solid customer base, not by technique, and other car salespeople are saying that honesty and straightforwardness sell cars; customer service is key.

The sales effort behind Toyota's Lexus is an example of a sophisticated modern sales effort. The company has been known to buy back cars from owners complaining about a problem as small as polishing marks on the paint finish. Lexus has devised a program that all dealers must pass, and Lexus salespeople are required to call at least one customer per week to see how recently purchased cars are per-

forming. In essence, Lexus salespeople go to great lengths not only to sell, but also to service after they sell. Today, effective marketers recognize that overly aggressive selling practices just don't cut it.

Questions

1. Why do you think selling cars has changed in the ways it has? Cite factors that could have been behind these changes.

2. Obtain promotional literature from an automobile dealership in your town. On what selling features does the literature focus? Is customer service emphasized?

3. Besides automobile sales, what are some other types of selling that have been criticized for the unethical behavior of salespeople?

CHAPTER 2

CAREERS IN PROFESSIONAL SELLING AND SALES MANAGEMENT

LEARNING GOALS

- Explain how sales management prepares someone for future career challenges.
- List and comment on the primary advantages of a sales career.
- Discuss how one goes about preparing for a sales career.
- Outline the major steps in a job search for students interested in a sales career.
- Identify and explain the dimensions of sales professionalism.

SALES CAREERS

Why would a new college graduate enter a career in sales? Well, there are many reasons. Salespeople are allowed to work more independently than most employees, they interact with many different types of people, and they have a large degree of control over their own financial destiny. Also, sales jobs are at most companies a well-recognized beginning of an upwardly mobile career path.

Just as salespeople have great opportunity, they also face substantial challenges. Long hours and undying energy are requirements. Competition is fierce in most industries and job-related travel takes time away from home. These less positive aspects of the sales job are sometimes harsh surprises for new salespeople, causing many to rethink their career choices.

The realities of a sales job are even harder to handle for someone who has been given an unrealistic job preview. Less-than-accurate job descriptions are a problem when recruiters are not completely familiar with a job, or when they are so anxious to fill a job opening that they gloss over the position's less desirable aspects. Such was not the case when Ron Bongo took a job selling stocks and bonds for the Hibbard Brown firm in New Jersey. The recruiter was actually a salesperson for the company, so he knew what the job would be like. He told Bongo that the position would be lucrative, but only with lots of hard work. Bongo, who is on 100 percent commission, does indeed face considerable pressure, working thirteen-hour days and taking a road trip every month. The recruiter was also responsible for Bongo's training, another incentive for him not to sugar coat the nature of the job.[1]

When sales managers talk with sales recruits or manage recruiting programs, they should be aware that it is in everyone's best interest for recruits to get an accurate job description. Chapter 2 discusses the sales career, including the initial job search. With its substantial challenges, selling is by no means a career for everyone. For those who relish the challenge, however, opportunity is limitless.

CHAPTER OVERVIEW

Sales in an excellent career choice for an aspiring marketer. In addition to putting a person at the forefront of a firm's competitive effort, sales management acts as a stepping stone to other types of managerial positions. A first-level sales manager has several options: to advance to the next level in the sales organization; to move to a higher position in another part of the marketing organization; or to enter a general management position. The essential point is that selling and sales management experience prepare a person for advancement in many areas.

Alan Schonberg, president of Sales Consultants International, the nation's largest recruiter of sales and marketing personnel, has noted:

> I have always felt that a sales career is the most success-oriented career in our business structure. The ability to sell, coupled with drive, attitude, and expectations, can lead almost anywhere an individual wants to go.[2]

In this chapter various aspects of a sales career will be discussed. In addition, suggestions for preparing for such a career and for the student's job search are provided. The chapter concludes with a discussion of sales professionalism.

ADVANTAGES OF SALES CAREERS

Careers in selling and sales management offer many advantages.[3] Figure 2-1 outlines the three major categories of sales career advantages: financial rewards, personal satisfaction, and opportunities for advancement.

FIGURE 2-1 Rewards of a Sales Career.

Financial Rewards

When most people think of sales careers, they think of the opportunity to earn a good living. This is true; successful salespeople and managers are well paid. However, as is the case in most professions, one has to work hard to realize the financial rewards. Regardless of whether a commission system is used or not, in few other occupations is one's compensation more closely tied to one's output than in sales.

Every year *Sales & Marketing Management* conducts a survey of selling costs. Compiled from many sources, this survey includes compensation information for all types of salespeople and sales supervisors and for all forms of sales compensation plans. Recently, an average sales trainee earned $26,036; a midlevel salesperson, $40,194; and a top-level salesperson, $59,955.[4]

Starting salaries are attractive for students who enter sales. Someone with a bachelor's degree in sales or marketing could expect a starting annual salary of $27,144 in 1992. Sales-oriented M.B.A. graduates would start higher, depending on prior work experience and undergraduate background. The starting salary for M.B.A.s with a nontechnical bachelor's degree was $44,796 in 1992.[5]

Financial rewards continue to grow if one is successful in selling. It is not at all unusual for a successful, experienced salesperson to earn $100,000 a year or more. Sales managers also can expect high earnings. The average annual compensation for a sales supervisor was $66,402 in a recent year.[6] The median annual compensation for top sales and marketing executives was $180,000.[7] Typically, this compensation is paid in both salary and a bonus based on sales force performance.

Indications are that sales and sales management careers will continue to provide college graduates with excellent potential for financial rewards. Sales is one of the top dozen career opportunities for middle-management positions in medium- and large-sized companies. The demand for people in international sales is strong.

People working in selling can expect to receive a company car, liberal expense accounts, sales incentives, and other rewards, as well as standard benefits like paid vacations, pensions, insurance, and so forth. An especially attractive benefit for salespeople and sales managers is a company car. In fact, people whose jobs require them to have company cars consider the cars their number one benefit.[8] New salespeople, in particular, are impressed by having a company car, and many firms are now using company cars as a tool to recruit young salespeople.

Personal Satisfaction

Regardless of the financial rewards one receives, personal satisfaction is also important in any career.[9] Successful salespeople and sales managers can take pride in what they do because they are providing an important service to their customers and employers' companies. Someone who has chosen sales as a profession knows that the sales force largely determines the firm's success.

Professional selling provides one with many opportunities to assist others as creative problem solvers. Salespeople are also crucial to the introduction of new products and technology. The professional salesperson of today is a well-trained, dedicated person who provides a special service to customers.

Successful salespeople gain considerable satisfaction from selling exciting products which meet buyers' needs. For instance, Jane Lee, who has a doctorate in education, left her position in the Georgia Department of Education to sell Apple computers to school districts. She is now manager of special education in the marketing department where she will help market computers designed to help disabled students. To illustrate the satisfaction she has gained from selling, Jane Lee cites how an Apple computer helped a young man with a severe muscle disorder overcome the academic limitations caused by his handicap. The young man is now about to go to school and sit in class with other students.[10]

Another interesting salesperson is Chuck Schupp, who sells Louisville Slugger baseball bats to professional ball players. A former college and minor league pitcher, he finds a lot of things interesting about his job. These include his workplace (clubhouses), his customers (Wade Boggs, Don Mattingly, and the rest of the 70 percent of major league players who use Louisville Sluggers), and being around a sport he loves. But most of all, Chuck Schupp enjoys the challenge of selling. "I'm a problem solver," he says. "If something is wrong with our product, I want to know what it is. If someone is not using our product, I want to know why."[11]

Three general aspects of selling contribute to one's personal satisfaction. First, selling is competitive. Good salespeople are stimulated by the excitement of intense competition. They want to win, and they are willing to work hard to be successful.

Sales careers also provide a person with independence. Outside salespeople are not confined to an office; they are able to travel and meet different types of people in different situations. The outside salesperson is his or her own boss and does not have to conform to the rigidity faced by other types of employees. When experienced salespeople are asked what they like most about their job, they often reply that it is the variety and diversity of selling that stimulates them most.

Finally, salespeople can be entrepreneurs. In fact, some observers suggest that selling is the last vestige of entrepreneurship in corporate America. As described in Chap. 1, many of the traits of successful salespeople are also the elements of entrepreneurship. Many successful entrepreneurs, like Sam Walton and Mary Kay Ashe, prove to be their firms' best salespeople.

Opportunities for Career Advancement

Sales is a recognized path to the top in many companies, and some studies have shown that more top executives come from sales and marketing than from any other business function.[12] For instance, John Akers started out as a sales trainee and in twenty-four years moved up through marketing to become chief executive officer (now retired) of IBM. Other prominent examples of chief executives with sales backgrounds are James W. Kinnear (Texaco) and Paul Fireman (Reebok).[13]

career path
Sequential steps in a person's career advancement

Most companies now think in terms of a *career path*, which is a series of steps a person goes through as his or her career advances. A person who enters a company as a sales trainee has the advantage of choosing from multiple career paths. For instance, National Semiconductor has dual career paths for its sales and marketing employees—one track for people who want to go into management and a parallel path for those who want to remain in the sales force.[14]

The major career-path options for salespeople are shown in Fig. 2-2. Depending on qualifications and interests, a person may choose to continue as a salesperson, select a career in sales management, or pursue a marketing staff career.

In addition to career advancement and flexibility for salespeople, there are numerous advantages of multiple career paths to the company. Sales recruiting is

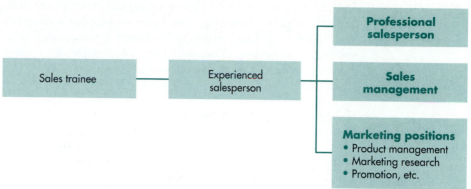

FIGURE 2-2 **Multiple Career-Path Options for Salespeople.**

enhanced when a firm can show that it has career opportunities to match any sales or marketing person's needs. Top salespeople are less likely to be frustrated because they can receive recognition and advancement without going into management. Money spent for training and development can be spent more wisely on specific individuals and their needs. [15]

SALES OPPORTUNITIES FOR WOMEN AND MINORITIES

Sales and sales management have become an especially attractive career option for women and minorities. Although field selling was viewed as "a man's world" in the past, this is no longer the case. For instance, a study of women in selling noted that sales offers women a career option with a high income, a great deal of freedom, a high level of training, and a high level of job satisfaction. [16]

In the past, blacks and other minority groups were not well represented in sales forces. This situation has also changed rapidly in recent years. Minorities now view sales as an option presenting excellent employment opportunities. Sales has always provided a means of achieving occupational and social advancement. It is now fulfilling that task again, and minority groups are increasingly seeing sales as an equal-opportunity field.

SALES OPPORTUNITIES IN GROWTH INDUSTRIES

Future sales career opportunities will reflect the changes taking place in the developed economies of the world. For example, in the United States and other industrialized nations, agricultural workers account for only a small percentage of the labor force. Manufacturing jobs have also declined, but service industries are on the upswing. Health care, information, energy, finance, high technology, and other services will provide the greatest opportunities for sales careers in the coming years. In this section some specific industry and company sales career opportunities are identified.

High Technology

Some of the best opportunities for creative salespeople are in high-technology sales. The use of technology in selling will be described in later chapters. Technological advances have helped to lower selling and management costs, improve communications, reduce selling time, and enhance customer satisfaction.

At the same time, major technological developments have created many sales career opportunities. Transportation, communications, information management, health care, and other advanced technologies must be sold. Salespeople who understand the technical details, uses, and possibilities of complex high-tech products are in demand.

Successful high-tech salespeople must be able to communicate effectively with demanding executives and to deal with highly sophisticated customers. They must have the desire to serve customers both before and after the sale and to act as consultants by troubleshooting clients' problems and helping expand systems.[17] The rewards are great for people who have the proper technical background and the desire to sell.

Service Businesses

At the same time that the number of sales opportunities is growing in high-technology firms, personal selling has become recognized as an important business-getting technique by many traditional service and nonprofit organizations. Some examples: Banks and other financial institutions have developed training programs in personal selling for branch managers and other employees; military recruiters have one of the most difficult jobs of all in selling young men and women on careers in the armed forces; the declining numbers of college-age people have made student recruiting an important activity for college enrollment departments; many hospitals have marketing departments and offer sales incentives to people who sell health maintenance and other health care services.[18]

Since personal selling is so new to most high-tech, service, and nonprofit organizations, sales management in these fields is in an early stage of development. These organizations draw heavily on managers and on sales management practices and techniques that have been successful in other industries. What is emerging are adaptations of successful sales management procedures taken from the long selling experiences of tangible goods manufacturers and retailers. This trend continues to be a very exciting development in the history of personal selling, and it offers students a chance to develop their selling skills in a challenging environment.

Outstanding Companies in the Field of Selling

There are many companies that have strong sales forces and provide excellent career opportunities for students. Some of these are *Fortune* 500 companies, while others are much smaller. In addition to companies in the industries described above, many other firms offer exciting, challenging career options in selling and sales management. A good source of information about these companies are business and professional publications, such as *Business Week, Fortune*, and *Sales & Marketing Management*.

For a number of years, *Sales & Marketing Management* has conducted a survey to rate America's best sales forces. Approximately one hundred sales executives in

TABLE 2-1 *Sales & Marketing Management*'s Top Sales Forces

Year	Company	Product
1992	Anheuser-Busch	Beverages
	Archer-Daniels-Midland	Food products
	Northwestern Mutual	Life insurance
	Bethlehem Steel	Metal manufacturing
	Eastman Kodak	Scientific and photographic equipment
	United Parcel Service	Shipping and delivery services

each of several industries are surveyed each year. The industry rankings are based on seven measures of sales force quality—recruiting top salespeople, ability to keep top salespeople, quality of training, opening new accounts, holding new accounts, product and/or technical knowledge, and reputation among customers. The top sales forces for 1992 and the industries they represent are shown in Table 2-1.

The editors of *Sales & Marketing Management* asked six earlier winners if there was one quality or characteristic they valued and stressed above all others. Their answers, which are shown in Table 2-2, emphasize the importance of recruiting top people and developing a good reputation with customers. For the student considering a career in selling and sales management, these responses suggest strongly that outstanding companies place the greatest emphasis on obtaining good people who are true problem solvers. It is up to the sales recruit to demonstrate the qualities that these outstanding sales organizations want.

SALES MANAGEMENT IN PRACTICE

SALES MANAGE-MENT

LOCTITE CORPORATION

There are outstanding companies and there are outstanding sales forces, and a combination of both is found in the Loctite Corporation, a Connecticut manufacturer of adhesives and sealants. Since 1987, Loctite sales have grown an average of 19 percent annually, and recently, with sales of $567 million, the company made the *Fortune* 500 list for the first time.

Loctite's success is largely due to its sales management efforts. Since Loctite's products are similar in price and quality to the products of its competitors, this firm sought to differentiate the offerings on the basis of customer service.

Most of Loctite's customers are independent distributors. The firm views them not only as customers but also as partners. The purchase of a Loctite product is only the beginning of the selling relationship. Loctite has developed what it calls the Loctite Partnership Program, under which distributors receive special visits (in addition to regular sales calls) from Loctite representatives and are shown financial sheets predicting Loctite products' potential benefits.

Loctite also holds around ten thousand classes for its distributors each year. The company devises individual marketing programs for its distributors in addition to offering cooperative advertising programs.

Loctite salespeople determine what distributors need, and they set out to satisfy those needs. The company does not expect its customers to change their activities to suit Loctite products; rather the company alters itself to satisfy customers. In this way, price wars are avoided. Products are only part of what is being sold; through Loctite's superb customer service, the company has set itself apart from the competition—and gained a spot on the *Fortune* 500 list.

TABLE 2-2　**What It Takes to Be the Best**

RJR Nabisco (food products)
"Recruiting is a number one priority for us—finding quality people who can analyze data from customers, see things from the consumers' eye, use available sales tools like laptops and syndicated data, and interface with the marketing people at headquarters."

Procter & Gamble (health and beauty aids)
"It's hard to separate recruiting top people and keeping top people. It doesn't matter how good your training or products are—if you don't have good people to begin with, you're nowhere."

Reynolds Metals (metal manufacturing)
"Our reputation among customers is most valuable to us. All seven categories are important, but if you've done all the right things to win a good reputation, all the other factors should fall into place."

United Parcel Service (shipping and delivery services)
"Our reputation among customers is the factor we value and pride ourselves upon the most."

Communications Satellite Corp. (telecommunications equipment and services)
"Keeping top people is most important to us. If you can keep your best people, that means you'll be opening new accounts and keeping them, and you're also assured of a good reputation among your customers."

CAREER PREPARATION AND DEVELOPMENT

How can a college student prepare for a sales career and be chosen by a company to enter its sales force? Of course, one strategy is to take sales and marketing courses in college. These courses help prepare students for the challenge of selling.[19] Well-prepared students take not only business courses, but courses in psychology, economics, speech, and written communications.

College courses in personal selling, consumer behavior, and sales management provide students with specific knowledge relevant to selling. These are courses that give the knowledge most desired by sales managers. But sales managers also want recruits who have developed their communications skills. That is why speech and writing courses are a necessity for anyone who wants a sales career.[20]

Other Activities

Work experience and extracurricular activities are also valuable to a student seeking a sales career. Many summer and part-time jobs provide the experience of dealing with people that is helpful in selling. Likewise, competitive athletics, student professional organizations and clubs (Pi Sigma Epsilon and American Marketing Association student chapters are examples), campus government, volunteer work, and other activities give students opportunities to work with people and to assume leadership positions.[21] Companies selecting sales recruits are more receptive to college students who have diverse experiences than to those who have done nothing but attend classes during their college years.

SALES MANAGEMENT IN PRACTICE

AT&T

AT&T's "Put It in Writing" advertising campaign, which defied competitors to commit their claims to paper, may have been merely promotional. The phrase is, however, telling of a recent emphasis on writing as a selling tool.

Perhaps no skill is more important to salespeople and sales managers than the ability to communicate. Only oral communications skills are needed in face-to-face selling situations; however, this type of selling is in many situations infeasible. With today's fierce competitive realities, many firms are looking for ways to cut selling costs. Especially when soliciting new business, the likelihood of getting sales is often too low to justify the high cost of face-to-face selling. In these situations, writing sales letters is a viable, cost-effective selling technique.

Besides their low cost, sales letters have other advantages. When the decision to buy takes a long time to make, a letter is a tangible and nonirritating reminder of the salesperson's product. Also, sales letters can serve as a way of describing technical features of goods or as a way of talking about services, which cannot be seen or touched, but only described.

AT&T, a service marketer in a competitive environment, possesses features that make sales writing advantageous. Also, since AT&T's offerings are similar to its competitors', sales letters serve to help differentiate AT&T. In today's environment, intense competition and service orientation are the rule. As students prepare themselves for a career in selling, they should take advantage of every opportunity to hone communications skills of all kinds. In the sales force, an ability to write clearly and persuasively will certainly be an advantage.

Extracurricular activities also provide early signs of career success potential. A study of the backgrounds of chief executive officers of large American firms revealed the following:

> Over half of them worked during their high school years; 38 percent of them participated in intercollegiate sports . . . and almost three out of four CEOs held at least one office in a campus organization during their college years.[22]

internships
Supervised work experience in a sales organization

Internships, in which students have supervised work experience while they are attending college, provide opportunities for students to learn about sales and marketing and to open the doors to sales careers. An internship helps a student learn to deal effectively with others. It shows students how firms function, and it helps students understand organizational dynamics.

Continued Self-Development

Self-development begins with learning from the experiences and knowledge of others. This is what a student can gain from internships, part-time employment, and extracurricular activities. Self-development continues, day in and day out, through individual experiences, observations, and personal insights. Specific self-development techniques include reading, observing, exchanging experiences with other salespeople and managers, and practice.

Reading. An effective marketer is always looking for ways to improve. One way is to keep up-to-date by reading business, industry, and professional books and journals. Lists of books and business, marketing, and sales publications with which a salesperson should be familiar are included in Chap. 4.

Observation.   This can also help one become a better salesperson or manager. Who was the best boss or professor you ever had? What made this person a good boss? A good teacher? How about your peers? What can you learn from them? We all can learn a great deal from others if we observe them carefully and make a deliberate effort to learn from our observations.

A specific form of observing and learning from others is *mentoring*, the development of a close friendship with an experienced salesperson or manager. A mentor can be a sounding board for ideas and can provide insights into company policies and politics.

mentoring
Association between a new salesperson and an experienced salesperson or manager who serves as a role model

A mentor can serve as a role model by providing the basic skill that is required to be successful in selling. It is estimated that a third of all major U.S. companies now have formal mentoring programs to provide personal counseling and career guidance to younger employees.[23]

Exchanging Ideas and Experiences.   Astute salespeople and managers also take advantage of every opportunity to exchange ideas and experiences with other sales professionals, both in and outside their company. Two ways to do this are by attending continuing education programs at colleges, universities, and professional associations and by joining trade and professional organizations.

Continuing education programs have important benefits for the salespeople and managers who attend them. These include learning new techniques, exposure to new ideas, reinforcement of basic knowledge, and exchange of ideas with other sales professionals. The latter is perhaps the most beneficial, especially to an inexperienced salesperson or sales manager. Most management seminar leaders stimulate the interaction of participants by using cases, role playing, group discussion, and similar participative techniques. Also, coffee breaks and meals provide seminar participants with additional chances to learn from each other.

Another means of learning about sales management practices is to join a professional or trade organization. For example, Sales and Marketing Executives International offers programs useful in selling and sales management. Also, most industries have trade associations that promote the interests of their members. Specific developmental programs and activities include newsletters, trade shows, seminars, and conferences.

Practice.   Another strategy for professional development is to take every opportunity to practice and challenge one's sales and management skills. There are many ways to do this. To suggest a few: Take on a leadership position in a community, religious, or professional organization; volunteer for special projects for the company (for example, to evaluate a new product idea); speak to a marketing or sales management class at a local college; write an article for a trade publication. Such activities give an aspiring sales manager a chance to practice business skills—to learn by doing.

JOB SEARCH GUIDE FOR STUDENTS INTERESTED IN SALES CAREERS

Sales personnel recruiting and selection will be covered in Chaps. 12 and 13, when the discussion will look at these areas from the sales manager's viewpoint. There is another side of these activities, however. This is the viewpoint of the sales recruit.

Many of the students reading this book will soon be taking part in their own job searches. How many times have you been asked, "What do you want to do when you graduate from college?" After graduation, you are haunted with the question: "Have you found a job yet?" Finding a job is not an easy task. If you are interested in a career in sales, this section may prove helpful.

Before You Start the Job Search

First, decide which factors are important to you. List your long-term versus short-term goals, personal versus career goals, and so on. You must do this to identify those factors which will define "the ultimate sales job" for you. However, you must realize that the word "ultimate" has different meanings for different people. By deciding which job factors are critical for you, the job search will be given direction and will help you make a wise decision.

There are many issues to be considered: salary, benefits, geographic location, the job description, growth opportunities, the training program, and so forth. Perhaps you want to work in an area close to your home, or perhaps you hope to receive the best possible sales training. Whatever your goals, however, don't think only about the salary and tangible benefits like a company car.

The next step is to focus your job search on a few specific industries. There are several concerns to think about when you pick an industry to evaluate. The industry you choose should be one that interests you. It should be one that allows for growth. You must become knowledgeable about the industry to know which firms offer the best career prospects. Finally, companies are interested in candidates who are motivated. Often the interviewer will ask about the other companies with which you are interviewing. If you were to answer that you were interviewing with General Foods, Dow, Pepsi, Xerox, and Metropolitan Life, you may not make quite the same impression on a recruiter from a computer company as you might have had if you said Apple, IBM, NCR, and Digital. The second response strongly conveys the message that you are focused on a sales career in the computer industry.

Starting the Search

Now you know what you are looking for and have identified the industries you would like to look into. Your resume is back from the printer and your suit is hanging in the closet. You're ready to begin.

Your school's career planning and placement office is a good starting point. A sizable portion of the scheduled placement interviews are for sales positions. Many large organizations, as well as smaller companies, come to campus looking for sales employees.

If you want to interview on campus, be sure that your schedule is free during the interview sign-up time. Competition is fierce for the choice interviews. If you are unable to sign up for a campus interview, put your name on the waiting list. Check back to see if there are any cancellations. If you are unable to arrange an interview, find out the name of the interviewer and call to explain your situation. Tell the interviewer that you are really interested in the company and try to arrange a few minutes early in the morning or after the person's interview schedule is completed. Try inviting the interviewer out to lunch or breakfast. If these tactics are not successful, be sure your resume is included in the interviewer's file. Finally, be sure not to sign up for an interview if you are not really interested in that company because you may be taking that slot away from someone who is interested. It is also wise to extend your search beyond the career services office.

Extending Your Job Search

Finding the first job in sales is just like selling itself. There are no easy shortcuts. A successful job search requires a lot of personal contacts with potential employers and others who might lead to job opportunities. As a result, a college student's job search must go beyond the campus.

An important means of extending your job search and obtaining information and referrals is through personal contacts. List all of the people you know in the field you have chosen. Include your family, friends, professors, neighbors, and former students. Often sources that you least expect to be helpful prove to be most invaluable.

Writing directly to the companies you are interested in is another method of obtaining interviews. Direct inquiries suggest initiative and allow you to demonstrate your communications skills. If you want a sales career, show potential employers you can sell by selling yourself! Research the company you are writing to, and then let them know you are interested in them. After writing several of these letters, the process gets easier.

What Sales Managers Look for in Candidates

Companies look for a myriad of qualifications in a sales recruit. Some organizations have formal criteria (specific degrees, minimum grades, work experience, and so forth). Others are interested in your involvement in outside activities and your goals for the future.

It is great if your resume states that you are a member of an organization, but that will not mean a thing unless you can elaborate on your involvement and commitment to the organization. Internships and jobs held are worth mentioning. If you financed your education through scholarships and part-time jobs, that fact should also be mentioned. If someone is willing to work sixty hours a week during the summer to pay tuition bills, companies may envision that person as a valuable employee.

Your personality and the impression you make during the interview are the most important determinants of whether or not you proceed to the next stage in the hiring process. It is important to project a pleasant, professional manner. If you cannot handle an interview satisfactorily, how will you be able to handle a cold call? Think of the interview as an opportunity to get to meet someone who has information about a company in which you are interested. The interview is a two-way communications process.

It is very important to prepare for every single interview. Research the company. Be prepared to ask questions. Be sure to have answers to the questions interviewers will probably ask. There is literature available that lists the interview questions most often asked. Get a copy of a list of such questions and rehearse your answers. An interviewer asking a simple question like "Tell me about yourself" does not want personal data, but wants to see how you respond. The interviewer wants to know what you have accomplished and how you are going to make a contribution to the organization. Believe in everything you say and be honest.[24]

Some Other Factors

There are a few other aspects of a job search that will be important to you. First, it is very time-consuming and frustrating. If you are committed to finding a job before graduation, be prepared to give up other activities. You will need plenty of free time for interviews. Campus interviews are convenient but second interviews usually require a visit to the company. Most of the second interviews include a half- or full-day regimen.

Do not catch the "I'll look for a job after I graduate" syndrome, because the best jobs are usually gone by then. Also, do not go to the other extreme and become obsessed with finding a job. Try to schedule a couple of hours every week solely for your job search. Do research, write cover letters, practice interview answers, and so on.

Having a set time for these activities will also help alleviate another job search symptom that is seldom talked about but often experienced—frustration. Job hunting can be very disappointing. Do not give up. Those who continue to search until they succeed are the people who land good positions. As frustrating as the job search may be at times, it can also be very exciting. Think about the experience in a positive way. You will be meeting all kinds of new people, and learning about different companies and types of businesses.

Finally, no one ever seems to mention that job hunting can be very expensive. Include in your budget the cost of the following: a suit(s), the printing expense of a resume, paper for cover letters, envelopes, stamps, typing services, long-distance telephone calls, and travel expenses. Although most companies pay for all expenses incurred on a company visit, the usual policy is that you pay all of the costs and then the company reimburses you, which creates a cash-flow problem for many college students.

Making a Job Decision

How do you choose from among the offers you receive? It is very easy to say that you will accept a position from the company that offers the most money, but think back to when you began your career search and you listed those job characteristics that were the most important. Think of the long-term benefits, not just the short-term ones. An opportunity for personal growth and advancement within a company and the company's training program may be the most important determinants.

In addition to the initial sales training program, you should look at the types of continuous programs a company offers. It is vital to be always on top of your product line, the marketplace, and recent sales techniques. Whether or not a company offers continuous training is important in the long run.

When making your initial career choice, you will undoubtedly consider compensation plans. Use caution here; often the most valuable benefits are overlooked. Sales representatives may be compensated by straight salary, straight commission, a combination of salary and commission, salary plus bonus, or a combination of the above. The forms of sales compensation will be discussed in Chap. 17.

Consider your lifestyle and your spending habits when you evaluate compensation plans. If you are paying rent, car payments, and student loans, some form of base salary may be necessary. On the other hand, commissions are very attractive and motivate you to sell. Another bonus many sales positions offer is a company car. Be sure to include the value of this benefit when comparing compensation plans. Most of the companies that do not provide a car offer some sort of automobile expense for the use of your own car. Also, consider the value of health care, profit sharing, flexible benefits, insurance, educational assistance, stock options, and vacations.

A final key decision factor is the manager for whom you will work. As will be discussed in more detail, the first-level sales manager is critical to a salesperson's success, especially a beginning salesperson. If possible, talk to the field sales manager. Find out about the manager's approach to leadership, feelings about training, developmental goals, and so forth. It may be better to take a sales job which offers fewer tangible rewards but provides an opportunity to work with and learn from a supportive field sales manager.

SALES PROFESSIONALISM

sales profession-alism Status concept based upon special training, personal dedication, and set standards of conduct

Before concluding this chapter about sales careers, a final topic must be discussed. The concept of *sales professionalism* includes three conditions: special training, personal dedication, and established standards of conduct. In the years to come there will be increasing concern for making selling and sales management more professional. Already public opinion and government regulations have imposed many controls and restrictions on sales practices and operations. In part, these have forced salespeople and managers to become more professional. There has also been substantial pressure from within selling for increased professionalism. This trend is destined to continue in the future.

Professionalism Enhances Sales Performance

There are two major dimensions of sales professionalism which must be attained. First, salespeople and managers must be informed, prepared, and dedicated to doing the best they can to satisfy the buyer's needs; in other words, the performance dimension of professionalism.

Much of the discussion in later chapters will concentrate on this aspect of sales professionalism. Changes in buyers, the widespread adoption of the marketing concept, and resulting changes in selling and sales management practices have led to enhanced sales performance and increased professionalism in selling and sales management.

Most important to this aspect of sales professionalism are changes in the buyers with whom salespeople and managers interact. Modern buyers are well educated, and they are knowledgeable about the goods and services they buy. As a result, contemporary salespeople and sales managers must adopt a more professional approach to their jobs. Admittedly, much of the increased professionalization of sales has come from within the selling profession; but a well-educated buyer is a safeguard that will eventually eliminate those salespeople who exhibit marginal professionalism.

All indications are that buyers will be even better informed in the future. Adult education classes, Junior Achievement, Distribution Education Clubs of America (DECA) chapters, improved business coverage in magazines and newspapers, and consumer economics classes are examples of how society's economic and business knowledge is being furthered. The consumer education process is expanding, and its various forms now reach many people, from preteens to adults. Sales managers applaud this trend, since one of its important byproducts is an improved sales function.

Perhaps just as significant as the improved consumer education process is the growing professionalism of industrial buying. Highly qualified, professionally trained buyers are responsible for most purchases of goods and services. It is also likely that several qualified people will participate in the process of buying complex industrial goods and services. Therefore, as buyers become better informed and more professional, it is reasonable to expect salespeople and managers to also become better informed and more professional.

Ethical Behavior Is an Important Factor in Professionalism

The second dimension of sales professionalism is ethics. Salespeople and managers are confronted often with situations that require ethical decisions. For example: A purchasing agent asks for a cash rebate paid directly to the agent when a large order is placed; a sales manager discovers an employee is "padding" the expense account; a salesperson is asked to divulge information about a direct competitor to a buyer; or a sales manager finds out that a salesperson has given an expensive gift which exceeds company limits to a customer.

"back-door" selling Less than ethical selling practice in which a salesperson bypasses the purchasing department of an organization and goes directly to the buying unit

A specific selling practice that has been studied from an ethical perspective is *"back-door" selling,*[25] a situation that occurs when a salesperson bypasses the purchasing department of an organization and goes directly to the buying unit in hopes of making the sale. Many salespeople do not consider this an unethical practice, but one study clearly indicated that purchasers believe back-door selling is unethical. Respondents also felt that the use of back-door selling would negatively influence a salesperson's chances of being chosen as the vendor.

As the above example illustrates, the issue of sales ethics is complex.[26] Many problems and major issues remain to be resolved. Although Sales and Marketing Executives International adopted a code of ethics for professional salespeople in 1963, there is still no widely accepted code of professional ethics. Marginal, and unprofessional, sales operations exist in many lines of business. For example, some telemarketing practices have come under attack in recent years by people concerned with privacy issues and the like.

Unethical sales practices can be very costly.[27] A growing number of lawsuits have cost businesses millions of dollars in recent years in terms of penalties, legal fees, and lost time. Moreover, sales are lost due to image damage and lost sales from adverse publicity. Marginal dealings and compromised ethical standards simply do not make good business sense.

The need for a professional code of ethics for sales is partly an outgrowth of the trend toward greater social responsibility. For a simple example of this trend, one only has to remember when sales managers could justify questionable sales tactics by asserting that the maintenance of sales volume preserved employment for many employees. Contemporary society questions whether or not certain sales tactics that are just concerned with making a sale are ethical. In general, the public's attitude toward marketers (and toward salespeople and sales managers in particular) is that they should adopt a more socially responsible orientation. Most salespeople and sales managers have already done this to a large extent, but even greater strides will be required in the future as the societal role of salespeople and sales managers expands.

Ethical responsibility needs to start at the top.[28] Senior management should concern itself with formulating a code of ethics, articulating corporate values, and establishing standards of action. Middle management should establish rewards to support behavior. Field sales managers should use workshops, sales meetings, and other training activities to teach sales ethics and should include assessments of ethical behavior as part of performance appraisal.

Recent studies have concentrated on the sales manager's role in curbing unethical sales practices. In one study sales managers were presented with four ethical issues and asked how they would respond to unethical salesperson behavior. The study indicated that a sales manager is most likely to use a harsh form of discipline when poor performance and negative organizational consequences are involved.[29]

Ethical Decision/ Action Process
Model of a moral decision structure and its related action process factors

Another sales researcher focused on how sales personnel arrive at ethical decisions and actions.[30] The resulting model—called the *Ethical Decision/Action Process*—is shown in Fig. 2-3. A moral decision structure is its key component. This structure involves (1) recognizing what actions are possible in a given situation, (2) determining the morally right alternative, (3) assigning priority to moral values, and (4) converting the intention into action, a decision, or behavior. The actions that take place within the moral decision structure are influenced by the decision maker's characteristics, situational moderators (corporate culture, peers, superiors, and so forth), and possible decision outcomes. The author feels that the model can help managers uncover possible causes of unethical problems resulting from the actions of salespeople or sales managers. In addition, the model may be used to suggest how unethical behavior can be counteracted or remedied.[31]

These and other studies indicate that sales ethics and professionalism will continue to be a major concern for salespeople and their managers. Recent studies have rated salespeople's most important attributes as honesty, integrity, and professionalism.[32] To instill these qualities in future salespeople and sales managers, colleges and universities are including ethics classes as part of their educational programs. Companies are also taking steps to limit unethical conduct. Human resources executives are screening job applicants more closely, and companies are including ethics in their training programs, as well as taking firm actions when confronted with unethical behavior.[33]

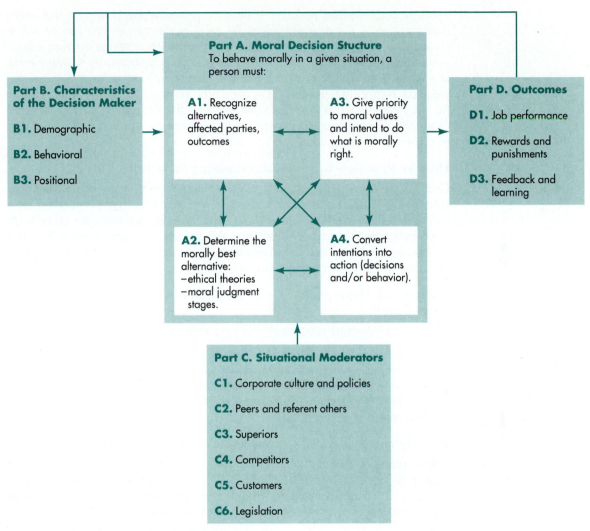

Part A. Moral Decision Stucture
To behave morally in a given situation, a person must:

A1. Recognize alternatives, affected parties, outcomes

A3. Give priority to moral values and intend to do what is morally right.

A2. Determine the morally best alternative:
−ethical theories
−moral judgment stages.

A4. Convert intentions into action (decisions and/or behavior).

Part B. Characteristics of the Decision Maker

B1. Demographic

B2. Behavioral

B3. Positional

Part D. Outcomes

D1. Job performance

D2. Rewards and punishments

D3. Feedback and learning

Part C. Situational Moderators

C1. Corporate culture and policies

C2. Peers and referent others

C3. Superiors

C4. Competitors

C5. Customers

C6. Legislation

FIGURE 2-3 The Ethical Decision/Action Process.

SUMMARY OF LEARNING GOALS

1. **Explain How Sales Management Prepares Someone for Future Career Challenges.**

    A sales position puts a person in the middle of a firm's competitive effort. Such a position acts as a stepping stone to higher positions in the sales organization, other parts of the marketing organization, or general management.

2. **List and Comment on the Primary Advantages of a Sales Career.**

    In terms of financial rewards, a good salesperson has the opportunity to earn an excellent compensation package. It must be remembered, however, that sales compensation is substantially based on sales performance whether or not a commission structure is used. Selling is also personally satisfying because it is so essential to the firm. Personal satisfaction is increased further by selling a good or service that involves creativity and assisting others. Also, many salespeople enjoy the competitive, independent, and entrepreneurial nature of selling. Finally, sales careers usually offer a choice among the recognized career paths of continuing as a salesperson, joining sales management, or moving into a variety of other marketing positions.

3. Discuss How One Goes About Preparing for a Sales Career.

College courses such as psychology, economics, speech, and written communications, in addition to sales and marketing, are very important preparation for a career in selling. Work experience and extracurricular activities are other ways to prepare for a sales career. In addition, people desiring a sales career should be continually focused on self-development through reading, observing, exchanging experiences with others, and practicing.

4. Outline the Major Steps in a Job Search for Students Interested in a Sales Career.

The sales job-hunting process involves the following:

- Deciding which job factors are critical
- Focusing the search on a few specific industries
- Interviewing through your school's planning and placement office
- Obtaining information and referrals through contacts
- Choosing among job offers

5. Identify and Explain the Dimensions of Sales Professionalism.

Sales professionalism includes a performance dimension, which involves the degree to which salespeople and managers are informed, prepared, and dedicated to satisfying the buyer's needs. Sales professionalism also includes an ethics dimension, an issue which has greatly increased in importance in recent years.

REVIEW QUESTIONS

1. Outline the advantages of a sales career. Cite specific data or examples to illustrate each advantage.
2. What is a career path? What are the major career path options for salespeople? What are the advantages of multiple career paths to the company?
3. Identify some of the changes taking place in the world that have affected sales career opportunities. What types of industries will provide the greatest opportunities for sales professionals in the coming years?
4. What effects have technological advances had on sales management? What sales career opportunities have been created by technological developments?
5. In what service or nonprofit organizations has selling recently become recognized as an important business-getting technique? From where are these new-to-selling businesses learning their selling techniques?

TABLE 2-3 **Periodical Library for Professional Selling**

Advertising Age	*Industrial Marketing*
American Salesman	*Industry Week*
Business Week	*Journal of Marketing*
Dun's Review	*Journal of Personal Selling & Sales Management*
Fortune	*Sales & Marketing Management*
Inc.	*The Wall Street Journal*
Industrial Distribution	

6. What are some of the things interviewers look for in a job applicant? What is the most important determinant of whether or not an applicant proceeds to the next stage of the selection process?

7. What are the factors that should be considered when choosing among job offers? Which factors would be most important to you?

8. How is the modern buyer different than buyers in the past? How has this affected selling?

9. What are some things that management can do to promote high ethical standards for salespeople? What have recent studies rated as salespeople's most important attributes?

10. What are some of the ethical dilemmas that salespeople face? How can compromised ethical standards cost businesses money?

DISCUSSION QUESTIONS

1. Go to your college's library and find the latest edition of any two of the publications listed in Table 2-3. Look over each of the publications carefully and read any articles of interest to you. Which publication do you prefer? Which one do you think would be most valuable to a salesperson or manager?

2. Look in your local newspaper's classified advertising and find the "Sales Positions Available" section. Read the ads and make a list of the adjectives used to describe the type of person desired. What personality traits seem to be most important in a person looking for a sales career?

3. Call your school's career planning and placement office or a local employment agency. Ask a counselor there what he or she thinks companies look for in a sales recruit in terms of personality, work experience, education, and extracurricular activities.

4. Prepare a practice resume geared toward getting a sales job. Do not worry about format but rather concentrate on content. What part of your resume would be the most appealing to someone wanting to fill a sales job opening? In what areas do you see weaknesses? Can you improve the weaker areas between now and the time you begin your job search?

5. Select a company with which you would like to interview for a sales job. Then use the resources discussed in the chapter to research the firm and prepare a list of questions to ask the firm's interviewers. Finally, prepare a cover letter and resume for the firm you selected.

ETHICAL DILEMMA

Jim Wybowski, a college senior, accepted a sales job with a regional company two weeks ago. Today he unexpectedly received a better financial offer from a large national corporation. He prefers the second offer. What should Jim do?

SALES MANAGEMENT CASE

The Job Search

Merck receives 200,000 resumes per year; AT&T, 100,000; Du Pont, 50,000; Coors, 40,000; and Nike, 35,000. IBM is inundated with 1,000,000 resumes per year. What the numbers for these companies and many others add up to is a very competitive job market. The recession of the early 1990s has forced many employers to reduce their work forces by hiring fewer applicants and laying off employees.

Even the once-revered M.B.A. graduate is having trouble finding a job these days. Managers have criticized M.B.A. schools for being irrelevant to the real world. There also seems to be an overly abundant supply of M.B.A.s; over 700 business schools graduate 75,000 M.B.A. students each year.

Many job seekers are taking a creative approach to the tough job market. At Washington University, for example, students developed baseball-like trading cards with their own pictures on front and "statistics" on back. Students who have found jobs through these cards say that the cards were a good way to stand out among the flood of resumes that companies receive.

The job market is least bleak for those who manage to stand out. Job searches should be tailored to the job being sought, and this involves researching companies thoroughly. Many recent college grads are starting out with part-time positions in order to prove themselves before being hired full time. Others have offered their services temporarily for free just for an opportunity to show what they can do.

Even those who find jobs will have to work hard to get where they want to be. Three recent graduates in New York were hired as management trainees by United Parcel Service (UPS); they are beginning their management careers by driving U.P.S. trucks for three months. In today's tough market, a substantial degree of diligence is needed to land the job you want.

Questions

1. Discuss a creative way in which a sales applicant could ensure that he or she stands out from the crowd.

2. Write a practice cover letter to a company demonstrating what you could do for it in a sales job.

3. In a tough job market, what ethical dilemmas might present themselves to the job seeker? To companies? To employment agencies?

PART

Two

THE PERSONAL SELLING
FUNCTION

CHAPTER 3

EVOLUTION OF PROFESSIONAL SELLING

LEARNING GOALS

- Trace the evolution of modern selling.
- Identify the major contributions of early American salespeople.
- Describe the role of personal selling today.
- Identify the various methods of classifying sales tasks and activities.
- Describe the unique challenges of selling in the 1990s.

THE COLLEGE TRAVELER

During the first half of the twentieth century, sellers of textbooks were known as "college travelers." These people usually had a territory of several states, and they were typical examples of traveling salespersons, living out of their suitcases for lengthy periods.

The college traveler represented a unique position in the publishing world. In addition to selling, the travelers also looked for new manuscripts their companies might be interested in publishing. They served an important public relations role and were a source of information for college professors; for example, travelers often arranged graduate students' first teaching jobs.

The college traveler's mode of transportation was typically by train (between towns) or by bus (within towns), and the time spent in just getting around was substantial. The modern-day publisher's representative's company car, cellular phone, and lap-top computer would have amazed the early college traveler.

Although the college traveler's job was difficult in some ways, in other ways it was less challenging than today's sales job in publishing. There were fewer competing titles, and many publishers could rely on a few staple books that sold predictably high numbers every season. During the summer, college travelers got three months off, or they could choose to work in their companies' offices.[1]

CHAPTER OVERVIEW

In this century, the profession of selling has changed dramatically, and it continues to do so. Understanding and appreciating the historical evolution of selling, the different theories of selling, and the selling process itself can help modern sales managers cope more effectively with the changes currently underway, as well as those they may face in the future.

This chapter describes the evolution of selling, from its ancient roots in medieval society, to colorful early American characters such as the Yankee peddler, to the sophisticated, professional sales forces of today. It has been said that a knowledge of the past can facilitate an understanding of the present. With this idea in mind, we begin a study of the history of selling.

EARLY HISTORY OF SELLING

Many current business practices can be understood best as modern outgrowths of developments that have been underway for decades, and even centuries. One of the clearest examples of such a development is the continuing professionalization of the modern sales force.[2]

Marketing's Early Development

The sales function has been an integral part of commercial activity for thousands of years. Marketing activity was the natural outgrowth of production surpluses. People left the subsistence stage of their economic existence by adopting the techniques of work specialization whereby each person concentrated on the activity in which he or she was the most efficient. This in turn created surpluses of goods, which necessitated the process of exchange.

Trading was the beginning of the modern marketing system. After purchasing their goods, the traders usually resold them in another geographical location. However, the chief marketing function of traders was the physical distribution of goods, not personal selling. In other cases, they (or their immediate families) actually produced the goods that were offered for sale. There was no significant separation of the production and marketing functions. For these reasons, the early traders cannot legitimately be classified as true salespeople. The marketing system characterized by these traders existed for many centuries, and it was not until medieval times that further changes occurred in the personal selling process.

Personal Selling Develops in England

town economy
Medieval economic organization in which commercial activities were concentrated in the population centers

The term *"town economy"* is often used to describe the economic organization of medieval society. Most commercial activities were concentrated in various local population centers because the existing political and social organization was quite fragmented and adequate transportation was not available. Each town (along with its surrounding trade area) became essentially a self-sufficient economic system, at the core of which was the local marketplace, where goods were exchanged on a barter basis. Traditionally, a specific day of the week was set aside as market day; but inadequate road networks prevented many farmers from bringing their produce to the central market. This led to the emergence of an important marketing intermediary: the *agricultural middleman*. These early businesspeople purchased staple farm products in the countryside and transported them to the town market for resale. The agricultural middlemen symbolized the final separation between trading and production, and the emergence of true personal selling.

agricultural middleman Early businessperson who purchased staple products from the countryside and transported them to a local market for resale

After the fall of the Western Roman Empire, England, along with the rest of Europe, was characterized by a fragmented and localized economic organization for centuries. Gradually, however, the chaotic conditions were replaced by a more stable business environment, one that was dominated by guilds (circa 1200–1500). The guild system provided the background from which the first industrial society emerged.

bagman Eighteenth-century salesperson who sold goods produced by the developing factory system

The first true salespersons appeared in the late eighteenth century during England's Industrial Revolution. They were called *bagmen* because they sold their goods from sample bags. They marketed the goods produced by the developing factory system. The first manufacturers to establish such sales forces were the Manchester (England) textile firms. As a result, the term "Manchester man" was often used interchangeably with bagman. Bagmen sold goods for firms in which they did not have an ownership interest. They were purely salespeople, and were the origin of professional selling as it is known today.

In the second half of the eighteenth century, the English pottery manufacturer Josiah Wedgewood was one of the first people to use advanced selling techniques to create a world-wide market for his products. This included establishing display rooms and warehouses in several cities, advertising and promoting his wares extensively, including the distribution of samples, and pricing to penetrate new markets. He hired a sales manager to supervise his sales and marketing efforts. In 1777, he decided that a field sales force was needed to sell his company's products. He was a pioneer in developing the modern approach to personal selling.[3]

The Early American Experience

Yankee peddler
Early American seller, traditionally based in New England, who sold to pioneers

American sales efforts began with the exploits of the *Yankee peddler* sometime during the late seventeenth century. These salespeople, often called "pack peddlers," were traditionally based in New England, but were soon selling on the nation's frontier. Wherever American pioneers went, peddlers soon followed. At first, upstate New York and parts of New Jersey were considered fertile sales territories. But, as competition increased, many peddlers moved on to the West and

JOHN H. PATTERSON

John H. Patterson thought he had made a mistake back in 1884. He had just bought control of National Manufacturing Company (later known as National Cash Register Company, then NCR, before merging in 1991 with AT&T's Computer Systems Division) for $6500. Patterson was so worried that he quickly offered to buy his way out of the deal. The seller refused, so Patterson set out to sell the firm's output—cash registers. At the time, the business community did not understand or want cash registers.

John Patterson changed that situation and, at the same time, introduced so many innovative sales and management techniques that he has been called the "father of modern salesmanship." He began by setting up a system of exclusive sales agents with guaranteed territories. Patterson established sales quotas and held people to them. He was one of the first top executives to allow commissioned sales agents to earn as much money as their abilities permitted.

Patterson also established the concept of the annual sales meeting to promote the exchange of information and ideas. His Century Point Club (so called because its members were those sales agents making 100 percent of quota) began in 1887 with nine agents. At one of the early sales meetings, he asked his brother-in-law, Joseph H. Crane, to discuss how he sold cash registers. Patterson was so impressed by the response that he asked Crane to write what became the first NCR sales primer (and the forerunner to today's sales training manuals).

Since Patterson firmly believed that a person could learn how to become a better sales representative, he made the sales manual that developed from this early effort the basis for NCR selling, and the company's agents were required to learn the principles it contained. The heart of the manual's content was a list of "Don'ts" and a shorter list of "Things to Remember." (See Table 3-1.) He also established the first formal sales training program and required every sales agent to attend.

Patterson did not restrict his managerial innovations to the sales force. He developed newsletters and brochures to communicate with employees and customers. He wrote employee job descriptions, and he established a procedure for employees to write suggestions and complaints to executives and managers. His factories offered good wages and working conditions. And, as a forerunner to today, he began hiring women in the early 1890s—placing some in administrative positions, including possibly the first woman to serve as a corporate lawyer.

---

to the South. By the time of the Revolutionary War, peddlers were operating near the Mississippi River.

Sometime after 1810, two different methods of personal selling developed in the United States. Some of the pack peddlers modified their selling methods by switching to the use of horse-drawn wagons capable of carrying several tons of merchandise. It was common practice for these salespeople, now called *wagon peddlers*, to leave home in the early spring to work their territories, and then to return by late summer. The wagon peddler was a well-known character on the American scene throughout the nineteenth century.

Other peddlers moved into retailing. One of the primary causes of this change was the increasingly strict local licensing requirements imposed on peddlers. Prior to

wagon peddlers
Nineteenth century salespeople, who covered their territories in covered wagons

TABLE 3-1   NCR's Early Sales Guidelines

Ten of NCR's "Don'ts" were:
 1. Don't fail to seat the prospect properly.
 2. Don't point your finger or pencil at him.
 3. Don't sit awkwardly on your chair.
 4. Don't have a calendar on the walls. It may remind him of an appointment or a note falling due.
 5. Don't put your feet on his chair.
 6. Don't smoke.
 7. Don't slap him on the knee or poke him with your finger.
 8. Don't chew gum or tobacco.
 9. Don't tell funny stories.
10. Don't talk fast—go easy and see that the prospect understands what you say and do.

The "Things to Remember" were:
1. Remember that you explain the register to customers for the purpose of securing their orders. The part of a salesman is to do and say that which will bring about this end.
2. Do not intrude your personality on the notice of the prospect, but try to make him forget you and become absorbed in studying the register. To do this, you must forget yourself.
3. You must interest the prospect in the register and what it will do for him, or he will not buy it. You must get him interested at the start, and hold and deepen that interest until you are through with him. Watch him carefully while you are talking and avoid long pauses.
4. The surest way for a salesman to arouse and keep up the interest of the prospect is to have a genuine interest in it himself. No matter how many times he has gone over the same ground, the salesman must not let the demonstration become an old story and so recite in a half-hearted, humdrum manner. Always demonstrate as if the goods were as new and wonderful to you as they are to your listener. Make every demonstration enthusiastic and fresh. This can be done, but it will require you to be always at your best and full of genuine love for your work.

John Patterson's NCR sales manual, his company's formal sales training program, and his other work in building the firm's sales force are now considered significant milestones in the development of contemporary sales practices.

the early 1800s, retail activities were performed by small shops operated by local crafts workers.

The growth of retailing led to the next era in personal selling, in which country stores were granted liberal credit terms by their suppliers. The financial panic of 1837, however, caused a tightening of these arrangements. As a result, the suppliers began to send out *credit investigators* who, in addition to evaluating a retailer's credit and collecting debts, were charged with developing good will. The credit investigators eventually began to sell merchandise to the rural stores.[4] The term "commercial traveler" later was used synonymously with credit investigators.

Rural and small-town store owners each usually made an annual buying trip to the nearest city to purchase merchandise for their stores. This led to the emergence of

credit investigators Supplier-employed people who evaluated retailers' credit and developed good will

greeters Supplier-employed sales representatives who solicited business from retailers on buying trips

early America's *greeters*. Greeters were salespeople who "greeted" the visiting retailers at their hotels by soliciting business for the various suppliers they represented. They later shifted their base of operations to the railroad stations. Greeters were permanent fixtures in nineteenth century trading centers.

As competition intensified, enterprising greeters started boarding the trains outside the city in order to make sales presentations before competitors had an opportunity to lure the prospective buyers away. Soon, the greeters simply journeyed to the merchants' places of business. At this point, "drummer" began to replace "greeter" in America's sales vocabulary.

drummers Nineteenth century salespeople who journeyed to merchants' places of business

The literature suggests two possible derivations of the term *"drummer."* According to one view, it came from the fact that these sales representatives "drummed up" trade for the manufacturers and wholesalers they represented. According to a second explanation, the term was derived from the large trunks carried by these sales personnel. The trunks—often weighing several hundred pounds—were used to transport samples, as well as personal items, during the long sales trips. The round shape of these trunks caused them to be called drums. Since the drums were closely associated with the traveling salesperson of the period, this explanation seems as plausible as the first. Many of these early salespeople went on to become prominent figures in business and public life. For instance, Marshall Field, Aaron Montgomery Ward, and King C. Gillette all started their careers as peddlers or drummers.

Contributions of Early American Salespeople

The territory that became the United States benefited in several ways from the selling carried on by its inhabitants during the years 1650 to 1900:

- The nation's standard of living improved. The goods sold were otherwise unavailable to people located away from the principal urban centers. A relatively efficient sales function allowed the rapid expansion of the country's emerging manufacturing sector.
- Personal selling served as a vehicle of upward economic and social mobility. This was certainly true for thousands of the immigrants who came to the United States.
- Selling also served as a rigorous training ground for future entrepreneurs. Peddling was dominated by young men who later went into other types of enterprises. Many of today's top marketing executives still continue to regard sales as the best management development program.
- The Yankee peddlers performed another essential function on the nation's frontier: They were the only source of information concerning important news events. The peddlers were also known for their storytelling, one of the most popular forms of entertainment in those days. They created considerable American folklore. The drummer later performed similar functions for rural America.

SELLING IN THE TWENTIETH CENTURY

The development of selling during the twentieth century parallels the growth of modern marketing. As businesses have moved from the production era, through the sales era, to widespread acceptance of the marketing concept, salespeople and their managers have adapted. But the essence of selling remains the same—people buy from people. Sales consultant Jack Falvey comments:

> Things were different in the 1890s, but people still bought from people (not from companies), and the salesmen's ability to produce new business, develop new markets, introduce new products, and find new customers (and keep old ones) was as necessary then as it is today.[5]

This section will review the changes that have taken place in selling during this century.

From Production to Sales

Personal selling underwent many changes during the first half of the twentieth century.[6] At first, selling was overshadowed by the tremendous growth of manufacturing. Business practice emphasized producing the product rather than marketing it. Selling was regarded as a secondary activity.

New manufacturing methods eventually led to production surpluses and a buyer's market in the 1920s. The net result was a re-emergence of the sales function and the beginning of what could be called the "era of the modern drummer." Others have called this period the "sales era," or the era of the "selling concept." Sales practices had changed very little since those used by drummers in the 1880s. Canned (or memorized) presentations, originally developed by John H. Patterson of National Cash Register, still dominated selling. The modern drummer, relying on a canned presentation, was characteristic of selling until the beginning of World War II.

Two significant events took place during the years before World War II. First, the Great Depression of the 1930s shook the free enterprise system to its very core. During this economic catastrophe, personal selling assumed a more aggressive posture. Industry favored expanding, or at least maintaining, the sales effort during a time when cost cutting and layoffs in other business areas were commonplace.[7] This marked a milestone in management's acknowledgment of the need for successful marketing.

The second event was the creation and rapid growth of corporate departments designed to support the sales effort, such as marketing research. Previously, many of these marketing support activities were performed by sales personnel who had no interest or ability in these areas. The recognition of the need for staff support was crucial to the development of professional selling.

Economic normalcy returned about 1948—meaning an environment in which sales professionalism continued to develop. The public had spent the excess liquidity built up from the war years 1941 to 1945, and the inflation of the immediate postwar era had begun to subside. This was the beginning of the "modern sales era," the time of the professional salesperson. Companies had to increase their sales forces, and, for the first time, college graduates were recruited extensively for sales positions. A greater emphasis was also placed on sales training, and efforts to raise selling to a professional status increased.[8]

Traditional Sales Approaches

During the modern sales era, the traditional view of the sales function, which has been called the "salesmanship approach," emerged. The salesperson's behavior was regarded as the key ingredient in the sales process. It was assumed that the success or failure of a sales call depended almost entirely on how the salesperson handled the prospect. Three variations of the traditional approach were canned sales presentations, the stimulus-response theory, and selling formulas.

canned sales presentation Structured sales script memorized by the salesperson

Canned Sales Presentations.   As noted above, NCR's founder, John Patterson, developed the first *canned sales presentation*, a prepared, structured sales script memorized by the salesperson. First used extensively in door-to-door selling and now employed by many telemarketers, canned sales presentations provide the salesperson with what a company considers to be the best way to sell.[9] However, the prospect is treated as essentially passive—the major weakness of canned sales presentations.

stimulus-response theory Sales approach that holds that the prospect will buy upon hearing the right sales message

Stimulus-Response Theory.   The premise of *stimulus-response theory* is that prospects are keyed to buy upon hearing a certain set of statements presented in the correct manner. If a salesperson says or does the proper things (i.e., provides the right stimulus), a prospect will respond to the stimulus by purchasing the good or service. This relationship is shown below:

$$\text{Stimulus} \longrightarrow \text{Response}$$
$$\text{[The correct selling} \qquad \text{[A successful sale]}$$
$$\text{statement or action]}$$

selling formulas Sales approach in which salespeople lead prospects through distinct stages of the buying process in a persuasive manner

Selling Formulas.   The *selling formulas* approach, a variation of the canned sales presentation, has salespeople lead prospects through various steps in a persuasive manner. An early example was Arthur Frederick Sheldon's formula published in 1902: AIDR (attention, interest, desire, resolve).[10] The Sheldon selling course, the first comprehensive course of its type, went through numerous revisions and became the accepted procedure for effective selling. The basis of Sheldon's argument was that the prospective buyer went through four identifiable stages—attention, interest, desire, and resolve—on the way to making a purchase decision. It is interesting to note that many modern marketing textbooks refer to the AIDA (attention, interest, desire, action) approach toward personal selling or advertising. AIDA is simply an update of Sheldon's AIDR concept and also emphasizes persuasive ability in that it proposes salespeople should be able to lead the prospect through each of the stages. A 1908 brochure entitled *What Is Salesmanship?* described the Sheldon method in this manner:

> You can take two men of apparently equal ability, teach them both the same facts about any line, send them out, and one man will sell twice as much as the other. The one . . . knew better how to appeal to the minds of his customers. He could persuade.[11]

In 1924, the Sheldon course defined successful selling as "the art of inducing conscious, willing agreement, resulting in a sale mutually beneficial to buyer and seller."[12] This definition again emphasized selling as an art that is performed by the salesperson. The phrase "inducing conscious, willing agreement" is descriptive of the traditional viewpoint of the sales function.

The only determinants of an effective sales presentation, according to the traditional viewpoint, are product qualities and customer needs. This approach is simplistic, since it ignores the fact that the sales function is performed within the context of changing environmental conditions.[13]

Emergence of the Marketing Concept

marketing concept
Philosophy of customer orientation that came of age during the 1950s and 1960s

During the 1950s and early 1960s, the *marketing concept* emerged as a framework for business. Best described as a philosophy of customer orientation, the marketing concept led to major changes in business organizations. All marketing functions were grouped under a top marketing executive. Sales remained the line function within the marketing organization, but now the service functions were coordinated to an extent not previously possible. The formation of technically qualified sales support departments aided in the professionalization of the field sales force.

As salespeople became more professional, they became more customer-oriented, in line with the customer orientation of the marketing concept. In the sexist language of the early 1960s, one writer described these changes in the following way:

> From bits and pieces of evidence in all sectors of U.S. business, it is now possible to discern the emergence of a new dominant type, a man with a softer touch and greater breadth, a new kind of man to do a new—much more significant—kind of job.
> Whereas the old-time salesman devoted himself primarily to pushing a product, or a line of products, the new-era salesman is involved with the whole distribution pipeline, beginning with the tailoring of products to the customer's desire and extending through their promotion and advertising to final delivery to the ultimate consumer.[14]

Selling continued to change in the 1970s. The problem-solving role of the salesperson received special emphasis. A *Business Week* special report described the salesperson of this decade:

> Today's supersalesman is far more than a seller of goods and services. In response to keener competition, savvier purchasing practices, and a growing recognition that you must satisfy a need rather than sell a product, the supersalesman must plug into nearly all facets of a prospect's business that bear on the product that the salesman is pushing. These might range from equipment amortization and inventory control to distribution.[15]

The emerging view of professional selling during recent years has emphasized helping customers to buy rather than attempting to sell them something. The focus of market-driven selling has shifted to an increased emphasis on solving customer problems and building long-term relationships. Effective salespeople have learned

SALES MANAGEMENT IN PRACTICE

F. G. (BUCK) RODGERS

Although the early 1990s have been difficult for IBM, during the 1970s and most of the 1980s, IBM was considered to be one of the finest sales and marketing organizations in the world. Much of the credit for this went to F. G. (Buck) Rodgers, who became IBM's senior marketing executive in 1974 when he was selected IBM Vice President of Marketing. This capped a career begun as an IBM salesperson in 1950 after his graduation from college.

Rodgers's sales and marketing approach reflected IBM's dedication to the customer. In his book *The IBM Way*, Rodgers wrote: "At IBM everybody sells! . . . Every employee has been trained to think that the customer comes first—everybody from the CEO, to the people in finance, to the receptionists, to those who work in manufacturing."[16]

Under Rodgers's direction, IBM developed comprehensive sales training and management programs that emphasized product and customer knowledge and, most importantly, a high level of service support after the sale. IBM's salespeople were taught to provide solutions to their customers in addition to selling equipment. Rodgers emphasized that "customers, rather than technology, establish the direction at IBM."

Rodgers's personal commitment to quality carried through to the IBM sales force. He believed in spending time and money to find quality salespeople. After finding these people, IBM provided them with a demanding sales training program. Role playing and other sophisticated training approaches were used to prepare sales trainees for marketplace conditions. Salespeople were taught to concentrate on what a product would do, not what it was. This enabled them to understand customers' problems and to offer sensible solutions. IBM rewarded its salespeople by providing them with meaningful and challenging assignments, paying salaries and incentives based on a "pay for performance" philosophy, and rewarding superior performance through honors and recognition.

Under Buck Rodgers's sales leadership, IBM became known as a company that maintained close working relationships with customers. Rodgers's and IBM's commitment to customer service and quality became the benchmarks by which many other sales organizations were judged.

that questioning and needs analysis have replaced the sales presentation as the most important step in the selling process.[17]

Many factors have contributed to the growth of professional, needs-oriented selling. These include the following:

Increased Sophistication of Buyers. This trend has resulted primarily from expanded efforts in the area of consumer education. The net result is a growing rejection of the modern drummer in the marketplace.

Further Professionalization of Purchasing Management. With a strict certification program, this occupational group has made great strides in enhancing professionalism in its ranks. This trend has also enhanced the professionalism of sales personnel who deal with contemporary purchasing management.

Wider Adoption of the Marketing Concept. The nearly universal acceptance of the marketing concept means that the sales force must update its policies, procedures, and practices. This is especially true for banks, telecommunications companies, and other service businesses that have had to become more competitive.

Better Training of Salespeople. Companies are providing salespeople with better, more extensive training. The well-trained salespeople of today are very different from those of the past.[18]

Teamwork in Selling

Perhaps the greatest change in selling in recent years has been the emergence of the salesperson as part of a team. In the past, field sales representatives were essentially loners. Such individuals had infrequent contact with their field sales managers, and salespeople in general had virtually no personal contact with other employees of their firms. Although often constituting a firm's only marketing effort, the sales force was typically isolated from the company's other parts.

Better communications and transportation helped alleviate this problem. But companies also began recognizing the role field salespeople played as integral parts of their marketing teams. They were given support from staff personnel and assigned responsibility for providing marketing information to staff members of the marketing team. Today's salespeople, instead of being loners, are far more likely to be part of a team working toward group goals. This involves coordinating sales and marketing efforts across product lines to customers, which requires an integrated approach.[19]

As noted earlier, most companies have expanded their sales and marketing capabilities by adding personnel to provide vital support activities to the sales force. Marketing research, distributor relations, marketing planning, sales promotion, and inside selling are examples of activities that now assist the direct selling effort. If the modern salesperson is to be a true problem solver, he or she must know how to use the expertise and knowledge of other company personnel.

systems selling
Team approach to selling that requires salespeople to bring all relevant components of the firm to bear in solving customers' problems

Systems selling, an approach developed in the 1970s to market computers, scientific instruments, machine tools, and other complex equipment, calls for a team approach to selling. In particular, it requires that a salesperson bring all the relevant components of the vendor's firm to bear on solving customer problems.[20] The process of systems selling begins with needs analysis, which assesses the prospective buyer's business and mode of operation. In the case of products like a computer system, the front-line salesperson may get support from technical personnel. But the systems approach to selling does not end there. Possibly even more important than the equipment capabilities the vendor provides to its sales force is the support it provides to the buyer directly, primarily in the form of training of operators and maintenance service turnaround time once the system has been purchased.

AT&T, IBM, and other information management companies use the team approach in developing effective sales techniques that involve sales support personnel. The sales representative has the primary responsibility for assigned accounts, but he or she must allocate other resources and support staff to meet the complex information needs of customers. Several major types of specialists assist sales representatives by providing sales support. Systems engineers design the systems, oversee their installation, and train customers in how to use them. Field engineers are specialists who serve as customer engineers to solve hardware problems, and product support representatives have responsibility for maintaining the software. These sales teams are important to sales success.

In general, there are three forms of team selling approaches. The first involves members of the sales force working together as a team. For instance, a field sales manager may accompany a salesperson on a joint call to a key customer. A second form of team selling involves integrating the efforts of other key personnel and departments with sales personnel. This is the approach used by IBM. The third form involves an even wider range of participants, including buyers and other vendors. Each form will require adjustments in the way a company conducts its sales and sales training activities. It is especially critical that sales training programs prepare individual participants for their specific roles and give them a clear understanding of how what they do affects the rest of the sales team.[21]

SALES ACTIVITIES AND TASKS

Sales tasks are the job activities carried out by salespeople. Another way to view the evolution of modern selling is to categorize salespeople by their tasks. Although the nature and extent of sales tasks and activities vary widely across industries and among companies, there are some activities that are common to most sales positions. Table 3-2 presents a list of the major sales activities and tasks.

Classifying Salespeople

creative selling
Arousing demand and influencing patronage
service selling
Aiding the customer in bringing a sale to completion

The simplest, two-way classification of salespeople is the division of selling into creative selling and service selling. *Creative selling* involves arousing demand and influencing patronage. *Service selling* aids the customer in bringing the sale to completion. An insurance sales agent who must make potential buyers aware of the need for insurance and convince them to purchase policies would be an example of creative selling. In contrast, retail salespeople who mainly assist their customers in the selection of purchases represent service selling.

TABLE 3-2   Sales Activities and Tasks

Activity	Representative tasks
Selling	Prospecting, planning and making sales presentations, handling objections
Handling orders	Writing orders, expediting orders, locating lost orders
Product servicing	Delivering and installing products, training customers
Information handling	Receiving customer feedback, providing technical information
Account servicing	Handling inventory control, stocking shelves, setting up promotional displays
Conferences and meetings	Attending conferences and sales meetings, setting up trade show exhibits
Training	Training new salespeople, traveling with sales trainees
Entertaining	Taking a customer to dinner, hosting a party, playing golf with customers
Traveling	Spending a night on the road, traveling out of town
Assisting distributors	Establishing relations with distributors, collecting past due accounts

A somewhat more extensive classification might include four types of sales tasks: development, missionary, maintenance, and support.[22] Sales development concerns the creation of customers through methods such as motivating buyers to change vendors. Missionary salespeople pull the product through the marketing channel by providing low-key personal selling assistance. Maintenance selling involves the generation of sales volume from existing customers. A support salesperson provides continuing service to the buyer. The support salesperson also sells directly by suggesting a replacement item rather than the repair of an older product. All of these tasks are important, and each makes a significant contribution to the total marketing effort.

These tasks can also be viewed as a series of selling situations. The field salesperson's job usually involves a blend of them. Salesperson A might spend 45 percent of the time in sales development work, 25 percent in missionary sales, 20 percent in sales maintenance, and 10 percent in sales support. Salesperson B might have a different mix of activities: development, 5 percent; missionary, 15 percent; maintenance, 60 percent; and support, 20 percent. While most salespeople perform all four tasks to some extent, they can be classified by the activity they spend the bulk of their time doing. Salesperson A would be a sales development specialist, and salesperson B would be classified as a maintenance salesperson.

Many companies try to expand the creative selling activities of maintenance and support salespeople. For instance, Averitt Express, a Tennessee trucking firm, has transformed its delivery truck drivers into salespeople. They carry business cards, solicit additional business from customers, pass out sales literature, and even call on new customers. They are also encouraged to look for outbound orders when they make a delivery.[23]

Extending the Sales Classification of Sales Personnel

Thomas Wotruba presents five distinct stages in the evolution of selling.[24] Although this analysis is similar to the above classification format, Wotruba's approach goes beyond other classification efforts and presents a more comprehensive overview of the various forms of salespeople and selling tasks. He notes that a cross section of sales jobs will include some at each stage of the evolutionary process because of the many competitive and market environments in which salespeople and their companies operate.

Wotruba defines the five stages in the evolution of selling as follows:

1. *Provider.* This is the earliest stage in the development of selling. The salesperson simply accepts orders from buyers and supplies the product desired. There is no effort to identify a buyer's needs or to tailor a sales presentation to the buyer's interest. Inbound telemarketing sales representatives who take orders called in by customers, route salespeople-drivers who service retail establishments, and sales clerks in self-service retail stores are examples.
2. *Persuader.* In this stage, the salesperson attempts to convince the buyer to purchase the seller's product rather than a competitive product. The success of the salesperson is dependent upon his or her ability to influence buyers. Insurance and automobile salespeople, outbound telemarketers, and door-to-door salespeople illustrate this stage of selling.

3. *Prospector.* In this stage, the salesperson seeks out selected buyers perceived to have a need for a product. The salesperson considers what the needs of the potential buyer might be and how they might be satisfied by the product being sold. A car insurance sales representative calling on a new car buyer and an office supplies salesperson calling on small business owners are examples.

4. *Problem solver.* This is the stage that most closely resembles the type of professional selling most commonly encountered today. The problem solver is a salesperson who is committed to diagnosing a customer's needs and concerns. The customer participates in defining these needs. The salesperson then presents a selection of available product offerings and helps the buyer select a product that meets the buyer's needs and solves the problem. "Adaptive selling," "consultative selling," and "sales negotiation" are terms used to describe this stage of selling. Team selling is also prevalent at this stage. Industrial salespeople and sales teams selling electronics, computers, telecommunications, and other high-tech products act as problem solvers.

5. *Procreator.* This is the most advanced stage of selling. In addition to defining a buyer's problem or needs and the possible solutions, it involves creating a unique offering to match the specific needs of the buyer. The procreator not only has the responsibility for overseeing the formulation of unique product offerings, but also can adjust price, credit terms, delivery, and other parts of the marketing mix to meet a specific customer's needs. "Systems selling" and "national account management" are terms used to describe this sales approach. A specific example of a procreator is a materials handling equipment salesperson who designs and sells a system to fit a buyer's manufacturing plan.

SELLING IN THE 1990s

Changes in professional selling continue as the year 2000 approaches. Sales researchers and consultants, like noted sales trainer Larry Wilson, point out that buyers will not be satisfied with a "product solution."[25] Customers are buying not only a product, but also a relationship with the salesperson. They are looking for salespeople who can serve as trusted consultants, and they want "value-added" service that exceeds their expectations.[26] To Wilson, this means giving buyers more service, more help, and more understanding than they thought possible.

In Chap. 1, some of the terms used to describe modern sales approaches were introduced. These included "partnering," "relationship selling," "team selling," "value-added selling," and "consultative selling." Each of them suggests that the focus of the selling process is to develop long-term relationships with customers. This depends on buyers having confidence in the salesperson's knowledge and ability. In other words, the sale is the beginning of the relationship—not its end.

There has been considerable research into the process by which salespeople develop relationships with buyers. These relationships involve a combination of situational, personal, and dyadic relationship factors.[27] In the buyer-seller dyad, two people interact. Modern research recognizes that many factors can affect this interaction between a salesperson and a buyer.[28]

Two researchers' views of the buyer-seller dyad reflect current thinking. In the early 1980s, Barton Weitz concentrated his analysis on the variables related to a specific situation. These included the interactions between sales behaviors (such as the type of sales message), the resources of the salesperson, the nature of the customer's buying task, and characteristics of the salesperson-customer relationship. Weitz stated that more attention should be paid to understanding the key characteristics of the salesperson-customer relationship, such as the relative power of each party, the level of conflict the relationship involves, and each party's anticipation of future interactions.[29]

More recently, Professors Kaylene Williams, Rosann Spiro, and Leslie Fine developed a model of the customer-salesperson interaction which focuses on communication as the essence of the interaction.[30] They emphasized that a salesperson interacts with customers and does not act on them. According to their model, salespeople must develop their interactive communications skills, such as careful listening and speaking with clarity, if they are to develop more effective salesperson-buyer interactions.

As the study by Williams, Spiro, and Fine suggests, selling involves an interpersonal communications process with a feedback mechanism. The overall communications process is outlined in Fig. 3-1. The sender (salesperson) transmits a message through a medium (sales presentation) to the receiver (prospect). The resulting interaction provides the necessary feedback mechanism and closes the communications system. While this description is admittedly simplified, it points out that the prospect is no longer viewed as passive, but is now seen as playing an active role in the sales process. The prospect responds, interacts, and communicates with the salesperson.

The view of selling as a communications process focuses on interpersonal factors that reflect the interaction between the dyadic parties. Research has indicated that the greater the similarity between seller and prospect, the greater the possibility of a sale. For instance, R. B. Evans' classic study of life insurance selling found that the more alike the salesperson and prospect are, and the more the prospect knows about the salesperson and the company, the more likely the prospect is to buy the insurance.[31]

Salespeople dealing with business-to-business and organizational purchasing situations face a special set of problems and must adapt the selling process to these

FIGURE 3-1 Selling as an Interpersonal Communications Process.

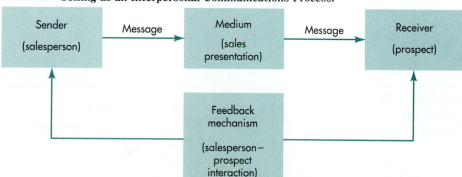

practices.[32] As a general rule, industrial buyers are more knowledgeable and more demanding than consumers. The buying process is usually longer and more complex.

Various studies of what industrial buyers expect from salespeople emphasize further the importance of building relationships through effective communication. Salespeople must have considerable knowledge, and they must possess the communications and selling skills to use this knowledge to solve customers' problems. The best salespeople are those who develop partnership relationships with their customers by continuously solving those customers' problems. Thoroughness and followup are also critical to developing satisfactory seller-purchaser relationships.[33]

Industrial purchasers go through three distinct stages in the buying process. First, they determine which product is suitable for the particular job. Next, they determine which vendors will receive trial orders. Third, they evaluate trial orders and decide whether to retain or drop a supplier.

At each stage in the adoption process, different parts of the buying organization make their influence felt. While purchasing and top management are always involved to some extent, the other participants vary from stage to stage. Many purchasing decisions stretch out over several months and involve many different people. Sales of capital equipment, high-tech products, or other complicated goods and services require significant preliminary work and may take many months or even years to close.[34] Salespeople must be able to identify and isolate the key buying influence in each stage. It is not difficult to visualize how a salesperson in such circumstances would have problems in identifying key buying influences. Some salespersons are simply unable to spot the decision makers. As a result, much of their activity and sales effort is wasted.

An instance of a very complex and drawn-out sales situation involved a salesperson of hospital equipment who had to wage a year-long campaign to sell $1.4 million worth of capital equipment. She had to convince the eighteen doctors who would use the equipment, the head technician who would operate it, the state regulators who had to approve the purchase, and the hospital's administration and board of directors. She participated in almost fifty meetings before the sale was completed.[35]

selling center
Group of salespeople and support personnel set up to meet a buyer's needs

buying center
People who participate in an industrial purchase decision

To meet the multiple demands and buying influences of organizational buyers, many industrial marketers are turning to sales teams, national account selling, and other methods of handling complex buying situations.[36] *Selling centers* consisting of sales and support personnel are set up to coordinate the sales and marketing activities of the vendor with the purchasing needs of the buyer. The goal is to identify and influence the various *buying center* participants, or those people who participate in an industrial purchase decision. This approach has important implications for sales strategy, organization, and training.[37]

SUMMARY OF LEARNING GOALS

1. **Trace the Evolution of Modern Selling.**

   The origins of selling started with the need to sell surplus goods. Ancient traders had as their chief task the distribution of goods, not personal selling, and oftentimes they produced the goods themselves. The production and personal selling functions eventually were separated by the medieval "agricultural middleman," who bought goods from farmers and then sold them in city markets. During the eighteenth century, England's Industrial Revolution produced the "bagman," and many companies employed sales forces of bagmen to market their factories' goods.

Early America had its own selling evolution, starting with the "Yankee peddler," who was based in New England but followed the movements of the pioneers westward. The years following 1810 saw the advent of the "wagon peddler." Modern retailing was born when strict licensing requirements began to limit the activities of the peddlers. Suppliers began to cater to the new retailers, hiring "credit investigators," "greeters," and "drummers" to make up their sales forces. As early as 1884, John H. Patterson, known as the "father of modern salesmanship," established sales territories, provided commissions, and used motivational tools such as handbooks and annual conventions.

2. Identify the Major Contributions of Early American Salespeople.

The major benefits that were derived from the first 250 years of selling in the United States were the following:

- An improved standard of living for the nation
- A vehicle for upward economic and social mobility
- A training ground for future entrepreneurs
- Dissemination of information

3. Describe the Role of Personal Selling Today.

Today, salespeople are customer-oriented and professional. They play a problem-solving role and emphasize the building of long-term relationships. This attitude toward selling is in marked contrast to that of the past, where the selling process was considered finished as soon as the good or service was bought by the customer.

4. Identify the Various Methods of Classifying Sales Tasks and Activities.

Sales tasks and activities can be classified in terms of the following categories:

- Creative selling versus service selling
- Development, missionary, maintenance, and support selling
- Provider, persuader, prospector, problem solver, and procreator

5. Describe the Unique Challenges of Selling in the 1990s.

Selling is more challenging than ever. Not only are salespeople required to sell their goods and services, they are also expected to sell a relationship and give more service, help, and understanding to clients than ever before. Modern salespeople must be creative in their efforts to satisfy customers, and they must have a thorough understanding of their own products and their customers' businesses, each of which is becoming increasingly complex.

REVIEW QUESTIONS

1. What development necessitated the process of exchange? How was early trading different from modern selling?
2. In terms of the evolution of selling, what did agricultural middlemen represent? Why are bagmen considered to be the first real salespeople?
3. What is the difference between a bagman, a Yankee peddler, and a wagon peddler? What was the stimulus for the move from peddling to retailing?
4. Who was John Patterson? What contributions did he make to selling?
5. What is meant by the "era of the modern drummer"? Describe two events that were significant for selling before World War II.
6. What is the major strength of canned sales presentations? What is this form of selling's major weakness?
7. According to the traditional viewpoint, what are the only two determinants of a successful presentation? Why is this approach considered simplistic now?
8. What factors have contributed to the growth of professional, needs-oriented selling?
9. Describe three forms of team selling. Which of these does IBM use? Also discuss "Buck" Rodgers's vision of "the IBM way."
10. How are industrial buyers different than general consumers? What three stages do buyers go through in the industrial buying process?

DISCUSSION QUESTIONS

1. Prepare a profile of someone who has contributed to the development of professional selling. Present the highlights of your profile in class.
2. There are many contemporary manifestations of early selling practices. Match each of the following terms to its modern counterpart.

   A. Early trader
   B. Agricultural middleman
   C. Bagman
   D. Wagon peddler
   E. Drummer

   1. Seller of popcorn from a trailer at a county fair
   2. Buster Brown representative who calls on clothing buyers at stores in which they work
   3. Quilter who sells her output at a monthly flea market
   4. Door-to-door salesperson who carries sample products and returns what he or she does not sell
   5. Teenager who buys newspapers and is unable to return what is not sold

3. The activities of street vendors operating out of shopping carts or automobiles have been restricted recently in Manhattan, New York; Elizabeth, New Jersey; and Santa Ana, California.[38] What early American sellers do these modern-day vendors resemble? What do you think public policy should be in regard to this activity? Justify your answer.

4. *Death of a Salesman*, by Arthur Miller, was published in 1947. The play, which won a Pulitzer Prize, was about a sixty-year-old traveling salesman named Willy Loman who just could not seem to make it anymore. Willy's speech in the play contains clues to his selling stance; phrases such as "personal attractiveness," being "well-liked," "making an appearance," and "creating a personal interest" are used to describe the way a salesperson "gets ahead." Describe the status of personal selling at the time of the play's publication. Was Willy Loman a product of his time? Explain.

5. United States Surgical has been selling surgical stapling equipment for over two decades, and the company is now planning to go into the suture market. Would you classify the selling effort that this new market will require as creative or service selling? As a development, missionary, maintenance, or support task? Explain.

ETHICAL DILEMMA

The purchasing agent for a large printing company has promised Judy Marshall, a new salesperson for a printing supplier, a large order if Judy gives the purchasing agent a kickback of one-third of Judy's commission on the sale. Even if Judy does this, she will earn over $1,000 on the sale. What should she do?

SALES MANAGEMENT CASE

Everybody's World

Personal selling has come a long way since John Patterson admonished his NCR sales force not to slap a prospect on the knee or "poke him with your finger." In Patterson's day, and for a long time to follow, sales forces were made up of a homogeneous group of individuals who sold to a similarly homogeneous customer base. In the 1990s, however, sales forces and customer groups are ethnically diverse, and a salesperson or a prospect is as likely to be a "her" as a "him."

Earl Middleton, a black real estate broker in South Carolina, runs a sales office that is a good example of modern-day diversity. All types of people make up Middleton's fourteen-member sales team, from black grandmothers to white farmers. The sales force appeals to a wide range of customers; as a rule, half of Middleton's customers are black and half are white.

Minorities and women are now an integral part of most sales forces, even in industrial selling, which has traditionally been considered a "man's" world. John Patterson probably would not have hired a women to sell cash registers, but today women are selling all kinds of industrial products. Goodyear Tire & Rubber is just one of the many companies with at least one women selling for its industrial division.

Employing a diverse sales force is a necessary element in modern selling. For one thing, discriminatory hiring practices are illegal; for another, a diverse sales force appeals to a diverse customer group. Finally, stereotyping significant segments of the population as unqualified to sell severely limits a company's competitiveness. For example, Cheryl Womak, who wanted to go on the road and sell insurance, was told by her employer to stay at home for her husband. Womak turned in her resignation the

next day and started her own business, which, 10 years later, is thriving. Her former employer, meanwhile, has gone out of business.

Questions

1. For women or minority salespeople whose presence is unusual in a field, which of John Patterson's "Things to Remember" might be difficult? Explain.

2. A key customer has requested that he not be serviced by one of your minority salespeople. You feel certain that the salesperson has done nothing wrong, but rather the customer is guilty of prejudice. You do not want to offend the salesperson, and, on the other hand, you do not want to lose the customer. How do you handle this situation?

3. Most women and minorities mention that, at first, they had to prove themselves to customers who did not expect them to do a good job. What can women and minority salespeople do to enhance the confidence of skeptics?

CHAPTER 4

PRELIMINARY STEPS IN THE SELLING PROCESS

LEARNING GOALS

- Understand the two basic steps in the personal selling process, prospecting and preparing, which are preliminary to the later steps of presenting, handling objections, closing, and following up.
- List the most common sources of prospects.
- Explain the MAN concept of qualifying a prospect.
- Understand the pre-approach activities needed to adequately prepare for a sales call.
- Understand the sequence of call planning activities needed to prepare for a sales call.

FINDING NEW BUSINESS

Of the many ways that salespeople can accomplish the preliminary steps of selling, one of the most effective is company-sponsored seminars. Sales organizations send prospects invitations to these events, where the emphasis is on general industry happenings but information is given out on the company's products. The technique is especially useful for technically complex products and for expensive items whose sales require a long time to close. Seminars are unique in the way they attract promising prospects; potential customers qualify themselves simply by responding to the invitation and showing up.

Almost every company that sponsors seminars focuses on a soft sell and the initial steps of establishing business relationships. The purpose is to inform and educate, not to make a sale right then and there. Some companies do not even involve their salespeople in the seminars at all. Rather, seminar leaders provide leads to the salespeople for followup after the session is over.

Gallagher Systems, Inc., a Virginia-based computer equipment seller, does use its salespeople to run its seminars, although the focus of the seminars is educational. The company uses salespeople rather than more technically oriented employees because its market is nontechnical.

The Gallagher seminars are objective overviews of the industry, with Gallagher products touted in a subtle manner. Each prospect is asked to fill out a questionnaire that both critiques the seminar and asks information about the future needs of the prospect's company. Gallagher salespeople use these questionnaires when they contact the most promising leads the following week. Here again, the approach is subtle; salespeople may maintain contact with prospects for several months before a sale is sought.[1]

There are an infinite number of places where new business can be found, and it is the job of all salespeople to recognize and seize opportunities when they arise. Chapters 4 and 5 will teach you how to do both by effectively implementing the preliminary and advanced steps of the selling process.

CHAPTER OVERVIEW

Experience in personal selling is a prerequisite for people seeking to advance to a position in marketing or sales management, particularly when the job involves direct customer contact. An understanding of the actual operation of the selling process is also vital to the study of its managerial aspects.

In fact, a number of corporate chief executive officers (CEOs) have emphasized that selling is an important part of any CEO's job. Harvey Mackay, chief executive officer of Mackay Envelope Company and popular author of many books and articles on selling including *Swim with the Sharks without Being Eaten Alive,* is one such proponent. Mackay has written that the top management of any company should be actively and visibly involved with a firm's sales force and selling programs. There are many reasons for this, including the need to learn whether salespeople know their prospects, whether they are effective negotiators, and whether they treat their customers in a consistent and equitable manner.[2]

A similar view was presented by James Koch, who founded The Boston Beer Company, which produces the popular Samuel Adams Beer. Koch wrote:

> . . . it's really selling that drives most businesses: the direct interface between the product and the customer, the crucial feedback loop. And if more CEOs had to go out and sell their products, day in and day out, they'd pay a lot more attention to what they were making. The more unwilling they are to put themselves in the middle of that transaction, the better chance they have of missing out on a critical element of their business. When you're out there selling, face-to-face with your customer, there's no place to hide. It's the acid test.[3]

Building on the evolution of professional selling presented in the previous chapter, Chaps. 4 and 5 describe the separate, but closely related, activities of the personal selling process. These include prospecting, preparing, presenting, handling objections, closing, and following up, as shown in Fig. 4-1.

Sales managers must have a thorough understanding of the selling process. They must continuously recruit and select people who can carry out their organization's selling process effectively. They must direct and advise their salespeople as they go

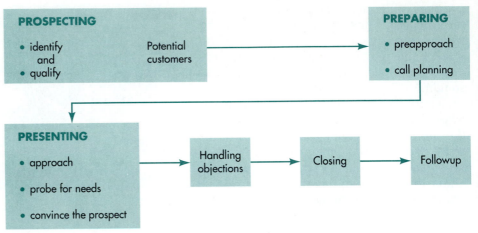

FIGURE 4-1 The Selling Process.

through these steps. Sales managers must also be prepared to assist salespeople when they encounter difficulties during the selling process, and they must praise and reward effective performance.[4]

The discussion of selling in Chaps. 4 and 5 focuses on practical sales techniques. Inherent in this "how-to" approach to selling is the belief that a salesperson can stimulate a prospect to buy if the selling process is skillfully handled.[5] Careful attention must be paid to each step in the selling process. In this chapter, prospecting and preparing to sell will be considered. For the reader who wishes to find out more about selling techniques and strategies, selected books and publications are listed in Tables 4-1 and 4-2.

TABLE 4-1   Selected Books about Selling

Chapters 4 and 5 provide a brief review of the selling process. For a more complete discussion, there are a large number of selling trade books and textbooks available. A short list of these books is presented below.

Anthony Alessandra, James Cathcart, and Phillip Wexter, *Selling by Objectives*, Englewood Cliffs, NJ: Prentice-Hall, 1988.

Porter Henry, *Secrets of Master Sellers*, New York: ANACOM, 1987.

Tom Hopkins, *How to Master the Art of Selling*, 2nd ed., New York: Warner Books, 1982.

David L. Kurtz and H. Robert Dodge, *Professional Selling*, 6th ed., Homewood, IL: Irwin, 1991.

Robert B. Miller and Stephen E. Heiman with Tad Tuleja, *Strategic Selling*, New York: Warner Books, 1985.

Neil Rackham, *SPIN Selling*, New York: McGraw-Hill, 1988.

Frederick A. Russell, Frank H. Beach, and Richard Buskirk, *Selling: Principles and Practices*, 12th ed., New York: McGraw-Hill, 1988.

Michael P. Wynne, *Sci-Tech Selling: Selling Scientific and Technical Products and Services*, Englewood Cliffs, NJ: Prentice-Hall, 1987.

TABLE 4-2   Sources of Articles about Selling

For up-to-date information on selling techniques and practices, the following publications often include articles about professional selling and sales management.

American Salesman
National Research Bureau, Inc.
424 N. Third Street
Burlington, IA 52601

Business Horizons
Indiana University Graduate
School of Business
Indiana University
Bloomington, IN 47405

Harvard Business Review
Harvard Business School
Soldiers Field
Boston, MA 02163

Inc.
Goldhirst Group
38 Commercial Wharf
Boston, MA 02110

Industrial Marketing Management
Elsevier Science Publishing Co., Inc.
52 Vanderbilt Avenue
New York, NY 10017

Journal of Marketing
American Marketing Association
250 S. Wacker Drive
Chicago, IL 60606

Journal of Personal Selling & Sales Management
Pi Sigma Epsilon
45 North Avenue
Hartland, WI 53209

Marketing News
American Marketing Association
250 S. Wacker Drive
Chicago, Il 60606

Personal Selling Power
P. O. Box 5467
Frederickson, VA 22403

Sales & Marketing Management
Bill Communications, Inc.
633 Third Avenue
New York, NY 10017

PROSPECTING

prospecting
Identifying potential customers and qualifying them to determine if they are valid prospects

The selling process begins with *prospecting*, or finding qualified potential buyers. In all types of selling except retail, it is unlikely that customers will come to the salesperson. Salespeople must seek out potential customers. Two major activities are involved in prospecting: identifying potential customers (sales leads), and qualifying these potential customers to determine if they are valid prospects.

The identification of potential customers is not an easy task. It can be very frustrating to beginning salespersons in particular. Immediate payoffs are often limited, and prospecting efforts are often met with rejection. Yet experienced salespeople and sales managers will point out that good prospecting frequently separates successful salespeople from mediocre ones. In a study of financial services salespeople, it was revealed that effective and ineffective salespeople differ in how they identify and assess potential customers. This, in turn, has important implications for the subsequent allocation of sales efforts. The study concluded that sales training should be directed toward helping new salespeople improve the efficiency of prospecting.[6]

Successful salespeople develop a strategy for prospecting that involves an organized and active system for generating sales leads and qualifying potential buyers. One approach that some successful salespeople use to develop and nurture sales

SALES MANAGEMENT IN PRACTICE

SANFORD CORPORATION

It has been said that you should not mix business and pleasure, but for salespeople, this adage does not always apply. John Layton is a sales representative for Sanford Corp., a marketer of office supplies, and he, for one, is a firm believer in the positive synergy of a business and pleasure mixture.

Layton is known for throwing parties to which he invites all the employees of a client company, from the lowest paid to the highest. Layton likes this indiscriminate invitation-giving for two reasons. For one thing, managers appreciate their employees—who are often ignored or taken for granted—being made to feel like an important and recognized part of the organization.

For another, you never know who will be promoted, and someday that hard-working secretary may have a substantial degree of control over what vendor the company uses.

Layton, like many effective salespeople, is as much an entertainer as a businessperson. He bought his house partly because it was able to accommodate parties. He has a policy of never lunching alone, and more often than not, he has business people over for dinner in the evenings.

If Layton shuns the idea of not mixing business and pleasure, he does seem to embrace at least one old wisdom: The way to a person's heart is through the stomach. In any event, business, pleasure, and Layton's gregarious personality are certainly a good mix, providing not only networking opportunities but also a lot of fun for a lot of people.

---

networking
Process of acquiring new contacts and cultivating existing ones

contacts is *networking,* an active process of acquiring new contacts and cultivating existing ones. As described by sales management consultant Gerald Michaelson:

> A solid network grows from continuous investments of time and resources. It is a combination of new acquaintances and deep friendships: good networking involves both getting those new acquaintances and developing them into lasting friends.[7]

The key steps involved in the prospecting process are shown in Fig. 4-2. The process begins with the target market identification—determining the type of person or organization that is most likely to purchase a given good or service. Marketing researchers, product managers, market planners, and sales managers can help a salesperson define the target market. Also, by networking and talking with members of the target market group, a salesperson can learn more about customer needs and further define the target market. A market survey can also be used to learn more about the target market.[8] For instance, a salesperson for medical equipment may carry out a simple survey of doctors, hospitals, and other health care facilities in an assigned territory to gain a basic understanding of the local market's dimensions and needs.

sales lead Firm or organization that might need a given good or service

The next step in the process is to generate sales leads. A *sales lead* is any specific person or organization that might need a given good or service. As will be discussed in the next section, there are many ways to generate sales leads. However, the most productive salespeople use those techniques that experience has

FIGURE 4-2 The Prospecting Process.

Define target market → Generate sales leads → Qualify prospects shown yield the best results. In general, the more a salesperson knows about the kinds of prospects desired, the easier it is to locate them.

The final step is to qualify the prospect. Qualifying involves making sure the person identified definitely has a need for the product, the desire to buy, and the financial resources to buy, as well as having the decision-making authority to do so. Of course, there will be other specific factors that may be relevant to a given good or service.[9]

IDENTIFYING PROSPECTS

Prospects come from many sources: friends and acquaintances, other salespeople, previous customers, suppliers, nonsales employees in the firm, and social and professional contacts. A number of sources and techniques for finding prospects are described in this section.

Present Customers

The best source of prospects is usually the salesperson's existing customers. It is much easier to sell additional goods and services to existing customers than to attract new customers. A person who has purchased a lap-top computer from an office supply firm and is pleased with it is usually more receptive than a novice customer to purchasing a fax machine or similar item from the same firm. For this reason, current customers should always be among those notified when new goods and services are introduced. If a salesperson is selling to an organization with several departments or business units, a buyer from one department may become an internal advocate for a salesperson and the company. This buyer can introduce salespeople to other departments' decision makers and can give them firsthand knowledge of a company's products and service record. Salespeople can develop internal advocates by providing current customers with a high level of service, by developing and improving their relationships with customers, and by asking their advice on new business opportunities.[10]

Former Customers

It may also be profitable periodically to reconsider former customers as prospects. A list of inactive customers can be compiled from company records. After deleting names of those to whom selling will be impossible (for example, buyers who have moved), the remainder may be considered as prospects. Former customers' needs may have changed in some way to again make them potential customers. Real estate salespersons are often able to sell new houses to former clients whose space needs have changed or who have a desire to "trade up" to a better home.

Cold Calling

cold calling Making unsolicited sales calls

Some salespeople rely heavily on *cold calling*, or unsolicited sales calls, as a prospecting technique. This approach simply involves knocking on doors. The salesperson makes contact with a potential customer, introduces himself or herself, and asks if there is a need for his or her product. Often, salespeople will cold call when they have time available between scheduled appointments. In real estate selling, this technique is known as "farming" when a salesperson canvasses a neighborhood in search of listings.

Given the high costs of selling, most salespeople and sales managers do not advocate extensive cold calling as a prospecting technique. It is more productive to prescreen sales leads prior to calling, or to use a less costly means to contact potential customers. For example, telemarketing is often used for this purpose.

Spotters

spotters People who identify and qualify sales leads

In some types of selling situations, salespeople use *spotters* to identify prospects. Sometimes known as "bird dogs," spotters are people who save a salesperson time by identifying and qualifying sales leads. Sales trainees are often used as spotters. Sales internships for college students also may involve extensive prospecting activities.

Directories and Mailing Lists

A wide variety of directories are full of prospects. The classified telephone directory is the most obvious one. City directories, state industrial directories, Thomas' *Register of Manufacturers*, Dun and Bradstreet's *Reference Book*, Moody's *Industrial Manual*, and Standard & Poor's *Register of Directors and Executives* are frequently used to identify prospects. A salesperson may also find that membership directories of trade associations, professional societies, and civic and social organizations are good sources for prospects.

Specialized companies also compile lists of individuals and organizations for direct marketing activities. For instance, R. L. Polk & Company, the world's largest mailing list compiler, markets extensive listings of consumer, professional, business, and institutional groups. Polk's business list file contains over nine million names. These lists may also be used to identify sales prospects. The major advantages of mailing lists are that they are often more current and more selective than directories. The best ones, however, are costly.

Prospecting Services

In addition to mailing list providers, there are specialized prospecting service companies that provide specific information on prospects. Dun's Marketing Services, a division of Dun and Bradstreet, is an example. Another service is *Sales Prospector*, a monthly publication of Westgate Publishing Company.

Referrals

Most salespeople feel that referrals from satisfied customers and other people familiar with their goods and services are one of the best sources of sales leads. As noted earlier, these may be internal advocates in a large company. However, referrals may come from other sources.

center of influence approach Prospecting technique using individuals with information about or influence on potential customers

A specific prospecting technique based on referrals is the *center of influence approach*. A "center of influence" is a person with information about other people or influence over them who can help a salesperson identify good prospects. Frequently used centers of influence are bankers, realtors, and attorneys.

endless chain prospecting
Prospecting technique in which a sales representative asks satisfied customers for the names of friends or business associates who may be potential customers

Another effective prospecting technique is to use satisfied customers as sources of referrals. *Endless chain prospecting* involves the sales representative asking customers for names of friends or business associates who might need similar goods or services. Then, as the salesperson contacts and sells these prospects, more referrals are solicited. The process can continue indefinitely.

Personal Contacts

Effective salespeople are active in professional, civic, and service organizations. The people they meet through these organizations may be prospects themselves or may provide helpful leads. Also, many people who are centers of influence are active in professional, civic, and service organizations.

Salespeople can identify many prospects through personal contacts. For instance, the real estate salesperson whose friend asks about the price of a house that just went on the market should be alerted to the person's possible interest in buying a new home. Helpful responses to such questions can lead to a prospect's further consideration of a good or service.

Trade Shows and Exhibits

A cost-effective way to make personal contacts and locate qualified prospects is to participate in trade shows and exhibits.[11] A company spends only about one-fourth the cost of an industrial sales call to meet a potential customer at a trade show since the potential customers absorb the travel expenses.

Trade shows are an especially cost-effective sales tool for small companies. But small firms, like all trade show participants, must prepare themselves to be fully effective at such shows.[12] Specific, realistic objectives must be established. If developing qualified sales leads is a specific objective, the firm must be sure that a trade show will attract the proper types of people. The firm's sales organization must also be prepared to follow up on the sales leads that are generated.

It is important that customers and prospects know about the trade shows and exhibits in which a company plans to participate. The company must promote their participation to maximize the payoffs of the shows and exhibits. Companies should encourage prospects to visit trade shows by mailing them invitations or promising them gifts. Advance announcements sent to trade publications may also help to attract prospects. With the rising costs of personal selling, trade shows have become an increasingly important source of sales leads.

Another key to using trade shows successfully is training salespeople for the parts they play in them. Unfortunately, salespeople at trade shows often are poorly prepared and do not represent their companies well.[13] Sales managers must provide training in booth etiquette, body language, communications skills, and other trade show selling skills. Salespeople must also understand the purpose of each trade show, its specific objectives, and their own responsibilities. During the show, short meetings should be held at the end of each day to review the day's activities.[14]

Direct Marketing

Many sales organizations have begun to use direct marketing techniques for prospecting.[15] Successful firms use a combination of advertising, direct mail, and

**lead management
systems** Programs
to generate better
leads and more pros-
pect information

telemarketing. These efforts are designed to generate sales leads and to obtain useful sales information about potential customers. Known as *lead management systems*, these programs generally provide the sales organization with higher-quality leads and more information with which to complete successful sales calls.[16]

An integrated direct marketing approach starts with the use of direct response advertisements and/or direct mail to attract inquiries about the goods and services featured. Companies often use reader cards in magazines, coupons, and 800 telephone numbers printed in advertisements or featured in radio and television commercials for this purpose.

In the past, a problem for many sales organizations was the failure of salespeople to follow up on inquiries. They ignored these sales leads because past experience showed that many leads generated by advertising were people who could not make a purchase or who were not planning on buying for some time. To deal with these problems, the lead management system uses telemarketing sales representatives to further qualify the leads before turning them over to the sales force. A more detailed discussion of telemarketing and its use as a sales tool is contained in Chap. 11. When properly handled, it is estimated that more than 20 percent of all sales leads and inquiries developed through advertising, promotion, trade shows, and direct mail will result in sales within six months.[17]

An effective prospecting technique that uses a combination of telemarketing and direct mail to generate leads for field salespeople and schedule appointments with qualified prospects has been developed.[18] The process begins with a prenotification phone call. The low-key presentation by the telemarketer is intended to determine if the prospect is willing to receive product information. If not, the call is terminated. If on the other hand, the prospect is receptive, the information is sent.

After enough time has elapsed for the prospect to receive and read the information, a followup telephone call is made. The caller first makes sure that the information has arrived and has been examined. Then the telemarketer tries to determine the prospect's reaction to the information. Questions are encouraged since they will lead to the prime goal of the call—the prospect's agreement to meet with a field salesperson.

Although somewhat more costly than conventional telephone canvassing for sales appointments, this approach has proven to be more effective. A significantly larger proportion of total contacts is converted into sales appointments. Further, the conversion rates of appointments into sales presentations and presentations into successful sales are significantly higher with this approach.[19]

QUALIFYING PROSPECTS

Once sales representatives have identified potential customers, they must qualify them to determine if they are valid prospects. Unless this is done, time can be wasted in trying to sell to people who cannot, or will not, purchase the product. A person with a $25,000 annual income may want a new Porsche, but the purchase is simply beyond this person's means. A secretary may want to purchase a new copy machine but be overruled by the manager who says a new copier is not in the budget. A college professor who wishes to adopt a new textbook may be prevented from

ANDREW CORPORATION

Andrew Corporation, an Illinois-based seller of telecommunications products, makes full use of its trade show time. At the recent National Association of Broadcasters' meeting, Andrew sold $2 million worth of communication products. This success was largely attributable to the firm's use of a "war room."

War rooms are separate spaces for sales managers to meet with their salespeople during trade shows. Strategy is discussed, customer requests and questions are analyzed, and the sales manager helps salespeople set goals and make plans before they head for the trade show floor again.

Traditionally, trade shows have been seen as a public relations device more than an aggressive prospecting tool. Now, however, sales managers are beginning to realize that it is possible to conduct some of selling's preliminary steps at trade shows.

Two keys to trade show selling are preparation and motivation. The shows are fast-paced and somewhat chaotic and it is easy for salespeople to get lost in the shuffle if they are not well organized and ready to hit the ground running. Trade shows, with their long hours and intense socializing, can also be rather exhausting.

The war room helps to lessen the probability of each of these potential disadvantages. Salespeople keep on track, and prospects are given quick, on-site answers to their questions. Finally, the war room's locker-room-like atmosphere is motivating and energizing.

Participation in trade shows is expensive and time-consuming for a company, and organizations like Andrew are striving to make them more profitable. Good personal selling skills are just one trade show weapon; in the future, specialized tactics like the war room will be part of every trade show participant's arsenal.

---

doing so because other faculty members vote to keep the same book for another year. These are all examples of prospects who are not qualified to buy.

To avoid selling to people who cannot make a buying decision, salespeople must learn to qualify their sales prospects. One way to do this is by asking a series of qualifying questions.[20] Table 4-3 presents a checklist for qualifying prospects in industrial sales situations.

As Table 4-3 indicates, there are many factors to consider when qualifying a prospect. Another approach to qualifying, often called the *MAN* (money, authority, and need) *approach*, involves answering three key questions about the prospect.

MAN approach
Qualifying method that involves answering questions about a prospect's money, authority, and need to buy

Money

Does the prospect have the money, or resources, to purchase a product or service? For example, does a potential homeowner have enough cash for the downpayment on a new home and sufficient income to meet the mortgage payments, or does a department manager have adequate funds in the departmental budget to purchase new office furniture? Since ability to pay is such a critical factor in qualifying prospects, salespeople must be familiar with their financial resources. It may be necessary to consult credit reporting agencies and other financial organizations to determine a prospect's financial resources.

Authority

Does the prospect have the authority to make a commitment? This is a particular concern when dealing with corporations, government agencies, or other large organizations. Even when selling to a married couple, it may be difficult to identify who

TABLE 4-3   Qualifying Checklist

Will they buy?	Yes	No	Unknown
1. Do they have good business reason(s) to buy?			
2. Have their needs (objectives) been identified?			
3. Is top management aware of these needs?			
4. Has funding been identified and approved?			
5. Have the decision criteria been established?			
6. Is the decision maker available to us?			
7. Will other key people give us time and information?			
8. Have they said they are definitely going to buy?			
9. Have all levels of management agreed to buy?			
Will they buy from me?	**Yes**	**No**	**Unknown**
1. Have I established a favorable image for us?			
2. Did I adequately describe our proven capabilities?			
3. Does (do) our product(s) provide solutions for their needs?			
4. Has genuine interest in our product(s) been expressed?			
5. Is the decision maker biased toward us?			
6. Have any preferences for us been stated by key people?			
7. Is (are) our solution(s) competitive?			
8. Does the competition have major advantages over us?			
9. Is a consultant (or other third party) involved?			
Will they buy from me now?	**Yes**	**No**	**Unknown**
1. Is there a pressing business reason to act?			
2. Does a sense of urgency exist with the key people?			
3. Has justification been presented and accepted?			
4. Have the key steps in the decision process been finalized?			
5. Has a decision date been determined?			
6. Is the competition making progress in the sales cycle?			
7. Has an installation or delivery date been established?			
8. Is a demonstration or benchmark required?			
9. Can we meet their implementation schedule?			

Source: Reprinted from Robert M. Goss, Jr., "How Valuable Are Your Prospects?" *Personal Selling Power,* (11) November-December 1991, p. 32.

actually makes the decision to purchase. A salesperson must identify the key decision maker early to make effective use of his or her selling time.

Need

Does the prospect want or need the good or service? This is, of course, the critical question. If a salesperson cannot establish that the customer will benefit from purchasing a product, there is no reason to waste a sales call. The prospect either will refuse the offer or will agree to buy but end up dissatisfied with the purchase. A salesperson should do as much as possible to learn about a prospect's needs and whether a specific need for the product in question exists. In some cases, this effort will identify needs of which even the prospect is unaware. Creative selling can only be effective if a salesperson fully understands the prospect's business.[21] The development of this understanding will be the subject of the next section.

PREPARING

After a prospect has been identified and qualified, the sales representative prepares for the sale. This stage involves the two key activities of pre-approach and call planning.

Pre-Approach

pre-approach Sales call preparation in which the salesperson seeks out additional information after the prospecting process is completed

In the *pre-approach*, or fact-finding, stage of sales planning, additional information is gathered about the prospect and his or her needs. It is necessary to go beyond prospecting information to plan the sales call. Additional information helps the representative choose the best strategy for the sales call. One writer described the importance of the information-gathering steps this way:

> Like a quarterback, the salesperson calls the signals in handling his [or her] accounts and prospects. But to sell more effectively, he [or she] has to gather basic information about them and develop an arrangement that results in more sales. This is the essence of a sales plan.[22]

There are certain questions that a salesperson must answer about customers.

Who Is the Customer? Buying is a complex process, especially in a large organization, and it may be difficult to identify the key decision makers. The sales representative needs to answer several questions:

- Who will make the actual decision to purchase the product?
- Who will influence the decision?
- Who actually will be responsible for using the good or service?
- With whom must the salesperson maintain a continuing, favorable relationship?

In some cases, all these people may be the same individual; in others, they may be different. Studies of organizational buying behavior have revealed that industrial salespeople must usually deal with several buying influences. This is because many organizational buying decisions involve a situation in which several people must give their approval before a commitment can be made. Marketers usually refer to all those involved in the purchase decision as the buying center. These individuals typically play different roles, such as the ones suggested in the questions above.

gatekeeper Buying center member who controls information or access to decision makers

The first buying center member encountered by the salesperson is often a *gatekeeper*—someone who controls information or access to decision makers. Secretaries, administrative assistants, and receptionists are examples. Sometimes the gatekeeper is the purchasing agent. Successful salespeople are skilled at identifying gatekeepers and "selling" them to gain access to decision makers.

economic buyer Buying center member who is the key decision maker

Once past the gatekeeper, an industrial salesperson must then analyze the various buying influences and their interests and needs. The *economic buyer* is usually the key decision maker. In fact, for many important purchases, the CEO is the economic decision maker.[23] This person will be most concerned with return on investment and other financial impacts of the purchase decision. Other key buying

users Buying center members who judge a potential purchase on the basis of the impact it will have on their job performance

technical personnel Buying center members who evaluate a potential purchase on the basis of whether it meets certain objective specifications

influences are *users*, who will judge the potential impact of a product on their job performance, and *technical personnel* such as engineers, who are concerned with whether a good or service meets certain objective specifications.[24]

In Chap. 3, the lengthy process involved in selling expensive medical equipment was described. This is exactly the type of complex situation many industrial salespeople face. Doctors, nurses, and technicians will use the medical equipment; they may also be concerned with the technical specifications. On the other hand, the hospital administrator will focus on the financial impact of the purchase. The salesperson must be skillful in identifying and meeting the needs of each type of buying influence.

What Are the Customer's Needs?　A sale will be concluded successfully only if the salesperson can demonstrate that the good or service will satisfy the prospect's needs, which the salesperson must identify prior to making a sales presentation.

dominant buying motive Major reason the prospect will purchase a good or service

The key to planning a sales call and successfully completing a sale is to identify the prospect's *dominant buying motive*—the major reason the prospect is purchasing a good or service. The dominant buying motive is related to the prospect's needs—emotional or otherwise. The seller must identify these needs and determine which are the most important.

Sometimes a sales representative is able to identify a prospect's needs through secondary information sources and other data obtained prior to the sales call. In other cases, the salesperson may need to use the first part of the interview to determine the prospect's needs. A mastery of questioning, observation, and listening skills is required.

What Other Information Is Required?　Depending on the situation, this may include personal information such as family background, hobbies, memberships in clubs and professional organizations, and business information, such as the credit rating, product line, and industry reputation of the prospect's firm. Information should be gathered on the customer firm's present suppliers and on potential competitors and the goods and services they offer. It is also important for customer files to identify anything that the salesperson should avoid when calling on the prospect. An example would be a day or time when the individual is extremely busy.

Mackay Envelope Corporation uses a detailed questionnaire to compile relevant information about customers.[25] By obtaining answers to a total of sixty-six questions, Mackay salespeople develop detailed profiles of the people to be contacted. Key information includes educational background, career history, family, special interests, and life styles. Harvey Mackay has observed: "Our overall goal is to know more about our customers than they know about themselves."[26]

Where Does One Obtain Information?　For current customers, the vendor company's internal records are the best source for much of the information needed prior to a sales contact. What products has the customer bought? What other relevant information is in the customer's file? What do the vendor's own employees know about the customer?

Other sources of information on business customers are annual reports, trade publications, advertisements, and catalogs. These and other public sources of information will give a salesperson insight into a business organization, its goals, philosophy, and performance record.

In addition to searching through written or published information, the astute sales representative also observes and listens. Much information can be gained from conversations with customers and other salespeople, as well as from talks with business and social contacts. Trade shows, industry conferences, and training seminars offer excellent opportunities to gather industry and customer information.

As the Mackay example suggests, many salespeople use a standard form of some type to summarize pertinent information about a prospect. An example of a checklist for planning an industrial sales call is shown in Fig. 4-3. This form outlines the major factors that an industrial sales representative needs to consider in preparing for an interview.

Call Planning

call planning
Sequence of precall
activities

Call planning involves a specific sequence of activities before the sales interview takes place. The sales representative must define the objective of the call, devise a selling strategy to achieve this objective, and make the appointment.

Specifying the Objective.   Prior to calling on a prospect, a salesperson must establish an objective. This involves determining the answers to three basic questions: (1) Why am I going on this interview? (2) What am I trying to make happen? (3) If the prospect says "Yes, I want to buy," what am I going to recommend?[27]

Like all business objectives, sales call objectives should be as specific as possible and have measurable outcomes. In addition, a time frame should be established to show when the sales action will be implemented. For example, a salesperson calling on the personnel manager of a commercial bank to present a group health plan could specify the sales objective as follows: "To convince the personnel manager to permit me to perform a needs analysis of the bank this week so I can present a group health plan for the bank by the end of the month." Another example might be a sales representative for a large resort hotel calling on a trade association executive who is planning a regional conference. The representative's goal could be: "To convince the prospect to visit the hotel next week to see the guest and meeting rooms, examine the recreational facilities, and sample the hotel's food."

As these two instances suggest, getting an order is not always a salesperson's immediate objective. Although that is the long-term goal of any sales effort, intermediate objectives may be required. In selling situations where multiple calls are needed, a specific objective should be set for each step of the selling process. Jack Falvey has suggested a typical sequence:

1. Telemarketing prequalifies a lead.
2. An appointment is "sold" to the prospect identified.
3. The salesperson holds a meeting with the purchasing manager and one or two people who will actually be using the product to learn the particular needs of the prospective customer.
4. A proposal is developed.
5. Another meeting is called, perhaps with a team from each side, to evaluate the proposal.

☐ **1.** Write down the name and address of the prospect company. _____
_____

☐ **2.** After you've made your survey of the company's needs and decide how you can accomodate them, jot down what you know about the company — its type of business, what it makes or does, how and to whom it sells, its annual sales, number of employees, etc. _____
_____

☐ **3.** Write down all you know about the company's buying policies and procedures — does it buy from competition, how much, on what terms? Can you submit a plan to save this company time and money? _____
_____

☐ **4.** Name and title of persons to call on: _____

☐ **5.** Write down the precise purpose of the call. _____

☐ **6.** Dates and results of previous calls (if any): _____

☐ **7.** Names of competitors: _____
_____

☐ **8.** Benefits offered by competition: _____
_____

☐ **9.** Compare and contrast your product with competitor's product. What are the advantages and disadvantages of each? _____
_____

☐ **10.** List all the things you sell that this company needs. _____
_____

☐ **11.** Make a list of the benefits you offer that will satisfy this company's needs. _____
_____

☐ **12.** What opening remarks will you use to arouse interest? _____
_____

☐ **13.** What questions will you ask to determine which benefits have the strongest appeal to your prospect? _____
_____

☐ **14.** Write down all the major points you plan to make in your presentation, in order. _____
_____

☐ **15.** Make a list of all the proof you'll use to back up your claims. _____
_____

☐ **16.** What major area of resistance do you anticipate? How will you handle it? _____
_____

☐ **17.** Give two or more answers to the objections you will encounter. _____
_____

☐ **18.** Write down a brief summary of your presentation. _____
_____

☐ **19.** Write down precisely how you plan to ask for your order. _____
_____

FIGURE 4-3 **Checklist for Planning an Industrial Sales Call.**

6. A contract is negotiated, setting forth the sale's terms and conditions.

7. The final order is signed.[28]

Developing a Strategy.   A salesperson must develop a strategy, or course of action, to achieve the sales objectives. The sequence described above suggests that each of the steps should be considered a separate sale leading to the final sale. If the overall sales plan is to succeed, each specific action and call must be individually planned and coordinated.

The prospect's background and needs must be carefully considered to formulate a tailor-made strategy appropriate for the prospect. The sales planner must also evaluate alternatives available to the prospect and attempt to predict actions of potential competitors. Contingency plans are usually a good idea, in case the competition does not react as predicted. A sales situation management guideline is shown in Fig. 4-4. This guide helps salespersons develop a strategy for each of their prospects.

Making an Appointment.   Sales calls are costly, so they should be arranged in advance. Cold calls—showing up without specific appointments—may be appropriate for introducing the salesperson or dropping off information, but are generally inefficient for selling most goods and services, and the practice is not consistent with modern professional selling. An appointment arranged in advance by telephone or letter will help assure the sales representative that the prospect will be available. Further, the salesperson may obtain additional data during a precall phone conversation that may assist in planning the interview itself.

Sales consultant Stephen Schiffman has emphasized that a salesperson should set a firm time and date for all appointments.[29] Arranging a specific time indicates to a prospect that the salesperson is a professional concerned about the work schedules of both parties. Arriving on time for appointments is also important, according to Schiffman. Arriving too early puts time pressure on the prospect, and arriving too late suggests a lack of respect for the prospect's time.

SUMMARY OF LEARNING GOALS

1. **Understand the Basic Steps in the Personal Selling Process, Prospecting and Preparing, Which Are Preliminary to the Later Steps of Presenting, Handling Objections, Closing, and Following Up.**

   The selling process begins with prospecting, or finding qualified potential buyers. After prospects have been identified and qualified, salespeople must prepare for the sale by gathering information. These two preliminary steps are followed by presenting, handling objections, closing, and following up (discussed in Chap. 5).

2. **List the Most Common Sources of Prospects.**

   Some of the most common sources of potential customers are present customers, former customers, cold calling, spotters, directories and mailing lists, prospecting services, referrals, personal contacts, trade shows and exhibits, and direct marketing.

SALES SITUATION MANAGEMENT
Marketing Services – New York

ESTIMATE OF THE SELLING SITUATION

STEP I
Consider the Customer's Objectives and Goals.

STEP II
Consider Your Objectives.
If multiple, set priorities.

STEP III
Compare Your Objectives and the Customer's.
Is there a conflict? If so, would you :
- re-examine your own objectives?
- attempt to change the customer's objectives?
- really try to keep this customer?

STEP IV
Consider Your Goals.
Short-range goals. Goal of today's call?
    Do they conflict with one another or with your objectives?
    Do they really enhance your objective?
    If not, which is right... your goals or your objective?

STEP V
Gather Intelligence.
(Essential Elements of Intelligence).
    Intelligence on the nature of your competition,
    Intelligence on products — yours and competition's.
    Intelligence on economic factors of the customer's business.
    Intelligence on psychological factors affecting the customer.

STEP VI
Analyze the Intelligence.
(Identify facts, make assumptions.)
    Consider assured advantages, possible advantages, effects.
    Consider assured disadvantages, possible disadvantages, effects.

STEP VII
Develop Your Sales Strategy.
    Consider possible courses of action, with alternatives.
    Consider customer's alternatives.
    Consider competitor's alternatives.
    Consider customer or competitor reactions to your alternatives.
    Choose the most promising in terms of your long-range objectives.
    Avoid attractive short-range methods that jeopardize objectives.

STEP VIII
Plan Opening Tactics.
    Same considerations as in Step VII.
    Exploit your advantages.
    Anticipate and meet disadvantages.
    Have alternate tactical plans ready.

FIGURE 4-4 Sales Situation Management.

3. **Explain the MAN Concept of Qualifying a Prospect.**

   The MAN approach to qualifying prospects involves answering three key questions about the prospect: Does the prospect have the money to purchase the good or service? Does the prospect have the authority to make a commitment? Does the prospect want or need the product?

4. **Understand the Pre-Approach Activities Needed to Adequately Prepare for a Sales Call.**

   The pre-approach involves finding out information about the prospect in order to better serve his or her needs. Specific questions need to be answered: (1) Who is the customer? (2) What are the customer's needs? (3) What other information is required? (4) Where does one obtain information?

5. **Understand the Sequence of Call Planning Activities Needed to Prepare for a Sales Call.**

   Call planning is focused on the sales call itself. The sales representative first determines the objective of the sales call. A selling strategy is then formulated. Finally, the salesperson makes an appointment with the prospect.

REVIEW QUESTIONS

1. What is prospecting? What are the two major activities involved in prospecting?
2. Why is the identification of potential customers sometimes frustrating to beginning salespersons? What are the key steps involved in the prospecting process?
3. What is usually the best source of prospects? How can salespeople develop internal advocates in the companies they sell to?
4. What is meant by cold calling? Cite some examples. How can the effectiveness of cold calls be increased?
5. List several examples of directories used by salespeople to find prospects. What is the advantage of using mailing lists? What is the disadvantage of mailing lists?
6. What is meant by the center of influence method of prospecting? What are some frequently used centers of influence?
7. How can a salesperson find out whether or not a prospect has the financial resources to buy? What other factors should be considered when qualifying a prospect?
8. What is meant by pre-approach? In preparing for a sales call, what questions must salespeople be able to answer?
9. What is a buying center? Identify the roles that exist within the buying center.
10. What sequence of steps is involved in call planning? Why should cold calls be avoided in this sequence?

DISCUSSION QUESTIONS

1. Interview a young salesperson about prospecting. Has this person found prospecting to be difficult? How does the person's employer teach sales representatives to prospect? Explain.
2. Some retail salespeople have been known to qualify prospects on the basis of their appearance. What is wrong with such an approach? Cite specific hypothetical examples.
3. Many companies that have traditionally relied on cold calling are changing their marketing strategy. The Fuller Brush Company, for example, is changing the orientation of the

famous Fuller Brush seller from a door-to-door approach to networking. What trends can you think of that have made cold calling a less favorable way to sell? Do you think cold calling is more appropriate for industrial selling or selling to individuals? Explain.

4. In an effort to increase sales to current customers, a consulting firm developed a client club. Members of the club receive a newsletter containing discounts and information. What are some advantages of this prospecting tool? How could the newsletter be used to achieve the organization's sales goals?

5. Social selling is an excellent way for salespeople to build relationships with prospects. Inviting a prospect to lunch is the classic form of social selling. What are the potential advantages of social selling? What are its disadvantages or potential pitfalls? What can salespeople do to increase the likelihood of getting into social selling situations?

E T H I C A L
D I L E M M A

Paul Robinson has been selling real estate for three years. He has worked hard and is now well established in the community. Last week he was approached by a mortgage lender with an offer of $200 for each customer Paul recommended that took a mortgage with the lender. What should Paul do?

SALES MANAGEMENT CASE

Any Prospects?

Chuck Piola, a sales representative for NCO Financial Systems, is a selling phenomenon. Piola sells NCO's receivable collection services largely through cold calls; for example, he may randomly pick a building, go in, and start chatting with secretaries. Before too long, these deceptively light conversations have provided him with valuable names and information, and made his call a lot less cold.

Piola makes around thirty cold calls and four presentations per day. He has been a salesperson for fifteen years, and he estimates that he has made over 15,000 cold calls during his career. His secrets to successful cold calling include, among other things, thinking fast and never assuming the person he's talking to is not a decision maker.

In contrast to NCO, prospecting at brokerage firm Shearson Lehman Brothers is nonrandom and streamlined, with various job levels responsible for different parts of the prospecting process. About forty lower-wage telemarketers have as their sole responsibility making unsolicited first contacts with potential customers. If callees are at all interested, they are transferred to another employee, called a "qualifier," who evaluates the prospect's investment

objectives, willingness to accept followup calls, and financial ability. Forty telemarketers making initial contacts can reach hordes of people; in one four-day period the callers contacted 18,004 prospects and opened forty accounts.

Many industries have been criticized for lead generation tactics such as massive telemarketing efforts. To make sure that consumers are protected, Congress is now putting limits on telephone and fax selling. The Federal Communications Commission is currently required to maintain lists of people who do not want to receive telemarketing calls, and companies are fined if they violate the wishes of those on the list. Autodialing is being critically reviewed, and legislation to ban autodialing to hospitals and other institutions that need open lines in case of emergencies has come before Congress. Some rule makers are pushing to ban unsolicited sales calls in any case where the callee has to foot the cost of the call (cellular phones, for instance); others want to ban all calls to homes.

There are those who say that cold calling is dead. Cold calls are often unpopular; however, they can also be quite effective if the benefit to the customer is legitimate and the salesperson sincere. At NCO, cold calling is based on dynamic personal selling. Organized technology is Shearson Lehman Brother's fo-

cus. For both companies, cold calling is, at least for the time being, very much alive.

Questions

1. Compare and contrast cold calling at Shearson Lehman Brothers and NCO.

2. Which of the two companies presented here is more likely to be affected by new regulations? Explain.

3. Would you rather be cold-called by Chuck Piola or a Shearson Lehman Brothers telemarketer? Explain.

ADVANCED STEPS IN THE SELLING PROCESS

LEARNING GOALS

- Discuss the various factors that go into making an effective sales presentation.
- Identify ways to open a sales presentation.
- Describe probing techniques used to determine prospects' needs.
- Explain features-benefits selling and other techniques used to convince prospects.
- Outline the types of objections encountered by sales personnel and explain how each objection should be handled.
- Identify the various closing techniques.
- Explain the importance of sales followup.

THE MAGIC OF IMPACT

Bill Herz is a professional magician who also happens to hold an M.B.A. His business, Magicorp Productions, is, like Herz himself, a unique blend of the monetary and the mystical. Herz performs magic for corporate events, and he also trains salespeople and executives to do magic tricks for use in their sales presentations.

Herz customizes his magic to fit the client's message. For example, an executive who wanted to convince his sales force of the importance of a new floppy disk learned how to make the disk turn into cash before their eyes. Herz also taught an insurance company vice president to tear an old policy into pieces and then put it back together to look like a new one. Not surprisingly, secrecy is of prime importance to Herz, who asks his clients to sign agreements not to tell others how to do the tricks.

Magicorp is not the only enterprise of its kind: Magic Touch in San Francisco; Magical Productions in Riva, Maryland; and Corporate Shuffle in Houston are examples of businesses similar to Magicorp. The common denominator for all of these services is a focus on the message. Sleight-of-hand, no matter how impressive, cannot take the place of a professional salesperson discussing the features and benefits of a good or service and taking a sincere interest in customer needs. Magic and other forms of entertainment should be used only to reinforce a seller's message, not to replace any part of the sales presentation.[1]

Chapter 5 discusses the advanced steps in the selling process. Certainly not all salespeople have the flair for and/or interest in all the techniques discussed here, nor should they. But in this chapter, you will learn the basics of good sales presentations, from the approach to closing and followup. Being confident in these basics will substantially enhance your ability to sell.

CHAPTER OVERVIEW

Chapter 4 discussed the preliminary steps in the selling process. Most of these activities take place prior to the actual sales presentation, the face-to-face meeting between the prospect and the salesperson. In this chapter, the focus will be on the steps involved in the sales presentation itself. A sales presentation consists of several interrelated activities. It begins with the approach, during which the salesperson obtains the prospect's interest and attention. Next the salesperson asks questions to identify and/or clarify the prospect's needs. The rest of the presentation involves efforts to direct the prospect's attention to a product's desirable features and to demonstrate its benefits. Prospects may offer sales resistance in the form of objections that must be addressed. Finally, the sales representative will try to get the order or reach some other goal, such as a followup phone call or meeting at a later date. This stage, the "close," is the culmination of the sales presentation. After closing the deal, the salesperson does whatever is necessary to complete the transaction. These activities are shown in Fig. 5-1.

A sales presentation guide that can be used to prepare for a sales call is presented in Fig. 5-2. The first portion of the guide contains information obtained during the preliminary steps of the selling process. Then, a series of questions are presented to assist the salesperson in developing the sales presentation. These questions relate to the specific activities of the presentation: (1) approach, (2) probing for needs, (3 and 4) convincing the prospect, (5 and 6) handling objections, and (7) closing.

It should be emphasized that Figs. 5-1 and 5-2 are intended to serve as general guidelines only. Today's professional salespeople must be able to tailor their presentation to the specific needs of the prospect and the unique aspects of the sales

FIGURE 5-1 Sales Presentation Activities.

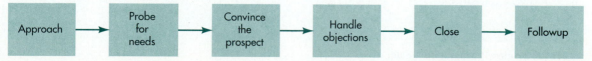

Approach → Probe for needs → Convince the prospect → Handle objections → Close → Followup

Prospect: _____   Location: _____

Key contact :

Title :   Phone :

Other contacts :

_____

Existing situation :

Possible needs :

_____

Sales call objectives :

_____

1. How should I develop/strengthen this relationship?

_____

2. What facts and questions should I discuss to find and clarify needs?

    Facts to review :

    Questions to ask :

_____

3. What tactics should I use to amplify the needs? What examples can I use to show feasibility of satisfying needs?

_____

4. What benefits should I stress to gain commitment?

_____

5. What resistance might I encounter?   **6.** How can I resolve it?

_____

7. What decision questions must I ask to get desired action?

    Recommended action:

    Decision questions:

FIGURE 5-2 Sales Presentation Guide.

situation. Modern selling is quite different from the structured sales approaches of the early phases of sales development described in Chap. 3.

adaptive selling
Adjusting a sales
presentation to fit
the customer or the
dynamics of the call

   The term *"adaptive selling"* has been used to describe the way in which salespeople modify their sales presentation during a sales call or use different approaches for different customers.[2] To do this well, salespeople and the sales managers who guide them must understand and know how to use many types of sales techniques and methods. They must also be skilled in asking questions and obtaining information to determine customers' needs.[3] These topics are addressed in what follows.

APPROACH

approach Selling
step during which
the salesperson ob-
tains the prospect's
interest and attention

The first portion of a sales presentation is a very critical part of the sales call. It is during this time, known as the *approach* (or opening), that the salesperson introduces himself or herself, outlines the purpose of the visit, tries to establish rapport with the prospect, obtains the prospect's attention, and attempts to build interest in the material that will be presented.

First Impressions Are Essential

A favorable first impression is not just important; it is crucial to the success of a sales call. Before buying a product, a prospect must first accept the seller. If one creates a poor first impression, the prospect's attitude toward one's company and its products will be damaged. As best-selling author John T. Molloy has pointed out:

> Salesmen fail—not when they open their mouths—but before they open them. Their appearances convey they are not likable, not honest, not trustworthy, not even sincere.[4]

To make a favorable first impression, a sales representative must look and act like a professional. Small things, such as sloppy clothing, poor grooming, a messy sample case, or a damaged business card, can detract from the total impression that one wants to project.[5] Some specific suggestions for making a favorable first impression include the following:

- Wear neat, conservative clothes.
- Be clean and carefully groomed.
- Know the prospect's name and pronounce it correctly.
- Be alert and pleasant.
- Let the prospect offer to shake hands.
- Forget about yourself and concentrate on the prospect.
- Avoid smoking or chewing gum.

For field salespeople who entertain customers and transport them to restaurants and other locations, the overall condition, cleanliness, and style of their automobiles is another important consideration.[6] Large, four-door models that provide easy access for several passengers are appropriate. The car should receive regular maintenance and repairs, and should be washed and vacuumed weekly. Finally, a salesperson should spot-check the car for any problems prior to picking up a customer.

Preparation

Another key to making a favorable first impression is adequate preparation. As discussed in Chap. 3, salespeople must do their homework. They must be knowledgeable about varied aspects of their prospects' companies such as their products, competition, and marketplace. They must carefully examine the prospects' sales-related wants and desires so they are sure they have selected the best selling approach for the specific selling situation. If the salespeople are familiar with all these factors surrounding any given selling situation, they are ready to approach a prospect.[7]

Beginning the Presentation

Many techniques for beginning the sales presentation exist. Each seller must choose the one that best fits his or her personality and the specific sales situation. Six proven techniques for getting favorable attention and stimulating a prospect's interest follow.[8]

Ask Questions.   A good question usually gets the sales presentation off to a good start. Questions that relate to the sales presentation are preferred. For example, if an insurance agent's call on a local business executive concerns a group life insurance plan, an appropriate question might be, "How many employees does your firm have?" Trite questions like "How's business?" must be avoided.

Use a Referral.   The name of another person is often an effective introduction: "Dr. Lopes recently purchased this new microscope and suggested that you might be interested in a demonstration."

Top salespeople feel that referrals are the best way to secure a new account. Some specific comments:

> A lot of the business I do is referrals. Before I go on a cold call, I check with the people I know who might know something about the prospect, then use their name to call someone at the prospect business.

> When I say I'm going to do something, I make sure it gets done because my best business card is referrals.

> Generally, if you're successful in a given geographical area, you use those successes as references to sell other accounts.[9]

Offer a Benefit.   This technique can provide an effective opening. Often it involves a startling statement: "Mr. Roberts, I have an idea that will cut your fuel consumption by 10 percent. Would you be interested?"

Offer a Service.   Most people are receptive to an offer of service: "Mr. Ricardo, I'd like to review your disability insurance program to determine if my firm can provide your employees with increased coverage at a lower cost."

Compliment the Prospect.   A compliment is a good way to establish rapport if the prospect has done something noteworthy or received some form of recognition recently: "Congratulations on your recent promotion, Mr. Lukas. I read in last Friday's paper that you are the new director of marketing."

Give Something of Value.   Accepting a small gift will usually make the prospect feel obligated to listen for a few minutes; however, the gift must be something appropriate to the company and the product sold. Also, many companies have guidelines covering the size and type of gifts that can be accepted by employees, and there are Internal Revenue Service limitations on the tax deductibility of such gifts. A salesperson must be aware of these guidelines and limitations when giving gifts to potential buyers.[10]

PROBING FOR NEEDS

In its most basic form, the selling process involves finding a need and filling it. To find needs, a salesperson must ask questions. According to one consultant:

> Questions are powerful selling tools. By asking questions, you give the customer an opportunity to get involved. You also give yourself an information gathering tool to help you close the sale.[11]

SPIN selling Selling approach that teaches salespeople to ask a logical series of questions to identify the needs of a prospect

Most corporate sales programs emphasize asking questions as a key part of the selling process. For instance, *SPIN selling* was developed after an extensive study of sales calls.[12] SPIN is an acronym for situation questions, problem questions, implication questions, and need payoff questions. SPIN selling teaches salespeople to ask a logical series of questions to identify the needs of a prospect. The sequence is: situation questions to obtain background and factual information; problem questions to determine specific problems or needs; implication questions to help the prospect understand the seriousness of the problem or need; and need payoff questions to focus the prospect on the salesperson's solution to the problem. This approach is most appropriate for sales that involve a long selling cycle, a large customer commitment, and the need to develop an ongoing relationship.

Understanding when and how to ask questions is essential to the success of a problem-solving approach to selling. And the salesperson's ability to identify and solve problems is the most important factor in successfully developing new business.[13] This means that salespeople must learn how to probe for needs so that they will focus on those problems that are most important to the prospect. Some specific tips for asking questions are presented in Table 5-1.

TABLE 5-1   Tips for Questioning

1. Is the question clear and concise?
2. Does the question require productive thinking before the client can formulate a response?
3. Does the question force the client to evaluate new information or concepts?
4. Does the question lead the client to draw from past experiences?
5. Does the question generate a response that the client has not thought about before?
6. Does the question relate directly to the client's current business situation?
7. Does the question relate directly to the client's objectives?

Salespeople must also develop active listening skills so they will understand what prospects are saying.[14] They must be able to project themselves into each prospect's position if they are to understand that person better, an ability known as *empathy*. Problem solving will be effective only if a salesperson fully understands the prospect's needs and concerns.[15]

empathy Ability to project oneself into the prospect's position

Benefits of Questions

Skilled salespeople use probing questions throughout a sales presentation.[16] As noted in Chap. 4, a salesperson must ask questions to qualify a prospect. Other major reasons for using questions during the sales process include the following:

- To learn about the prospect's needs. By asking questions and listening to a prospect's answers, a salesperson will develop an understanding of those needs. This will allow the salesperson to present a solution and emphasize the benefits that the prospect will receive through the purchase.
- To maintain control. The person who asks the questions controls the sales presentation. Thus, asking questions is a subtle way of controlling a sale without making the prospect feel controlled.
- To involve the prospect. Asking questions will help a salesperson get and keep a prospect's attention. Questions will involve the prospect in the sales presentation from the start.
- To build relationships. Questions about a prospect's business, interests, needs, and other relevant topics will provide a salesperson with a deeper understanding of the prospect. This information can be used to develop a long-term relationship with the prospect.
- To establish trust. Questions show that the salesperson has a sincere interest in the prospect and the prospect's needs.

Types of Questions

There are many types of questions that a salesperson can ask during a sales presentation.[17] In general, these questions fall into three basic categories.

open-ended questions Broad questions asked early in the sales presentation

Open-Ended Questions.   Broad questions that are asked early in the sales presentation are *open-ended questions*. They are used to encourage the prospect to talk and to build rapport by showing the prospect that the salesperson is interested in the prospect's needs and point of view. Examples of open-ended questions include: "Tell me a little about what you want in a new house." "What projects are you working on?" "What type of car do you want?"

reflective questions Questions asked in response to a prospect's comments

Reflective Questions.   Questions used in response to a prospect's comment are *reflective questions*. Their purpose is to ask for more information that will help the salesperson prepare a response. Reflective questions will also help the salesperson clarify the prospect's feelings. Reflective questions are used most often to respond to sales objections. For instance, when a prospect says "Your price is too high," the reflective response is "Our price is too high?" Then the salesperson waits for a response which clarifies the prospect's price objection.

**directive ques-
tions** Leading
questions designed
to point the prospect
toward areas of
agreement

Directive Questions.   As a sales presentation moves forward, the salesperson uses *directive questions*, or leading questions designed to point the prospect toward areas of agreement. Directive questions are closed-ended questions that call for a specific response. These questions put pressure on the prospect to make a decision and are used to determine if the prospect is ready to close. They are questions like: "This is what you want, isn't it?" "Would you prefer model A or model B?"

CONVINCING THE PROSPECT

After identifying a prospect's needs, the salesperson moves to convince the prospect that the good or service will satisfy these needs. This portion of the sales presentation should be clear, concise, and well prepared.[18] Even though the sales presentation must be adapted to the particular selling situation, specific actions and techniques that have been successful in the past can be incorporated into sales presentations in a standardized format.[19]

Persuasion is a key aspect of any sales presentation.[20] A salesperson must use personal communications skills to convince the prospect to purchase the product. The usual format involves the seller outlining the item's major features, citing its benefits, and concluding by reporting on the successful use of the product by others.

The salesperson should seek verbal agreement from the prospect on key points. For example: "Do you like this particular option on the equipment?" In addition, the salesperson should try to get the prospect to narrow the selection. The salesperson, of course, has already assessed what the prospect wants and needs in the purchase. The usual approach is to ask the prospect to narrow the choice based on an analysis of the various features of the alternatives. Eventually, the selection process settles on the preferred choice.

Salespeople are also called upon to be skilled negotiators during the sales presentation. The real skill in negotiating a sale is to work out a settlement that gives each party enough to make both willing to agree to its terms. There can be no loser when negotiations are successfully completed. Therefore, salespeople must learn and develop the necessary negotiating skills so that their presentations will result in "win-win" conclusions.[21]

Features-Benefits Selling

**features-benefits
selling** Type of sell-
ing in which the
seller relates to a
prospect's needs by
emphasizing the ben-
efits received from
the seller's product

feature Desirable
characteristic of a
product

benefit Satisfaction
that the buyer will
obtain through the
purchase and use of
a product

Most professional sales trainers emphasize *features-benefits selling*. The seller relates to a prospect's needs by emphasizing the benefits a prospect will receive from the features of a good or service. A *feature* is a desirable characteristic of a product. It is what the good or service has or does. A *benefit*, on the other hand, is related to the customer's needs and desires. It represents a satisfaction the buyer will obtain through the purchase and use of the good or service. The benefit is what the product gives to, or does for, the customer. Benefits are the result of features. For example, in an insurance sales situation, the agent might say: "This group insurance policy has a double-indemnity clause for accidental death. This means that your employees will have added protection while traveling on company business." Here, the feature was stated first, followed by the benefit. Another approach is to reverse the two: "This life insurance policy will provide extra protection when your

SALES MANAGEMENT IN PRACTICE

FARAH, INC.

Oh, fickle fashion. When Farah, Inc., moved heavily into double-knit slacks in the 1970s, little did company executives know that the consumer would soon grow tired, even disdainful, of double-knit clothing. With Farah's unfortunate timing, inventories rose, and in 1976 the company lost $24 million.

Although Farah survived the double-knit debacle by revamping its line, it soon ran into other problems, including slipping quality, late orders, and, again, growing inventories. The problems were blamed in part on overexpansion of the company.

In 1989, after the Farah line was dropped by Dillard Department Stores, the Farah board of directors put Richard Allender in charge of running the company.

Allender made drastic cost cuts in order to improve Farah's profitability, and he focused on winning back former customers and gaining new ones.

Dillard Stores, for one, was difficult to convince. It took Allender a year and a half to get an appointment with Dillard chairman William Dillard. In early 1990, however, the leaders of the two companies met. Allender showed up with Farah slacks and competitor slacks, literally "laying it on the table." With some persuasive selling, Allender convinced Dillard to give Farah another chance, and by the fall, Farah clothing was back at Dillard's.

Farah is not the only company whose CEO is unafraid to get out and sell. At Xerox, Chairman Paul Allaire is prone to stepping in and meeting with the top executives at companies that the Xerox sales force is having trouble selling to. Evidently, a sales-oriented CEO can be a pretty powerful weapon.

---

employees travel. That's because this policy has a double-indemnity clause for an accidental death."

Finally, the salesperson may actually point out the benefit to the customer. The use of connecting phrases is illustrated by the hypothetical dialogue that follows. Sharon Ricci, a marketing representative for a bank, is discussing an employee payroll savings plan with Arthur Rubinsky, president of Fantasy, Inc., a toy manufacturer. The dialogue resumes after she has asked Rubinsky how many employees his firm has.

Rubinsky: We have some seasonal employment, but right now, we have about 250 people.

Ricci: Mr. Rubinsky, would you like to provide your employees with an employee benefit that would cost you almost nothing?

Rubinsky: How could I do that?

Ricci: Let me explain our payroll savings plan. This plan would permit your employees to make direct savings deposits to their accounts at our bank. Their savings would be fully insured, and they would earn a fair return on their money. This means that you can provide them with an added benefit. And industry studies prove that savers make better employees.

Rubinsky: That sounds very interesting, but won't this plan involve a lot of paperwork?

Ricci: Everyone worries about paperwork these days, so you will be happy to know that your accountant would have to do very little. That's because the payroll savings plan works just like a group health or life insurance plan. Once the plan is established, we take care of the administrative details.

Rubinsky: And you're sure that this plan won't cost me anything?

Ricci: Yes . . . that is a good question. In fact, the plan may save you money. That's because your employees will have money available for emergencies, and you won't have to make as many payroll advances. Henderson Company established a payroll savings plan two years ago and this is one of the benefits they have reported.

Rubinsky: Sounds good; let's go talk to my accountant.

Presentation Techniques

The sales dialogue above contains examples of techniques a sales representative can use to prove how an item will benefit a customer. Prospects buy benefits as well as items, and they must be convinced that they will receive those benefits. To convince her prospect, Ricci cited industry studies in addition to a plan established at another local firm. Other techniques for convincing the prospect include visual aids, testimonials, examples, guarantees, and demonstrations.

Visual Aids.   Charts, graphs, slides, flip-charts, videos, and other visual aids increase the impact and believability of what is being claimed. They are used as cues to provide an image that is keyed to a particular point in the presentation.[22] For instance, Ricci could have shown Rubinsky a chart of data from companies using the payroll savings plan, and the number of employees participating in each company, to demonstrate its popularity.

Many salespeople now use audiovisual equipment in their sales presentations. They feel this technique allows them to make better-prepared, more lively, and less-distorted presentations than other methods. Furthermore, buyers are more likely to recall points made visually.

Testimonials.   Reports from satisfied customers can be very persuasive. Ricci stated the satisfactory experience of another business customer in her presentation. Experience has proven that written testimonials shown to prospects have the greatest impact.

Examples.   Ricci used two examples to illustrate the benefits of the payroll savings plan: the industry study that savers make better employees, and the insurance example to illustrate the ease of establishing such a plan. Examples provide additional evidence of how purchasing a product will benefit the buyer and add credibility to the sales presentation.

Guarantees.   If a prospect is unsure about the benefits of a service, a guarantee can be used to relieve the anxiety. Ricci provided a modest guarantee when she assured Rubinsky that his accountant would have to do very little.

Demonstrations.   Demonstrations can be a powerful sales tool, but they require adequate planning. A salesperson should double-check all parts of a demonstration before attempting it. Even a minor failure or malfunction at a critical point may convince the prospect that the product (as well as the company it represents) is totally undependable.

Demonstrations supplement and reinforce the sales presentation. They allow the prospect to take an active role in the sales situation. A basic rule in demonstrating a product is to let the prospect touch, feel, or operate the product. For example, an industrial sales representative might arrange to demonstrate an item before the purchaser's technical personnel.

HANDLING OBJECTIONS

sales resistance
Actions or statements by a prospect that postpone, hinder, or prevent the completion of a sale

objection Outward expression of a prospect's doubts or negative feelings about a sales proposal

All salespeople encounter *sales resistance*—actions or statements by a prospect that postpone, hinder, or prevent the completion of a sale. Normally, sales resistance takes the form of an *objection*—an outward expression, usually verbal, of a prospect's doubts or negative feelings.

Objections are reasonable and should be expected. People naturally tend to postpone, delay, or avoid making purchase decisions. Many prospects are unable to deal with the uncertainty involved in a buying decision. They are never completely sure whether a purchase will work out as well as they think or hope.[23]

Objections Represent Sales Opportunities

Some salespeople experience considerable difficulty in identifying objections. Either they become so involved in their presentations that they simply overlook objections, or they treat their customers' actions or remarks as complete rejections of their products. Both reactions are wrong.

Although sales objections present an obstacle to the completion of a sale, experienced salespeople view most objections as opportunities. They are aware that buyers will have fears and concerns. They have learned to expect sales resistance and prepare themselves to deal with buyers' objections. One writer has pointed out: "A salesperson has nothing to fear from objections per se; they only pose a problem to closing a sale when they are not countered or answered properly. In fact, the rule is that objections should be welcomed in the sales presentation."[24]

In many cases, objections are really disguised requests for additional information. Objections usually indicate that the prospect has at least some interest in the product. This is an opportunity for the alert salesperson to further stimulate the prospect's interest. For instance, a prospective buyer observes that an office building would require some renovation to make it suitable for the firm's needs. The salesperson might counter this objection by pointing to the high cost of new construction and the lower cost of remodeling.

Types of Objections

Although a salesperson encounters many types of objections, most are related to four concerns—timing, price, source, and competition.

Timing. Most people wish to delay making decisions, especially important decisions dealing with money. For this reason, a sales representative is likely to encounter objections like the following: "Your proposal makes sense, but I think I should discuss it with my partner." "I'm sorry, but I don't have time to discuss this with you now." "There's plenty of time. I don't have to make a decision today."

How should this type of objection be handled? In most cases, the best approach is to find out the reason for the delay and then point out the advantages of making a decision immediately. The salesperson will usually find that the delay hides another objection of some kind. Once the true reason for not making a decision is resolved, the customer may be more willing to act.

Price.   This form of objection arises when the prospect feels that he or she has financial constraints or can get a better price from a competitor. Examples might include the following: "I think I can get a better deal elsewhere," or "Your competitor is two cents per unit cheaper."

Price objections can be handled best by pointing to quality and other benefits the customer will receive. For instance, the customer who complains about the higher price of a copier can be told about its greater durability, its longer warranty, and the convenience of repair facilities.

Source.   This type of objection results from negative feelings, which may be real or imagined, that the prospect has about the product or company. Examples include: "I'm impressed by what you've said, but I've heard that your firm has a poor delivery record." "Two years ago, one of your company's salespeople misled me about your product's performance record. What's changed to make me want to buy now?" "I've heard that your company has a poor reputation for aftersales service."

When confronted with a source objection, salespeople must make sure they understand the true concern. A question such as "Can you tell me why you feel that way?" will help clarify the objection. When responding, salespeople must be careful not to become too defensive and argumentative. If the objection has validity, the salesperson may be better off to admit past difficulties and then demonstrate how conditions are now different. If the concern has no merit, the salesperson must use facts to point out the fallacy of the source objections.

Competition.   The fourth type of objection is frequently encountered when calling on new customers. These prospects find their present suppliers satisfactory and they are unwilling to change. Examples of this objection include the following: "I've done business with DeLuxe for many years. Why should I change?" "It's too much trouble to change suppliers." "I like Joan [the competitor's salesperson], and she has done a good job for us."

Competition objections can be offset if the salesperson points out the additional benefits the company provides. One might describe a new feature or benefit that a competitor does not have. This requires that the salesperson possess adequate competitive information. A sales representative may also ask questions to identify some dissatisfaction with the customer's present supplier; the salesperson can then point out that his or her company can alleviate the problem.

Responding to Objections

A suggested four-step approach for responding to sales objections is shown in Fig. 5-3. After an objection has been raised, the salesperson must make sure the true nature of the concern is understood. This involves listening carefully and asking

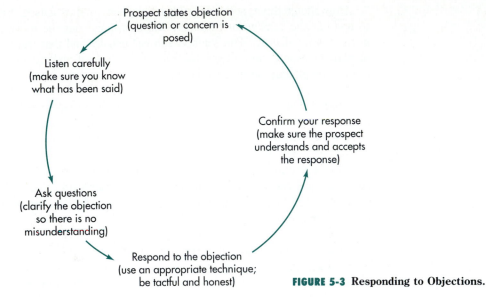

FIGURE 5-3 **Responding to Objections.**

questions to clarify the issue. The salesperson then uses an appropriate technique to respond to the objection, and afterward makes sure the prospect understands and accepts the response.

This procedure suggests two basic rules for handling objections: ask questions, and respond directly to a prospect's concerns.

Ask Questions.   Often a prospect's objections are unclear and the salesperson must probe to determine the real reason for the resistance. Consequently, most experts suggest that the first step in handling an objection is to turn it into a question: "Evidently, you have a reason for saying that. Do you mind if I ask what it is?" This helps both the seller and prospect identify and clarify the problem.

Respond to the Objection.   Once a salesperson has identified the true objection, it must be answered. In most selling situations, an objection is an opening for an effective salesperson to expand the presentation and to strengthen the selling points of the item or service. The best sales tactic is to meet an objection directly.[25]

Product knowledge plays an important role in handling objections, especially timing or price objections.[26] If a customer says that the price of a product is too high, the sales representative can explain the reasons for the price and emphasize the product's added features and quality. One must be very careful not to contradict or argue with a customer. In the long run, no salesperson has ever won an argument with a customer.

In addition to the general guidelines for responding to an objection, there are a number of specific techniques used by experienced salespeople.[27] The *yes . . . but method* is the most popular. The salesperson agrees with the prospect's objection, but then makes a statement that offsets the objection: "Yes, Mr. Swanson, our prices are slightly higher than our competitors, but we use higher-quality materials so our product lasts longer, and you actually save money in the long run."

yes . . . but method Sales technique in which the salesperson agrees with the prospect's objection, but then makes a statement that offsets the objection

SALES MANAGEMENT IN PRACTICE

TOWN & COUNTRY

Real estate sellers often face objections from potential home buyers who are not sure they can afford the house they want. To help solve this problem, the sales staff at Town & Country, a Chicago home builder, has been provided with computers to use in responding to such objections.

After a salesperson plugs in information about a prospect's income, savings, and debt situation, specially designed software determines whether the prospect can handle a mortgage. The prospect is given a printout that includes, in addition to data on the ability to afford a home, rent or buy comparisons and available options for all the homes the prospect is interested in.

Once a prospect knows a new home is affordable, continuing with the sales process is usually much easier.

Another advantage of the computers is their speed. Without the computers, salespeople had to perform calculations by hand, and they were often distracted from the sale itself. Equipped with computers, salespeople are able to make a more seamless presentation.

The Town & Country computers are no substitutes for good personal selling, but they are very useful to agents faced with the "I don't know if I can afford it" objection. With the computers, salespeople are able to respond to this objection quickly and efficiently, and greatly increase their chances of getting to the next phase of the selling process—the close.

---

boomerang method Sales technique that converts a prospect's reason for not buying into a reason for buying

comparison method Sales technique that minimizes the prospect's objection by comparing it with something that is acceptable

compensation method Sales technique in which the salesperson recognizes the prospect's objection, but then points out advantages that compensate for the problem raised

case history method Sales technique in which the salesperson uses an example of a satisfied buyer to offset the prospect's objection

The *boomerang method* involves converting a prospect's reason for not buying into a reason for buying. For example, Bob Mason, a young father, has indicated that he cannot afford a life insurance policy. The agent responds: "Bob, I realize your concern. But that's the very reason you should buy life insurance. Things are tight now, but what would happen to your family if you were not here to support them?"

The *comparison method* involves an attempt to minimize the prospect's objection by comparing it with something that is acceptable. "Mr. Morales, I realize that these special radial tires cost $150 more for a set of four than the tires you now have on your car. But you'll probably drive 45,000 miles on these tires during the next two years. It will cost you less than $1.50 per week to provide the added safety of these tires. That is less than most people spend for newspapers during a week."

The *compensation method* is similar to the yes . . . but method. The salesperson recognizes the prospect's objection, but then points out advantages that compensate for the objection: "Yes, Ms. Larsen, delivery of our machine will take six weeks longer, but the added care we take in filling your order will mean that the machine will not have to be modified to meet your specific needs."

The *case history method* uses an example of a satisfied buyer to offset the prospect's objection: "I know how you feel, Mr. Armstrong. Bob Watson of AVCO Company was also concerned about our meeting delivery commitments. We have not only met our commitments to AVCO, but we are two weeks ahead of schedule. If you'd like, I can call Bob so you can discuss this with him."

CLOSING

The final part of the sales presentation is the *close* or requesting the order. After a salesperson has established rapport with the prospect, demonstrated the product's features and benefits, and handled any objections, he or she is ready to ask for the

close Culmination of the sales presenta-tion—when the sales representative tries to get an order or achieve some other goal

order. The entire sales effort has been wasted unless the prospect agrees to buy the product.

Many salespeople fail to close a sale because they do not understand its role in the selling process. This point has been explained as follows:

> Well planned and structured closing techniques move the prospect into making a deci-sion after he [or she] is convinced that he [or she] wants and needs the product. Closing is the sum total of the steps . . . from the time you first contacted the pros-pect until he [or she] is satisfied with the purchase.[28]

As this quotation suggests, closing is the natural culmination of the sales process. It is an agreement to do business. It is not an attempt to trick the customer into buying a product. Being honest and straightforward about what is wanted is the best approach to closing the sale.[29] The alert salesperson will know when the prospect is ready to make a commitment. The two key aspects of closing are knowing when to close and how to close.

When to Close

Trying to close a sale too early or too late will generally result in a lost sale. If a close is attempted too soon before the prospect is convinced, the seller will give the impression of being overly aggressive. Closing too late, after the person's interest has peaked, may result in the prospect's becoming bored or impatient. Salespeople determine when to close by observing buying signals and using trial closes.

Looking and Listening for Buying Signals.   It has been said that buying signals are like clues in a mystery novel: The clues may not be noticed by others, but they are clear to a professional. *Buying signals* are indications that tell an observant salesperson that the prospect is ready to buy. These signals can be verbal or nonverbal.

buying signals Indications that the prospect is ready to buy

Verbal Buying Signals.   The prospect may make comments that suggest a readiness to make a commitment. These may be in the form of statements or questions. Some verbal buying signals are: "How soon can the order be processed?" "I would like to have our attorney review this proposal." "I understand your company is the innovator in this field."

body language Facial expressions and physical action that may act as buy-ing signals

Nonverbal Buying Signals.   Facial expressions and physical actions, known as *body language,* also act as buying signals. Much has been written about how people communicate through their body movements.[30] Astute salespeople understand and use nonverbal communications; they know how and when to react to a prospect's body signals, such as gestures, expressions, and movements.[31] Positive actions include moving forward in the chair, nodding one's head up and down, using open-handed gestures, and stroking one's chin. A friendly gesture, such as offering the salesperson a cup of coffee, is also a positive buying signal. On the other hand, arms crossed over the body, clenched hands, or movement away from the salesperson may signal defensiveness or some other form of negative reaction. The salesperson must then try to put the prospect at ease and reverse the negative feelings.

trial close Sales technique that asks for an opinion

Using a Trial Close.   The salesperson must not move too fast, even if a prospect appears to be sending positive buying signals. The prospect's opinion should be tested. There is an important difference between a *trial close* and a close. A trial close asks for an opinion; a close asks for a decision.

Many types of questions can be used to determine the prospect's readiness to buy. For example, one might ask: "How does this sound so far?" "Do you think this proposal has possibilities?" "Was there something you wanted to ask?" Or "In your opinion, do you think . . .?" Most people believe that the last question is best because it clearly asks for the prospect's opinion. The prospect is forced into commenting.

alternative pro-posal close Closing technique in which a salesperson offers the prospect a choice between details

How To Close

Closing is simply asking for the order. There are many ways to do this. The professional salesperson knows several techniques from which to select a close that fits the specific prospect and selling situation. Some effective closing techniques are described below.

assumptive close Close that assumes the prospect will make a commitment

The *alternative proposal close* offers the prospect a choice between details: "Do you prefer truck or rail shipment?" "Will the standard drill suit your needs, or would you prefer to go with the superior model that you have been examining?" The philosophy of this close is to ask for a relatively minor decision.

gift close Closing technique that provides the prospect an added inducement for taking immediate action

The *assumptive close* assumes that the prospect will make a commitment. After receiving a positive buying signal and verifying this with a trial close, the salesperson proceeds to write up the order or complete a shipping form. Then the prospect is asked to "sign your name here so that I can process the shipment."

The *gift close* provides the prospect with an added inducement for taking immediate action. "If you sign the purchase order today, I'm sure we can have the order delivered to you early next week."

action close Closing technique that suggests the sales representative take an action which will consummate the sale

The *action close* suggests that the sales representative take an action that will consummate the sale. "Let me arrange an appointment with your attorney to work out the details of the transaction."

one-more-yes close Closing technique in which the salesperson restates the benefits of the product in a series of questions that result in positive responses, then asks for the order

The *one-more-yes close* is based on the principle that saying yes can become a habit. The salesperson restates the benefits of the product in a series of questions that will result in positive responses. The final question asks the person to complete the sale.

balance sheet close Closing technique in which the salesperson and the prospect list the reasons for acting now against the reasons for delaying, aimed at pointing out the advantages of prompt action

The *balance sheet close* is an effective technique to use with procrastinators. The salesperson and the prospect list the reasons for acting now on one side and the reasons for delaying action on the other. If the salesperson has built a persuasive case, the reasons for immediate action will outweigh the reasons for delaying. Then the salesperson can ask for the order.

direct close Closing technique in which the salesperson simply asks the prospect for a decision

The *direct close* is clear and simple. The salesperson asks for a decision. Many salespeople feel that this is the best approach, especially if there are strong positive buying signals. Frequently, the salesperson will summarize the major points that were made during the presentation prior to asking for the sale.

A direct, nonthreatening close is to simply ask: "How should we proceed from here?" or "Where do we go from here?" This type of close is most applicable when the salesperson feels that all the prospect's relevant needs have been identified and product benefits have been thoroughly explained.

Many other closing techniques are available to resourceful salespeople. The crucial point is that the salesperson should try several closings throughout a presentation. Experienced salespeople always try to close early. If they are not successful, they continue the presentation and then try a different close. Good salespeople know that if they have successfully completed all of the earlier steps, then the prospect is worth an extra effort at closing. In most cases, this simply means switching to a different type of close. Closing is the most important aspect of selling. Unless the salesperson can close the sale, the other steps in the sales process are meaningless.

FOLLOWUP

followup
Salesperson's after-sales activities

Many sales representatives make the mistake of assuming that the selling process has been completed when the sale is made. This is a critical mistake. The term *"followup"* is used to describe the important aftersale activities. Effective sales followup reduces the buyer's dissonance, or doubt, and it improves the chance that the person will buy again in the future. Sales representatives must always follow up on the sale.

Long-term customer relationships are built on integrity and effective followup. It is especially important that salespeople be perceived as honest, dependable, and concerned with their customers' long-term needs and problems. Customer trust grows as the salesperson demonstrates dependability, competence, and other desired traits over time.[32]

A leading sales representative for Xerox has described the importance of followup:

I'll be there after the sale because after I've sold something to someone, I can sell them more. I just don't disappear. You see me as much after the sale as you do before the sale. . . . I want to be sure that my competitor doesn't get in the door.[33]

Postsale Action

The most important part of the followup is to make sure that the item or service sold to the customer has been received in good condition. Salespeople should check back with buyers to determine whether they are satisfied with their purchases and to remove any sources of discontent. These callbacks also allow the salesperson to gather valuable market information and to sell additional items.[34]

To assist salespeople in the required followup activities, many firms are making their technical staff and resources an integral part of the selling effort. Technical support staff can assist in building long-term relationships. They can also help identify new sales opportunities and generate repeat sales. Although technical support personnel are helpful throughout the selling process, they are especially critical for installation, training, and other after-sales service activities.[35]

Another important reason for followup is that satisfied customers become good salespeople for the products they bought. For example, buyers often reduce their dissonance by promoting their purchases to their peers. Any major purchase decision creates a considerable degree of anxiety in the buyer. This anxiety can be reduced by promoting the item to others. So, it is important that the salesperson initiate a procedure for following up on all customers to remove postpurchase doubts.

Top automobile salesman Jim Dailey attributes much of his success to followup. He has been quoted as saying: "It doesn't take but 10 minutes to check out the car to see if everything's in order. I don't just throw them the keys with a casual 'thank you'!"[36] Dailey works hard to establish a long-term relationship with his customers. He sends thank you cards, makes service arrangements, and even lends his own car to selected customers when their own are being repaired.

Customer Relations

In addition to postsale activities, salespeople are also required to maintain good customer relations. Several specific policies should be instituted and practiced consistently to ensure that customers' needs are not neglected.

Handle Complaints Promptly and Pleasantly.   No matter how efficient a company is, there are always some customer complaints. These reports should be taken seriously and handled with concern. The customer must know that the company cares about maintaining good customer relations. Therefore, sales managers must develop policies and procedures for handling customers' grievances and train their sales personnel to use these approaches effectively.[37]

Maintain Contact with Customers.   Reasonably frequent contacts with existing customers are an expected part of the sales representative's job. For important customers, personal visits are appropriate. Letters, notes, and telephone calls are also good ways to keep in touch with customers. Many companies also offer customer newsletters.

Keep Serving the Customer.   Successful salespeople never stop serving customers. In addition to handling complaints, they keep customers informed, fulfill reasonable requests, and provide other forms of assistance as needed.

Show Appreciation.   There are many ways to thank customers for their business. Small gifts can be given after the sale and at appropriate times during the year. Also, saying thank you by actions as well as words will let customers know that they are appreciated.

Self-Analysis

self-analysis
Continual personal evaluation of a salesperson's own performance and methods

A final followup task is *self-analysis*—a continual evaluation by sales personnel of their own selling performance and methods. A salesperson should analyze every call to determine what factors influenced its eventual outcome. Self-analysis is very useful in improving overall sales effectiveness.

Specific questions a salesperson should ask after completing a call include the following:

1. Were the planned sales objectives achieved?
2. What could I have done better?
3. What did I learn from this call that will contribute to my future success?

1. **Discuss the Various Factors That Go into Making an Effective Sales Presentation.**

   Effective sales presentations begin with the approach, during which the salesperson obtains the prospect's interest and attention. Then the salesperson asks questions to identify and/or clarify the prospect's needs. The rest of the presentation involves efforts to direct the prospect's attention to desirable product features and to demonstrate the product's benefits. From there the salesperson handles any objections, tries to reach his or her overall goal (this is known as the "close"), and performs followup activities.

2. **Identify Ways to Open a Sales Presentation.**

   The following are effective ways of starting a presentation:

   - Asking questions
   - Using a referral
   - Offering a benefit
   - Complimenting a prospect
   - Giving something of value

3. **Describe Probing Techniques Used to Determine Prospects' Needs.**

   Probing techniques that salespeople can use to determine prospects' needs include open-ended questions to encourage prospects to talk, reflective questions used in response to prospects' comments, and directive questions used to point prospects toward areas of agreement and determine if they are ready to close.

4. **Explain Features-Benefits Selling and Other Techniques Used to Convince Prospects.**

   Features-benefits selling is a technique in which a seller relates to a prospect's needs by emphasizing the benefits a prospect will receive from the features of a good or service. Other techniques used to convince prospects include citing industry studies and using visual aids, testimonials, examples, guarantees, and demonstrations.

5. **Outline the Types of Objections Encountered by Sales Personnel and Explain How Each Objection Should Be Handled.**

   The following are types of objections encountered by sales personnel:

   - *Timing objections.* Salespeople should find out the reason for the delay and point out the advantage of making a decision immediately.
   - *Price objections.* Salespeople should handle these by pointing to quality and other benefits the customer will receive by purchasing the good or service.
   - *Source objections.* Salespeople should address these by making sure they understand the prospect's concerns. Then they should demonstrate how things have changed or point out the fallacy of the objection.
   - *Competition objections.* These can be offset by pointing out the additional benefits the vendor company provides.

6. **Identify the Various Closing Techniques.**

   Closing techniques available to salespeople include the following:

   - Alternative proposal close
   - Assumptive close
   - Gift close
   - Action close
   - One-more-yes close
   - Balance sheet close
   - Direct close

7. **Explain the Importance of Sales Followup.**

   Sales followup is crucial because it reduces the buyer's dissonance and it improves the chance that the person will buy again in the future. Effective followup shows that a salesperson is honest, dependable, and concerned with the customer's long-term needs and problems.

REVIEW QUESTIONS

1. How is modern selling different from the structured approach of earlier days? What skills must salespeople possess in order to be adaptive sellers?
2. What sort of gifts should be used to open a sales presentation? What limitations must be remembered when giving gifts?
3. List the sequence of steps in SPIN selling. When is SPIN selling most appropriate?
4. Why is understanding when and how to ask questions essential to the success of salespeople? Explain the concept of empathy.
5. When should a salesperson ask questions during the sales process? Cite some examples of questions that can be used.
6. Name the advantages of using audiovisual aids in sales presentations. How do guarantees influence prospects? What benefits do demonstrations provide?
7. Describe two wrong reactions that are sometimes characteristic of salespeople and their handling of objections. How do experienced salespeople view objections?
8. What are the basic rules for handling objections? What specific techniques can be used to handle them?
9. What are the two key aspects of closing? Explain the difference between a trial close and a close.
10. What is the most important part of sale followup? How can companies maintain good customer relations?

DISCUSSION QUESTIONS

1. While image is not really everything, it is important. Many managers are afraid to approach a salesperson about being poorly dressed or less than socially skilled for fear of offending the individual with these touchy issues. Spend some time thinking of innovative and sensitive ways for managers to prevent such situations or to handle them when they do arise.
2. List a possible feature and possible benefit of each of the following:

   - A stereo
   - A puppy
   - A pair of sunglasses

- A magazine subscription
- A coat

3. Deborah Tannen is a best-selling author who has studied the different communication styles that exist between men and women. Women, Tannen says, are more likely than men to take sales objections personally because women are usually not used to dealing with challenges as much as men are. Other differences, according to Tannen, are that men are concerned with being respected, while women want to be liked; when being talked to, women are more likely to nod their heads and say "uh-huh" than men are; and women make direct eye contact more than men do.[38] Make an informal analysis of Tannen's assertions by watching the communication styles of men and women around you. Do Tannen's statements seem true? How could the traits Tannen mentions cause miscommunication in a sales call?

4. The American Medical Association allows pharmaceutical salespeople to offer gifts to doctors if these gifts are small or helpful to patients. Recently, a government study found that eight out of ten doctors are offered gifts by pharmaceutical salespeople. These range from pens, prescription pads, meals, and trips to research funding.[39] Which of these gifts would you consider "small"? Which are helpful to patients? Should an ethical standard be set for accepting such gifts?

5. Recall a recent sales presentation made to you. Which closing technique did the salesperson use on you? Why do you think this technique was selected? Discuss.

E T H I C A L
D I L E M M A

There is a tendency for some salespeople to oversell by exaggerating the benefits of their offerings. As a result uninformed buyers may purchase a product which does not perform as well as promised. How can sales managers make certain their salespeople do not misrepresent products?

SALES MANAGEMENT CASE

Selling to Businesses

Businesses that sell to other businesses face special challenges—one of which is trying to determine who in a prospective company actually makes the buying decisions. Business-to-business marketers now segment industrial markets on the basis of geography, demographics, business personality, and behavior in order to make their selling efforts more efficient. Salespeople who sell to businesses also desire to organize themselves efficiently; to do so, many use a method called "strategic selling."

Strategic selling provides a methodology for all members of a salesforce to use in analyzing sales opportunities. This methodology ensures that everyone speaks a common language; for example, an "economic buying influence" is a person with authority to buy. A "coach" is someone who guides a sales-

person through the customer's organization. A "technical buying influence" judges how well a product meets technical specifications, and a "user buyer influence" is a person who will use the product on a day-to-day basis. Each of these influences can be in an "even keel," "growth," "trouble," or "overconfident" mode. A "Blue Sheet" is provided for every prospect; this form serves as a source of information about the progress being made and the direction in which the selling effort is going.

Companies selling products that are very expensive or very technical can especially benefit from strategic selling. For expensive or technical goods or services, the decision to buy is difficult to make because it is economically consequential or complicated. For example, an organization that sells satellite-based communications networks for an average of $7 million each uses strategic selling. The firm has shortened its sales cycle in a number of cases, and some sales have been directly attributable to the strategic selling system.

Questions

1. How can strategic selling help salespeople make more effective presentations?

2. Select a product and describe the features and benefits you would emphasize to the following individuals:

    a An economic buying influence
    b. A technical buying influence
    c. A user buying influence

3. In selling the product you selected, what objections would you expect from each of the influences listed? How would you react to such objections?

CHAPTER 6

TERRITORY DEVELOPMENT AND TIME MANAGEMENT

LEARNING GOALS

- Understand the nature and scope of territory management.
- Identify the reasons for establishing and revising territories.
- Describe the objectives, criteria, and basis for territory formation.
- Outline a model of territory management.
- List and discuss routing patterns and scheduling issues.
- Explain the concept of time management and how it relates to sales territories.

ASSIGNING TERRITORIES

When Dictaphone began experiencing high sales force turnover and decreasing productivity, its management began paying closer attention to the exit interviews of departing salespeople. These interviews indicated that many of them were unhappy with the company's territory assignments.

This situation concerned Dictaphone's management, since one of the main purposes of territories is to motivate salespeople. Motivation is hampered, however, if territories are not fairly or efficiently assigned.

Dictaphone changed its territory assignments through the use of a sophisticated computer program. Historical sales data by type of business, the number of employees working at the business, and market potential, along with the 80/20 rule (80 percent of

a company's business comes from 20 percent of its customers), were combined to come up with efficient and fair territories. The benefits of this new system included reduced sales force turnover and increased productivity. Also, the system allowed better control.

The difficulty of territory development and time management increases with the size of the business. When the task of territory assignment becomes very complicated, technology provides a way to determine optimal assignments.[1]

Chapter 6 discusses time and territory management. The options available to sales managers are numerous. Territories can be based on geography, market potential, servicing requirements, and workload assign-

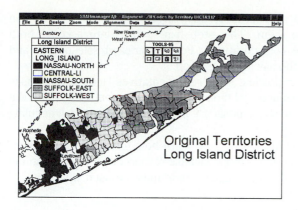

Original Territories
Long Island District

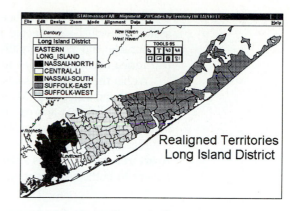

Realigned Territories
Long Island District

ments. They can be developed through one of several allocation methods, and salespeople can cover their territories using one of several patterns. The number of ways in which salespeople can spend their time are equally numerous. A major responsibility of the sales manager is to increase the efficiency of time and territory management by sales personnel.

CHAPTER OVERVIEW

Salespeople are not only responsible for individual customers (account management), but they are also responsible for a group of accounts (territory management). This is the first step in moving from selling to managing. A sales manager must learn to use time efficiently and must provide guidance to salespeople so that they will also make the most productive use of their time. Establishment of sales territories is the starting point for this critical management activity.

Ideally, sales territories are structured in a way that facilitates planning and control of the sales effort. Calling patterns can be adjusted to reflect differences in account potentials. Improved sales force control is achieved by setting quotas and other sales objectives on a territory-by-territory basis and comparing actual performance against these targets. Morale is improved when salespeople receive credit for the results.

Territories are well suited to most selling situations. Exceptions include certain nonrepetitive sales situations and highly specialized technology applications. Similarly, a firm may exempt given types of accounts from territorial coverage.

Sales territories are established for a number of reasons, ranging from account servicing to managerial control. Occasionally, changes in environmental conditions or managerial philosophy prompt a review and possible revision of territorial boundaries. By and large, however, territories are a long-lasting structural arrangement.

Territorial boundaries can be determined by dividing the company's total market into smaller parts. Or they can be decided by taking the smaller units of that market—the individual accounts—and assembling them into larger territories. In either case, each territory must be cohesive in a way that promotes the efficiency and effectiveness of the sales effort.

Once territories have been appropriately structured, sales management can assign individual salespeople to them. This step has to take into account both measurable and nonquantitative considerations. Poorly matched salespeople and territories become liabilities to the sales organization.

Within their assigned sales territories, sales representatives face the dual tasks of routing and scheduling. Minimizing travel time and maximizing contact time are the objectives; different approaches to these goals are possible. Routing and scheduling involve constant decision making.

Finally, salespeople and their managers must learn how to manage their time. Apart from talent, time is a salesperson's most valuable resource. To yield maximum benefit to both the salesperson and the company, time must be used wisely.

THE NATURE OF TERRITORY MANAGEMENT

When sales representatives are placed in charge of their own territories, the scope of their activities broadens. Instead of merely taking and executing orders from both their superiors and their customers, they assume responsibility for making things happen. Since sales territories are microcosms of a firm's total market, this involves scaled-down managerial duties.

Defining Territory Management

sales territory
Configuration of current and potential accounts for which responsibility has been assigned to a particular sales representative

A *sales territory* is a configuration of current and potential accounts for which responsibility has been assigned to a particular sales representative. Although geographic considerations play a role in setting boundaries, sales territories are primarily based on customer groupings. This is particularly true in the case of significant accounts with multiple plant locations that buy centrally but require on-location servicing. Occasionally problems arise in assigning territories. For instance, a salesperson has developed a strong personal relationship with a customer who relocates out of the salesperson's service area. Should the salesperson who invested a great deal of time in cultivating the account continue servicing it, or should the account be reassigned for geographic reasons—at the risk of losing it?[2] Assignment issues can also arise when buying professionals change employers, but prefer to continue doing business with their favorite sources, or even when salespeople are given new territories. These problems must be resolved for a sales organization to function smoothly.

Every conceivable variation of territory organization can be found in actual practice, ranging from rigid geographic setups to situations that disregard all geographic factors. Strict geographic boundaries are typical for cigarette and other types of grocery sales, in which intensity of coverage and restocking frequency are overriding determinants. The other extreme is represented by high-technology firms, whose highly trained and specialized sales engineers freely roam the country, or even the globe, in search of a very limited number of customers.

major accounts
Customers whose significance to the company's business requires special attention and experience

Other companies use mixed systems that employ geographic boundaries mainly for convenience but exempt selected accounts. Exempted accounts tend to fall into either of two categories: major or direct accounts. *Major accounts*, sometime called "key accounts," are customers whose significance to the company's business re-

direct accounts
Large accounts involving special arrangements in terms of pricing, credit, or product design

quires special attention and experience. They are usually called on either by special sales personnel, variously labeled "senior sales representatives" or "key account managers," or by the appropriate district or regional sales manager. *Direct accounts*, sometimes called "house" or "national accounts," are those serviced by home office personnel or executives. These accounts are generally very large—such as central buying offices of national or multinational firms, fleet buyers, and exporters—and often involve special arrangements in terms of pricing, credit, or product design. The special servicing of both types of accounts can cause resentment among regular sales force members unless they understand that territories are groups of customers, not geographic areas.[3]

territory management Planning, implementation, and control of salespersons' activities with the goal of realizing the sales and profit potentials of their assigned territories

Territory management can be defined as the planning, implementation, and control of salespersons' activities with the goal of realizing the sales and profit potentials of their assigned territories.[4] As territory managers, salespeople must first be planners. It is the responsibility of sales representatives to plan their activities in their territories: "Territorial planning has been described as a predetermined course of action that involves establishing objectives, estimating the resources needed, and designing strategies which utilize these resources for the most efficient accomplishment of the stated objectives."[5] The implementation phase of territory management puts the plan into action while the control component activates a feedback mechanism to keep territorial performance on course.

The Scope of Territory Management

Salespersons may be viewed as scaled-down sales managers since they bear the ultimate burden of managing parts of the customer base. But there is one important difference between them: In managing their territories, salespeople manage only themselves and their time, not the activities of other people. No subordinates report to them.

At its core, territory management involves making the best use of one's time. A supportive, cooperative relationship with one's superiors and the home office is essential to good territory management. Successful territory managers must also practice continuing professional development.

Table 6-1 presents a checklist showing the extensive range of territory management. A territory manager must carry out a large number of specific responsibilities related to a given group of customers. This requires a broad range of skills: analytical thinking, comprehensive planning and preparation, careful decision making, human relations skills, effective communications, and efficient time management.

SALES TERRITORY DESIGN

Designing sales territories involves breaking down a firm's customer base so that accounts can be well serviced by individual salespersons. This assignment of accounts ranks as one of the most important responsibilities of sales management. Poor territory design has severe repercussions, such as inadequate market coverage, unequal workloads, lack of control over the sales force, and depressed morale.

A company's sales territories represent basic accountability units at the lowest level of aggregation. Several territories are usually combined into a district, several

TABLE 6-1 Territory Management Checklist

Analyze a territory

1. Maintain constant analysis of territory with sales supervisor to determine the following:
   A. When and where new accounts are needed.
   B. What must be done to meet volume and dealer development objectives.
2. Carefully select potential new accounts, based on the following considerations:
   A. Character.
   B. Capacity.
   C. Credit.
   D. Competition.
3. Continually evaluate current accounts to ensure that you have the best possible accounts.
4. Allocate received territory potential and quota to current and prospective accounts.
5. Set short- and long-range objectives for each account to achieve territory quotas.

Prepare

1. Work closely with your sales supervisor to develop the basic proposal.
2. Develop new account presentation based on your research of account sales and operating activity.
3. Arrange meetings with all account personnel concerned.

Present

1. Bring out all the advantages of carrying and using your products.
2. Explain cooperative advertising or other programs.
3. Explain the terms and extent of your company's credit policies.
4. Sell planned programs tailored for the account.
5. Make the recommended opening order for the products and merchandising materials.
6. Secure the order and arrange for followup on the delivery and display of products.

Service

1. Train personnel to sell or use the products.
2. Set up and assist continuing advertising or other "use" plans.
3. Arrange for adequate display or storage.
4. Follow through with extra attention for the first ninety days.

Schedule for best use of time

1. Organize time, work, and materials to achieve the maximum time for selling.

districts into a region, several regions into a zone, and a number of zones into the national marketplace.

The factors that motivate and govern the formation of sales territories are as multifold as the companies influenced by them. However, they can usually be classified into three categories: customer-related, salesperson-related, and managerial. Conditions in the different territories and information about them change over time. Most structures need revision periodically.

Reasons for Establishing Territories

Companies form sales territories mainly to maximize sales and profits. Sales territories make this goal more achievable because they reduce it to reasonable

TABLE 6-1 *(Continued)*

   A. Analyze your territory to establish the frequency of calls for all accounts, based on the importance of account classification and your allocation of potential to each.
   B. Apportion the time you will devote to each account, based on potential. Work with the sales supervisor to arrive at the most efficient coverage.
   C. Establish routing patterns to achieve maximum coverage with a minimum of call-backs.
   D. Establish progressive objectives for each account to secure continuing development.
   E. Maintain a file on each account including the following data:
      1. Names of personnel.
      2. Buying history.
      3. Progressive objectives.
      4. Merchandising ideas.
2. Perform nonselling tasks during nonselling hours.
   A. Fill out reports and orders.
   B. Plan calls and promotions.

Coordinate with headquarters

1. Apply company policies, principles, and procedures to your everyday operations.
2. Submit accurate reports—on time.
3. Review your performance with your sales supervisor and set plans for improvement.
4. Work with your sales supervisor to establish account potentials.
5. Help your management direct field selling efforts effectively.
   A. Keep your sales supervisor informed of territorial trends, productwise.
   B. Keep your sales supervisor posted on account attitudes.
   C. Keep your sales supervisor informed of competitive promotions or of your local promotions that proved effective.
6. Suggest areas of improvement in the overall operation.

Maintain personal development

1. Maintain good personal appearance and deportment.
2. Maintain car appearance and upkeep.
3. Keep informed on industry trends; know what the competition is doing.
4. Keep up to date on product knowledge.
5. Be constantly on the lookout for new sales and merchandising ideas you can adapt to your job.

proportions. Individual salespeople then can make it their personal mission to improve territory yield. More specifically, however, there are three pairs of guiding principles that cause sales management to employ territories in their operations. They are listed in Table 6-2.

The list of reasons for sales territories is headed by customer-related purposes. Accounts that are inadequately covered yield less than their true potential and may be won over by competitors. Conversely, proper territory design yields maximum sales and profits. This means that each territory should contain just the right account mix—neither too many nor too few of any account type. Customer service benefits are another result of proper territory design. Personalized customer service produces immense mutual satisfaction.

TABLE 6-2 Reasons for, and Benefits of, Sales Territories

Reasons	Benefits
CUSTOMER-RELATED	
Provide intensive market coverage	Produce higher sales
Provide excellent customer service	Produce greater satisfaction
SALESPERSON-RELATED	
Foster enthusiasm	Lead to less turnover
Facilitate performance evaluation	Offer rewards related to effort
MANAGERIAL	
Enhance control	Reduce expenses
Coordinate promotion	Give more "bang for the buck"

A second set of reasons for territory establishment involves the salesperson in charge. Territories can act as morale builders, motivating salespeople to give their best, since everything that happens in an individual's territory is a direct reflection on him or her. Salespeople feel able to shape their own destinies. Individuals who experience this sense of entrepreneurship will be less inclined to move on to other employers. Sales territories also make it easy to evaluate individual performance and reward it appropriately. Most sales compensation plans contain an incentive component tied to territory results.

The third set of factors related to territories is of particular concern to sales management. Sales supervisors have to keep a tight handle on selling expenses, and this is easiest to accomplish when costs are related to territories. Expenses can best be kept in line and linked to sales efforts at the level of individual territories. The careful review of calling patterns, allocations, and territorial reports, as well as periodic field visits, allow sales management to exercise effective control over the field effort.

Reasons for Revising Territories

When a company first approaches the task of dividing its customers into territories, it typically possesses inadequate information about sales potentials. If it puts little effort into seeking this information, its original territory breakdowns will be the product of arbitrary decisions. But even if a company systematically examines the potential of its customer base, markets are dynamic and conditions change. Major accounts open or close down facilities, move into or out of an area, or shift the nature of their business. Sometimes they become subsidiaries of other companies, resulting in an alteration in their buying policies. Similarly, competition may have intensified in a territory, requiring a redoubling of the sales effort. Sales management may have overestimated the potential in a territory, or maybe an entire industry closes its doors, leaving the salesperson without adequate earnings potential.

Among the customer-related reasons for territory revision are shifts in a customer's business, which may be geographic or technological in nature or which may relate to the firm's product policies. More aggressive domestic and international competition can also necessitate changes.

Salesperson-related revisions can be triggered either by physical or psychological changes. A sales representative may display a reduced energy level. Family problems of various kinds can affect territory performance significantly. A salesperson may also simply be frustrated due to the inadequate challenge posed by a specific territory. Any of these situations may call for a territory realignment.

Management misjudgment heads the list of managerial reasons for territory revision. If a territory's sales potential was underestimated, the salesperson will be forced to skim an oversized territory rather than work it thoroughly. Underestimating sales potential is more common than its opposite of overestimating, which leads to the undersizing of territories. Managers can also find they need to realign territories as new product lines are introduced into the company's product mix and the presentation and servicing burdens become too great under the old arrangement. Or the maturing of a product line can cause an intensification of the personal selling effort, which in turn may require smaller territories. Similar developments can occur as entire firms grow and mature.

Reasons for Not Establishing Sales Territories

There are three instances in which territory formation is not appropriate: when a company is small, when friendship sales are important, and when high-technology selling is involved. A small business is not in a position to draw rigid territorial lines. It has to be quite flexible about who will handle a particular account. Social relationships or personal friendships are often the basis of sales in the financial services field. It would obviously be counterproductive to place territorial restrictions on such relationships. This would tend to drive salespeople to seek employment elsewhere and to take their following with them. In high-technology applications, there are often a very limited number of potential customers nationwide that require highly specialized advice. To restrict the kind of specialist salesperson who can effectively deal with such accounts to any type of territorial boundaries would be foolhardy.

Dealing with Territory Management Problems

Even the most carefully designed plan is bound to encounter problems when put into practice. Changing environmental conditions, inadequate insight into territorial parameters, and unanticipated behavior on the part of territory managers are among the reasons why difficulties occur. Sales management must see to it that problems are detected early and overcome before they become serious.

A list of typical territory management problems is presented in Table 6-3, together with capsule suggestions on how to correct them. The most frequent serious challenge caused by territory design is inadequate coverage. This problem is not necessarily avoidable, since financial, sales force, data, or geographic limitations may dictate a certain territory structure. Inadequate coverage results when a salesperson is given too many accounts or a territory whose geographic dimensions are too large to handle. The company does not realize its full sales potential because its territory managers cannot call on all of their accounts with sufficient frequency. The need to split some territories in order to cover them better should be anticipated when the original structure is laid out.

TABLE 6-3 Territory Management Problems and Remedies

Problems	Remedies
Inadequate coverage	Split territories
Inadequate size	Enlarge territories
Revision	Prepare salespeople
Shifting accounts	Revise territories
Direct accounts	Clarify at hiring
Inadequate support	Assist salespersons
Territory jumping	Eliminate practice
Overlapping territories	Minimize crossovers
Selling cost variations	Review cost figures
High turnover	Rectify causal factor

The opposite problem surfaces if territories offer inadequate potential and challenge. This can be solved by reassignment if it involves strictly personal issues. Certain differences in territory potentials can be intentional and even healthy, but one type of territory may appeal to a particular salesperson more than another. If the problem is structural and counterproductive to selling efforts in general, the need to redraw territorial boundaries is indicated.

Whenever territory revisions take place, personnel problems are commonplace. If a number of accounts are reassigned, the territory manager formerly in charge of them will fear a reduction in income. The possibility of such occurrences should be announced to job candidates during the hiring interview. If reassignments actually take place, the salesperson should be counseled on ways to increase sales volume and income through improved coverage of the remaining accounts.

Direct, house, or national accounts are a sore point in many sales organizations. Major customers are exempt from territorial assignment and are serviced directly by headquarters. Territory managers tend to resent the loss of such a substantial amount of business within the geographic boundaries of their territories. At the very least, they should be informed about this arrangement at hiring time. The number of such accounts should also be minimized, or the territory managers should be given overrides on this additional business. Sales representatives should also be involved in servicing these accounts.

It is essential to establish and maintain close communications with the inside organization at the home office. Commitments are sometimes made in good faith to customers, but are not followed through promptly by the internal organization, leading to friction with account contacts. Home office visits to shore up team spirit and bridge any communications gaps are useful and relatively inexpensive tools for effective sales management.

Salespeople occasionally invade each other's territories. The only sensible way to deal with this problem is to eliminate it. If insufficient territory potential, rather than greed, prompted the practice, territory revision may become necessary. The principle of the inviolability of sales territories should be upheld.

When a territory is divided, complaints by the former territory manager or account contacts can cause sales management to grant exceptions and allow the former territory manager, rather than the new territory manager, to service selected accounts. But this arrangement should be permitted for only a very short transition period.

Significant differences may be observed in selling costs between sales territories, suggesting vastly different potentials. High-potential territories are characterized by relatively low selling costs, whereas low-potential territories are plagued by high selling cost burdens. Excessive travel costs can also be a symptom that boundaries have been misdrawn in territory design.

An unusually high turnover of salespeople also indicates trouble. High levels of dissatisfaction and frustration drive territory managers to seek more fulfilling employment elsewhere. Business deteriorates as the continuity of coverage is threatened. Enlightened sales managers are sensitive to early warning signs, investigate the causes of discontent, and correct them immediately.

PROCEDURES FOR DEVELOPING TERRITORIES

When forming territories, there are certain objectives to be considered, such as workload and opportunity equalization. A variety of approaches are available to the sales executive, all of which are quantitative in nature. In applying these methods, a given sequence of steps has proven to be particularly effective. The process begins with the selection of an appropriate unit (or base) of aggregation and involves several points at which adjustments are made to refine the initial division of the firm's customer base.[6]

Objectives and Criteria for Territory Formation

Drawing up territories ranks among the most important responsibilities of sales managers. It profoundly affects sales force morale and performance. Results may be measured by absolute sales volume, relative market share, or profits. Consequently, the primary objective for the sales manager is to determine both the optimum number of territories to be formed and their configurations. If an insufficient number of territories are formed, the sales potential of the firm will not be realized for lack of coverage. If too many territories are created, the account base of the business will become fragmented. High turnover may result since salespeople will perceive little opportunity for personal growth in such a situation.

This leads to another major objective: the equalization of territory potentials. To be fair to all members of the sales force, all territories should possess equal potentials. Theoretically, this can be done by redistributing accounts until the optimum point is reached.[7] The result would inevitably be territories of different sizes, since accounts and geographic areas will differ with respect to sales potential. Because of variations in travel requirements and coverage difficulty, this often results in territories with unequal potentials. The problem is compounded by the fact that it is difficult to assess any territory's sales potential at a given time.

It may, however, be desirable for sales management to have territories with differing potentials. Limited-potential territories can be used as training grounds for new members of a sales force, or as less-demanding settings for senior members. Salespeople can be assigned to more challenging territories in accordance with their performance. A more appropriate objective in many cases may be adequately challenging territories, formed by taking into consideration coverage difficulty, salespersons' varying abilities, and territorial sales potentials.

The coverage objective is related to territory potential, since the latter will not be fully realized unless salespeople call on customers with the appropriate frequency. Adequate coverage is necessary for the firm to be able to achieve and defend a sizable market share in the face of vigorous competition. Ideally, coverage should be both effective and efficient: effective so that no significant sales opportunity in the territory remains unexploited, and efficient in that neither money nor time is wasted.

Another important consideration in establishing territories is the sales representative's workload and nature of the job. A person whose job is to prospect and sell can make more calls in a given day than a representative who must service each account (take inventories, write reorders, train personnel in products, and so forth). A prospecting salesperson can handle a larger territory assignment than a person who must provide full service for each account.

The type of product can dictate territorial size as well. The more selective the product, the larger the territory. Other factors affecting territorial configuration and size are the selling and organizing abilities of the sales representatives, the type of competition faced by the company, the desired intensity of market coverage, the stage of development a particular market has reached, the channels of distribution available, and the types of transportation used.

Bases for Territories

The objectives and criteria for sales territory formation are directly related to the bases used in creating the territories. The actual division of a firm's customer base into individual territories can be achieved by means of several methods, depending on which of four alternative types of bases is most important: geography, potential, servicing requirements, and workload. These bases are described below.

Geography.   The establishment of geographic territories—the most frequently used basis—is simple because it tends to adopt existing geopolitical boundaries such as states, counties, or cities. The major advantage of the geographic approach is the ready availability of secondary data from such sources as the U.S. Bureau of the Census, A.C. Nielsen's Retail Index, or *Sales & Marketing Management* magazine's Buyer Power Index. In terms of the sales opportunities existing for a particular kind of product, however, strictly geographically based territories tend to become quite arbitrary.

The use of trading areas can help overcome this problem. Trading areas mirror natural traffic and shopping flows to and from hub cities. They differ from one product category to the next. Some of the companies using trading areas lose some of their realism by arbitrarily adjusting their outlines to fit existing political boundaries. This is done primarily to use available statistical data.

Potential.   The potential approach refers to splitting up a firm's customer base according to sales potential. It would seem to provide equality of opportunity and thus bring out the best in salespeople. The procedure is relatively simple. First, management has to estimate the sales potential for the entire company, typically by applying an expected market share percentage to the projected market potential. Next, it has to determine what sales potential will be appropriate for the average salesperson. This average sales potential is divided into the organization's overall sales potential to arrive at the number of territories needed. The sales potentials of all the territories should be identical. However, the approach ignores the differences in coverage difficulty. Topography, customer density, and competitive intensity are among the factors that require modification of the equal-potential principle. So, while potential has to be taken into account, other aspects related to each individual territory must be considered too.

Servicing Requirements.   Among these aspects are the servicing requirements of current and prospective future accounts. Assume that a firm has estimated its total sales potential at $10 million for a given year. Sales management has further determined that each salesperson can handle a personal sales potential of $500,000. This would mean that twenty territories would be formed, all of which would have identical sales potentials of $500,000 each. However, the customer base constituting these potentials could differ from one territory to another. To contrast two possible extremes, one salesperson might have a single customer worth $500,000 a year, whereas another might be asked to work with 500 accounts doing $1000 worth of business annually.

A refinement of this approach classifies all accounts according to their annual potentials. The best known of these classifications distinguishes between A, B, and C accounts based on their annual volumes and established call frequencies. A accounts are cultivated aggressively and may receive weekly or even more frequent calls; they represent the mainstay of the business, but are also most vulnerable to competitive efforts. B accounts are solid, steady business. They are serviced regularly, perhaps at monthly intervals. C accounts are marginal and may warrant only quarterly visits. Depending upon the account mix, servicing requirements will differ from one territory to the next unless adjustments are made to achieve an equitable distribution.

Workload.   The fourth sales territory base, workload, goes one step further. It not only considers individual account potentials and servicing requirements in creating territories, but also reflects differences in coverage difficulty caused by topographical features, account locations, competitive activity, and so forth. A single urban area is likely to represent several sales territories, whereas a rural state may not offer enough potential for even a single sales representative. A rural salesperson may only be able to carry out two or three sales calls a day; his or her urban counterpart may easily accomplish ten or even fifteen visits daily. This raises complex issues of equity in workload and compensation.

Some companies try to attain equity by assigning finite numbers of accounts and establishing average call frequencies. For instance, a firm may give every territory manager two hundred accounts to service and prescribe an average frequency of ten calls per day. This would mean that all accounts are visited once during a month's twenty working days. Although this procedure is simple, it fails to account for the different servicing requirements of the various account categories and neglects new account development.

Other firms design territories to fit products or product lines. In high-technology companies in which highly specialized product knowledge is essential, there may only be one or two persons available who understand the complexities involved. They are often matched by a sparsity of accounts involving this kind of highly specialized technology. It is best to have these product specialists cover substantial areas in pursuit of a limited number of customers and prospects.

Methods of Designing Territories

buildup method Designing territories through combining enough pieces of a company's overall market to create units that offer sufficient sales challenge

The *buildup method* of designing territories involves combining enough pieces of a company's overall market to create units that offer sufficient sales challenge. To use this approach, actual and potential customers have to be identified and their individual sales volumes assessed. After classifying them according to desirable call frequencies and determining how many calls a salesperson can reasonably be expected to make, account mixes can be created to satisfy the dual goals of adequate sales challenge and adequate customer coverage. This method is favored by many consumer goods manufacturers looking for intensive distribution.

breakdown method Determining the number of territories by dividing projected average sales per salesperson into an overall sales forecast

The *breakdown method* proceeds in the opposite direction. It starts with the overall sales forecast for the entire company, which is in turn derived from a projection of the total market potential and an estimate of the company's likely share of it. The method then sets an average sales figure per salesperson that is subsequently divided into the overall sales forecast. The result is the number of territories to be formed. Such an approach may prove satisfactory for industrial goods producers that desire selective distribution. The method, however, suffers from a severe conceptual paradox: Instead of viewing sales as a result of salesforce effort and then forecasting sales accordingly, the number of members in the sales organization are determined by the expected overall sales. This can lead to a self-fulfilling prophecy.

incremental method Establishing additional territories as long as the marginal profit generated by the territories exceeds the cost of servicing them

The *incremental method* is conceptually the most appealing. With this approach, additional territories are created as long as the marginal profit generated exceeds the cost of servicing them. Administrative difficulties, however, hamper the method's applicability since it requires a cost accounting system capable of determining sales, costs, and profits associated with various levels of input. If a company can determine this kind of information, however, profits can be maximized by increasing the number of territories up to the point of negative returns.

Assigning Salespeople to Territories

The same salesperson can succeed in one territory and fail in another—with the same amount of effort. These differing outcomes may result from differing account mixes.[8] To succeed in a given territory, a salesperson has to relate well to the majority of the company's customers it contains. This vital rapport occurs most readily if the sales representative's personal charactertistics correspond closely to those of key contacts at major accounts. Sales managers should attempt to match salesperson and contact characteristics to the extent possible.

SALES MANAGEMENT IN PRACTICE

HYATT HOTELS

The selling of relationships goes right along with the selling of goods and services in the 1990s. Salespeople must be able to show that they understand a customer's needs better than the competition to be successful today.

The effects of the new relationship-oriented selling are apparent in territory management. Many sales forces that were once organized on a product or regional basis, for example, are now being reorganized on a customer basis. Salespeople who were expected to be product or regional experts are developing expertise in dealing with particular customers.

In 1990, Hyatt Hotels reorganized the way it sold reservations for its hotels in Hawaii. Before the change, a salesperson who worked for a particular Hawaiian Hyatt called travel agents, meeting planners, and corporations to pitch only that hotel at which he or she worked. Many organizations were called too often by too many salespeople in this uncoordinated effort, and potential customers sometimes felt annoyed.

Hyatt reassigned most of its Hawaii-based sales force to central selling offices in Chicago and Omaha. To convince disgruntled representatives that this was the right move, Hyatt's management told the newly assigned salespeople not to worry about how much they sold for the time being. They were instructed to spend their time getting to know their customers and how they made decisions. The process was dynamic; salespeople provided information to Hyatt, which in turn gave them comprehensive customer profiles to use in their selling efforts. Hyatt's salespeople slowly began to accept the new customer-based structure. Currently, it is still too early to tell how successful the new organization will be, but in one recent quarter bookings in Hawaii were up 25 percent from what they were in the same quarter of the previous year.

Success is further achieved if territorial assignments are kept stable over time so that salespeople closely identify with their territories. If individual desires and preferences are reflected in assignments, salespeople will be positively motivated to achieve higher performance levels. Frequent territory turnover, on the other hand, is highly disruptive to steady customer relationships, demoralizing to the salesforce, and frequently harmful to profits and sales volume. Building business requires continuity of effort. Some companies, bent on avoiding transfers at all costs, may even redesign territories to fit entrenched salespeople, thus reversing the logic of territorialization.

The ideal practice is to assign each salesperson to that territory where the person's relative contribution to the company's profits will be highest. This approach redirects managerial thinking from a volume orientation to a profit orientation. Its use is dependent on the availability of adequate cost data. Where the focus is on profits, territories with unequal potentials are assigned according to the perceived abilities of different sales personnel. Generally, this means that top performers are given the best territories, whereas beginners get the weakest. The top-down method allows new members of the sales organization to work their way up or older members to phase into retirement, but a rigid application of this method will not necessarily maximize profits. Since outstanding salespeople may not be adequately challenged if assigned to the territories with the highest potentials, higher profits may result from placing them in second-tier territories. To avoid demoralizing individuals assigned to territories with low potentials, differences in those potentials should be reflected in different sales quotas.

A MODEL OF TERRITORY MANAGEMENT

Having defined and explored the concept of territory management, and explored the scope of its activities, we can now design a model of the territory management cycle. This model is shown in Fig. 6-1. It reflects the cyclical nature of territory management and highlights the three major responsibilities emphasized earlier when it was defined: planning, implementation, and control.

The flow diagram of territory management activities necessarily begins with the planning phase because it governs the entire process. It is made up of four components: analysis, objectives, strategies, and tactics. The success of territory management hinges upon the analytical skills that the salespersons in charge possess or, alternatively, on the analytical assistance and support they receive from their superiors. The analysis component deals with three key concerns: account load, account potentials, and servicing requirements. The term *"account load"* refers to the number of actual and potential customers assigned to a given salesperson. Sales records provide a reasonable indication of each account's total purchase volume in a certain product category. From this information, the territory manager can project *account potential*, or the share of an account's business that the firm can reasonably expect to attract. New business potentials must also be considered. Established and new accounts have servicing requirements that are based on both their past volume with the company and their unique needs and problems.

Careful study of a territory's data base enables the sales representative to proceed to the next step of the planning phase—the setting of objectives. The first concern here should be sales volume and market share goals in the territory, which should be derived in a top-down manner, starting with corporate objectives. Volume targets in and of themselves are of little value; profit objectives are essential to keeping territory performance on track. New business targets should also be part of every territory plan. They include both the introduction of new product lines with established accounts and the conversion of selected prospects into buyers.

The territory manager next proceeds to map sales strategies. The volume of business obtained from the territory during the planning period is affected by the frequency with which the sales representative calls on the various accounts. In order to optimize the calling pattern, the accounts making up the territory have to be categorized according to their potentials. Each account type A, B, and C (large, medium, and small) is then assigned an appropriate call frequency, such as weekly, monthly, or quarterly.[9]

Familiarity with customer characteristics is helpful when the salesperson selects the items from the firm's overall product mix to be emphasized within the territory. Pricing policies, including promotional pricing and payment terms, are also part of the strategic approach to territory management.

The final component of the planning phase deals with tactical issues, such as intensity of territory coverage and the minimization of nonproductive time. The latter is an issue of time management and involves routing and scheduling tasks. *Routing* refers to a salesperson's travel plan, or the sequence of locations to be visited. The term *"scheduling"* refers to the sequencing of appointments or unannounced visits for maximum contact time. Both routing and scheduling are concerned with time management. Considerable economies and sales results can be achieved by effective time planning.

account load
Number of actual and potential customers assigned to a given salesperson

account potential
Share of an account's business that the firm can reasonably expect to attract

routing Establishing the sequence of locations a salesperson will visit

scheduling Sequencing of appointments or unannounced visits for maximum contact time

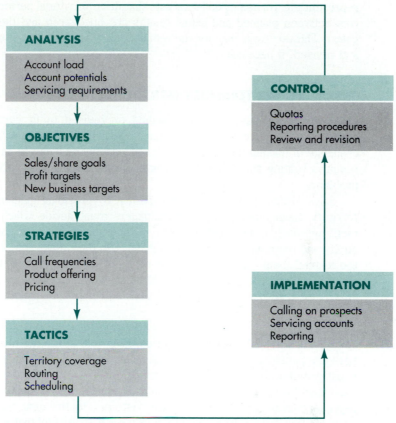

FIGURE 6-1 Model of the Territory Management Cycle.

Sales representatives do not make these decisions in isolation from the rest of the company. Their immediate supervisors, as well as the entire sales management hierarchy, become involved in this process. Individual territory plans have to be coordinated and integrated into the total planning structure.

In the implementation phase of the cycle, the territory manager attempts to achieve new business targets. To compensate for account turnover and provide for growth opportunities, new business development should be a continuous undertaking. The mainstay of each territory, however, is its established customer base. Selling and servicing these accounts has to be the principal thrust of territorial activity. Maintaining the satisfaction and expanding the purchase volume of established customers are among the foremost concerns of the territory manager. The third ingredient in the implementation package is reporting, that is, maintaining a steady flow of reports to the home office about sales results, problems, and competitive activity. Without these reports, sales management would be missing an essential link to the marketplace.

A feedback mechanism is required to ensure compliance. In the control loop of the territory management cycle, a comparison takes place between intended and actual results, with a view toward taking corrective action where needed. Quotas represent the volume or dollar targets that drive territorial performance. Discrepancies between planned and actual results are uncovered and their reasons investigated. The territorial plan for the remainder of the planning period is then reviewed and revised, if necessary.[10]

OPERATING THE TERRITORY MANAGEMENT SYSTEM

Once territories have been established or revised to fit current needs and all members of the existing sales force have been assigned, sales management faces the challenge of making the system work successfully on a day-to-day basis. This effort requires routing and scheduling programs and dealing with territory management problems.

Sales managers assist their salespeople by providing guidance and controls for territory management; however, managers must decide which territory management approach works best for each salesperson. Too much control can limit creativity and result in losing a top performer. On the other hand, if a sales manager is too relaxed about territory management, he or she may not be able to spot a problem while it can still be resolved easily. Most managers try to combine "hands-on" and "hands-off" approaches so that flexibility and results are maintained.[11]

Routing

Having established sales territories using one of the methods mentioned, sales personnel must now be routed. Decisions have to be made concerning the geographic pattern of account coverage. Length of visits to customers, as well as frequency, must also be spelled out. Without specific guidelines and instructions, some sales representatives simply go from one customer to the next making no distinction between how long or frequently they visit each. They feel that this is "covering" the territory.

Calling sequences must be laid out that satisfy the dual objectives of minimizing travel time and maximizing frequency of visits. Taking into account both daily call rates and the classification of the territory's customer base, a travel pattern must be established that guarantees complete and predictable coverage of all accounts. If done properly, routing ensures effective and efficient servicing of all accounts.

The process begins with account identification. The geographic locations of actual and potential customers have to be put on a detailed map of the territory. A wall chart using different colored pins to indicate potential and desired call frequencies can be used. Topographical features must be considered if these account locations are to be organized into an orderly succession of calls. Climate may play a role if areas are inaccessible during certain times of the year. Where using an automobile is impractical, modes of public transportation and their departure frequencies have to be studied. Finally, it may be important to reflect trading area boundaries in the route-planning effort.

The principles applied in connecting the customer locations on the map into a routing plan are obvious. Travel distances between two calls should be minimized, and backtracking on the same route and crisscrossing back and forth across a territory should be avoided. Since daily or weekly routes tend to start and end in the same location (the salesperson's home or office), a definite pattern begins to emerge.

straight-line method Routing pattern in which the salesperson begins with a call at the outer perimeter of his or her territory and then works back to the home base by calling on accounts located in the interior portion of the territory

cloverleaf pattern Routing method made up of four or more adjoining circular sequences

hopscotch pattern Hub-and-spoke-like sales routing pattern in which the salesperson starts a calling sequence at the outer end of a spoke and works back to the hub

This pattern is often achieved by identifying customer locations that are situated at the outer perimeter of the territory. The salesperson begins with a call on a customer located at that perimeter and then works back to the home base by calling on accounts located in the interior portion of the territory. This is known as the *straight-line method* of routing. If size and diversity of the territory prevent its use, a *cloverleaf pattern* of four or more adjoining circular sequences can provide the desired intensity of coverage without sacrificing economy. These individual routes represent one week's list of calls to be made. In a four-leaf clover, this would mean that every account is visited once every four weeks. A *hopscotch pattern*, on the other hand, follows more of a hub-and-spoke, rather than a circular, traveling route. Several spokes radiate from the hub (salesperson's residence). Each calling sequence starts at the outer end of a spoke, and the salesperson works back from there toward the hub in a zigzag manner. The three basic routing patterns are outlined in Fig. 6-2.

Responsibility for route planning depends largely on the nature of the product and the account mix as well as on a company's managerial philosophy. At one extreme, headquarters does all the routing—possibly with the help of computer models. At the other extreme, territory managers are left to their own devices in developing calling patterns. In between these extremes is the possibility of the district sales manager deciding the calling sequence. Headquarters routing is typical and appropriate in product categories that require the regular servicing of large numbers of accounts at identical frequencies, such as routes covered by a driver/delivery person in the tobacco and bakery products industries. By contrast, if differentiated call frequencies are indicated by the account mix and sensitivity to changes in local market conditions is essential, it is best to leave territory planning to the territory manager.

As a general rule, routing approaches that involve participation by salespeople are more likely to be successful than those imposed by sales managers. Salespeople understand their customers and territories, and they know about travel conditions and customers' time demands. Salespeople will also be committed to the routing method if they have had a role in establishing it.[12]

FIGURE 6-2 Three Basic Routing Methods.

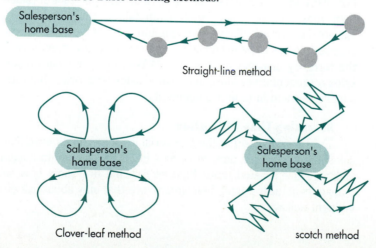

Straight-line method

Clover-leaf method

scotch method

Salesperson's home base

Scheduling

Whereas geographic and account potential considerations predominate in routing decisions, proper use of a salesperson's time hinges on careful scheduling. This takes into account all the activities performed by the representative during a day, a week, or a month.

Scheduling refers to the task of allocating the salesperson's time asset. In scheduling a particular time unit's activities, estimates have to be developed for the customer contact, waiting, and travel times involved with the specific accounts that form the agenda for the upcoming call sequence. Although averages based on historical data and experience will provide approximations, they have to be modified and adjusted to reflect the circumstances of the specific planning period. Depending on the person or persons that must be seen at each customer's offices and the subjects that must be addressed during the meetings, more or less time may be needed than in previous visits. Waiting times on customer premises may also vary according to the time of year, the day of the week, or even the time of the day, as well as according to the number of people involved. Travel time between accounts tends to be fairly stable unless conditions such as rush-hour traffic or road construction interfere.

Building some buffer time into the daily program permits flexibility to deal with unexpected events such as car trouble, new business openings, and the like. When there is no breathing room on a salesperson's schedule, even a little emergency can make a simple challenge seem impossible.[13] Time also has to be set aside for planning and support activities. The success of scheduling is enhanced if appointments are set up ahead of time.

Each territory manager's planned use of time should be compared with the time actually consumed during the week. Reasons for divergence should be investigated to sharpen future scheduling. These and additional time management suggestions will be covered in the next section.

TIME MANAGEMENT

For many sales managers, managing their time and that of their salespeople is one of their most crucial tasks. Apart from talent, time is a sales professional's most valuable resource. To yield maximum benefit to both the salesperson and the company, it has to be used wisely. Individual achievement levels depend on how well the territory manager utilizes time.[14] Well-managed sales organizations do not turn sales representatives loose in assigned sales territories, but rather direct, guide, and supervise them in time management.

Assessing Time Utilization

time management
Structuring a sales-person's time resources so as to maximize productive time and minimize wasted time

Time management at the territorial level has as its objective the structuring of a salesperson's scarce time resources in such a way as to maximize productive time and minimize wasted time. Figures 6-3 and 6-4 show how salespeople and sales managers actually spend their time. Note that only about half of a salesperson's time is spent selling.

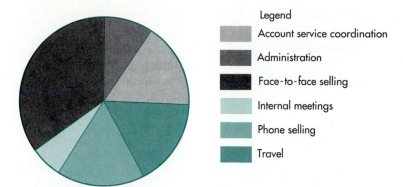

Legend

■ Account service coordination

■ Administration

■ Face-to-face selling

■ Internal meetings

■ Phone selling

■ Travel

FIGURE 6-3 How Salespeople Spend Their Time.

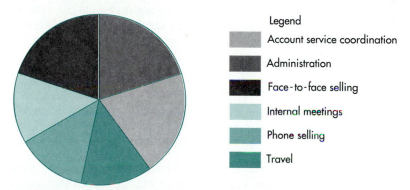

Legend

■ Account service coordination

■ Administration

■ Face-to-face selling

■ Internal meetings

■ Phone selling

■ Travel

FIGURE 6-4 How Sales Managers Spend Their Time.

To develop effective time management strategies, it is useful to classify alternative time uses with regard to their productivity, as has been done in Fig. 6-5. The most important use of a sales representative's time is customer contact such as face-to-face and telephone selling and servicing.[15] It would be wrong, however, to consider all other uses of time unproductive. Customer contact effectiveness is greatly dependent upon the salesperson's preparation for each individual sales call. Time invested in planning presentations, anticipating objections, and developing appropriate answers for them is time well spent. Support activities represent an equally important function. They involve paperwork, including sales reports, order followup, and professional development through self-study programs.

Whereas the above activities ought to be maximized—with particular emphasis on customer contact—the remaining two time uses of travel and waiting listed in Fig. 6-5 should be minimized, since they fail to produce benefits for anybody. For example, most waiting time is wasted unless it can be used to elicit useful information on customer needs and practices or on industry trends.

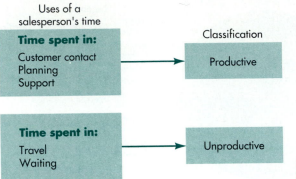

FIGURE 6-5 Taxonomy of Time Uses.

Although maximization of customer contact time may be the most efficient use of a salesperson's time, it probably does not represent the most productive application of available time. The latter comes about only if profitability is taken into account. Toward this end, the following formula has been suggested:[16]

$$ROTI = \frac{GM}{CTI}$$

where ROTI = return on time invested
      GM   = gross margin
      CTI = cost of time invested

Since productivity measures relate output figures to input figures, the gross margin in the above equation represents the output measure, and the cost of time invested is the required input. The gross margin is computed by deducting manufacturing costs from sales revenues. Cost of time invested, on the other hand, reflects only a sales representative's direct costs: salary, bonus, and travel and entertainment expenses. ROTI can be determined on an account-by-account basis so that those with the highest ROTI can be favored in the allocation of a territory manager's time.

Territory time management can also deal with time distribution between current account coverage and new account development. This task translates into the choice between a short-term and long-term perspective of territory development: How much time should be devoted to selling and servicing existing customers as compared to identifying and courting new customers? The issue of field work versus office work also has to be addressed. A proper balance has to be found because a salesperson who sells without followup will quickly run out of satisfied customers, whereas a territory manager who spends more time in the office than on customer premises will generate more paperwork than sales.

Leaving salespeople to their own devices when it comes to planning the coverage of their territories is unlikely to result in optimum time utilization. Sales managers must assist their staff in routing and scheduling activities. Managers must also help them develop their individual time management skills.

Time Management Skills

Three keys to managing time well are planning, organization, and discipline.[17] These skills are described below.

Planning.   All salespeople and managers must plan for the optimum use of the limited time that they have. Some suggestions for better time planning include the following:

1. Establish priorities for sales management activities. One author suggests a "to do list" on which the manager ranks activities according to A, B, or C priorities. The manager concentrates on completing the A priorities before turning attention to the B and C activities.
2. Anticipate major tasks that will come up in the future. By thinking ahead, a manager or salesperson will spend less time on "fire fighting" and more on "fire prevention."
3. Establish deadlines for management tasks and for salespeople and adhere to them.
4. Make sure plans and schedules are flexible. Develop contingency plans to facilitate readiness for changing conditions and emergencies when they arise.

Discipline.   Good time management is based on self-discipline and the development of good work habits. There must be a sincere desire to avoid bad work habits and to manage time effectively. Some suggestions:

1. Do not procrastinate. The person who is going to do something tomorrow never seems to get it done.
2. Be alert to unnecessary interruptions such as casual visitors and unimportant telephone calls.[18] One must have blocks of uninterrupted time to accomplish major tasks such as writing a report or preparing a sales forecast.
3. Learn to be brief. Too frequently managers and salespeople waste time on unnecessary details when writing or speaking.
4. Avoid requests for special favors. Quite often special requests have no relation to the employee's or the company's goals.

Organization.   The third characteristic of effective time managers is organization. Salespeople and managers must carefully study the tasks they must perform and get organized to accomplish them. One trick is to prepare a daily or weekly work schedule to organize one's work. Other suggestions for organization:

1. Consolidate activities whenever possible. For example, it may be better to take one long trip to visit customers in the field than several short ones.
2. Delegate tasks to subordinates. A manager who tries to do everything will discover that there is never enough time remaining for important management responsibilities.
3. Concentrate efforts on major tasks whenever possible. In particular, do not try to do several things at once.
4. Identify the key problems so time is not wasted on less important matters.

Time Management in Action

The following example illustrates how selected territory and time management techniques can be used by a salesperson. Mary Stewart, a sales representative for New England Business Systems, is preparing her territorial sales plan for the coming year. Mary's personal goal is to earn $35,000. Her expected direct selling expenses for the coming year are $15,000. Since Mary is paid a commission of 10 percent of sales and is required to pay all of her direct selling expenses, she must achieve a sales level of $500,000 to reach her earnings goal. Since this represents a 10 percent increase over her past year's sales, Mary realizes that she must allocate her time wisely if she is to reach her projected goal.

Mary begins by analyzing the accounts in her territory, which includes Hartford, Connecticut, and the surrounding area. At the present time, Mary's territory has three hundred prospects and active accounts. Mary recognizes that she cannot provide the same coverage for each account, so she decides to take her sales manager's suggestion and use the ABC rule to classify her accounts.

Classification	% of accounts	Number of accounts	% of sales	Sales volume
A	15	45	65	$325,000
B	20	60	20	100,000
C	65	195	15	75,000
Totals	100	300	100	$500,000

As discussed earlier, grading of customers for frequency of calling is important so that a sales representative can use scarce time efficiently. An A account, for instance, would represent a major or key account that provides a considerable amount of business. Level A accounts justify more frequent calls and more attention than B or C level accounts. Usually, C accounts represent only an occasional order.

Based on past experience, Mary expects to work 240 days during the coming year and to have an average of five hours per day for direct selling activities. For the year, she will have 1200 hours available for sales calls. She uses this information plus her prior ABC analysis to prepare a preliminary call plan for the coming year. She allocates her time as follows:

Classification	Number of accounts	×	Number of calls	=	Total calls per year
A	45		12		540
B	60		4		240
C	105		2		390
Totals	210		18		1,170

To provide further guidance for specific account coverage, Mary also decides to compute her expected return on time invested for each prospect and account. Mary's cost per call hour is calculated by dividing her selling costs ($50,000) by the

SALES MANAGEMENT IN PRACTICE

ELECTRONIC LIQUID FILLERS, INC.

At Electronic Liquid Fillers, Inc. (ELF), absolutely nobody has time to waste. The Indiana-based company established a marketing niche in the bottling and equipment industry by promising its customers a ten-day turnaround, a drastic reduction in the industry average of four months. With its middle-of-the road prices, ELF has based its competitive strategy on time, and this effort must be pursued by every employee in every aspect of the business, including the sales force.

The custom-made machinery for bottlers and packages that ELF sells are basic models that the company alters to fit customer specifications. Since the machines go through production and are delivered within ten days, it is imperative that every detail be set before production begins. Such detail is accomplished with an eighteen-page production form filled out by the salespeople. These forms literally serve as surrogate supervisors for the production workers, and so the salespeople must have extensive product knowledge and no small amount of mechanical know-how. All employees are required to serve as equipment installers before they are eligible to go into sales. In this way, they acquire the necessary hands-on skill.

ELF prospecting procedures are also designed for speed. Salespeople call on potential customers by performing demonstrations in trucks filled with $80,000 of equipment. The expense of the trucks is justified by ELF's belief that prospects who see the performance of the equipment are likely to commit on the spot. The desire for quick commitments stems from ELF's own production speed; the company keeps no back-log of orders, and if orders are not coming in, production workers have nothing to do.

ELF also expects expediency from its customers. No payment is received until the equipment is up and running, but as soon as the equipment is performing satisfactorily, ELF expects a check in the mail. In fact, customers are encouraged to make their payment to the installer on the day of delivery. Herein lies another motivation for ELF's straight-commission salespeople to hurry, hurry, hurry; they do not get their paychecks until the job is done.

number of call hours available (1200), which yields a cost per call hour of $41.67. Mary can use this calculation to assess the potential profitability of each account.

For instance, Apex Manufacturing Company usually gives Mary an order which provides here with an average gross margin of $250. Mary calculates her return on time invested (ROTI) as follows:

$$\text{ROTI} = \frac{\text{Average gross margin}}{\text{Cost per call hour}}$$

$$= \frac{\$250}{\$41.67}$$

$$= 6$$

A second customer is Smalltown Office Supply, which provides only an average gross margin of $35 per order. Mary's calculated ROTI for this account is only 0.84 ($35 ÷ $41.67). Clearly, Apex is a far more profitable account than Smalltown. In fact, Mary should find a less expensive way to deal with Smalltown (perhaps by phone or direct mail) since the ROTI for this account is less than 1.

What this analysis shows Mary is that her selling time is worth over $40 per hour. She must do enough business with an account to offset the cost of her time. She can also use this approach to establish calling priorities and frequencies.

Mary must also build some flexibility into her schedule to meet new sales opportunities and emergency situations. And she must use her past experience as a guide. For instance, Mary, like most experienced salespeople, is familiar with the 80/20 rule, which suggests that 80 percent of sales come from 20 percent of a salesperson's accounts. She will have to keep this rule of thumb in mind and decide which of her accounts fall into which category when planning the coverage of her sales territory.

THE CHALLENGE OF SALES PRODUCTIVITY

Declining sales productivity has become a key sales management concern.[19] According to the Dartnell survey of sales force compensation for the period 1977 to 1987, selling costs for many companies have risen faster than sales volume, and sales force productivity has suffered, both individually and collectively. While pressure from competitors, purchasers, and distributors has had an effect, the bottom line is that the sales force is selling less.[20] As a result, senior executives in many companies are looking to the sales organizations to improve their performance.

Improving sales productivity presents a great opportunity for potentially significant gains. For instance, a top-level task force in one company found that a 10 percent improvement in the time its sales force spent selling could generate a more than 5 percent increase in sales volume.[21] Companies are attempting to improve sales productivity in a number of ways. They are providing salespeople with more and better sales training to teach them to use their time more effectively. They are experimenting with new selling methods, such as telemarketing, demonstration centers, seminars, and industrial stores, in an effort to lower overall selling costs.[22] Companies are also developing revised sales compensation and incentive plans which provide greater control over selling costs. These new incentive plans are designed to focus sales efforts on strategic accounts and products.[23]

Many of the efforts to increase sales productivity focus on providing salespeople with more time for selling. In large part, sales force productivity has declined because salespeople sometimes spend too much time on nonselling activities such as administrative tasks, internal meetings, and travel. To resolve this problem, companies are turning to sales automation. In fact, one of the most dramatic changes in selling during the 1980s was the greatly increased use of personal computers and laptops in sales. They are being used to improve selling efficiency and productivity as well as to reduce sales cycles and administrative tasks. In addition, improved customer service, more accessible information, and better internal communications are other benefits realized by companies that have automated their sales organizations.[24]

Investment in automation has resulted in real gains in sales force productivity. In one study it was reported that companies have increased sales anywhere from 10 percent to more than 30 percent by automating sales and marketing functions.[25] Other case studies also report substantial success in achieving sales advances through automation.[26]

Many companies, large and small, have taken steps to automate their selling and sales management activities. These include DuPont, Levi Strauss, Hercules Chemical, Hewlett-Packard, General Foods, and many, many more. In fact, modern selling is all but impossible without the aid of the computer.

Sales force automation systems are designed to increase sales by providing sales personnel with a wider range of current information and by reducing administrative time, allowing more time for selling activities. For example, Shell Chemical Company's manager of systems development points out that Shell's system is a "laptop computer based 'tool-kit' of integrated software applications." Specific functions include electronic mail, daily sales information, account management, administrative forms, word processing, and time management.[27]

Individual salespeople have sometimes pioneered their companies' sales force automation efforts. For example, Marc Clausen moved from Xerox's 285th-best sales producer to number one in a single year. He did this by developing computer programs to make his selling efforts more effective:

- A prospect management system that finds, adds, deletes, and changes prospect information, indexes prospect data bases, and prints out a master file listing of prospects
- An activity reporting system that adds accomplished activities and prints out a weekly report
- A daily time management system that keeps track of activities, lists them according to priority, and deletes completed activities
- A reference account management system that adds reference accounts to the file, searches by reference type, and displays a master list
- A sample generation system that automatically prints customized or generic mailing sample sets
- A letter master correspondence system that writes letters and prints out mass mailings and envelopes

Xerox recognized Clausen's territory management expertise by asking him to develop a three-day training session in the use of his program.[28]

Based on their study of sales automation, Al Wendell and Dale Hempeck[29] have concluded that a comprehensive sales force automation program must include the following elements:

- Remote access with portable computers to branch office or company headquarters' computer systems for up-to-the-minute information on order status, product price and availability, and competitive data to answer customers' questions on the spot
- Electronic mail for internal communications, eliminating phone tag with hard-to-reach people and storing phone-in messages from customers
- Word processing and spreadsheet software for customizing sales letters and automating call reports, preparing budget quotas and proposals, and developing sales forecasts
- Time management software to plan activities and automatically update call reports
- Suspect, prospect, and customer data-base files for precalling, planning, call-back notification, and account profiles
- Cellular phones for creating productive time from often wasted driving time

TABLE 6-4   Guidelines for Sales Force Automation

- Sales and management must both agree on system objectives. This is best accomplished by first providing functions for the sales reps and then integrating the needs of management.
- Expectations should be realistic. Things will go wrong. Alternatives should be prepared.
- Define one or two needs quickly and get the system to the field in some form. A few early successes are important. Delays will lead to a loss of interest.
- Provide effective hands-on training. Give sales reps basic training on PCs. It is important not to overwhelm them with too much information.
- Always provide user support or a HELP function. Nothing will destroy your efforts faster than failing to "hold the hands" of reps who need assistance when they need it. Help should always be available during your normal workday.
- Finally, improvise and experiment. Improve applications that produce results. Modify or eliminate those that do not. Automation is an ongoing process and should continually grow to meet the changing needs of your sales organization.

- Support from management encouraging consistent and complete usage of productivity tools
- Adequate training to overcome "computerphobia" and to teach new skills of sales efficiency

Before introducing personal computers and other forms of sales automation, sales management should examine what it expects these changes to do for the sales force. Management must also consider how personal computers will fit into the overall sales process.[30] Specific guidelines for automating a sales force are presented in Table 6-4.

Many companies also use computer-based support systems to facilitate the sales management process. Analyses of salesperson, territory, product, or customer performance can be obtained in short order. These analyses provide the bases for simulations aimed at determining the consequences of alternative combinations of marketing variables. Mathematical sales models for both established and new products can forecast likely market response and guide purchasing and production. The computer can also be of major assistance in designing and assigning sales territories, determining call norms and schedules, and setting sales quotas and commissions. Effective routing is also frequently determined according to a computer model.

SUMMARY OF LEARNING GOALS

1. Understand the Nature and Scope of Territory Management.

Territory management implies responsibility. Sales representatives in charge of their own territories are responsible for making things happen. A territory can be thought of as a scaled-down version of a firm's total market, and so a sales representative in charge of a territory has many sales management duties.

2. Identify the Reasons for Establishing and Revising Territories.

The reasons for establishing and revising territories can be customer-related, salesperson-related, or management-related.

3. **Describe the Objectives, Criteria, and Basis for Territory Formation.**

The primary objective of territory formation is to determine both the optimum number of territories to be formed and their configurations. Equalization of territory potentials is another consideration. Results of territory formation are measured by sales volume, market share, or profit criteria. The basis for territory formation may be geography, sales potential, servicing requirements, or workload.

4. **Outline a Model of Territory Management.**

Territory management can be defined broadly in terms of planning, implementation, and control activities. More specifically, planning includes analysis, objectives, strategies, and tactics components. Implementation involves the achievement of new business targets. Both business development and selling and servicing of current customers are emphasized. Also, reporting is part of the implementation phase. Finally, the control function compares intended and actual results, with a view toward taking corrective action where indicated.

5. **List and Discuss Routing Patterns and Scheduling Issues.**

One routing method is the straight-line method, in which the salesperson begins with a call on a customer located on the outer perimeter of his or her territory and then works back to the home base by calling on accounts located in the interior portion of the territory. A cloverleaf pattern is four or more adjoining circular sequences that represent a week's list of calls to be made. A hopscotch pattern involves "spokes" radiating from a "hub" (the salesperson's residence). Each calling sequence starts at the outer end of a spoke, and the salesperson works back toward the hub in a zigzag manner.

Scheduling involves the allocation of a salesperson's time. Time estimates are developed for customer contact, waiting, and travel. These estimates may be based on historical data. Buffer time should be built into the schedule, and substantial differences between scheduled and actual times should be investigated.

6. **Explain the Concept of Time Management and How It Relates to Sales Territories.**

Apart from talent, time is a sales professional's most valuable resource. As such, it must be used wisely. At the territorial level, time management has as its objective the structuring of a salesperson's time in such a way as to maximize productive time and minimize wasted time.

REVIEW QUESTIONS

1. Under what situations are strict geographic territory boundaries typical? When should geographic boundaries be disregarded?
2. What is the difference between territory managers and sales managers? List skills that are essential for a territory manager.
3. What negative repercussions stem from poor territory design? List the three categories that motivate and govern the formation of sales territories.
4. List examples of the customer-related, salesperson-related, and managerial benefits that can arise from good territory design.

5. What happens if an insufficient number of territories are formed? If too many are created?
6. Is it ever desirable for sales management to have territories with differing potentials? Explain.
7. Why is the buildup method for designing territories popular? Describe the conceptual paradox of the breakdown method. Why is the incremental method used infrequently?
8. In time management, which activities should be maximized? Which should be minimized?
9. Name the principal thrust of territorial activity. What other goals should territory managers pursue?
10. What skills are used in time management?

DISCUSSION QUESTIONS

1. Interview a salesperson who is a territory manager. What does this person like about his or her job? What features does the individual dislike?

2. According to *The Wall Street Journal*, more and more companies are encouraging their salespeople to stay longer in the same territory.[31] What would you suspect is behind this development?

3. Nestor, Inc., a company that specializes in artificial intelligence, started a sales and marketing department in 1988, after "only" thirteen years in business. The additional staff increased the number of Nestor employees from twenty to thirty. Newly developed computer applications that can read handwriting were the incentive for the change.[32] Do you think the company should have developed territories? If not, why not? If so, on what basis should territories be developed?

4. Debbie Breed, list sales manager for *Consumers Digest*, believes she can cut order processing time by two-thirds if she can purchase and implement a list management software package called Market Knowledge List Fulfillment System.[33] If you were Debbie's supervisor, what questions would you ask her to determine whether or not to automate order processing? Relate your decision to the material in Chap. 6.

5. Write a general weekly schedule for your own activities as a student. How good a time manager are you?

E T H I C A L D I L E M M A

Sales managers often realign territories in response to market and competitive changes. For example, sales gains may result in an increase in the number of sales territories. Salespeople who have spent years building sales in their territories may find these territories cut back and customers lost. How should sales managers deal with salespeople who have lost portions of their territories?

SALES MANAGEMENT CASE

For Automated Sales Forces, There Is No Time to Waste

Computers are a time management tool; they can maximize productive time and minimize wasted time. Spalding Sports Worldwide is just one of the many companies that have provided lap-top computers to their sales forces with the goal of improved time management.

Spalding provides official basketballs to the National Basketball Association. Each team has a standing order of fifty basketballs per year; however, most of Spalding's sales are not so predictable. Salespeople often need to find out quickly whether or not a certain quantity of a product is on hand. With their laptop computers, they can dial into the firm's data base, which tells them exactly how many units are in stock. If there are enough available, the salesperson can type in a code that reserves a certain number for his or her order. If there are not enough in stock, the salesperson can find out when more will be produced. This process is much more efficient than a nonautomated system in which several phone calls would be required. Also, automation provides a timeliness of data impossible to obtain without a centralized data base.

Spalding's computer automation saves time in other ways. Through a "messaging" feature, a manager who has just attended a sales meeting can sit down with his or her lap-top computer and compose a letter describing what was discussed. The letter can then be sent electronically to the entire sales force.

Computers are an invaluable tool for managing salespeople who are geographically dispersed. Sales personnel can use their lap-tops to monitor sales, and managers can keep tabs on how particular salespeople and/or territories are performing. Spalding pays $5000 for its fully loaded lap-tops. If time is money, Spalding is certainly getting a positive return on investment.

Questions

1. How can laptops help salespeople maximize productive activities? How can they minimize unproductive activities?

2. Describe ways that sales force automation benefits each of the following:

   Salespeople
   Sales managers
   Support staff
   Customers
   Production managers
   Marketing managers

3. Assume that Mary, who was described in this chapter, is able to increase her annual sales by 5 percent using a $5000 lap-top. Should New England Business Systems invest in the lap-top?

PLANNING
THE SALES EFFORT

CHAPTER 7

SALES MANAGEMENT ENVIRONMENT

LEARNING GOALS

- Differentiate between the internal and external environment.
- Identify the major components of the external environment.
- Discuss the meaning of environmental opportunities and threats.
- List the response modes to environmental opportunities and threats.
- Explain how each facet of the environment impacts upon sales management.

DAVID KESSLER: HOW ONE MAN CHANGED THE FOOD AND DRUG INDUSTRY'S SELLING ENVIRONMENTS

On February 25, 1991, David Kessler took over as commissioner of the Food and Drug Administration (FDA). Since that time, he has been showing some of America's biggest companies how one person in a position of responsibility can drastically change selling environments.

The FDA, like many federal regulatory agencies, was criticized for inefficiency, and Kessler came into his new position with an aggressiveness that is perhaps in part an attempt to save the agency's reputation. Under the law, the FDA can ban not only false but also misleading selling activities related to food and drugs. Kessler has declared war on potentially misleading labeling practices. Especially endangered are questionable health benefits that have been advertised by many marketers since the 1980s health craze.

Drug industry practices that push the limits of honesty also are being strictly regu-

lated under the Kessler regime. For example, Ciba Geigy Corporation markets a gallstone-dissolving drug called Actigall. There is, however, a new type of minor surgery available that can solve the same problem in far less time than Actigall, and in Kessler's opinion, Actigall ads that do not mention this fact are not adequately informative.

The promotion by drug companies of unapproved uses for their products are also being curtailed. For example, Upjohn Company's baldness drug, Rogaine, cannot be promoted to women because the drug has been approved only for men. The Upjohn sales force is forbidden to mention Rogaine as a baldness treatment for women.

Drug companies have also been known to produce magazines that look like medical literature but are actually little more than advertisements, or to sponsor "medical conferences" that are sales-oriented. These practices fall under Kessler's definition of misleading.

The new FDA stance has greatly affected the practices of food and cosmetics giants who sell a wide variety of regulated products. The claims, "fresh," "natural," "high fiber," "low fat," and "no cholesterol" are not taken lightly by Kessler. Procter & Gamble (P&G), for example, was publicly chastised by the FDA for its use of the word "fresh" on its Citrus Hill orange juice, which is made from concentrate. After several unheeded warnings, the FDA actually seized a shipment of Citrus Hill, forcing an embarrassed P&G to alter its label. Companies that produce potato chips, cookies, cake mixes, margarine, and cooking oils will have to be very cautious of their no cholesterol claims; FDA studies show that many consumers think "cholesterol-free" means fat-free, which it does not.[1]

David Kessler is one person heading one

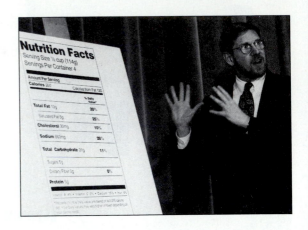

regulatory agency, yet his influence has implications for the selling activities of many corporate giants. As Chap. 7 indicates, if there is one constant fact about the selling environment, it is that the environment is constantly changing. Effective sales managers must make every effort to enable their sales forces to deal with these changes.

CHAPTER OVERVIEW

The planning process for selling would be quite simple if a sales manager had only to set a goal and then deploy a sales force to achieve it. In this ideal situation, all variables that impact the selling process would be accounted for, leaving no room for unexpected events. Control would rest entirely with the sales manager, who would be able to determine the exact nature of the selling situation. Unfortunately, such ideal situations do not exist. A host of unexpected variables, most of which arise from outside the company, interfere. The totality of these external forces that affect the sales management process is called the *environment*.

environment
Totality of the external forces that affect sales management

The most distinctive feature of the environment is its dynamic nature. All managers, but most especially sales managers, work under constantly changing conditions. New products are introduced, a competitor cuts its price, new government rulings that affect a particular business are issued, new territories are opened —change never stops.

Sales success depends on a firm's ability to adapt quickly to changes in its selling environment. One writer described this aspect of sales management as follows:[2]

> Marketing and sales organizations play a pivotal role in adjusting to change. They provide early reconnaissance and must signal changes to other operations such as manufacturing, engineering, or logistics. . . .

A MODEL OF THE ENVIRONMENT FOR SALES MANAGEMENT

internal environment Factors within the organization that impact the selling process

There are two basic types of environments that must be considered by the sales manager. The first is the *internal environment*, which consists of those factors within the organization that impact upon the selling process. Corporate resources, the sales budget, the number and types of products offered, and sales force structure are among the components of this internal environment. The sales manager will negotiate the sales budget and help to determine the sales structure. Likewise, new products are often developed using input from the field sales force.

external environment Factors beyond the control of the organization that impact the selling process

The *external environment*—factors that are beyond the control of the company in most cases—presents a different challenge. Unexpected changes in the external environment—for example, soaring fuel costs, new government regulations, or rising interest rates—may present opportunities or threats to the sales organization. At the senior management level, these factors are considered during the corporate planning process. This aspect of planning, known as "situation analysis," will be discussed in the next chapter.

Field sales managers must try to understand how external environmental forces will affect the sales organization. Then, they must develop and implement tactics to deal with these forces. For instance, they may be required to realign sales territories and calling patterns to cope with higher travel costs, or they may have to institute temporary price discounts to meet the challenge of a competitor's lower prices.

Figure 7-1 shows how the external environment is subdivided into several components:

1. The social and cultural environment, which includes such demographic factors as the average age of the population, its geographic distribution, birthrate, and level of educational attainment; and the persistence of values and norms and their effect on the selling process.

FIGURE 7-1 Model of the Environment for Sales Management.

2. The technological environment, which involves human modifications of the natural environment.
3. The economic environment, which considers the ways in which scarce resources are used and distributed.
4. The competitive environment, which involves the nature and types of competition the sales manager will encounter.
5. The political and legal environment, which includes the actions taken by government to regulate the selling process.

While careful evaluation of both types of environments is crucial to the success of the selling efforts, the remainder of this chapter will focus on the second aspect—the external environment.

COPING WITH ENVIRONMENTAL CHANGES

How does the sales manager assess the nature of the environment? What courses of action should be taken once these factors have been studied?

environmental scanning Identification of the major environmental factors of interest to sales management, the assignment of responsibility for each area, and the development of methods for collecting and disseminating the information that has been gathered

Environmental scanning involves the identification of the major environmental factors of interest to sales management, the assignment of responsibility for each area, and the development of methods for collecting and disseminating the information that has been gathered. This process will result in the identification of environmental opportunities and threats.

Environmental Opportunities and Threats

environmental opportunity Comfortable situation favoring positive action that affords a relatively high probability for success

The concepts of environmental opportunity and threat, or stimulus and challenge, have received increased attention in recent years as firms have realized the importance of environmental analysis in the planning process. A stimulus, or *environmental opportunity*, may be defined as a comfortable situation favoring positive action that affords a relatively high probability for success. A stimulus may then be seen as an impetus for action, where such action will generally result in the successful attainment of desired goals. For instance, a major competitor with labor difficulties is struck by its union, limiting its ability to supply the needs of its customers. Quick response to this situation may enable a firm and its salespeople to develop account relationships with some of the competitor's customers who are concerned about supply shortages.

environmental threat Unfavorable situation that, if not accounted for and acted upon, would lead to severe decline in selling effectiveness

An *environmental threat* (or challenge) is an unfavorable situation that, if not accounted for and acted upon, would lead to a severe decline in selling effectiveness. A challenge also calls for action. Here the sales manager will act to reduce or counteract the negative consequences of the threat. In fact, many sales managers thrive on challenge and do their best work under these circumstances.

Responding to Challenges.   Perhaps the easiest response to environmental challenges is to do nothing—a situation often characterized by apathy or "foot dragging." This response, however, may be fatal to the future of a company and its sales force. More appropriate is one of three other possible responses to change—adapting to the change, moving against it, or trying to modify it in some way. This is the kind of thinking that successful sales managers display in their responses to the constantly changing environment of sales.

Adapting to Change.   Usually the safest course of action is to try to adapt sales operations to changes in the environment. If a leading competitor is having success with a product-based sales organization, you could reorganize your sales force into a similar pattern.

Moving Counter to the Change.   This course of action involves more risk, but it can have a greater payoff. For example, suppose there is a trend toward using telemarketing and other direct marketing techniques to sell to smaller accounts in a particular industry. To counter this trend, a firm might expand its sales force to provide personal attention to these accounts in an attempt to strengthen customer loyalty and increase market share.

Trying to Modify the Change.   In some situations, moving counter to a change is not possible because the change stems from large-scale economic or cultural factors, or from decisions by the government, which an individual firm cannot overcome. In other situations advertising, public relations, and personal selling can influence, or modify, the change in a firm's favor. Consider the case of a large producer of industrial chemicals that hires recent college graduates as salespersons. Several purchasing agents refuse to deal with these representatives, claiming they lack industry experience. The firm might develop a series of seminars in which the new salespeople present current industry and product information. The doubtful purchasing agents would then realize that the new salespeople had the industry knowledge and insights to meet their needs.

Several specific suggestions for adapting to changes in the sales environment are presented in Table 7-1. Flexibility, open-mindedness, and preparation are the keys to coping successfully with environmental changes.

TABLE 7-1   Adapting to Change

To be fleet-footed and adapt successfully to change, a marketing and sales organization must have the following characteristics:
- A simple organizational structure that permits fast response times
- Field-level managers who have the authority to execute account-by-account strategies and make appropriate distribution, pricing, and promotion decisions
- Simple pricing schemes
- Experimentation that has provided experience with alternative forms of advertising and promotion
- Sales force continuity involving continuous training, continuous leads fed to sales reps, continuous focus on customer-related activities, and continuous teamwork among all sales teams

THE SOCIAL AND CULTURAL ENVIRONMENT

People are the most important part of a company's selling environment. Successful salespeople and managers know their customers intimately: who and where they are; how, when, and why they buy; their needs and operations; even their personal histories and idiosyncrasies. They also understand the organizational dynamics and corporate cultures of their customers—the quality orientation at AT&T and the emphasis on innovation at 3M—and aim at appealing to particular customer values.

In large part, the needs and buying behavior of customers are determined by the social and cultural environment. Factors such as the size and average age of the population, its geographic distribution, the birthrate, the emerging importance of ethnic subcultures as consumers and employees, the changing notion of the household, cross-cultural similarities and differences, and the evolution of social values must be carefully considered by sales managers. These factors contribute to the success or failure of the selling process. The social and cultural environment also determines the type of people who will become salespeople and sales managers in the future. Finally, sales managers must understand the impact of these factors on international as well as domestic markets.

Population Characteristics

The U.S. population is expected to continue to grow at a moderate rate for at least the next fifty years. But this does not mean that sales management can expect to enjoy continued prosperity by maintaining current selling strategies during this period. Like all aspects of the environment, the population is constantly changing.

Unequal Rate of Growth. The rate of population growth is unevenly distributed both in the United States and abroad, with the greatest increases generally occurring in the least prosperous areas. For example, poorer nations have experienced a tremendous population explosion relative to more affluent nations. In the United States the birthrate is generally higher for the poor than it is for the affluent. For middle- and upper-income families, the birthrate has declined, as women from these economic sectors have elected to marry later, work longer, and have fewer children. This situation poses a unique problem for sales management, which must reevaluate the demand for certain types of products and the nature of the selling strategies to be employed.

Increase in Average Age. The average age of the U.S. population has increased dramatically during this past century. The average life expectancy is expected to reach 74.0 years by the year 2000. At the same time, the declining birthrate among large segments of the population has pushed the median age to over 30 years. As a result, the 39 million workers aged 35 to 44 will dominate the U.S. labor force in the year 2000. The share of workers aged 45 to 54 will also rise, so that by 2000 one in two workers will be 35 to 54 years old.[3]

Changing Geographic Distribution. The U.S. population is also shifting geographically. First, regional shifts have resulted in increased numbers of people in the South and the West, while some northeast areas have experienced population declines. Second, since the onset of the Industrial Revolution, Americans have flocked to the cities, where opportunities for employment and advancement are greater. Beginning shortly after World War II, many Americans elected to move to suburban areas where they can enjoy the comforts of the suburban lifestyle with the convenience of the city close at hand.

Increased Education Attainment. The level of educational attainment in the U.S. population has increased steadily throughout this century. Fifty years ago, a high school education was a luxury not available to all. By 1970, census figures showed that 50 percent of the population had a high school diploma; this number increased to more than 68 percent by 1980. This better-educated population has sought even higher levels of education. Americans are attending college in record numbers. The growing popularity of continuing education programs, ranging from leisure crafts to personal enrichment to career advancement, emphasizes the desire for increased knowledge. Unfortunately, not all Americans are taking advantage of increased educational opportunities. Many minority persons, who represent a growing share of the youth population, drop out of high school.

Increased Number of Working Women. One of the most important aspects of the social and cultural environment is the dramatic increase in the number of women in the American labor force. It is projected that 63 percent of women aged 16 or older will be in the labor force in 2000.[4] This trend has led to more day-care centers, longer store hours, more efficient and convenient household appliances, fast foods, and a host of other new or expanded goods and services.

The Changing Nature of the American Household. Sales organizations that attempt to cater solely to the suburban married couple with children fail to recognize the importance of the ever-increasing number of nontraditional households. Twenty percent of all children in the United States currently live in single-parent households; 50 percent of our children will have spent four or more years in a single-parent household by the end of this decade.

Other nontraditional households have also become more common recently. Single-adult households, for example, now number almost 20 million; these are composed largely of the divorced, the widowed, and the young adult population. Cohabitant couples now account for approximately 3 to 6 million people. Group household arrangements, especially among young adults, are also popular. Each of these variations represents unique opportunities for the sales manager. For example, the popularity of single-serving food packages is a direct result of the trend toward living alone.

The Impact of Population Changes. Population changes and shifts affect sales managers in various ways. First, the demand for specific products is affected. All marketers including sales managers must constantly reassess the viability of the markets they serve. Sales personnel and other resources must be redeployed periodically to reflect marketplace shifts. An aging population, for instance, will increase the demand for retirement communities, medical services, travel, and other types of recreation. A well-educated public will be more demanding, since it will be more aware of quality and the various product options that are available. In addition, better education and increased awareness contribute to increased affluence, which, in turn, increases the demand for quality products and improved customer service. This means that sales training programs must be improved and that customer service and quality must be emphasized.

Recent sales and marketing changes made by Avon Products reflect the impact of population shifts on sales strategy. Avon and other direct sales companies have been especially hard hit by the increased number of women working outside the home; however, Avon continued to use its established door-to-door sales strategy until 1983 when its new chief executive officer began to make major changes. The firm revised its door-to-door approach by reducing the number of cold calls and making appointments to be sure that customers would be at home. New sales support techniques, such as catalogs, direct mail, direct-response advertising, and 800 numbers, were also introduced to supplement the direct sales effort. Sales contacts are being made at work, and about 25 percent of Avon's sales now take place in the work setting. Finally, Avon has diversified by selling upscale beauty products in retail stores and by acquiring Foster Medical Corporation and Mediplex Group to enter the growing health care market.[5]

Sales organizations are also impacted by the effects population changes have on their own salespeople and those who manage sales personnel. Today, there are more salespeople with college educations, changed attitudes toward work in relation to recreation and other uses of time, and different concepts of marriage and the family. As a result, sales managers' roles today are different from that of their predecessors. Managers must spend more time getting to know their people—their likes and dislikes, attitudes, personal goals, strengths, and weaknesses. They must be prepared to provide training, feedback, and support to a diverse sales force. According to one writer:[6]

> The major challenge of tomorrow may not lie in balancing employers' needs with workers' skills, but in balancing workers' personal needs with job demands.

The Importance of Cultural Considerations

culture Basic way of life and core of values that are passed between generations

Each society has a *culture*, or a basic way of life and core of values that are passed between generations. In addition, there are a host of secondary values that are more flexible. The sales manager must distinguish between these two types of values before attempting to develop the proper strategy. Efforts to alter core beliefs will generally be unsuccessful, while changes in secondary values can be achieved.

Within each culture, there are generally a number of different subcultures, each with its own set of secondary beliefs. Subcultures pose a unique set of opportunities and challenges for sales managers. Several marketers have also noted buying differences between generations and between lifestyle groups. A lifestyle group may be defined as a group of people sharing similar beliefs, attitudes, and values. Such groups can be expected to share similar buying patterns.

In the United States and Canada, cultural diversity has become a key issue for sales managers. Companies have begun to recognize the value of developing multi-cultural work forces which take into consideration the increasingly diverse labor pool and customer base. A striking example is Levi Strauss & Company, the clothing manufacturer best known for its jeans and other casual attire. Over half of Levi's employees belong to minority groups, and its top managers were 14 percent non-white and 30 percent female in a recent year. The company has a "Valuing Diversity" educational program which teaches managers and employees how to become more tolerant of differences among people. In addition to the benefits it derives from its improved, culturally diverse work force, Levi's also benefits from its ability to design and develop merchandise for diverse consumer markets.[7]

Cross-cultural differences must also be taken into account by the sales manager. Consider, for example, the role of women in different societies. In the United States and most Western cultures women have been fully integrated into the work force, including sales organizations; however, a saleswoman calling on customers in Middle Eastern countries and certain other cultures would not be accepted in her sales role.

Attitudinal factors are equally important to the sales manager. The strong desire for achievement, for example, has been cited repeatedly as a motivating factor in the American work force; however, traditional attitudes toward work are changing as Americans seek nonmonetary rewards and a better quality of life. At the same time, many large corporations have altered their employment practices so that employee loyalty is not valued as it once was. These and other factors have moved many American workers away from the work ethic and toward a more satisfaction-oriented society. The basic respect for established institutions is not as prominent as it once was. These attitudinal aspects of the social environment have a profound effect on all phases of the selling process, especially salesperson selection and retention.

As the brief discussion of global sales in Chap. 1 indicated, the importance of social and cultural factors goes far beyond the national boundaries of the United States. As increasing numbers of American firms have become involved in international markets, more and more sales managers find themselves dealing with salespeople and customers abroad. The cultural aspects of international sales management will be discussed in Chap. 18.

THE TECHNOLOGICAL ENVIRONMENT

technology Methods by which people use their knowledge and available resources to produce goods and services that improve the quality of life

invention Creation of something brand new

innovation Redesign or adaptation of ideas or products to better fit consumer's needs

Technology involves the various methods by which people use their knowledge and available resources to produce goods and services that improve the quality of life. These products and services come about through one of two processes: invention and innovation. *Invention* involves the creation of something brand new, while *innovation* is the redesign or adaptation of ideas or products to better fit consumer needs. Most of the products introduced today are of the latter category, representing minor improvements as opposed to major new technologies.

Rapid technological changes will make today's most modern equipment and products obsolete by tomorrow. The one dominant characteristic of the modern technological revolution is its rapidity of change. New products are being developed at an extremely fast pace. Many new products fail, and others become obsolete as quickly as the relevant technology improves.

Consider, for example, the remarkable advances in telecommunications technology and the impact on international communications. Fiber-optic cables are quickly replacing copper cables and satellites for international communications. A single fiber-optic cable can carry more than 8000 conversations, compared with 48 for a copper wire. Fiber-optic cable calls are also faster and much clearer than those made on copper wire. This technological advance has stimulated demand tremendously. In 1977, people in the United States made 580 million minutes of overseas calls; ten years later in 1987 they made 4.7 billion minutes—an eightfold increase in a decade.[8]

John Naisbitt and Patricia Aburdene recently commented on this phenomenon:[9]

> In telecommunications we are moving to a single worldwide information network, just as economically we are becoming one global marketplace. We are moving toward the capability to communicate anything to anyone, anywhere, by any form—voice, data, text, or image—at the speed of light.

An important consideration in the face of changing technology is sales management's role in these changes. The field sales organization is expected to provide vital input into product innovation decisions. This role will probably expand in the future. In addition, sales personnel must remain constantly aware of the prevailing, and proposed, technology in their field. Their customers depend on them as information sources for new innovations related to their business. A technologically uninformed salesperson is a poor investment for a firm. Sales management must provide the educational leadership needed for a vital, modern sales effort.

Another important consideration deals with the application of new technology to the selling process itself. As discussed in Chap. 6, sales managers are especially concerned about finding ways to increase sales productivity since selling costs are rising rapidly. Many types of products can no longer be profitably promoted via personal selling.

Sales management's task is to find new ways of coping with this situation. As selling costs escalate, so must the level of sales productivity. Sales management's job is to discover how to make the sales effort more effective. Better sales training, new sales strategies and tactics, and the adoption of the latest technology, such as personal computers and telecommunications systems, are required to deal with cost escalation.

In the past, salespeople have become more productive because of major improvements in transportation and communications. These two areas will continue to be important technologies as will a third, computers.

Transportation

Salespeople of the early 1900s never would have understood what the automobile could do for more effective selling. The early salesperson's territory was dictated by the location of railroads, whereas today's salesperson covers a far wider area. Also of particular importance is the emergence of air travel as the primary means of intercity business travel. Today, a British sales executive can leave London on the Concord, fly to New York for a meeting, and return to London on the same day.

Unfortunately, advances in transportation are not without problems. The cost and availability of transportation will continue to pose real or potential problems for business. The rapid expansion of air travel has been a two-edged sword. Deregulation has resulted in higher fares for business travel, crowded airports, and delayed flights. And the congested streets of London, New York, Tokyo, Hong Kong, and

SALES MANAGEMENT IN PRACTICE

COACHMEN INDUSTRIES

The automobile, the telephone, the computer: Each of these technologies has changed dramatically the nature of selling. Coachmen Industries, a seller of recreational vehicles, has joined one essential selling tool, the automobile, with other modern-day selling devices. The result has been a "mobile office" that can greatly enhance some types of selling.

Coachmen equips its custom-made vehicles with desks and chairs for boss and secretary, and cellular phones are also included. The vehicles can be electrically wired to handle computers, fax machines, photocopiers, and VCRs. The recreational vehicles are large enough to carry a substantial amount of merchandise, and so they serve as both an office and a showroom.

There are serveral advantages of using the Coach-

men vehicles. Salespeople can spend less time in their offices, and so the amount of work space that companies must provide their employee is decreased. Also, salespeople have merchandise and information available on a sales call, so customer questions can be answered immediately. By giving sales presentations in the vehicles themselves, customers can listen with undivided attention, uninterrupted by coworkers or phone calls. Finally, salespeople save travel time between sales calls and their offices.

There are many new products on the market designed to support the mobile salesperson, but Coachmen Industries' custom-designed mobile offices are unusual in the extent to which they mobilize salespeople. The mobile office/showroom, a melding of modern-day technologies, is a powerful tool for salespeople and can greatly enhance sales performance and efficiency. With a sticker price of $50,000, the vehicle may prove to be a sound investment for sales forces.

---

other major metropolitan areas make travel to sales appointments difficult and expensive.

Communications

Modern communications have enhanced the selling process in many ways. Flexible communication devices, such as audio and video cassettes, special slide projectors, and portable computers, have become effective selling tools. Also, as will be discussed in Chap. 14, audiovisual aids have become an integral part of sales training. Perhaps the greatest impact on selling, however, has come from the telephone.

The rapid development of modern telecommunications systems has provided sales and marketing managers with a flexible time- and cost-saving tool. At first, telephones were used primarily by salespeople to assist them in the personal selling process. The telephone became an effective aid in making initial sales contacts and scheduling appointments. With the rapid rise in the cost of sales calls made in person, the telephone has helped firms improve their sales productivity.

Another early use of the telephone in sales work was to improve customer service. For instance, if a customer complained about a delay in delivery, the salesperson could often resolve the difficulty with a quick call to the factory. The wide availability of efficient, inexpensive telephone service was a significant improvement over the telegraph and mail services used by earlier sales representatives.

As technology has improved, so has the application of telecommunications to selling and sales management. Sales communications have been improved and speeded up through worldwide networks, facsimile machines, electronic data transfer, priority mail services, and other advances. Customers can make purchases and obtain information through telemarketing, facsimile machines, video and electronic shopping, and other direct marketing approaches. The discussion of new selling structures in Chap. 11 covers telemarketing and telecommunications technology in more detail.

There is no question that many salespeople are using the new telecommunications technologies. A survey by Dartnell Corporation revealed that 15 percent of salespeople in the United States have home facsimile machines and 35 percent use car phones.[10] However, there are questions about whether or not salespeople and managers are using these tools effectively. Although cellular phones are ideal for field-to-office communication, they are not especially effective for customer calls. Likewise, answering machines can be helpful in internal office communications, but subjecting customers to recorded messages should be avoided.[11]

Computers

As the discussion of sales productivity noted, computers have already had a significant impact on selling and sales management, and this trend is likely to continue and accelerate. Traditionally, marketers have been slower than others to adopt computers. But now that their use has been accepted, marketers have become some of the computer generation's strongest proponents.[12] As covered in Chap. 6, sales applications of computers include prospecting, sales analysis, promotional budgeting, aligning of sales territories, and routing of sales personnel. As a result, individuals planning a career in sales management should become familiar with the uses of computers and related data processing equipment.

marketing information systems (MIS) Computer-based systems that provide decision-oriented information to marketing and sales executives

One of the most important applications of computers to sales and marketing has been in the development of *marketing information systems (MIS)*. The marketing information system, which will be covered in more detail in Chap. 8, is a computer-based system that provides decision-oriented information to marketing and sales executives. The MIS provides management with the current or projected future status of the market. It also provides indications of market responses to company actions as well as to the actions of competitors.

In addition to their value in collecting and analyzing vast amounts of information, computers are also extremely helpful to individual salespeople and managers. Computer support systems enhance sales force productivity, customer account management, and communications between the field and office.[13]

THE ECONOMIC ENVIRONMENT

Economic trends and forecasts are of critical importance in strategic sales and marketing planning because they influence both the size and attractiveness of the various markets served by particular firms and their potential profitability. Information concerning the current and projected status of the economy is available from both government and industrial sources and will be discussed further in Chap. 9.

The relationship between general economic conditions and sales is relatively obvious. However, the economic condition of a specific industry, geographical area, population group, or distribution level can be quite different from general economic conditions at any particular time. Sales managers must recognize and deal with the differences in economic conditions between the various elements of the economy that pertain to them. For instance, rising fuel prices have a greater impact on the economy of New England than that of the Southwest. As a result, sales managers in New England must look for more efficient, cost-effective selling approaches during times of rising fuel prices.

Many factors must be considered by sales managers when assessing the economic environment. Factors that affect demand are income level and purchasing power, the impact of inflation, changing patterns of savings and debt, and unemployment. In addition, sales managers must be aware of production costs and their impacts.

Income Level and Purchasing Power

The income level of consumers influences demand in that it helps to determine consumers' ability to purchase various goods and services, which, in turn, affects the demand for industrial products. *Purchasing power* may be defined as the ability of the consumer to buy various goods and services for personal consumption. It is a function of several variables: income level, the prevailing price structure, savings versus debt patterns, and the availability of credit.

purchasing power Consumer's ability to buy various goods and services for personal consumption

Purchasing power has a decided impact on personal selling strategy. Times of reduced purchasing power may call for more aggressive sales efforts. By contrast, rising purchasing power may suggest an expansion of sales personnel.

The Impact of Inflation

Inflation is defined as a rising price level that reduces consumer purchasing power. Continued inflation dampens incentive and may cause curtailed business investment. It may lead to the introduction of government policies that will reduce spending, decrease income, and contribute to increased unemployment.

inflation Rising price level that reduces consumer purchasing power

Inflation presents another dilemma for buyers. Should products be purchased now to reduce the risk of even higher prices in the future? Should purchases instead be put off until some future date in the hope that inflation will ease? The way that customers answer these questions is critical to sales managers, since it will determine the rate of purchases for various product types. In most durable goods industries, buyers will tend to delay big purchases in lieu of more urgent items. Clearly, there is a need for careful planning to offset the problems posed by inflation.

Savings and Debt Patterns

The increased availability of credit has had a significant impact on the growth of the American economy as buyers purchase more than their means would normally permit. This increase in expenditures enhances the demand for various goods and services, creating new job opportunities and stimulating even greater demand. This increased impetus toward spending may be channeled into a demand for specific products. At the same time, there is a growing challenge spurred by such spending. High levels of debt mean that buyers must spend more of their money to pay off existing debts. The result is a negative impact on future buying trends in selected industries, most notably heavy durable goods purchases.

Unemployment

Perhaps one of the most serious economic challenges sales managers must face is unemployment. Expenditures among the unemployed are largely curtailed, with the exception of immediate necessities. Pricing strategies and the presentation of value at fair cost become increasingly important as methods of attracting the unemployed consumer. The market for luxury items diminishes. Aggressive selling efforts are required to encourage purchases, since even those who are presently employed often feel threatened by work-force cutbacks.

In prosperous times, however, price considerations are less critical. Nonprice considerations and luxuries assume greater importance in the purchasing process. The selling effort emphasizes increased customer service, the development of long-term vendor-buyer relationships, and the like.

Cost of Sales

A thorough understanding of the economic concepts of costs is essential for successful sales management. On a per-customer-contact basis, personal selling is by far the most expensive promotion technique of all those available to sales and marketing planners. In many companies, sales managers are responsible for their controllable costs and, therefore, the profits that are generated by their units. When this is the case, sales managers must fully understand the nature of the costs for which they are responsible. They must manage their units as profit-generating centers. Cost analysis concepts and techniques will be covered in Chap. 20.

Because of the growing cost of personal selling, many sales organizations are searching for more cost-effective ways to reach their customers. As discussed earlier, telemarketing, seminar selling, and trade show selling are a few of the techniques being used. In addition, Chap. 6 described how management techniques are being employed to improve the productivity of salespeople and sales managers.

THE COMPETITIVE ENVIRONMENT

competition
Struggle among various firms for market share

Competition—the struggle among various firms for market share—is a fundamental aspect of a free economy. Buyers are generally able to select from among a number of similar products marketed by different firms.

In general, sales managers have virtually no control over the actions of competitors, who are a major limiting constraint on company sales and profits. Sales managers must therefore see to it that they and their reps know everything they possibly can about competitors' activities.[14] Further, they must be keen "market intelligence" sources for higher management.

Complexity of Competition

Competition in today's world is far more intense and complex than ever since the buyer's purchasing decision really concerns how to best allocate funds among numerous alternative uses. This new concept of competition is one of the most significant influences on the selling environment in several years. It has been spurred on by the major shift in government policy toward deregulation of business and by increased global marketing.

SALES MANAGEMENT IN PRACTICE

SCHWEPPE & COMPANY

Recent economic trends have not done a great deal of good for the real estate industry. Fewer new households have been formed in the past few years, credit has been tight, land for development has been in short supply, and many consumers have been too concerned about their income or job security to consider making major purchases. The goal of owning a home is out of reach for many; the National Association of Realtors' index of housing affordability was in a recent year at its highest level since 1974.

While many bemoan their plights, at least one realtor, Jay Schweppe of Montclair, New Jersey, is making the best of a tough situation. Schweppe and his agents create opportunities by pursuing aggressively both buyers and sellers. For example, houses bought during a specific time frame within a certain price range would turn a reasonable profit if the current owner sold now. Schweppe's agents have searched through the records to find such desirable time/price houses. The agents consult tax records to determine the owners'

names, and then they cold-call the owners, asking if they would like to sell their houses. The basic theme is, "If you sell now you could still come out OK, but if you wait until next year. . . ."

Schweppe woos his clients who are looking to buy, staying in touch often and informing buyers immediately when interesting houses go up for sale.

Schweppe uses other methods as well. His salespeople, who work on a commission-only basis, are expected to earn a minimum of $40,000 per year. He advertises in a way that verges on the obnoxious, showing bar charts comparing Schweppe sales to competitors' sales, for example. His classified ads for homes are known for their glaring omissions—a description might not include the number of bedrooms, forcing potential clients into calling Schweppe's office for the information.

Like Jay Schweppe or not (and most of his competitors do not), his unorthodox tactics have ensured his survival. Montclair had twenty-one real estate offices in 1986. Today, the town has only eleven. Schweppe & Company is one of the few realtors that has thrived in the face of such adverse economic conditions.

Although it is obvious that competitors are a critical force in the sales manager's environment, it is not always clear who the competitors are. For example, banks and other traditional financial institutions face competition from Sears, Roebuck and Company (with subsidiaries Allstate Insurance, Discover Card, Dean Witter Investments, and so forth), General Electric, American Express, AT&T, and many other nonbank competitors.[15]

Many banks and other traditional financial institutions are taking a sales-oriented approach to meet the challenges of new competitors. They must develop a quality-oriented, customer-focused sales system to compete with nonbank financial services firms that have longstanding sales cultures. However, as some banks are discovering, it is not easy to make a banking organization sales-minded.[16] Shifting to a sales culture requires strong support from senior management and a commitment to selling as a way of doing business. Major investments in sales planning, training, incentives, and other sales support activities are also required.[17]

Another dimension of competition is technological development. A firm's products and services can be quickly replaced in the marketplace by improved technology introduced by competitors. Typewriters have been replaced by personal computers; adding machines have been replaced by calculators and personal computers; the use of conventional ovens and unprepared foods has been reduced in many homes by the advent of microwave ovens and prepared foods. Sales managers who do not keep pace with technological advances will soon find themselves at a competitive disadvantage.

Finally, sales managers must contend with aggressive competitors from other nations. Goodyear's major competitors in the U.S. tire market are Michelin (France) and Bridgestone (Japan). AT&T's Network System Group, which sells telecommunications equipment to phone companies throughout the world, must contend with Northern Telecom (Canada), Siemens (Germany), NEC (Japan), and other global producers.

Strong foreign competition has important implications for the sales manager, who must aggressively promote the firm's products through a combination of price and nonprice strategies. Where foreign prices for competing products are lower due to differences in labor costs, the sales manager must promote customer service and demonstrate the quality of domestic products. This concept is also tied to the economic environment, for an inability to successfully market domestic products in the face of foreign competition contributes to a poor balance of payments, unemployment, and other economic ills.

Models of Competition

Economic theory provides another approach to competitive assessment. The four basic models of competition are pure or perfect competition, monopoly, oligopoly, and monopolistic competition. The following discussion comparing these market structures is summarized in Table 7-2.

Perfect competition is a situation where there are so many buyers and sellers in the marketplace that no one firm will make a great difference in the price. It is best illustrated by agricultural products. Consider the case of corn. Farmers who produce corn create a homogenous product; one farmer's crop is a perfect substitute for another's. There is no distinct advantage enjoyed by one farmer's product over

perfect competition Market where there are so many buyers and sellers that no one firm will make a great difference in the price

TABLE 7-2 A Comparison of Market Structures

Market characteristics	Type of competition			
	Pure or perfect competition	Oligopoly	Monopolistic competition	Monopoly
Type of product	Homogeneous	Somewhat heterogeneous		Unique in the marketplace
Numbers of sellers	Large number	Few	Few-many, depending on product	One
Price	Market price	Price leaders and followers	Price competition influenced by nonprice factors such as brand loyalty	Pricing freedom due to lack of competition
Selling effort required	Aggressive effort, as products are perfect substitutes; emphasis on nonprice factors	Price and nonprice factors important; brand differentiation important; emphasis on distinguishing characteristics; aggressive marketing effort, through advertising and other promotional methods		Limited due to solo source situation

another's. Selling effort is minimal. With the exception of agriculture (when there are no government supports and controls), there are few examples of perfect competition.

monopoly Market dominated by one firm offering a product for which no close substitute exists

Monopoly is the other extreme form of competition. Here, one firm dominates the market and no close substitute for the product exists. Price is set by the monopoly firm, which charges whatever the traffic will bear. The selling effort is not critical, since no other options are available to customers. With the exception of a few temporary monopolies or those sanctioned by public policy, this market does not exist in our economy.

oligopoly Market dominated by relatively few large firms

An *oligopoly* exists in those instances where relatively few large firms dominate the market. A common price often emerges for the good or service. Should one manufacturer decide to lower the price in an effort to gain market share, competitors will quickly follow suit. Should the firm attempt to raise the price, however, its market share will deteriorate as buyers purchase the product at the lower price offered by the competition.

monopolistic competition Market in which several competitors offer products that are relatively heterogeneous to the consumer

In *monopolistic competition*, several competitors offer products that are relatively heterogeneous to the consumer. Each firm attempts to gain market share through a combination of price and nonprice factors. Brand loyalty or perceived quality differences are critical, since the consumer has several available options from which to choose. Price is generally a function of perceived quality.

Most instances of competition in the U.S. economy are of the latter two types. It is important for a sales manager to distinguish the factors that characterize a selling situation and act accordingly. In situations of oligopoly, price considerations are not crucial in the selling effort; instead, nonprice considerations, such as customer service and quality, must dominate a sales manager's strategy. Under monopolistic competition, a sales manager may use a combination of pricing and nonpricing strategies. Product quality and reputation and awareness through advertising and other promotional strategies, as well as relative price, must be used by a sales manager in marketing a firm's products.

THE POLITICAL AND LEGAL ENVIRONMENT

Closely tied to the notion of the competitive environment is the political and legal environment, especially the extent and complexity of laws that govern all selling and interstate commerce. These are aimed at preventing monopoly and deceptive and unfair trade practices.

Other laws are intended primarily to protect consumers. These include federal laws for specific industries, such as food, drugs, and cosmetics. There are also state laws regulating sales transactions. Under these laws, salespeople are considered the agents of their companies, and the penalties imposed on a company and one or more of its salespeople individually for violation of these laws can be substantial.

The cardinal rule here for sales managers is: Managers and their sales reps must know enough about the law to recognize situations in which they need legal advice. The laws are so numerous and complex that anytime sales reps or managers make amateur legal decisions on borderline transactions, they court disaster for their companies and themselves.

Antitrust Legislation

The major U.S. antitrust laws are outlined below:

Sherman Antitrust Act (1890) Oldest federal law regarding monopoly and conspiracy in the restraint of trade

- The *Sherman Antitrust Act (1890)* is the oldest federal law regarding monopoly or conspiracy in the restraint of trade. Judicial interpretations over the years have rendered practices such as price fixing or deliberate restrictions of production illegal. Under present regulations, fines of up to $1 million may be levied against firms found to be in violation of the Sherman Antitrust Act. In addition, individual violators may be fined up to $100,000 and may face up to three years in prison.

Clayton Act (1914) Antitrust legislation that restricts practices whose effects might be to substantially lessen competition or to tend toward creating a monopoly

- The *Clayton Act (1914)* is an extension and clarification of the Sherman Antitrust Act. Its purpose is to restrict practices whose effects might be to substantially lessen competition or to tend toward creating a monopoly.

Federal Trade Commission Act (1914) Federal law that prohibits unfair competitive practices; also set up the Federal Trade Commission

- The *Federal Trade Commission Act (1914)* prohibits "unfair competitive practices." As a result of this act, the Federal Trade Commission (FTC) was established as a quasijudicial agency to monitor various laws dealing with business operations. Initially prosecution was difficult to obtain due to the need to demonstrate "injury to competition." This standard was changed with the enactment of the Wheeler-Lea Amendment (1938), which banned all deceptive or unfair marketing practices, including deceptive packaging, branding, pricing, or advertising.

The FTC often uses company or industry consent agreements and conferences rather than formal legal action. The consent method secures a specific agreement from the offending company to abandon an unfair practice, while the conference method seeks voluntary compliance from a company with mutually acceptable rules and regulations.

The Regulation of Pricing Practices

Robinson-Patman Act (1936) Amendment to the Clayton Act that prohibits price discrimination not based on a cost differential and selling at unreasonably low prices to eliminate competition

Pricing practices have also been regulated through federal legislation. The *Robinson-Patman Act (1936)*, an amendment to the Clayton Act, prohibits both price discrimination not based on a cost differential and selling at an unreasonably low price to eliminate competition. This bill was based on the premise that large purchasers might be able to secure discounts not readily available to others. The Robinson-Patman Act remains an important part of the sales manager's legal and regulatory environment.

Deregulation

An important trend in recent years has been the movement toward fewer government restrictions on business. In part, deregulation has resulted from dissatisfaction with the regulatory system, which imposes limitations on businesses and prohibits the natural evolution of competition. Deregulation is also the result of technological innovation that has introduced many new forms of competition into some "old," stable industries. Most affected by deregulation have been transportation, communications, financial institutions, and professional services. In general, deregulation has increased competition in these industries and given sales and marketing managers greater flexibility. This trend has also led to increased emphasis on sales and marketing by traditional service businesses. The development of a sales culture by banks is an illustration.

The Impact of the Legal Environment on Sales Management

All of these laws and regulations are important to sales managers, for they restrict discretionary power either by defining the limitations of pricing strategy or by otherwise regulating or promoting competition. In examining the impact of these laws, sales managers must consider three types of issues:

1. What corporate and marketing strategies are constrained by law?
2. What kinds of costs might be incurred due to changes in applicable regulatory procedures and policies?
3. What opportunities and challenges are presented by changing laws or regulatory actions?

In addition to the regulations mentioned, three other legal areas have become increasingly important to sales managers: equal employment opportunity, buyer protection legislation, and laws dealing with salespersons' actions and statements.

Equal Employment Opportunity

There are several laws that specify the right to equal employment opportunity. The U.S. government, most states, and many counties and cities have laws that are directed toward preventing discriminatory practices.

Civil Rights Act of 1964 Federal law banning discrimination on the basis (Title VII) of race, color, religion, sex, or national origin

Title VII of the *Civil Rights Act of 1964* is one of the most important pieces of legislation regarding equal employment opportunity. This provision prohibits discrimination on the basis of race, color, religion, sex, or national origin by employers, employment agencies, unions, and committees controlling apprenticeship or training programs. Since its inception, other laws have been enacted to protect the handicapped, the elderly, and veterans. All phases of employment are covered in Title VII. Discrimination is prohibited except in cases of "bona fide occupational qualification."

sexual harassment Unwelcome sexual advances, requests for sexual favors, and other verbal or physical conduct of a sexual nature

Sexual harassment is a form of discrimination that violates the Civil Rights Act of 1964. Unwelcome sexual advances, requests for sexual favors, and other verbal or physical conduct of a sexual nature constitutes *sexual harassment*. When submission to this conduct is made a condition of employment, or is used as the basis for employment decisions, or affects an individual's work performance, or creates an intimidating, hostile, or offensive work environment, an employer is guilty of sex discrimination.

Equal Employment Opportunity Commission Government agency that deals with the Equal Employment Opportunity Act and related legislation

Many laws have expanded upon the provisions outlined in Title VII. For example, the Equal Employment Opportunity Act of 1972 amended Title VII and expanded coverage to include civil service employees as well as employees of educational institutions.

The *Equal Employment Opportunity Commission (EEOC)* was initially established under the provisions of Title VII to resolve grievances and to interpret Title VII's provisions with regard to specific cases. In 1972, this power was expanded to include the ability to prefer charges against employers in federal courts.

Pregnancy Discrimination Act Federal law that prohibits employment discrimination on the basis of pregnancy, childbirth, or related medical conditions

Recent amendments to the Civil Rights Act have added protection for pregnant women and people of different national origins. The *Pregnancy Discrimination Act* prohibits employment discrimination on the basis of pregnancy, childbirth, or related medical conditions. Pregnancy must be treated like any other short-term medical disability; the same rights and benefits must be extended to pregnant workers as to other temporarily disabled employees. For instance, insurance and employee benefits including seniority, vacation leave, and pay increases must be the same for pregnant employees as for any other temporarily disabled employee.

Immigration Reform and Control Act of 1986 (IRCA) Federal law that requires employers to verify that everyone hired after November 6, 1986, is legally authorized to work in the United States

The *Immigration Reform and Control Act of 1986 (IRCA)* requires employees to verify that all hirees (after November 6, 1986) are legally authorized to work in the United States. The IRCA also prohibits discrimination based on national origin or citizenship status. Therefore, an employer who singles out for employment verification individuals of a particular national origin or individuals who appear or sound foreign may have violated IRCA, Title VII, or both. Under Title VII no one can be denied equal employment opportunity because of birthplace, ancestry, culture, or linguistic characteristics common to a specific ethnic group. Under IRCA employers may not impose citizenship requirements or give preference to U.S. citizens in hiring unless there are legal or contractual requirements for a particular job; however, where two individual applicants for a job are equally qualified, IRCA allows preference for citizens.

Penalties for noncompliance are severe. The EEOC and similar state agencies may take legal action against employers. Substantial financial penalties such as back pay and salary adjustments can be levied by the courts. In many cases, an employer and the EEOC will negotiate a settlement. Such was the case when AT&T agreed in 1973 to make payments of $15,000,000 to 15,000 employees to compensate for past discriminatory practices. Specific hiring problems and guidelines for meeting EEOC provisions will be discussed in Chap. 12.

Buyer Protection

Legislation designed to protect consumers has been in existence for decades at the federal, state, and local levels. In 1872, for example, the federal government declared that it was illegal to use the mails in an attempt to defraud consumers. Later, the *Pure Food and Drug Act of 1906* was enacted as a result of public outrage over the practices taking place in the Chicago stockyards. This act prohibited the adulteration and misbranding of food and drugs in interstate commerce.

Pure Food and Drug Act of 1906 Law banning the alteration and misbranding of food and drugs sold in interstate commerce

Many recent laws have been concerned with the prevention of consumer deception and fraud. Telemarketing and other new technologically advanced sales techniques have been misused to dupe consumers. As a result, laws requiring full disclosure of sales offers, the provision of a "cooling-off" period for the buyer, and other buyer protection measures have been passed. In addition, the concern for consumers' privacy has led to the passage of many laws that restrict the sending of direct mail and limit telephone sales contacts.

What are the implications for sales managers? Very simply, awareness and vigilance must be the watchwords. Because of the nebulous wording of some consumer protection legislation and the tendency toward stricter enforcement, sales managers must be certain to work within regulations. Violations may be costly in terms of fines and other financial consequences, as well as because of the negative publicity that is generated.

Salespersons' Actions and Statements

Salespeople who overstate the capabilities of their products may also inadvertently create liability problems for their firms. Improper use of promotional mate-

TABLE 7-3 Sales Practices That Can Create Legal Obligations for a Firm

Legal issue	Example of misstatement
Creation of unintended warranty	Chemical salesperson inadvertently overstates product's technical capabilities
Dilution of warning effectiveness	Securities salesperson tells client that warnings in prospectus are unimportant
Disparagement of competitive offerings	Industrial equipment salesperson makes unverified negative statements about rival's products
Misrepresentation of own offerings	Real estate salesperson lies to buyer about condition of a house
Tortious interference with business relationships	Sales agent makes false accusations about franchisee before franchisee's customers

rials, misrepresentation of samples, and even silence in the face of a prospect's questions are other ways that salespeople can create an unintended warranty or misrepresent a product's features and benefits. These actions clearly violate standards of ethical behavior for professional salespeople. Further, they may result in negative publicity for the firm, and, depending on the circumstances, could result in significant financial penalties.[18]

Based on an extensive review of a legal data base, the authors of a study of the legal dimensions of salespersons' statements have identified five categories of sales statements or actions that may have legal consequences. These are presented in Table 7-3. To avoid these legal problems, a proactive sales management program is recommended. To make sure that salespeople comply with legal guidelines, managers must do the following:

1. Include specific legal guidelines in sales training programs for beginning salespeople.
2. Provide updated information to salespeople about legal developments related to communications with prospects and customers.
3. Use incentive compensation packages that reward salespeople for appropriate behavior.
4. Review salespeople's performance to identify any actions or practices that might lead to legal problems.
5. Lead by example by always following legal guidelines when accompanying salespeople in the field.[19]

SUMMARY OF LEARNING GOALS

1. **Differentiate between the Internal and External Environment.**

   The internal environment consists of factors within the organization, while the external environment consists of factors outside the company that are out of the company's control. It is the external environment that top management considers in its planning process.

2. **Identify the Major Components of the External Environment.**

   The external environment is made up of the following:

- The social and cultural environment
- The technological environment
- The economic environment
- The competitive environment
- The political and legal environment

3. Discuss the Meaning of Environmental Opportunities and Threats.

Environmental opportunities are positive stimuli for action that will generally result in the successful attainment of desired goals. Environmental threats present the negative challenge of unfavorable situations that, if not accounted for and acted upon, could lead to declines in selling effectiveness.

4. List the Response Modes of Environmental Opportunities and Threats.

Potential responses to opportunities and threats include the following:

- Adapting to the change
- Moving against the change
- Trying to modify the change

5. Explain How Each Facet of the Environment Impacts Upon Sales Management.

- The cultural and social facets of the environment impact upon sales management through changes in population characteristics such as growth rates, age distribution, geographic distribution, education levels, number of minority and women employees, changing types of households, and changes in values.
- Technology, especially that involving transportation, telecommunications, and computers, greatly affects sales management.
- The economic environment affects sales management by altering consumer income levels and purchasing power; the economic environment also determines savings and debt patterns, raw material costs, prices, and the inflation rate.
- The competitive environment a firm faces determines the prices that can be charged for products and also the types and extent of selling effort that will be required.
- Political and legal environmental factors affect sales management through antitrust laws, regulation of pricing practices, equal employment opportunity regulations, buyer protection, and laws that deal with salespersons' statements and actions.

REVIEW QUESTIONS

1. Differentiate between the internal and external environments for sales management. Cite examples of each category.
2. Define environmental scanning. What is its objective?
3. What is meant by an environmental threat or challenge? How can sales managers respond to such challenges?
4. What is the difference between an invention and an innovation? Under which category do most of today's new products fit?

5. What technologies have had the greatest effects on sales management? How has each such technology been used?

6. How do inflation and unemployment affect the selling process? What techniques are being used to sell in a less costly manner?

7. What selling strategies are appropriate in an oligopolistic environment? In monopolistic competition?

8. What industries have been most affected by deregulation? How has deregulation impacted sales management?

9. Outline the major federal legislation that affects sales management. Which law do you regard as the most significant?

10. What legal issues are involved in selling practices? What must sales managers do to make sure that salespeople comply with legal guidelines?

DISCUSSION QUESTIONS

1. When the Atlanta Braves were closing in on baseball's National League Western Division title in the summer of 1991, foam-bedding salesperson Paul Braddy had an inspiration: to design a foam tomahawk to go with Braves fans' trademark hand chop. Braddy designed and marketed his tomahawk, and within a few months he had quit the foam-bedding business, hired 23 employees, and sold 200,000 tomahawks.[20] What potential threats might Braddy face as he continues to market his product?

2. The number of environmental factors that can affect the selling process is almost limitless. Choose any recent social, technological, economic, competitive, or political/legal trend and prepare a short report on how it has affected sales management.

3. How should a sales manager respond to the following environmental threats?

   a. Your major competitor just moved a second salesperson into one of your key territories. Your representative is now outnumbered 2 to 1.

   b. Your voice mail system is down because of a fire. You can no longer get messages out instantly to your far-flung sales force.

   c. A competitive rep tells an important customer that your firm has been guilty of unethical behavior in the past. While true, this behavior was corrected long before you joined the firm.

4. As public health awareness has increased in recent years, there has been a louder and louder outcry against the marketing practices of some companies, especially those who sell alcohol and cigarettes. If you were a sales manager in one of these industries, how would you respond to the critics? Explain how the criticism would affect the way you manage your sales force.

5. Interview a local sales manager. What steps does this individual's employer take to avoid legal errors by the sales force? Discuss this approach and compare it to the material presented in Chap. 7.

ETHICAL DILEMMA

In very competitive industries there are likely to be some companies that resort to unethical practices, such as kickbacks and misrepresentation, to obtain orders. How should sales managers and salespeople respond when they become aware of these unethical practices by competitors?

SALES MANAGEMENT CASE

Threats, Opportunities, Response

Effective sales managers are able to respond quickly to environmental threats and opportunities. Chapter 7 designated environmental influences as social and cultural, technological, economic, competitive, and political and legal. Examples of these influences abound.

Lap-top computers are arguably the hottest topic on the current sales management technology front; it seems as though anybody who is anybody is "automating the sales force." Salespeople at London Fog, for example, hook their lap-top computers up to phone lines that automatically check in with London Fog's central data base during the night. The salespeople always have access to the most accurate and current data. The importance of sales force automation to sales management is indisputable; the area will triple in size between the years 1991 and 1994.

The health of the economy has many repercussions for sales managers. Incentives represent only one of the issues to be considered. When times are tough, one might expect companies to reduce their incentive programs. During the recession of the early 1990s, however, many companies took the opposite approach. FTD, for example, actually expanded participation in its incentive program by offering more incentives to a greater number of florists. The types of incentives that are effective also vary with the health of the economy. Merchandise, travel, and cash tend to be more popular in tough times than recognition awards, which are of long-term value.

Change in the legal environment must be monitored constantly by sales managers. In all states except California and Florida, it is illegal for insurance salespeople to cut out part of their commission in order to make policies less expensive for a customer. Salespeople have been known to fly to California or Florida in order to make commission-reduced sales.

Changes in the environment continually alter the way salespeople sell and sales managers manage. An

United States Virgin Islands
St.Croix St. John St.Thomas

ability to adapt to change is one of the most important skills for business people, determining which companies succeed, and which are left behind.

Questions

1. Which of these environmental situations are opportunities? Which are threats?

2. Do you agree that incentive requirements should be lowered during tough times? Why or why not?

3. A recent study reported that, while high-technology equipment increased salesperson productivity, it did not necessarily increase the amount of time salespeople spent with customers. Is this a problem? Why or why not?

SALES MANAGEMENT PLANNING

LEARNING GOALS

- Understand the role of sales planning in the corporate context.
- Explain the importance of the marketing information systems (MIS) and marketing decision support systems (MDSS) to sales management.
- Outline the steps involved in the sales management planning process.
- Describe the content of the analysis phase of sales management planning.
- Identify key sales objectives.
- Discuss the significance of strategy selection.
- Highlight the role of tactical decisions in sales planning.
- Put the implementation and control phases of the sales management planning cycle into perspective.

HOME DEPOT—A SALES PLAN BASED UPON TRAINING

Home Depot, the king of the hardware do-it-yourself market, has grown to a 188-store chain with 30,000 employees. Sales volume in a recent year exceeded $5 billion.

The success of Home Depot can largely be credited to its retail sales team and the sales strategy employed by the firm. Home Depot's sales plan is based on sound recruiting and training. New sales employees are typically experienced carpenters, electricians, tile-layers, and the like. Home Depot sales personnel have the practical skills to teach someone how to do a household repair or similar project. For example, Ernie Palisin, the floor coverings department manager in Orlando, Florida, organized a Saturday afternoon tile class on his own.

New sales hires go through a five-day training program in which the company's history and culture is explained. Nothing is left to chance. Sales personnel are taught to ask about the projects on which shoppers are working. The objective is to go through the customer's project lists to see how Home Depot can help.

Sales personnel are then assigned to a department where they go through three additional weeks of training under the direction of the department manager. The emphasis is on ordering, stocking, and selling. Learning

Home Depot's 30,000-item inventory is quite a job. Product seminars are part of the training.

Building sales skills in its personnel is the key to Home Depot's sales plan. Chris Brumfield, an assistant store manager, tells new hires: "Never just point to another aisle. Walk the customer over and find someone to help." Home Depot sales personnel do not fight for customers since the firm refuses to use commissions. The emphasis is on helping the customer find a solution to his or her problem.[1]

Chapter 8 discusses sales management planning. As you will see, planning involves setting objectives and determining ways to achieve them. Planning is long-term-oriented, it is strategic, and it is essential to

the sales function. Home Depot's efforts to build a well-trained sales team are the basis of its overall sales plan.

CHAPTER OVERVIEW

Effective sales managers are planners. They formulate objectives to guide the efforts of the sales force, they map courses of action in the pursuit of these objectives, and they evaluate the actual performance of their salespeople by measuring it against objectives. Planning is essential to the sales function. Without it, sales managers lack the benefit of a long-term perspective. They also lack the means to coordinate the diverse components of the selling process. As one experienced sales and marketing manager put it: "Without a plan . . . your sales and marketing efforts are likely to be random, unfocused, even pulling in several different directions."[2]

Sales planning does not occur in a vacuum. Sales managers must consider the environmental forces affecting sales management and the environment's impact on sales plans. They must also recognize that sales management planning is governed by company-wide considerations and has to be coordinated within the corporate context. Schedules, quantities, and cash flows projected in the sales plan have to align with other plans, such as the general marketing plan.

To achieve this kind of fine-tuning, sales managers require a great deal of information. They rely in part upon input from the field sales organization, and they also need a system that feeds them a steady flow of relevant information to help them devise and update sales plans.

Sales management planning consists of a series of cyclical steps. These steps lead from analysis to decision making, implementation, and control, and they closely mirror the sequence that characterizes the sales management cycle. An understanding of the complexities of the sales planning process is vital to the successful management of the sales function.

THE NATURE AND IMPORTANCE OF SALES PLANNING

planning Deciding what to do in the future

Planning means deciding what to do in the future. It involves setting objectives and determining ways to achieve them. Sales managers engaged in planning must examine where their company is currently, how it got there, and where it is going. A popular homily expresses the importance of planning as follows:

> Poor managers work on
>   yesterday's problems.
> Good managers work on
>   today's problems.
> Excellent managers work on
>   tomorrow's problems.

sales planning Anticipating environmental developments and preparing to meet or capitalize on them

Sales planning involves anticipating environmental developments and preparing to meet these developments or capitalize on them. Planning means controlling events instead of being overwhelmed by them. As discussed in Chap. 7, environmental forces can act as threats or opportunities for a company's sales and marketing activities, and what is a threat to one firm is an opportunity to another. While adaptation is the most frequent mode of coping with environmental changes, environmental modification should not be overlooked.

Sales planning is particularly crucial and challenging when it comes to the introduction of new products. The very newness of an item requires additional selling effort and produces buyer resistance. Close cooperation between sales and production management is crucial to the successful launching of innovative products.

Sales planning is important to all members of the sales organization. A well-conceived sales plan generates excitement and enthusiasm when put into action. It provides the direction and framework for sales activities. It helps sales personnel understand where the sales organization is headed, how it is expected to get there, and what specific actions are to be undertaken, by whom, and when.

SALES PLANNING IN THE CORPORATE CONTEXT

Sales management planning must be implemented in concert with other components of a company's planning system. Fine-tuning is best achieved by means of a corporate planning department or planning committee.

corporate mission Beginning of the planning process: a statement giving a company's reason for being

As shown in Fig. 8-1, the corporate planning process begins with a statement of the *corporate mission,* or the organization's "reason for being." A company will only function well if all its components operate in concert with each other. Sales managers have to be familiar with their company's mission statement. Corporate marketing, and, ultimately, sales objectives are all derived from this statement of the firm's aims, strengths, and uniqueness.

Marketing research and other information sources are used to identify markets to be served and to predict likely future environmental conditions. Projections of trends form the assumptions governing the overall corporate planning system. Strategic business and marketing plans will be based upon this analysis. The analysis

FIGURE 8-1 Planning Hierarchy.

also leads to the preparation of the sales forecast that represents the cornerstone of the corporate planning process.

The sales forecast must, in turn, be reconciled with the company's mission statement. This reconciliation process may suggest further analysis to give new direction to a firm mired in mature markets with little growth potential. This may lead to a restructuring of the sales effort by de-emphasizing or abandoning less profitable businesses in favor of more attractive ones.

Based on analytical information, sales managers will develop sales strategies and tactical action plans. These sales plans specify how home offices and field resources will be employed. The sales plans are part of the strategic marketing plan, which includes related support activities such as product management, advertising, and sales promotion. In conjunction with the marketing plan, the company plans its production. Production depends on the purchasing department to procure the necessary equipment and flow of materials. All three of these major component plans—the marketing plan, production plan, and purchasing plan—must tie in with the finance plan, because none of them will come to pass unless funding is available. Taken together, the plans make up the company's or business unit's *strategic plan*, an outline of how resources will be allocated to market opportunities.

strategic plan
Outline of how re-
sources will be
allocated to market
opportunities

Important similarities and differences between corporate and sales planning are shown in Table 8-1. Sales managers must take their lead from corporate plans. The activities of the sales organization must be coordinated with the company's marketing strategy and other business plans.

Consider, for example, the impact of sales planning on production planning. First, quantities have to be matched so that the number of units projected to be sold can be produced and delivered in time. Second, schedules have to be related to each other in such a way that component activities feed smoothly into each other. Finally, cash flows must be coordinated with one another so that the firm is able to meet its obligations.

TABLE 8-1   Corporate versus Sales Planning: Similarities and Differences

	Corporate planning concerns	Sales planning concerns
Scope	Business in which to engage—broad expansion, diversification, acquisition guidelines	Development of new sales opportunities constrained by corporate scope and sales resources
Policies	Constituent policy (employee, stockholder, government) Broad marketing policies (share, distribution, pricing) Broad product policies (commodity, quality, breadth of line)	Following basic policies handed down by corporate management Broad description of the conduct that sales management will support to at least maintain the viability of the business—for example, product line emphasis, sales strategies, systems selling, and so forth
Financial objectives	Broad corporate aspirations Business-level aspirations	Plan to achieve sales and profit objectives set by corporate management
Resource allocation	Selection of business areas to receive resource infusions	Recommended sales resource expenditures based on (1) competitive position and industry attractiveness for existing products and (2) added lines that have synergy with present operations
Organization	Melding, separation, and sharing of existing and newly acquired plant and personnel resources across businesses	Melding, separation, and sharing of existing sales resources within the business

Sales obligations represent a key link in the corporate planning context, since they affect all other planning efforts. If this responsibility is taken lightly, the company is likely to be out of step with the marketplace. If sales management underestimates the demand for certain items, it will be unable to supply sufficient quantities, which will invite competition. On the other hand, if anticipated demand levels do not materialize, the company can be caught in a cash squeeze caused by excessive inventories. So an adequate information base is a prerequisite of successful sales planning.

INFORMATION FOR SALES PLANNING

information
Processed data

secondary data
Data originally collected for a purpose other than the one at hand

Modern sales management planning has to be information-based. *Information* is processed data. *Secondary data* are types of information already in existence, but originally collected for another purpose. Census data are an example. *Primary data* are collected for the purpose at hand; mall intercept interviews with shoppers are an example. Data, in and of themselves, do not constitute information; to be useful, they have to be processed, analyzed, interpreted, and made actionable.

primary data Data
collected specifically
for the purpose at
hand

Information for better decision making is supplied to sales managers by their firm's marketing information system (MIS) or marketing decision support system (MDSS), which monitor the environment for relevant trends, report on internally generated data, and investigate the market for sales opportunities. An effective information system will enable sales managers to respond to sales problems and issues promptly and effectively. This is especially important when sales managers must deal with strategic problems and issues.[3]

SALES INTELLIGENCE

Salespeople are expected to provide information for sales planning and management, and there is a growing need for better sales intelligence from the field. While salespeople have always provided competitive data from the field, much of this information was never formalized, systemized, or made effective. The salesperson's role as an information gatherer has been much expanded in recent years.[4] Salespeople possess vital information about the market that can be used to develop sales forecasts and quotas, to assess new products, and to formulate marketing strategy.

The need for information from the field poses two important sales management planning issues. First, salespeople must be encouraged to provide needed marketing information. Some field personnel claim that this new aspect of their job takes too much time away from selling activities. Most salespeople can devote some part of their time to collecting sales intelligence for analysis by staff personnel; however, management must provide the training, incentives, and supervision to encourage them to provide relevant information. Sales managers must also make sure that the marketing intelligence process is a two-way street. Once the data have been analyzed, it is essential that relevant facts are communicated back to the field force in order to improve their selling efficiency.

The second management planning issue concerns developing procedures for using information obtained from salespeople. This is a concern because, even though salespeople may know a great deal about their markets, they may have biased or incomplete knowledge, or they may not understand the complexity of their markets. Information obtained from salespeople must be properly assimilated with information obtained from other sources. Sales managers must work with staff specialists to develop a procedure for incorporating information from the field into the marketing planning process.[5]

Several other sources of information can be used to assess and supplement information from salespeople. As noted earlier, secondary data sources can be used. Trade publications, government documents, statistical reports, and the like can provide extensive insights into market conditions and competitors. Sales force reports should also be weighed against a comprehensive analysis of internal sales data. Internal records allow sales managers to trace the histories of individual products, accounts, territories, and seasons. The identification of product life-cycle patterns, as well as the identification of the fluctuations, growth, and decline of specific customers or customer groups, is possible. This information can also be used to detect changes in different areas and at different times throughout the year. Relationships, trends, and reasonable projections can be made concerning likely

SALES MANAGEMENT IN PRACTICE

SALES MANAGEMENT

PROGRESSIVE INSURANCE

Being selected by *Sales & Marketing Management* as one of the nation's six best sales forces is no small honor. Progressive, a member of this elite group in 1991, has carved out its niche in the insurance industry by specializing in automobile insurance for high-risk drivers. The company has made it easier for customers to make claims by providing a 24-hour accident hotline. The amount of time required for claims settlement has also been reduced from thirty to seven days.

These services are designed for the benefit of current customers; they are not expected to attract a large number of new customers. For this purpose, Progressive relies on a salesperson intelligence system that is used widely for planning purposes.

Progressive's compensation plan for salespeople, which is high for the industry, gives little weight to incentives because the company does not want to discourage salespeople from spending time finding out what competitors are doing. If compensation were based only on volume considerations, the salespeople might not be as willing to spend time gathering the data that is critical to the company's welfare.

It is one thing to ask salespeople to provide competitive information, and another thing altogether to provide a system in which salespeople are motivated to do so. Progressive's achievement of overall selling excellence is based in part on its ability to collect vital competitive data.

future occurrences. Another information source is provided by marketing research, which concentrates on project-oriented activities.

USING THE MARKETING INFORMATION SYSTEM

marketing information system (MIS) Information system that provides actionable information to sales and marketing managers

The *marketing information system (MIS)* serves to collect, report, process, analyze, and interpret sales and marketing data and present actionable information to sales and marketing managers. It highlights possible future conditions, pinpoints potential courses of action, and describes what will probably happen if these actions are undertaken. This means that the MIS does not make planning decisions—sales and marketing managers do. A well-run MIS, however, will enable managers to make better-informed decisions.

The information generated by a marketing information system should not be overrated. If information alone were the key to success, computers could be programmed to perform the entire sales planning process. But computers can only provide alternatives, not decisions. Decisions require the human qualities of judgment, commitment, and risk assessment. Information is a tool, not a substitute, for decision making. It is useful in situations where past and current facts offer a reasonable glimpse into the future, but true growth opportunities do not possess this comforting quality of continuity. Growth opportunities create completely new markets or substantial changes in buyer behavior patterns.

Sales managers are not usually called upon to engage in this kind of guesswork, since they usually deal with annual schedules. A desire and an ability to look further into the future and to develop a long-term perspective of their company's business does, however, demonstrate their commitment to sustain growth rather than to settle for only short-term progress.

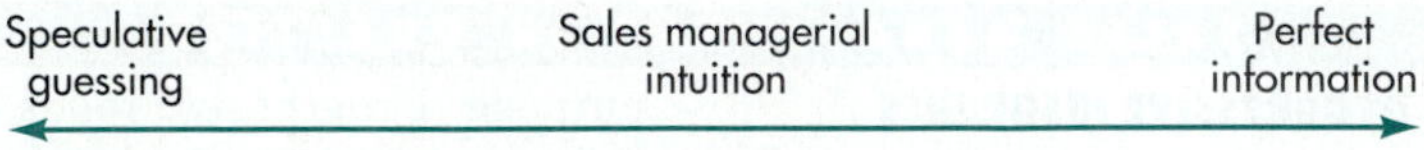

Speculative	Sales managerial	Perfect
guessing	intuition	information

$\longleftarrow\!\!\!\longrightarrow$

FIGURE 8-2 The Information Continuum.

Midway on the continuum between perfect information and speculative guessing is sales managerial intuition, which uses experience to guide speculation (see Fig. 8-2). *Intuition* involves judgment as well as creative interpretations of facts. It can separate sales managers from mere sales administrators.

intuition Judgment plus creative interpretation of facts

The MIS acts to reduce uncertainty and render it manageable, but it cannot eliminate uncertainty. The sales manager must still answer a number of questions. How much data gathering can the sales force reasonably be expected to do? How much time can the firm afford to divert from selling responsibilities? Is the firm willing to pay the price for this restructuring of priorities? How much computer time can be allocated to the processing of internal sales data? How timely and accurate will the information be? Is it worth conducting a special research project to gain a more thorough understanding of a particular sales problem or opportunity, or would it be better to make a decision now and take a chance?

THE GROWING IMPORTANCE OF MARKETING DECISION SUPPORT SYSTEMS

marketing decision support system (MDSS) Information system that links sales and marketing managers with relevant data bases

The latest twist in marketing information systems is what is known as the *marketing decision support system (MDSS).* Here, the marketing decision maker is linked via computer to known data bases. This arrangement, shown in Figs. 8-3 and 8-4, provides sales and other managers with more complete, up-to-date information.

Many of the nation's largest retailers have established so-called partnerships with their vendors. Retail buyers share information with vendors' sales and vice versa. These electronic data interchanges allow the retailers to reduce their inventories, as well as assisting the sales planning of their suppliers.

Dillard's Department Store now requires any new vendor to establish an electronic data interchange within 90 days. Dillard's estimates that this computer linkage saves it $16 million a year in paperwork.[6]

THE SALES MANAGEMENT PLANNING PROCESS

Sales management planning is an essential and demanding process that calls upon the full range of a sales manager's capabilities. It takes place in a logical series of stages

FIGURE 8-3 General Format for an MDSS.

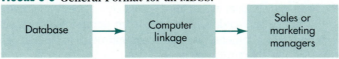

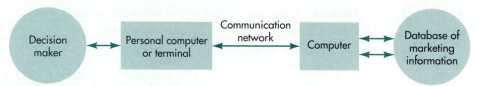

FIGURE 8-4 Model of a Marketing Decision Support System.

that are cyclical in nature and parallel to those of the sales management cycle (the sales management planning process is outlined in Fig. 8-5.

The analytical phase examines what happened in the past, looks at the present situation, and predicts what is likely to transpire in the future if current trends continue. The goal-setting phase spells out the direction that the sales effort should take during the planning period. Sales strategies translate these objectives into an action framework. The action details within this framework are filled in during the tactical phase. The plan is then executed during the implementation phase. The control stage serves to compare actual outcomes with planned results, in order to examine the need for plan revision.

Another way to look at the sales planning process is through a series of specific steps. The steps in this process can be carried out by securing detailed answers to the following specific, although broadly stated, questions:

1. Where do we stand now?
2. What will the future be like for our sales organization?
3. Where should we be heading?
4. How can we get there?
5. Who is going to do what, and when?
6. How much will the plan cost, and what do these costs cover?
7. What are the results?
8. What changes need to be made?

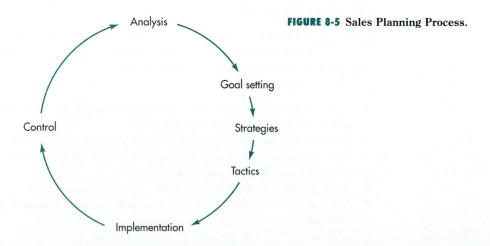

FIGURE 8-5 Sales Planning Process.

TABLE 8-2   **Questions Asked in the Sales Planning Process**

Step	Question	Response factors
1	Where do we stand now?	Situation analysis or sales force audit: present position with respect to markets, products, costs, competition, and other environmental factors
2	What will the future be like?	Trend analysis: future condition for our sales organization. The same areas addressed in step 1, including: (a) forecasts and assumptions, (b) opportunities and threats, and (c) potential surprises
3	Where should we be heading?	Sales objectives and strategies required to respond to opportunities and threats
4	How can we get there?	Sales action program (tactics) required to realize the objectives and strategies recommended in step 3
5	Who is going to do what, and when?	Assignment of responsibilities and deadlines
6	How much will the plan cost? What do these costs cover?	Preparation of a sales budget and financial plan
7	What are the results?	Collection and analysis of data required to monitor the sales strategies and actions chosen
8	What changes need to be made?	Revisions in sales strategies and actions if the sales organization is not on its planned course or if changes in conditions have occurred.

Table 8-2 suggest the factors, listed as steps 1 through 8, that are associated with the answers to each of these planning questions. As the table indicates, the strategy and tactics steps (steps 3 and 4) in the sales planning process depend completely on a thorough evaluation of the business's present position and an understanding of the trends affecting the business. The more complete the situation analysis or audit done in step 1 and the trend analysis done in step 2, the clearer will be the issues that the strategy and tactics steps must address. A complete discussion of the sales force audit is contained in Chap. 20.

THE ANALYSIS PHASE

In the first stage of their planning effort, sales managers need to get the facts about past and current market trends and the company's sales performance. They have to examine where their firm stands, how it got there, and where it is going. Many questions should be asked:

- Over the past five years, how have specific products, territories, and accounts developed in terms of sales profitability?
- How has the market in general evolved during this time span?
- How does our track record compare with those of competitors?
- What has happened to our market share?
- What can be learned from the past?
- Are values and behavior patterns of our clientele undergoing any significant changes?

- What new technologies appear on the horizon?
- Is the political-legal and/or economic climate changing?
- What new initiatives are competitors taking?
- What are our strengths and weaknesses?
- What emerging opportunities could we profitably seize upon?
- What new capabilities should we develop?

SWOT analysis
Sales management's evaluation of strengths, weaknesses, opportunities, and threats faced by the sales organization and the firm

The situation analysis has to be conducted in a factual and objective manner. A useful format many managers use is called *SWOT analysis*. The acronym stands for strengths, weaknesses, opportunities, and threats. Strengths and weaknesses relate to the sales organization's internal situation while opportunities and threats result from environmental factors.

To assess internal strengths and weaknesses, sales managers examine the company's sales records, market share, product applications and benefits, and target markets on a product-by-product basis. They look to the past and present price structures, both of their own products and of competitive items. They investigate availability and product life-cycle positions, and consider the advisability of promotional pricing or price deals. They also analyze the effectiveness of their channel policies. Sales managers may consider augmenting their distributors' sales organizations with missionary salespeople of their own, and they may institute training or promotional programs for distributor personnel. They also evaluate the impact of past advertising campaigns on product demand, and include reviews of promotional aids for retailers, as well as reviews of the relative importance of trade versus consumer advertising.

Sales managers also look at profiles and buying patterns of their various customer groups. They divide these groups according to purchase volume, and then they determine the level of effort each warrants, as well as the frequency with which each will be called upon. They review other relevant breakdowns, for example, by industry, or geography, or lifestyle. They may study the dynamics of group buying decisions to better direct personal selling efforts toward key decision makers. Awareness research highlights the level of product knowledge and brand identification among potential users and clarifies the need for aggressive advertising and promotion.

Sales managers must assess competitors for tactics to avoid or adopt. They must compare their own managerial caliber, technological capabilities, financial resources, and distribution systems against those of leading competitors. They must analyze competitive advertising media, themes, and spending levels, and they must acquaint themselves with their competitors' pricing practices and trends in market shares.

The analysis phase of sales planning also involves the consideration of environmental factors. Although much of this portion of the analysis will be done by marketing planners at the corporate level, sales managers must also become aware of major environmental issues and trends that will affect the sales function.

macroenvironment Technological, economic, political-legal, and sociocultural factors affecting a sales organization

Environmental factors are important in the analysis stage. The environment can be subdivided into the macroenvironment and the market. The *macroenvironment* is made up of technological, economic, political-legal, and sociocultural factors. Of more immediate concern to a sales planner, however, is the firm's *market*, which consists of actual and potential buyers (both ultimate and intermediate), as well as actual and potential competitors.

market Buyers, potential buyers, actual competitors, and potential competitors relevant to a sales organization

The firm's market is subject to frequent and rapid fluctuations. A well-managed MIS should monitor the market on a continuous basis to spot impending changes early. Buyers' and prospects' incomes, budgets, needs, and lifestyles vary over time. Competitors also enter and leave the market.

As discussed in Chap. 7, sales managers also have to keep up with changes in the macroenvironment. More advanced technologies make older products obsolete and have often doomed antiquated industries that did not change with the times. Likewise, economic conditions can substantially alter the sales outlook for a firm. Political and legal developments can also modify the nature of the game. Nowhere is this fact more evident than in the telecommunications industry, where MCI Communications won a landmark ruling against the Federal Communications Commission in 1978, and has since become a billion-dollar company. As a result, AT&T has been forced to dramatically change its sales strategies. Finally, the social and cultural environments are characterized by changing values, relationships, and influence patterns.

Macroenvironmental factors take effect primarily in the form of threats or constraints placed upon a sales manager's decision-making freedom. Threats usually come from current or prospective competitors. Opportunities, on the other hand, are more specifically related to markets.

Analysis of external and internal forces and trends leads to a sales forecast. Chapter 9 notes that the forecast represents sales management's best projection of sales revenues, assuming that the company's current practices are pursued unaltered. The forecast is then reconciled with the corporate and marketing objectives. The latter govern sales objectives, which are checked for feasibility against the sales forecast and other information sources.

SETTING SALES OBJECTIVES

objectives Desired ends, conditions, or occurrences that provide motivation and orientation for purposeful action

Upon completion of the situation analysis stage, management can address the task of setting sales objectives. *Objectives* are desired ends, conditions, or occurrences that provide motivation and orientation for purposeful action. They provide the specific direction for the sales organization's activities and answer the question: "Where do we want to go?" Clearly, a sales organization's objectives must be consistent with the mission and marketing objectives of the company.

Objectives channel resources toward their most productive uses. Sales objectives serve as guidelines and yardsticks for sales managers and salespeople. The level of objective attainment is then used to evaluate the success of the firm's sales effort.

Sales objectives not only express sales management's expectations, they also represent standards against which actual sales performance will be measured and evaluated. The setting of sales objectives is a structured, step-by-step process, as shown in Fig. 8-6. Based upon the corporate mission, top management sets the corporate objectives for the planning period. These objectives, in turn, trigger marketing objectives, which are also used in the sales forecast. The national sales manager then sets the national sales objectives, regional sales managers formulate objectives for their respective regions, and district or division managers determine their units' sales objectives and decide on objectives for their representatives. These objectives, which are usually referred to as sales quotas, will be discussed in more detail in Chap. 9.

As Fig. 8-6 shows, objectives serve as the focal points for the development of strategies and tactics. In the case of regional and district sales objectives, national sales strategies are the guiding forces for setting objectives. Personal sales objectives, or quotas, provide guidance for the preparation of personal sales plans such as selling schedules and territory coverage plans.

For the individual salesperson, sales objectives act also as directives, preferably indicating the consequences of compliance and noncompliance. Rewards can be monetary, such as bonuses or raises, or nonmonetary, such as recognition and/or honorary plaques. For the sales manager setting the sales objectives, rewards serve as a means for placing sales emphasis and exercising control. Good field managers use the participative method of formulating objectives, whereby they and subordinates jointly develop action guidelines. In this case, the process of setting sales objectives involves a combination top-down and bottom-up approach.

When formulating sales objectives, several guidelines should be followed. Most important, objectives must be specific and provide a precise statement of what is to be accomplished by the sales organization's strategy. Objectives should be stated in simple, understandable terms so that everyone involved in carrying out the strategy knows exactly what is to be achieved. Further, objectives should be measurable; that is, they should be stated in quantitative terms. Finally, sales objectives should be related to time so that everyone knows when the objectives are to be achieved.

A classification scheme for sales objectives can follow a number of different lines. It can distinguish between aggregate and individual objectives, broad and specific

FIGURE 8-6 **Process for Setting Sales Objectives.**

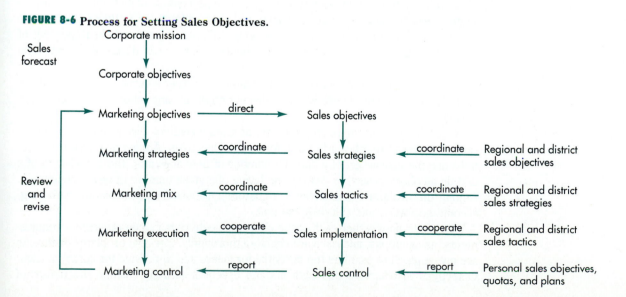

goals, and quantitative versus qualitative targets. Aggregate objectives are concerned with the entire sales function, whereas individual objectives direct the effort of one person. Broad objectives give a general direction for sales activities, specific objectives spell out particular accomplishments that should occur. The attainment of quantitative objectives is easily measurable. Qualitative objectives, on the other hand, are difficult to evaluate, since they can only be measured indirectly, such as by the level of returns or complaints.

Some sales managers have planning difficulties because they state their objectives in vague, difficult-to-measure terms. "To increase sales" and "to provide better service" are not satisfactory objectives. For this reason, sales managers must formulate quantitative objectives that are related to sales volume, market share, or profitability.

Sales volume objectives are often specified in terms of the number of units or dollar sales that are targeted to be sold in a given selling period. For example, the business might wish to sell 400,000 units of product A and 250,000 units of product B during the coming year. These sales volume objectives would be set in accordance with the unit's financial goals.

For some sales organizations, market share is a meaningful goal to pursue. Increased market share reduces vulnerability and increases pricing flexibility; it facilitates new product introductions and is positively correlated with profitability. In fact, the Profit Impact of Market Strategy (PIMS) model developed by the Strategic Planning Institute reveals that, the higher a business's share of its served market (the segment of the total market in which a business actually competes), the more likely it is to have above average profits and cash flow.[7]

Maintaining market share is a conservative and defensive goal, whereas expanding market share is an aggressive or offensive target. For instance, a major airline might state the following as a goal: "To increase our market share of the Chicago to Los Angeles route from 21 percent to 24 percent of total passenger miles by the end of the year." Attaining representation in a certain percentage of distribution outlets is another way to express a market share goal. For example, a producer of shampoo and hair conditioner might state the following: "To place our brands in 40 percent of the retail drug and food outlets in the Middle Atlantic area during the next fiscal year."

When it comes to profitability, it is common to target a certain minimum rate of return on investment. There will be a discussion of this and other financial concepts in Chap. 10.

In addition to the three major forms of sales objectives discussed above, some sales managers use other criteria to formulate objectives. Among quantitative objectives are the acquisition of a specific number of new accounts, the completion of a certain number of calls per day, or the hiring of a given number of new salespeople. Among the qualitative objectives are customer satisfaction, information gathering, account servicing, and self-development.

To ascertain whether each of the chosen objectives is indeed attainable, requirements, assumptions, and risks are checked thoroughly. Possible problems or threats are investigated to examine the potential for failure and to provide for contingencies. Objectives that survive this rigorous and essential scrutiny assume the nature of commitments. These commitments also involve the assignment of responsibility and accountability, so that it becomes evident who is at fault if the objectives are not realized.

FORMULATING SALES STRATEGIES

sales strategies
Blueprints for action that reconcile sales management's resources with environmental constraints

Sales managers next have to choose the avenues that will lead to success. *Sales strategies* are blueprints for action that marshal and reconcile the sales function's resources with environmental constraints. Strategies answer the question: "How do we get there?"

It is unlikely that sales managers, except those in small companies, will be involved in developing corporate marketing strategies. All sales managers, however, must understand these strategies and how they are formulated. Further, they must understand the implications of these strategies for the sales organization.

Michael Porter has suggested three generic approaches that can serve as a good starting point for strategic thinking:[8]

1. *Overall cost leadership.* A firm strives to achieve the lowest production and distribution costs so that it can price its products lower than those of competitors and capture a large share of the market. To do this, a firm must be efficient at engineering, purchasing, manufacturing, and physical distribution. Sales and marketing skills are less important. Hence, sales managers will be most concerned with cost-cutting strategies that result in the fewest resources being allocated to sales development activities.

2. *Differentiation.* In this case, a firm tries to achieve superior performance in an important customer benefit area that is valued by the market. For example, the company can strive to be the quality leader, the style leader, the technology leader, and so forth. To do this, a firm must use its strengths to create a competitive advantage in the chosen customer benefit area. A differentiation policy will have significant implications for sales strategy, especially if customer service is identified as the criterion for differentiation.

3. *Focus.* Here a firm concentrates on one or more specific market segments rather than going after the entire market. It identifies the needs of the chosen segment or segments and develops a targeted marketing strategy. As a result, the sales strategy must also focus on the target market, and salespeople must become sales specialists rather than generalists.

Building on Porter's strategic options and other approaches, Orville Walker and Robert Ruekert have developed a conceptual framework that helps explain marketing's role in the implementation of business strategies. Their analysis suggests strategic implications for all components of the marketing mix including sales and other forms of marketing communications.[9] As shown in Fig. 8-7, two major dimensions are used to form the conceptual framework—(1) the business unit's desired rate of new product-market development and (2) its intended method of competing (low cost or high differentiation through higher quality or better service). The sales organization will be most important for those firms that are pursuing a "differentiated defender" strategy. Walker and Ruekert's analysis is based on three ideas:

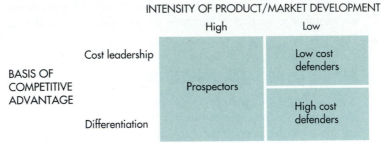

FIGURE 8-7 A Hybrid Typology of Business Unit Strategy.

1. The business strategy of a "prospector" is based on the business unit's desire for rapid new product or market development. The focus of marketing will be to develop relatively broad, technically sophisticated product lines. Because a prospector must generate awareness, stimulate trial, and build primary demand for new and unfamiliar products, its marketing communications policy will involve relatively high advertising and sales promotion expenditures.

2. A differentiated defender, in contrast, is concerned with maintaining the loyalty of customers by adapting to their needs and providing good service. In most cases, this will be accomplished by an extensive, well-trained, well-supported sales force. As a result, a policy of high sales force expenditures in relation to those of competitors will be appropriate.

3. A "low-cost defender" attempts to appeal to its customers primarily on a price basis. Thus, it will have relatively low expenditures on advertising, sales promotion, and sales force activities.

A third way to look at the development of sales strategies is to consider the linkages between sales strategies and the four basic market share strategies—"build," "hold," "harvest," and "divest."[10]. Each market share strategy suggests a primary sales objective and emphasis on specific sales tasks:

1. The primary sales objective for an organization with a "build" marketing strategy is to increase sales volume. This often involves securing distribution outlets for the product. For the sales force, the primary activity is calling on prospective and current accounts to introduce and sell the product. Salespeople will also be expected to provide high levels of customer service and to assist in collecting product and market intelligence information.

2. In a "hold" marketing strategy, maintaining sales volume by consolidating the organization's market position is the primary sales objective. Salespeople are asked to provide service to current targeted accounts to solidify the organization's position with these customers.

3. Reducing selling costs is the primary sales objective in a "harvest" marketing strategy. This is so the organization can "milk" the product for greater cash flow to be used elsewhere. Salespeople call on only the most profitable accounts and eliminate calling on smaller, unprofitable customers. In addition, service levels are reduced except in those areas where salespeople can work with the most profitable customers to develop greater efficiencies in serving them.

SALES MANAGEMENT IN PRACTICE

SALES MANAGEMENT

CAMPBELL SOUP COMPANY

In the mid-1980s, the Campbell Soup Company developed a strategy of focusing on geographical areas of the United States to market its over 1000 food products. Formerly, all products had been marketed to all parts of the country. Campbell's new policy greatly affected the company's sales force by dividing it into twenty-one autonomous regions; all of a sudden, field salespeople were known as "brand sales managers." They were also given control over large budgets, a fact that caused no small amount of confusion for the salespeople and resentment from others whose budgets had been reallocated.

The implementation of the new strategy was accompanied by in-house encouragement and support in the form of motivational meetings and much needed marketing information for the salespeople. After the sales force had fully adopted the plan, Campbell management organized its manufacturing on the same basis as the sales force, and the plants were expected to become responsible for the segments they represented. Also, the twenty-one regional offices assumed their own profit responsibility, and executive bonuses were tied to company or division performance.

The Campbell segmentation strategy is an example of how a company can focus its sales and marketing efforts to meet the particular needs of a large, segmented population. The strategy has proven effective; shortly after the plan was implemented, revenues, unit sales, and profits all improved. The regional focus at Campbell Soup, and at many companies that are following Campbell's lead, should only grow stronger.

4. In a "divest" marketing strategy, cutting selling costs to the minimum and clearing out inventory are the primary sales objectives. Salespeople will attempt to "dump" inventory at liquidation prices.

TACTICAL DECISIONS

sales tactics
Activities required to implement sales strategies and achieve sales objectives

The term *sales tactics* refers to the day-by-day activities that are required to implement sales strategies and achieve sales objectives. It is at the tactical level that most field sales managers become involved in the planning process. Every level of the sales organization must have an internal plan of action. A field sales manager who fails to do any planning and chooses instead to operate by "the seat of the pants" can cause a lot of problems.[11] It is especially important that field sales managers' plans fit into the company's overall plan. Field managers have to engage in a great deal of decision making at this stage to coordinate their tactics with the other elements of the marketing mix.

Sales managers have to determine which products to emphasize, when to emphasize these products, and which customer groups to target. They should have input into product deletion decisions as well as some involvement in new product planning. Products that make no significant contribution to the bottom line can drain resources, including sales force time, and should be dropped unless they leave product line gaps that make the rest of the product mix less salable. Sales managers know what their clientele demand, and they can provide valuable input into pruning decisions. New products, on the other hand, are a firm's lifeblood. Sales forces need the excitement of newness to keep up their selling enthusiasm. Production information manuals and selling tools such as audiovisual aids are designed to inform and assist representatives in introducing new products. Special training programs may also be necessary if a product is technically complex.

Some sales managers face situations in which their brand encounters resistance due to its relatively high price. In such instances, it is often advisable to practice a multiple-brand policy. For example, liquor manufacturers sell both high-priced, heavily advertised prestige brands and moderately priced, unadvertised brands simultaneously through the same outlets. Multiple brands afford sales management considerably more flexibility than a single-brand approach.

Decisions must also be made regarding the type of customer that the sales force is to call on (i.e., whether to call on ultimate or intermediate buyers), the customer's industry classification and size, the nature and extent of customer credit evaluation, and the use of single or multiple distribution channels. Sales management has to set priorities for time allocation between established and new accounts. It should specify the rules regarding calling frequencies and patterns for various types of accounts. Managers may even want to spell out customer-specific sales targets. In any event, one of a sales manager's tasks is the setting of sales quotas. Sales managers must take into account territory potential, competition, economic conditions, and so forth in setting sales quotas. They must also attempt to make the goals fair, realistic, and challenging.

Sales managers have to contemplate what kind and what level of sales support personnel will need. A further set of tactical decisions relates to the compensation system, which may feature either straight salary, straight commission, or some combination of salary and incentive pay. And policy regarding reimbursement of expenses must be determined.

Salespeople also need to be informed about the company's pricing policies. They have to understand their firm's degree of pricing flexibility, as well as its discount policy. Availability of credit, applicable interest rates, and management's attitude about leasing must also be communicated to them.

Sales managers have to coordinate their tactical choices closely with the rest of the promotion component of their firm's marketing mix. For instance, advertising can be used for generating inquiries that can be turned into leads for the sales force. Trade magazines typically offer reader inquiry card services through which interested parties can request specified promotional materials. Serious prospects can be identified by means of the qualifying process, and sales visits can be initiated.

push tactics Use of advertising and other promotional tools to move merchandise into the distribution channel

pull tactics Creation of end-user demand that forces the trade to carry and keep restocking a firm's products

Push tactics refer to utilizing advertising and other promotional tools to "push" merchandise into the distribution channel or—in the parlance of the trade—to "fill the pipeline." *Pull tactics*, by contrast, aim to create end user demand that will force the trade to carry and keep restocking the company's products. Retail grocery buyers want to know the nature and level of advertising support that they will receive and will order products accordingly. Many salespeople carry tear sheets of print advertisements to show prospective dealers, and some even bring audiovisual equipment to their sales presentations and play upcoming television commercials.

Sales promotion encompasses a multitude of techniques that attempt to stimulate sales on a short-term basis, as opposed to the long-term perspective of advertising. Promotions can be used to stimulate selling by the sales force as well as buying from dealers and ultimate end users. Sales managers frequently use contests and other performance incentives to motivate their sales forces. It facilitates representatives' jobs greatly if such contests are accompanied by simultaneous advertising to, and deals for, both intermediaries and end users, so that they do not end up unnecessarily loading dealers with excess inventory and creating ill will in the trade. Brochures, fliers, posters, samples, coupons, and point-of-purchase materials are commonly used. Participating in trade shows is another tool that can be of considerable assistance to the sales organization. The primary purpose of trade shows is not necessarily to book orders, but to identify prospective customers.

SALES PLAN IMPLEMENTATION

If a sales plan is to be implemented successfully, it has to be communicated properly. The first task is to prepare a written sales plan. A suggested outline for a sales and marketing plan is shown in Table 8-3. How much of this plan should be communicated to whom is a matter of sales management policy.

TABLE 8-3 Elements of a Sales and Marketing Plan

1. Introduction
2. Mission
3. Company outlook
   A. Strengths
   B. Weaknesses
   C. Opportunities
   D. Threats
4. Market status
   A. Industry
   B. Market(s)
   C. Key factors
   D. Purchase criteria
   E. Price analysis
   F. Competition
5. Objectives and strategies
   A. By market segment
   B. Target product/service mix
   C. Promotional program
      1. Publicity
      2. Direct mail
      3. Advertising
      4. Trade shows/receptions
      5. Presentations
6. Sales plan
   A. Forecast by market segment
   B. Target accounts
   C. Distribution
   D. Current account status
7. Organization
   A. Administrative
   B. Sales/account service
   C. Marketing support services
8. Financial

Sales meetings and conferences are the common means for communication with the sales force. Senior sales managers should address sales representatives and sales supervisors and explain the sales objectives for the upcoming period, the strategies chosen, and the tactics to be used in their implementation. Each of the attendees should come away from such a meeting with enough information to do an effective job and contribute to the overall sales effort.

Sales meetings also serve a second important purpose: They are used as motivational tools to build up enthusiasm for the sales plan. Sales management can appeal to the enlightened self-interest of sales representatives by offering special incentives related to the level of quota attainment.

Communication and persuasion are still not enough to make the implementation phase succeed. Additional training of the entire sales organization may be needed to make the plan work. Further, while they carry out their assigned responsibilities, representatives need the assurance of continuing support from their managers. They need backup and follow-through, advice and assistance, and information and commitments. Salespeople should be assured that they can call on the resources of the entire firm in their efforts. Last, but not least, sales managers must truly manage during this phase. More specifically, they must direct and supervise their subordinates. No matter how carefully strategies, tactics, and policies have been planned, situations occur that require choices and decisions. Salespeople have to schedule their time, map out their call patterns, respond to competitive challenges, service accounts, deal with transportation problems, evaluate credit risks, expedite shipments, consider price concessions, and so on. Without proper, steady guidance, they may stray from the established sales plan.

THE CONTROL PHASE

The control phase of the sales management planning process closes the feedback loop by comparing planned and actual results. Where they differ, the control stage also involves an examination of the reasons for the divergences. Ultimately, this investigation may trigger a revision of the original sales plan to adapt sales operations to an altered set of circumstances, or it may suggest that an alternative contingency plan be put into effect.

Sales control, which will be discussed in more detail in Part VI, involves more than passive reporting of actual figures. It also entails active intervention to make sure that sales plan objectives are met. An early warning system has to be put in place to help detect environmental challenges and threats before sales performance veers off course. To realign expected and actual sales performance in midcourse, two basic options are open to the sales manager:

1. Initiate correcting action that counteracts the reasons for the differences and restores the sales effort to its rightful course
2. Adjust the sales management plan, including sales objectives, strategies, and tactics, to correspond more closely to the reality of the sales environment

This decision about which course to follow rests on the causes for the differences between the planned and actual results. Were the sales estimates and objectives unrealistic? Were the planning assumptions unsound? Did demand shift or competition intensify? Is the company lagging in technology, or is it ahead of its time? Are the problems rooted in the firm's operations? Do shipments arrive late? Is product quality inadequate? Is the product mix insufficient? Are prices too high? Are targeted customers aware of the company's offerings? Is advertising effective and adequate? Are sales representatives properly trained and motivated? Answers to these and other similar questions provide clues to the changes that are necessary.

management by exception Decision to alter sales plans only if significant deviations occur in key data

To make sales control more effective, current data reporting has to be timely, and accountability must be clearly assigned. *Management by exception* should be practiced. Under this procedure, sales plans are altered only if significant deviations occur in key data, such as the level of sales quota attainment. Correcting such problems is a primary task of sales management.

SUMMARY OF LEARNING GOALS

1. **Understand the Role of Sales Planning in the Corporate Context.**

   Sales planning is governed by company-wide considerations and has to be coordinated within the corporate context in order to align sales schedules, quantities, and projected cash flows with the organization's overall mission. Also, marketing research, especially that which results in the projection of future trends and sales forecasts, greatly affects the organization and represents the cornerstone of the overall planning process.

2. **Explain the Importance of Marketing Information Systems (MIS) and Marketing Decision Support Systems (MDSS) to Sales Management.**

   Modern sales management planning is based on information, and information is supplied to sales managers by the marketing information system. The MIS monitors the environment for relevant trends, reports on internally generated data, and investigates the market for sales opportunities to enable managers to respond to sales problems and issues promptly and effectively.

   One type of MIS is the marketing decision support system (MDSS). The MDSS is an information system that links sales and marketing managers with relevant data bases.

3. **Outline the Steps Involved in the Sales Management Planning Process.**

   These steps are the following:
   a. Analysis   d. Goal setting
   b. Strategies   e. Tactics
   c. Implementation   f. Control

4. **Describe the Content of the Analysis Phase of Sales Management Planning.**

   The analysis phase of sales management planning may be broken down into a situational analysis of strengths, weaknesses, opportunities, and threats. Internal strengths and weaknesses may be assessed through an examination of market share, price, structures, product life cycles, or distribution channels, among other things. External opportunities and threats may be determined through the development of customer tactics and environmental factors (both macroenvironmental and market). Through such analysis, an appropriate forecast is determined.

5. **Identify Key Sales Objectives.**

   Examples of key sales objectives are those based on any of the following:

   a. Sales volume
   b. Profitability
   c. Calls per day
   d. Customer satisfaction
   e. Account servicing
   f. Market share
   g. New accounts acquired
   h. New salespeople hired
   i. Information gathering
   j. Self-development

6. **Discuss the Significance of Strategy Selection.**

   The strategy that an organization chooses has implications for the sales organization. A cost leadership strategy demands that sales managers be most concerned with cost-cutting strategies, while a differentiation strategy requires a performance orientation, and a focused strategy requires salesperson specialization. Prospector, differentiated defender, and low cost defender strategies have their own requirements, and a company's decision to build, hold, harvest, or divest is also a typical basis for strategy selection. Any strategy that a company chooses, however, will have major implications for the activities and goals of the sales force.

7. **Highlight the Role of Tactical Decisions in Sales Planning.**

   Sales tactics are the day-by-day activities needed to implement sales strategies. Tactics are usually devised by sales managers and involve the formulation of sales hiring practices, sales training programs, sales incentives and compensation, sales support activities, performance appraisal measures, and the coordination of sales activities with other marketing mix components.

8. **Put the Implementation and Control Phases of the Sales Management Planning Cycle Into Perspective.**

   The implementation phase of the sales management planning cycle determines the plan's success. Implementation involves communication of the sales plan through meetings or conferences, additional training if necessary, assurances of support to salespeople, and sales managers' supervision of their subordinates. The control phase keeps sales efforts on course; it involves the comparison of planned and actual results and the actions to be taken when divergences between those results occur.

REVIEW QUESTIONS

1. How is sales planning linked to the corporate planning process? Trace the various steps in the corporate planning process.
2. What are the differences between information, primary data, and secondary data? Cite examples of each.
3. How is information from salespeople used in the sales planning process? What two

management planning issues are involved with this information? What other sources of information may be used to assess and supplement information from salespeople?

4. Differentiate between marketing information systems and marketing decision support systems. How is each used by sales management?

5. What questions should be asked during the sales planning process? How should each be answered?

6. What is meant by SWOT analysis? Cite an example for each letter in the acronym.

7. What guidelines should be followed in the formulation of sales objectives? How can sales objectives be classified?

8. Within Walker and Ruekert's framework, explain the differences between the prospector, low-cost defender, and high-cost defender approaches to sales strategy.

9. What are the primary sales objectives and specific tasks involved with the build, hold, harvest, and divest market share strategies?

10. What two options are available to sales managers when sales performance veers off course? What are some of the reasons that sales performance may differ from what was planned?

DISCUSSION QUESTIONS

1. Prepare a report on salesperson attitudes toward information gathering based on short interviews with at least three salespeople in your community. Do the salespeople desire more input into management strategy decisions? In what ways, if any, are they encouraged to provide competitive data? In what format are they expected to provide information? Do they feel that information gathering takes too much time away from selling? Discuss any opinions you developed as a result of conducting these interviews.

2. Search through news publications for articles that have implications for a particular company or industry. Collect as many articles as you can. Do the articles involve macroenvironmental or market issues? What advice would you give to the company or industry based on the information you obtained?

3. Cyprus Semiconductor makes hundreds of kinds of chips, turns out small lots, and can switch rapidly from one product to another in its manufacturing process. Which of Porter's strategies might be inferred from these activities? Justify your answer.

4. Select a firm employing a multiple-brand strategy at a retail store. What are the differences between the brands? Talk to a salesperson or manager. Which brand is selling better? From which does the store make a higher profit? Can you spot anything about the store that would explain why one brand is selling better than others? Finally, what is sales management's role in a vendor's use of a multiple-brand strategy?

5. Flip through a popular magazine or watch television commercials to find a product that is heavily advertised. On what basis do marketers attempt to separate their products from the competition? Do you think these claims are, for the most part, legitimate? What is the role of personal selling in this effort?

ETHICAL DILEMMA

Abdul Shah, a district sales manager for Magna Corporation, is preparing his district sales plan for the coming year. His supervisor, the national sales manager, has urged Abdul to increase each salesperson's sales objective by 15 percent. Abdul feels that this is unreasonable, since this increase will put too much pressure on his salespeople. How should Abdul resolve this situation?

Curad—Converting a Marketing Strategy into a Sales Gain

When you cut your finger, what do you put on it to stop the bleeding?

If you said, "a band aid," welcome to the club.

Naturally, the use of the trade name Band-Aid® as a generic term is bad news for the lawyers at Johnson & Johnson who struggle to maintain the Band-Aid trademark. But it's even worse news for Paul Amatangelo: He's the guy in charge of marketing "that other bandage"—Curad.

Ironically, Amatangelo left a position as senior brand manager for Band-Aid in 1988 to become director of personal care products for Kendall-Futuro, the Newport, Ky., maker of Curad. Upon arriving at the company, he was presented with a situation that would make any marketers' blood run cold. Curad's slice of the $260 million adhesive bandage market had hemorrhaged 10% a year since 1985. Meanwhile, Band-Aid had remained buoyant, and private label brands were on the upswing.

The solution: "If children are using sixty percent to seventy percent of adhesive bandages, as our research showed they are, we figured, why not design a small bandage especially for kids?" says Amatangelo.

Not that the idea hadn't been tried before. Adhesive strips imprinted with Mickey Mouse and the ubiquitous Teenage Ninja Mutant Turtles already dotted the shelves. And the ⅝" strip—the cornerstone of Amatangelo's proposed children's line—had been around for years.

Still, the 45-year-old marketer was convinced the idea was the perfect antidote for Curad's ailments. So in March 1990, Amatangelo debuted Curad Kid Size, an array of adhesive bandages imprinted with animated characters and scaled down to fit pint-sized cuts and scrapes.

Of course, arch rival Johnson & Johnson quickly launched a counter strike. As Curad rolled out Kid Size, J&J entered the market with a similar line bedecked with Sesame Street characters—but in regular adult sizes.

Amatangelo still had a few aces up his sleeve, however. For one thing, Curad had an exclusive licensing agreement with McDonald's to imprint the Ronald McDonald character on Kid Size strips. The agreement also called for 7.5 million samples and coupons to be tucked into Happy Meals during the first two months of the launch.

"I think if we had tried to sell the product on just the size element, we wouldn't have been as successful," say Amatangelo. "The most important thing we did was the McDonald's piece of it."

He may be right. According to McDonald's data, Ronald McDonald is the second most well-known character in America (the first being Santa Claus). Moreover, 85% of children aged 4 to 7 eat at McDonald's at least once a month.

Besides whetting consumer demand, the McDonald's tie-in also helped win back retailers. "Once they got wind of the samples in Happy Meals, they made sure they had Kid Size on the shelves," says Amatangelo.

Price gave Curad yet another edge. Because J&J's children's line was packaged in its infamous tin containers, a 30-strip package cost around 25% more than Kid Size's cardboard box.

Also, Curad focused on a consumer other bandage-makers had overlooked: school nurses. Throughout the fall of 1990, Curad's PR agency, New York-based G.S. Schwartz & Co., met with four major nursing associations and conducted a poll of 1,000 nurses nationwide to determine how Curad could better serve their needs.

Eventually, the agency hit upon the idea of a brochure, which school nurses could obtain in bulk, that would teach kids to care for their own bumps and scrapes. The approach was low key, using a "Carrie Curad" character and illustrated, step-by-step instructions on cleaning and covering a wound.

These three elements—the McDonald's tie-in, pricing, and the school nurse program—thrust Curad into an unfamiliar position. After years of idling in the No. 2 position, the company currently holds a commanding 36.1% of the children's bandage market (which is itself 15% of the total bandage market), according to Nielsen figures. Band-Aid trails at 26.6%, with "all other" brands accounting for an additional 37.3%.

Curad's recuperation will undoubtedly continue in the capable hands of Amatangelo, who was recently named vice president of marketing for Kendall-Futuro. In the future, he'll be nursing along new kid-oriented adhesive bandages and first-aid products such as adhesive tapes and topical antibiotics.

To borrow a phrase from one increasingly well-known brand, Curad's future look "ouchless" indeed.

Questions

1. Relate Paul Amatangelo's actions to the information continuum. Explain the basis for your classification.

2. Perform a SWOT analysis on Curad, or of the time Amatangelo moved to Kendall-Futuro.

3. Outline the specific sales strategies that would support the marketing strategies discussed in this case.

CHAPTER *9*   SALES FORECASTING

LEARNING GOALS

- Understand the importance of sales forecasting to the firm.
- Differentiate among market potential, sales potential, sales forecasts, sales quotas, and sales budget.
- Explain the concepts of market and sales potentials.
- Discuss economic, industry, company, and product forecasts.
- Outline the various qualitative and quantitative methods of sales forecasting.
- Discuss who is responsible for sales forecasting.
- Relate forecast exactness, accuracy, and assumptions to the forecast time period.
- Understand how to evaluate sales forecasting effectiveness.

PIZZA DELIVERY? CATFISH?

Events of the past few years suggest pizza deliveries as an indicator of political upheaval. On the day of the Soviet Coup, for example, 260 pizzas were delivered to Boris Yeltsin and crew, and on the day that Operation Desert Storm began, the Pentagon ordered 25 pizzas (it averages only three a night). While pizza deliveries as an indicator of political upheaval may seem far-fetched, you may think it equally strange that, in Japan, many believe that catfish can predict earthquakes.

Sales forecasters, while not relying on catfish and pizzas for data, have been accused of being just about the equivalent of witch doctors in the methods they use. In a survey conducted by the National Science Foundation, a majority of the research users questioned said that industrial marketing is more of an art than a science. Also, research has shown that most forecasters are loathe to predict bad news, because the opportunity costs of such a prediction can be high if sales are higher than expected.

Despite its limitations, sales forecasting is an integral part of the business world. An example of a company that used forecasting to steer a long period of sustained growth under differing market conditions is Alltel Corporation, whose basic business is cellular phone service. In the mid-1980s, signing up new subscribers was becoming more difficult for the cellular industry. Revenue growth for the industry slowed from 71 percent in 1989 to 36 percent in 1990. Also, people who did subscribe were using their cellular phones less, and they were disconnecting at a higher rate than in past years.

These trends told Alltel to keep diversifying, and the company is now into manufacturing, long distance, cable, and computer software. Alltel is particular about the cities to which it takes its cellular service; it has chosen growing cities in the sunbelt, such as Atlanta and Savannah, Georgia, and Charlotte, North Carolina, for expansion.

Things have picked up in the cellular phone business, and the subscriber rate has doubled since 1989. The industry has increased its profitability, provided better customer service, and produced new technologies. Recently, Alltel forecast a 50 percent annual growth rate.[1]

Chapter 9 discusses sales forecasting, a process that is imperfect, yet essential to the sales effort. As you read on, you should keep in mind the dichotomy that was addressed in the National Science Foundation

Cellular Customers
The Timeline of Growth

SOURCE CTIA

June 1983	0 Million
June 1984	.04 Million
June 1985	.2 Million
June 1986	.5 Million
June 1987	.9 Million
June 1988	1.6 Million
June 1989	2.7 Million
June 1990	4.4 Million
June 1991	6.4 Million
June 1992	8.9 Mil.
Nov. 1992	

10 Million Customers

survey. Sales forecasting involves both art and science, and company decision makers should be skilled at both.

CHAPTER OVERVIEW[2]

Many executives have compared sales forecasts to the predictions that emanated from the soothsayers of ancient times. Magically, it seems, forecasts of the next period's sales come pouring out of corporate headquarters. To the field sales force, these estimates often appear to be about as dependable as crystal ball prophecies.

sales forecast
Estimate of company sales for a specified future period

In most cases, however, this view of sales forecasting is far too critical. A *sales forecast*—an estimate of company sales for a specified future period—is an important aspect of sales management. These forecasts are the result of painstaking efforts by a number of individuals and departments in the firm, and their development should be no more mystical than any other type of organizational planning.[3]

As this chapter shows, sales forecasting is an integral part of the marketing information system. Forecasts aid sales managers in improving decision making. As will be discussed, however, no one sales forecasting method is suitable for every situation. Sales managers must be familiar with the various forms of forecasting and their use. Particular attention must be given to matching the sales forecasting method to the decision-making situation.[4]

IMPORTANCE OF SALES FORECASTING

Forecasting of sales provides the starting point for assumptions used in various planning activities and for the development of short-term financial control systems. [5]

For example, financial budgets are variable in that they show different expense patterns for varying levels of production. A firm's production level is linked closely to its sales output. The financial budget, therefore, is dependent upon the sales forecast for the projected revenue figures.

Consider also the examples of human resources planning, financial budgeting, and production scheduling. All functional areas of an organization have a planning task, and all their projections and future estimates depend upon the forecast level of sales. Human resources executives use sales forecasts to project staffing needs, financial executives use them as aids in establishing and controlling operating and capital budgets, and production managers use them to schedule purchasing and production and to control inventories. Sales forecasting is the most important planning task within any company—large or small.

SALES QUOTAS AND BUDGETS

sales quotas Sales goals sought by management

Two of the most vital managerial uses of the sales forecast are the setting of sales quotas and the developing of sales budgets. As stated in Chap. 8, *sales quotas* are the sales goals and objectives sought by management. They are the performance standards for the sales force; comparison of actual sales with assigned quotas is the basis of much of the sales function's evaluative effort. Consequently, the establishment of realistic quotas is one of the most critical tasks faced by a sales manager.

A sales forecast is the most reasonable foundation upon which quotas can be set. The forecast is the company's actual prediction of what sales will be in a forthcoming time period. If sales forecasts are realistic, they are the best and fairest method for setting sales quotas.

sales budgets Expenditure plans used to accomplish sales goals

Sales budgets are another important evaluative technique. A sales budget is a management plan for expenditures to accomplish sales goals. It is a blueprint for sales force action. Since a sales forecast is the revenue component of a sales budget, sales budgeting is a natural extension of the sales forecasting function. The sales budgeting process will be covered in Chap. 10.

SALES FORECASTING CONCEPTS

A large company, such as Du Pont, is concerned with several types of sales estimates. For instance, Du Pont would be interested in knowing how much nylon could possibly be sold in the United States during March. Since the textile business is characterized by stiff competition in all geographical regions, Du Pont would also be concerned about how many units it could possibly sell in the Southeast during March. In other words, Du Pont would like to be able to determine what its maximum market share would be. Finally, the company would want to know how much nylon it is likely to sell in a given region during this time period. This estimate might be used to establish a sales goal for its regional sales managers.

Du Pont's situation suggests that there are three levels of concern in sales forecasting: market potential, sales potential, and the actual sales forecast. Sales goals, or quotas, are also frequently derived from sales forecasts. These concepts are illustrated in Table 9-1.

TABLE 9-1 Forecasting Concepts

Concept	Example
Market potential	Estimated sales of antifreeze in New England during the coming winter
Sales potential	Prestone's expected New England sales
Sales forecast	Prestone's actual sales estimate based on potential and marketing plans
Sales quota	Quota for Connecticut is 1 million gallons

market potential
Highest possible expected industry sales of a good or service in a market for a given time period

sales potential
Firm's share of the market potential

market share
Percentage of a market controlled by a company or product

Market potential is the highest possible expected industry sales of a good or service in a specified market segment for a given time period. The market potential for the sale of antifreeze in New England, for example, might be 20 million gallons annually. This means that the entire antifreeze industry would expect to sell a maximum of 20 million gallons this year in New England. Market potential might be described as the capacity of a sales segment.

Sales potential refers to an individual firm's share of the market potential. It can be expressed as:

$$\text{Sales potential} = \text{market share} \times \text{market potential}$$

where *market share* is defined as the percentage of the market controlled by a particular company or product. The sales potential of Prestone antifreeze might be 5 million gallons, or a market share of 25 percent. Sales potential is the maximum sales that the firm could hope to obtain.

The sales forecast, by contrast, is the sales estimate that the company actually expects to obtain. It is based on marketplace circumstances, company resources, and the firm's marketing plan. The sales forecast is less than the sales potential, since the latter is based upon an ideal set of circumstances. For example, limited raw materials might prevent the manufacturer from producing 5 million gallons of Prestone for the New England market, so the company's sales forecast might be 4 million gallons, or 1 million less than its sales potential.

A sales quota is a sales goal assigned to a salesperson, region, or other marketing unit for use in managing sales efforts. Sales quotas are frequently derived from sales forecasts. For instance, Connecticut has approximately one-fourth the population of New England. So, the sales quota assigned to Prestone's Connecticut sales manager would be 1 million gallons.

ESTIMATING MARKET AND SALES POTENTIALS

Continuous assessment and monitoring of market and sales potentials is important to effective sales forecasting. A company must keep track of trends in sales and market share. It must also remain alert to basic shifts in product offerings and competitive marketing programs. Market and sales potentials assume that the current product offerings are relevant to a particular market. For instance, if a major competitor were to come out with a greatly improved product, Prestone's sales would be affected.

Market potential is dependent upon two major factors: buyers' ability to buy and their willingness to buy.

Ability to Buy

The ability to buy refers primarily to whether or not a buyer has the financial resources to purchase a product. For example, in a study of the market potential for grinding machines in the machine tool industry, a forecaster estimated buying ability by considering (1) the number and size of plants using such machines, (2) the need for additional equipment, (3) the need for replacement equipment, and (4) the funds available for such purchases. Sales potential is also dependent upon the buyer's ability to purchase the good or service.

Willingness to Buy

The willingness of customers to buy also influences market potential, but is far more difficult to assess. The *Index of Consumer Sentiment*, published by the University of Michigan's Survey Research Center, is probably the best-known effort to measure consumer attitudes toward purchasing. This index combines consumers' responses to questions about their present and future financial status, expectations about present and future business conditions, and purchasing plans for consumer durables. The index is best used as a general indicator of consumers' economic expectations.

There are also surveys of business purchase plans. Plant and equipment expenditure forecasts published in the *Survey of Current Business* are based on the U.S. Department of Commerce's *Securities and Exchange Survey of Spending Plans*. Another well-known survey of projected plant and equipment expenditures is the McGraw-Hill *Survey of Spending Plans*. Specific forecasts based on this survey are published in *Business Week*.

Marketing research studies are the most common method of estimating the effect of customer willingness to buy upon sales potential.[6] Marketing research methodology is quite varied; it ranges from simple mail questionnaires to focus groups to actual test marketing of a product in selected localities. For example, a pharmaceutical company might establish a panel of doctors to evaluate possible new products. If 15 percent of the panel indicated a willingness to prescribe a new form of medication, then the sales potential of the new product might be estimated at 15 percent of pre-established market potential. In this case, the market potential would probably be based upon the average usage of similar products over the past several years.

test marketing
Forecasting approach that measures sales in a selected area, then projects the results onto a broader area

Although test marketing is expensive in terms of time and money, some firms are turning to it as a way of estimating market and sales potential.[7] *Test marketing* involves marketing a product in a limited geographic region, measuring sales, and then using the results to predict the product's sales over a larger market area. The most frequent use of test marketing is to estimate demand and project sales for a new product. Test marketing can also be used to assess different product features, marketing options, and sales strategies.

WASTE ENERGY, INC.

Keith Burnett has a new product, a new company, and a new industry, and under these circumstances, sales forecasts can be a ticket to success. Goldfire, Burnett's brainchild, converts trash and waste oil into electricity. The invention is environmentally beneficial, and practically eliminates monthly electric and trash bills.

Goldfire produces more electricity than a typical customer can use, and electric companies are required by federal mandate to buy excess electricity produced by private individuals. Goldfire users actually make money from these sales. Also, there are large liability issues involved with handling waste oil, which are avoided by using Goldfire. The most apparent market for the invention are the quick-lube franchises and service stations. But Burnett has also developed adaptations aimed at large buildings such as supermarkets and building complexes such as shopping malls, as well as machines geared toward farmers that convert cornstalks and other farm refuse into power. All in all, Burnett estimates Goldfire's market potential to be 600,000 customers. His sales potential is equal to his market potential, since the patented Goldfire is the only machine of its kind.

Projected Goldfire sales are $46 million for the first year, $161 million for the second year, and $394 million for the third year. Burnett forecasts that the total U.S. market will eventually approach $22 billion.

Burnett was definitely thinking big with his idea, but he was not at first financially equipped to achieve all of Goldfire's potential. He hired a salesperson named Sunny Decker to look for investors. Look for investors Decker did, and he came back with $140,000 in limited partnership shares. With this working capital, Burnett opened a factory, and Waste Energy, Inc., was born. Decker, now southeast regional sales manager, is planning a commission-only sales force made up of 600 people.

A good, marketable product and a defensible sales forecast were needed for Burnett to see his inspiration turn into reality. Without these two things, the partnership units would not have been bought, and commission-only sales jobs would not have been filled.

THE PRODUCT LIFE CYCLE

product life cycle
Sales planning and control tool that projects the changes in a product's sales and profits over time

When estimating market and sales potential, sales managers must also take into account the stage the product has reached in its life cycle. The *product life cycle*—shown in Fig. 9-1—is an important sales planning and control tool, since it projects the changes in a product's sales and profits that will occur over time. It provides a conceptual framework for developing sales objectives and strategies for different stages of a product's life. The sales forecaster will encounter different problems and consequently use different forecasting techniques depending on where a product, company, or industry is in its life cycle.

The most difficult stage of the product life cycle to forecast is the introduction. There is no historical sales record, and new products have a high failure rate. It is important for the sales forecaster to prepare a realistic estimate of potential sales so that management can assess the risks of introducing the new item.

Most firms use marketing research techniques such as focus groups, surveys, and test marketing to project sales of new products. If a new product gains market acceptance and enters the growth stage, traditional sales forecasting methods can be

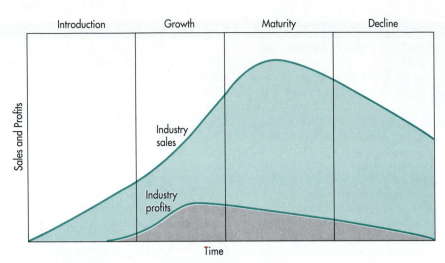

FIGURE 9-1 Industry Sales and Profits Shift over the Product Life Cycle.

used. The forecaster must be aware of the adoption rate for the new product, and of the potential impact of competitive products.

Sophisticated mathematical models are now used to simulate the buyer adoption process, project market share, and estimate sales. These models are expected not only to provide useful sales forecasts, but hopefully to reduce product development time and speed introduction.[8]

During the maturity and decline stages, traditional forecasting techniques are appropriate. Historical data can be analyzed statistically to project sales. The sales forecaster must also be alert to other factors, such as new uses for the product, that may suggest significant changes in the sales trend.

INFORMATION SOURCES

The U.S. Bureau of the Census is a very useful source of information in determining the ability to buy. The *Census of Population*—published every ten years—provides extensive demographic information such as the numbers of U.S. individuals and households, residence data, average family size, and other related information that can be used to establish market potentials in consumer markets. The *Census of Business* (wholesale, retail, and service industries) and the *Census of Manufacturing* can be used to estimate the market potentials for many industrial products. These censuses, which are conducted every five years, provide information such as the numbers, sizes, and basic characteristics of firms in various categories.

Sales & Marketing Management's "Survey of Buying Power" is another useful source of information. It provides population, income, and retail sales estimates for all major metropolitan areas in the United States and Canada. It also presents a "Buying Power Index," which combines these three basic elements into a weighted index measuring a market's ability to buy. This index is useful in estimating the potential for mass-marketed products sold at popular prices.

Sales & Marketing Management also publishes two other annual survey issues—"Sales Manager's Budget Planner" and "Survey of Media Markets." In addition to sales forecasting, other sales management uses of these surveys include setting sales goals and quotas, analyzing sales territories, setting up sales budgets, developing sales strategies and distribution channels, and measuring sales performance.[9]

In addition to these information sources, there are a number of commercial organizations that provide economic forecasts. Although these forecasts will not be directly related to a firm's own sales forecast, they can be used to provide background data for preparing economic assumptions upon which the sales forecast is based. Before purchasing information or the services of such an organization, however, a sales manager should carefully review studies concerning the accuracy and economic usefulness of its forecasts.[10]

SALES FORECASTING PROCEDURES

There are three sequential steps in the sales forecasting process: (1) preparing a forecast of general economic conditions, (2) preparing a forecast of industry sales, and (3) preparing a forecast of the product or company sales. A general outline of each is presented below.

Forecasting General Economic Conditions

gross domestic product (GDP) Value of all goods and services produced within a country during a given year

Sales forecasting is based upon an assessment of general economic conditions. The standard yardstick for measuring general economic activity is the *gross domestic product (GDP)*, which is the value of all the goods and services produced within a country during a given year. Some other frequently used measures of general economic conditions are the Dow-Jones index of common stock prices, personal income, personal consumption expenditures, level of employment, and the consumer price index. For many sales forecasters, estimates of general economic conditions are difficult to evaluate because of problems in determining their accuracy and their economic usefulness.

Few firms actually predict national economic activity, since these forecasts are readily available from various government agencies, trade associations, private foundations, and universities. The sales forecaster in an individual firm, however, has to be informed of the existing general forecasts. They form much of the background information upon which more specific industry and company estimates are made.

Estimating Industry Sales

Many firms attempt to predict industry sales. The development of industry forecasts seems to be related to the size of the firm: Smaller firms are apparently less concerned with, or less able to develop, such forecasts. They often rely on industry estimates available from trade associations and government sources. Some of the estimates are based upon the relationship between industry sales and a national economic indicator such as GDP or national income. In other cases, more sophisticated quantitative techniques are used.

TABLE 9-2   Classification of Forecasting Methods

Qualitative Methods	Quantitative Methods
Jury of executive opinion	Continuity extrapolation
Delphi technique	Time series analysis
Sales force composite	Exponential smoothing
Survey of buyers' intentions	Regression and correlation analysis
Factor listing	Multiple-regression analysis
	Leading indicators
	Econometric models

Large organizations are likely to have a corporate economist who provides support and information for sales forecasting. For instance, Dow Corning Corporation's corporate economist is charged with analyzing and communicating information about worldwide economic conditions and recommending corporate reactions to these conditions. In addition, the economist's staff also develops long-range sales forecasting models.[11] At Inland Steel Company, the chief economist is part of corporate planning and a member of the CEO's staff. Although sales forecasting is carried out elsewhere in the company, the economist forecasts the economic environment for the firm. This information is communicated to managers at all levels within the corporation.[12]

Projecting Company and Product Sales

Company and product sales estimates are the major areas of concern for a firm's sales forecasting function, since they are the revenue forecasts upon which other planning activities throughout the company are based. Forecasting methods can be classified as either qualitative or quantitative. Qualitative methods rely upon subjective, but informed, opinions or judgments, whereas quantitative forecasting applies mathematical and statistical techniques. Both are useful in the sales forecasting function. Table 9-2 classifies a number of possible approaches as either qualitative or quantitative. Each forecasting method is discussed in the sections that follow.[13]

QUALITATIVE METHODS

Qualitative, or judgmental, methods can make an important contribution to sales forecasting because they consider factors that simply cannot be quantified. These methods also typically make wider use of expertise in all areas of the organization. Qualitative methods, however, should always be used in conjunction with some other approach; few executives would suggest the use of any of these methods by itself.

Jury of Executive Opinion

jury of executive opinion Panel charged with developing a sales forecast

The *jury of executive opinion* is probably the oldest approach to forecasting, and is used by many firms.[14] Its basic premise is to establish a committee charged with the development of a sales forecast. This group typically has a varied membership consisting of people from sales, marketing research, accounting, production, and advertising. Each member is asked to provide an estimate of future sales. A written justification of the estimate is often required. These forecasts are usually made for only the most aggregate of the sales categories, such as districts, product groups, or customer classes. The opinions are then pooled and analyzed at a group meeting. Variations are synthesized through the collective judgment of individual estimates.

The obvious advantage of such a forecasting procedure is its simplicity. But the jury of executive opinion also has its limitations. The sales forecast is only as reliable as the judgments of the people involved. There is concern that it may take up too much executive time. Breaking down an aggregate sales forecast into more detailed estimates of expected sales is difficult. And finally, like other management decisions, accurate executive opinion sales forecasts depend on sales and other executives having sufficient current information upon which to base their forecasts.

Delphi Technique

Delphi technique Group of experts used to make long-range projections

An approach similar to the jury of executive opinion is the *Delphi technique* developed by the Rand Corporation. Most often used to make long-term projections, a group of "experts" is assembled to give their views on such issues as the future direction of business conditions, business activities, technology, new product development, and market changes. The experts are often leading authorities from universities, private foundations, industry, and government agencies.

Although dealing with long-term, often complex issues, the procedure used to make the projections is relatively simple. To make sure that opinions are formed independently, the experts are kept apart. They prepare individual anonymous forecasts, which are then compiled and returned for a second round of projections. The experts are also informed of the "average" or "typical" opinions. This process continues until a consensus forecast of the future emerges. The person in charge of the Delphi forecasting process is responsible for reviewing and compiling the opinions of the experts and deciding when a consensus has been reached. The Delphi technique has the advantage of eliminating the group pressures of a committee meeting. Honeywell, Exxon, and Weyerhaeuser Company are examples of firms that have used this method. When used in conjunction with exponential smoothing and regression analysis (concepts explained later in this chapter), the Delphi technique has resulted in much lower sales forecast errors. The Rand Corporation has concluded that the Delphi technique is a useful sales forecasting tool.

Sales Force Composite

sales force composite Forecast arrived at by combining salespersons' estimates of expected sales

The *sales force composite* approach is based on the assumption that individual salespeople are best qualified to estimate sales figures for their territories. Salespeople forecast their expected sales, and those forecasts are then combined to prepare a composite forecast. Many large companies use this approach to prepare sales forecasts.[15] For example, General Electric Company has used it for forecasting the sales of some industrial products. Other users include Pennsault Chemical, Harris-Intertype, and Otis Elevator.

The sales force composite method is useful in setting sales quotas. Field representatives will be more apt to accept sales quotas if they know that information they supplied played a role in their derivation. It has also been suggested that a salesperson's compensation be based partly on the accuracy of his or her forecast.[16]

There are several disadvantages associated with the sales force composite method. Salespeople are sometimes poor judges of future sales levels. Their emotional involvement may color their forecasts. It can be argued that field sales personnel are "too close to the marketplace" to provide an objective approximation of future events. Forecasting also may be viewed as a secondary activity by field personnel, so that they fail to invest the time and effort necessary to prepare the best possible forecasts. Another disadvantage of the sales force composite is that salespeople may deliberately understate their estimates if the forecasts are to be used in setting sales quotas. In contrast, some salespeople may be overconfident and present forecasts that are too optimistic. These unrealistic forecasts can lead to excess production, inventory surpluses, and reduced margins.[17]

To offset these difficulties and improve the accuracy of sales forecasts by salespeople, several actions can be taken. First, salespeople must be provided with adequate information and enough time to prepare their forecasts. They must be trained in how to carry out their forecasting responsibilities. Most importantly, they must be given clear, precise instructions. Providing incentives for accuracy will also improve the forecasts. Finally, sales managers must carefully review all forecasts and make any needed adjustments.[18]

Survey of Buyers' Intentions

survey of buyers' intentions Forecast survey of a limited and well-defined group of buyers

The *survey of buyer's intentions* method is particularly applicable to situations in which potential purchasers are well defined and limited in number, such as industrial markets. In such cases, a forecast has the advantage of being based on direct contact with the marketplace. The sophistication of these surveys can vary from the simple recording of customer responses to the application of advanced sampling and probability concepts.

American Airlines has successfully used consumer sentiment polls to predict air passenger traffic. American's forecasters used passenger polls to develop a monthly index of consumer expectations regarding future travel. The index proved to be closely correlated with changes in air traffic. Consequently, the forecasters were able to predict critical turning points in air traffic, and to adjust American's operations to changing market conditions.

Despite American's success, this approach has several limitations. The most obvious is that customers do not always do what they say they plan to do. Second, the respondents to such a survey may deliberately overestimate their future needs so as to assure a continued flow of supplies or materials. Finally, buying plans—particularly for industrial goods—can change rapidly in response to changes in the operational environment.

Factor Listing

Factor listing was originally formulated to alleviate an obvious flaw in the jury of executive opinion and sales force composite approaches. While these latter methods may ask participants to justify or explain the reasoning behind their forecasts, they do not attempt to analyze the importance of the variables that were considered in making the forecasts.

For instance, the marketing research director of an electric utility company may justify her forecast of a $40 million sales increase by saying that she expects greater

TABLE 9-3 A Factor Listing Balance Sheet for a Suburban Electric Company

CURRENT SALES = $510 MILLION	
Positive factors	**Negative factors**
Increased industrial activity (+$22 million)	Below average temperatures during summer months, meaning decreased usage of air conditioning (−$4 million)
Expanded new housing starts (+$14 million)	
Construction of large government installations (+$3 million)	
Increased sales to neighboring utility company (+$5 million)	
Total = +$44 million	Total = −$4 million
Forecasted sales = $510 million + $40 million = $550 million	

industrial activity in the utility's geographic area and an expansion of new housing starts. However, she may not place a dollar value on either expectation. The *factor listing* method forces forecasters to quantify the reasoning behind their judgments. A balance sheet, showing positive and negative influences on future sales, is set up. Relevant factors affecting sales are then listed, and estimates of their influences on sales are noted. The positive and negative sales factors are then summed, and the difference in the sums is added to, or subtracted from, current sales to produce the sales forecast. This process is illustrated in Table 9-3.

factor listing Identificaton of factors affecting sales and their specific impact in the forecast period

While the factor listing approach has the advantage of forcing the forecaster to quantitatively justify a prediction, it still suffers from the fact that its validity depends on the accuracy of the people involved. This is the primary limitation of most of the judgmental approaches to forecasting.

QUANTITATIVE METHODS

Quantitative methods of sales forecasting have the advantage of an impartial objectivity not possible with the qualitative methods. The basic disadvantages and limitations of quantitative methods concern the nature and the validity of the assumptions used, the lack of data, and the fact that mathematical forecasting techniques tend to generalize on the basis of past experience. Sudden shifts in environmental circumstances, for example, can best be evaluated through judgmental insight. It is especially difficult to use statistical forecasting techniques in high-technology industries that are subject to dramatic changes. [19]

Continuity Extrapolation

continuity extrapolation Projection of the last increment of sales change into the future

The *continuity extrapolation* technique attempts to project the last increment of sales change into the future. Continuity extrapolation can be done on either an absolute dollar basis or a percentage basis. Suppose that a firm had current sales of $310 million and previous year's sales of $290 million. On an absolute dollar basis, the last increment of sales change would be $20 million. This would then be added to current sales to produce an estimate of $330 million for the next year's sales. On a

SALES MANAGE- MENT

SALES MANAGEMENT IN PRACTICE

AMERICAN GREETINGS

Sometimes, intuition is the only tool needed to make an accurate sales forecast. When the Persian Gulf War began in 1990, Alan Soirefman, an American Greetings sales manager, got his sales force out selling yellow ribbons. Within two months, sales of the decorations for oak trees, car antennas, mailboxes, and home doors had increased by 20 percent in Soirefman's region.

American Greetings was not the only company to respond to the situation. The Coca-Cola Company sent 2000 free cases of Coke to troops, who also received Artesia and Evian bottled water, Circus Circus playing cards, and 20,000 cases of Gatorade.

American Greetings does not, of course, rely on qualitative sales forecasting methods alone. Regional sales managers are provided with demographic data on a neighborhood-by-neighborhood basis, and they are constantly kept informed of local activities in their territories. In this way, they are able to make good sales forecasts and help their salespeople respond quickly to selling opportunities of all kinds, from earth-shattering events like the Persian Gulf War to local events like parades and music festivals.

percentage basis, the last increment of sales change was $20 million/$290 million, or 6.9 percent. Next year's predicted sales would then be calculated as $310 million + 6.9 percent of $310 million, or $331.4 million.

For short-term forecast periods, this method may prove to be fairly reliable. The continuity extrapolation approach is limited, however, because it assumes that there will be no directional change, and the last increment of sales change approximates the average increment of sales change, which is not always true.

Time Series Analysis

The origin of time series analysis can be traced back to the early 1920s. It is based on business cycle theory, and involves the construction and interpretation of the business cycle.[20] The crucial challenge to forecasters is to analyze and anticipate the business cycle and its impact on the firm's sales.

time series analysis Projection of the average increment of sales change into the future

Time series analysis is best used for long-term company forecasts and industry sales projections. It assumes a continuation of the firm's or industry's sales history and, in fact, extrapolates that average increment of sales change. Utilities, such as Georgia Power Company, have used this method to forecast sales.[21] The Coca-Cola Company is another firm that uses time series analysis extensively. Ten years' annual data for each time series make up the data base for Coca-Cola's sales forecasts.[22] Sears, Roebuck and Company, Jantzen, and Joseph E. Seagram and Sons are examples of other companies that have used this technique.

A time data series is determined by four basic elements of sales variations: trends, or long-run changes (*T*), cyclical changes (*C*), seasonal variations (*S*), and irregular or unexpected factors (*I*). The analysis is based on the assumption that these elements are combined in the following relationships:

$$Sales = T \times C \times S \times I$$

The four basic elements are then projected. This is done by extrapolating the trend with adjustments for the cyclical and seasonal factors. The irregular factors are acknowledged, but not forecast separately. The interrelation of these variables is shown in Fig. 9-2.

Most forms of time series analysis use a moving average to analyze and project sales. This technique helps the forecaster identify the seasonal components of a data series and smooth out the effects of random variables. The computation of a moving average is relatively simple: The average moves progressively forward in time as data from the earliest period to be included are dropped and data from the latest period are added. The problem of uneven sales patterns (such as when one specific day dominates total weekly sales) can be accounted for with a special type of moving average technique usually called the "Box-Jenkins model." This approach is often more accurate than more complex techniques, especially when used for short-term forecasts. [23]

Exponential Smoothing

exponential smoothing
Weighted average time series analysis technique

A popular modification of time series analysis is *exponential smoothing*, a weighted-average time series analysis technique. Actual sales of recent periods are weighted more heavily than the average sales of earlier periods. Exponential smoothing is best suited to short-term forecasting in relatively stable markets. It is particularly useful in updating quarterly forecasts. Further, exponential smoothing techniques are easier to use and maintain than Box-Jenkins models and other sophisticated mathematical models. [24]

Regression and Correlation Analysis

One of the simplest mathematical forecasting models is regression and correlation analysis. This approach has been used to forecast sales by such companies as Eli Lilly and Company, Eastman Kodak, and Vendo Corporation. It involves the following three basic steps:

FIGURE 9-2 Components of a Time Data Series.

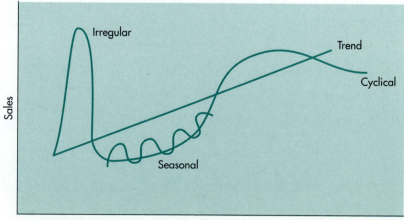

Determine the Factors That Affect Sales.   The aim of regression analysis is to identify factors that influence, or are closely associated with, changes in sales. A preliminary analysis can be accomplished by plotting a scatter diagram, as shown in Fig. 9-3. A significant relationship can be observed between company sales and gross state product. This is an example of *simple regression*, since there is only one independent variable. The use of two or more independent variables is called *multiple regression.*

With a single independent variable, the relationships in a regression model are typically determined by the least-squares method. The basic formula is

$$Y = a + bX$$

where Y = the dependent variable (sales)
       X = the independent variable (gross state product)
       a = the Y-intercept value (the value of Y when X equals zero)
       b = the average increment of sales change (the slope of the equation)

Using this formula, the statistical procedure involves determining the average increment of change in Y (sales, the dependent variable) resulting from one increment of change in X (gross state product, the independent variable).

Measure the Degree of the Relationship between Sales and Other Variables.   This measurement is done through a statistical procedure known as correlation analysis. A coefficient of correlation (designated as r) is determined. The coefficient ranges from -1.0 (perfect negative correlation) to $+1.0$ (perfect positive correlation). An r value of $+1.0$ would mean that for each one-unit change in the independent variable, there would be a one-unit change in sales in the same direction. An r value of -1.0 would mean a proportionate change in the dependent and independent variables, but in opposing directions. If the independent variable went up one unit, then the dependent variable would go down one unit. Assume that the

FIGURE 9-3 **Scatter Diagram of Sales and Gross State Product.**

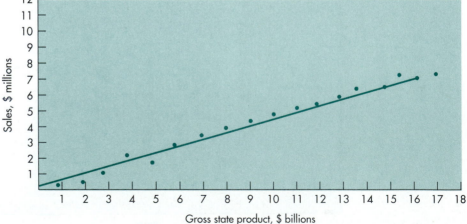

Gross state product, $ billions

Side notes:

simple regression Forecasting technique using only one independent variable

multiple regression Forecasting technique using two or more independent variables

coefficient of correlation from Fig. 9-2 was .80. This would be considered relatively high, and the firm would be able to use gross state product as a predictive variable in its sales forecast.

Forecast the Dependent Variable (Sales) from the Independent Variable. The relationship identified in the first step is then used to predict sales. An estimate of the independent variable is required to project further sales.

Multiple-Regression Analysis

Most forecasting models include more than a single independent variable. In the current example, a multiple-regression analysis would determine the relationship (if any) between sales and several different variables. The general form of such an equation would be

$$Y_F = a + b_1X_1 + b_2X_2 = b_3F_3 + b_nX_n$$

where $X_1 \cdots X_n$ would represent the different independent variables.

Consider the variables that might affect the sale of service station equipment. Replacement rates, highway construction, changes in automobile registrations, the availability and cost of capital funds, and general economic activity are some of the variables that might be related to the sales of new gasoline pumps. Multiple-regression analysis assumes that such variables would continue to be related to sales in the future.

Leading Indicators

leading indicators Time series of an economic activity whose movement leads changes in sales volume

Sales managers sometimes use *leading indicators* to predict sales volume. These are the time series of an economic activity whose movement leads changes in sales volume. Some of the best leading indicators are the "Index of Net Business Formation," "Stock Prices, 500 Common Stocks," and "New Orders, Durable Goods Industries."

The primary value of this forecasting procedure is to predict the timing of changes in sales. For example, data on the number of building permits issued might be a lead indicator of lumber and building materials sales. The key to using this technique is to select an economic data series which is a reliable leading indicator. Since there is not always a relationship between the indicator and sales, however, the accuracy of this method is limited.

Econometric Models

input-output models Models showing that the output (sales) of one industry is the input (purchases) of another industry

Many of the more complex forecasting models include several variables and are known as econometric models. An example is *input-output models*, which show that the output (sales) of one industry is the input (purchases) of another industry. Input-output models have been developed that show the impact on vendors of increased production in the industries they supply. Any sales forecasting situation that can be mathematically replicated can be put into a computer program. For instance, a methodology has been developed to forecast sales of an ethical drug prior to test marketing and then to adjust the forecast when early data become available. The parameters of the model are based on physicians' perceptions of the drug, the appropriate range of ailments, and the expected frequency of prescriptions. The model is used to project the drug adoption process.[25]

It is evident that most of business's future progress in sales forecasting will come in the area of mathematical model building. New techniques are being explored every day.[26]

MANAGING THE FORECASTING FUNCTION

As noted earlier, sales forecasting is a complex, challenging task. Sales managers who become involved in forecasting—and most do—must deal with the following key issues:

- Who should be responsible for forecasting?
- Which forecasting methods should be used?
- What should the lengths of forecasts be?
- How should forecasts be evaluated?

Responsibility for Forecasting

Although it varies among firms, the organization of the sales forecasting function tends to be viewed as either a marketing, a sales, or a finance/accounting function. Accounting professionals originally became involved in this activity because of their natural interest in, and control over, much of the internal data required to forecast sales. In some cases, the marketing function may have lacked the necessary interest or analytical sophistication to perform the sales forecasting task. But times have changed! Today, marketing has assumed responsibility for developing the sales forecast in most companies.[27]

Sales managers are not always responsible for preparing the sales forecasts, but they certainly have significant input in all cases. Some companies have elected to make the marketing research department responsible for sales forecasting, particularly in regard to its quantitative analysis aspects. But even in these situations, the sales manager must provide a judgmental evaluation. Sales forecasting remains an important part of the sales manager's job. It is essential that sales managers, and everyone else who will help develop the sales forecast, understand the procedures used in forecasting.

Selecting Forecasting Methods

The best approach to sales forecasting is the use of a combination of methods. It is particularly important to balance a forecast derived from a quantitative approach against one developed by qualitative methods, and vice versa. In fact, most companies use several different sales forecasting techniques, which vary by time horizon, size of firm, and type of product.[28]

Combining sales forecasting techniques improves forecasting accuracy.[29] A combination approach allows a firm to counteract most of the deficiencies inherent in using a single method. If there is a substantial deviation among the forecasts emanating from each method, then the entire process should be repeated. Forecasters should strive for a consensus among the results of the various approaches employed.

Lengths of Forecasts

Most firms develop sales forecasts of varying lengths, ranging from a week or a month to several decades. An appliance manufacturer might prepare monthly, quarterly, and annual forecasts, as well as long-range projections of periods from two to ten years. Short-term forecasting is necessary to formulate production, human resources, and sales plans. Long-term forecasting is critical in capital expenditure decisions.

A major timing concern is that all forecasts are based on numerous assumptions. An annual forecast for an electric utility is based on certain assumptions concerning weather conditions, industrial activity, and residential and commercial construction. Short-range forecasts are likely to be more accurate than long-term predictions simply because basic assumptions are usually more correct over the short run. Since market position is often slow to change, substantial changes in the sales forecast are not likely to occur from one quarter to the next.

The importance of the assumptions upon which future sales estimates are based cannot be overly stressed. Sales managers should pay particular attention to this aspect of the forecasting procedure. Ill-founded assumptions can seriously bias sales estimates, and sales planning is ineffective if it is based upon faulty forecasting.

Figure 9-4 shows that there is likely to be greater divergence between actual sales and predicted sales as the time period of a forecast increases. The exactness required of forecasts usually depends upon the time period involved.

Consider how Ford Motor Company might develop sales estimates. Figure 9-5 shows that a short-range forecast of one year might specify estimates at the corporate, division, and product line levels. An intermediate forecast of two or five years might warrant only corporate and division breakdowns. In the long run, perhaps only a corporate estimate would be realistic.

If management requires greater detail for longer forecasts, then the assumptions upon which these forecasts are based should be clearly stated. There might even be

FIGURE 9-4 Impact of Time on Forecast Accuracy.

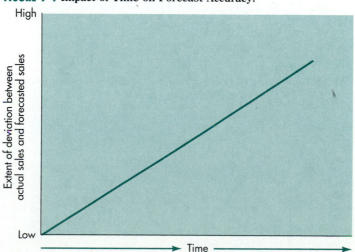

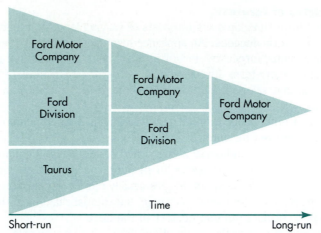

FIGURE 9-5 Forecast Exactness as a Function of the Time Period Involved.

several long-range forecasts, depending upon which assumptions are chosen. The number of assumptions that are required tends to vary according to the length of the forecast period, as demonstrated in Fig. 9-6.

The above discussion also points toward the need to continually revise sales forecasting methods. Sales forecasting models must be routinely updated to be truly effective. Re-evaluation is needed if sales forecasts are to be the key to planning throughout the organization.

Evaluation of Sales Forecasts

The sales manager is often given the responsibility for periodically evaluating the sales forecast. In other cases, higher-level management is charged with this duty. Three objective criteria can be employed for assessing the accuracy of sales forecasts:

1. *Comparison with total sales*. This approach matches sales performance forecasts with actual sales performance.

FIGURE 9-6 Number of Forecasting Assumptions as a Function of Time Period Involved.

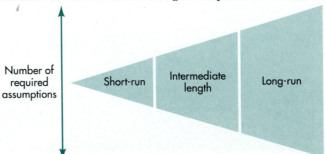

2. *Comparison with actual change in total sales.* Here, the forecast's anticipated change is compared with the actual change. For example, if sales are expected to increase from $200 million to $230 million, but only go up to $215 million, then the sales forecast has failed to predict 50 percent of the real change.

3. *Comparison with other forecasting techniques.* Another evaluative approach is to compare a firm's actual sales forecast with the results obtained through some naive method of estimating future sales such as extrapolating the last increment of change in sales. This third approach allows the firm to assess whether or not a more sophisticated technique is beneficial.[30]

Assessing the accuracy of sales forecasting is important to business planning, but the measurement of the economic consequences of forecast error may be even more crucial. As in many business contexts, the degree of acceptable error in forecasting varies from situation to situation. For instance, a 0.0001 percent error may be intolerable in medical research, where a loss of human life might result. By contrast, a 5 to 10 percent error in an IQ test administered by an educational psychologist might be permissible, since it would probably cause little harm to the future education of the child involved.

In the case of a sales forecast, the degree of acceptable error really depends upon the costs associated with that error. Did the firm make an expensive commitment to buy new equipment because of the forecast? Can corrective action be taken immediately? Are these expenditures sunk? Are they recoverable?

It is crucial that sales managers understand how sales forecasts have been developed if they are to evaluate and use them properly. They must also have input into the forecasting process. If not, a sales manager's lack of knowledge and input may result in a communications gap. To bridge this gap, sales managers must make sure that forecasters understand the key organizational issues and sales variables and their relationships. They must also use common sense when judging sales forecasting methods and results.[31]

SUMMARY OF LEARNING GOALS

1. **Understand the Importance of Sales Forecasting to the Firm.**

   All organizational planning is dependent upon an accurate projection of future revenues to the firm. Sales forecasting is the most important planning task within any company, large or small, since it is the basis of all other planning.

2. **Differentiate Among Market Potential, Sales Potential, Sales Forecasts, Sales Quotas, and Sales Budget.**

   Sales forecasts—or the actual estimate of company sales for a specified period— must first determine market potential (expected industry sales of a good or service in a specified market segment for a given time period) and sales potential (the share of market potential that a company or brand expects to achieve). Market potential is dependent upon both the buyers' ability and willingness to buy. Market and sales potentials set the limits within which forecasts can be developed. Two of the most common uses of forecasts are to set sales quotas (the goals and objectives sought by sales management) and the sales budget (management's plan for expenditures of money to accomplish sales objectives).

3. **Explain the Concepts of Market and Sales Potentials.**

   Market potential is the highest possible expected industry sales of a good or service in a specified market segment for a given time period. Sales potential refers to an individual firm's share of the market potential. It is equal to market share (the percentage of the market controlled by a particular company or product) times market potential.

4. **Discuss Economic, Industry, Company, and Product Forecasts.**

   The sales forecasting process consists of three sequential steps: preparing a forecast of general economic conditions; preparing a forecast of industry sales; and preparing a forecast of product or company sales. Gross domestic product, or GDP, is the standard measure of general economic conditions. Industry estimates are typically based on the relationships between industry sales and national economic data. Finally, product and company forecasts can be determined through qualitative or quantitative methods.

5. **Outline the Various Qualitative and Quantitative Methods of Sales Forecasting.**

   Forecasting methods can be classified as either qualitative or quantitative. Qualitative techniques include the jury of executive opinion, Delphi technique, sales force composite, survey of buyers' intentions, and factor listing. Quantitative techniques include continuity extrapolation, time series analysis, exponential smoothing, regression and correlation analysis, multiple-regression analysis, leading indicators, and econometric models.

6. **Discuss Who Is Responsible for Sales Forecasting.**

   Responsibility for sales forecasting varies among firms. The forecasting function can be handled either by marketing, sales, or finance and accounting personnel. In most organizations, marketing has replaced finance and accounting as the function responsible for forecasting. In all cases, sales management provides valuable input to the process.

7. **Relate Forecast Exactness, Accuracy, and Assumptions to the Forecast Time Period.**

   Sales forecasts can be classified as either short range (one year or less), intermediate (two to five years), and long range (over five years). Forecast accuracy decreases with the length of time covered by the forecast. Forecast exactness also varies inversely with the forecast time period: The longer the time period, the less exact the forecast. It addition, the number of assumptions required for accurate and exact forecasts increases as the time periods involved lengthen.

8. **Understand How to Evaluate Sales Forecasting Effectiveness.**

   The effectiveness of sales forecasting can be evaluated by three methods:

   a. *Comparison with total sales.* This approach matches forecast sales performance with actual sales performance.

   b. *Comparison with actual change in total sales.* This method compares the forecast's anticipated change with the actual change.

c. *Comparison with other forecasting techniques.* This approach compares a firm's actual sales forecast with the results obtained from a naive forecasting approach.

REVIEW QUESTIONS

1. Explain the importance of sales forecasting. How are sales forecasts used by different managers in the organization?
2. What are sales quotas and sales budgets? What role do sales forecasts play in the development of sales quotas and sales budgets?
3. Distinguish among market potential, sales potential, and sales forecasting. How is market share linked to these items?
4. Identify and explain the variables that influence market potential. Cite an example of each variable and its impact on market potential.
5. Relate sales forecasting to the product life cycle. How is the product life cycle used as a forecasting tool?
6. Why should sales forecasts be concerned with economic and industry forecasts? How are these forecasts developed?
7. Define each of the following qualitative methods: jury of executive opinion, Delphi technique, sales force composite, survey of buyers' intentions, and factor listing. What are the advantages of qualitative methods of sales forecasting? The disadvantages?
8. Contrast continuity extrapolation, time series analysis, exponential smoothing, regression and correlation analysis, multiple-regression analysis, and econometric models. What are the advantages and disadvantages of quantitative sales forecasting methods?
9. How are forecast exactness and accuracy related to the forecast time period? How are assumptions affected?
10. What options are available to sales management in evaluating the effectiveness of a firm's sales forecasting effort? Discuss each of these approaches.

DISCUSSION QUESTIONS

1. Interview a salesperson in your community. Ask this person how sales forecasts affect his or her job.
2. DATS (digital audio tapes) are still a recent innovation in recorded music. How would you estimate the market potential for this product?
3. Shortly after the failed Soviet coup of August 1991, Procter & Gamble (P&G) announced a new joint venture in the former Soviet Union. How would you estimate the market potential and sales forecast for the sale of P&G products in the Soviet Union?
4. Prepare a report on a recent economic forecast for your area or state. Discuss what this forecast could mean to local sales personnel.
5. Study the history of a product that failed. Do you see any reasons that the company's sales forecast missed the mark? What could have been done to spot potential problems?

ETHICAL DILEMMA

Some salespeople and sales managers forecast sales for their territories at lower levels than they expect to achieve. This allows them to look good at the end of the forecast period when they exceed their projections. In what ways does this practice cause problems for companies?

Where's the Camera When You Need It?

Cardboard cameras are a product with enormous potential. With film included, they do not have to be loaded or unloaded. After the roll of film is used, the entire camera is turned over to a photofinisher for processing.

When first introduced in 1987, cardboard cameras were not well received. Environmentally conscious consumers did not approve of this most recent development in throw-away technology, and photography enthusiasts did not believe that a disposable camera could produce good pictures.

Eastman Kodak Company, whose current U.S. market share of the camera market is estimated at 80 percent, worked to turn these problems around. First, it instituted a cardboard camera recycling program. Then it gave the cameras away in promotions and increased advertising so consumers would begin to see they were capable of taking quality pictures.

Kodak's efforts paid off, and it was not long before consumers began discovering novel uses for a product costing only the $8 to $12: It is the ideal solution for someone who "forgets to bring the camera." Such cameras can be distributed to wedding guests, who have fun taking pictures that are later dropped off with the bride and groom. Other niches are senior citizens and children (who may find regular cameras daunting to use or too expensive), sports fans, and water enthusiasts.

Some 22 million cardboard cameras are now sold annually in the U.S. The new product is providing growth in an otherwise stagnant market, and one thing seems clear—the forecast for cardboard camera sales is up, up, up.

Questions

1. At what phase of the product life cycle is the cardboard camera? Discuss.

2. Could continuity extrapolation be used to forecast sales in this situation?

3. What other forecasting methods could be used in this situation?

CHAPTER 10

SALES BUDGETING

LEARNING GOALS

- Explain what is meant by sales budgeting and show how it is used by sales management.
- Identify and explain the major types of selling expense budgets.
- Explain how sales budgeting levels are determined.
- Outline the steps in the sales budgeting procedure.
- Describe actual sales budgeting practices.

THE VALUE OF INFORMATION

Information has value, and, like most things with value, it costs money. When developing budgets, companies must find cost-effective sources of information.

Consultants are one source, but their services can be expensive. Small businesses, especially, are often unable to justify the cost, so they must turn to innovative ways to get information.

The Alternative Board, known as TAB, was formed in 1989 to provide an opportunity for small business owners to come together and meet for the generation and exchange of ideas. Today, the company has 543 clients in St. Louis, Chicago, Los Angeles, and Colorado. Membership in TAB is limited to the chief executive officers of non-competing businesses, and members pay from $1000 to $3000 a year for the TAB service.

There are other sources of inexpensive information. Some colleges have programs

through which students advise businesses as part of their coursework. Advanced students are typically used in such programs.

The U.S. Small Business Administration runs the Service Corps of Retired Executives (SCORE) program. SCORE advice if free, and offices are located across the country.

The efficient use of resources is usually crucial for the survival of small companies. But even in large companies, there is competition between departments for budget dollars. In either case, the cost of information, which often does not contribute directly or immediately to sales volume, must be justified.[1]

Chapter 10 discusses sales budgeting. After reading this chapter, you should have a good grasp of how sales organizations allocate and justify expenses of all kinds, including those incurred for seeking information.

CHAPTER OVERVIEW

Budgeting is a key task of sales management. Effective budgeting demands both the sales manager's involvement and his or her understanding of the budgeting process and the reason it is necessary.[2] The manager must be aware of the types of expenses that are incurred both before and after the sale as well as the sales revenues generated.

Consequently, it is essential that sales managers know how to use analytical concepts to estimate and measure the financial consequences of their sales plans. In particular, they must assess the financial implications of their plans prior to implementation. For example, Pioneer Electronics U.S.A. made a number of sales and marketing changes that impacted the firm's sales, costs, and profits in important ways. These changes included combining the company's three separate home audio, home video, and car stereo operations into a single business; shifting the product mix focus to higher-margin, high-end equipment; doubling the firm's national advertising expenditures; and replacing independent agents with the company's own sales representatives. Each of these moves affected the firm's revenues and costs and, to some extent, had an impact on selling.[3]

Assessing the potential financial impact of sales and marketing changes like these involves the process of budgeting. Profits can only be achieved on a continuous basis if they are pursued in a planned fashion. Sales management planning is vital to a company's success and growth over the long run. Sales planning, in turn, is structured around the sales forecasts—the projection of future levels of sales. These anticipated sales volumes affect sales budgeting in two ways: (1) Units sold translate into sales revenue, and (2) the sales targets contained in the sales forecasts require appropriate selling efforts and selling expenses.

What Is Sales Budgeting?

sales budgeting
Estimating future levels of revenue, selling expenses, and profit contributions of the sales function

Sales budgeting involves estimating future levels of revenues and selling expenses and consequently the profit contributions made by the sales function. The outcome of sales budgeting is seen in the form of two documents: the sales budget and the selling expense budget. The sales budget starts with the sales forecast, which projects future sales volumes.[4] The revenue objectives are then prepared. The selling expense budget shows the expenditures necessary to reach the revenue objectives. Through sales budgeting, sales management can reconcile these revenues and expenditures with the firm's hierarchy of objectives.

A sales budget is expressed in financial terms, so it could be called a "financial plan" or "financial statement of revenue and expense flows." Sales budgeting is concerned with cost reduction and improved selling efficiency.

TYPES OF BUDGETS

budget Financial statement that outlines a firm's intended actions and the resulting cash flow consequences

A *budget* is a formal statement that spells out in detail a firm's intended financial activities and their cash flow consequences. It is an authorized blueprint for action that translates tactical decision into dollars and cents. Most sales budgets cover a period of one year, but they are often broken down into quarterly, or even monthly, targets. A budget's individual figures should always be compared to actual results; this comparison may well prompt a revision while the sales effort is in progress.

Sales budgeting is a process that results in a number of different budgets. These can be classified in several ways: on whether they contain only expenditures or also contain revenues; on the kind of expenditures they include; on the rigidity of their figures; or on the reasons for their development.

Allocating Sales Costs

fixed costs Costs that do not vary with output level and are incurred whether or not a sales effort is made

An essential prerequisite for successful sales budgeting is an accounting system capable of segregating costs and revenues so they can be allocated to particular products, orders, customers, territories, or periods. *Fixed costs,* such as base salaries or equipment depreciation, do not vary at all with the output level, and are incurred whether or not a sales effort is made. Changes in the level of fixed costs are nonetheless possible over the long run. Switching to a commission plan, or selling tangible assets to investors and leasing them back, can reduce fixed costs markedly. A sales manager, however, should view fixed costs as basically unalterable during the budget period.

variable costs Costs that fluctuate directly with the level of sales activity

Variable costs, such as commissions or travel expenses, fluctuate directly with the level of sales activity. These costs are controllable and deserve constant managerial scrutiny. They expand and contract in direct proportion to the sales volume, shrinking to zero when there is no sales activity. While variable costs can be reduced to increase sales efficiency, excessive zeal in this direction can boomerang, with an emphasis on short-term order getting overshadowing longer-term company interests in the areas of account servicing and development. Variable costs are determined by multiplying the anticipated product quantities by the variable cost per unit.

semivariable costs Costs that vary, but not in direct proportion to sales volume

The third group of costs represents a mixture of the other two. *Semivariable costs* move somewhat with volume changes, but they do not vary in direct proportion to them. Encompassing both fixed and variable components, semivariable costs move at a less-than-proportionate ratio. Because of their fixed ingredients, they return to a level that is higher than zero when volume drops to zero. These costs are less controllable than variable costs, but more manageable than fixed costs.

Major Budget Categories

As noted earlier, two types of budgets are the principal outcomes of sales budgeting: the sales budget and the selling expense budget. Both are related to the

sales budget
Projection of revenue computed from forecast unit sales and average prices

sales forecast. The *sales budget* projects revenues computed from forecasted unit sales and average prices. The firm's entire budgeting system revolves around the sales budget. The sales budget has to be differentiated not only according to product, but also according to period and territory. Customer differentiation is also often used. For instance, an auto accessories manufacturer may have separate sales strategies and budgets for auto manufacturers, auto parts distributors, specialty retailers, discount stores, and general merchandisers.

selling expense budget Approved amounts that management will spend to obtain the revenues projected in the sales budget

The *selling expense budget,* by contrast, documents approved spending levels and details what management is prepared to spend to obtain the revenues anticipated in the sales budget. Some firms prefer to subdivide the selling expense budget into before-sale and aftersale expenditures, whereas other firms structure them as fixed, semivariable, and variable. Sales management will occasionally establish a separate administrative or advertising budget. But for the most part, the selling expense budget is simply designed as a list of natural cost categories grouped together, as shown in Table 10-1.

TABLE 10-1   **Major Selling Cost Categories**

1. **Selling**
    A.   **Compensation (salary, commission, bonus, incentives, fringe benefits)**
    B.   **Travel and entertainment (lodging, meals)**
    C.   **Prospect seminars**
    D.   **Discounts and allowances**

2. **Promotion**
    A.   **Cooperative advertising allowances**
    B.   **Catalogs, brochures, price lists**
    C.   **Fairs and exhibits**
    D.   **Samples, models, displays**
    E.   **Selling aids (audiovisual equipment and materials, flipcharts, manuals, kits)**
    F.   **Contests and deals**

3. **Fulfillment**
    A.   **Packaging and shipping**
    B.   **Billing**
    C.   **Credit**
    D.   **Warranty**
    E.   **Returns**

4. **Servicing**
    A.   **Distributor and customer training**
    B.   **Technical counseling**

5. **Support**
    A.   **Recruitment and selection**
    B.   **Training and development**
    C.   **Sales meetings**
    D.   **Customer service**
    E.   **Warehousing**

6. **Administration**
    A.   **Office expenses**
    B.   **Telephone and postage expenses**

SALES MANAGEMENT IN PRACTICE

ELAN FROZEN YOGURT

What does a young consumer goods company do when its selling budget will not allow the large expenses normally associated with consumer goods promotion? For some companies, product sampling has proven to be a very effective way to promote new products. The Elan Company, for one, has taken its frozen yogurt from a home-made-from-scratch recipe in 1986 to sales in more than twenty states at the present time. Elan's success is largely attributable to product sampling, the only promotional effort that was affordable during the firm's early years.

Product sampling is normally done through direct mailings or through in-store demonstrations. There are companies that specialize in providing in-store demonstration setups; normally, around $100 is charged for the day-long use of a card table and a trained demonstrator. In addition to the demonstration company's fee, Elan also had to pay for the yogurt that was sampled and the coupons that were distributed with the samples. The entire in-store demonstration cost, however, is cheap when compared to other sales methods. In-store sampling is also less expensive than sampling through direct mail, which in addition lacks the benefit of targeting shoppers already in the store and ready to spend.

Elan is an example of a company that took a small budget and made the most of it. Although in-store demonstrators were trained by the demonstration companies, Elan took special care to educate them in the specifics of its product. It provided the demonstrators with uniforms and replaced the demonstration company's card tables with specially designed Elan yogurt tables. The company also worked closely with supermarkets to obtain demographic information and focused its sampling efforts only on the most appropriate stores.

Elan is no longer a fledgling company. While it is now using some other types of advertising, the company's promotional efforts still emphasize product sampling. Considering the nature of Elan's product, sampling makes perfect sense: A television advertisement telling consumers how good Elan Yogurt tastes is less convincing than an actual taste of the yogurt in person. Considering the effectiveness of Elan's product sampling efforts, its current we-could-pay-more-but-why philosophy is very understandable.

---

profit budget
Merged sales budget and the selling expense budget to determine gross profit

The sales budget and the selling expense budget usually remain separate and distinct from each other. Occasionally, they are merged into a *profit budget,* in which gross profit is determined by deducting planned selling expenditures from expected sales revenues.

DETERMINING THE BUDGET LEVEL

A key sales management decision involves the setting of the overall level of spending on personal selling activities. Once this total figure has been determined, the sum is then allocated between the various natural cost categories that make up the selling expense budget.

Sales Force Funding

The amount of money that will be made available for personal selling depends on the relative role that personal selling plays in the promotion mix and in the broader marketing mix. Selling's role will vary considerably from industry to industry and from company to company, according to marketing practices and corporate philosophies. As a general rule, personal selling is more significant in an industrial marketing mix than for consumer marketing. Marketers of consumer convenience goods, for instance, often rely on a combination push/pull strategy that assigns a more substantial role to advertising and sales promotion. The amount spent on personal selling also depends on whether management subscribes to an expense mentality or an investment philosophy of selling, whether it is content with passive order takers or wants aggressive order getters, whether salespeople find it difficult to obtain orders, and what mode of distribution the company uses.

The sales function may have to compete for funds with advertising and sales promotion, marketing research, product management, customer service, research and development, and production, among other nonmarketing functions. The selling expense level is also affected by the relative influence of sales management in promoting the importance of an aggressive sales effort, salesperson training and development, selling aids, aftersale service, and so forth to the higher levels of company management.

The task of obtaining funds for sales activities and programs is especially difficult during hard economic times. Adjustments must be made when sales managers are confronted with budget restrictions resulting from recessions, industry shakeouts, or the fallout from mergers and acquisitions.[5] Cuts sometimes must be made in sales and marketing communications, especially trade advertising and public relations programs, training and other sales support activities, and other costs that may not always appear to contribute to the bottom line. However, major cuts in sales communications, customer service, and sales development activities may have negative long-term effects on the sales organization.

During tough economic times sales managers must place even more emphasis on the sales budgeting process. They may be able to postpone some expenses such as the printing of new sales literature. They may also be able to reduce travel and entertainment expenses. In extreme cases, layoffs of salespeople and managers may be necessary; however, most sales executives consider this extreme action their last resort.[6]

Methods of Funding Sales Forces

There are several methods by which to fund sales forces. These parallel the approaches to the appropriation of advertising funds and are characterized by the same strengths and weaknesses. Regardless of the method used, sales managers should be involved in the budget development process since they will be held responsible for sales expenses. For this reason, the most practical sales budgets are usually those that are developed from the bottom up.[7] The major methods used to budget sales expenses are discussed below.

affordable method
Sales budgeting method in which management decides what share of revenues above and beyond the cost of goods sold it is prepared to spend on selling and administrative costs, after achieving a predetermined profit level

Affordable Method. With the *affordable method,* management first decides what share of revenues above and beyond the cost of goods sold it is prepared to spend on selling and administrative costs, after achieving a predetermined profit level. The resulting appropriation for selling and administrative costs is then allocated as follows: Administrative or overhead costs are deducted from the overall appropriation to arrive at a promotion fund, which, in turn, is then split between advertising and personal selling.

The amount that a company can afford to spend on personal selling is an arbitrary figure. It may exceed, but will more typically fall short of, the true funding needs of the sales function. This approach neglects the differential yields of selling expenditures. The economic *law of diminishing returns* states that additional units of input (selling expenditures) will first produce increasing, then diminishing, and finally negative, returns (sales revenues).

law of diminishing returns Additional units of input will first produce increasing, then diminishing, and finally negative returns

percentage of sales method Sales budgeting method in which the funding level is found by multiplying sales revenues by a given percentage.

Percentage of Sales Method.

The *percentage of sales method*—the most popular of the budgeting techniques—determines the overall level of funding for personal selling by multiplying sales revenues by a given percentage. Therefore:

$$\text{Selling expense budget level} = \text{a percentage of sales revenues}$$

The sales revenues may either be those of the past period or of the planning period. In the latter case, budgeting is based on anticipated, rather than historical, revenues. The sales forecast, then, not only determines the sales budget, but also the selling expense budget. A weighted average of past and future sales might also be used.

The advantage of the percentage of sales method of selling expense budgeting is its simplicity. No additional decisions are needed to expand or contract the budget. This method can also be a time saver if past conditions can reasonably be expected to persist throughout the planning period.

There is, however, a serious flaw underlying this approach. It perverts the cause-effect relationship by suggesting that the levels of sales effort should be derived from sales results. In actuality it is the effort that produces the revenues. The percentages chosen vary widely by industry, and even by company. This method depends more on managerial judgment and the stature of personal selling in the firm than on rational decision-making criteria. The percentage figure is also a function of the competitiveness of an industry and the relative size of the company. A small competitor will tend to spend a high percentage of its sales revenues, and a large firm a lower percentage, on personal selling.

Unique opportunities exist for those daring to be different during times of economic adversity. Bad economic times may indicate that promotional activities would be reduced according to the percentage of sales method. But increases may set the stage for a spectacular recovery. This suggests that some companies should consider raising spending levels rather than lowering them.

competitive parity method Sales budgeting method based on the competitive practices in an industry

Competitive Parity Method.

Adherents of the *competitive parity method* use competitive practices in an industry as their guide to setting sales spending levels.[8] They refer either to specific competitors or to the industry average. In determining their selling expense budgets, they can use either absolute figures (dollars budgeted) or relative figures (percentage of sales). Use of the latter is more frequent. The reasoning behind this practice is that the collective wisdom of an industry exceeds that of a single firm, or that a company should not surrender the field to more aggressive rivals.

The technique is unlikely to produce lasting advantages and may even represent a disservice to the firm's true interests since it means surrendering management's decision-making authority to outside competitive factors. Sales management should set and live by its own priorities, not those of others.

Objective and Task Method.   All of the above approaches to budgeting for selling expenses share a major deficiency: They lose sight of the company's objectives. They can lead to budget figures that bear no relationship to selling targets.

objective and task method Sales budgeting method in which appropriations are based on the costs of the tasks necessary to accomplish agreed-upon objectives

The most meaningful budgeting approach is the *objective and task method,* also known as zero-based budgeting. Unlike the simplistic affordable, percentage of sales, and competitive parity methods, this approach starts with the sales objectives to be accomplished and arrives at the budgetary appropriation in four steps, as shown in Fig. 10-1. It starts by spelling out the objectives to be accomplished by the sales effort during the planning period.

This budgeting method will also help a sales manager defend the sales budget.[9] The more closely the budget is related to the company's strategic plan or mission, the more likely it will be accepted by senior management. In addition, a firm's priorities are set through selling expenses by demonstrating their relationship to those priorities.

The budgeting process begins with the establishment of mutually agreed-upon objectives for every member of the sales force, possibly on an account-by-account, product-by-product, or quarter-by-quarter basis. In the second step, selling tasks or activities that have to be carried out to achieve the specified objectives are identified. In other words, sales management now pinpoints the means, or inputs, required to reach the objectives. In the third step, the tasks or activities are translated into expenditures by asking the question, "What will it cost to get the job done?" The activities derived from the objectives are converted into projected cash outflows by planning interval. The final step involves adding all selling costs mandated by the objectives according to territory, product, and quarter to obtain the total selling expense budget level. One problem with this approach is that objectives may be specific without concern for their profit impact. If a number of different objectives are to be pursued simultaneously, the thrust of the sales force may be diluted. Sales managers, therefore, have to carefully evaluate, prioritize, and select sensible objectives before incurring expenses. A second problem arises because it is often

FIGURE 10-1 The Objective and Task Method.

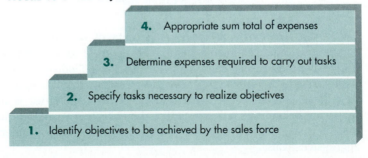

4.   Appropriate sum total of expenses

3.   Determine expenses required to carry out tasks

2.   Specify tasks necessary to realize objectives

1.   Identify objectives to be achieved by the sales force

difficult to compute precisely what it will cost to execute a certain task. Still, the objective and task method represents a significant improvement over the preceding techniques.

Other Methods.   Every company wants to deploy its resources in the most productive fashion, and sales managers are challenged to find new methods to establish and justify their budgets. Zero-based budgeting, which involves the objective and task approach, is becoming more popular. Some firms employ a *bidding system* in which the sales function competes with other functions for limited funds on the basis of expected payoff. The *return-oriented method* relates sales-generated profits to selling expenses and generates financial support for personal selling up to the point at which alternative capital uses become more attractive. This approach is difficult to put into practice, since the profit attributable to individual sales activities defies precise measurement.

The economic resource allocation approach, also known as marginal analysis, could theoretically yield the optimum selling expense budget by setting its level in accordance with the sales volume, where marginal cost equals marginal revenue. Although conceptually sound, this method has little practical merit, since it would be expensive to administer, and would strain the capabilities of most accounting systems.

One of the most promising approaches to sales budgeting involves rate-or-return thinking. Some sales managers have begun to use this financial management concept to choose between alternative courses of action. *Return on investment (ROI)* is the simplest calculation. This is determined by dividing net income by total assets employed to earn the income. This measure is also known as return on assets (ROA) or return on total assets (ROTA). For managers who have limited control over the assets managed, the calculation may be limited to determining the *return on assets managed (ROAM),* which is the most appropriate measure for sales managers.

A return-on-investment technique such as ROAM can help sales managers visualize the total financial impact of sales budget decisions. For instance, new sales territories not only represent expanded sales potential, but require additional incremental investment.[10] This added investment comes in the form of new accounts receivable and the need for increased inventories to service orders promptly. Two separate ratios are computed: profit divided by sales, and sales divided by investment. In the ROAM formula, these two ratios are multiplied together, which reduces the equation to profit divided by investment. The major benefit of this technique is that it points out the importance of the relative profit contribution of a decision option. It assumes that the incremental investment required can be estimated with a reasonable degree of accuracy. However, a limitation of this approach is that it cannot be applied across the board to the entire sales function.

Accordingly, return on investment can be used most effectively to assess the impact of a specific sales cost allocation on sales revenues and profits. For example, many organization are considering the costs and potential benefits of automating the sales force. The total costs of sales force automation are much greater than the prices of hardware and software. In addition to the costs of hardware, software, and applicable supplies (approximately $5000 per salesperson), operational costs (insur-

bidding system
Sales budgeting method in which functional areas compete on the basis of expected payoffs

return-oriented method Sales budgeting method based on the profit attributable to individual sales activities

(ROI) return on investment Rate-of-return approach to sales budgeting determined by dividing net income by total assets employed to earn the income; also known as return on assets (ROA) or return on total assets (ROTA)

return on assets managed (ROAM) Alternative to ROI used by managers whose control is limited to assets managed

ance, software upgrades, warranties, etc.) and implementation costs (consulting and training services, etc.) must be included. On the average, these expenses will add another $2000 per salesperson to costs. Thus, the total cost of automating the sales force is approximately $7000 per salesperson.

Return-on-investment analysis for sales force automation could be used to estimate the payoff as follows:

1. National statistics show that a salesperson spends about fifteen hours per week selling, fifteen hours per week on administrative tasks, and ten hours per week servicing existing accounts.
2. Sales force automation will reduce the amount of time spent on administration by three hours per week. This implies an increase of three hours of selling time per week.
3. Assume the average salesperson is responsible for $2,000,000 in sales and the average gross margin is 10 percent, or $200,000 per year. Since there are 750 selling hours per year (50 weeks × 15 hours per week), the profit per selling hour is $267 ($200,000/750).
4. If a sales person spends three more hours per week selling, which adds up to 150 more hours per year (50 weeks × 3), he or she will contribute an additional $40,050 ($267 × 150) in gross profits to the company.
5. The return on investment from sales force automation would be a whopping 579 percent ($40,050/$7,000)![11]

SALES BUDGETING PROCEDURE

Sales budgeting is a sequential decision-making process that involves a series of orderly steps.[12] The steps involved in this procedure are shown in Fig. 10-2, which relates closely to the stages of sales management planning discussed in Chap. 8. It also incorporates the sequence of events inherent in the objective and task method of sales budgeting (see Fig. 10-1).

Situation Analysis

As a first step, sales managers engaged in sales budgeting have to get the facts. They will want to take a look at the magnitude of past differences between budgeted and actual figures and the reasons for these differences. The learning experience resulting from the previous year's mistakes allows for a refinement of both procedural and conceptual aspects of sales budgeting. Budgets can be changed. Fine-tuning the sales and selling expense budgets is an art whose practice benefits from past mistakes.

Identification of Problems and Opportunities

The problems and opportunities that present themselves to sales management emerge from the situation analysis. These actual and potential threats and challenges have to be assessed and addressed to determine their probabilities of occurrence and the severity of their impacts. What is viewed by one sales manager as a problem may appear to another as a fascinating challenge. Whichever the case may be, this second step of sales budgeting is one of realism: facing the facts.

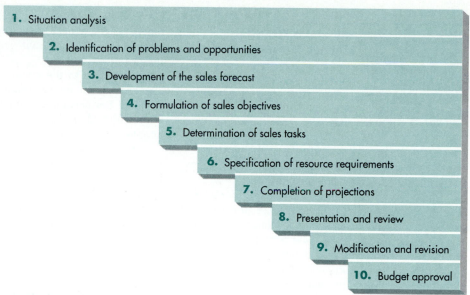

1. Situation analysis
2. Identification of problems and opportunities
3. Development of the sales forecast
4. Formulation of sales objectives
5. Determination of sales tasks
6. Specification of resource requirements
7. Completion of projections
8. Presentation and review
9. Modification and revision
10. Budget approval

FIGURE 10-2 Steps in Sales Budgeting.

Development of the Sales Forecast

Sales management is now equipped to forecast sales, the third step in the sales budgeting process. As described in Chap. 9, the forecast methods employed differ from one firm to the next. In fact, several methods may be used by the same firm, and a combined effort is not uncommon. Projections are made about the anticipated levels of sales by territory, product, and type of account, based on planning assumptions about future environmental conditions.

The sales forecast that results is typically a blend of the broader picture supplied by the marketing information system and the estimates put forth by individual salespeople. It is expressed both in units and in dollars so that later comparisons against actual results can help managers analyze whether variances observed are due to quantity or price differences. The sales forecast is at the very core of the sales budgeting procedure because it determines not only budgeted sales revenues, but also the appropriate level of sales effort required.

Formulation of Sales Objectives

Once the sales forecast has been developed, the sales force has to be told what sales targets to strive for and what objectives to pursue. These sales objectives have to be developed in a participatory fashion, giving all the individuals affected an opportunity to get involved and to be heard. But mutual agreement on sales objectives is not sufficient for a successful sales operation. Objectives have to be prioritized, validated, and supported by adequate resources. Prioritization means that a desirability index has to be developed that indicates the order of importance in which the different objectives are to be pursued. This includes an examination of their likely profit consequences. When looked at from a cost/benefit perspective, many objectives that originally appeared very important may have to be discarded. Validation

MID-STATES TECHNICAL STAFFING SERVICES

Between sales and cash flows lies a very important function—collections. Traditionally, companies have performed collection activities through their accounting departments. Recently, however, they have been giving this responsibility to their salespeople.

Mid-States Technical Staffing Services, a leaser of engineering services, has performed collections through its sales force since the company's beginning in 1986. Mid-States' revenues have grown to $4 million annually. The company averages a twenty-day collection cycle and has only failed to collect on two invoices.

Mid-States sends out invoices once a week, and salespeople get copies of all bills mailed to their clients. Salespeople are expected to know the paying peculiarities of their clients, so they have a good idea about where payment bottlenecks may occur.

In addition to the invoices, each salesperson also receives a weekly report on the statuses of all his or her accounts. Commissions are affected by how quickly payments are received, so salespeople stay very attuned to those statuses.

Mid-States and other companies have found that many salespeople and sales managers prefer to have salespeople involved in the collection process. If a salesperson has established a good relationship with a client, he or she does not want that rapport jeopardized by accounting personnel who may or may not be sensitive to a client's situation. The diplomacy inherent in the selling process comes in handy for the sticky situation of collecting on overdue bills. Salespeople are uniquely qualified to perform this budget control function without jeopardizing future business.

refers to an investigation of the attainability of the surviving objectives, which may render additional objectives unacceptable. At the end of this fourth step of the sales budgeting procedure, only sales objectives judged valuable, worthwhile, and feasible remain.

Determination of Sales Tasks

Sales management and the sales force have to carry out a broad array of sales activities, ranging from recruiting to evaluation, and from prospecting to aftersale servicing. The purpose of the fifth step of the sales budgeting process is to identify tactical tasks. This assignment represents a remarkable challenge; it is one thing to know where you want to be and another thing to know how to get there. Options have to be examined, their sales and profit impacts have to be projected, and their likelihood of success has to be considered.

Specification of Resource Requirements

The sixth step of the sales budgeting process spells out the resources that will be required to implement the specified activities and achieve the desired objectives. These resources include the salespeople to be employed either temporarily or permanently and the items necessary to support them, ranging from automobiles, lap-top computer, and audiovisual selling aids to manufacturing plants and inventories. Sales objectives will not be realized unless the firm is in a position to provide sufficient support. If this is not the case, the program will have to be revised.

Completion of Projections

Sales objectives, tasks, and resources can now be tied together into one cohesive and coherent whole. All the inputs and requests from the various units of the sales function are assembled and integrated into a comprehensive package. This seventh step is the last in the sales budgeting procedure that is internal to the sales organization. It requires careful review and coordination of the ingredients of the total and selling expense budgets to make the final product sound.

Presentation and Review

In step 8, sales management has to present and defend its budget proposal to top management. It has to justify its request for scarce funds by competing with other parts of the organization. Top executives would be remiss in their duties if they did not challenge sales management's budget proposal. Some sales managers deliberately ask for more funding than they expect to receive. Although the ethics of such an approach are questionable, inflated initial requests may be a necessity in some firms. In any event, the sales and selling expense budgets have to be fitted into the corporate master budget and coordinated with its other components, such as the production and procurement budgets. Some specific suggestions for presenting the sales budget to upper management are presented in Table 10-2.

Modification and Revision

Sales management may have to engage in a series of compromise sessions. In step 9 of the sales budgeting process, sales targets and budgets may be adjusted by management, reflecting its assessment of both the needs of the corporation and the true potential of the marketplace. Such modifications also influence selling expense budgets. Top management may decide to channel disproportionate support to research and development or toward the acquisition of new businesses, rather than to fund fully the sales organization at the level requested in the sales budget. The sales function, therefore, may end up with less than it asked for in its original request.

Budget Approval

Final levels are eventually approved and authorized for both the sales and selling expense budgets. This tenth and final step in the sales budgeting process enables sales management to proceed as the new planning period takes effect. Allocation of the approved amount for specific tasks is implied in the authorization. At regular intervals actual and budgeted figures are compared to each other. Deviations are noted and investigated. Budget revisions may become necessary if sales results or costs are substantially off course. For instance, rising fuel costs, safety concerns, and a slow economy after Iraq's invasion of Kuwait in August 1990 caused many firms to revise their sales travel budgets. Although the entire sales budgeting procedure occurs as an annual ritual, the process supporting it is continuous and cyclical. Findings from one year's periodic progress reviews feed into the next year's situation analysis.

TABLE 10-2   Tips for Winning the Budget Wars

1. *Get the facts.*
   - If a project, campaign, or other program is instrumental to the department, prove it.
   - Prepare figures to show how past advertising campaigns worked.
   - Provide documentation that sales increased as the result of trade show participation.
   - Research and justify expense outlays.

2. *Put things on hold.*
   - Do not include new projects and ventures in the budget during a slow business period.
   - Do not try new, untested programs.
   - Set priorities and stick with them.

3. *Be realistic.*
   - If cuts have to be made, make them.
   - Show management that you are willing to do your part.
   - It is better for *you* to make the cuts than for someone outside the department to mandate them.

4. *Be flexible.*
   - If management wants still more cuts, be prepared to bargain.
   - Find out what management thinks is most important.
   - Be willing to compromise.

5. *Avoid confrontation.*
   - Try to understand upper management's point of view.
   - Do not disagree with them on every issue.
   - Remember to save your best arguments for the really important projects.

6. *Stay lean.*
   - If you allowed yourself to get "fat" during good times, look for management to come down hard on you.
   - By being lean—and staying that way—you can avoid big cuts.

7. *Sell it.*
   - Sales is your forte.
   - Your budget is your product or service.
   - Upper management is your customer.

bottom-up budgeting Buildup approach to sales budgeting

top-down budgeting Breakdown approach to sales budgeting

The sales budgeting procedure described here reflects what may be called *bottom-up budgeting,* or buildup budgeting. This approach is rooted in market conditions. Alternatively, some enterprises choose *top-down sales budgeting,* also called breakdown budgeting. Beginning with corporate objectives and fiscal abilities, sales objectives and budgets are formed in a derivative manner. Since input from the marketplace represents an afterthought, this approach will sometimes backfire. The bottom-up method is superior in most circumstances. The actual practice of sales budgeting involves a number of additional issues that will be addressed in the following section.

PRACTICE OF SALES BUDGETING

The success of sales budgeting depends largely upon the level of commitment and cooperation obtained from everyone involved in it. Sales budgeting problems are mostly human relations issues. Hostility and dishonesty are serious problems. There is a great deal of resistance to sales budgeting in many organizations because sales personnel often resent being tied down by precise figures. Successful sales budgeting requires a commitment by salespeople to sales objectives. They must take sales forecasts seriously since management measures actual performance against forecasts. Similarly, success in budgeting selling expenses means sales personnel must accept the constraints imposed when upper limits are placed on those expenses. Participation in sales budgeting is considered by some salespeople to be a waste of time, since it involves nonselling activities and produces no revenues per se. Some of these negative attitudes can be alleviated by rewarding sales personnel for their accuracy in forecasting and for attaining their sales quotas.

Honesty in Sales Budgeting

Lack of honesty in sales budgeting is another problem. As mentioned earlier, budget requests may be inflated in anticipation of their reduction during the review process. Sales managers often take an extreme position at the outset and prepare for compromises during the review leading to approval. Another less frequent, but even more dangerous, ploy is to deliberately understate the financial needs of the sales function to look good and avoid arguments at budget approval time. The assumption underlying this attitude is that higher actual spending levels can later be explained, or will not be questioned at all.

Budget Discipline

The sales budgeting process is only as good as its enforcement. Will there be a followup process to hold the various units to the authorized levels and to compare actual versus planned figures for control purposes? Will there be an analysis of variances investigating volume versus price deviations and fixed-versus variable-cost variations? Will sales management be held accountable for all fluctuations? Are the budgets tight (designed for maximum efficiency with little room for error), or loose (formulated for normal efficiency levels, allowing for some margin of error)? Tight budgeting can frustrate even the most motivated sales manager, because it is all but impossible to realize sales objectives while spending only the approved amounts.

If there is no reward for bringing in the budgeted sales revenues at a cost below the expected level, sales managers may make little effort to cut expenses. Below-budget expenditures can backfire in the form of reduced budget allowances for the subsequent budgeting period. There may be a scramble to spend leftover monies during the final weeks of a planning interval to preserve current budget levels for the future. This is particularly true if future budgets are determined by adding a given percentage to past budget amounts.

Intervals for Sales Budgets

Depending upon management preferences and philosophies, sales budgeting intervals differ from one firm to the next. The most common interval is annual budget preparation, but semiannual, and even quarterly, budget periods can be found. A monthly budgeting format is usually impractical since it takes time away from other sales management responsibilities. Where monthly budgets exist, they are usually translations of longer-term budgets into monthly terms.

rolling budget
Budget using periodic updates that eliminate the immediate past period; the budgets for the following period are modified as needed, and another period is added at the end of the cycle

flexible budgeting
Budgeting process in which a base budget geared to average conditions is drawn up and then adjusted in accordance with actual sales results

A typical one-year planning and budgeting cycle is illustrated in Fig. 10-3. Also shown are the specific tasks and levels of responsibility for corporate, marketing, and sales management.

To increase the flexibility of the budgeting process, some firms have adopted other budgeting approaches. A *rolling budget* involves periodic updates whereby the immediate past period is eliminated, the budgets for the following period are modified as needed, and another period is added at the end of the budgeting cycle. This approach is hampered by the difficulty of judging whether or not the observed deviance between the previous month's budgeted and actual results is structural in nature or simply a temporary situation.

Another tool used to adapt sales budgeting figures to the evolving sales environment is *flexible budgeting,* where a base budget geared to average or normal conditions is drawn up and then adjusted in accordance with actual sales results.

A further option—one that is more theoretical than practical—is *alternative budgeting,* in which sales management envisions three possible sets of market

FIGURE 10-3 Planning and Budgeting Cycle.

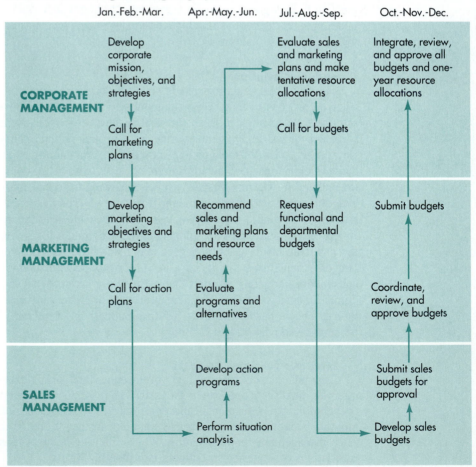

alternative budgeting Budgets based on envisioned best-case, most likely, and worst-case scenarios in order to achieve emergency preparedness

sales productivity Ratio of output (sales revenues) to input (selling expenses)

conditions: a best-case scenario with little competitive activity, a most likely scenario with the usual level of competitive action, and a worst-case scenario that assumes severe competitive interference. This method of emergency preparedness involves preparing several alternative budgets.

Sales Productivity

A major concern of all sales managers is improving *sales productivity*, which can be expressed as the ratio of output measures to the appropriate input figures:

$$\text{Sales productivity} = \frac{\text{output}}{\text{input}}$$

Ideally, productivity would relate physical measures to each other such as physical units sold related to hours spent by the sales force in obtaining the sales.[13] In the typical sales force situation, though, it is difficult to compare physical units of advertising, sales promotion, and personal selling. Dollar values are used to achieve compatibility and comparability. Sales productivity cannot be added, and it is a comparative term that should be expressed in terms of either current performance versus another period or entity, or actual versus planned results.

Comparability is attained by multiplying the physical units involved times their respective prices. Thus, the above equation can be restated as follows:

$$\text{Sales productivity} = \frac{\text{sales revenues}}{\text{selling expenses}}$$

This formula can be applied at any level, from the company as a whole to individual sales territories. It can be used to compare actual and planned outcomes for the same entity. If period-to-period comparisons are undertaken, there must be adjustment for price changes over time. Other things being equal, sales productivity can be improved in two ways: (a) improved effectiveness = same input, more output; and (b) improved efficiency = same output, less input.

The sales force will be more effective if it generates more sales for the same selling expenses. For example, money spent on training will be considered well spent if the increased sales generated exceed the costs of training. On the other hand, higher efficiency also results if the same sales revenues are realized at a lower level of spending on selling. Advocates of telemarketing point to lower selling costs as a major reason for selling to smaller accounts through telemarketing sales representatives rather than field salespersons.

As sales budgeting makes managers more aware of opportunities for greater efficiency and improves sales productivity, it also improves profitability. Sales budgeting creates cost consciousness and profit awareness in sales managers. However, the increased concern for sales productivity may backfire if too much emphasis is placed on controllable cost elements such as travel and training expenses. This may result in an expense mentality, rather than an investment philosophy, of sales budgeting. Selling expenditures are expenses in the year in which they are incurred, instead of being capitalized and depreciated over a longer time period, even though their value may extend over a longer period of time. Therefore, it is advisable to moderate sales management's short-term concern with sales efficiency by keeping in mind the firm's long-term objectives, and by occasionally sacrificing current profitability for future returns by building the business through investment and training and other sales development activities.

Sales budgeting is a device for planning profits both in the short run and the long run. It helps to identify weaknesses and pinpoint opportunities for improvement. It serves to measure how well objectives are being realized to highlight emerging problems, and to suggest remedies. It should be a continuous process and steering mechanism of the sales operation, constantly updated for maximum impact.

SUMMARY OF LEARNING GOALS

1. **Explain What Is Meant by Sales Budgeting and Show How It Is Used by Sales Management.**

   Sales budgeting refers to the estimation of future levels of revenues and selling expenses and, consequently, the profit contributions made by the sales function. Sales management uses the sales budgeting outcomes—sales budgets and selling expense budgets—to reduce costs and improve selling efficiency.

2. **Identify and Explain the Major Types of Selling Expense Budgets.**

   The types of selling expense budgets can be differentiated based on the methods by which they are developed. Examples of the different methods available for budget formulation are the *affordable method,* in which management determines what to spend on selling after accounting for the cost of goods sold and desired profit level; the *percentage of sales method,* in which the level of selling expense funding is a certain percentage of revenues; the *competitive parity method,* in which competitive practices in an industry determine sales spending levels; and the *objective and task method,* in which the budget allocation is based on the objectives of a firm, the tasks necessary to achieve these objectives, and the expenses related to these tasks.

3. **Explain How Sales Budgeting Levels Are Determined.**

   Sales budget levels are determined by studying past differences between budgeted and actual figures, evaluating the present situation, and forecasting. The objective and task method is used in sales budgeting, and the level of funding received is influenced by the effectiveness of the budget request presentation.

4. **Outline the Steps in the Sales Budgeting Procedure.**

   The steps in the sales budgeting process are the following:

   - Situation analysis
   - Identification of problems and opportunities
   - Development of the sales forecast
   - Formulation of the sales objectives
   - Determination of sales tasks
   - Specification of resource requirements
   - Completion of projections
   - Presentation and review

- Modification and revision
- Budget approval

5. Describe Actual Sales Budgeting Practices.

The effort to establish a commitment to the budgeting process from all those involved can be thwarted by dishonesty and hostility. To alleviate these problems, rewarding the accuracy of forecasting and the attainment of quotas is important. In addition, procedures must be used to ensure budget discipline.

REVIEW QUESTIONS

1. How is sales budgeting linked to sales forecasting? What is the role of sales management in this linkage?
2. What is the difference between a sales budget and a selling expense budget? On what basis can a sales budget be differentiated? How can selling expense budgets be subdivided?
3. Differentiate among fixed, variable, and semivariable costs. Cite an example of each.
4. What are the major selling cost categories? What factors determine the amount spent on personal selling?
5. What is the disadvantage of the affordable method of budgeting? How is the law of diminishing returns related to this method?
6. What is the advantage of the percentage of sales method? What are its disadvantages?
7. What specific figures determine the basis for competitive parity budgeting? What is the reasoning behind the use of this method?
8. What are the steps in the objective and task funding method? What advantage does this method have over other methods described in this chapter? What are the potential disadvantages of this method?
9. How can dishonesty come into play in the sales budgeting process? In what ways can adherence to the sales budget be enforced?
10. Explain the concept of sales productivity. How is comparability attained? How is effectiveness improved? How is efficiency improved?

DISCUSSION QUESTIONS

1. Develop a yearly budget for your own financial activities. What variable costs go into your budget? What fixed costs are included? Would you say that your budget is "loose" or "tight"?

2. The business press often report changes in the sales budgets of major firms. Select one of these reports; then explain how this change has affected the firm's revenues and profits.

3. An argument can be made for procyclical, as opposed to countercyclical, sales budgets. How would you present such a case to management? What major points would you raise in your argument?

4. Sales force automation is one way in which selling costs can be reduced. Name ways in which the selling effort can be automated. From the customer's viewpoint, would you rather have your business solicited in an automated or nonautomated fashion? Explain.

5. Talk with a sales manager in your community. Ask this person how the budgeting process works in his or her company. Is the manager satisfied with the budgeting process? Has the manager encountered problems in the development of budgets? Identify these problems.

E T H I C A L
D I L E M M A

Linda Archer has just taken over as central regional sales manager. While reviewing her budget for next year, she notices that the allocation for travel and entertainment is much higher than she expected. Although Linda feels that she should bring this to the national sales manager's attention, she is reluctant to do so since the result may be a reduced regional sales budget. What should Linda do?

SALES MANAGEMENT CASE

Weathering a Recession—and Coming Out of One

The recession of the early 1990s caused the revamping of many sales budgets. Sales organizations deal with recessions in various ways. One common strategy is to centralize the sales forces from different parts of the firm. In 1991, Time Inc., for example, combined the advertising sales forces of *Entertainment Weekly, Fortune, Life, Money, People, Sports Illustrated,* and *Time.* Time officials claimed the restructuring was in response to its advertisers, who wanted to deal with just one representative. Whether or not cost savings were the goal, they were certainly the result.

Other companies have taken an approach similar to Time. Bell Atlantic combined the sales force of its Bell Atlanticom Telephone Equipment unit with those of seven other units. The move affected 2000 salespeople, but no layoffs resulted. After the change, some salespeople concentrated on existing customers. Other focused on gaining new customers.

Archive Corporation provides another example of consolidation. After the company acquired Cipher Data Products Corporation, the sales forces of each were combined. This move, along with similar activities in the administrative and engineering departments, resulted in the reduction of Archive's work force by 150 employees.

Other companies have had to resort to layoffs. Model American Computer Corporation recently laid off almost all of its manufacturing staff and cut its sales force by one-third.

Chrysler Corporation took a different approach to the recession. In 1992, it put $35 million into teaching new sales and service tactics to the 115,000 employees of the company's 5000 dealerships. Surveys, undercover shoppers, and other marketing strategies were also included in Chrysler's budget.

The budgeting process has been likened to a battle, with various departments fighting over scarce funds. In difficult economic times, funds become

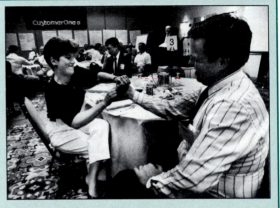

scarce, and the battle gets bloodier. In good times and in bad, however, sales managers must fight for what they believe is best for the company. The budgeting process is, when it comes right down to it, an ongoing sales call, and sales managers responsible for their departments' budgets must be prepared to do what they do best—sell.

Questions

1. Of the companies discussed here, which came out of the recession in the best shape? Did any company (or companies) weaken itself for healthier economic times? Explain.

2. Consider Time Inc's consolidation decision. Do you see weaknesses in selling magazine advertising through a commodity approach? If so, describe the weakness. If not, discuss the strengths of Time's restructuring.

3. Choose an item below and write a short report that would convince upper management not to reduce the expenses involved during a recession:

    a. Sales force training
    b. Sales force travel
    c. Sales force seminars

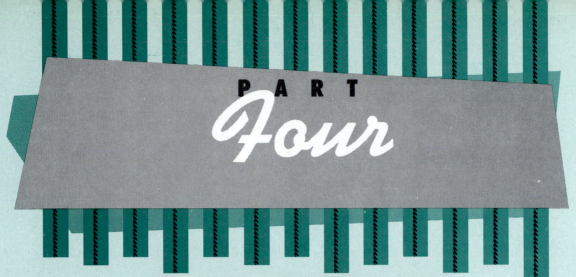

PART
Four

DEVELOPING THE
SALES FORCE

CHAPTER *11*

ORGANIZATION OF THE SALES FORCE

LEARNING GOALS

- List the major tasks of the sales organization.
- Outline the primary organizational issues that need to be addressed when setting up a sales organization.
- Identify the basic types of sales organizations.
- Understand the importance of maintaining effective liaison between the sales organization and other units of the company.
- Discuss the major organizational trends that impact sales management.

PILOT PEN CORPORATION ORGANIZES ITS SALES FORCE

Young or small companies often use independent sales reps rather than their own in-house salespeople. The issue of which type of sales force to employ poses the same cost/benefit dilemma as many farm-out-or-bring-in-house decisions. Starting a sales force is expensive, and it requires sales management talent that many young or small companies have not yet acquired. Independent reps, on the other hand, are not under direct company supervision, and they divide their energies and efforts among several clients.

Pilot Pen used independent reps until 1988, when it decided its sales were getting so large an in-house sales force was needed.

Once this decision was made, however, comprehensive planning was required to determine how the transition would take place. Handling the reps was a delicate issue. Pilot did not want to damage their reputations by any hint that they were being discharged because they had not done good jobs. But most of all, the company wanted to avoid the damage to its own reputation that would be caused if disgruntled reps criticized the firm's actions to customers once they were let go.

Pilot handled the problems by devising an appealing severance package. The reps would not compete with Pilot for a six-month period, and, in return, would receive full commissions for the first month. Over the next five months, their commissions would gradually be reduced to zero.

The reps accepted the offer. At this point Pilot had a unique opportunity to organize its own sales force precisely the way it wanted. No time was wasted. The company divided the country into five sales regions, each of which was supervised by a regional sales manager. Managers were assigned the task of hiring their own salespeople. A support staff was planned, and then a sales administration manager and a sales analyst were hired before the sales positions were filled.[1]

As you read Chap. 11, keep in mind all the issues that managers must address when they organize their selling personnel. In Pilot's case, the decision to develop in-house selling was consistent with the company's growth. For a company with a different agenda, another organizational strategy might be more appropriate.

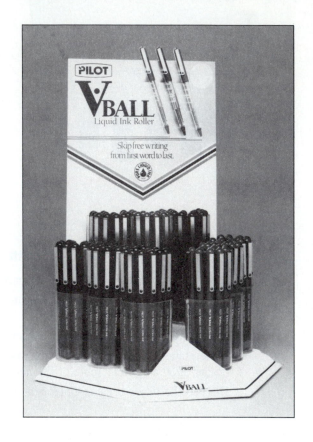

CHAPTER OVERVIEW

organization Basic management functions of arranging the firm's sales activities

Organization is the basic management function of arranging the firm's work activities. It is performed by all managers regardless of their other responsibilities—by controllers, production managers, quality control supervisors, and sales managers alike. Top management supervises and coordinates the overall organizational function for the entire company.

Unfortunately, organization is often viewed as merely the determination of structure. Some executives treat the task as a one-time effort that is finished as soon as the organizational structure is established. This is far from the case: Organization is a continuing task requiring constant management attention.

Organizing the sales force is a crucial sales management task, since it has a direct impact on the field manager's job performance. This chapter explores the organizational responsibilities of the sales manager, beginning with the overall tasks of the sales organization itself. Next, the various issues involved in developing a sales organization are discussed, and the basic types of sales organizations are described. The relationships of sales to other company departments are considered, and current major trends in sales organization are identified. The chapter concludes with a brief description of evaluating the effectiveness of a sales organization.

TASKS OF THE SALES ORGANIZATION

The nearly universal adoption of the marketing concept has meant that most companies have reorganized their sales and marketing activities to reflect the stronger commitment to their customers. This trend has enhanced the importance of sales force organization.[2] Three basic tasks must be accomplished by organization:

1. Maintenance of order in achieving sales force goals and objectives
2. Assignment of specific tasks and responsibilities
3. Integration and coordination with other elements of the firm

structure Division of activities into tasks and the related coordination

Organization represents a continuation of the company's strategic planning process. An effective sales force organization provides the structure for achieving sales objectives by carrying out the firm's sales strategy. *Structure* involves the ways in which an organization divides its activities into distinct tasks and then achieves coordination among them.[3] Without structure, the sales force will tend to languish in confusion and turmoil, goals and objectives will be misunderstood, the selling effort will often be misdirected, and channels of communication will be blocked and inoperative.

Effective structure allows the maintenance of order, which is a fundamental task in any organization, whether its province is business, the military, religion, government, or social service. Organizational structure also permits the assignment of specific tasks to a position whose incumbent is then charged with responsibility for accomplishing them. An effective organization does not permit buck passing. Integration and coordination is another aspect of sales force organization. The organizational structure allows the coordination of the various functional areas of the firm. Functional goals and objectives can be integrated to accomplish the primary corporate or company goals.

The many changes that are taking place in business, marketing, and sales are causing managers to reconsider the traditional tasks and forms of business organization. According to Peter Drucker:

> The typical large business 20 years hence will have fewer than half the levels of management of its counterpart today, and no more than a third the managers. In its structure, and in its management problems and concerns, it will bear little resemblance to the typical manufacturing company, circa 1950, which our textbooks still consider the norm. Instead it is far more likely to resemble organizations that neither the practicing manager nor the management scholar pays much attention to today: the hospital, the university, the symphony orchestra. For like them, the typical business will be knowledge-based, an organization composed largely of specialists who direct and discipline their own performance through organized feedback from colleagues, customers, and headquarters. For this reason, it will be what I call an information based organization.[4]

Drucker goes on to define and describe his view of the information-based organization in detail, with its fewer levels of management and many more specialists. Those specialists will be found in operations, not at corporate headquarters. In many cases, specialists from many functions will come together as a team to develop, produce, and market products, working out of operational divisions, not corporate headquarters.[5]

Some businesses have already moved in this direction. For instance, Gillette has formulated an organizational approach that concentrates its sales and marketing activities at the regional level. This is in response to the large "superaccounts" created by the mergers of giant retailers. Gillette's regional sales managers have seen their jobs expand beyond overseeing the activities of the company's sales force into being responsible for the overall sales planning and merchandising efforts of their geographical areas.[6]

DEVELOPING A SALES ORGANIZATION

Developing a sales organizational structure is not an easy task. Sales managers must recognize, and then deal with, the following basic organizational issues:

1. Formal and informal organizations
2. Horizontal and vertical organizations
3. Centralized and decentralized organizational structures
4. The line and staff components of the organization
5. The size of the company

Formal and Informal Organizations

formal organization Management-created relationships between departments and between individuals

informal organization Communications pattern formed from the social relationships existing within the formal organization

grapevine Another name for the communications patterns of the informal organization

Every firm has a formal organization and an informal organization. The *formal organization* is a creation of management, whereas the informal organization is often developed from the social relationships existing within the formal organizational structure. The *informal organization* is basically a communications pattern that emerges to facilitate the operations of the formal organization; it is sometimes called the *grapevine*. Most formal organizations would be totally ineffective without this supporting informal organization.

Figure 11-1 shows an informal communications pattern that might exist in a marketing organization. Actual communications do not usually follow the formal organizational structure. Some communications cross functional, as well as organizational, lines. This situation allows the formal structure to operate efficiently.

Consider the case of a field salesperson who is responsible for collecting certain kinds of information, such as the prices and trade discounts of competitors. If this information were forwarded through the formal organization shown in Fig. 11-2, there could be a delay before it reached the relevant decision maker. The informal communications system, however, allows the information to be transmitted in a more direct fashion. Similarly, consumer complaints over delays in correcting billing errors can be eliminated more quickly when the district sales manager contacts the head of accounts receivable directly.

The development of an effective sales organization requires a recognition that informal relationships and communications patterns are useful in accomplishing sales force objectives. The grapevine should be encouraged to the extent that it improves organizational efficiency.

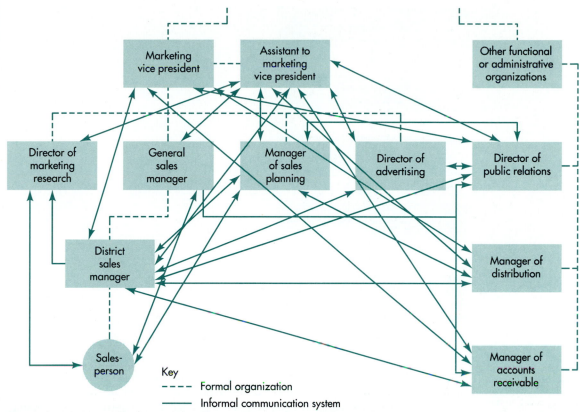

Key

- - - - Formal organization

———— Informal communication system

FIGURE 11-1 Informal Communication System in a Marketing Organization.

Horizontal and Vertical Organizations

vertical sales organization
Organization that has several levels of management all reporting upward to the next level

horizontal sales organization
Organization in which the number of management levels is small and the number of managers at any particular level is large

Sales forces can have either horizontal or vertical organizational formats. The arrangement varies among companies, even within the same industry.

A purely *vertical sales organization* would be similar to the structure represented in Fig. 11-3. Within it, there are several layers of sales management—all of which report vertically.

The opposite extreme is the *horizontal sales organization*, shown in Fig. 11-4. Here the number of management levels is reduced, but the number of managers at any particular level is increased. Instead of two or three district sales managers, there may be seven or eight.

FIGURE 11-2 Lengthy Formal Communications Channel.

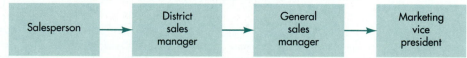

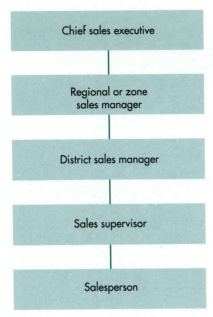

FIGURE 11-3 Vertical Sales Organization.

span of control
Number of employees reporting to the next higher level in the organization

The factor that determines whether a vertical or horizontal organizational structure should be employed is the effective span of control. *Span of control* refers to the number of employees who report to the next higher level in the organization. Horizontal structure tends to exist where larger spans of control are acceptable, while vertical organizations characterize cases in which closer managerial supervision is required.

It is difficult to generalize about setting guidelines for appropriate spans of control. However, it appears that many firms are increasing their spans of control as they continue to focus on "lean and mean" types of organizations. Of course, the type of selling task is an important consideration. The optimum span of control is reduced

FIGURE 11-4 Horizontal Sales Organization.

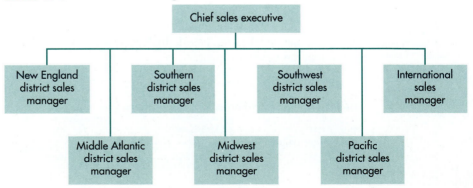

as the type of selling becomes more technical or complex. Approximate guidelines for setting reasonable spans of control are the following: trade selling, 12 to 1; consumer service selling, 10 to 1; missionary selling, 10 to 1; and technical or industrial selling, 6 to 1.

It must be remembered that these ratios are only guidelines. Each company must determine the span of control that works best for its sales organization. Once set, the span of control should be monitored periodically in order to assure maximum effectiveness.

Centralized and Decentralized Organizations

The degree of centralization in sales organizations is an important issue that has to do with the organizational location of the responsibility and authority for specific sales management tasks. In a *decentralized sales organization*, responsibility and authority are delegated to lower levels of management. In a *centralized sales organization*, the responsibility and authority for decisions are concentrated at higher levels of management.

There is usually a higher degree of decentralization as an organization grows in size. Increased size results in top executives being less able to deal with the range of decisions that they handled when the organization was small. By necessity, responsibility for making these decisions is then shifted downward in the organization.

A decentralized organizational structure is ineffective unless the assignment of decision making to lower levels of sales management is accompanied by a commensurate authority to carry out the decisions. A classic mistake is for top management to charge a field sales supervisor with the responsibility for performing a particular task, but then fail to grant the authority to accomplish the assigned objective. It is a mistake because it both results in a failure to achieve the objective and destroys the morale of the personnel involved.

decentralized sales organization
Organization in which responsibility and authority are delegated to lower levels of management

centralized sales organization
Organization in which responsibility and authority are concentrated at higher levels of management

Line and Staff Components

Marketing organizations also feature line and staff components. A *line function* is a primary organizational activity, and a *staff function* is a supporting organizational activity. In a marketing organization, the selling function is the line component, whereas advertising, marketing research, marketing planning, sales training, and distributor relations are usually considered staff roles.

Although the use of the terms "line" and "staff" in regard to marketing organizations has been criticized in many quarters, the basic premise behind that use remains valid. A modern sales force has to receive various types of support to accomplish its objectives. Advertising and sales promotion precondition the prospect to accept the salesperson's presentation; marketing research and sales planning are required because they allow field representatives to concentrate their efforts on the largest potential markets; in-house sales correspondents relieve the field force of activities that detract from their basic efforts; and distribution, credit, and maintenance personnel assure that customers are satisfied with their purchases.

Some firms operate with a simple line sales organization, such as the one shown in Fig. 11-5. Here, the marketing organization is simply the sales organization. This type of arrangement may be satisfactory for small firms in basic industrial markets.

line function
Primary organizational activity

staff function
Supporting organizational activity

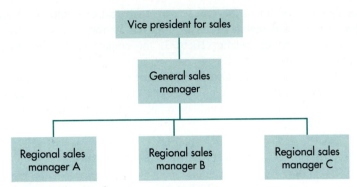

FIGURE 11-5 Line Marketing Organization.

If the needs of the marketplace become more complex, or if the company expands, then there is usually a need to add specialists prepared to deal with these problems. Over time, these specialists become members of the staff departments found in most large organizations.

Figure 11-6 demonstrates several key aspects of a large-scale marketing organization. First, the chief marketing officer is typically called the vice president for marketing rather than the vice president for sales. The title change is indicative of the person's added responsibilities under a line and staff structure. The vice president for marketing is in charge of more than just the field sales force. The line and staff organization shown in Fig. 11-6 indicates that all marketing activities have been

FIGURE 11-6 Line and Staff Marketing Organization.

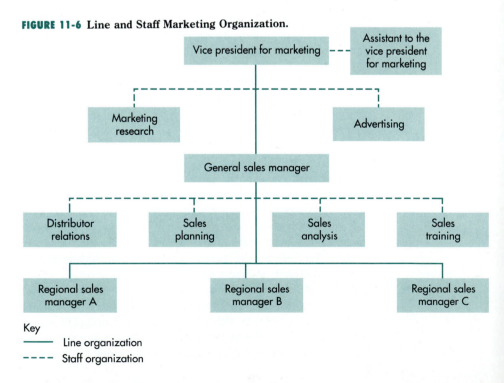

grouped together, suggesting that the basic tenets of the marketing concept have been accepted.

Second, staff activities report to the line position that they support. Distributor relations, sales planning, sales analysis, and sales training are considered to be directly supportive of the field sales effort, so these departments report to the general sales manager. By contrast, marketing research and advertising are broader functions, and they report to the vice president for marketing.

Finally, Fig. 11-6 shows a position titled assistant to the vice president for marketing. This is also a staff position. The fact that the position is diagrammed

suggests that this is usually a single individual rather than a department. The *"assistant to . . ."* is responsible solely to the vice president and does not have line authority over anyone in the organization. The individual is usually a staff person who performs specific tasks (often nonrecurring in nature) for a line executive.

assistant to . . .
Staff person who performs specific tasks for a line executive without having any line authority himself or herself

Company Size and Organization

The above discussion suggests that the size of a company is a major factor influencing its organizational structure. For a small company there is likely to be no formal organizational structure. Rather, the owner/manager is involved in all aspects of the business—accounting, manufacturing, operations, personnel, sales, and so forth.

The attention given to sales as a distinct function depends upon the owner/manager's abilities and interests. In some cases, the owner/manager will have a strong sales background and, in fact, he or she may be the company's top (perhaps only) salesperson. In other cases, the owner/manager will not have a sales background and will hire one or more salespeople. These salespeople are often not given the direction and guidance they need. As a result, sales management is often a neglected activity in a small company.

If a company grows beyond the small-scale entrepreneurial stage, the owner/manager must devote more attention to overall policy and planning and less time to daily operations. A level of management below the owner/manager has to be recruited or developed to take over the specialized functions of the growing business. This will be a gradual process. The owner/manager who has little interest in sales may hire five salespeople over a period of several years. Then, realizing that these people are not being adequately supervised, he or she may decide to hire a sales manager or to promote one of the salespeople already on staff. In this way the small company may evolve into a *functional organization*, one organized by the various activities performed within the firm.

functional organization Organizational format based on primary activities

A very simple functional company organization is shown in Fig. 11-7. This structure is appropriate for most small and medium-sized companies. These compan-

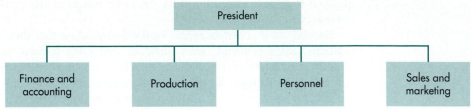

FIGURE 11-7 Functional Company Organization.

ies have relatively few products or services and use a limited number of distribution channels. As each functional area becomes larger, the functional organization is extended. A functional marketing organization is shown in Fig. 11-8.

Coordination of a functional organization becomes more difficult as a company's growth continues. In part, this is because the manager of each functional specialty tends to think only in terms of his or her function's own problems and needs. For example, the human resources department, in its desire for a uniform compensation plan for all employees, fails to recognize the need for a different compensation plan for salespeople. Or an organization that has undergone expansion may be unresponsive to the changing needs of its customers because no one has an overall responsibility for assessing the demand for each product. As a result of these and other difficulties, growing businesses are likely to move toward a more sophisticated form of sales organization.

BASIC TYPES OF SALES ORGANIZATION

The very existence of a field selling organization, as well as the circumstances surrounding its operation, depend on a variety of factors. These factors determine the nature and complexity of the organization. As noted in the previous section, the

FIGURE 11-8 Functional Marketing Organization.

size of the sales force is a determining factor, since larger sales forces create the basic need for a field organization. Firms that place a higher emphasis on personal selling in their promotional mix tend to have more extensive field systems. The physical location of customers served by the sales force is another crucial factor. The amount of account servicing that is required partially determines the existence and extent of the field organization. If customer needs require that accounts be serviced by a salesperson every week, then a sophisticated field organization is necessary.[7]

Most company sales forces are organized on the basis of geography, customers, or products, or some combination of these factors. Each of these bases has positive and negative features.

Geographic Specialization

Geography is the simplest and most widely used basis for organizing a sales force. Nearly all companies use it at some level in their sales organization. Some firms carry specialization based on geography through several organizational levels (see Fig. 11-9).

geographic specialization Sales organization in which selling personnel are given the responsibility for direct-selling activities in a given geographical area

According to *geographic specialization*, field sales personnel are given the responsibility for direct selling activities in a given geographical area, or territory. The sales representative is responsible for selling the firm's full line of products. Many firms prefer their field sales personnel to operate as territorial managers with complete responsibility for sales in given areas. Territories are treated as separate profit centers for purposes of analysis and for the evaluation of sales personnel.

Geographic specialization is the most commonly used method of sales organization. Its simplicity probably explains its popularity among sales executives. It also offers the advantages of adaptability and of improved coverage at the local level. Customer and product specialization approaches are usually more complex, and

FIGURE 11-9 Geographic Specialization in a Sales Force.

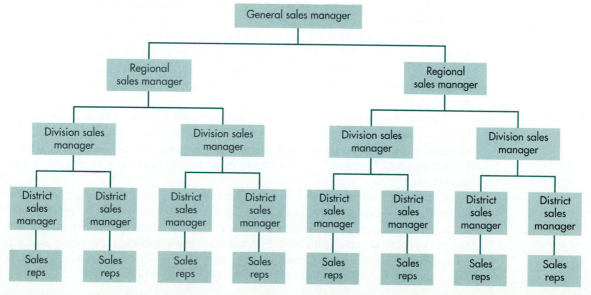

should only be used if their specific features are critical to the firm's sales effort. Even if the sales force uses them at higher levels, geographic specialization is common at the district and territorial levels in many sales organizations.

Campbell Soup Company reorganized its field force from a product line basis to a geographic basis in order to simplify its sales operations. Product-line division managers were eliminated, regional brand managers were added, and decision-making authority at all levels of the sales organization was increased. Prior to these changes, there was a Campbell sales manager and sales organzation for each product line, and some retail stores had as many as five Campbell salespeople calling on them. The revised organization was designed to lower sales costs and to provide better service to retailers.[8]

Customer Specialization

customer specialization Sales organization in which selling personnel are organized by particular customers or industries

Sales forces may be organized in terms of customers for various reasons, a concept referred to as *customer specialization*. The firm's customers may require a specialized knowledge of their industry. IBM is an example of a company that uses specialized sales forces for different classes of customers. Office equipment manufacturers often have sales specialists who deal only with educational institutions. Some textbook publishers have sales forces that specialize by discipline. One salesperson might handle only the behavioral sciences and humanities, while another might cover the physical sciences, mathematics, engineering, and business administration. The publishers that use this type of organization believe it allows them to serve their customers better because each salesperson is a specialist in the area he or she serves.

According to proponents of customer specialization, organizing around customers is necessary if the sales force is to focus on customers' needs and build the best possible relationships with clients. For example, U.S. West, one of the regional telecommunications companies created by the Bell System breakup, has created marketing and sales organizations that focus on specific groups of customers such as government and education services.[9]

Another company that has reorganized its sales force to concentrate on specific groups of customers is Joy Manufacturing. A producer of industrial fans for a number of industries, Joy was unsuccessful in its niche marketing strategy until it refocused the efforts of its sales force so that each individual called on specific market segments.[10]

Another factor leading to customer specialization in sales forces is that some industries exhibit significant geographical concentration. The petroleum, aircraft, and electronics industries are examples. In such cases, geographical sales specialization is meaningless. Customer specialization may be the best way to approach the marketplace.

Figure 11-10 shows several types of customer specialization arrangements. The approach can be implemented by industry, by distribution channel, or by general type of customers. Specialization by type of industry might be used by a manufacturer that has to deal with diverse industries. Specialization by distribution channel is useful if customers within the various channels have significantly different needs. For example, domestic consumers and export sales require specialized product and sales

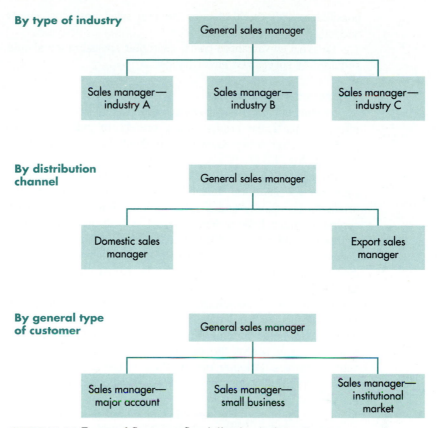

By type of industry

By distribution channel

By general type of customer

FIGURE 11-10 Forms of Customer Specialization in Sales Forces.

appeals. Finally, there is specialization by type of customers or markets in which the company operates. An office machine manufacturer, for example, might organize its sales force by major accounts, small business, and institutional markets. This topic will be covered in more detail in a later section.

Champion Products, a manufacturer of sports uniforms and athletic wear, had to restructure its sales force to serve different markets. For most of the company's history its sales personnel had sold to team coaches. This approach had alienated sporting goods stores, which meant Champion was not in a good position to profit from the recent fitness boom. The solution was to create two sales organizations, one to call on coaches and campus bookstores and the other to call on retail accounts.[11]

The primary disadvantage of customer specialization is that territories typically overlap. There may be three, four, or more of the company's sales representatives covering the same geographical area, but serving different clients. The result is often higher selling costs.

Another possible disadvantage of customer specialization is its lack of flexibility. Sales specialists in boom-bust industries such as computers, aerospace, chemicals, and oil cannot easily be redeployed in times of industry downturn. Even if it is possible to shift them to more general sales positions, costly retraining may be needed.[12]

To avoid unwarranted costs, customer specialization should be used only if it is required by specialized buyer needs.

Product Specialization

product specialization Sales organization in which selling personnel concentrate their efforts on particular product lines, brands, or individual items

Product specialization allows salespeople and sales managers to concentrate their efforts on particular product lines, brands, or individual items. In most cases, it implies that the entire sales force is divided by product groupings, such as those shown in Fig. 11-11.

Product specialization shares many of the advantages and disadvantages of customer specialization. In most cases, product sales specialists are used when a product's complexity limits other options. For example, marketers of mainframe computers must have product specialists who understand the specialized needs of customers and can use their detailed product knowledge to identify and develop specific applications. Also, because of the high dollar value of an installed sale, mainframe manufacturers can afford the higher costs associated with such specialists.[13]

The primary disadvantage of product specialization is that, in many cases, two or more salespeople from the same company call on the same customer. Although clients reap the advantage of the specialized knowledge provided by each salesperson, they may resent the extra time they must spend dealing with two vendor representatives. Another disadvantage is the expensive duplication of sales effort that results from having more than one salesperson operating in the same geographical locality.

These problems have caused some companies to reorganize away from product specialization. For instance, a large company's consumer products division went from fifteen separate product-oriented sales forces to a single national sales force. The sales organization was originally structured around the various plants producing the division's many products, ranging from peanut butter to turkeys, sausage, and other meat products. In addition to the fifteen separate sales forces, the division also used a network of food brokers to sell its products.

The new, unified sales organization provided that each account would deal with only one salesperson who represented the division's entire line of processed foods. The objective of the reorganization was to have a single sales representative call on a customer and take a consolidated order for all the division's products.

FIGURE 11-11 Sales Force Specialized by Product.

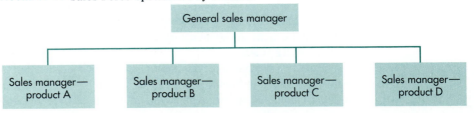

Although most sales forces organized along lines of product specialization have not undergone changes as dramatic as the one just described, the disadvantages described earlier have resulted in several modifications of this approach. For example, strict product specialization may not be practical in marginal geographical areas, which may require the use of individuals who sell the full line of a firm's products (see Fig. 11-12). Some firms prefer to use *manufacturers' representatives*, or brokers, in such regions. These are independent commissioned sales agents who sell for several manufacturers of noncompeting products. They are paid on commission, which means they represent variable selling costs to the firms whose products they sell. Manufacturers' representatives allow firms to obtain sales representation in sparsely populated, low-volume areas.

Some companies prefer to organize staff specialists who assist sales personnel according to product classification. In these instances, the sales force may be organized geographically or by customers, while the sales support personnel are organized by product groups. This is often used by companies that view sales planning, sales promotion, and advertising as product-related.

Product or brand managers are normally the terms used to describe these staff specialists who support specific product groups. Procter & Gamble, Pillsbury, General Mills, and many consumer goods companies use the product manager form of organization, along with large commercial banks and other service organizations. Even some industrial goods producers, such as Uniroyal, have accepted the product management concept.

Product managers are responsible for many aspects of product development, sales planning, and coordinating the total promotional package for a given product. This type of organization arrangement is shown in Fig. 11-13.

The advantage of this system is that it allows product specialization in the area where it is most often needed—sales support activities. At the same time, it avoids the duplication of sales effort that often accompanies strict product specialization.

Combination Organizations

Geographic, customer, and product specialization are the basic approaches to sales organization. But as earlier examples indicated, the structures of most sales

manufacturers' representatives Independent commercial sales agents who sell for several manufacturers of noncompeting products

product or brand managers Staff personnel who support specific product groups

FIGURE 11-12 Sales Force Employing Both Product Specialization and Full-Line Selling.

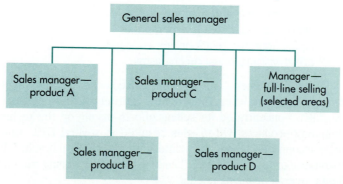

Key
—————— Line organization
– – – – Staff organization

FIGURE 11-13 **Use of Product Managers in the Sales Organization.**

forces combine two or more of them. An industrial product company may have separate sales forces for its two product lines: say, shears and fasteners. Each of these groupings may then be organized by geographcial location, such as by district or regional office. Finally, within each district, the salespeople may specialize by types of customers. Some may call on the canning industry, while others may concentrate on consumer products. This type of combined organizational structure is shown in Fig. 11-14.

Some of the most complex and difficult challenges are being confronted by high-tech companies. Traditional approaches to sales organization have not been effective in the rapidly changing, high-growth markets in which these firms compete. As a result, many high-tech companies are attempting to develop new organizational strategies. These new "combination organizations" can be characterized by the following traits:[14]

- Market, product, and function
- Decentralized staff and line personnel
- Complex staff-line relationships
- Overlaid organizational mechanisms

Digital Equipment Corporation (DEC), the world's second-largest computer company, provides an example of how high-tech firms are changing. Until a few years ago, DEC concentrated its selling efforts mainly on the technical end users of its computing products. Often, this resulted in several DEC salespeople calling on a single account, each handling a different product. As a result, DEC was relating to its customers on a sale-by-sale basis without developing an understanding of their clients' overall business needs.

PROCTER & GAMBLE

SALES MANAGE-MENT

"Team building" is synonymous with modern management. Sales organizations have promoted a team atmosphere, making efforts to realize the competitive gains and better customer service that team selling can bring.

Procter & Gamble (P&G) is no exception to this general trend. Traditionally organized on a product basis, the company's selling efforts suffered from the inefficiency caused by different salespeople calling on the same customers. To remedy this situation, salespeople and departmental specialists some time ago were consolidated into teams that worked together, so that fewer people were needed to visit customers.

Then recent changes in P&G's marketing strategy made team selling less advantageous. Most consumer goods giants such as P&G cater to retailers by offering them substantial volume discounts and co-op promotion dollars. Such incentives have proven extremely costly, however,

and P&G recently decided to replace this approach with an everyday low-pricing strategy. The plan is designed to stabilize demand and allow operations to run more smoothly. Team selling, which is helpful for complicated and/or relationship-oriented selling situations, is not as useful for this new, more straightforward approach.

In addition to the new marketing strategy, P&G also has a new chairman, Edwin Artzt. A firm believer in individual accountability, Artzt is changing the sales force's focus from relationship building to volume and profit building. Teams are not being eliminated, but team members are being given distinct responsibilities.

Artzt is seeking to find a middle ground for P&G's sales force. He is attempting to blend the advantages of team selling (efficiency, competitiveness) with the advantages of old-style product specialization (individual accountability). To achieve this balance, and to achieve it within a new marketing strategy and Artzt's own management style, would be a significant accomplishment.

FIGURE 11-14 Organizational Structure Employing All Three Approaches to Organizing Sales Forces: Organization by Product, Geography, and Customer.

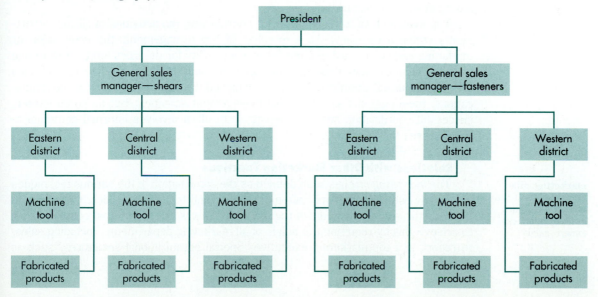

DEC's newly formed Industry Marketing Group is designed to resolve this problem. Each of the company's three industry marketing units has two key objectives: to provide DEC with an external, industry-oriented, customer viewpoint, and to communicate to customers that DEC understands their needs. Specialists with specific industry knowledge and/or experience provide the focus and coordination for DEC's relationship-building sales efforts.[15]

RELATIONS WITH OTHER DEPARTMENTS

A key concern for sales managers is the relations between their own and other departments. According to the marketing concept, all the activities of a business should be coordinated in order to satisfy customers' needs. Sales is the key link to customers, so coordinating the sales effort with other departments is absolutely essential.

There are two types of departments with which sales must have good working relationships. The first are those connected with other marketing activities— advertising, marketing research, sales promotion, product management, and so forth. The second are those with nonmarketing functions such as human resources, manufacturing, and finance. Substantial difficulties can arise if there is a breakdown in the coordination between sales and other departments. For example, a printer of bank checks developed a new style designed for the business customers of banks that were superior to the business checks provided by competitors. However, the new checks did not go over well at first. Why? Their designer failed to provide the company's sales force with adequate information about the competitive advantages of the checks. Since it is more difficult to sell a new product than to fill reorders for existing products, most of the field personnel did not push the new checks. Only after the national sales manager realized the advantages and explained them adequately to the sales force did its members begin to sell the checks. Of course, special selling incentives also helped.

Top management is responsible for coordinating the activities of all the departments within a company. As a member of top management, the chief sales or marketing executive must assume this responsibility for the sales force. A thorough understanding of other departments' functions, and how these relate to the sales effort, is required. Coordination may be achieved through policies, written communications, meetings, and similar formal management activities. But as noted earlier, successful coordination between departments often involves informal communications as well.

Relations with Other Marketing Functions

marketing mix
Combinations of the various techniques used to satisfy customers' needs

The *marketing mix* has been defined as the combination of the various techniques a company uses to satisfy its customers' needs and to stimulate sales. Coordination between the various elements of the marketing mix is essential. Most companies try to achieve this by requiring the heads of all marketing departments, including sales, to report to a top marketing executive. Special organizational structures, such as product management, are also used to coordinate sales with other marketing functions.

The relations between sales and advertising are of special concern. Both forms of promotion have the same purpose—to inform the public and persuade people to buy the company's products—and they often overlap. Thus sales managers must be aware of the advertising department's plans and activities so that sales activities can be complemented by advertising. For example, advertising may be a good source of sales leads, but there must be a procedure for informing salespeople of the inquiries generated by advertising.

There are many other ways by which sales and advertising can help one another. Salespeople who have daily customer contacts can provide feedback on advertising themes and media. They can also obtain dealers' support for cooperative advertising efforts. On the other hand, the advertising department can assist salespeople by developing sales aids, by helping to presell goods and services, and by generating sales inquiries.

Another key facet of the sales department's relations with other marketing functions involves the flow of information. Information obtained by marketing researchers can assist the sales force and, as discussed in Chap. 8, salespeople themselves are good sources of market and competitor information used in marketing planning and analysis. Product planners and managers also need information from the field sales force.

Relations with Nonmarketing Departments

The sales department must also work smoothly with the company's nonmarketing departments. The most critical are its relationships with research and development, production, human resources, and accounting and finance.

Research and Development.   Most companies now have a research and development (R&D) function. R&D may be organized as a separate staff department, or responsibility for it may be assigned to marketing or production. Regardless of its location within the company's departmental structure, its primary function is always the same—to perform basic research and engineering activities needed to develop new products and improve existing products.

The sales department can assist R&D efforts in two primary ways. First, salespeople are excellent sources of new product and product modification ideas. (Remember the boundary-spanning concept discussed in Chap. 1?) In addition, salespeople can serve as sounding boards for new product ideas. Field personnel have valuable insights into whether or not a new or revised product will meet customers' needs.

As noted earlier, the relationship between the sales force and the research and development function is crucial in high-tech firms. Field sales managers often find themselves dealing with several product development groups working out of their company's headquarters. Issues arise such as how headquarters staff should interact with field sales management and with final customers and whether salespeople should be trained in each product's technology. These have been termed "technical-marketing interface" issues.[16]

account control concept Idea from the high-tech sector which says that the authority and responsibility for handling the account rests with field sales management

To solve these problems, high-tech companies have developed what has been called the *account control concept*, in which the authority and responsibility for handling, or controlling, each account rests with field sales management. When specific technical product knowledge is needed, product specialists accompany salespeople. However, field sales still has overall responsibility for the sales effort.[17]

Production.　The production, or operations, function is concerned with preparing products for sale. Often there are conflicts between sales and production people. These usually result from misunderstandings about the roles and responsibilities of the two functions. Production executives tend to be concerned with minimizing costs through product standardization, long and continuous production runs, long production lead times, and so forth. On the other hand, sales executives want many types of products, frequent product changes, customer special orders, short production lead times, and so forth.

Joint planning is the best way to achieve cooperation between manufacturing and sales.[18] The sales department can assist manufacturing by providing realistic sales forecasts that take into consideration product changes and modifications. The forecasts provide the basis for determining which products to produce, the quantities and qualities needed, the production schedule to be followed, and the cost structure required to price the items competitively.

The critical way in which production helps sales is to provide technical knowledge. The check vendor example above illustrates the type of detailed knowledge salespeople need to be able to sell a product. The production department should provide information on special features and characteristics, manufacturing costs, product limitations, and delivery schedules.

Human Resources.　This department, sometimes also called the personnel department, is responsible for the people, or human resources, of an organization. The unique aspects of managing people who sell often lead to conflicts between sales and human resource managers. Some human resource departments do not understand the problems involved in managing people who are located away from the home office. As a result, they perform the routine sales personnel functions, such as recordkeeping, while the sales departments themselves handle the more complex tasks of selecting, training, and evaluating their own personnel.

However, sales managers often need to consult human resource specialists for guidance. For rapidly changing issues like affirmative action and occupational health and safety, a sales manager would be unwise not to seek advice from experts.

Accounting and Finance.　These functions are concerned with company funds. The three major areas of cooperation between sales, accounting, and finance are budgeting, cost control, and credit.

As described in Chap. 10, budgeting begins with the sales forecast. The sales department can provide short-range sales estimates to serve as the basis for financial

SALES MANAGEMENT IN PRACTICE

LOTUS DEVELOPMENT CORPORATION

In selling high-tech products, the relationship between sales and engineering is critical. The benefits of particular computer hardware and software, for example, are not immediately apparent; a product may be so cutting-edge or so complicated that extensive customer education is needed if its features are to be fully understood.

Lotus's Lotus Notes software package presented such a scenario. Although not hard to use, it was complicated from an engineering standpoint, and consumers had to be educated if all the benefits of the package were to be understood. The minimum price of Lotus Notes was $62,500, so organizational buyers did not take the purchase lightly.

Salespeople alone could not sell Lotus Notes; they simply were not qualified to explain its complex features to technically expert buyers. On the other hand, Lotus engineers were not necessarily very effective sellers. Since neither salespeople nor engineers could be all things to all people, the answer was clear: Technical expertise was involved in the selling process, and it was essential that technical competence and selling ability be melded in Lotus's customer education and sales effort. Engineers and salespeople would have to go on sales calls together.

Six teams made up of one representative each from both groups were formed, and specific compensation and incentive programs were developed. Although the compensation of both salespeople and engineers was tied in part to sales volume, pay for the former was more heavily commission-based. The salesperson's job was, after all, to sell; the engineer's job, although essential to the selling process, was education-oriented. The selling of Lotus Notes would not have been successful without this blending of two complementary sources of expertise.

---

planning and budgeting. Long-range sales forecasts are also needed to prepare plans for capital expenditures.

Accounting specialists can assist sales managers in their efforts to control costs by providing data for selling cost analyses. These data can be used to establish sales quotas, develop compensation plans, prepare pricing and discount structures, and monitor and control all forms of selling expenses. These topics will be covered in more detail in Chap. 20.

Finally, credit plans are a major concern for sales as well as accounting and finance. The sales department should not establish credit policies, since sales executives are usually more concerned with making sales than with collecting accounts. However, since credit terms are a key facet of selling, sales executives should have input into establishing credit policies. Salespeople can also provide current credit information about their customers and, in turn, receive credit information on prospects and customers prior to sales calls. Most importantly, everyone responsible for sales and credit needs to be in regular communication so that uniform credit guidelines are conveyed to all the firm's customers.[19]

MAJOR TRENDS IN SALES ORGANIZATIONS

The traditional forms of sales organization are undergoing careful scrutiny, as companies search for new and better ways to serve their markets. For consumer goods and service companies, the new approaches involve efforts to modify the product manager form of organization. Industrial manufacturers are looking closely at strategies that will help them adapt to changes in buying behavior and develop more specialized sales forces. For many firms the major challenge is to change from a product- to a customer-driven orientation.[20]

Further, important changes in industrial buying brought about by corporate mergers, acquisitions, and reorganizations (for example, the breakup of the Bell System and the subsequent restructuring of AT&T and the "baby bells"), by different kinds of corporate financing, by the increasing size and complexity of businesses, and by new environmental factors have changed industrial selling. Salespeople are expected to learn different skills, and the costs for this retraining as well as those associated with servicing industrial accounts have increased dramatically. Likewise, many sales organizations are faced with the need to downsize and restructure when they themselves are involved in mergers or acquisitions.[21]

Finally, increasing competition from international marketers has forced many firms to reconsider their sales structures. They have realized that they must complement high-cost direct sales forces with a more extensive range of distribution and sales options including direct mail, telemarketing, and electronic computer-to-computer selling.[22]

These changes in the selling environment and their implications for selling strategies and sales organizations were first identified by Benson Shapiro and John Wyman.[23] They noted that evolving sales communications approaches—national account management, demonstration centers, industrial stores, telemarketing, and new forms of catalog selling—"offer opportunities to improve the precision and impact of the marketing program, sometimes at great cost savings over the traditional methods."[24] To a large extent, the options suggested by Shapiro and Wyman have become part of the sales and marketing strategies of many companies. National account management and telemarketing in particular have had a dramatic impact on many sales strategies and organizations. In addition, many companies have turned to indirect sales channels as alternatives, or supplements, to direct selling.

Telemarketing

Telemarketing, or the use of telecommunications technology in personal selling, has been mentioned in earlier chapters. As technology has improved, so has the application of telecommunications to selling and sales management.[25] Telemarketing units are now part of most sales organizations. Sometimes they are set up as separate regions or divisions within the formal sales structure.

telemarketing Use of telecommunications technology in personal selling

As discussed in Chap. 7, the effective use of the telephone as a sales tool goes back to the early 1900s. However, only since the early 1960s have technological advances led to the widespread growth of telemarketing. It was in 1960 that AT&T introduced WATS (Wide Area Telephone Service), a bulk discounted call service. This provided the means for lower-cost long-distance calling, a stimulus for outbound calling. The introduction of 800-number inbound WATS telephone lines in 1967 provided the impetus for inbound telemarketing. Increased competition and deregulation over the last decade and a half have also stimulated technological changes and the growth of telemarketing.

At the same time, computer technology has also been undergoing significant change (see Chap. 7). The result has been a proliferation of microcomputers and minicomputers and the development of applications software to drive them. Combined with modern telecommunications systems, the new computer technology has led to automated telemarketing. Today most firms with large telemarketing operations support telemarketing sales representatives with systems that feature autodialers, screen prompting, and data-base access.

While the cost-effective technology of telemarketing was being developed, the costs of personal selling were increasing dramatically. For instance, it has been shown that a personal sales call can cost up to 30 times more than a telemarketing call.[26] Many companies can no longer justify the time and expense of servicing marginal accounts by field salespeople. In addition, sales managers began to recognize ways that telemarketing could assist and support field selling efforts.

As it has evolved, telemarketing is more than just using the telephone to sell. It has been defined as "a new marketing discipline that utilizes telecommunications technology as part of a well-planned, organized, and managed marketing program that prominently features the use of personal selling, using non face-to-face contacts."[27]

direct marketing
Marketing approach that bypasses intermediaries to deliver goods and services directly from seller to buyer

Modern telemarketing is part of a broader range of marketing tools and techniques known as *direct marketing*, an emerging form of promotion and distribution that combines elements of advertising and personal selling. Direct marketing bypasses intermediaries to deliver goods and services directly from seller to buyer. The greatest strength of direct marketing is its ability to deliver individual selling messages to specific prospects or customers at an affordable cost. The development and maintenance of a customer data base is the key to successful direct marketing.

Many forms and applications of telemarketing exist. Perhaps the easiest way to differentiate them is to distinguish between inbound and outbound telemarketing. The basis for these terms is the party who actually makes the call; the prospect contacting the company (*inbound telemarketing*) or the salesperson contacting the prospect (*outbound telemarketing*). Order processing, which is the least complex of telemarketing applications, is usually accomplished through inbound telemarketing. A somewhat more complex application of inbound telemarketing is customer service. By contrast, outbound telemarketing includes lead generation, call scheduling for field sales representatives, and various followup activities. In some cases, outbound telemarketing involves the total selling process—initiating and completing all sales activities by telephone.

inbound telemarketing
Telemarketing efforts in which potential customers contact the selling company

outbound telemarketing
Telemarketing efforts in which the selling company contacts prospects and customers

Sales executives are primarily interested in telemarketing for two reasons. First, a firm's telemarketing manager is most likely to report to the sales vice president or manager, and sales and/or marketing executives will have the greatest influence on telemarketing activities and programs.[28] Most importantly, however, is the growing recognition that telemarketing has become an important aspect of selling strategy. Sales managers must understand the various roles of telemarketing in selling strategy and how to manage the interrelationship between telemarketing and face-to-face salespeople.[29]

Although the use of telemarketing has grown rapidly in industrial sales organizations, many sales and marketing executives have not yet learned how to successfully apply this tool.[30] In particular, a key sales management issue is how to coordinate telemarketing with the field sales force. For example, in a study of one firm's telemarketing and field sales forces, it was observed that telemarketers often feel they are perceived as inferior to field salespeople. In contrast, many field salespeople feel threatened by telemarketing.[31] These perceptions and concerns must be dealt with by sales managers.

A telemarketing job classification scheme is shown in Table 11-1. This conceptual framework defines the four major telemarketing job types. The prospector job type was cited above as an example of outbound telemarketing. The customer relations aspects of telemarketing were discussed as part of both inbound and outbound telemarketing. So let us turn our attention to the account manager and backup sales types of jobs.

Account managers perform all stages of the selling process in the same way as field sales personnel. Many large industrial marketers, such as A.B. Dick, IBM, 3M, and Xerox, use telemarketing to reach and sell to small or marginal accounts or to sell specific products, such as copying paper and other office supplies.[32] Some business-to-business marketers have gone so far as to conduct all their sales efforts by telemarketing. Ellett Brothers, a South Carolina distributor of sporting goods, began its telemarketing program as a supplement to field sales. Management soon discovered that telemarketing sales representatives were more effective than the company's field salespeople. Today all of Ellett Brothers' sales efforts are conducted by telephone, and the company's sales are nearly sixty times what they were at the time telemarketing was initiated.

In terms of sales backup, many companies use telemarketing to support the field sales force. For example, Amoco established a telemarketing unit to assist its field salespeople to sell tires, batteries, and accessories (TBA) to its service stations. Field sales representatives had paid little attention to these products, since their major concern was selling gasoline. The telemarketing unit has increased TBA sales and has lowered selling costs. In addition, Amoco's sales representatives have time to take on more of a consulting role with dealers since the telemarketers handle the order taking and other supportive activities.[33]

TABLE 11-1   Telemarketing Job Types

Job Type	Major Job Activities
1. Account manager	Account responsibility Post-sales service Order taking Problem solving
2. Prospector	Prospecting
3. Backup	Field sales support
4. Customer relations specialist	Information transfer Handling complaints/inquiries Conducting research Promotion inquiries (1-800 numbers) Customer service

The above applications and examples indicate telemarketing's potential. In some cases, such as selling to marginal accounts, telemarketing may be the only way to profitably serve a particular market segment. However, using telemarketing with a firm's largest accounts may be counterproductive, especially if competitors are willing to invest in a national account team of field sales personnel. The nature of some products, such as journal subscriptions and low-cost office supplies, may also determine where telemarketing can fit into a firm's marketing mix.

National Account Management

This approach has been developed because companies have recognized that a few large accounts comprise a disproportionately large percentage of their sales. In some industries, sales to major customers represent 25 to 40 percent of company revenues.[34] Known also as "key account" or "major account" marketing, national account management involves sales teams that combine both sales generalists and specialists. AT&T, IBM, and Pitney Bowes are among the companies that have established national account programs.[35]

national account management
Special sales force dedicated to obtaining and/or maintaining large accounts

The concept of *national account management* is relatively simple. A special sales force is dedicated to obtaining and/or maintaining major accounts. A national, or major, account is defined by Jerome Colletti and Gary Tubridy as follows:[36]

- A customer that involves several people in the buying process before a sale takes place
- A customer that purchases in significant volume, both in absolute dollars and as a percentage of a supplier's total sales
- A customer that buys centrally for a number of geographically dispersed organizational units
- A customer that desires a long-term, cooperative working relationship with the supplier
- A customer that expects specialized attention and service

To meet the unique demands of national accounts, a national account manager is responsible for coordinating the efforts of a sales and support team to serve their needs. This may involve people who work in other divisions of the selling company or in other functional areas. Most companies view their national account managers as coordinators of sales, support, and operations personnel who report to different profit centers or divisions. However, some companies give national account managers line authority over large, dispersed sales and support teams. In fact, some firms have gone so far as to create separate manufacturing operations for selected national accounts, with the national account team serving as the profit center.[37]

Eastman Kodak's national account management group, which was established in 1984, is an example of a support organization. Known as the corporate accounts organization, it is not a profit center and does not compete with Kodak's business units in any respect. In fact, Kodak's business units have their own national account organizations. As described by Kodak's Director of Corporate Accounts:[38] "Our role is to assist the business units and make it easier for our corporate customers to have an enhanced business relationship with Kodak." Within Kodak's corporate accounts organization, account executives are assigned to specific accounts and given world-wide responsibilities for them.

As with telemarketing, a major challenge of developing and managing a national account management program is coordinating it with the rest of the sales effort. The sales structure of Pitney Bowes' U.S. business systems' sales force is illustrative of the approach many firms use. Approximately fifty national account managers sell to Pitney Bowes' four hundred largest customers. About one hundred senior sales representatives call on fifteen hundred multilocation customers that have centralized purchasing. All of the firm's other customers (approximately a million) are served by the remaining thirty-five hundred area sales representatives who cover the full line of Pitney Bowes' mailing and copier products. When justified by sales potential and economics, sales representatives are supported by specialists in copier, inserter, advanced weighing, or shipping applications. In addition, full-time managers also assist trainee sales reps.[39]

Indirect Sales Channels

indirect sales channels Independent sales representatives or agencies used by a company in place of its own field sales force

In some instances, sales managers are replacing their own direct sales forces with dealers, agents, brokers, or manufacturer's reps, the so-called *indirect sales channels*. IBM's decision to use agents and independent retailers to sell its personal computers is an example. Throughout most of its history IBM relied totally on its own sales force to sell its products, from giant mainframe computers to typewriters. However, because the company's minicomputers and microcomputers had smaller profit margins, selling them through its own sales personnel did not meet the firm's profit objectives. Further, in too many cases, even IBM's mainframe computer salespeople were spending their time selling low-margin products. Finally, the company's sales force was not able to serve small-business customers that were geographically dispersed and did not require large amounts or large pieces of equipment. In 1981 IBM began to change its sales approach, and by 1985 a full 10 percent of its sales volume was generated by agents and independent retailers.[40]

As the IBM example suggests, independent sales representatives or agencies are often viable alternatives to a firm fielding its own direct sales force. This is particularly true for small companies with limited resources. Independent representatives are frequently less costly than a direct sales force and enable a company to realize an advantageous "fixed-cost-to-sales ratio."[41] Independent reps are also an effective, low-cost way to open up new markets, since they have established contacts in local market areas.[42] In addition, many of them can offer marketers long-term customer relationships, in-depth territory knowledge, and community goodwill not easily acquired by a company on its own.

When a manufacturer relies on independent reps, however, it relinquishes some degree of control over the selling process. Independent agents follow their own rules about what to sell, how to sell, when and how to service customers, and so forth. The sales manager who decides to use independent reps must understand what they can and cannot do and what must be done to select, train, and support them.[43]

Recruiting and selecting independent reps poses special problems because they are established businesspersons rather than individual job applicants. Not all independent reps are good or professional, and some that are good may not be appropriate for a specific product line.[44] Even if excellent independent reps are selected, strong efforts are required to make the relationship work. According to the owner of one agency, "more than anything else, respect, support, and a team relationship—not an adversarial one" is what reps expect.[45]

EVALUATING THE SALES ORGANIZATION

The effective organization of a sales force relies on many of the concepts and principles common to the organizational effort in any functional area. A sales organization must provide for a reasonable span of control for each management position. Responsibility for performing a sales management task must carry with it the authority to take the actions necessary to accomplish the particular goal. The sales organization should be built around activities, rather than around the specific people involved in the activities.

It is essential, however, to understand that both people and structure influence organization effectiveness. Statements such as "ABC Enterprises is a good organization" reflect this truth. What is really meant is that ABC Enterprises is represented by good people. The structural aspects of the organization may in fact be very weak. The reverse is also true: Many difficulties attributed to organizational problems can instead be people-related.

People who work for an organization influence its structure. Owners influence small business situations, and top management influences the structure that exists in larger firms. The most complex problem faced by those who attempt to assess structural effectiveness is to account for the human factor.

The key to evaluating organizational effectiveness successfully is to be able to define what one wants the organizational structure to accomplish. In other words, what are the organization's goals and objectives? Is it sales maximization? Lowest operating cost? Increased market share? The problem then becomes whether or not the organization is flexible enough to satisfy these objectives. The answer can emerge only after careful study and analysis by sales management.

SUMMARY OF LEARNING GOALS

1. **List the Major Tasks of the Sales Organization.**

   Major tasks of the sales organization are maintaining order in achieving sales force goals and objectives, assigning specific tasks and responsibilities, and integrating and coordinating the sales force with other elements of the firm.

2. **Outline the Primary Organizational Issues That Need To Be Addressed When Setting Up a Sales Organization.**

   The sales manager must recognize and deal with the basic issues of formal and informal organization, horizontal and vertical organization, centralized and decentralized organization, line and staff components of the organization, and size of the company. The way these issues are resolved will have a profound impact on the way the organizational structure eventually emerges.

3. **Identify the Basic Types of Sales Organization.**

   Sales organization can be divided into geographic, customer, or product lines, or some combination involving more than one of these approaches. Each format has its own advantages and disadvantages.

4. **Understand the Importance of Maintaining Effective Liaison between the Sales Organization and Other Units of the Company.**

   Since the sales force is a company's key link to its customers, it is essential that sales managers maintain coordination between their own and other departments, both marketing and nonmarketing. The nonmarketing units that are especially crucial to sales are research and development, production, human resources, and accounting and finance.

5. **Discuss the Major Organizational Trends That Impact on Sales Management.**

   There are three major organizational trends that directly influence sales management in terms of both people and structure: telemarketing, national account management, and indirect sales channels. Telemarketing refers to the use of telecommunications technology in personal selling. National account management is a special sales force dedicated to obtaining and/or maintaining large accounts. Finally, indirect sales channels refer to the use of independent sales representatives or agencies by a company instead of its own field sales force.

REVIEW QUESTIONS

1. What are the major tasks of a sales organization? Define structure.
2. Compare and contrast formal and informal organization. How is each formed? Is the grapevine valuable to the organization?
3. What is span of control? How does it determine whether a vertical or horizontal organizational structure should be used?
4. What is the relationship between centralization and company size? How is a discrepancy between responsibility and authority a problem for decentralized organizations?
5. Describe how the selling function is supported by advertising and sales promotion, marketing research and sales planning, in-house sales correspondents, and distribution, credit, and maintenance. Which of these is a line component? A staff component?
6. Under what conditions is geographic specialization an appropriate way to organize a sales force? When are customer specialization and product line specialization appropriate choices?
7. How can companies encourage communication between sales and other marketing departments? Do sales personnel have conflicts with other departments? Explain.
8. Differentiate between inbound and outbound telemarketing. What is the role of telemarketing in the overall sales effort?
9. What is meant by national account management? Cite examples of firms that use this concept in their sales organizations.
10. Give some examples of different types of indirect salespeople. What are the advantages of such indirect sales channels?

DISCUSSION QUESTIONS

1. Peter Drucker envisioned the "information-based organization." Do you see evidence of his predictions in the organizational trends discussed in this chapter or in any organizations you have been involved with?

2. Interview a sales manager about his or her sales organization. Describe how the manager's sales force is organized. Try to find out why it is organized in this format.

3. What experience have you had with the grapevine of any organization? Was the grapevine more accurate or less accurate than more official sources of information?

4. Interview a salesperson and their interface in another department or unit. Ask each to describe a situation in which conflicting goals caused problems between the salesperson and employees in the other department.

5. Describe your most recent experience with telemarketing. Did it involve inbound or outbound telecommunications? Was this telemarketing effort effective? Why or why not?

ETHICAL DILEMMA

As described in this chapter, many companies have implemented national account management programs. Large customers, known as key or national accounts, are assigned to senior salespeople. Often these national accounts have been taken away from salespeople who have serviced and developed them for several years. How should a firm compensate salespeople for the loss of large customers?

SALES MANAGEMENT CASE

Telemarketing—Better Than License Plates?

Look in the classified advertising section of a local newspaper, and chances are that there will be several jobs available for telemarketers. Many companies operate with an ongoing shortage of them. Companies also have a greater need for them at peak selling times. In either circumstance, some companies, including Best Western, Super Valu stores, and TWA, are going to an unusual source to find telemarketers: state prisons.

The way businesses use inmate telemarketers sounds more like a government-sponsored prisoner reform program than a private business endeavor. Typically prisoners are paid the same as the companies' other telemarketers and are allowed to participate in the same incentive programs. A certain amount of inmate income, usually 25 to 30 percent, goes to pay for room and board at the prison. In some cases, inmates are required to send money home to dependents or to donate a percentage of their paychecks to funds such as those to help crime victims.

Beyond these deductions and after normal taxes, the prisoners are allowed to keep the rest of the money they earn.

Inmate telemarketing benefits companies whose selling efforts might otherwise suffer from a shortage of labor. Inmates earn an income and learn a skill, and upon their release many are hired by the companies for which they did the telemarketing in prison. Government and taxpayers alike benefit from the various deductions taken out of inmate paychecks. And the programs seem to cause no concern among consumers; most of those contacted never know that the person on the other end of the line is a convict. If asked from where they are calling, the inmates are instructed to give a noncommittal answer like "Chicago."

Currently, about five thousand prisoners in the United States work for private companies, and that number is expected to increase. It is hard to find fault with these programs, which provide so many benefits for so many people.

Questions

1. Do you think a company should conceal the fact that it employs prison inmates as telemarketers? Why or why not?

2. Discuss activities or personality traits associated with certain types of criminals that, if properly channeled, would make a good salesperson.

In what ways would a telemarketing department made up of prison inmates be easier to manage than a sales force made up of regular employees? What problems would sales managers face in using this labor source?

CHAPTER 12

SALES PERSONNEL PLANNING AND RECRUITING

LEARNING GOALS

- Identify the three major steps in the sales force staffing process.
- Explain how a firm can determine its optimum sales force size.
- Describe how job descriptions are developed and used in sales management.
- Relate job descriptions to job qualifications.
- Discuss the need for planning and coordination in sales force recruiting.
- Identify the various sources of sales recruits.
- List problem areas related to equal employment opportunity and suggest procedures for recruiting women and minorities.

ATTRACTING THE RIGHT PEOPLE

Advantage Refreshment Systems, Inc. (ARS), which leases food and beverage vending machines, recruits a special kind of salesperson. Vending machines are leased to companies' middle managers, and it is ARS policy that deals can be closed only in the presence of the buying company's president. The ARS selling job therefore requires an ability to develop a rapport with managers so they become allies in a joint effort to sell company presidents on leasing ARS products.

ARS became focused on recruiting in 1986, when the company found it was having difficulty attracting the kind of smooth, confident salespeople capable of achieving this rapport in their sales calls. The firm had to become more creative in its recruiting ef-

forts. This meant it had to provide significant incentives to lure the type of people it wanted to join its sales force, and then provide the training necessary so they could succeed in meeting the company's sales goals.

ARS devised a deal that was very attractive to salespeople. First, the company rewarded them immediately in cash upon signing up customers to lease vending machines. Second, it gave them a stake in the company's success through franchising. Third, it offered them residual income from continuing leases. Finally, it gave them the freedom to do nothing but sell. ARS assumed all the administrative burdens.

The company also trained them in a specific selling strategy geared toward its products. While based on fundamental selling ideas, this strategy emphasized the basic principles behind the ARS corporate selling philosophy.[1]

Good recruiting practices can mean the difference between a company's making it or not making it. In Chap. 12, you will learn how sales managers should approach the recruiting process. In analyzing personnel needs, recruiting candidates, and selecting applicants, effective sales managers continually seek to draw the best employees from a competitive labor pool.

CHAPTER OVERVIEW

Sales managers are only as good as the salespeople reporting to them. Staffing is the crucial first step in building an effective sales organization. The success of any sales force hinges on how well this task is performed. The sales manager must be both a good salesperson (recruiter) for the company and a good judge (selector) of the ability or potential of new hires. A systematic approach for recruiting and selecting salespeople includes three major steps: (1) analyzing sales personnel needs, (2) recruiting sales candidates, and (3) screening and selecting applicants.

Sales personnel planning involves two important activities: determining the number of salespeople required, and identifying the type of personnel desired. A realistic understanding of both needs enables management to develop recruitment, selection, and training programs that will make optimum use of the company's existing sales force and meet the sales organization's human resource needs of the future. *Recruiting* involves identifying potential salespeople and attracting them to the company. Managers must be aware of the best sources for sales recruits. They must cultivate these sources through personal and indirect recruiting techniques. *Screening* is a negative process of elimination. Unqualified and undesirable applicants are weeded out until only qualified candidates remain. *Selection* is the positive process of choosing the particular people desired from this group of qualified candidates.

recruiting Identifying potential salespeople and attracting them to the firm

screening Negative process of eliminating unqualified and undesirable sales job applicants until only qualified candidates remain

selection Positive process of choosing from among a group of qualified sales applicants

This chapter will examine the planning and recruiting aspects of the staffing process. In addition, it will discuss the important topic of equal employment opportunity. The screening and selection aspects will be covered in Chap. 13.

ANALYZING SALES PERSONNEL NEEDS

Like most labor pools, the availability of sale personnel fluctuates somewhat with economic conditions. As a result, there is a need for thorough sales personnel planning. A hiring mistake can cost companies between $40,000 and $50,000 in recruiting, selection, and training expenses.[2] At that rate, they cannot afford to make too many such mistakes. Careful planning can help avoid hiring more salespeople than needed, or hiring the wrong kind of personnel.

Timing is also important in the staffing process. Those in charge of hiring should be able to forecast the company's needs for salespeople well in advance of the time they will be required. Applicants must also be hired in plenty of time to provide them with the proper training.

Another concern relates to the recruitment approach. Those doing the hiring often need to convince young people that a sales career presents attractive opportunities. This is especially the case in regard to college students, whom more and more companies want to hire but whose education often points them in another direction. One of sales management's greatest challenges is to convince qualified candidates—regardless of gender or race—that selling is an attractive professional career field.

QUANTITATIVE REQUIREMENTS USED IN SALES PERSONNEL PLANNING

Chapter 11 dealt with organizational issues of sales forces. Another critical question for sales and marketing managers is the size of the sales force a company needs. Traditionally, scant attention has been paid to this matter. Field sales forces are often expanded or contracted with minimal evaluation on the part of sales management. Smaller firms, for example, are often grossly understaffed, and some large firms are overstaffed in their sales positions beyond the point of economic feasibility.

Sales force size is crucial to companies in two ways. First, it establishes the total level of selling effort available to the sales organization.[3] Second, it is a prime determinant of sales organization structure. The discussion of span of control in Chap. 11 pointed out that larger field sales forces require more levels of sales management.

Determining Sales Force Size

marginal analysis
Approach that compares the cost of the last salesperson hired to the profit that will be obtained from that individual to determine the optimum size for a company's sales force

One of the oldest and best-known methods for determining sales force size was developed by Walter Semlow.[4] This so-called *marginal analysis* adds salespeople until the cost of adding the last additional person equals the profit of the sales volume the person is expected to produce. Semlow expressed his approach in a simple formula:

$$S(p) - C = 0$$

where S = sales volume that each additional salesperson is expected to produce
p = the expected profit margin on the sales volume
C = the total cost of maintaining the salesperson in the field

If new salespeople were expected to achieve a \$240,000 sales volume each with a 15 percent profit margin, then the firm should continue to hire sales personnel up to the point at which the cost of maintaining each salesperson in the field (including salary) was equal to \$36,000. Sales force expansion beyond this point would be unprofitable.

A company's accounting records provide the necessary information about its profit margin on each dollar of added sales volume and the total cost of maintaining a salesperson in the field. But estimates of sales volume that an additional salesperson would produce must be based upon a sales manager's judgment. This is a potential weakness of the marginal analysis approach.

incremental approach Term used to describe collectively the quantitative approaches that can be used to determine optimum sales force size

More recently, various quantitative methods for determining sales force size have been developed. These have been called collectively the *incremental approach.*[5] They are similar to Semlow's method in that they compare the marginal profit contribution for each additional, or incremental, salesperson to the marginal costs associated with that person. But they also often provide a format for designing sales territories.[6] Another model combines determining sales force size with allocating sales effort to particular products and various market segments.[7] Unfortunately, these methods are complex and the relationships they deal with difficult to develop.

Predicting Sales Personnel Needs

Since sales force size is so important, we now describe in more detail an objective approach that can help sales managers predict the personnel needs of their organization. The procedure starts with the estimation of the number of salespeople needed.

Sales Personnel Needed.   Any forecast of sales personnel needs must rest upon a factual base. The most useful base is a reasonably accurate projection of the firm's long-range sales. Usually, a five- or ten-year forecast is an appropriate planning base.

trend analysis Projection of historical data into the future

Trend analysis is a technique that can be used to predict sales personnel needs.[8] Historical data relevant to sales personnel requirements are obtained from company records, and significant trends are identified and projected into the future. The sales personnel forecast is derived from the projected trend.

To illustrate this technique, suppose that Dexter Company has collected data on its sales and the number of its sales representatives over the last twenty years. The relationship between these two sets of data can be determined mathematically or graphically. Figure 12-1 shows the graphical relationship. By projecting the trend line, management can derive the sales personnel requirements for future sales levels. For example, if sales are expected to be $150 million, 600 salespeople will be required.

A similar approach is to compute the sales-per-salesperson ratio and project this trend. Suppose Dexter Company now employs 400 representatives and has sales of $100 million. The current sales/salesperson ratio is $250,000 ($100 million/400 salespersons). The company predicts sales of $150 million at the end of a 5-year planning period. An approximation of the number of sales personnel that the firm will require at the end of 5 years is 600 ($150 million/$250,000).

Trend analysis has two major weaknesses. One is that it assumes operating conditions will remain the same in the future as they were in the past. This may be unrealistic in today's fast-changing business world. Personnel requirements are affected by increases in productivity, by the introduction of new products, by promotional strategy shifts, and by other changes in marketing policy. Also, trend analysis assumes a linear relationship between sales force size and sales generated. This linearity is not necessarily accurate.

For example, suppose that Dexter's management decides to increase the advertising support given the sales force because it expects this to improve the sales-per-salesperson ratio by 2 percent per year. If this happens, sales per representative will be approximately $275,000 in 5 years. When this is divided into $150 million, the revised estimate of salespersons needed is 545.

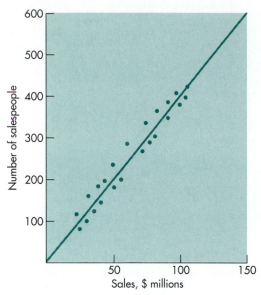

FIGURE 12-1 Using Trend Analysis to Predict Sales Personnel Needs.

Sales Personnel Available.   Next the sales planner must determine how many salespeople will be available within the firm. The starting point for this task is a comprehensive inventory of current sales personnel. A person-by-person approach is recommended, in which the abilities, promotability, and retirement status of each salesperson are determined. The losses of staff that will occur are highlighted in this way. The task has been simplified in recent years by the introduction of computerized payroll and personnel coding systems.

Trend analysis can also be used to predict the number of salespeople available at some future date. Here too historical data on the retirement, turnover, and promotion rates of current salespeople are assembled. Then a total loss rate is calculated and projected into the future.

Assume that Dexter Company's total loss rate is computed as 5 percent a year. If no interim hiring is done, the company will have slightly more than three-fourths (311) of its original sales force available in 5 years. This year-by-year loss is shown in Fig. 12-2.

The final step is to compare the available sales personnel with the forecast need for salespeople. To achieve its sales goal of $150 million in 5 years, Dexter Company will need an additional 234 sales reps assuming that the new advertising support policy is implemented and the annual loss rate of 5 percent continues.

Other Factors.   Other factors may also modify the number of salespeople needed. Changes in company promotion policies, retirement plans, and transfer procedures will affect sales personnel planning. For example, if a company stresses maximum promotion from within, planners must make sure there are qualified salespersons who can be upgraded to management positions. They must also take this policy into consideration when estimating the potential sales personnel available.

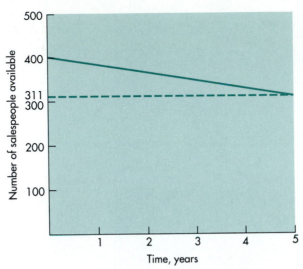

FIGURE 12-2 Using the Total Loss Rate to Predict the Number of Salespeople Available at Some Future Date.

Economic conditions facing sellers and potential buyers are also important. An industry that has gone through a period of consolidation may require fewer sales personnel; similarly, tough economic times may mean buyers suspend their purchase of certain items, which again will impact on the number of sales personnel a vendor requires.

Other factors must also be considered. These include the overall level of economic activity, the situation vis-à-vis competitors, labor relations, and government economic policies. Suppose, for example, that a major competitor decides to double its sales force. It is quite likely that other firms in the same industry will lose experienced people if the competitor offers higher salaries.

QUALITATIVE REQUIREMENTS USED IN SALES PERSONNEL PLANNING

A second task of sales personnel planning is to determine the type of salesperson desired. This involves three activities: (1) job analysis, (2) preparation of a job description, and (3) identification of job qualifications.

Job Analysis

job analysis Study and written summary of a specific sales job

The first step in determining the type of salesperson desired is *job analysis*—a careful, objective study and written summary of the selling job in question. Company records, direct field observation, and other supporting information (such as government statistics and trade association studies) may be used to assess the sales job in terms of a variety of critical issues.

Environmental Factors.   What is the nature and extent of the competition salespeople will encounter? What are the general business conditions? What industry structures and practices must be taken into account, such as traditional channels of distribution and industry credit policies? In short, what is the business and social framework within which salespeople will have to sell and in which their work will be supervised and evaluated?

Performance Factors.   How do salespeople currently spend most of their time—traveling, selling, filling out reports, securing sales promotion support, waiting around for appointments, and/or entertaining? What specific selling functions do they perform? How much time do they spend on each function and activity? On what factors will they be judged? Regardless of how this is finally summarized, it amounts to a time-and-motion study, much like those used in a plant to study the performance of production workers. When completed, it shows in detail just how salespeople spend their time.

A large western liquor wholesaler handles this part of the job analysis process particularly well. In its annual review of sales force performance, the wholesaler sends several specially trained supervisors into the field for two days with its sales personnel. Each supervisor notes on a carefully designed form everything that his or her sample of salespeople do, along with approximate time required for each activity. These reports are summarized at headquarters and the results compared to the existing sales job descriptions. This process keeps the descriptions current with environmental and market changes.

critical analysis
Study of how a salesperson should be spending his or her time

Critical Analysis.   The last stage in the job study is the *critical analysis* of how salespeople should be spending their time. Should they continue performing the functions they are currently performing? Should they continue to place the same relative emphasis on the various functions? Are they dealing effectively with competitor and environmental factors? Should they be doing more, less, or the same amount of entertaining? By critically analyzing all the performance and environmental factors affecting each sales job in an objective, careful way, management develops a meaningful understanding of what the selling job should be.

Job Description

job description
Statement of the specific functions a salesperson must perform

A systematic job analysis allows the sales manager to prepare a detailed, written *job description,* which is a statement of the specific functions the salesperson must perform that includes guidelines about the relative importance of each function.

The job description provides the focal point for the hiring process. It is the basis for preparing job application forms, interview forms, appropriate psychological tests, and other selection tools. When these tools are not used, sales managers tend to hire people who reflect their own abilities and qualifications. They also tend to hire on the basis of a single outstanding physical, mental, or personality trait to the exclusion of other important considerations.

A detailed job description will save both the company and job applicants time and money. Some applicants will eliminate themselves if the job description and their own expectations do not coincide. A comprehensive description also provides the sales manager with a good understanding of what to look for in applicants. This saves time in preparing for interviews, and often results in more organized interviews.[9]

A good sales job description is also important in other aspects of sales management. Without one, it is difficult, if not impossible, to do a good job of training and motivating salespeople, to assign salespeople to territories, or to plan effective marketing strategy. Job descriptions are also the key to a good sales evaluation program.

To summarize, the sales job description specifies the following:

1. The precise components of the sales job: the functions or specific activities that the seller must perform, such as prospecting for new customers, traveling, selling, setting up displays, providing service assistance, and filling out reports.
2. The ideal or desired division of the salesperson's time between each function: how the rep should divide efforts among the job's many activities, stated in measurable, relative terms.

Characteristics of a Good Job Description

A good job description has five important features. It must be (1) in written form, (2) accepted, (3) specific, (4) inclusive, and (5) detailed, but terse.

Written Form.   A job description must be committed to paper. Informal, verbal job descriptions are virtually useless in managing salespeople, and often lead to misunderstandings and friction. In short, job descriptions that are not written out are usually worse than no job description at all.

Accepted.   To be of any use at all in its many applications to sales management, a job description must be understood and accepted by salespeople, their immediate managers, and other sales executives. Unless the job description is agreed to by everyone affected by it, problems will result when it is used in any of its applications—selecting personnel, training hirees, or evaluating job performance. A situation where each sales representative and each manager formulates and acts upon his or her own private understanding of the job and the relative priorities of its various functions must be avoided.

Specific.   The job description must be specific. It must not be vague or general in delineating the various sales functions the job encompasses or the relative emphasis that should be placed on each function. Task coverage must be defined in measurable terms, such as number of calls per day, dollars brought in or units sold per fiscal period, number of displays set up, or number of new accounts opened. An example of the kind of statement that is too vague and general to be of use is the following: "An important part of our salesperson's job is to make regular calls on the trade." No one except the original writer can know what is meant by "important," "regular," or "call." An example of a better description might read as follows:

> Our sales reps must call on Class A customers 50 times a year; on Class B customers, 25 times a year; and on Class C customers, as frequently as their duties allow. Our salespeople do not call at all on Class D customers, who are serviced entirely through wholesalers. Each class of customers is established by dollar volume with Class A being. . . .

Inclusive.   To be useful in the management of the sales force, the job description must be inclusive. It must identify and furnish priorities for all the functions the salespeople are required to perform. Nothing can be overlooked or assumed to be evident. If opening new accounts, or controlling expenses, or maintaining a certain average order size are important, the job description should specifically identify them as such. Part of the inclusiveness involves the use of effective measures or standards of performance for all important functions, such as an average of new accounts to be opened or the amount of dollar sales expected per week or month, or the dollar range for average order size.

The need for job description inclusiveness places a high premium on the careful study of the sales job in the first stage of its development, and on the later careful study of the effect the job description has on sales performance in case revision is needed.

Detailed, But Terse.   The job description must be detailed, but terse. One that is too brief will be so generalized that it is useless for management purposes. The first example above is an illustration of this. It describes the sales function in very few words, but it says nothing that can be used in managing salespeople.

At the other extremes, there are job descriptions that includes too much detail. In these cases, the sales functions are analyzed so minutely that it is difficult, or impossible, for salespeople or managers to use them. Job descriptions must be only as detailed and specific as is absolutely necessary to serve as effective management tools and to show salespeople what is expected of them.

In summary, a job description should be a realistic and detailed statement of the salesperson's job functions. It is a profile of the sales job, highlighting the functions one must perform and the amount of time, effort, attention, and emphasis one should place on each activity. A good job description for a sales representative is shown in Fig. 12-3.

Job Qualifications

Once the job description has been prepared, it serves as the basis for identifying *job qualifications*—the characteristics or traits that one looks for when recruiting and hiring sales candidates. Selection of these criteria is difficult, because there is no clear-cut agreement on what are the best qualities for selling.

Profiling, a technique that sales managers can use to identify desired job qualifications, sets up a skill profile, or composite of traits, skills, and characteristics of the top achievers in a sales organization.[10] The profile provides a checklist, or benchmark, with which to evaluate sales job candidates. By comparing the qualification of each candidate with the qualities of the organization's best salespeople, the sales manager can avoid hiring decisions based only on subjective criteria and hunches.

Much research has gone into determining specific personality factors that contribute to sales success. One study of the pharmaceuticals industry suggested that successful pharmaceutical salespeople are warm in manner, outgoing, and cooperative in attitude. It also found them to be empathetic toward the needs of others,

job qualifications Characteristics or traits one looks for when recruiting or hiring sales candidates

profiling A benchmark technique used to evaluate sales candidates; comparison of their qualifications versus those of the firm's top sales producers

TITLE:	Sales Representative/ Senior Sales Representative
REPORTS TO:	Regional Manager
PRIMARY DUTIES:	Sells division products to customers in assigned territory. In addition to selling product line, provides customer service, managing assigned territory/customers as a business. Is a source of data to the marketing organization. Receives assistance from the division as a member of the field "selling team."
DESCRIPTION OF DETAILS:	Identifies and interprets customer's requirements, shaping these requirements to fit the division's capabilities and communicates these to customers. Applies the division's products to customer's needs. Influences preparation and presents proposals, quotations, and bids, and negotiates and closes sales. Provides technical assistance, consultation, and problem solving as necessary, and expedites orders. Serves as the focal point of the division's contact with customers, a responsibility requiring a broad knowledge of the division and an attitude that is in tune with its goals. Functions as a businessperson, aware of and responsive to the conditions that affect the business. These conditions include knowledge of competition (their products, pricing, procedures, and personnel); of customers (their organizations and procedures); and of the industries represented by customers. Is responsive to the customer's needs as well as to conditions and trends that affect them.
	Serves as a channel of information to the division about customers, markets, and competition. Receives guidance concerning markets, prices, products, deliveries, and competition from the division. Utilizes divisional resources in the performance of all responsibilities.
PERFORMANCE CRITERIA:	The Sales Representative and Senior Sales Representative differ only in the degree of responsibility. Judged objectively on: performing selling and customer service functions in order to maximize the return from the assigned territory/customers and/or market in terms of sales volume, product line mix, penetration, and growth; managing and developing the territory, as well as cultivating and developing new customers and new applications for mature products; and the attitude with which one handles the job.
	Judged selectively on establishing and maintaining smooth working relationships with marketing and the division.

FIGURE 12-3 Job Description of Sales Representative.

socially oriented, and approval-seeking.[11] Another study had salespeople, sales managers, and physicians comment on a list of fourteen characteristics considered desirable for success in selling pharmaceuticals. Six of the traits—the abilities to learn, to communicate effectively, to be adaptable, to comprehend new information easily, to ask questions skillfully, and to show enthusiasm—were identified as necessary by all three groups.[12]

Sales managers can use the findings of such studies to help them identify the traits needed by the sales people on their own staffs, and thus to screen job applicants more effectively during interviews and other phases of the hiring process.

Research suggests that the traits of successful salespeople vary, in part, by industry, company, and type of sales position. However, there are some qualities that every salesperson must possess. These include the following:[13]

- The ability to collect a wide range of facts that can be brought to bear in making a sale
- The ability to make clear, effective, presentations
- A personal sensitivity to the feelings of others and how these feelings are communicated
- The ability to establish and maintain strong, positive relationships with a wide range of people
- A basic technical knowledge of the field in which one is selling, which must be used to cultivate business relationships and promote sales

SALES RECRUITING GUIDELINES

Once human resource needs are projected for the sales force, plans must be made for recruiting applicants. The establishment of an effective sales recruiting function should be the goal of every business organization. Salespeople, sales management, top management, and most writers on the subject seem to agree on the following general guidelines for doing so.

Plan and Coordinate Sales Recruiting

crisis hiring
Practice of thinking about recruiting only when vacancies occur, which leads to poor selection decisions

Too often a sales manager thinks about recruiting only when a vacancy occurs. This practice, which has been called *crisis hiring,* only leads to poor selection decisions. In their rush to fill vacancies, the manager is likely to overlook many applicants, and to ignore the shortcomings of those applicants on hand.

Successful sales recruiting is an ongoing process that must be thoughtfully planned for and organized. Some of the most common reasons for poor sales recruiting are directly related to a lack of coordination among the different parts of the process: (1) deficiencies in the overall organization of the program, (2) lack of feedback to recruitment personnel, (3) little continuity in the recruiting staff, and (4) lack of status of the recruiting function within the company. Every firm should reassess its existing procedures with the objective of strengthening the coordination aspect of its recruiting program.

One way to avoid a hurried search for sales applicants is to maintain a file of potential candidates. This is similar to a salesperson's prospect file. Every sales manager comes in contact with many potential sales applicants. A prudent manager finds out something about these people, records this information, and files it for future reference. When a vacancy occurs, the manager then already has a list of recruits who have been prescreened.

Use Several Recruiting Sources

Sales managers typically have favorite sources of sales recruits. A skillful manager will continue to use those that have proven fruitful in the past; however, it is desirable to maintain contact with anyone who might be able to suggest potential candidates since word of mouth can also provide important leads. Referrals can come from contacts outside the company, such as friends, customers, and suppliers, as well as from internal company sources.

Select and Train Qualified Recruiters

Sales managers often view recruiting as an alien task. Top sales management should stress the need for effective recruiting in their discussions with field sales managers and emphasize this important task in all promotional decisions. Further, the recruitment staff should be thoroughly trained in recruiting methods and in what to look for in a sales job applicant. Without that training, they will not be able to find and select the very best candidates. They will also not be able to relate well to applicants. Recruiters must have the knowledge and ability to discuss factors associated with job satisfaction, employee morale, internal company communication paths, job training programs, compensation, and other considerations that applicants use to determine their own "fit" with a sales job and a company.[14] The need for careful training is especially evident in the case of sales job recruiting among college graduates.[15]

Review the Recruiting Program

The data generated from recruiting activities should be analyzed and reported. Offer-rejection questionnaires and exit interviews are examples of procedures that supply meaningful data, but many companies fail to study this information. Also, records should be kept on the number and quality of sales applicants that come from various recruiting sources. For example, how many qualified applicants responded to an advertisement in a trade journal? These records help a sales manager judge the effectiveness of recruiting sources. Another review procedures is to follow the progress of successful applicants. How many became outstanding salespeople? How many left the company? Are there any significant characteristics of successful and unsuccessful recruits?

An especially useful technique is to question those applicants that refuse job offers. Why are they refusing? Perhaps they feel that the compensation is too low, that the job does not provide a challenge, or that they need more job security. These and many other possible responses may suggest needed changes in a firm's recruiting program.

Periodic review of the sales recruiting program can pay real dividends to a company. Consider the case of a large pharmaceutical company that abandoned its requirement that all of its sales representatives possess a biology, chemistry, or pharmacy degree when it discovered its highest sales producers were the few business administration graduates the firm had hired as a stop-gap measure to staff some newly created sales territories. This example shows that periodic reviews are a necessity for improving sales recruiting practices.

SOURCES OF SALES RECRUITS

Many sources for sales recruits exist.[16] These include educational institutions, internal company sources, company salespeople, suppliers and customers, competi-

SHOPSMITH, INC.

Shopsmith, Inc., a $43 million producer of woodworking equipment, sells its products through Shopsmith retail outlets and through demonstrations performed in shopping malls. In recruiting its sales force, the company seeks out individuals who not only have good sales experience or sales potential but are experienced woodworkers. Shopsmith's customers often come into the retail outlets needing advice about how to solve particular woodworking problems, and so employees must be knowledgeable about woodworking techniques and the firm's products if they are to satisfy these customer needs.

Another type of Shopsmith salesperson, the demonstrator, must be so comfortable with the company's equipment that he or she can turn out impressive wood products while at the same time presenting a believable sales pitch. The demon-strator's job is to show that anyone can turn out a wood masterpiece with Shopsmith equipment.

To find such uniquely qualified individuals, Shopsmith uses a simple recruitment source—its own customers. Shopsmith recruits by direct mail, which it has found to be both more targeted and less expensive than classified advertising in newspapers. On average, each direct mail piece is sent to around 3000 customers.

Besides being an effective recruiting method, contacting customers about job openings has other advantages. For one thing, being asked to apply or interview for a job is flattering; so, in a way, the method also functions as a marketing tool. For another, hiring people who like woodworking allows Shopsmith to use its own products and discounts on products as part of the employee compensation package. A disadvantage is rejection: What if a very good customer interviews for a job and turns out to be a not-so-good candidate? At the very least, Shopsmith better keep a sugary rejection letter on file.

tors, professional associations, local business and civic organizations, government agencies, the armed forces, job fairs and seminars, unsolicited applicants, advertisements, and employment agencies. The specific use of each of these sources is considered below.

Educational Institutions

All types of institutions for higher learning—colleges, universities, community colleges, business schools, and adult evening education programs—are fertile sources of sales recruits. Of course, the institution contacted will depend on the job qualifications required.

Some salespeople need a technical background, so colleges and universities are a primary source of recruits. Moreover, a college education has become a prerequisite for many sales jobs. This is especially true when a company has a promote-from-within policy and sales positions are the entry level point for advancement to middle, then upper, management positions within the company.

When recruiting college students, contacts with professors, placement officers, and administrators will pay off. In particular, professors who teach students in sales and marketing classes can help recruiters identify students who have the aptitude and desire for sales careers. Sales managers can establish relationships with professors by offering to guest-lecture on some aspect of the firm's business. This can lead directly to the identification of potential sales recruits as well as to additional contacts with faculty and students who can also serve as sources of information.

Once faculty relationships have been established, it is not unusual for professors to call sales managers to recommend outstanding students.[17]

Contacts with university placement centers are also an important aspect of college recruiting. A placement center is cost-effective since it provides many of the same services as an employment agency but does not charge for them. A placement center also offers economies of scale in the interviewing process. On may campuses, a sales manager can prescreen applicants and then interview only those who possess the desired qualifications. A sales recruiter can conduct as many as sixteen personal interviews with prescreened applicants in a single day.[18]

To stimulate students' interest in sales opportunities, many companies place recruiting ads in college newspapers and other college media. Advertising prior to interviewing sign-up deadlines can encourage students to apply. Posters placed in appropriate campus locations may also be effective. In addition, many companies have developed special college recruiting brochures and other promotional materials that explain the company to students and the challenging opportunities available in sales careers.

Another effective strategy for recruiting and screening college students is to offer internships or part-time jobs in selling. Students are always interested in an opportunity to find out what the "real world" of business is like. Providing work-study opportunities gives the company a chance to attract qualified sales recruits and observe them on the job. Students in cooperative programs are often effective in missionary and similar promotion tasks, and many become interested in full-time sales employment as a result of their experiences.

S. C. Johnson & Sons (the manufacturer of Raid, Johnson Wax, and other home and personal-care products), AT&T, and many other companies have developed summer sales internships for college students. Interns usually participate in sales meetings and other company activities. At the end of the summer, students who are considered potential full-time sales representatives are given letters of intent to hire. Both parties benefit from this approach. The company has someone who has been evaluated and will be motivated to work for the company, and the student has a job offer and a more relaxed senior year.[19]

Northwestern Mutual Life Insurance Company has developed a very successful internship program for college students. Excerpts from Northwestern's internship booklet describe this program:

> Launching a professional sales career while still in school will push you ahead of your peers. As an NML college intern you're involved in more than just a part-time job.
> . . . You'll get a feel for the business world in general, and the life insurance business in particular. . . . As a college intern, solving problems is your job . . . like designing a savings program for somebody. Or providing just the right kind of protection for some guy's wife and kid.[20]

Since its establishment at the Universities of Rhode Island and Connecticut in the late 1960s, Northwestern's college internship program has provided thousands of students with an opportunity to learn about selling on a firsthand basis. It is not unusual for a college intern to earn several thousand dollars in commissions while still a full-time student. From Northwestern's viewpoint, the program is successful because almost two-thirds of the college interns go on to become full-time insurance agents with the company.

Sales recruiters should also consider community and junior colleges. These two-year institutions, which have multiplied rapidly in recent years, offer a rich source of potential sales recruits. For example, many older men and women enroll in two-year programs. These students often have dependents and are eager to begin work as soon as possible. Many firms report that two-year graduates are effective in selling and are very loyal employees.

Another rich source of sales recruits is the evening programs of colleges. People enrolled in them are usually employed but searching for ways to advance themselves. Courses in public speaking, personal selling, and marketing are logical places to locate people who have an interest in sales careers. One way a sales manager can meet and interest these people in sales jobs is to speak to their classes.

Finally, sales recruiters should not overlook school alumni. Most college placement centers maintain active alumni files. Experienced salespeople often contact the placement directors of their alma maters when they decide to change jobs. Some colleges and universities publish alumni directories listing names, addresses, telephone numbers, dates of graduation, degrees and major fields of study, and brief descriptions of the graduates' current employment. These directories, particularly of colleges and universities that offer programs in areas applicable to a specific organization, are another excellent source of sales recruits.

Internal Company Sources

Employees within the firm should not be overlooked as potential sales recruits. Those already working in manufacturing, maintenance, or warehouse jobs may have latent sales talent. The company's human resources department should be made aware of sales personnel needs. Since the human resources manager continuously evaluates the qualifications of all employees, he or she may be able to supply candidates with the qualifications for sales positions.

Company Salespeople

Like field sales managers, salespeople become acquainted with many potential sales recruits. They should be encouraged to refer qualified applicants to the company. Referrals from company salespeople can save thousands of dollars in advertising and recruiting costs. Also, company salespeople are sources of high-quality referrals because they know the job and are unlikely to recommend anyone unsuitable for it.

Some firms offer bonuses as incentives to salespeople to recruit others; however, such referrals must be handled tactfully. To make sure they do not cause hard feelings among those hoping for financial rewards, job eligibility rules, reasons for rejection, and the type or amount of reward offered for successful referrals should all be clearly stated.[21]

Suppliers and Customers

Recruiters should look upon salespeople who call on their own companies as possible candidates. Sometimes they are dissatisfied with their current jobs and looking for something new. Also, a company's distributors, dealers, and customers may have suggestions about salespeople who call on them.

Competitors

Some of the best candidates may be those salespeople who work for competitors. They have a knowledge of the firm's products, the industry overall, and the customer base, and they know what it takes to be successful at selling the products in question. These people can be contacted at conventions, trade shows, and customer locations. It is imperative, however, that any approach be discreet and confidential so as not to jeopardize the candidate's position with his or her current employer.

Professional Associations

Technical, trade, and professional sales organizations usually maintain informal employment listings for members. They may also publish and distribute listings of job opportunities. Sales managers can contact the executive directors of these associations for information.

Local Business and Civic Organizations

Participation in community organizations will often provide recruiting leads. Civic organizations, local business associations, and service organizations are all possible sources of sales recruits.

Government Agencies

Public employment centers provide listings of qualified applicants for certain types of sales positions. These offices may be particularly helpful to companies seeking technical persons displaced by technological or economic changes.

Armed Forces

Personnel at "mustering-out centers" for the military may know of men and women interested in selling careers. Some military personnel may have had prior selling experience. Others may have leadership experience and may possess selling potential.

A related source of sales talent is military recruiters. These people, who are trained to persuade young men and women to enroll in the Army, Navy, Air Force, and Marines, know how to function in an environment much like that of a sales organization. They must make presentations to both individuals and groups. They must overcome objections, educate and inform, and "close deals." Military recruiters must meet quotas, and they receive performance rewards for signing up more personnel than other recruiters in similar positions.

Job Fairs and Seminars

State and local chambers of commerce, professional organizations, civic groups, and government agencies sponsor job fairs, which bring applicants and employees together. These job fairs have the major advantage of providing a large number of initial contacts at very little cost; however, they may not be appropriate for certain types of sales jobs.

Some companies have been successful in running their own job fairs. The American Banker's Life Assurance Company uses a series of "opportunity seminars" to attract and evaluate job applicants. During three evening sessions, interested persons are provided with general and specific job information and are screened for further consideration.

A hiring seminar can be a highly efficient method of locating large numbers of prospective sales recruits at a modest cost. The sales manager's energy is not wasted by having to repeat the same message to twenty or thirty people throughout the day. Instead, by conveying the information to one large group all at the same time, he or she is able to maintain a level of excitement about the sales opportunities within the organization that is easily communicated to all the applicants. Another benefit is that the exchange of information stimulates questions from the group, which can lead to a healthy exchange of views. The more serious candidates express their interest in the job through their questions, and are likely to pursue the opportunity further.

Unsolicited Applicants

Sales candidates frequently contact companies directly. This action shows that the applicants have initiative, but unsolicited applicants must be checked out carefully. Why did these applicants elect to skip the other recruitment channels?

Advertisements

Advertisements placed in newspapers, professional newsletters, and trade journals may produce many qualified sales applicants. If a technically qualified or experienced person is needed, advertising in trade journals or professional newsletters is appropriate. For more general sales jobs, newspaper advertisements are adequate.

Sales recruitment ads must be appealing and informative. Those that simply list the requirements and responsibilities connected with jobs will turn off many applicants because they contain only demands and no benefits. Like a sales presentation, a recruitment ad must sell; it must be interesting, persuasive, and benefit-oriented.[22] A strong headline that states a benefit ("We want a pro who wants to be part of the industry's top sales team") along with interesting visuals will help sell the company's sales opportunity to potential recruits. The body of the ad should include information about the company, the nature of the job, the specific qualifications required, the amount of compensation and fringe benefits offered, and any opportunities for advancement. To make it easy for an applicant to reply immediately, a telephone number or a mailing address should be included.

On the other hand, a recruitment ad must not promise too much. It should be written in a manner that discourages applications from those not qualified. Unqualified applicants encouraged by a vague advertisement to apply for a sales job will result in an unnecessary screening and selection burden. High rejection rates can also cause considerable ill will toward the company.

Placement of sales recruitment ads in the appropriate media is also important. Advertisements in trade and professional publications should usually be located in their employment sections. A newspaper ad will reach more potential sales recruits if it appears in the employment section of the Sunday edition.

Some companies have begun to recruit sales applicants through radio and television spots. Brief radio announcements of sales openings during early morning and late afternoon driving times (or commuting hours) have drawn well. Although television ads are expensive, they reach large numbers of people and have a great impact. The sales manager who wishes to use radio or television advertising should consult an experienced advertising professional before preparing and placing the ads.

Duro-Test Corporation used a national radio advertising campaign to recruit salespeople. The campaign cost $64,000, asked listeners to call a toll-free number, and attracted over forty sales recruits. The company felt the campaign attracted better-qualified applicants than its newspaper ads.

For examples of well-written ads for various kinds of sales positions, see Fig. 12-4.

Employment Agencies

If a sales manager needs recruiting help, he or she might use an employment agency. Many agencies specialize in sales jobs and render a valuable recruiting service. The following guidelines are suggested for using an agency to the best advantage:

1. Select one with experience in recruiting salespeople. One indication of an agency's professionalism is whether or not it is a member of the National Employment Association (NEA). Membership means that it subscribes to the NEA's Code of Ethics.
2. Visit the agency personally. Study its facilities and personnel in an effort to determine whether or not it is able to screen applicants effectively.
3. Make sure the agency knows what is wanted. Provide its recruiters with a comprehensive description of the job and of the required qualifications. Supportive literature about the company is also helpful.
4. Develop continuing relationships with agencies that provide good results and eliminate those that do not.

Many companies have turned to executive recruiters when searching for sales executives and highly specialized salespersons. Unlike employment agencies, which normally represent job seekers, executive recruiters represent their client companies. They work closely with their clients to fully understand the needs of the position, and then conduct a search for the best qualified candidate. Often these candidates are already employed and not actively seeking new positions. Executive recruiters charge approximately one-third of the new hire's first year's compensation plus expenses for their services.[23]

EQUAL EMPLOYMENT OPPORTUNITY

Equal employment opportunity is a crucial ethical and legal issue for sales managers. As discussed in Chap. 7, the federal government, the individual states, and many counties and cities have laws directed toward preventing discriminatory employment practices. As a result, all major companies doing business in the United States have adopted a policy statement that reflects the legal requirements with regard to Equal

The sales recruiting ads you run depend on the job, speed needed to fill it, availability of the applicant, and competition.

If you want specific experience in your industry, business publications are effective. However, need for speed may rule this avenue out.

For faster results, advertise in newspapers. Sundays are effective for classified. Provide a telephone number the reader can call on Sunday, if possible. Answer inquiries right away before they cool off. Display ads in the business pages are good for sales management and top selling posts.

If the newspaper groups sell ads, don't start your ad with SALES. Flag them down with the experience required:

APPLIANCES

```
Major nationally advertised firm seeks salesperson for established
territory to sell electrical appliances to department and discount
stores. Experienced required. Salary plus expenses plus company car
plus commission. Call (XXX) 555-2939.
```

If you are more interested in markets sold to than product sold, play that up in the headline:

VARIETY CHAINS

```
If you have sold to variety chains and have merchandising, POP, co-op
advertising experience, here's opportunity to take over growing territory.
Heavy travel. Company car. Draw against commissions. Phone Mike Thomas at
800-555-6543 for appointment this week.
```

If you estimate earnings, do not exaggerate. Puffed-up estimates cause distrust. If inexperienced applicants are fair game, advertise for sales trainees:

SALES TRAINEE: WE WILL TRAIN ...

```
In sales techniques and product knowledge if you are college graduate with
some technical or mechanical background. Nationally known manufacturer of
valves and fittings sold to original equipment manufacturers offers $XX,XXX
starting salary plus expenses and bonus. Send resume to Sales Manager, Acme
Valve Co., 111 Second Street, Mineola, NY 11501.
```

This ad shows you want someone interested in learning sales. Copy shows established, well-known firm, starting salary, bonus opportunity. Restrictor—college grad with technical or mechanical background—prevents you from being flooded with unqualified trainees.

Here's how to attract trainees from another field:

ACCOUNTANTS

```
Tired of working with figures? If you have accounting background or education
and prefer dealing with people rather than ledgers, we will train you to sell
business forms and systems. Our training program includes a step-by-step
approach to mastering selling of our products which will lead to high
earnings on a commission basis. Salary $XXXX per month during training
period. Phone Rod Matthews at (215)555-0987.
```

Using a box number allows you to screen unwanted applicants. They won't be able to bother you with phone calls or surprise visits. Disadvantage: Many employed people won't answer box number ads.

FIGURE 12-4 Writing Help-Wanted Ads for Salespeople Positions.

Employment Opportunity. An example is the policy of a large pharmaceutical manufacturer:

> The management of this company hereby specifies this policy not to discriminate against any employee or applicant for employment because of race, color, religion, sex, age, or national origin. This includes, but is not limited to, the following: hiring, placement, transfer, demotion, recruitment, advertising, or solicitation for employment.

Since they lack legal training and experience, many sales managers are confused about the EEOC's requirements for the selection of women and minority personnel. It has been suggested, however, that the most critical aspects of the EEOC's guidelines can be summarized in one sentence: "An employer is required to validate his selection procedures only if his present selection procedures have an adverse impact on minority groups."[24]

four-fifths rule
EEOC-required minimum selection rate for any minority group when compared with the nonminority group

The three key terms in the above statement are "adverse impact," "selection procedures," and "validate." "Adverse impact" is defined as a substantially different rate of selecting minority personnel compared with the selection rate for nonminority personnel. One way of evaluating this is the *four-fifths rule:* A selection rate for any minority that is less than four-fifths of the selection rate for the group with the highest selection rate indicates discrimination in the selection process. "Selection procedures" include all the activities used to make hiring decisions.

The key issue for sales managers is to have a sales selection process that is ethically sound, legally valid, and managerially useful. This can be done by developing a sequential selection process, such as the one described in Chap. 13, and by carefully validating each selection tool. This will permit sales managers to make good hiring decisions while complying with governmental regulations.[25]

Avoiding Costly Mistakes

Mistakes are sometimes made because recruiters and sales managers do not understand equal employment opportunity law, or are careless in using selection procedures. The key point for sales managers to remember is this: If you have any doubt about a recruiting or selection technique, you should seek qualified legal advice. The penalties are too severe to risk a mistake. Areas of specific concern under the law are application forms, interviews, and employment tests.

Application Forms.   As discussed in Chap. 13, application forms must ask only for information related to the sales job. Personal information, such as marital status, number of children, and age, should not be requested, since it could be used to prevent or restrict employment. Questions about military discharges and arrest records can also be considered discriminatory. Likewise, questions about the applicant's financial status, such as the number of credit accounts, whether the individual rents or owns his or her home, or whether she or he has ever declared bankruptcy, should not be asked since the information might result in different treatment for different groups of people. The basic guideline is to seek only that information which

SALES MANAGEMENT IN PRACTICE

VALUING DIVERSITY AT MONSANTO

Most people are familiar with Monsanto for the products it makes—Nutrasweet, for example, Monsanto is also known, however, for its reputation as an excellent employer of minorities and women. The reputation is well deserved; for years Monsanto has made consistent efforts to change the corporate culture and not merely to satisfy government-mandated quotas and affirmative action laws.

Monsanto's emphasis on equal employment opportunity is both defensively and offensively motivated. Defensively, good EEO programs save thousands of dollars per year by cutting back on litigation, recruitment, and turnover costs. From an offensive standpoint, Monsanto hopes to use its well-nurtured diversity as a fierce competitor; having many people with many outlooks on its side is a good way for the company to understand a diverse customer base.

Monsanto began its "Value Diversity" program in 1989 as a way to change its corporate culture, not merely to assimilate nonwhites and women into the culture that already existed. To accomplish this goal, it began by establishing work teams made up of volunteers from all levels and all departments of the company. These team members participated in awareness training and sensitivity courses, where they confronted their own prejudices and were taught effective ways to work with others.

Valuing diversity at Monsanto goes much further than the immediate work place; for example, to enhance the safety of its Round-Up weedkiller, Monsanto sales representatives, accompanied by interpreters, regularly visit the Spanish-speaking workers who are its main users. This fact is especially impressive considering that the weedkiller is bought usually by white males.

Monsanto has developed a "consulting pairs" program that places employees in race- or gender-matched pairs. The pairs discuss discrimination issues and serve as consultants to other employees, and they are constantly on the lookout for discriminatory practices. By providing a format to discuss and solve discrimination problems and by setting a good example through its selling activities, Monsanto is making great progress in helping its employees face their own prejudices and grow to respect the differences between themselves and their co-workers.

---

bona fide occupational qualifications
Information about a job applicant directly related to potential job performance

is related to what the EEOC calls *bona fide occupational qualifications,* that is, information directly related to potential job performance.

Personal Interviews.   The most popular sales job selection tool, personal interviews, provides information about applicants and their qualifications for sales positions. EEOC experts want sales managers to be particularly careful in conducting interviews. The same restrictions on information that can be requested on application forms applies to interviews. Further, sales managers must not express personal opinions or value judgments about women or minorities to interviewees.

Tests.   Tests have been criticized because some observers feel they discriminate against minorities. In fact, court cases and guidelines issued by the EEOC have caused some companies to discontinue testing as a selection technique. This may not be necessary, but a company must be prepared to prove its tests are job-related and do not illegally discriminate. If a test is used, it must be validated by a qualified professional. An authority on sales selection tests says: "The key point for the sales manager is to insist on a professionally developed test battery which measures characteristics which are demonstrably job relevant."[26]

Recruiting Women and Minority Applicants

It is essential that sales recruiters make special efforts to hire women, minorities, and older persons for sales jobs. Besides blacks and females, ever-increasing numbers of Hispanics, Asians, Native Americans, and other minorities are entering the sales field. Modern sales management must expedite and facilitate this crucial adjustment process.

While the labor force participation rate of men is expected to remain stable throughout the 1990s, the rate for women is predicted to grow from 45 percent to 47 percent. The black labor force is expected to grow nearly twice as fast as the white labor force, and the number of Hispanics in the labor force could grow at more than four times the pace for non-Hispanic whites.[27] There is no doubt that women and minorities will represent larger portions of future sales forces. The hiring and equal treatment of women, minority persons, and older people is simply good business practice.

Perhaps the strongest support for hiring all types of people for sales has come from noted sales selection researchers Herbert Greenberg and Ronald Bern. In their landmark study, based on observations of thousands of salespeople, they concluded the following:

> Our experience shows that a man of 50 may have more openmindedness and youthful vigor than a man half his age; that women have the same ranges of business talents as men; that race has nothing to do with ability to sell.[28]

Additional research by Herbert and Jeanne Greenberg further strengthens the position that successful salespeople do not fit any stereotype. They also note that there is a large pool of sales talent among older people, women, and minorities that is waiting to be tapped.[28]

With some modifications, the recruiting sources discussed earlier in this chapter can also be used to recruit women and minorities. However, an effective affirmative action program cannot rely on traditional sources of sales recruits alone. Sales managers must develop new recruiting messages and expand into different media to reach specific populations and subgroups. Consider the following suggestions:

Consider Present Women and Minority Employees for Sales.

It is likely that some of the company's present minority and female employees have sales potential. Women and minority persons in secretarial, clerical, manufacturing, and similar positions should be considered when sales openings occur. The human resources manager is a good source of information on current employees. A sales manager can also ask minority and female employees for referrals.

Contact Specialized Employment Agencies and Organizations.

There are many employment agencies that specialize in placing women and minorities. Sales managers should make a special effort to seek out these recruiting sources.

Contact Women's and Minority Educational Institutions.   Although times are changing, there are still a number of educational institutions that have predominantly minority or female student enrollments. Also, most large colleges and universities have minority administrators and student advisers who are useful sources of referrals. College instructors of sales and marketing courses are also likely to know women and minority students interested in sales careers.

Use Targeted Advertising Messages and Media.   Certain newspapers, radio and television programs, magazines, and other media appeal to minority and female populations. Recruiting ads placed in these media should be designed to appeal to such special groups. For instance, if photographs are used, females and minorities should be featured in them, and copy should be in the appropriate language if English is not used.

Develop Personal Contacts.   Personal contacts are an effective affirmative action recruiting technique. A female executive is an excellent source of information about women interested in sales and marketing careers. Similarly, a minority professor may know minority students who are interested in business careers.

SUMMARY OF LEARNING GOALS

1. Identify the Three Major Steps in the Sales Force Staffing Process.

The three major steps in the sales force staffing process are (1) analyzing sales personnel needs, (2) recruiting sales candidates, and (3) screening and selecting applicants.

2. Explain How a Firm Can Determine Its Optimum Sales Force Size.

Marginal analysis is one way to determine optimum sales force size by comparing the cost of adding another salesperson to the profit that person is expected to generate. Salespeople are hired until the cost of an additional salesperson equals the profit that individual is predicted to generate. Another way to determine optimum sales force size is the incremental method, which is a term used collectively to describe various quantitative techniques. Trend analysis, which involves studying historical data to determine future needs, is also an important method that can be used in determining sales force size.

3. Describe How Job Descriptions Are Developed and Used in Sales Management.

Job descriptions are statements summarizing various job functions and the relative importance of each function. They are developed through a systematic analysis of job tasks and the amount of time that must be allocated to each. They are used by sales managers as a focal point in the hiring process; used properly they save both the company and job applicants time and money; and they serve management as good tools for training, motivating, and evaluating sales staff members.

4. **Relate Job Descriptions to Job Qualifications.**

Job descriptions, which detail the various functions jobs entail and the relative emphasis that should be placed on each of those functions, serve as the basis for identifying job qualifications, or the traits needed for a person to be able to do the job effectively.

5. **Discuss the Need for Planning and Coordination in Sales Force Recruiting.**

A lack of planning and coordination in sales force recruiting practices can lead to "crisis handling," or recruiting only when vacancies occur. This is likely to cause qualified applicants to be overlooked and nonqualified applicants to be hired. A company needs to continually update its sales force recruiting practices and see that the various elements of the program remain coordinated for optimum effectiveness. Files of job applicants should be kept current.

6. **Identify the Various Sources of Sales Recruits.**

Sources of sales recruits can include educational institutions, internal company sources, suppliers and customers, competitors, professional associations, local business and civic organizations, government agencies, the armed forces, job fairs and seminars, unsolicited applicants, advertisements, and employment agencies. Sales managers should use all of them, and should maintain contact with anyone who can provide leads to potential candidates.

7. **List Problem Areas Related to Equal Employment Opportunity and Suggest Procedures for Recruiting Women and Minorities.**

Recruiters and sales managers sometimes make mistakes because of carelessness or a lack of understanding about the law. In general, sales managers must be prepared to defend the job-relatedness of the applications, interview processes, and testing procedures they use. Women and minorities may be recruited for sales jobs through specialized employment agencies and organizations, women's and minority educational institutions, targeted advertising messages and media, and personal contacts.

REVIEW QUESTIONS

1. Outline a systematic approach for recruiting and selecting salespeople. Define all the relevant terms involved in the process.
2. Why is timing important to the staffing process? Cite another challenge that sales management faces in the sales staffing process.
3. Describe Semlow's classic method for determining sales force size. What name is usually applied to this approach?
4. How is trend analysis used to predict sales personnel needs? What are the weaknesses of trend analysis as a sales staffing tool?

5. What is a job description. What happens if a job description is too detailed or too brief? What are the characteristics of a good job description.
6. What are the qualities that every salesperson must possess? Define each of them.
7. What are some of the most common reasons for poor sales recruiting? How can these problems be overcome?
8. Identify the sources of sales recruits.
9. What are the traits of a good recruitment ad? What are the advantages and disadvantages of television advertising?
10. What is the one sentence that summarizes the EEOC's guidelines about the hiring of women and minority personnel? Explain what is meant by "adverse impact" and "selection procedures."

DISCUSSION QUESTIONS

1. Pick a firm with a large sales force. Make some general projection of future sales personnel needs. Report your conclusions to the class.

2. The baby boom was a well-known increase in the birth rate between the years 1946 and 1964. Demographically, the baby boom has provided a large population of middle-aged people for the nineties and will lead to a large elderly population in the future. Compared to their parents, baby boomers are better educated, but fewer are marrying, more are divorcing, and they are having proportionally fewer children. Consider the goods and services that "boomers" will require in the future. What types of companies may need to reduce or increase their sales force hiring rates as the general population gets older? Justify your response.

3. Obtain a sales job description from any company in your area. Does it possess the characteristics of being in written form, specific, inclusive, and detailed but terse, as described in this chapter? Make a phone call to a salesperson in the company who actually holds the position described. Does the job description seem to be accepted by this person?

4. While competitor firms may be excellent sources of new job hires, companies must be wary of using the inside information about a competing firm's policies or plans that a salesperson newly hired from that company might possess. Do some research into this topic. What constitutes an "insider"? Cite examples of inside information that could be provided by a salesperson.

5. Interview an employment agency that lists lots of sales jobs. What types of people are being sought for the positions? What else can you learn about sales job selection procedures? Report your findings to the class.

E T H I C A L   D I L E M M A

Although age discrimination is illegal, some sales executives feel that older people cannot handle the physical and mental demands of selling. How should you respond to this skepticism?

SALES MANAGEMENT CASE

Dow Chemical Company—Walking the Walk

A few years ago, Dow Chemical Company's sales force was chosen by *Sales & Marketing Management* as one of the six best in America. To achieve such a high honor, an organization must exhibit excellence on many levels. Dow's recruiting efforts are no exception to the company's overall standard of excellence.

Dow recruits from thirty-five college campuses, and it treats each school like a business partner, getting to know its administrators and goals. Such relationship building, so successful in selling, is equally appropriate for recruiting.

Although Dow's relationships with schools are very important, effective recruiting tactics alone are not enough to attract the best recruits. Dow offers its salespeople enormous opportunity. New recruits go through a year-long training program that prepares them to go into the field. They are given the opportunity to sell for their entire career yet still advance within the company. Evaluations are geared toward both professional and personal goals, and Dow's "Achievers Club" program rewards around 35 percent of its sales force each year with merchandise gifts and trips. The company also does an excellent job of giving its sales force the backup selling tools they need. For example, it has streamlined its information systems so that salespeople can access information in any Dow data base throughout the world.

When it comes to management, there are companies that "talk the talk" and there are companies

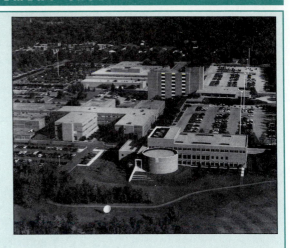

that "walk the walk." *Sales & Marketing Management*'s selection of Dow's sales force as one of the best in the country is recognition of Dow's excellence in all of its sales management efforts.

Questions

1. Dow recruits almost exclusively from colleges. Do you think this source is appropriate for the company? Explain.

2. In your opinion, what questions should potential recruits ask companies? Which would be appropriate for an interview with Dow?

3. As a sales manager, if you thought that your organization truly offered many advantages to its sales force, how would you prove it to recruits?

CHAPTER *13*

SALES PERSONNEL SELECTION PROCESS

LEARNING GOALS

- Describe the sales personnel selection process.
- Outline the questions that must be answered in evaluating a salesperson selection program.
- Explain why a systematic approach to selection is important to salesperson hiring decisions.
- Identify the major selection tools used in staffing a sales force.
- Explain the correct way to extend an offer of employment or to reject a candidate.

THE BEST PERSON FOR THE JOB

Effective sales managers make every effort to hire the best sales personnel available to them. Poor selection procedures cause expense and heartbreak to both employees and employers. Hiring mistakes cost the organization considerable training monies. The costs to the wrongly selected trainees themselves are in the form of missed opportunity: What other jobs could they have taken?

An organization's turnover rate shows the effectiveness of its selection procedures, although it also points to other possible problems, such as accuracy of job descriptions. A poorly chosen salesperson is likely to leave the company on his or her own or, in the worst case, to be fired. Such short stints of employment waste the company's training and recruiting dollars, but also look bad to customers, who lose faith in and grow impatient with a company that cannot keep its sales force.

Merrill Lynch recognizes the detrimental effects of high turnover and encourages its newly hired brokers to stay by offering them $100,000 if they are still with the company after ten years. Also, managers' compensation is based in part on the turnover rate of the employees under them. Similar tactics are being used by car dealerships which pay salespeople a bonus for every car they sell, but pay them only after a given length of time.

While the above approaches may be effective in reducing turnover, they do not improve selection procedures, which, if wrongly developed, can predispose employees to leave a company. PSS, which sells medical supplies door to door at physicians' offices, altered its selection procedures as a way of reducing its unacceptable turnover rate. The company developed a profile of its best salespeople and formed a sales inter-

view guide with questions aimed at determining whether or not candidates fit that
profile. The interview format has lowered
turnover and provides an efficient and systematic guide for evaluating candidates.[1]

Reducing turnover is only one reason
that sales organizations must develop effective selection procedures. Chapter 13 also
discusses the other factors that make sales
personnel selection so critical to sales managers. In addition, it describes techniques
for establishing good procedures. As you
read, you should be aware of both these issues so that by the chapter's end you will

understand both the why and the how of
sales personnel selection.

CHAPTER OVERVIEW

Chapter 12 dealt with sales personnel planning and the recruiting of sales applicants.
Once a pool of potential talent has been generated, it is necessary to select the
individuals who best fit the needs of a particular company. The sales personnel
selection process refers to the steps sales management goes through to staff a sales
organization. The development of an effective sales screening and selection process
is the topic of this chapter.

Recruitment and selection present interesting problems for the sales manager,
especially for one who has advanced from the ranks of selling. In purchasing the
services of people for the company, the manager must reverse roles, putting aside
the strategies he or she learned as a seller to become, instead, an astute buyer.

Prediction Is Risky

Like most purchases, the selection of salespeople involves risk. When hiring a
sales applicant, the sales manager is predicting that the individual will be an effective
salesperson.

Both the company and the applicant have much to gain or lose from whether this
prediction is accurate or not. The company incurs costs for recruiting, hiring, and
training each applicant, and sales losses can be expected if the wrong person is
chosen. From the applicant's viewpoint, the gamble involves part of his or her
working life. If the wrong job is selected, the applicant has lost a portion of a career
that cannot be recovered.

Adding further risk to the usual employee selection process is the complexity of
selling. Unlike many jobs, success in selling does not depend solely upon intellectual
qualifications. The emotional demands that sales jobs impose mean that sales job
selection techniques must go beyond the concepts of managerial psychology to
emphasize personality and temperament, as well as ability, experience, and apti-
tudes.

Is Salesperson Selection an Art or a Science?

Selection is both an art and a science. The process of sales personnel selection is scientific in some of the tools it uses, but is an art in the interpretation of the information obtained by means of those tools. Accurately predicting an applicant's future job performance involves experience, and usually more than a little luck. The objective is to reduce the probability of making a poor hiring decision.

Sales managers cannot rely solely on their experience and luck, however. Critics of sales job selection methods argue that many sales managers fail to follow a tested, systematic procedure when hiring, falsely believing they can recognize a good salesperson without using proven selection tools. The result is a tendency for managers to seek and hire people like themselves.

Unfortunately, no company can expect to do a perfect job of selection. People are too complex, and not everyone is cut out for the rigorous demands of selling. But a systematic screening and selection process is far superior to relying only on one's instincts and feelings when hiring salespeople. By following a logical procedure, a sales manager can expect to improve the selection performance rating. This is the science of selection.[2]

WHO IS RESPONSIBLE FOR THE SALESPERSON SELECTION PROCESS?

In the past, most companies placed the responsibilities for recruiting, screening, and selecting people who sell with field sales managers, since these managers are ultimately responsible for the success or failure on the job of those hired. However, many field sales managers have proven to be poor recruiters and selectors.

A busy field sales manager often fails to use proven hiring practices. Preoccupied by pressing day-to-day operations, he or she frequently does not devote sufficient attention to the vital activity of personnel selection. A manager may settle for the first available applicant to fill a territory, or may hire someone who seems to be in his or her own image while rejecting anyone who does not seem to fit this view of a good salesperson.

Many field sales managers also lack the training and experience needed to do a good job of selection. Techniques like interviewing and testing require a certain background. Unless field sales managers have received the proper training in their use, it is unlikely that they will be able to use them effectively in predicting job success.

Some companies now involve experienced salespeople in the selection of hirees. For instance, FSG, Inc., the sales and marketing subsidiary of Financial Services Group, has sales recruits try the job under the supervision of experienced agents as the final step of its hiring process.[3] Other companies have salespeople interview sales recruits. The inclusion of salespeople in the hiring process also provides additional insights into candidates from the perspective of those already performing the job.

Most large companies have now centralized their sales selection activities to some extent. Professional recruiters are used to relieve field sales managers of preliminary hiring chores. Applicants are recruited, tested, and screened by trained

TABLE 13-1   Who Hires the Sales Recruit?

National sales manager	43.0%
Regional/district manager	28.5
First-level sales manager	24.2
Personnel manager	2.7
Sales trainer	0.4
Campus recruiter	0.4
Outside agency	...
Other	7.0

Note: Based on 256 responses. Multiple answers make total more than 100 percent.

specialists. However, most companies still leave the final selection to members of sales management.

This shared arrangement is probably desirable. In a large company having a human resources department, recruiting and preliminary screening should be turned over to experts. Of course, they should receive guidance from the sales department. Final selection decisions should also remain with sales management. Consequently, it is necessary for field sales managers to understand the complete selection process and to be able to interpret test scores and the recommendations of human resources specialists. In a small company, which may lack such trained specialists, it is imperative that field sales managers understand the selection process.

Current practices regarding the selection of new salespeople are shown in Table 13-1. As this table indicates, the final hiring decision usually remains with the sales organization.

EVALUATING A SELECTION PROGRAM

When is a company's selection program in need of revision? If employee turnover is excessive, or if the selection process is too time consuming, the program may be deficient and require modifications.

Is Turnover Excessive?

Sales turnover is a problem for almost every company, and it cannot be eliminated entirely. There will always be some who quit the company for other positions, and other who are considered unfit for selling and must be discharged. There is also turnover that occurs for positive reasons—sales positions opened by promotions of salespeople to management or their transfer to larger territories, for example.

turnover rate
Number of salespeople who quit or are discharged divided by the average size of the sales force during a given period of time

Turnover rate equals the number of salespeople who quit or are discharged divided by the average size of the company's sales force during a given period of time (usually one year). One study by Learning International revealed that more than half of all salespeople had been with their companies for five years or less, and only one in five had at least ten years with his or her current employer.[4]

What is "normal" turnover? Turnover varies according to company, industry, and type of selling. It is also affected by the quality of the firm's products, pricing, delivery, and compensation programs. Salespeople soon leave companies plagued with poor-quality products which they are forced to sell at high prices. Moreover, if salespeople feel that sales goals and management expectations are unrealistic, they become discouraged. Resignations soon follow.

For most companies and most types of selling situations, a turnover rate between 10 and 20 percent a year is considered normal. However, higher turnover rates are found among first-year employees and in certain types of selling jobs. For example, it is not unusual for direct sales organizations like Avon and Amway to have sales turnover rates which approximate 100 percent a year. Likewise, many tele-marketing sales centers experience high turnover rates because the sales tasks are dull, repetitious, and require cold calls to unknown prospects.

What Are the Costs of Turnover?

The out-of-pocket costs of turnover are startling; they include costs in time, energy, and the money spent on recruiting, selecting, training, and supervising people who ultimately fail to sell. The compensation paid to these salespeople must also be counted. Often, salespeople work for a year or more before they become productive and begin to repay the company (in sales and profits) for the costs of hiring, training, and supervising them.[5]

The Learning International study revealed that the average corporation loses five salespeople a year. In dollar terms, turnover costs the average company approximately $50,000 per lost salesperson or almost $250,000 per year.[6] These figures include the lost investment in salespeople who leave the company and the costs of hiring and training their replacements.

Suppose Essex Company estimates that the average cost of hiring and training a new salesperson is $20,000. If Essex has 200 salespeople, and if turnover is 10 percent per year, then the firm will incur an expense of $400,000 per year. By cutting the turnover rate in half, Essex could save $200,000 per year.

Turnover costs may also be viewed another way. Again, assume expenses of $20,000 to recruit, select, and train a salesperson. If Essex has a turnover rate of 10 percent, the cost of each retained salesperson is approximately $22,000 ($20,000/0.9). If turnover can be reduced to 5 percent, the cost per retained salesperson falls by almost $1,000 per individual ($20,000/0.95 = $21.053).

In addition to hiring and training expenses, there are indirect costs of sales job turnover. When a salesperson leaves, the impact on sales volume is immediate. If the departed salesperson has switched to a competitor, he may take some customers with him. A customer's loyalty is often to the salesperson rather than to the company or its product.

Even if customers remain loyal to the company, excessive turnover may result in lost sales. It is hard to convince customers that they are dealing with a reputable firm with quality products if they see a different salesperson every few months. Further, the buyer's ordering routine is interrupted during the time needed to recruit, select, and train replacements. These incremental costs of turnover may be more costly in the long run than the initial out-of-pocket expenses.

Coping with Turnover

Sales force turnover is a perplexing, costly problem for sales management. Unfortunately, many sales managers do not understand why their salespeople leave. Nor do they know how to develop a logical approach to deal with high turnover. Fortunately, researchers have begun to study turnover and its causes.[7]

One group of researchers has arrived at the following recommendations for sales management:[8]

1. Managers should focus more on recruiting, training, and supporting salespeople and less on attitude adjustment if they wish to reduce turnover. This is because turnover appears to be related more to tenure and age than to attitude.
2. Managers must try to anticipate changes in their external environments and take actions to minimize turnover due to these changes. This is because general economic conditions and industry job opportunities are more likely to affect sales turnover than are job or attitudinal factors.
3. Managers need a better understanding of the individual circumstances of salespeople who leave. Systematic exit interviews can provide information that may suggest reasons for turnover unique to a firm.
4. Managers should understand that not all turnover is "bad" for a firm. Low-performing salespeople who leave can be replaced by stronger people capable of higher levels of performance. Also, sales managers may wish to focus special retention efforts on specific groups of salespeople (e.g., recently hired, high-performing salespeople).

Is the Selection Process Too Time-Consuming?

Unnecessarily long selection procedures result in numerous indirect costs to a company. Sales management's time is expensive, and its use must be equated with the benefits that accrue to the organization. In addition, an inefficient hiring procedure can lead to an extensive loss of goodwill for the firm. And sales managers who do not move quickly enough to fill vacancies will incur lost sales and profits.[9]

Unfortunately, many organizations have an inefficient selection process that is too time-consuming. One-fourth of the salespeople in one survey said that their own hiring took between 2 and 4 weeks. Another 20 percent indicated that their hiring took between 4 and 6 weeks. Certainly, no one would advocate speeding up the hiring process to a point that renders selections standards meaningless, but simplification and improved efficiency should be goals of any sales selection procedure.

SYSTEMATIC SELECTION PROCESS

Most experts agree that poor selection is perhaps the major contributing factor to high sales force turnover. A comprehensive study of sales force selection puts it this way:

The selection of salesforce members is a critical function for sales managers, not only because of the real costs of hiring and training but also because of the consequences of increased turnover. Frequent replacement of salespersons can diminish customer goodwill, translating into lost future sales. With high turnover, management must allocate time and money to additional hiring and training efforts instead of working with the salesforce to increase its effectiveness.[10]

Avoiding Hiring Mistakes

The company's sales job description provides the framework for screening and selection. It is the basis for preparing application blanks and interview forms, and for picking psychological tests and other selection tools. When these tools are not used, sales managers tend to hire people who reflect their own abilities and qualifications. Or they select on the basis of a single outstanding physical, mental, or personality trait. For example, one study revealed that sales managers in the life insurance industry believe that tall people make the best salespeople. Or a sales recruiter might perceive a very articulate (or attractive or dapperly dressed) recruit to be hard-working, intelligent, diligent, and responsible, when in fact the person possesses none of these characteristics.

halo effect
Selection based on a single quality

Selecting someone on the basis of a single quality has been called the *halo effect*. This practice has resulted in many costly hiring mistakes. It is most likely to occur when other characteristics that need to be to be taken into account are hard to observe. Since most of the traits on which recruiters evaluate sales job candidates are difficult to observe in terms of behaviors, they are particularly subject to errors of judgment resulting from the halo effect.

A leading sales management periodical warns sales recruiters about a similar error, which it calls "cloning":

> Cloning is a good bet to replace nepotism as the most common form of corporate suicide, especially in smaller companies. What happens is that sales managers tend to hire in their own image, believing they can best relate to people who share their values, interests, and background. However, duplicating yourself may simplify interpersonal relations, but it does nothing to ensure sales effectiveness. You need some people who think differently from you—even if they're harder to manage.[11]

A Systematic Approach to Salesperson Selection

Overcoming these hiring errors requires a systematic approach to selection. One model is a sequential selection process that involves three phases: preliminary screening, initial interview, and intensive interview and testing leading to the selection of a sales candidate.[12] This model is shown in Fig. 13-1.

A systematic approach involves use of the following selection tools:

1. Application forms and resumes
2. Interviews
3. References
4. Psychological tests
5. Medical examinations
6. Trial periods

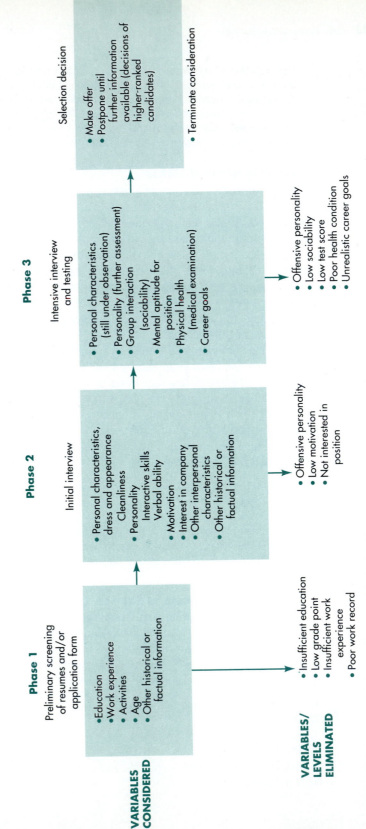

VARIABLES CONSIDERED

Phase 1

Preliminary screening of resumes and/or application form

- Education
- Work experience
- Activities
- Age
- Other historical or factual information

Phase 2

Initial interview

- Personal characteristics, dress and appearance
  Cleanliness
- Personality
  Interactive skills
  Verbal ability
- Motivation
- Interest in company
- Other interpersonal characteristics
- Other historical or factual information

Phase 3

Intensive interview and testing

- Personal characteristics (still under observation)
- Personality (further assessment)
- Group interaction (sociability)
- Mental aptitude for position
- Physical health (medical examination)
- Career goals

Selection decision

- Make offer
- Postpone until further information available (decisions of higher-ranked candidates)

- Terminate consideration

VARIABLES/LEVELS ELIMINATED

- Insufficient education
- Low grade point
- Insufficient work experience
- Poor work record

- Offensive personality
- Low motivation
- Not interested in position

- Offensive personality
- Low sociability
- Low test score
- Poor health condition
- Unrealistic career goals

FIGURE 13-1 Sequential Selection Process of Industrial Salesperson.

SALES MANAGEMENT IN PRACTICE

BODY SHOP

Anita Roddick, owner of 709 U.K.-based Body Shop units, is a strong believer in Amnesty International, re-cycling, animal rights, and Greenpeace. Her sales force is, too; or at least they had better be. Body Shop employees are expected not only to sell but to disseminate information on the social, political, and environmental causes in which Roddick believes.

Body Shop sells, through its own stores and by mail-order, cosmetic products made from natural ingredients that have not been tested on animals in the past five years. Product labels go into detail about their environmentally friendly ingredients, and product information manuals are available at all the stores. While shopping, customers can pick up literature about various environmental concerns. Packaging is minimal, recycling is encouraged, and if customers bring back empty Body Shop containers, they get a twenty-five cent refund on their next purchase.

The salesperson job description includes, in addition to selling, sending postcards and enlisting members for Amnesty International. To ensure that her employees will be loyal to and enthusiastic about her causes, Roddick has a rather unique application procedure in which prospective employees are asked about such things as their personal heroes and literary tastes. She even once turned down a candidate, whom she had planned to hire, when she found out the person liked to hunt.

Political activist or cosmetics seller? Anita Roddick is both, and fervor for certain causes, along with selling ability, is an occupational qualification for Body Shop sales recruits.

New England Mutual Life Insurance Company uses a salesperson selection program which includes several of these tools. Known as STEPS (selection, training, evaluation, performance system), this systematic process has significantly improved New England Life's selection/retention results.[13] It involves five major tasks:

1. A first interview involves matching candidates against New England Life's successful agent profile, screening candidates by making observations about their interpersonal skills, and identifying job-related information from a candidate's work, education, personal history, and test results.
2. Work-related and personal references are checked to verify information the candidate has supplied.
3. A second interview focuses on the candidate's qualifications in relation to the position to determine the person's potential for success.
4. A third interview determines which candidate is most likely to succeed at the job and identifies the best training and managing strategy for the person and the manager.
5. Performance followup involves checking the person's performance over time to determine how well the selection decision worked out and to decide whether or not changes should be made in the selection process.

The New England Life procedure suggests that several screening and selection tools should be used. No single technique is superior. Each sales manager and company must choose the combination of selection tools that is most appropriate for the specific sales job involved.[14]

In a survey of sales management practices, top sales executives were asked which selection tools their companies used.[15] As shown in Table 13-2, personal

TABLE 13-2   Usage of Sales Job Selection Tools

Selection tool	Percentage of small firms "extensively" using tool	Percentage of large firms "extensively" using tool
Personal interviews	91	96
Application blanks	73	70
Personal reference checks	70	62
List of job qualifications	34	45
Job descriptions*	30	51
Psychological tests*	22	32
Credit reports*	15	36

* A statistically significant difference ($p < .05$) exists between the percentage of small and large firms that extensively use this sales management tool.

interviews, application blanks, and personal reference checks are used by a majority of the firms that responded. Other selection tools are used less frequently, especially by smaller companies.

APPLICATION FORMS AND RESUMES

If properly constructed, a written application form is an important source of information about a candidate's background and qualifications. Most companies use application forms for two purposes: to collect pertinent background information and to aid interviewing. Even though most sales applicants submit personal resumes, most companies still require completion of an application form that asks specific employment questions. Sales managers typically use application forms as one of the first steps in the selection procedure.

Application Forms Used as Background Review

application form
Selection tool that a sales manager uses to check an applicant's background

An *application form* provides a sales manager with a means of reviewing the applicant's background without being influenced by the individual's appearance or personality. A typical form records facts about an applicant's educational background, business experience, and other activities. Other facts pertinent to job success can also be included. This information is then used to eliminate candidates who are not qualified. Since there are legal limits on the types of information that can be requested on application forms, it is advisable for a firm to clear them with its legal department.

Some companies deem applicants unqualified if certain factors show up that the firm believes would prevent them from being successful salespeople. For example, a company might look for evidence of job hopping, or an unexplained gap in employment. The danger with this approach is that such factors may not always mean the people exhibiting them would be ineffective at selling. As a result, some potentially good salespeople may not be hired. Sales managers should also be certain that eliminating candidates on the basis of these factors complies with federal, state, and local regulations.

Application Forms Used as Interviewing Aids

Information provided on application forms also provides sales managers with the insights needed to prepare for personal interviews. Specific questions for use in an interview are determined by carefully reviewing an applicant's written responses. For example, if the person indicates an active involvement in a civic organization, the interviewer might be prepared to ask what the applicant's personal role is, and what he or she expects any future role to be.

As suggested above, the application form also points out possible difficulties that should be pursued in the personal interview. Have there been gaps of several months between jobs? Has the applicant changed jobs several times during his or her career? These and similar issues require further investigation.

Types of Application Forms

Each company must prepare its own application forms. Only information that will be used in the selection process should be requested. Some companies have found a short application form useful for initial screening, followed by a comprehensive form to be completed by applicants who make it to the next level. Another variation is a weighted application form. This involves specific weights assigned to the information requested; the sales manager can then mathematically determine how an applicant compares to the minimum qualifying score, and unsatisfactory candidates can be eliminated. However, when weights are assigned, a sales manager must be careful not to discriminate on the basis of age, sex, race, or other factors specifically protected by federal, state, or local legislation. Sales manager should also be careful that the weights they apply to individual cases do not adversely impact the hiring of protected classes as a whole.

Resumes

resumes Personal data sheets or vitae

As noted above, most sales applicants submit *resumes,* also called "personal data sheets" or "vitae." Often, resumes contain much of the same information requested on application forms. However, firms still typically prefer to have applicants complete their own application form, because resumes can be misleading. The best resumes do not always belong to the best candidates. With the proliferation of resume shops that offer writing services, layout and design, typesetting, and printing, even mediocre candidates can appear outstanding.

Evaluating personal resumes involves the same considerations as evaluating application forms. In fact, even greater care and thoroughness is required since applicants may omit information, enhance activities and accomplishments, list incorrect information, and do other things to mislead the sales recruiter. For example, educational qualifications are sometimes misrepresented on personal resumes. This information can be easily verified by a phone call to the registrar's office of the designated college or university. Other data that should be considered carefully are excessive extracurricular activities, unusual job progression and accomplishments, and exceptional statements of job responsibilities and authority. For instance, a candidate who states that she was "totally responsible for implementing company marketing strategies within assigned territory" is probably just indicating that she "followed orders."

INTERVIEWS

Interviews are the major source of evaluative information about a sales applicant, and most sales managers agree that the interview is the single most important step in the selection process. The study of sales management practices cited earlier in this chapter verified this belief that personal interviews are the most extensively used sales selection tool.[16] However, there is evidence that interviews lack reliability and validity and are a poor predictor of sales job success.[17] This may be because interviewers are poorly trained and do not ask the correct questions. In this section interviewing techniques and approaches will be described, and suggestions will be made for effective interviewing.

What Is an Interview?

interview Conversation with a purpose

An *interview* is a conversation with a purpose, normally involving two people. The general function of an interview is to exchange information. The interviewer's role is to obtain information about the interviewee and to furnish the interviewee with information about the company. The interviewee's role is to furnish information about his or her qualifications and to seek information about the company and the job being considered.

Types of Interviews

Interviews vary in format and style, depending on the company involved, the type of salespeople desired, and the specific purpose of the interview. Screening interviews are useful as a preliminary step, and more extensive interviews are very important as part of the final selection process. Each sales manager must decide which interviewing techniques work best for his or her company. A major choice is between patterned and unpatterned interviews.

patterned interview Interview in which the interviewer uses a set list of questions

The *patterned interview,* sometimes called a "guided" or "structured interview," is the easiest to use. This method employs a list of questions that the interviewer asks to obtain the required information. The set list serves as a control and helps the inexperienced interviewer to cover all the factors relevant to the applicant's history, qualifications, and goals. Written notes of the applicant's responses are taken. As an interviewer gains skill and confidence with this method, he or she can go beyond the prepared list of questions to explore other areas of interest.

For example, a patterned interview was prepared to help in hiring route salespeople because a firm's sales managers were not successful at distinguishing between potentially good and bad performers. The interviewing approach involved reviewing the nature of the job, identifying what top performers did and what they did not do, and then designing specific interview questions. The questions were assigned point values so that the interviewer could score applicants.[18]

unstructured interview Interview with no set format; sometimes called an "unpatterned interview"

The *unstructured interview,* sometimes called an "unpatterned interview," requires more skill and experience to conduct successfully. This method has no set format or plan; instead, it involves a relaxed discussion in which the interviewee is encouraged to talk about whatever is on his or her mind. The interviewer assumes that the interviewee will reveal much information during the discussion. The unstructured interview is limited as a fact-finding device by the skill of the interviewer. Unless an interviewer is trained in using this technique, a patterned interview is a better choice.

semistructured interview Interview in which the interviewer has an outline of topics to be covered, but the questions are stated in the interviewer's own words

The *semistructured interview,* sometimes called an "outline interview," combines characteristics of both patterned and unpatterned interviews. The interviewer has an outline of topics to be covered, but the questions are stated in the interviewer's own words. The interviewer also has the freedom to determine the depth and order in which outline topics will be pursued. Many sales managers prefer this intermediary approach.

Screening Interviews

screening interview Interview used to interest applicants in a position and to determine whether or not they should continue to the next level of the interview process

An early step in the selection procedure is a preliminary *screening interview*. It has two purposes: to interest applicants in sales positions with the company and to screen these applicants. An applicant wants to know about the company and the job, and the interviewer wants to know about the applicant. The interviewer must maintain a fine balance between generating enthusiasm for the job and questioning the ability of the applicant.

Screening interviews should be patterned. They should also be short; thirty minutes or less is a desirable length of time. The main purpose is to quickly eliminate applicants who are not interested in the job, or whose qualifications do not meet the job's basic requirements. This can be done by briefly describing the job and by asking each applicant a few pertinent questions. Frequent reasons for eliminating applicants at this stage are inadequate experience, unsuitable training or educational background, and inappropriate personality.

Screening interviews are often done by personnel specialists. Recruiting teams who visit college campuses are trained to prescreen applicants. Higher-level sales executives enter the selection process only after the initial screening.

Telephone interviews are often used to screen applicants and determine who should continue on to the next level of the selection process. The director of sales personnel for an international pharmaceutical company suggests the following three guidelines for telephone screening interviews:

1. Obtain a brief history of the applicant—both academic and work-related.
2. Take no more than three minutes to complete the interview.
3. Determine whether or not the applicant should be given an initial personal screening interview.

This company's telephone interview screening guide is shown in Fig. 13-2.

Even though the sales manager does not actually see a candidate during a telephone interview, he or she can learn a great deal about the person. For example, the candidate's voice (tone, pitch, delivery, use of language, and so forth) can give the manager insights into the person. Does the candidate's tone of voice convey enthusiasm? Does he or she seem genuinely excited and interested about the opportunity to discuss the position? A monotonous, dull voice, lacking in enthusiasm, can reveal a candidate's possibly poor attitude.

Does the candidate sound intelligent and professional over the phone, or does he or she use colloquialisms or cliches excessively? If a customer were listening to this voice, would his or her attention be favorably or unfavorably directed at this salesperson?

Does the candidate attempt to ask questions of a sales closing nature: "What is the next step?" "When can I meet with you in person?" "Do I have the experience

Date _____

I. Name _____

Address _____

Phone _____

II. Do you have a degree ? ____ In what subject ? _____ B.S. ☐ B.A. ☐

What college did you attend ? _____

When did you graduate ? _____

III. Are you willing to be away from home _____ nights per month ? _____

What is the minimum annual salary you would be willing to accept ? _____

IV. Would you give me a brief history of positions you have held in the past five years ?

Company _____ From _____ To _____ Income _____

Duties _____ Reason for leaving _____

Company _____ From _____ To _____ Income _____

Duties _____ Reason for leaving _____

Company _____ From _____ To _____ Income _____

Duties _____ Reason for leaving _____

V. Interviewed by _____

Appointment time _____

Applicant rejected _____ List reasons _____

_____

_____

NOTE: IN COMPLIANCE WITH EQUAL EMPLOYMENT OPPORTUNITY REGULATIONS, REASON FOR REJECTION MUST BE ENTERED AND THIS RECORD MUST BE RETAINED.

FIGURE 13-2 Telephone Interview Screening Guide.

you are looking for?" Closing questions from a candidate during a phone screening interview convey assertiveness, confidence, and a desire to make things happen. These are desirable qualities in a sales representative. A candidate who is meek, nonassertive, or passive may not be strong enough to make appointments with customers by phone either.

Name _____   Date _____

Address _____

_____

Phone: Home _____   Work _____

1.   Tell me about yourself start with high school and bring me up to date.
                (Record general information only. Specific dates, etc. can be recorded later.)

High school _____

_____

_____

College _____

_____

_____

Employment _____

_____

_____

Personal _____

_____

_____

Comments (Does person meet specifications required to receive application?)

_____

_____

_____

Rejected: _____   Application given: Yes _____   No _____

Followup: _____

Interviewed by: _____

FIGURE 13-3 Initial Screening Interview.

The pharmaceutical firm follows its telephone interview with another screening interview. The purpose of this interview, as indicated by the questions shown on the form in Fig. 13-3, is to obtain a more detailed history of the applicant and to look for patterns of success that may be suggested by increases in the applicant's past earnings, increases in his or her job responsibilities, and greater involvement in his or her previous jobs. The interview, which is relatively unstructured, takes about thirty minutes. At its end, the interviewer decides whether or not to ask the applicant to continue on to the next level in the selection process and to complete a detailed application form.

Selection Interviews

selection inter-
views Interviews
conducted by sales
management to make
actual final hiring de-
cisions; sometimes
called "employment
interviews"

After candidates have progressed through the preliminary selection steps, in-cluding a screening interview, they are interviewed in depth. The *selection inter-views,* sometimes called "employment interviews," are usually conducted by sales management for the purpose of making actual hiring decisions. Table 13-3 shows that more than one sales manager, typically, interviews a candidate.

The selection interview is a continuation of the screening and selection process. Only qualified applicants are sent to selection interviews. During the selection interview, the sales manager tries to make sure the applicant has the intelligence, education, and experience to perform the job. The manager determines whether or not the applicant's attitudes and personality will permit her or him to become an effective member of the sales organization.

Selection Interview Formats

There are several techniques used for selection interviews. The most common is a background interview, in which the interviewer employs a structured format to discuss the experience, education, interests, and outside activities of the applicant. An example of a structured interview is shown in Fig. 13-4, which is the third interview that the pharmaceutical company mentioned earlier conducts with its sales applicants.

Some sales managers prefer a discussion interview involving an informal and flexible format with no set questions. But, as noted earlier, this approach requires an experienced interviewer.

job-question inter-
view Interview that
poses job-related
problems to an appli-
cant and asks how
these problems
should be handled

Two other variations on interview format are the job-question interview and the stress interview. The *job-question interview* involves posing a job problem to an applicant and asking how it should be handled. It is assumed that the response will reveal the way the applicant would handle similar problems on the job. Performance-based questions help the interviewer determine how a candidate's experiences

TABLE 13-3   Who Interviews Potential Sales Recruits?

National sales manager	56.3
Regional/district manager	44.5
First-level sales manager	34.0
Personnel manager	23.0
Sales trainer	3.1
Outside agency	3.1
Campus recruiter	1.2
Other	9.4

Name _____   Date _____

WORK HISTORY

1. How did you get your job with your present or last company?_____
    (Did he/she show self-reliance in getting job?)
    _____

    _____

2. Will you describe your responsibilities and duties on that job?_____
    (Did work require energy and industry?)
    _____

    _____

3. How did you spend an average day on the job?_____
    (Was he/she on top of the job?)
    _____

    _____

4. What were some of the things you particularly enjoyed when working for this company? _____
    (Has he/she been a contributor?)
    _____

    _____

5. What did you enjoy less? _____
    (Did he/she get along with the people? Were dislikes justified?)
    _____

    _____

6. What do you consider your chief accomplishments in your present or last job? _____
    (Is there a pattern of success?)
    _____

    _____

7. Did you have any setbacks, disappointments, or things that turned out well? Tell me about them._____
    (Applicant's confidence and maturity.)
    _____

    _____

8. In which way did your job change since you originally joined the company? _____
    (Was there increase or decrease in responsibility?)
    _____

    _____

9. What were your reasons for leaving the company? _____
    (Were they justified?)
    _____

    _____

10. In the past, for what things have your superiors complimented you? For what things have they criticized you?
    (Major or minor?)
    _____

    _____

FIGURE 13-4 Depth Interview Guide.

11. What were some of the things about your job you found difficult to do? _____
    (Clues to motivation?)

    _____

    _____

12. How long have you been looking for another position? _____
    (Did he/she try to obtain sales work? Reasonable time on job market?)

    _____

13. For what types of jobs have you taken interviews? _____
    (Were they sales?)

    _____

    _____

ACADEMIC HISTORY

1. Why did you choose the particular college that you attended? _____
   (Direction?)

   _____

2. What determined your choice of major? _____
   (Knew what he/she wanted, interest in this field or easy path?)

   _____

   _____

3. How would you describe your academic achievements? _____
   (Pattern of success?)

   _____

4. How did you spend your summers while in college? (high school) _____
   (Did he/she keep busy?)

   _____

   _____

5. What were your career plans at the time of college (high school) graduation? _____

   _____

   _____

   _____

PERSONAL HISTORY

1. In general, how would you describe yourself? _____

   _____

   _____

   _____

FIGURE 13-4 (Continued)

2. What do you regard to be your outstanding qualities? _____
_____
_____
_____

3. What do you regard to be some of your shortcomings? _____
_____
_____
_____

4. In which areas do you feel you would like to develop yourself? _____
_____
_____
_____

5. None of us is perfect. If I were to talk with your spouse (parent or best friend), what are the areas in which he/she would say you need improvement? _____
_____
_____
_____

6. What has contributed to your career success up to the present time? _____
_____
_____
_____

7. What disappointments, setbacks, or failures have you had in your life? _____
_____
_____

8. How might you further your own business career? _____
_____
_____

9. What were some of the major problems or decisions that you have had to make up to the present time?
_____
_____
_____

10. If you had to do it all over again, what changes would you make in your life and career? _____
_____
_____

FIGURE 13-4 (Continued)

11. What would you want in your next job that you are not getting now? _____

_____

_____

12. What kind of position would you like to hold in five years? In ten years? _____

_____

_____

13. What are your present salary expectations? How have you arrived at this figure? _____

_____

_____

FIGURE 13-4 (Concluded)

compare with the sales position's critical job dimensions.[19] Examples of performance-based questions are the following:

- How do you handle difficult accounts?
- How do you deal with crisis situations, such as demanding client requests and crash programs?

stress interview
Interview in which stress is used to determine how the applicant would react to similar situations on the job

In *stress interviews*, stress is placed on an applicant through interruptions, criticism, or silence. The applicant's reactions are studied by the interviewer to determine how he or she would respond to stress on the job. The downside to stress interviewing is that it can turn applicants off to the organization. On balance, however, stress interviewing is deemed appropriate for salesperson selections. Another form of stress interviewing puts the applicant in an unusual, unexpected situation such as many new sales representatives will encounter. For example, the sales manager may select an object (such as a pen, stapler, or book) and ask the applicant to "sell" it. Or the manager may be less obvious and pose a challenge such as: "Why didn't you participate in extracurricular activities in college?" or "What do you think your major weakness is?"

Sales Consultants, the leading sales recruitment and placement firm in the United States, has prepared a list of questions in seven key areas: attitude, motivation, initiative, stability, planning, insight, and social skills. These questions, and the insights they are expected to provide the interviewer, are presented in Table 13-4.

Guidelines for Interviewing

Poor interviews are a complete waste of time for sales managers and applicants alike. Nevertheless, many busy sales executives fail to give serious thought to

TABLE 13-4   Interviewing Guide

Ask yourself	Ask the candidate
I. Attitude	
1. Can compete without irritation?	Ever lose in competition? Feelings?
2. Can bounce back easily?	Ever uncertain about providing for your family?
3. Can balance interest of both company and self?	How can the American way of business be improved?
4. What are life priorities?	Do you feel you've made a success of life to date? How?
5. Is there a loyalty level?	Who was your best boss? Describe the person.
6. Takes pride in doing a good job?	What duties did you like most in your last job? Least?
7. Indications of cooperativeness—a team player?	How do you feel about working with other employees?
II. Motivation	
1. Is settled in choice of work?	What ambitions does your spouse (or others) have for you?
2. Works from choice, or necessity?	What have you done on your own to prepare for a better job?
3. Makes day-to-day and long-range plans?	What mortgages, debts, etc., press you now?
4. Uses some leisure for self-improvement?	How will this job help you get what you want?
5. Is willing to work for what he/she wants in face of opposition?	What obstacles are most likely to trip you up?
III. Initiative	
1. Is he/she a self-starter?	How did you get into this line of work?
2. Completes own tasks?	Do you prefer to work alone or with others?
3. Follows through on assigned tasks?	What do you like and dislike about your kind of work?
4. Works in assigned manner without leaving own "trademark"?	Which supervisors let you work alone? How did you feel about this?
5. Can work independently?	When have you felt like giving up on a task? Tell me about it.
IV. Stability	
1. Is this person excitable or even-tempered?	What things disturb you most?
2. Impatient or understanding?	How do you get along with people you dislike?
3. Does he/she show likes and dislikes freely?	What children's actions irritate you?
4. Does candidate use words that show strong feelings?	What were your most unpleasant work experiences?
5. Is candidate poised or impulsive; controlled or erratic?	Most pleasant work experiences?
6. Will this person broaden or flatten under pressure?	What do you most admire in others?
7. Is candidate enthusiastic about job?	What things do some people do that are irritating to other people?
V. Planning	
1. Ability to plan and follow through? Or will he/she depend on a supervisor for planning?	What part of your work do you like best? Like least?
2. Ability to coordinate work of others?	What part is the most difficult for you?
3. Ability to fit into company methods?	Give me an idea of how you spend a typical day.
4. Ability to think of ways of improving methods?	Where do you want to be five years from now?
5. Will he/she see the whole job or get caught up in details?	If you were the manager, how would you run your present job? What are the differences between planned and unplanned work?

TABLE 13-4   (Continued)

Ask yourself	Ask the candidate

VI. Insight

1. Realistic in appraising self? . . . . Tell me about your strengths/your weaknesses.
2. Desire for self improvement? . . . . Are your weaknesses important enough to do something about them? Why or why not?
3. Interested in problems of others? . . . . How do you feel about these weaknesses?
4. Interested in reaction of others to self? . . . . How would you size up your last employer?
5. Will this person take constructive action on weaknesses? . . . . Most useful criticism received? From whom? Tell me about it. Most useless?
6. How does he/she take criticism? . . . . How do you handle fault finders?

V. Social Skills

1. Is this person a leader or follower? . . . . What do you like to do in your spare time?
2. Interested in new ways of dealing with people? . . . . . Have you ever organized a group? Tell me about it.
3. Can get along best with what types of people? . . . . . . What methods are effective in dealing with people? What methods are ineffective?
4. Will wear well over the long term? . . . . What kind of people do you get along with best?
5. Can make friends easily? . . . . Do you prefer making new friends or keeping old ones? Why?
   How would you go about making friends?
   What must a person do to be liked by others?

interviewing techniques. They can also have difficulty applying those techniques; interviewing is both a science and an art, and applying rules rigidly is not an effective approach. The Sales Consultants' interview guide shown in Table 13-5 provides some specific suggestions for conducting an interview.

Some other general guidelines that will assist one in becoming a better interviewer are listed on the following page.

TABLE 13-5   Suggestions for Interviewing

Meeting the candidate

At the outset, act friendly but avoid prolonged small talk—interviewing time costs money.
- Introduce yourself by using your name and title.
- Mention casually that you will make notes. ("You don't mind if I take notes, do you?")
- Assure the candidate that all information will be treated in confidence.

Questioning
- Ask questions in a conversational tone. Make them concise and clear.
- Avoid loaded and negative questions. Ask open-ended questions which will force complete answers: "Why do you say that?" (who, what, when, where, and how?)
- Do not ask direct questions that can be answered "Yes" or "No."

Analyzing
- Attempt to determine the candidate's goals.
- Try to draw the candidate out and allow him or her to talk.
- Don't sell—interview.
- Try to avoid snap judgments.

Prepare for the Interview.   To evaluate a candidate accurately and to save interviewing time, adequate preparation should be done prior to the interview. This involves reviewing the job description, the company's personnel policies and procedures, and existing data on the applicant. This will enable the interviewer to identify goals for the interview and to determine exactly what she or he wants to know about the candidate. A complete application form and/or resume are effective interviewing aids since they can be used to prepare questions and to eliminate areas for discussion. Asking the candidate questions that have already been answered in writing is an inappropriate use of interviewing time.

Select a Suitable Environment.   The interviewer should make sure the setting is appropriate for interviewing. If the interview takes place in an office, the interviewer should avoid interruptions from others, accept no phone calls, and postpone routine office work. If it takes place in the field, one should select a quiet hotel or motel room and make sure that there will be no interruptions.

Establish Rapport.   A pleasant, relaxed atmosphere must be established early during the interview. The interviewer and the interviewee must be at ease with one another. Perhaps the simplest way to do this is to open the discussion by asking about a topic of mutual interest. A quick review of the interviewee's application form may suggest a suitable opening question. Another approach is to review the steps taken so far in the hiring process with the applicant.

Listen and Observe.   Most authorities recommend that the interviewee should do about two-thirds of the talking. To make sure the interviewee does the talking, ask probing questions. Questions that can be answered by a simple yes or no do not tell much about the applicant. It is also important not to prejudice the applicant's responses by expressing approval or disapproval.

Successful interviewers also learn through observation. They begin to learn about an applicant as soon as the person enters the room. Does the interviewee project a businesslike appearance? Is he or she dressed appropriately? Poised and confident? Alert? Observation will provide many clues about how the applicant is likely to behave in a selling situation. For instance, clasping and unclasping the hands, fidgeting, not maintaining eye contact, and crossing the legs and arms are signs of nervousness, uncertainty, and lack of confidence.

Take Few Notes.   Most interviewers will need notes to refer to when evaluating an applicant after an interview. However, taking notes during an interview distracts the applicant and slows down the tempo of the interview. Skilled interviewers will develop unobtrusive methods of taking notes. Another technique is to use a simple evaluation form that can be completed after the applicant has left.

Use Two or More Interviewers.   It is unwise to rely on a single interview or interviewer. In the words of an experienced sales executive: "Anyone who hires someone after one interview is foolish. You should have three to five interviews, and you should feel better about the candidate with each interview. If you don't, don't hire the person."

Several interviews are crucial if inexperienced interviewers are involved. These interviewers may be unduly influenced by an applicant's appearance or personality; this danger is reduced by multiple interviews.

REFERENCES

Reference checks yield several benefits to the selection process. First, and most important, they provide evaluative information. No matter how promising a candidate may appear, there may be flaws that go unnoticed. Information provided on application forms or in interviews can be verified by checking an applicant's references. Reference checks may also provide some indication of the candidate's future sales performance. In fact, it has been shown that they are more accurate than psychological tests, formal simulations, and prehiring interviews in identifying outstanding salespeople.[20]

Reference checks also have public relations value. They indicate that a company has a sincere interest in picking the right people for job openings. The company's name becomes familiar to key persons in the community. Further, reference checks reveal to applicants that the company is sincerely interested in them.

When checking personal references, a sales manager has two concerns. First, he or she must be aware of legal constraints. Legislation designed to protect the privacy and civil rights of individuals places limitations on the use of references as selection tools. As a result, many companies place less emphasis on them than they did in the past because they may lead to privacy or discrimination lawsuits. As one sales recruiter observed: "Today it's very, very difficult to get a true perspective on a person's background. You have to spend an awful lot more on good interviewing skills. You can't depend on reference checking any more."

Line managers often refer requests for information about present or past employees to their companies' human resources departments. If this happens, it is likely that only the dates and nature of past employment will be disclosed, unless the applicant has given written permission to release more detailed information. Even if permission has been granted, there is disagreement among lawyers about whether or not personal information can be released to outside parties. Educators are also limited in what they can reveal about a present or past student unless the individual has provided written authorization.

The second concern is finding the best references for sales applicants. A sales manager should not contact just the applicant's listed references. These persons may not be objective sources of information. Furthermore, many times people listed as personal references may not be able to judge the applicant's potential for sales success.

Despite these limitations, personal references are still an important part of the sales selection process. The best source of information about a person is a previous superior. More than anyone else, a former boss should know what the person is really like on the job. Previous employers can answer important questions about the applicant's job performance from personal experience: How well does the individual get along with others? What are his or her strengths and weaknesses? What is the applicant especially good at doing? Perhaps the key question is whether or not the superior would rehire the candidate.

If the candidate has had experience in sales, past customers are another valuable source of information. They may also be more candid in their assessment of the candidate's sales performance than former bosses. Among the questions that need to be answered:[21]

- Has the candidate been able to keep customers, and for how long?
- How loyal are customers to the candidate personally, as opposed to the product or the company?
- Was the candidate seen as efficient, dependable, and genuinely interested in customers?

For younger applicants who have little or no job experience, educational references are important. Factual data (dates of attendance, courses taken, grades, and degrees received) can be verified by the school's registrar's office only with the written consent of the applicant. Other information about the applicant's character and performance may be obtained by contacting instructors and faculty advisors.

It is generally most effective to interview references in person. If personal visits are too difficult to arrange, or too costly, a telephone call is more effective than a letter. People are reluctant to say anything bad about someone else in writing. A telephone call is a prompt, efficient way to get an accurate assessment of an applicant. To be sure all items are covered, it is a good idea to have a checklist or interview form to follow. Another method of improving reference checks is to ask the applicant to provide five, six, or seven references. Some companies have found that the last two references listed under such a system are the most unbiased ones.

Some companies are turning to specialized data vendors to check the backgrounds of job applicants. Using various data bases, providers of pre-employment data produce summaries that describe an applicant's financial condition, criminal and driving records, and business relationships. A background report can cost several thousand dollars for a corporate officer or as little as a hundred dollars for a lower-level employee.[22]

PSYCHOLOGICAL TESTS

Psychological testing is an attempt to measure a person's behavior. Industry uses these tests to predict employment success. It is assumed that a test is representative of a person's past behavior and a valid predictor of future employment behavior. As a sales selection technique, psychological tests are used to measure attributes that cannot be measured by other selection tools. They are concerned primarily with aptitude, interests, mental ability, and personality.

Psychological testing of sales applicants first began shortly after 1940. Since then, research into what makes a good salesperson has resulted in a proliferation of tests. By the late 1960s, a large number of companies were using psychological tests in sales selection. Some of the reasons for the increased emphasis on testing were the greater importance of selection, the rising costs of selection and training, the increased knowledge of psychological tests, and the greater availability of tests for industrial use. Many companies also reported that testing reduced turnover by providing an objective means for evaluating sales recruits.

However, the use of psychological tests declined dramatically during the 1970s. This was mainly because firms were concerned about the legal implications of making selection decisions based on test results. As one testing authority has said: "The people . . . didn't stop using tests because of their inability to predict performance, but because the corporate legal departments were saying it wasn't worth the hassle."[23]

In recent years, there has been a growing demand to use tests again, and there is convincing evidence that they may be the most powerful tool managers have for selecting salespeople.[24] Testing takes some of the risk and expense out of the hiring process. When properly used, psychological tests can help identify potentially high-performance salespeople.[25]

Principles of Testing

To effectively measure and predict behavior, a test must be constructed using four major principles:

1. Job analysis reveals the type and degree of specific qualifications required for successful job performance. Each test should be designed to match the person to the job.

reliability
Consistency of test results

2. *Reliability* refers to the consistency of a test's results. A test is reliable if a person taking it again under the same conditions would achieve approximately the same score. Inconsistent results mean it is doubtful that the test provides a true representation of the candidate's behavior. Selection decisions cannot be based on highly variable results.

validity Authenticity of a test as a measure of behavior

3. *Validity* refers to the authenticity of the test as a predictor of behavior. A test is valid if it actually measures what it is supposed to measure. To accurately predict job success, a test must be valid. Tests must be validated by a trained psychologist or other qualified professionals. There are two ways to validate a test. One is to give it to currently employed salespeople and to compare the results with actual job performance. If there is a high correlation, the test will probably be a valid predictor of job success. The second method is to give tests to new salespeople, but to withhold the test scores from interviewers. After the salespeople have begun work, their performance is compared with their test scores. Again, the degree of correlation will reveal the validity of the test.

4. Standardization implies a uniform procedure for administering and scoring a test. Any deviation from this procedure will impair the reliability and validity of the test.

Types of Tests

There are many kinds of tests available for screening and selecting salespeople. Sales managers should seek the advice of experts when choosing tests for their companies.

intelligence tests
Tests of mental ability

Intelligence tests are useful for determining whether or not an applicant has sufficient mental ability to become a salesperson. General intelligence tests are designed to show how well a person reasons, thinks, and understands. They provide a rough guide to the applicant's overall mental abilities. Other more specialized tests have been designed to measure certain types of intelligence, such as speed of learning, facility with numbers, fluency of ideas, accuracy of memory, and verbal skills.

sales aptitude tests Measures of what a person knows about selling

Sales aptitude tests are designed to measure what an applicant already knows about selling. This form of test may be useful if applicants have selling experience. However, many sales managers doubt that it is possible to measure a special aptitude for selling. It is also important to note that an aptitude for selling does not mean that someone will be a successful salesperson. An applicant must also have the interest and desire to succeed in selling.

A sales aptitude test that has proven effective is the Personality Dynamics Inventory Test, which was developed in the early 1960s by Marketing Survey and Research Corporation. This test assumes that empathy (the ability to know what the other person feels or is thinking) and ego drive (a fierce desire to conquer) are the two traits most vital to successful selling. Forced-choice questions are used to measure these two traits. The designers of the test feel that anyone who has an abundance of these traits can be taught to sell.

Selected questions from another sales aptitude test are shown in Fig. 13-5. These questions are adapted from the Diagnostic Sales Intelligence Test developed by Sales Aptitude Corporation, a division of Personnel Sciences Center. This firm has evaluated over 27,000 sales applicants for such companies as Emery Air Freight and Thom McAnn.

personality tests Assessments of personality

Personality tests assess personality variables. They have value, provided that they indicate people who will fail in selling. Personality tests are not considered to be as reliable as other kinds of tests. Since the accuracy of their results depends on skillful interpretation, those results should never be analyzed by an untrained person.

interest tests Tests of whether a person wants to do a job

Interest tests determine if a person wants to do a job. If the information obtained is reliable, it can be quite helpful. An applicant who has little interest in selling as a career cannot be expected to perform up to potential. On the other hand, a person with strong motivation to sell may be able to overcome a lack of natural ability. The tests are limited, however, by the fact that they can be faked by clever applicants.

One of the most widely used interest tests is the Strong Vocational Interest Blank. This test asks questions about likes and dislikes in order to measure the similarity between an applicant's special interests and the interests of those who are successful in a given occupation. Some companies have found this type of information helpful in screening sales applicants.

Assessment Centers

assessment center Testing situation that places the sales candidate in a realistic problem-solving setting

A variation of psychological testing is the *assessment center,* an intensive testing situation that places the sales candidate in a realistic problem-solving setting. The candidate must prioritize activities, and make and act upon decisions. Judges, who are experienced managers or other knowledgeable persons, observe the applicant and evaluate his or her performance. AT&T and Merrill Lynch are two companies that use this approach.[26]

In essence, an assessment center attempts to simulate the sales job. Situational exercises and job simulations (business games, discussion groups, reports, and presentations) are used, and the process can last from one to three days. In addition

WHAT'S THEIR/YOUR SALES INTELLIGENCE?

How well would you do on a test that's aiding sales executives in selecting salespeople? Take the test to find out.

Presented here are 10 questions adapted from the 40-question Diagnostic Sales Intelligence Test being used by Sales Aptitude Corp., a division of Personnel Sciences Center of New York, for recruiting salespeople. The company has evaluated over 27,000 salespeople for such companies as Emery Air Freight, E.F. Hutton, Almay, Inc., Sun Chemical, Hilti, Inc., and Melville Corp. and its Thom McAn division.

The best score is 11 (the final question requires a double answer); the worst possible score is 0.

PREPARATION

1. As a salesperson of complex industrial equipment, which of the following would be most important to you?
   a. A full understanding of the equipment
   b. An ability to cite exact figures about the equipment's efficiency, life span, production capacity, etc.
   c. Information about companies that have used this equipment
   d. Memorizing a standard sales presentation covering all important features of the equipment

2. The salesperson should try to understand the prospect in order to (check the <u>worst</u> answer) —
   a. Show an interest in the prospect
   b. Make the sale as fast as possible
   c. See the prospect's viewpoint regarding the product
   d. Quickly establish rapport with the prospect

OPENING

3. Prior to your presentation, your prospect, whom you have just met, is talking to you about something not related to your product. While this is going on, the worst thing you could do is—
   a. Listen attentively
   b. Mentally review your presentation but appear attentive
   c. Attempt to politely interrupt so that you can start your presentation
   d. Try to get some clues about the prospect's personality

4. You have found out that your prospect wants very much to impress his/her boss. The best way of establishing your relationship with your prospect would be to —
   a. Mail him/her a news clipping in which his/her boss is mentioned
   b. Put in a good word for the prospect to his/her boss.
   c. Give him/her ideas he/she can present to his/her own management
   d. Ask the prospect what you can do to help him/her impress his/her boss

PRESENTATION

5. When presenting information about your product, advertising material is best used —
   a. As an initial attention-getter
   b. In the middle of the presentation to break up whatever boredom there may be
   c. As a visual aid, to be referred to from time to time
   d. At the end of the presentation, and left with the prospect

6. During the course of a presentation, a prospect inquires about his/her competitor's plans, with which you are familiar since the competitor is also one of your customers. Which would be the worst course to take?
   a. Show how ethical you are by refusing to answer such a question
   b. Help the sale along by telling what you have learned
   c. Avoid answering by saying that you are not aware of the plans
   d. Impress your prospect with the idea that he/she wouldn't want you to divulge such information about his/her organization

OVERCOMING OBJECTIONS

7. When a prospect points out that in certain areas your competitor's product is better, the worst thing you can do is —
   a. Show how your competitor's product is lacking in other areas
   b. Point out that this is only a very minor advantage compared with the advantages of your product
   c. Point out the benefits of your own product
   d. Subtly deny that his statement is valid

8. Your prospect is a "yes" person who agrees with every point you make. However, when the close is attempted, he/she says that he/she needs more time to think it over. When you call on the prospect again, the same situation occurs. What should you do on the third call?
   a. Continue your presentation, but inform your prospect that you can't call again
   b. Attempt to close the sale, but if this is not successful, leave and forget this prospect for the time being
   c. Make a far-fetched claim about your product to see if your prospect is listening
   d. Ask your prospect directly why he/she is not giving you the order

CLOSING

9. What should you do if the buyer of a company constantly refuses you?
   a. Alter your presentation
   b. Study the methods of your competition
   c. Don't call on him/her for a while
   d. Attempt to influence the buyer's subordinate personnel

10. After completing a rather lengthy presentation which included most benefits and features of your product, — you should (check both the best <u>and</u> the worst action)
    a. Summarize the features in which the person has shown interest
    b. Suggest that the person think a minute before making a decision
    c. Ask the person when he/she thinks he/she can make a decision
    d. Ask the person how much of your product he/she wants to order

FIGURE 13-5 Diagnostic Sales Intelligence Report.

to selection, the results of assessment centers can be used for promotional purposes, evaluation of sales training programs, and identification of managerial potential.[27]

Merrill Lynch, the giant brokerage firm, uses a sales simulation as part of its selection process for account executives. During this exercise, which simulates an account executive's day, applicants carry out all the normal tasks of an account executive. Sales applicants prospect for new customers, open accounts, call established customers, buy and sell stocks, learn about new products, handle paperwork, and interact with other account executives and an officer manager. The simulation, which follows filling out an application form, taking math and business knowledge tests, and undergoing a personal interview in the selection process, has been successful. It has allowed Merrill Lynch to hire applicants who have a lower turnover rate and earn higher commissions.[28]

Another successful assessment center was developed for the selection of life insurance salespeople. Techniques used include an "in-basket" exercise during which the candidate is confronted with a set of problems in the form of letters, memos, reports, and similar material that have accumulated in the in-basket of a manager. The assessment process also includes three telephone role-playing exercises that take place while the candidate is completing the in-basket exercise. The assessment center appears to be successful in predicting who will survive in the life insurance industry and who will drop out.[29]

Using Tests Intelligently

There is no magical shortcut for finding good salespeople. Tests are relevant only if they are part of the total screening and selection program, and if they are directly applicable to an individual company's needs. Professional testers feel that the most important factors in a salesperson's success are the desire to persuade others, an ability to empathize with customers, and the ability to bounce back after losing a potential sale.[30]

A manager who uses tests should be aware of their limitations, the greatest of which is perhaps that they are suited for group, rather than individual, predictions. Tests that attempt to predict sales success based on what is "normal" are dubious. They may eliminate innovative and creative people who do not conform to normal expectations about what is correct behavior.

Many tests developed to predict sales success have not been scientifically and statistically proven valid for measuring what they are supposed to measure. If you use them you open yourself to legal challenge and much expense, to say nothing of wasted effort. Great care must be used in choosing tests.

Another problem with many standard tests is that reasonably intelligent applicants can fake their answers to make themselves look good. This is especially true of aptitude and personality tests. Since applicants want the jobs they are seeking, they may answer the questions as they think the company wants them answered.

The best advice for sales executives is to use tests with caution. They should not be relied upon to the exclusion of other selection tools. When used with discretion, however, and with competent professional help, tests may provide information not available from other sources. Test results may help a sales manager avoid a serious error, but they must not make the selection decision for the manager.

PERFORMANCE FACTORS, INC.

Employee drug testing poses a dilemma involving two issues that are sometimes hard to reconcile: employee privacy versus workplace safety. Urinalysis traditionally has been the most common form of drug testing, but it has been criticized because, in the opinion of some, it compromises employee privacy. Urinalysis does not evaluate performance ability, but rather whether or not an employee has been using drugs; the results do not indicate where the drugs were taken, nor do they directly show whether job performance will be hampered. Probably most employers would prefer to hire employees who do not use drugs at all, but should businesses have the right to monitor what employees do on their own time?

A small, California-based company, Performance Factors, Inc. (PFI), has developed a unique solution to the drug-testing problem. Called Factor 1000, the procedure comes in the form of a computer software system that tests hand-eye coordination to measure whether or not employees are fit to work. When the software is first installed at a company, employees are tested repeatedly to establish their individual averages. They are then later routinely tested and the results compared to these scores; a substantial deviation from an initially established average indicates that an employee is not at his or her best, for whatever reason. It is up to the employer to establish a policy regarding what action to take in this situation.

Sales managers must be concerned about both the welfare of their companies and the rights of their salespeople. Surely most sales managers are loathe to violate salespeople's rights, but, on the other hand, consider the damage to a company's reputation that could be done by a drug-abusing telemarketer making customer or potential customer contacts for an entire day, or the risk to human life arising from a drug-abusing salesperson driving a company car.

Clearly, the drug-testing issue is difficult for sales managers who need to be responsive to the needs of several parties. With the increase of innovative drug-testing procedures such as PFI's Factor 1000, however, managers will be aided in their search for new approaches to handling it.

MEDICAL EXAMINATIONS

Most sales managers consider medical examinations a necessary selection tool. Salespeople often travel for long periods of time, make numerous calls, and may be required to perform some strenuous physical work. To cope with the stresses of selling, they cannot be hampered by illness. Consequently, complete medical examinations of applicants may be required, despite the relatively high costs involved. Many companies also require medical examinations because the insurance companies handling their group insurance programs offer lower rates if such examinations are given.

A company physician should be used, or the sales manager should designate the physician. The company should provide information to the medical practitioner about the physical requirements of the job. Extraordinary travel requirements and the like should be highlighted. The physician must make sure the applicant has no chronic diseases, hearing ailments, digestive troubles, or respiratory difficulties. It is essential that those applicants who will be unable to stand the physical strain of selling be eliminated. Medical exams also serve to point out existing medical problems that may be excluded from company insurance benefits.

Drug abuse should also be considered at this stage of the selection process. Drug problems are especially sensitive in sales because salespeople represent their companies and must be mentally and physically fit to perform their jobs well. As a result, many employers require a drug test as part of the sales selection process.[31] However, there are serious ethical and legal issues related to the use of drug-testing procedures, and care must be taken. Legal precautions must also be taken when using a medical exam as a selection tool. The job description must be specific regarding the physical qualifications needed for the job, and the company, if challenged, must be able to prove that these qualifications are real and necessary. Further, an employer must be able to show that disabled persons were not eliminated simply because of their disabilities. Finally, to comply with the ideals of equal employment opportunity, if a medical examination is required it should be the last step before hiring, and it should be administered to all recruits.

TRIAL PERIODS

A recent employment trend is to try out sales applicants before permanently hiring them. In fact, it may be wise to hire all salespeople on a probationary basis. It is easier to replace someone who is on trial than someone who is a permanent employee.

Trial periods, also called "auditioning" for jobs, have grown in popularity as more and more experienced salespeople and managers are eliminated through corporate mergers and acquisitions. Corporate reorganizations and reductions in personnel have also contributed to a growing number of excess sales personnel. As a result, placement specialists expect auditioning to become an important aspect of the selection process.[32] One specialist commented: "The really big benefit of auditioning is the chance to learn if the 'marriage' is going to work in the long run. You never know what it's going to be like working with your boss day-to-day or what the company will be like unless you've lived together for a while."[33]

Moore Business Forms uses its training program to screen out unfavorable sales recruits.[34] New recruits have a four-week "forward training program" during which they take fourteen tests. If an individual fails any of these tests, he or she is terminated. Recruits are told about this policy before they are asked to audition so that there are no surprises.

Frequent progress evaluations should be made to determine whether or not to continue the employment of an auditioning salesperson. At some point a definite decision must be made. The timing varies from employer to employer. Life insurance companies have found that a three-month trial period is usually sufficient to discover whether or not a new sales agent will be successful. In a large retail shoe chain the trial period is shorter. Store managers claim they know within a month whether a new recruit will be a good salesperson.

HIRING A CANDIDATE

All of the planning, preparation, and effort to recruit and select sales candidates is a waste of valuable time if the result is that nobody is hired. Once a candidate is selected, the task of hiring becomes a special form of sales activity. Sales managers must understand that actually hiring a qualified candidate is as important as selecting the person.[35] Critical issues are timing the offer, extending an offer, and rejecting candidates.

Timing the Offer

There comes a point in the selection process when there are no other questions to be asked, either of the candidate or of the employer. This is the point when the sales manager must decide either to eliminate or to hire.

It is crucial that a decision be made at this time. A firm should not postpone a hiring decision for an unspecified period of time, although many sales managers do this in the hope that another candidate will come along who might be better. When this is done, managers leave qualified candidates "hanging"—waiting endlessly for a decision. A postponement of even a few days seems like weeks, and weeks seem like months to eager, prospective sales candidates. Indecision may cause the candidates to rationalize ("It probably wasn't a good job anyway") and lose the enthusiasm they initially had for the position. This can be damaging, particularly if the sales manager returns to a finalist two or three weeks later to extend an offer. Frequently, the candidate has "cooled off" and lost interest in the position, or is no longer available because an offer from another company has been accepted.

In the final analysis, sales managers must keep in mind that they are not the only persons doing the evaluating during the selection process. Many sales candidates are sophisticated buyers in their own right. They read indecision in a manager during the selection process as a weakness of the manager and the company. Candidates may question what it would be like to work for such a company and manager in situations where they need an important decision to be made or decisive action to be taken. Would the company and sales manager waver then as well?

Extending an Offer

One of the happiest moments for sales candidates and managers alike is the extending of an offer of employment and its acceptance. This should be done in an upbeat and positive manner, establishing the groundwork for a happy and productive working relationship. It is best to extend the offer in person, but if time and distance dictate, doing so over the phone is acceptable. In either case, following up a verbal offer with a confirming letter is always appropriate.

When the offer is made, it is wise to review the details it includes (compensation, benefits, expenses, company vehicles, and so forth), as well as the job's starting date, time, and place, and the training program schedule. The new hire should be provided with a copy of the job description; along with a company policy handbook and any other pertinent materials relative to his or her employment.

When extending an offer, a sales manager should be prepared for the candidate who does not accept on the spot, but would like a few days to make a decision. This is considered customary, particularly when a spouse is involved or relocation is necessary. In other instances, a candidate may be considering more than one job offer. Candidates should be given the time, but should be kept to the agreed-upon decision-making timetable. If a candidate returns with no decision and asks for much more time, the person is most likely trying to find a better offer, or is doubtful about making the job change. In such cases, having another qualified candidate as a backup is always wise. It is then easier to encourage the initial candidate to say "No" if necessary, since there is another individual who might accept the position.

Rejecting Candidates

When sales candidates are eliminated during the selection process, they must be told promptly. To not inform or to postpone informing them is unfair. Further, this unprofessional behavior may create negative public relations for the firm that could hinder future hiring efforts.

Candidates should not be told specifically why they were rejected. For this reason, some sales managers do not like to tell candidates in person that they were eliminated. They prefer to send letters thanking rejected candidates for their interest in the company, the opportunity to consider them, and the time that they spent in interviews and other selection activities. Other managers prefer phone contacts or personal meetings. Regardless of the method used, rejections should be done succinctly and always with expressions of "thank you" and best wishes for the candidate's future career success.

SUMMARY OF LEARNING GOALS

1. Describe the Sales Personnel Selection Process.

Sales personnel selection, the final step in the sales staffing process, involves the various tools that a sales manager may use to select individuals who best fit the needs of the company. The salesperson selection process puts the manager in a buyer's role.

2. Outline the Questions That Must Be Answered in Evaluating a Salesperson Selection Program.

For this type of evaluation, the following questions must be answered:

- Is turnover excessive?
- Is the dollar investment lost on people who have left the company excessive?
- Are sales lost because salespeople leave the company?
- Is the selection process too time-consuming?

3. Explain Why a Systematic Approach to Selection Is Important to Salesperson Hiring Decisions.

A company that uses a systematic screening and selection process avoids costly hiring mistakes. The use of appropriate selection tools helps determine whether or not the candidate and company can form a successful union.

4. Identify the Major Selection Tools Used in Staffing a Sales Force.

Application forms, interviews, references, psychological tests, medical examinations, and trial periods are some of the major selection tools used to hire new salespeople.

5. Explain the Correct Way to Extend an Offer of Employment or to Reject a Candidate.

As with many sales activities, timing is a critical concern in the hiring process. A company that does not extend an offer of employment reasonably quickly hurts itself by alienating the candidates it wants and hurts all the candidates by keeping them anxiously "hanging." In addition to timing, companies should also be concerned with making sure offers are extended in an upbeat and positive manner and rejections are done in an appreciative manner but without explaining why the candidate was not chosen.

REVIEW QUESTIONS

1. In what ways is the salesperson selection process an art? How is it a science?
2. What problems are associated with having field sales managers responsible for the salesperson selection process? What are some companies doing to solve these problems?
3. The Fairway Corp. has a regular sales force of 105 reps. The company lost twelve salespeople to retirement and other jobs last year. They also terminated three sales representatives last year. What is Fairway's turnover rate?
4. What are some of the costs involved with salesperson turnover? What can managers do about this problem?
5. Identify the selection tools that have been most used to screen and select sales personnel. Which of these are used most extensively?
6. What purposes are served by the use of application forms? Why should an application form be completed even though an applicant has submitted a resume?
7. Outline the various types of sales interviews and briefly describe each.
8. What are some general guidelines for effective interviewing? Who should talk more during an interview, the interviewer or the interviewee?
9. What benefits does reference checking provide? Why has reference checking become more difficult in recent years? Who is the best source of information about an applicant?
10. What advantages are there in using psychological tests for evaluating applicants? Discuss the current status of such tests. Identify the different types of tests.

DISCUSSION QUESTIONS

1. Have you or has anyone you know ever had a job at a company that suffered from very high turnover? To what do you attribute the turnover? Do you think the turnover was something with which the owner or manager was very concerned? Why or why not?
2. Collect some salesperson application forms. Why types of information are requested in these forms? What generalizations can you make about the application forms you collected?
3. Have you ever been through any kind of job interview? If so, did the interviewer follow the suggestions and guidelines discussed in this chapter? Discuss your interview in class.
4. The issue of job applicant drug testing has been debated heatedly in recent years. Even more recently, however, companies have begun to show a preference for hiring those who do not smoke, who exercise, and who have good diets. Do you see differences in drug testing and testing for the other "vices" mentioned? What types of testing should be permitted?
5. Of the tests used to screen and select potential employees, which do you think are the most appropriate for evaluating salespersons? Think of a time you participated in or witnessed a sales situation. On which of these tests would the salesperson in this situation have done well? Which tests would the salesperson have probably failed?

ETHICAL DILEMMA

Bob Foster, a district sales manager, has heard that an applicant he is considering for a sales position had a drug abuse problem in college several years ago. Bob likes the applicant and feels that this person would be an asset to the sales force. However he does not want someone who may have a serious personal problem. What should Bob do?

SALES MANAGEMENT CASE

Finding Salespeople Who Write Right

A person whose handwriting is straight and vertical is object-oriented, while one whose writing is slanted is more feeling-oriented. Believe that? Many people do, and managers, in greater and greater numbers, are using handwriting analysis as a tool for selecting employees.

Graphology is the examination of handwriting characteristics to determine personality traits. An estimated one thousand U.S. firms are using graphology to make employment decisions, especially for occupations like sales, in which employee personality and integrity are important.

Graphology has its skeptics, but it does have at least one advantage in that it gets around the liability issues associated with some other employee selection techniques. In an interview, asking an applicant about medical history, arrest record, or former drug use is an illegal invasion of privacy. Asking about age or national origin is discriminatory. More subtly, asking a woman any questions that would not be asked of a man is illegal. Reference checking has been especially limited by the modern legal environment—employers, fearing slander suits, are oftentimes unwilling to say anything negative about former employees. These legal restrictions make it very difficult for managers to find out anything about applicants, especially regarding their integrity.

Used in conjunction with interviews and reference checking, graphology is becoming a recognized employee selection tool. The International Graphoanalysis Society, located in Chicago, trains people to be graphology specialists. The U.S. Labor Department recently changed "graphologist" from the "amusement and entertainment" category to the "miscellaneous professionals" category. Specialized companies analyze handwriting for client firms. One such company, based in New York, calls itself A New Slant and claims to be working with three hundred companies.

A substantial number of sales managers are turning to graphology to measure applicants' personal characteristics. Although the technique is unconventional, it just might allow sales managers to gain a greater selection precision, while minding their legal p's and q's.

Questions

1. Does graphology make salesperson selection more of an art or more of a science? Explain.

2. In Rhode Island recently, a legislator tried to have graphology banned as a selection tool. What unfairness might exist in using handwriting to evaluate job applicants?

3. The vertical/slanted criterion for handwriting analysis was mentioned earlier. Take a creative guess at what graphologists would say about the distance between letters, the pressure on the page, or the consistency between different occurrences of the same letter. How would this relate to the sales personality?

CHAPTER 14

SALES TRAINING AND DEVELOPMENT

LEARNING GOALS

- Differentiate between formal and informal sales training.
- Relate training to the salesperson's career cycle.
- Identify the reasons for training sales personnel.
- Discuss the educational principles upon which a sales training program should be based.
- List the questions that sales management must answer in designing a formal sales training program.
- Explain how formal sales training programs should be evaluated.
- Discuss informal sales training and sales management's field coaching role.

PROGRESSIVE TRAINING AT PAYCHEX, INC.

No one should ever accuse Paychex, Inc., of not being progressive. In 1971, the company found its niche in the payroll accounting service business by designing its services for small clients. Until this time, other payroll accounting companies had virtually ignored the small-client market and had instead focused on building high-volume business with a few large companies. More than half of Paychex's clients have fewer than fifteen employees.

Since its auspicious beginning, Paychex has reached annual sales of $137 million. Currently, the company serves 125,000 clients and is increasing its offerings to include tax services and personnel services such as writing employee handbooks and advising

clients about new laws and regulations. These new tax and personnel services are a natural for the company and are marketed to current customers.

Paychex's sales training and development program is consistent with the company's general overall excellence. New hires go through seven weeks of training at a professionally staffed school at Paychex headquarters. During the first three weeks, trainees learn about tax law and accounting principles, and they must pass a comprehensive exam over the material in order to continue in the program. The next two weeks of training are spent at Paychex branches getting hands-on experience and accompanying seasoned salespeople on calls. After this, the salespeople go back to the school for another week, during which they learn about selling skills.

The Paychex school is staffed by former teachers and by its own salespeople. The salespeople who teach are rotated in order to keep a fresh-from-the-field perspective. Paychex estimates that it spends $3500 on every trainee. These costs, however, are recovered by reduced turnover expenses and increased productivity.[1]

Paychex is one of many progressive companies that believe in the positive cost/benefit tradeoff of comprehensive sales training and development. Chapter 14 discusses training options available to the sales manager, from informal, ad hoc opportunities to comprehensive programs such as Paychex's.

CHAPTER OVERVIEW

A common misconception about personal selling is that "salespeople are born not made." In other words, salespeople must have certain attributes or qualities that they are born with or that are developed during their formative years. But just as a gifted natural athlete needs coaching and practice to become a top professional, so must a person with sales aptitude be trained to become a skilled salesperson. The focus of this chapter will be sales training and its role in developing professional salespeople.

Once sales recruits have been selected, a sales manager must turn to the tasks of training and developing these new people. There are two distinct forms of sales

formal sales training Planned training programs for new sales personnel

training: formal and informal. *Formal sales training* in most companies involves carefully planned programs complete with schedules, lesson plans, visual aids, other teaching devices, and systematic reviews and evaluations. There are three distinct phases in formal sales training: designing the sales training program, managing its operation, and evaluating its success.

informal sales training Continuous professional development of sales personnel

Informal sales training involves the continuous professional development of salespeople. These activities are as important for the maintenance of an efficient sales force as formal training. Informal training is a prime responsibility of the sales supervisor and includes working with individual salespeople, guiding their daily activities, and advising on improvements that should be made. Informal training has been characterized as curbside training, or field coaching. Unlike formal sales train-

coaching Informal, on-the-spot instruction; also known as "curbside training"

ing, *coaching* involves informal on-the-spot instruction on how to improve performance. Although it does not utilize formal training methods, curbside training plays a vital part in the development of salespeople. This chapter will explore coaching and customer contacts as informal training activities.

TRAINING AND THE SALEPERSON'S CAREER CYCLE

Since salespeople have varied educational backgrounds, experience levels, learning abilities, and so forth, they also have their own training needs. A major training determinant is where the salesperson is in his or her career development.

salesperson career cycle
Career stages a salesperson goes through

The *salesperson career cycle*, a conceptual framework that describes the stages a salesperson goes through during his or her career, is shown in Fig. 14-1.[2] Since the salespeople reporting to a field sales manager will be in different career cycle stages, they must be treated differently in terms of training, supervision, and evaluation. The four stages of this cycle, preparation, development, maturity, and decline, can be described as follows:

1. Preparation is the first stage in a salesperson's career. Since the person is new to selling or at least new to the company, the emphasis is on orientation and training. New sales recruits must be made aware of their duties and functions, and of the environment in which they will perform. New hires must receive product and company knowledge and, if they are new to selling, instruction in basic sales techniques. Even an experienced salesperson who is new to a company will need instruction on how the company sells its products.

2. Development, the second stage, occurs when a new salesperson's productivity begins to rise. The emphasis here is on supervision. The developing salesperson needs field coaching to identify and correct sales problems and to prevent him or her from acquiring bad habits.

3. Maturity occurs when a salesperson's productivity begins to level off. It has been said that mature salespeople work "smarter rather than harder." Although this may be desirable, many mature salespeople begin to take shortcuts that hurt them in the long run. As a result, they need to be retrained. Sometimes they simply need to be reminded of the basic selling skills that made them successful. One way to do this is to provide them with new challenges, such as transferring

FIGURE 14-1 The Salesperson's Career Cycle.

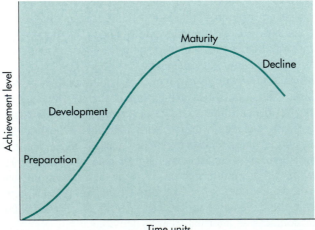

them to a new territory, asking them to assist management as field coaches or sales trainers, or promoting them to management positions.

plateauing Stage in which career growth ends

This stage, which has been called *plateauing*, is perhaps the most difficult career development phase with which to deal. Mature salespeople have reached a point in their sales growth where they have stopped developing, stopped improving, and perhaps even stopped showing an interest in their work. This scenario usually occurs when salespeople feel that their career growth has come to an end.[3]

Another important reason behind career plateauing is inadequate training. When salespeople are given new sales responsibilities, companies assume that they can "hit the floor running." Consequently, companies provide little or no training in handling those responsibilities. Over time, the lack of relevant training limits the salesperson's growth and development. The person also feels more stress and becomes vulnerable to burnout.[4]

4. Decline, the final stage, also represents a difficult sales management problem. It is very challenging to reverse the steady decrease in productivity of a salesperson in the decline stage. Retraining and motivation are needed, but it may be too late to reverse the negative trend.

REASONS FOR TRAINING SALES PERSONNEL

Salespeople need training during all stages of their careers. Unfortunately, many people assume it is necessary and possible only in large companies with many salespeople and large operating budgets. This is not true. Although extensive formal programs exist less frequently in smaller enterprises, various types of sales training are carried out successfully on a modest scale and with minimal outlays in small companies with few salespeople.[5] Whatever the size of an organization, the training needs of salespeople are virtually universal. There are two basic justifications for this extensive training effort:

1. *To develop the right work habits.* Salespeople's patterns of work habits depend upon what and how they are taught. They learn how to cover their territories, how to approach customers, in what style to live while traveling, what sort of records to keep, and how to plan and execute their sales calls. Salespeople learn to do these things well and efficiently, or poorly and at substantial expense to their companies. If sales recruits are trained properly, they learn the right work habits and patterns, at the right time, and from the right learning sources.

detraining Learning the wrong things from field experience

2. *To offset the effects of detraining.* Salespeople are constantly exposed to *detraining*—that is, learning the wrong things—through their field experiences. They adopt undesirable shortcuts, gravitate toward ineffective ways of selling, and often become discouraged and dispirited from the constant buffeting of the competitive marketplace. Both new and experienced salespeople must be trained to offset the negative effects of their field sales experiences.

Effective training pays for itself in a number of important ways:

1. It improves sales representatives' relationships with their customers by showing them the right way to do business.

2. It motivates salespeople to develop themselves and raises their morale because they see their company as concerned with their personal development.
3. It reduces the costs and the lost sales that result from high turnover of salespeople.
4. It makes salespeople more flexible and innovative in meeting changing competitive conditions.
5. It reduces the costs incurred by inefficient territory coverage, by poor use of company-supplied sales tools, or by the wrong application of company policy (credit terms, for instance) or of operating procedures (delivery schedules).
6. It increases sales volume.
7. It reduces the costs of supervision: Well-trained salespeople are more economical to supervise because they require less attention from their managers.
8. It increases the efficiency of controlling sales activities. A well-trained salesperson needs less direct control by a supervisor.

The net effect of training is to develop proper work habits and to offset the negative effects of field detraining, so that sales expenses are reduced and sales volumes are maximized. Both of these are critical management objectives.

EDUCATIONAL PRINCIPLES AND SALES TRAINING

Like all forms of management training, sales training must be based on educational principles. So, before considering the design of a formal sales training program, one must understand the characteristics of the process by which people learn. In the basic learning situation at least one of three things is true: (1) The learner knows nothing about the subject being taught, (2) the learner knows something but not a sufficient amount, and/or (3) what the learner knows is incorrect. The mission of the training process includes transmitting knowledge and skills, creating positive attitudes, and/or enhancing these things if they already exist. Training people to do anything effectively and efficiently is, in the last analysis, really the application of basic principles of education. An effective sales training program is based on the educational principles discussed below.

Clearly Recognized Purpose

It is a poor trainer indeed who does not clearly recognize the purpose and mission of the training program. But this is not enough. Trainees must also be given a clear understanding of why they are being trained, toward what goals their instruction is directed, how they will use what they learn, and how they will personally benefit from the instruction. Training can never be successful if trainees feel they are simply being "walked through" the program because it is a matter of company policy. This means a sound training program involves a carefully planned pretraining orientation period, in which trainees are shown the purposes and payoffs of the training they are about to undertake, and are allowed to question any purposes or methods that may be unclear to them. It is also useful to remind the trainees of the purposes and uses of their training during the entire course of the program.

Clarity of Presentation

Trainers too often know the company, industry, products, sales problems, and technical jargon of the business so well they forget that trainees do not. If trainers assume too much, the trainees are likely to become quickly lost among unfamiliar language, concepts, or procedures. Every effort must be made to make the training material simple and clear, and to present the material in terms that are understandable to the trainees.

Planned Repetition

Few people fully grasp a new idea or concept the first time they are exposed to it, no matter how clearly it is presented. This is especially true if the idea or concept is complicated, or if it varies in form or application between different selling situations. In addition, repetition is necessary if the trainee is trying to unlearn some previously learned wrong notions or techniques.

To overcome this difficulty, the good trainer builds restatement and repetition into the program. Important ideas or concepts are repeated at relevant places in the training program, either in their original or in different forms. In this way trainees have the opportunity to reinforce their understanding of the concepts and to examine them in several different applications or contexts. Planned repetition is a required characteristic of good learning and training, and it will be welcomed by trainees.

Systematic Review

Reviewing, and highlighting material already covered, has several advantages. It allows the trainees to check their understanding of what has been covered. It shows them what they have failed to learn, and where they must shore up their knowledge by extra work. If they have been applying themselves, review bolsters their morale because it demonstrates to them what they have correctly learned. Finally, a periodic review sets the stage for the training material that is to follow.

Orderly Development of Material

The major difference between learning by experience and learning by training is that training is orderly and can be repeated, while experience is random and uncontrolled. Suppose a sales manager wanted to teach a trainee how to deal with a common objection raised by customers. If the trainee were to learn how to handle this objection by experience only, he or she might make dozens of calls before encountering a customer who raised it. Even then, experience alone would probably not indicate whether the trainee handled the objection well or poorly. Orderly training can demonstrate the proper handling of objections and allow trainees to practice the proper responses as many times as necessary to master them.

The training program should be designed so that learning has a logical and meaningful sequence, flowing from topic to related topic and avoiding random skips. In this way trainees are not confused by being asked to study what appears to be unrelated material, and are able to relate individual steps or activities to those that logically precede or follow. For example, assume the trainer wants to discuss how to prospect for new customers. The logical order or flow of the topic would be (1) how

SALES MANAGEMENT IN PRACTICE

KRAFT USA

The Kraft company uses a training program that bends with the needs of its trainees in terms of both what is learned and how fast learning takes place. The training program lasts for twelve weeks (more or less), ending when supervisor and trainee each agree that the trainee is ready to manage a sales territory.

Responsibility for the successful training of new sales representatives is not placed on the trainee's supervisor alone but rather is shared with "district support teams," members of which are selected on the basis of their training abilities. Team members periodically evaluate how far sales trainees have progressed and sign a "learning contract" when trainees have mastered a particular task and are ready to move on to a new learning phase.

Other features of the Kraft training program are "thought provokers," periodic assessments, and "skill development managers." Thought provokers are issues brought out in the training process that are designed to encourage creative thinking. The sales trainees themselves are encouraged to come up with their own thought provokers as well. Sales managers and support teams are periodically assessed by their superiors and the trainees, and skill development managers are available to help trainees with special concerns or needs.

Kraft's approach to training new salespeople has the advantage of melding training expertise (from the district support team) with the sales manager's responsibility for and interest in the new sales recruits. This and the individualized support provided through a flexible learning pace and skill development managers are important aspects of Kraft's efforts to prepare its new sales recruits.

to locate new potential customers, (2) how to identify the particular buyer to be visited, (3) how to arrange to meet the prospect, (4) how to plan the introductory call, (5) how to initiate a continuing relationship with the prospect, and (6) how to follow up.

Sensible Pace

People learn at different rates of speed, and it is important to remember that the pace at which an individual learns has little relationship to how well he or she retains and uses what has been learned. Fast learners can be quick forgetters or poor users of what they have learned, whereas slow learners may remember what they have learned for long periods of time and use the information well. The trainer must be sure that the training is not proceeding at a pace too fast for slower learners, and that fast learners are retaining the information they absorb so quickly. One useful device for checking these conditions is periodic tests—verbal or written—during the training program. These tests should cover not only the material recently learned, but also material learned earlier.

Trainee Participation

Research in learning has established that people retain a very small portion of what they passively see or hear, but a much greater portion of what they see and hear in relation to doing. Implementing or performing what one is learning reinforces the message that the memory at first receives by sight or sound. Effective trainers explain, then they demonstrate, and then they have the student perform what is being taught. Skilled sales trainers realize the importance of reinforcing oral and visual instruction by action, and they devise ways by which trainees may participate in their own training by actually doing what they are learning. A later section on teaching techniques suggests ways by which this can be accomplished.

ORIENTATION OF SALES RECRUITS

Before turning to the development of a formal sales training program, brief mention must be made of the importance of an orientation program for sales recruits. Proper orientation of new salespeople is an essential first step in any formal sales training program.

Some sales managers view orientation as the last step in selection, whereas others see it as the first step in training. Regardless of how orientation is considered, it is an important activity. Sales managers must help new salespeople make the transition from recruits to employees as smoothly as possible.

Consider the orientation needs of college students, women, and minority persons entering selling. In regard to students, colleges are providing more courses in sales and sales management, but they have limitations.[6] College students must learn what a selling career involves so that they can prepare themselves. The comments of a recent college graduate in his first sales job illustrates the difficulties a sales recruit can encounter:

> My first job showed me the importance of having the sales manager available when and if questions regarding information on the products arise. Since I was new to industrial selling and placed in a brand new sales territory, I felt lost without my boss being nearby. He was so busy with his own selling, that he neglected the newly formed sales staff. I should mention that the manager was based in another state where the company was better known. This was the major reason why I decided to try my fortune elsewhere.

In regard to female or minority recruits entering a predominantly white, male sales organization, it is especially important to provide a strong orientation program. These hirees may have unique adjustment concerns that require extra attention during the first few months on the job.[7] Managers and other salespeople should be sensitive to these concerns.

Although sales recruits are usually enthusiastic about their new jobs, they are also apprehensive and have unrealistic expectations about selling. New salespeople complain that their jobs are more difficult than they expected, that they were not adequately prepared for handling rejection, and that they were not clearly apprised of the techniques and frustrations associated with selling.[8] An effective sales orientation program will provide new recruits with more realistic expectations and can help relieve their apprehension and anxieties.

Orientation should begin with an enthusiastic welcome to the company and the sales force. The formal orientation program is then used to help the new person become a contributing member of the sales organization, to maintain his or her enthusiasm at a high level, and to foster a commitment to the firm's sales goals and policies.

The following key activities should be part of every company's orientation program for new salespeople:

- The sales manager or human resources specialist should make sure that all employment records and forms are completed and processed.
- Each new salesperson should be provided with all the necessary employment information, especially that concerning expense accounts, vacation policies, payroll procedures, and other important policies and procedures.
- Each new sales representative should be informed of formal and informal office practices and special company events or activities such as office parties or gift funds.
- The sales manager should make sure that the new salesperson's office space is ready, and that samples and office supplies are available. If a car is provided, the company's policies about maintenance, insurance, and personal use should be explained.
- Someone should introduce the new representative to the other salespeople, immediate supervisors, clerical and secretarial workers, and anyone else with whom he or she will have contact.
- The sales manager should make a special effort to keep in touch with the recruit. This may be as simple as stopping in and asking, "How are things going?" It is also essential that the sales manager provide frequent feedback on job performance. This is especially important for inexperienced recruits so that they do not develop bad selling and work habits.

Perhaps the most critical element in a new salesperson's orientation is the sales manager's own attitude and behavior. The sales manager is the role model. If the manager appears indifferent to job responsibilities and his or her work habits are sloppy, the recruit will soon decide that the company's performance standards are low. On the other hand, a professional manager will show by example what is expected from a professional sales representative.

DESIGNING A FORMAL SALES TRAINING PROGRAM

Clearly, the benefits of sales training cannot be attained unless the program is well designed to fit a particular company's needs. In a survey of sales managers in manufacturing companies, five critical training variables were identified—objectives, content, training techniques, ability of trainers, and the skills and backgrounds of trainees.[9] As a result, the design of a formal sales training program involves answering four critical questions for each sales group:

1. Which salespeople should be trained, and at what points in their careers?
2. What should the training program cover?
3. How should the training be done?
4. Who should train salespeople, and where does training fit into the organization?

WHICH SALESPEOPLE SHOULD BE TRAINED, AND AT WHAT POINTS IN THEIR CAREERS?

Successful salespeople and their managers recognize the need for continuous training. All salespeople need training at all stages of their careers.

Training New Salespeople

After the basic orientation of sales recruits, the question of when to begin their formal training must be addressed. On the one hand, training is more efficient and meaningful if they have already had some firsthand selling experience. Consider the example of new salespeople for a computer manufacturer. Their training is more interesting, efficient, meaningful, and economical if, before they begin it, they are familiar with such things as the language of the trade, the problems and practices common to the computer industry, and the objections often raised by computer buyers.

On the other hand, it is difficult to provide selling experience for untrained salespeople, since, by doing so, a company risks sales losses and damaged customer relations. As a result, a minimal amount of field selling experience is usually provided for sales recruits before they are given basic sales training.

Retraining Experienced Salespeople

It is often necessary to retrain experienced salespeople. Refresher sales training builds on and adds to previous experience.[10] For instance, State of the Art, an accounting software firm, provides its sales representatives with up to four hours of training weekly plus periodic supplementary training sessions.[11]

Some of the specific situations that call for retraining are the following:

- When new products are to be introduced
- When new kinds of customers are to be solicited
- When a salesperson is to be assigned to a new territory
- When new reporting or other new sales operating procedures are to be introduced
- When a salesperson is to be promoted to a supervisory position
- When there is evidence that the salesperson has adopted improper selling habits
- When competition, economic conditions, governmental regulations, or other environmental conditions change in such a way that they drastically affect the company's selling operations

These or similar conditions call for substantial changes in the knowledge, skills, and attitudes required of experienced salespeople, and retraining is usually indicated. For instance, there is a growing need for assimilation training for sales forces which must be bonded together as a result of mergers and acquisitions. An even more important area is the many changes taking place in selling which make followup sales training essential for all sales organizations.

WHAT SHOULD THE TRAINING PROGRAM COVER?

The successful sales representative for any company, regardless of the company's size or industry, must know the company's products and its policies and procedures. Salespeople must possess the necessary sales and territory management skills, and must have a positive, constructive attitude toward the products they sell, their customers, their jobs, their companies, and themselves.

In setting up a training program, the first decision concerns content, or what the training program should cover. What must sales representatives do, and how well must they perform, to reach the organization's goals? The answers to these questions will provide a unified approach to the sales training program and its role in the total sales management system.[12]

Figure 14-2 shows the process by which the program's content is determined. To illustrate it: All salespeople need to know the technical specifications of a company's products, but new salespeople will not know them. So new hires must be trained in product specifications, whereas experienced salespeople may only require a brief review. This same sort of analysis applies to every sales training program, whatever the company or its products.

Determining the Optimum Content

needs assessment
Analyzing what knowledge, skills, and attitudes are required for sales success in a particular company

Designing the content of a formal training program for a particular company is a matter of analyzing what knowledge, skills, and attitudes are required for sales success in that particular company, a process known as *needs assessment*. Sales training programs should be designed with the help of suggestions from senior sales executives, field sales managers, successful salespeople, sales trainers, and outside professionals.[13] Interviews with customers and observed sales calls can also be used to determine training program content.

The dramatic changes currently taking place in sales and marketing are bringing about changes in the content of sales training programs. To be specific, when sales managers are asked to indicate what should be included in a sales training program, they tend to emphasize effective listening and other selling skills in addition to product knowledge and company policies and procedures. Other preferred topics are closing and gaining commitment, maintaining self-motivation, cold-calling, managing time efficiently, what to do when the client says no, making a presentation, and opening the call.[14] Many other studies also emphasize that salespeople must acquire a broad range of selling, communications, and interpersonal skills needed to develop long-term relationships with customers.[15]

Training program orientations vary. For instance, computer firms that are marketing-oriented have sales training programs that emphasize selling skills and marketing topics. In contrast, product-oriented firms often spend most of their training time on products, which does not prepare their sales personnel adequately for the selling situation.[16] Many firms that have become more customer-focused are also providing sales training for employees who do not sell but who are part of the selling process. This training also emphasizes listening and other interactive selling skills.[17]

A checklist for determining the content of a sales training program is presented in Table 14-1. A step-by-step analysis of this sort against the job description will show specifically what each sales group's training requirements are, and what the skill,

FIGURE 14-2   **Training Program Content.**

| Knowledge, skills, attitudes salesperson must have | less | Knowledge, skills, attitudes attained | equals | Training needed to be more effective |

TABLE 14-1   Checklist for Training Program

PRODUCT KNOWLEDGE

1. How much technical knowledge, and of what sort, do salespoeple need to know about the products (for example, how they work, what they will and will not do, how they are made, their expected life)? What do they not need to know about the products?
2. What do they need to know about how the product fits into the customer's technology, production, use, or resale processes?
3. What do they need to know about competitors' products—their strengths and weaknesses, characteristics, use features?

KNOWLEDGE OF COMPANY POLICIES AND PROCEDURES

1. What must salespeople know about internal policies and procedures, such as expense accounting, retirement, sick leave, vacations, and transportation?
2. What must they know about marketing policies and procedures, such as credit, terms of sale, delivery, product guarantees, advertising and promotion support, service and technical assistance?
3. What must they know about marketing operations, such as order and report forms, territory coverage, personal records?

REQUIRED SELLING SKILLS

1. Must they know how to prospect for customers?
2. Must they be able to plan each call?
3. Must they know how to handle customer objections?
4. Must they be skilled in identifying customer needs and matching them with product features and benefits?
5. Will they need to entertain their customers?
6. What social skills are required?
7. What communications skills will they need?

ATTITUDES

1. What positive attitudes must they have toward their customers, the company, their jobs, their supervisors?
2. What sort of relationship will they have with their customers and what attitudes will this require?

knowledge, and attitude content of the training program should be. This should be the basis for establishing sales training objectives which indicate (1) what sales trainees should be able to do at the end of their training, (2) the conditions under which they will have to perform, and (3) the performance standards they will have to achieve.

HOW SHOULD THE TRAINING BE DONE?

The next consideration in designing a formal sales training program is the learning policies and methods to be used.

Learning Basics and Training Policy

Formal sales training is based on one of two basic educational philosophies or policies. The best alternative for a particular sales group depends on the specific conditions involved—on the characteristics of the salespeople, product, markets, competition, and customers. Both approaches are well suited to certain conditions but not to others. The first policy discussed below is the historical basis for sales training, whereas the second is relatively new.

conditioned response Sales training approach in which salespeople are taught in advance to make the proper responses to any and all problems, conditions, and objections that they may encounter

Conditioned Response.   Under the *conditioned response* approach, salespeople are trained in advance to make the proper response to any and all problems, conditions, and objections that they may encounter. The selling job is carefully analyzed. Prospecting for new customers, the approach, the sales presentation, the close, and the followup are carefully combined into a general model representing all selling situations. Salespeople are expected to learn premade instructions and responses, and to adhere to them strictly. Under carefully prepared conditioned response policy, no salesperson is ever in a situation that has not been anticipated, or in which he or she is not fully prepared with a reaction provided by the training program. Conditioned response is a generalized response, which the training program is designed to transmit.

cognitive scripts Training concept that describes the sequence of activities to be followed in a specific situation

Consider how sales organizations use this approach to prepare salespeople to deal with common field situations. *Cognitive scripts*, which describe an appropriate sequence of activities or events to fit a specific selling situation, are prepared. These scripts are based on how an experienced, effective salesperson would handle a particular selling situation (for example, an initial sales call on a buyer for a larger business). These cognitive scripts are then used to teach the complex skills and behaviors of selling to novice or less experienced salespersons.[18]

insight response Sales training approach in which salespeople are taught to respond to selling problems on the basis of their personal insights into the nature of each selling situation

Insight Response.   The *insight response* approach entails an opposing stance: Salespeople are expected to respond to selling problems on the basis of their personal insights into the nature of each individual selling situation. The training is aimed at helping salespeople develop their insights and analytical skills. Insight response is an individualized approach.

Developers of sales training programs that use this approach place their emphasis on applying and expanding behavioral concepts to selling strategy.[19] Training is based upon the assumptions that selling involves an influence process and that a salesperson must use an influence strategy that is appropriate for the specific selling situation encountered.[20] Desired selling techniques are fostered through the development of specific behavioral strategies, skills, and tactics. For example, salespeople may be taught how to manipulate their communications (tone of voice, body signals, facial expressions, and so forth) to create a certain impression on buyers.[21]

Deciding Which Approach to Use.   It is useful to consider two completely different selling situations in deciding which training policy is best-suited for a given sales group. If the product is atomic power generation equipment, for example, the selling situation is complex and highly technical. Customers are knowledgeable and their requirements are varied. Salespeople must be highly trained and sales force turnover is generally low. At the other extreme, there are situations such as door-to-door selling, in which the selling job is fairly simple and nontechnical. Customers know little about the products, and their requirements are standard. Salespeople need not be highly trained and sales force turnover is high.

In the first selling situation, insight response is indicated; in the second, conditioned response is favored. In general, a decision concerning whether to use conditioned response or insight response will be based on questions such as the following:

- Is it feasible to condition the salesperson's response? In complex, changing sales situations involving knowledgeable buyers with various requirements, it is not possible to do so effectively because the customer's individual needs and requirements are so varied that it is impossible to anticipate them. When these conditions are reversed, conditioned response is possible.
- Is it desirable to condition the salesperson's response? The kinds of customers, their knowledge, and their needs dictate the answer to this question. Are customers best persuaded by a conditioned or an insight response?

In extreme cases, such as the examples given above, the choice between these two training policies is not difficult. The selling conditions of a great many companies fall between the extremes, however, and do not clearly demand either conditioned or insight response approaches. For these companies, the decision about which to use involves weighing the advantages and disadvantages of both policies, along the lines suggested in Table 14-2.

TABLE 14-2   **Advantages and Disadvantages of Conditioned and Insight Response Philosophies**

Advantage	Disadvantage
CONDITIONED RESPONSE	
Expert experience and advice is brought to bear on all of the problems the salesperson encounters.	Salesperson may overlook particular interests or problems of individual customers while adhering to the conditioned response pattern.
No problem, procedure, or situation the salesperson will encounter is overlooked.	Salesperson is not allowed to adjust to unique selling conditions.
Training is economical once the response program has been developed.	Customer may resent a standardized selling process as manipulation, or as a high-pressure tactic.
All salespeople in the group react in the same way, making it easy to transfer individuals between territories within the same company.	Some salespeople may resent absence of initiative and opportunity, thus affecting morale.
Customers are supplied all information the seller wants them to have.	
INSIGHT RESPONSE	
Salesperson is flexible to adjust to changing market and customer conditions.	Training is slow, difficult, and expensive.
Salesperson's focus is on an individual situation, not on a generalized situation.	
Customer's individual conditions and problems are central in the sales call.	
Salesperson's morale is raised by active participation in his or her own work.	

Training Techniques

Sales trainers have adopted a variety of teaching devices and techniques from the field of education. Each has its own special purposes and applications. Most companies use a combination of these devices and techniques rather than relying on a single method.

Lectures.　A lecture is a formal, structured, verbal presentation of information to trainees by expert trainers and company executives. This technique economizes trainees' time and makes top-flight trainers and executives available for training efficiently and at low cost. It is a very effective method of transmitting straight factual information. It is the most frequently used presentation method because much of the time in sales training sessions is devoted to product knowledge.[22] The major difficulty inherent in the method is that, unless lecturers are carefully prepared, planned, and rehearsed, trainees will not be receptive to the information presented. Since lectures must be generalized, the method is also poorly adapted to the transmission of the specific information needed for dissimilar selling conditions.

Discussions.　Under the guidance of a skilled conference leader, discussions permit trainees to examine a common problem, procedure, company policy, or case history. Discussions are well suited to teaching trainees how to handle selling problems that involve individual judgment, personal decision, and adjustment to specific selling situations. They have the further advantage of directly involving trainees in their own training. A limitation of this technique is that it requires skilled, experienced conference leaders. Such people are in short supply.[23]

Lanier Business Systems' training sessions for new sales representatives involve highly interactive classes. In fact, lectures are rare. It is felt that discussing topics rather than listening to speeches helps Lanier's sales trainees remember the basics better. For instance, a discussion of prospecting brought out the point that others within the company may be a good source of prospects, especially since Lanier has an incentive program that gives employees a commission for valuable sales leads.[24]

Panels.　A panel consists of a small group of trainees and sales managers—or a combination of both—who make short prepared presentations on a training topic. Presenters are then questioned by other panel members and by the trainee group. Advantages are that the panel is an economical way to make experts available to trainees; trainees can ask individual questions; and trainers can observe the trainees' responses. The panel also adds interest to the training program through the give-and-take exchanges between panelists, and between panelists and trainees. One weakness of panel discussions is that the differing opinions and points of view of panelists may confuse trainees. In addition, it is sometimes difficult to control the interchange between trainees and panelists so that a clear, consistent message comes across. This is especially true when one panelist monopolizes the presentation or the question-and-answer period.

Role Playing.　In role playing, a realistic situation is stated and several trainees play out the buyer and salesperson roles in the problem.[25] Other trainees, trainers, and executives observe the role-playing session and later make suggestions and offer constructive criticism. The advantages of this technique are that it adds realism and interest to the training program and increases the trainee's skills in reacting immediately to selling problems in a face-to-face sales situation. Because trainees take an active role in the learning process, they gain a better understanding of the dynamics of a sales situation. The weaknesses of the technique are that trainees sometimes feel awkward and embarrassed and the role-playing skills of individual trainees vary widely. Both of these conditions can detract from its effectiveness.

In recent years, the availability of inexpensive, easy-to-operate videotape technology has enhanced role playing as a sales training tool.[26] Video enables salespeople to view instructional tapes and to use on-camera role playing to improve their personal selling skills. A study of Prudential Insurance Company confirmed that video equipment contributes significantly to the development of new sales agents' selling skills and increases sales productivity.[27] Perhaps the greatest benefit is that a sales trainee has an opportunity to see and review the role play immediately after completion of the exercise. Trainees can see how they performed and what they did or did not do correctly.

There are certain role-playing guidelines to follow to ensure that the trainees gain the maximum benefit from the role-play experience and that they are not embarrassed or degraded by the training. Specific suggestions for using role playing as a training tool are: to (1) give each session a specific subject, (2) have the featured salespeople critique their own performances, (3) make sure observers comment on the things a salesperson did well, and (4) do not attempt to teach a certain way to react to a selling situation.[28]

Dramas and Skits.   In live dramas and skits, a script is produced that highlights the training points to be emphasized. Actors, in the appropriate stage setting and with the appropriate props, act out the script before the trainee audience. The main advantage of this technique it that is can be used as a change of pace and to add interest to the training program. Dramas and skits facilitate learning and allow trainees to associate themselves with the situations being presented. Since no one's feelings are involved, dramas can be used to introduce humor, criticism, and satire, which might not be acceptable in lectures or discussions. The disadvantage of the approach is that the skits are difficult to design, and are, therefore, expensive. It requires a specialist to prepare a script that is interesting, entertaining, and engrossing, and that at the same time gets the message across. Such specialists must usually be found outside the company. The actors also are usually hired from outside the company. As is the case with other training materials, however, there are companies that specialize in planning, producing, and presenting training dramas and skits.

Visual Aids.   These include films, tapes, flip charts, chalk and flannel boards, personal computers, closed-circuit and playback television, and overhead slide projection. It is an established fact that learners retain much more of what they both see and hear than of what they only hear. Other advantages of visual aids are that they add color, motion, and drama to the training sessions. They can be repeated as often as necessary for review and reinforcement of the message, and for rechecking by the trainees. Since visual aids are prepared in advance, their form, content, sequence, and organization can be completely preplanned and controlled. There need be no unrehearsed presentation mistakes.

The main disadvantage of visual aids as a training device is that they are often expensive to develop or purchase. Recently, however, technological advances have reduced their costs and greatly increased their flexibility. Further, companies that specialize in producing visual aids have become proficient in the presentation of selling techniques and skills.

A successful producer of management and sales training films and videotapes is Video Arts, which features the British actor John Cleese in many of its productions. These films and tapes use carefully structured humor to present the sales training message and to offer examples with which trainees can identify.[29] According to Cleese, a "key to a training film is to involve the audience at a gut level . . . create situations that will carry sort of an emotional conviction." Humor is used, he notes, to "get people involved in the gut."[30]

For companies that want to produce their own visual aids, an advertising agency may be able to provide the necessary artistic talent and technical competence. In addition, there are a number of firms that specialize in the planning and production of visual training aids for specific clients. Many companies have developed their own in-house expertise. For instance, Amway produces videocassettes in a TV studio located at company headquarters. These are mailed to Amway's distributors for in-home use. Massachusetts Mutual Insurance Company and ComputerLand also make extensive use of videos as sales training tools.[31]

Audio Tapes. The rapid growth of videos as training tools has pushed audio sales training tapes into the background. However, audio tapes continue to be useful in training, especially for those outside salespeople who travel a great deal.[32] Salespeople can listen to cassettes while they are in their cars or on airplanes. In addition to the ease of listening to audio cassettes, their relatively low cost is another advantage. Pfizer Labs, Moore Business Forms, Scott Paper, Johnson & Johnson, and Gillette are just a few of the firms that use audiocassettes extensively as a sales training tool.[33]

High-Tech Training Methods. Many of the recent advances in sales training have come from the expanded use of high technology. The major forms are computer-assisted instruction, interactive video, and video conferencing. Among the benefits that these advanced technologies provide are time savings, reduced selling expenses, better problem-solving skills, and enhanced sales training.[34]

In one study of high-tech approaches to sales training, researchers found that high-tech tools have not yet been widely adopted in sales training.[35] Interactive video is the most frequently used, but even this method has limited applications. However, respondents to the survey indicated that the usage of all forms of high-tech training methods will grow rapidly. According to the researchers:

> . . . in general, high-tech methods deemed most effective at achieving . . . training objectives have the combined attributes of high-tech and (interaction) as their basis. For example, simulation games, problem solving exercises and interactive video typically involve not only interaction between the trainee and the computer, but also allow for

flexibility, creativity, and human interaction during the training exercise. Firms using interactive video have found that the method facilitates the simulation of realistic sales situations, allows critique of trainee performance upon completion of training exercises and results in higher retention of knowledge.[36]

The three major forms of high-tech training methods and some applications are described below.

Computer-Assisted Instruction.   Begun in the late 1950s as a method of training computer programmers, computer-assisted instruction has become a popular sales training technique. As used today, this approach involves the interaction between the sales trainee and a microcomputer on a one-to-one basis. Use of a microcomputer to present sales training allows materials to be customized to the trainee's needs. Flexible training materials enable the trainee to move along at an individual pace, to skip over materials with which the person is already familiar, and to return to specific materials for review. Thus, a new salesperson can learn basic concepts and skills while an experienced salesperson can refresh and reinforce important skills.[37]

Computer-assisted instruction also offers many cost-saving opportunities to sales trainers. Publishers of packaged microcomputer-based sales training programs claim that training can be achieved for 10 percent of the cost of conventional methods. These savings come from the elimination of the cost of instructors, the cost of travel to and from the training sessions, and the cost of classroom facilities.[38]

One of the earliest sales training uses of computers was the development of business games. Also called "simulation exercises," these began as "pen-and-paper" exercises, but most are now computer-based. Competing as individuals or as teams, trainees must make a series of decisions, which are then scored against the moves of competing units. One unit eventually emerges as the winner on the grounds of such standards as profit, return on investment, or penetration of new markets. For example, many companies use a simulation exercise to teach time and territory management techniques to their salespeople. Trainees are required to allocate their sales efforts to customers and products using a computer-designed matrix and a computer-generated chart of accounts.

The advantages of business games are that they are realistic and interesting, and they give trainees a genuine sense of competition in the market. They also allow the exposition and demonstration of business and selling problems that are not always readily demonstrable through the use of other teaching techniques. A business game is, however, usually expensive, and games applicable to some industries and selling situations are not available unless specially prepared.

For individual sales training, programmed learning approaches are used. In programmed learning, the total body of knowledge that trainees are to learn is broken into small segments, each of which consists of explanatory material and questions. These segments are presented to the trainees in sequence. Each trainee answers a set of questions on each module of the work, and is directed either to restudy the explanatory material and take the test again, or to proceed to the next lesson.

Most computer-assisted instructional programs use the following approach. Trainees first complete an assessment test which measures their current level of knowledge. The computer then directs each trainee to the appropriate material in the training program based on the results of his or her assessment. Upon completing each section, the trainee participates in a question-and-answer drill whose results indicate whether or not the material has been mastered. A postassessment test provides immediate feedback and measures the trainee's new level of understanding. Examples of this form of training are MasterPOINT, a software program developed and marketed by Applied Learning Systems,[39] and Sell! Sell! Sell!, published by Thoughtware, Inc.[40]

Some computer-based training approaches use expert systems, sometimes called "knowledge systems." An expert system is a computer system that behaves as a human brain. The key to the development of an expert system for sales training is the involvement of master salespersons in the creation of the knowledge that is the heart of an expert system. When this is done properly, new salespeople will be exposed to a vast amount of experience. Expert systems can also be used to train people in specific tasks, such as risk management, claims adjusting, and financial planning.[41]

Interactive Video.   This approach involves the presentation of video segments followed by computer-generated questions. The combination of video and computer technology offers the opportunity for total interactivity. Trainees' responses allow for the "branching" of video presentations and computer questioning into a number of selling situations. NCR, AT&T, Caterpillar, and Bell South are among the firms that have used interactive video technology to teach their salespeople negotiation skills, presentation finesse, basic sales techniques, and methods of trade show selling.[42]

Interactive video instruction provides salespeople with a convenient risk-free opportunity to practice selling skills and approaches. Because the equipment can be set up in a field sales office, salespeople can participate in the training at their own convenience. The most involved format is the simulated sales call, which allows sales trainees to make the key decisions about what to say or do next. And, because trainees are practicing their selling skills with a computer, not in the field, mistakes will not result in lost sales.[43]

When IBM shifted over 20,000 employees from manufacturing and administration into marketing and programming, it was faced with the challenge of teaching plant employees, laboratory technicians, and managers how to sell. The firm, which has the most comprehensive sales education program in the computer industry, developed an interactive video training system. This self-study approach combined a laser video disk and a personal computer. Fewer than 100 of the people who undertook the sales training program failed to complete it.[44]

Videoconferences.   These are electronic meetings, or video teleconferences, that allow participants in one location to interact with instructors and participants at other locations. Also known as "business TV" (BTV), this method combines advances in telephone and telecommunications technology. Although companies use videoconferencing for a number of long-distance communications purposes, fully 75 percent of all corporate broadcasts are for training purposes. It is an ideal method for training because trainees can interact with other trainees and instructors.[45]

There are a number of sales training applications for videoconferencing. Texas Instruments has used it to introduce new products to its salespeople and distribu-

SALES MANAGEMENT IN PRACTICE

AETNA LIFE & CASUALTY

Aetna has learned a thing or two about business television since 1987, when it installed its own television network linking 235 field offices with its home office in Hartford, Connecticut. Currently, the network broadcasts seventeen hours of programming each month, most of which is for training purposes.

BTV is interactive, combining one-way video with two-way audio. One of its main advantages over more traditional training methods such as classroom teaching or videotape is immediacy—employees all over the country can get the same message at the same time. Also, Aetna has found that BTV entails a lower cost per pupil than in-person training because transportation and lodging expenses are eliminated and employees are not taken away from their jobs for long periods of time. Reduced costs allow a greater number of employees to be reached; for example, Aetna uses BTV to provide an orientation workshop for new first-line managers.

Only about four hundred managers actually attend the workshop in person, but over a thousand managers participate through BTV.

Using BTV instead of in-person training does have at least one disadvantage, however. Aetna found that television instructors cannot hold students' attention for as long as in-person instructors can. In response, the company developed a special format for BTV courses. Taught in a traditional classroom setting, the workshops are often conducted in six-hour segments over two days. If televised, they are taught in weekly ninety-minute sessions. Between segments, participants apply what they have learned. At the next session, students all over the country are able to share their experiences and get feedback from the instructor and from each other.

BTV has been characterized in the past few years by better technology, increased awareness of telecommunications, and greater cost-effectiveness. In the future, networks and programs such as Aetna's will become widespread as more and more companies begin to embrace this training-conducive medium.

---

tors; Aetna Life & Casualty Company has linked its salespeople, customers, engineers, and consultants through videoconferencing; and ComputerLand has used a videoconferencing network to connect its 650 stores to train salespeople, introduce merchandising programs, and conduct seminars for customers. The growth of videoconferencing is due to many factors, including improved transmission quality and lower prices.[46]

One of the most extensive sales training applications of videoconferencing took place in early 1990. The sales forces of 200 American and 20 Canadian television stations participated in an interactive sales training teleconference presented by the Television Bureau of Advertising.[47] Programs similar to this are the wave of the future. As one leading consultant has said: "There's still a lot of innovation to be tried, and eventually prospective users are going to make business TV a daily part of their corporate lives."[48]

WHO SHOULD TRAIN SALESPEOPLE, AND WHERE DOES TRAINING FIT INTO THE ORGANIZATION?

Who should train salespeople? Where does training fit into the organization? As with the other questions relating to this topic, there are no easy answers. One of the difficulties is that many companies do not see a need for professional sales trainers.

Professional Teaching Skills Are Critical

Most company sales trainers are selected from the sales force.[49] Union Carbide, Metropolitan Life Insurance Company, and other firms select top salespeople to serve as sales trainers for a few years. It is felt that these individuals will project credibility, will have a better feel for the market, and will bring new ideas to the training program. After they have spent several years in sales training, they are promoted into some form of management position.

This approach is not without problems, however. It takes a great deal of time and effort to coordinate an effective training program, and there is a time lag as salespeople learn to become good trainers, which sometimes they never do. This is because in sales training, as in other forms of education, the skills of teaching are different from the skills of performing the job being taught. However, there is a prevalent fallacy in all fields of human endeavor that anyone who does something well is automatically an outstanding teacher-trainer of that same skill. Actually, the skills involved in making a sale are completely different from the skills needed to teach or train someone how to make a sale.

Some skilled salespeople and sales managers are top-flight trainers, but others are poor. Some mediocre salespeople are good trainers. Some professional sales trainers were, or would be, poor sales representatives, others excellent. This condition has an important bearing on the questions of who should train salespeople and where the training should take place in the organization.

The general feeling of sales trainers is that teaching skills are more important to the success of a sales training program than is knowledge of the subject matter being taught.[50] Interpersonal skills are especially important. In a study of sales training participants, almost half of the respondents felt that interest in and enthusiasm for the subject matter are the most important positive attributes in a trainer. Good communication skills came next, while practical experience was the third most important attribute.[51] The trainer must create an environment conducive to learning. An effective trainer also has the ability to adapt training to the needs of each individual trainee, and to interact with each trainee so that he or she is motivated to learn. In effect, trainers are salespeople who sell learning to the trainees.[52]

The Sales Trainer and the Training Location

In regard to the question of who should train salespeople, the alternatives are (1) in-house training specialists, (2) field sales managers and experienced salespeople, or (3) outside training specialists. As to location, training can take place either in a single, central training location or in field sales units.

A number of combinations of these alternatives are possible. However, field sales personnel cannot generally afford the time away from their sales work to participate in centralized training at another location, while training experts are too expensive to be employed at different field locations. As a result, most companies must choose between three more realistic alternatives: (1) sales training by company training specialists in a central training location, (2) training by outside experts in a central training location, or (3) training by field salespeople at field sales locations. Each of these has its merits and its limitations, which are considered in Table 14-3.

Sales managers must use the kind of analysis summarized in this model to deciding the best training choice for their own companies. This requires weighing the relative importance of program specifications against each training alternative. For

TABLE 14-3 Evaluation of Three Training Alternatives by Type of Trainer and Training Location

Merits	Limitations
TRAINING BY COMPANY TRAINING SPECIALISTS IN A CENTRAL TRAINING LOCATION	
Provides specialized training knowledge and experience.	Training cannot be directly related to real-life selling situations and problems.
Does not take line salespeople away from their work or distract their attention from their sales job.	Trainees learn nothing about the markets in which they will be working.
Training is the main purpose of the operation—hence, there is no dilution of the training activity by the pressures of selling problems.	When trainees are sent to the field after training, their managers may belittle centralized training as being unrelated to real market conditions.
	Adds overhead costs of staff, special equipment, and meeting rooms.
TRAINING BY OUTSIDE EXPERTS IN A CENTRAL TRAINING LOCATION*	
Provides ideas and techniques from training in other industries and companies; offers broader experience and viewpoint.	Danger exists of leaking company trade secrets to the outside training experts.
	Expert may not know or may not be able to master important problems or conditions unique to the particular company.
TRAINING BY FIELD SALESPEOPLE AT FIELD SALES LOCATIONS	
No added overhead costs for training personnel, since line salespeople are already on the payroll.	Does not provide specialized training knowledge and experience.
Training can be related to real selling situations.	Takes line salespeople away from selling and managing.
Trainees learn about conditions in the actual market.	Training emphasis is likely to be diluted by the pressures of everyday sales activities.
Field salespeople are themselves involved in the training, so they are less likely to deny or downgrade its value.	

* This alternative shares the merits and limitations cited above for training by company training specialists in a central location, except that training by outside experts has an additional advantage and two potential limitations.

instance, decentralized training by field personnel reduces expense, adds realism to the training, orients trainees in their future territories, safeguards company trade secrets, and focuses on company problems and procedures. However, it does not provide specialized training skills and experience, does not utilize full-time trainers, and may not be particularly creative.

A Combination Plan

Combination plans used by Pitney Bowes and other companies involve sales training in the field by field salespeople who are assisted in a staff capacity by training specialists from headquarters.[53] In such instances training specialists assist the field trainers in planning the program, participate in the program, counsel field trainers, and assist in evaluating the program. A mix of line people having product knowledge along with people knowledgeable in personnel development is obtained. Although this is not necessarily the ideal solution, it does have all the merits of training in the field by field people. At the same time, it lessens the problems posed by the lack of special training know-how and by the diversion of sales personnel from their selling jobs.

Selecting Outside Trainers

Although the majority of the average company's sales training is provided by inside trainers, there are times when a firm has to go outside for training. Small companies often have special needs for outside training; they typically cannot afford to maintain their own sales training staff.

Training specialists can be brought in from the outside, or salespeople can be sent to outside programs, seminars, and college courses.[54] Sources of information about outside trainers and training programs include professional and trade associations, business associates, sales training professionals, marketing faculty members, and professional journals.

Evaluation of outside training options is not easy.[55] Although promotional literature and sales representatives are a good source of information, it is always wise to obtain personal information about an outside training program. Sales training vendors can be asked to provide a list of clients who can be contacted. Personal observation of the training approach, materials, and methods is also recommended.

EVALUATION AND FOLLOWUP

The costs of sales training are astounding. It is no wonder that evaluation of sales training programs has become a major sales management issue. In particular, sales executives are concerned that the money spent on sales training should lead to added sales or new accounts.[56]

Evaluating the Immediate Impact of Training

In some respects, evaluation of a sales training program is not difficult. A key question is whether or not trainees felt it was well taught. Written questionnaires can be used to assess participants' reactions during and after the training program. Informal verbal feedback from trainees also provides insight into their feelings toward the instruction they received.

It is also relatively easy to determine if the program has succeeded in imparting the necessary factual information. Trainees can be tested to find out if they know the pertinent facts about products, company policies, and sales operations. Some firms use incentives to determine whether or not salespeople have learned product information and to reward those who have. For instance, Smith Kline Bio-Science Laboratories' salespeople participated in a contest to reward the learning of product knowledge about nine new medical tests. Information about the new products was provided by technical updates, test information brochures, service manuals, and sales training materials.[57]

In the areas of sales skills and personal attitudes, the evaluation of sales training is difficult and inexact. There are three major reasons for this:

1. Skills and attitudes are difficult to observe and to evaluate objectively.
2. One can never be sure which skills and attitudes have been acquired through training and which may have existed in the trainees before going through the program.

3. After training, one cannot be sure which skills, attitudes, and knowledge the trainee has learned from sales experience, and which have come from the training program itself.

As a result of these factors, sales training evaluation is an inexact and only semimeasurable activity. The effectiveness and efficiency of sales training can never be determined completely accurately. And since people develop and apply selling skills and attitudes over relatively long periods of time, evaluating sales training is also a long-term activity. In spite of the known inaccuracies, the training program must be subject to constant evaluation, and possible revision, if training dollars are to be spent well and efficiently. In addition, sales managers must go beyond traditional subjective forms of evaluation to objectively determine the training program's contribution to the firm.[58]

Evaluation Issues

Two training authorities have suggested that there are four critical training evaluation questions:[59]

1. To what degree does the training produce appropriate learning?
2. To what degree is learning transferred to the job?
3. To what degree is the knowledge or skill level maintained over time?
4. Does the value of participants' improved performance meet or exceed the cost of training?

They point out, however, that these questions are difficult to answer because of constraints on time, resources, and access to personnel.

Training Evaluation Methods

Companies use various methods to evaluate their sales training program. Table 14-4 presents a list of the most frequently used measures as determined by one

TABLE 14-4 **Sales Training Evaluation Measures Ranked According to Frequency of Use**

Course evaluations

Trainee feedback

Teaching staff comments

Supervisory feedback

Performance tests

Supervisory appraisal

Self-appraisal

Knowledge tests

Bottom-line management

Customer appraisal

study. As the authors of the study comment, most of these measures are "internal" and may not provide a complete picture of the effectiveness of a sales training program. They suggest greater use of "external" measures such as supervisory appraisal, self-appraisal, bottom-line measures, and customer appraisals.[60]

Several techniques which are used by many companies are discussed below.

Observe Salespeople at Work. After training, skilled observers who know the training program and its objectives can accompany recent trainees on their sales calls. They can observe how the new hires are, or are not, applying what was taught in the program. They can thus evaluate the training techniques used and change or improve them to better fit market conditions.

Ask Customers. Customers can be contacted personally or by mail for their opinions about a salesperson's performance before and after training. In many instances, customers' reactions indicate strengths or weaknesses in the sales training program. Further, customers have unique insights into their own needs that can be included in the sales training program.[61]

Review Sales Performance against Standards. Some companies establish one set of performance standards—such as new accounts opened or promotions arranged with customers—for salespeople without training, and another set for those who have been through the training program. By comparing the performance of trained and untrained people against these standards, they can achieve some evaluation of the training program.

Interview Trainees. Carefully planned pretraining interviews can be compared with matching posttraining interviews to indicate what effect training has had on attitudes, skills, and knowledge. Another version of this evaluation device employs written tests taken by trainees before and after their training.

Seek Managers' Opinions. Sales supervisors who have undergone training can be a useful source of information about the value of the program. Since sales managers have probably been successful salespeople themselves, they can provide helpful information about what selling techniques and information should be taught. Key questions include: Do the newly trained people have positive, constructive attitudes? The necessary selling skills? The necessary company and market information? Perhaps more than anyone else, a trainee's immediate supervisor can supply valuable insights into these and similar issues.

Redesigning the Sales Training Program

What if an evaluation of the sales training program indicates that it is inadequate? What if evaluation shows that salespeople do not possess the proper attitudes; that their product, company, or industry knowledge is insufficient; or that they lack the required selling skills? In this unhappy event, management is confronted with the necessity to redesign the training program. This process begins with a reexamination of the training objectives, program content, teaching methods, location of the training, and training personnel.

On the other hand, what if an evaluation of the sales training program indicates that it is a good one, and that it is satisfactory in all respects? Should a firm discontinue further regular evaluations? Definitely not! The marketplace is in a constant state of change: Competitors introduce new products, new uses for the good or service appear, new competitors enter the market, economic conditions shift, new customers appear, and old customers disappear. Consequently, the skills, knowledge, and attitudes required for successful selling are also in a constant state of change, and the form and content of sales training are always subject to alteration. Evaluation must continue, because training that is successful today may be inadequate tomorrow. Certainly, at some point in time market and economic changes will necessitate the redesign of even the best sales training programs.

Limitations of Formal Sales Training

Whether sales managers are developing a new sales training program or revising an existing one, they need to realize that a formal training program cannot do everything.[62] It cannot impart all of the necessary skills, attitudes, and knowledge to all of the company's salespeople. Consider the following points:

Not All Skills and Attitudes Can Be Acquired through Training.   Some skills and attitudes are fixed and unchangeable when a person is hired. Others can be imparted or changed through training, but the company cannot afford to undertake the project. An electronics company, for example, might require its sales reps to have extensive technical training. When certain required skills, attitudes, or knowledge cannot be acquired through any formal program, or when the company cannot afford the training needed to impart them, the recruiting and selection system must choose people who already possess the qualities that are desired.

Success Requirements Vary among Sales Groups.   The skill and knowledge required for sales success differ according to the product, the industry, and the specific competitive conditions. Therefore, the content of training programs must vary also. No single program can fit all selling conditions.

Individual Salesperson Training Needs Vary.   Among new salespeople, one can assume a certain consistency of background. For instance, all graduates of reputable business programs can be assumed to have had at least basic accounting. On this level, one can safely presume that sales recruits will require the same general content in their training. Frequently, however, individual training needs vary, so firms should individualize training to the greatest degree possible. Further, sales managers must encourage salespeople to read, listen to tapes, and pursue other individual self-development activities.

Informal Training Can Accomplish Much.   A major responsibility of sales supervision is continuous informal, curbside training of salespeople. Much of the knowledge, skills, and attitudes needed by the successful salesperson do not have to be included in a formal training program. They can be imparted on the job by the superivsior or by contacts with customers. This is the subject matter of the final section of this chapter.

INFORMAL TRAINING

Although most companies have formal sales training programs, there is still much learning that occurs on the job. Sales training also involves self-development, and each salesperson, no matter how experienced, must receive continuous guidance and training. It is the first-line sales manager who has primary responsibility for a salesperson's informal training, since he or she has the most direct contact with field personnel. This training is accomplished through field coaching and customer contacts.

Field Coaching

"Field coaching," another term for curbside training, is actually a sales training, motivation, and evaluation tool because coaching, or helping salespeople to develop themselves, is the heart of the sales manager's job. This involves a process of sharing what each has learned through past experience. An experienced sales trainer has suggested that coaching "bridges the gap" between the classroom and on-the-job application of selling skills.[63]

The major advantages of this training technique are that it provides a realistic learning experience as well as the immediate opportunity to correct bad selling habits and techniques. Effective coaches foster a give-and-take process that provides an opportunity to share sales ideas and experiences. However, this process takes time, and many sales managers do not have the background to be effective field coaches. A poor coaching effort can be worse than none at all.[64] Furthermore, coaching is expensive, and the selling situations encountered are random and cannot be fitted into any sort of predetermined trainee experience.

observed sales call Field coaching technique in which a sales manager makes a joint call with a salesperson

The focal point for field coaching is the *observed sales call*, or a situation where the sales manager makes a field call with a salesperson. The supervisor observes the individual's sales techniques and later coaches the person on methods for improvement. To minimize the expense and randomness of coaching, sales managers must carefully plan and oversee the coaching process.[65]

Prior to the coaching session, the manager must review the sales job description to identify key points to look for. A review of the salesperson's past performance should also be carried out to note any problematic aspects that should be emphasized. For instance, if a salesperson has had past difficulties with closing, the sales manager will probably wish to concentrate on that skill during the coaching session.

During the precoaching briefing, the manager shares the coaching objectives with the salesperson and should reinforce the beneficial aspects of the process to create a positive atmosphere for the learning experience. This is also the time for the salesperson to express his or her own specific concerns and goals for the coaching session.

During the actual sales call, the coach's role is to observe, not to take part in the sales presentation. The focal points for observation are the specific issues identified during the precoaching planning. Many sales managers use a checklist to evaluate sales performance. However, it is wise to complete the checklist after a call, not while observing the sales presentation.

At the conclusion of the sales call, the manager and salesperson review how it was handled. This is known as the "curbside conference." It should involve a dialogue between the manager and the salesperson and should cover both positive as well as negative aspects of sales performance. Most sales managers like to begin by commenting on something positive to relax the salesperson's anxieties. Then they ask the salesperson to assess the call in terms of what went well and what could have been done differently. This usually leads to a discussion of ways the person can improve his or her sales performance.

At the end of a day of coaching, the salesperson and manager summarize strengths and major improvement opportunities. These will form the basis for an action plan for continued development. Specific steps and followup dates to review progress should be agreed upon. A written memo should be sent to the salesperson to summarize the steps that have been agreed upon.

Customer Contacts

The best way for any salesperson to learn about customers, their needs, and how to sell to them is through contacts in the field with customers. This is also an excellent way for salespeople to learn how to apply their product knowledge to many specific selling situations.[66] Many companies use a "buddy system" to provide sales trainees with customer contacts and exposure to field selling. They pair each trainee with a salesperson, usually someone who has just completed the training process or who has only a year or two of sales experience. Participating as an observer and asking questions between sales calls gives the sales trainee a realistic view of what it takes to succeed in selling.

SUMMARY OF LEARNING GOALS	**1.** **Differentiate between formal and informal sales training.** Formal sales training involves established training programs, whereas informal training refers to the continuous professional development of salespeople.

2. **Relate training to the salesperson's career cycle.**

During the preparation stage of a salesperson's career, the individual receives product and company knowledge and learns basic sales techniques. In the development stage, the emphasis is placed on supervision and field coaching in an effort to prevent bad habits from forming. During maturity, retraining is often required. The decline stage presents the challenge of reversing the steady decreases in a salesperson's productivity.

3. **Identify the reasons for training sales personnel.**

Sales personnel are trained in an effort to help them develop the right work habits and to offset the effects of detraining.

4. **Discuss the educational principles upon which a sales training program should be based.**

These principles include clearly recognized purpose, clarity of presentation, planned repetition, systematic review, orderly development of material, sensible pace, and trainee participation.

5. **List the questions that sales management must answer in designing a formal sales training program.**

Sales managers must ask themselves: (1) Which salespeople should be trained, and at what points in their careers? (2) What should the training program cover? (3) How should the training be done? (4) Who should train salespeople, and where does training fit into the organization?

6. **Explain how formal sales training programs should be evaluated.**

Sales training programs are, in some respects, very difficult to evaluate, but some evaluation techniques often used are:

- Testing trainees after they complete the training program
- Observing salespeople at work
- Asking customers for their opinions
- Reviewing sales performance against standards
- Interviewing trainees
- Seeking managers' opinions

7. **Discuss informal sales training and sales management's field coaching role.**

Informal sales training and field coaching involve an interactive, give-and-take approach that tries to help salespeople avoid bad selling habits and techniques. Informal methods are geared toward self-development and on-the-job training.

REVIEW QUESTIONS

1. Are salespeople "born" or "made"? Use the material in Chap. 14 to defend your position.
2. What is "plateauing" in terms of the salesperson's career cycle? What are two reasons behind plateauing? What have some companies done to prevent this problem?
3. What are the advantages of training new salespeople after they have had some on-the-job experience? The disadvantages?
4. Under what circumstances is the need for retraining indicated. What have sales managers emphasized as being important in sales training programs?
5. Under what kind of selling conditions is a conditioned response approach appropriate? When is an insight response method better suited?
6. What are some of the teaching tools that sales training uses? List an advantage and a disadvantage of each.
7. What are the three alternatives when deciding who should train salespeople? Where does training usually take place with each of these kinds of trainers?
8. Why is it so difficult to evaluate sales training in the area of sales skills and personal attitudes? What methods can companies use to evaluate sales training programs?
9. When does management need to recycle or redesign the sales training program? Why should management constantly evaluate its training program, even if the program seems adequate in all respects?
10. Who is responsible for the informal training of salespersons? What are the major approaches to informal sales training?

DISCUSSION QUESTIONS

1. Consider your current or most recent job. What type of training did you receive? Did this training follow the general guidelines developed in this chapter? Discuss.

2. Sales training is similar to the general education process. Think of a class you have taken in which you learned a great deal (or very little). Which education principles did the instructor follow (or fail to use)? Which techniques of education were used?

3. Develop a logical flow of instructions for any task that you know how to do. Assume your "trainees" know nothing at all about the process. Under this condition, is it difficult to avoid "jargon"?

4. The banking industry, in response to today's difficult business climate, has trained many of its employees to be more sales-oriented, turning some of its "bankers" into "market development officers." Some critics are now saying, however, that this transformation has damaged the banking industry. What problems can you see with training bankers to be salespeople? Do you see ways to alleviate or reduce these problems? In what other industries would management need to be wary of making its employees too sales-oriented?

5. As mentioned briefly in this chapter, many companies are taking what might be called a "synergistic" approach to sales; that is, they are combining different products, people, companies, or even industries to form alliances that make possible bigger sales than ever before. What does such a trend imply for sales training? Do you see particular educational techniques or principles that seem especially relevant to preparing a new salesperson to operate in a "synergistic" selling environment?

ETHICAL DILEMMA

Beta Corporation, a leading high technology firm, uses a product applications test to make sure that its sales trainees have adequate product knowledge before they move into the second phase of the sales training program. After grading this test, the sales training manager believes that the company's top two sales recruits have cheated. What should the training manager do?

SALES MANAGEMENT CASE

Developing Creativity

When Gay Balfour of Cortez, Colorado, had a dream in which he saw himself putting a hose into the ground and sucking out prairie dogs, he followed his inspiration, bought a converted septic tank and a hose, and started a new business, called, appropriately enough, Dog-Gone. Balfour's system, which captures prairie dogs unharmed and sets them free in another location, has been used throughout the Southwest. Happy with newfound success, what Balfour may or may not realize is that his product development process is a testimony to the ideas behind "creativity training," an increasingly popular training tool that, among other things, advises people to listen to their dreams.

The "cut-and-paste technique," "image streaming," "brain writing," "guided fantasies," and the "six-hat method" may sound more like grade school projects than legitimate sales training techniques, but

they are all methods to be found in a typical creativity training session.

Creativity, an important asset for any salesperson, is essential when salespeople are expected to take on new roles or when they are in the "hot seat" and have to respond quickly to customer questions. Recognizing this, many companies are making deliberate attempts to train their salespeople to be creative.

The cut-and-paste technique, for example, involves trainees making two collages of photographs—one symbolizing their own company and one representing customers' or potential customers' companies. Differences and similarities between the selling organizations are then more easily recognized. The six-hat method requires trainees to wear different colored hats, each of which represents a particular mental process. The goal is to train people to separate their emotions.

Frito-Lay, Milton Bradley, Xerox, AT&T, and other companies have invested in creativity training with techniques that range from using employees known for their creativity sharing how they do it, to reading books, to hiring specialists. Not surprisingly, the costs of these techniques escalate quickly—modestly priced creativity training by a specialist is about $500 a day.

In the challenging field of selling, creative thinking is not only a way to do a better selling job but also a generator of ideas a company can use. With the unique perspective salespeople have on customers, their insights, with a creative twist, just might be the start of something great.

Questions

1. Some creativity consultants bring children into boardrooms, taking advantage of the fact that young people are highly creative and also unembarrassed to tell their ideas to others. Gay Balfour's Dog-Gone, in fact, is almost childlike in its simplicity. Use your own creative skills to develop an idea for a product that, like Dog-Gone, is innovative and unusual.

2. Why would you suspect that creativity training is a hot topic today? Why do salespeople need to be more creative than ever?

   In your opinion, is creativity training more appropriately used within a conditioned response or an insight response training approach? Explain.

DIRECTING THE SALES FORCE

CHAPTER 15

SALES LEADERSHIP AND SUPERVISION

LEARNING GOALS

- Understand the elements of sales motivation.
- Describe the various needs that influence the behavior of sales personnel.
- Describe the development of motivation theory in sales management.
- Outline the basic concepts of sales leadership.
- Explain the leader-follower relationship.
- List the leadership roles that sales managers are required to play.
- Identify the individual leadership and human relations skills important to sales management.

GETTING SALESPEOPLE TO DO THEIR JOBS WELL

The power of the individual is immense, and leadership at its finest taps this power. Enlightened management is characterized by an appreciation of the value of individuals, a vision of employees as assets to be cultivated and nurtured, not as necessary evils needed only to get a job done.

PepsiCo, Inc., was chosen by *Fortune* magazine as one of the ten most admired companies in the nation, and Wayne Calloway, PepsiCo CEO, by *Sales & Marketing Management* as one of its "superstars of selling." Calloway, who has been with Pepsi since 1967, is a strong believer in employee empowerment, advising employees to act like owners, not "hired hands." Through Pepsi's "SharePower" program, all 300,000 employees have been given stock options.

Employees are encouraged to contribute to innovation at the company through programs such as the "Great PepsiCo Brainstorm," in which prizes are given for usable ideas.

PepsiCo salespeople are given tremendous latitude, and Calloway sees mistakes as a natural feature of that latitude and a necessary part of the learning process. Freedom to seize opportunity is the benefit of employee autonomy, as evidenced when a Moscow Pizza Hut manager, acting on his own, sent 150 free pizzas and 20 cases of Pepsi to Boris Yeltsin and his supporters during the failed Soviet coup.

Bill Gates, founder of Microsoft Corp., is another leadership success story who believes in his employees. At Microsoft, employees can send messages directly to Gates through an electronic mail network. In this way, he benefits from a constant inflow of ideas.

Huge companies like Microsoft and Pepsi do not have a monopoly on leadership. Telecom Library, a sixty-employee publishing company, was on the verge of layoffs until it started seeking sales-increasing ideas from its employees. All departments contributed, and six months later the company's sales were improving and it did not have to resort to layoffs.[1]

In Chap. 15, we will study sales leadership and supervision. Every sales manager has his or her own tried and true methods. In general, however, good managers' respect for the ideas of others is part of their ability to get salespeople to do their jobs well. Long-term vision rather than a more short-term focus on the next sale, the ability to be

a coach rather than a player and a conductor rather than a soloist—these are part of what makes an effective leader in a sales organization.

CHAPTER OVERVIEW

The most difficult task any sales manager faces is the supervision of subordinates. Salespeople may be scattered across a large geographical area; they may offer a broad product line to several diverse markets; their selling jobs are often technical and highly competitive; and they control large business expenses. Nor can a sales manager assume that sales personnel are strongly motivated day in and day out. Failure to identify the needs of subordinates and to provide effective leadership will result in increased turnover, lower productivity of the sales force, and unnecessary selling expenses.

Stewart A. Washburn, a management consultant, describes the importance of sales supervision and leadership as follows:

> All the elements either come together or fall apart through field supervision. Teams do not get to the Super Bowl or win pennants with unsupervised players. Coaches play a critical role—coaches who identify strengths and weaknesses and suggest better ways, who provide training and encouragement and who, on occasion, decide who can't make it and who can become a star.[2]

To a great extent, sales success depends upon the quality of management provided by the first-line sales supervisor. Most supervisors come from the ranks of the sales force. Their jobs change completely when they are promoted. Unfortunately, too many new sales managers have difficulties making this transition because they do not understand the role of sales leadership and supervision.

Salespeople are evaluated and rewarded, or punished, on the basis of how they do—how well they sell, cover their territories, service customers, and so forth. In short, they stand or fall on their own personal sales performance records. On the other hand, sales managers are evaluated not on how well they themselves sell, but on how well their salespeople perform. The job of salespeople is to sell. The job of sales managers is to supervise the selling activities of their personnel. If salespeople do a good job, the sales manager is successful. If they do a poor job, the manager has failed.

Chapter 15 examines sales leadership and supervision to provide a better understanding of why salespeople do or do not follow their superiors well. Effective sales leadership requires a thorough understanding of human behavior and the concepts of motivation. The chapter also identifies important leadership and human relations skills and indicates how they can be improved for greater efficiency and lower cost in sales force operation. The following two chapters will then discuss the specifics of sales motivation. Chapter 16 will describe various forms of sales incentives, and Chap. 17 will cover sales compensation.

MOTIVATION

motivation "How-to" aspect of getting salespeople to do their jobs well

Motivation—the heart of sales management—is simply the "how-to" aspect of getting salespeople to do their jobs well. Motives are the "whys" of behavior. A sales manager must understand the "whys" of salespeople's behavior before taking steps to lead and motivate them. Incentives, or stimuli, must be developed to fit the specific needs of people who sell.

To determine the proper incentives to use, sales managers must understand the needs of their salespeople. This is not easy because each salesperson is different and has different needs. For instance, as discussed in Chap. 14, the career stage an individual has reached influences job attitudes and performance. Research also suggests that salespeople's psychological and sociological needs differ according to career stage. In general, sales managers can expect more difficulties in motivating and supervising salespeople early and late in their careers.[3]

Types of Needs

How can a sales manager identify the specific motives of subordinates when every person's needs and life goals are unique? Fortunately, there is general agreement that human needs fall into a universal pattern.

primary needs Physical needs that must be satisfied immediately

secondary needs Needs that can be satisfied at a later time

Primary and Secondary Needs.   Psychologists differentiate between primary and secondary needs. *Primary needs* are physical needs that must be satisfied immediately. Examples are hunger and vulnerability to excessive heat or cold. *Secondary needs* are those that can be satisfied at a later time. Frequently, secondary needs are psychological or have been learned from others. The needs for recognition and love are secondary needs.

rational needs Needs based on reason

Rational and Emotional Needs.   Another useful distinction is between rational and emotional needs. *Rational needs* are those based on reason. A person's desire to purchase a compact car because of its relatively low price and economy of operation illustrates the dominance of a rational buying motive. On the other hand, another

emotional needs
Needs based on
emotion rather than
reason

person's purchase of a luxury car, which may result from desires for status and prestige, are referred to as *emotional needs*. It is often quite difficult to identify exactly which needs are based on emotion and which on reason.

Hierarchy of Needs

hierarchy of needs
Abraham H. Maslow's arrangement of
needs in order of importance

Much of the understanding of motivation comes from the early work of Abraham H. Maslow, who developed a theory of motivation that arranges needs in the order of their importance.[4] This theory, known as the *hierarchy of needs*, suggests that needs on the lowest level must be satisfied before higher-level needs become important motivating forces. When a need is satisfied, it ceases to be a motivator of behavior.

Figure 15-1 shows Maslow's hierarchy of needs. As a theory of motivation, its contribution is to identify and rank motivating forces in the order in which they must be satisfied for those on the next level to become effective motivators. These need levels are physiological, safety and security, social, ego, and self-actualization.

1. Physiological needs include the basic requirements for food, clothing, shelter, and the like. Also called the "tissue needs," these are built-in needs that the body requires to function normally. Needs at this first level must ordinarily be satisfied before those at higher levels will significantly influence a person's behavior. Praising a salesperson's performance (an ego need) has no motivating power if the person is not earning enough to feed the family. However, physiological needs cease being motivating forces when they are totally satisfied.

2. Safety needs stem from the desire for protection from various kinds of threats, dangers, and deprivations. They are not being met when people are uncertain of or fearful for their own well-being, that of their families, or their job. In today's fast-paced world, many working people are especially concerned with being prepared for what the future may bring. Life insurance, pension plans, and health and accident policies are a few of the incentives that appeal to this level of needs.

3. Social needs are satisfied by significant relationships with other people. Almost everyone has a desire to belong, to be accepted, and to give and receive friendship and love. Company bowling teams, department picnics, and golf outings serve to enhance the social aspects of a job.

4. Ego needs are directed toward enhancing or gratifying the ego or self-image. They include feelings of self-esteem, self-respect, self-confidence, and achievement. A person wants to feel like a somebody. Also, people desire the esteem of

FIGURE 15-1 Maslow's Hierarchy of Needs.

Self-actualization needs

Ego needs

Social needs

Safety needs

Physiological needs

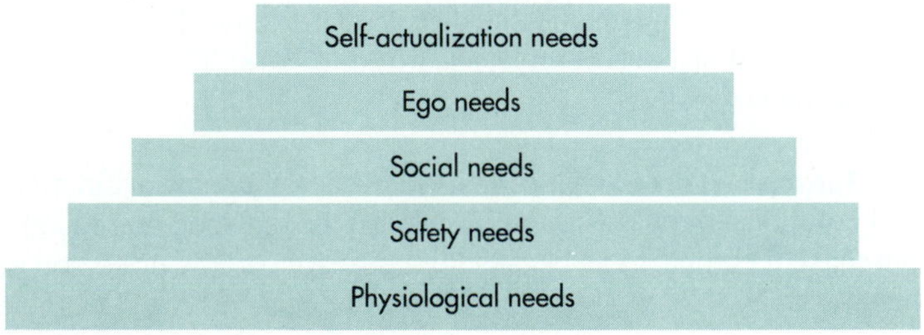

others—that is, they want status, recognition, and appreciation from their peers. Status in an organization may be conveyed by a person's title, office size and furnishings, and special privileges and responsibilities.

5. Self-actualization needs involve the desire for self-fulfillment and a wish to succeed simply for the sake of accomplishment, not for material gain or recognition. Successful artists, writers, and other creative people are driven by their desire to satisfy self-actualization needs.

Maslow's hierarchy is a useful tool for analyzing human motivation.[5] In fact, many other behavioral scientists and management theorists have used Maslow's work as a starting point for their studies of behavior.

It shows that a need is an effective motivator only when it is activated; that frustration of an activated need acts negatively on productivity and morale; and that satisfaction of an activated need acts positively on productivity and morale. Research on sales force motivation has shown that salespeople tend to be driven by Maslow's two upper levels of needs—ego and self-actualization.

People who have a high level of ego needs tend to select sales as a career. In fact, salespeople have stronger needs for self-esteem and the approval of others than those in most other occupational groups.[6] Successful salespeople are also driven by their need for achievement. Stephen Doyle and Benson Shapiro have found that "the degree of a person's need for achievement is directly related to salesforce motivation. As need for achievement increases, so do efforts and motivation."[7]

In particular, there is evidence that salespeople are more likely to be driven by self-actualization needs than are most other workers. In a study of motivational characteristics of salespeople based on Maslow's hierarchy, the authors found that slightly over half of the respondents were high actualizers. They describe these salespeople as individuals who:

> Seek opportunities to self actualize in their work. Seek opportunity for personal growth and self improvement. Enjoy creative self-expression and challenging assignments. Low interest in job or income protection and securing. Enjoy working with other people, but have low desire for social and recreational activities. Do not appear to seek recognition for doing a good job or that work is important.[8]

Whether or not a salesperson's job is challenging and interesting is critical to motivation. It is very difficult to motivate people who find their jobs dull, boring, and endless. Fortunately, the challenge of selling is an effective motivator for sales personnel. Most salespeople rise to the competitive aspects of the job. They are motivated by factors intrinsic to selling, such as achievement, responsibility, growth, enjoyment of the work, and earned recognition. These job features appeal to the ego and self-fulfillment needs.

Morale

morale Employees' attitudes about their jobs and their attitudes about themselves

Morale and motivation are closely related. *Morale* relates to salespeople's attitudes about their jobs—their feelings toward their supervisors, pay, fellow employees, and other job-related components—and their attitudes toward themselves. Factors contributing to morale include company policy and administration, work conditions, pay, relationships with peers, and the salespeople's personal lives.

Although not necessarily powerful motivators in themselves, these situations may affect job satisfaction.

Positive feelings about one's job and company also lead to loyalty. When considering morale and overall job satisfaction, it is important to consider everything that binds employees to a company, from corporate culture to the personal management style of individual sales managers. A manager should take advantage of every opportunity to build sales force loyalty.[9]

Morale has two sides to it. Creating good morale will not necessarily motivate salespeople. However, unless salespeople are generally content with their jobs, they will not be receptive to attempts to motivate them.

SELECTED VIEWS OF SALES MOTIVATION

As one would expect, the motivation of salespeople has been the focus of considerable study by sales consultants and researchers. In this section, the results of some of this research are discussed briefly.

Expectancy Theory

expectancy theory
Theory that people decide how much effort to put into their work based upon what they expect to get out of it

Many studies of the motivation to work have concentrated on *expectancy theory*, which proposes that people decide how much effort to put into their work based on what they expect to get out of it. Salespeople will be motivated to do well if they believe that their efforts will result in appropriate rewards. The expectancy model shows promise as a framework for understanding sales force motivation.[10]

Figure 15-2 shows a simplified model of expectancy theory. This theory portrays a causal sequence of motivation, level of performance, and outcome. High motivation occurs when a salesperson values the specific outcomes (or rewards) that result from successful performance, expects that the desired outcomes will be contingent on successful performance, and expects that a high level of effort will lead to successful performance.

Expectancy theory has two significant implications for sales managers. First, they must learn which rewards are important to their subordinates. Managers must discover salespeople's feelings about work requirements, career goals, monetary needs, and so forth. Then, they must strive to implement the sales organization's reward system properly. The manager's role is to help salespeole in their efforts to work at a level that will allow them to achieve their desired rewards.[11]

Organizational Commitment and Climate

Although expectancy theory has become a popular model for studying sales force motivation, there are ongoing research efforts to further refine and clarify the relationships between motivation, performance, and other behavioral outcomes.

FIGURE 15-2 Model of Expectancy Theory.

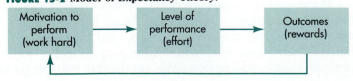

Much of this effort has concentrated on developing a better understanding of the importance of organizational commitment. Some salespeople are more likely to be influenced by commitment to the sales organization. Hence, a salesperson's effort will be dependent upon motivational influences and the degree of organizational commitment. [12]

An extensive study concluded that conceptual and empirical differences do exist between commitment variables and expectancy-based motivational variables. Specifically, job commitment and, to a modest extent, organizational commitment are related to a salesperson's effort and performance. The study noted that organizational commitment might have greater impact on motivation and sales performance in other cultures such as Japan. [13]

Other studies of sales force motivation have concentrated on the dimensions that form the organizational climate for selling. These include the characteristics of the sales job, the characteristics of sales leadership, and the extent to which salespeople identify themselves with their organizations. As one study put it, these factors make up the perceptions, or cognitive map, that salespeople have about the situations in which they are performing. [14] The study also revealed that these factors influence salespersons' perceptions of the desirability of rewards. Job challenge and variety, considerate leadership, and organizational identification are particularly important in this regard. [15] Relevant characteristics of the organizational climate impacting sales force motivation are presented in Table 15-1.

Organizational Behavior Modification

organizational behavior modification Concept that a behavior followed by a favorable consequence is more likely to be repeated than a behavior followed by an unfavorable consequence or by no consequence at all

Another suggested approach for explaining sales force motivation is *organizational behavior modification*, the concept that a behavior followed by a favorable consequence is likely to be repeated. [16] The theory also says that behavior followed by an unfavorable consequence or by no consequence at all is less likely to be repeated.

As a result, according to this approach, behavior is determined by subsequent consequences, which means rewards or punishment shape behavior. Positive reinforcement, where desired behaviors are rewarded, encourages the continuance of

TABLE 15-1 **Organizational Climate Characteristics**

Variable name	Description
Considerate leadership	Extent to which salespeople feel that their ideas and opinions are sought by the supervisor and taken into consideration in designing jobs which affect their performance
Job challenge and variety	Extent to which a job gives salespeople a chance to use their skills and abilities, and calls for them to engage in a wide range of behaviors
Job autonomy	Extent to which salespeople have freedom to decide what steps should be taken to complete a given task or how a problem should be handled.
Organizational identification	Degree to which salespeople feel that the organization provides vehicles for development of personal goals
Perceived inequity	Extent to which salespeople perceive that their reward/performance ratio is inconsistent with other salesperson's reward/performance ratios

those behaviors. An example would be the payment of a bonus for acquiring a new customer. In contrast, negative reinforcement, where undesirable behaviors are punished, also encourages desirable behaviors, but by making people seek to avoid the negative consequences of the punishment. For instance, a salesperson will make more sales calls each month to avoid an unfavorable performance review. The theory also says extinction of an undesirable behavior can be achieved by offering no reward for that behavior.

Sales managers can use organizational behavior modification to stimulate sales performance. Sales reports, travel in the field with salespeople, and other information sources will provide insights into behavior that should be changed. The manager can then assess the frequency of the behavior and why it is happening. The next step is to select a behavior modification strategy depending upon whether the manager wishes to increase a desirable or reduce an undesirable behavior. Most sales management applications involve positive reinforcement, for example, favorable performance reviews, sales incentives, and other rewards designed to encourage positive behavior. The final step is to evaluate whether the behavior modification strategy has worked.[17]

Attribution Theory

In a study of over twelve hundred salespeople, Professor Harish Sujan concentrated on another aspect of sales motivation.[18] His study was different from other research on sales force motivation in that it examined the motivation to "work smarter" in contrast to the motivation to "work harder." Salespeople can work smarter by choosing sales approaches that are effective for particular customers or by increasing their mastery of different sales approaches.

attribution theory Theory that people are motivated not only to maximize their rewards, but also to attain a mastery over the situation and environment in which they work

Attribution theory says that people are motivated not only to maximize their rewards, but also to attain a mastery over the situation and the environment in which they work. Salespeople who attribute lack of success to poor strategy will be motivated to work smarter. Salespeople who are stimulated by intrinsic rewards related to their work, such as the satisfaction obtained from influencing customers and learning more about their products, are likely to be more concerned about working smarter. The results of Sujan's study suggest that salespeople's motivation to work smarter has a significant impact on their performance, perhaps even greater than their motivation to work harder.

Role Clarity

role clarity Extent to which a sales supervisor clearly defines the tasks and performance levels required for a job

role ambiguity Lack of clarity in what is expected from an individual or in how he or she will be evaluated

Another critical aspect of sales motivation that has received much attention is role, or job, clarity. It is extremely important that a salesperson understand his or her role in the company. *Role clarity* refers to how clearly a sales supervisor defines the tasks and performance levels required for a job. In contrast, *role ambiguity* is a lack of clarity in the definition of what is expected from an individual or in how he or she will be evaluated. If a salesperson feels that his or her role or job is ambiguous, there will be a negative impact on that individual's performance and feelings of satisfaction with the job.[19]

Sales managers who wish to increase their personnel's satisfaction levels must place more emphasis on leadership styles and behaviors that help reduce the role

path-goal theory
Concept that a sales-
person's motivation
stems from a super-
visor setting the
tasks and expected
performance levels,
then providing the
support required for
their accomplishment

conflicts of salespeople, or at least help them cope with conflicts. *Path-goal theory* is a leadership model that says the supervisor's establishment of tasks and expected performance levels and the provision of the needed coaching, guidance, support, and rewards will motivate subordinates toward higher levels of performance and greater job satisfaction.[20]

Equally important in motivating salespeople is making them feel like integral parts of their companies. To be motivated, they must be sold on their companies, their colleagues, their customers, and the goods or services they sell. If salespeople understand their roles in their companies, they will make their companies' goals their own and think in terms of "my company."

THE ESSENCE OF SALES LEADERSHIP

leadership Day-to-
day manner in which
a sales manager
supervises and stim-
ulates subordinates
to achieve desired
levels of productivity

Leadership—sometimes described as motivation theory in action—is the day-to-day manner in which a sales manager supervises and stimulates subordinates to achieve desired levels of productivity.[21] Since the job of a salesperson is fairly autonomous and nonroutine, sales managers must provide subordinates with structure, direction, and support. People must recognize, however, that true motivation comes from within themselves. The sales manager's major task is to provide a motivational climate that will foster self-motivation.

Larry Wilson, a leading sales training consultant, described the sales manager's leadership challenge as follows:

Effective leaders capture attention and inspire people by proposing exciting ideas. They know how to share and communicate the vision. They try to make everyone feel he's part of the team. Every team member understands his role. Leaders see their jobs as facilitating and running interference for and empowering the team members so that each person can work on his part of the vision. Finally, leaders lead by setting an example and by providing constancy. They inspire people with integrity, accountability, patience, and growth.[22]

Another view of leadership is suggested by management consultant Gary Couture, who has written:

Leadership is identifying the missing link in people—helping them discover their own uniquely personal characteristics. And leadership is developing in people a willingness to utilize their communication strength to produce better results. Leaders understand the need to spend a lot less time studying product and a lot more time studying people.[23]

Some authors and researchers of executive leadership claim to be able to prescribe formulas of leadership that are applicable to all supervision problems; however, the truth is that current knowledge of sales leadership and motivation is inadequate. Little is known about what is involved in effective sales supervision. Further, sales leadership problems are essentially unique unto themselves and no two sales supervision problems are exactly the same.[24]

Sales managers are very aware of the difficulties of dealing with different types of salespeople. At one extreme are the outstanding sales performers—the superstars. Top salespeople are highly competitive, aggressive people, and this makes them difficult to supervise. It is especially challenging to find ways to make them partici-pate as part of the sales team.[25]

At the other extreme are the problem salespeople and those that are in a sales slump. The challenge is to find ways to make these people productive again.[26] Sometimes disciplinary action is called for, but often the sales manager will be expected to use training, coaching, and counseling skills to resolve the problem. What a sales manager cannot do is do nothing at all. Ignoring a problem in the hopes that it will go away usually results in a more serious problem.

Understanding leadership and developing skill in it depend upon the sales super-visor having an understanding of why salespeople follow (or do not follow) to the full extent of their capacities, an ability to play the roles required of a sales supervisor-leader, and a mastery of the creation and maintenance of ardent followership—the individual and human relations skills of leadership.

SALES LEADERSHIP AND COOPERATION

As a leader of people who sell, the sales manager must deal with such critical questions as the following:

- What determines the degree to which salespeople cooperate with their super-visors?
- What are the conditions under which the supervisor must be an effective leader of people?
- What roles must the supervisor play in leading?
- Why do some salespeople follow their supervisor-leaders enthusiastically and to the best of their capabilities, while others are stubborn, reluctant, and unpro-ductive?
- What are the results of poor leadership by sales supervisors?

The Critical Importance of Cooperation

In leading and supervising people who sell, the degree to which they cooperate with their supervisors is of critical importance. Imagine a line that measures the degree of cooperation a salesperson gives to a manager. Such a cooperation scale is shown in Fig. 15-3. The line extends from zero (no cooperation at all) to 100 percent (complete cooperation). Somewhere on the line is a cutoff point, the absolute minimum amount of cooperation that the supervisor will tolerate. If a salesperson does not cooperate at least to that degree, the person will be fired. If the person cooperates to a satisfactory degree—that is, between the cutoff point and 100 per-cent—the rep will be retained. Above the cutoff point, it is largely the salespeople

FIGURE 15-3 Cooperation Scale.

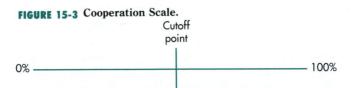

who elect the degree to which they will cooperate. The amount of cooperation attained is a result of the quality of the sales manager's leadership.

Costs of Incomplete Cooperation

Since salespeople choose the degree to which they will cooperate with their sales managers, does it make any real difference if they elect a low or a high level of cooperation? If there is no dollar-and-cents difference between minimum and maximum cooperation, does a manager need to be concerned with leadership and supervision as an important determinant of the level of cooperation?

When salespeople elect a low level of cooperation because they are poorly led, they generate real costs that could be avoided by good leadership and supervision. When they choose minimum cooperation—just above the cutoff point—they generate such costs as lost business, damaged customer relations, impaired corporate image, increased sales expenses, and customer complaints. In short, anything less than 100 percent cooperation by salespeople lowers sales, increases costs, and reduces profits.

A Contractual Relationship

As noted, salespeople choose the degree to which they cooperate with a manager. The degree of cooperation a salesperson chooses depends, in large part, on what the person expects to receive in return.

A contract is an agreement between two or more parties. In this sense, the leader-follower relationship is a contract. It is not a written contract, nor is it always even consciously recognized. It is, nevertheless, a contract under which the leader and the follower each give something of value in return for receiving something of value. The contractual nature of the leader-follower relationship is critical to understanding why salespeople choose the degree of cooperation they do.

What Salespeople Give

In the leader-follower contract, the things salespeople give that the supervisor values are time, energy, skills, attention, loyalty, interest, extra effort, imagination, knowledge, and devotion. These can be given completely or partly withheld at the individual's discretion. In a sense, these are the qualities and activities the follower has for sale under the contract.

What Salespeople Want

If salespeople give the values they have to offer under the contract and do not receive what they desire in return, they are frustrated and dissatisfied. They produce at low levels, generate avoidable costs, and possibly quit. If, however, they receive a full measure of what they desire, their job satisfaction and productivity are high, and they do not generate the avoidable costs of less than complete cooperation. Typically, salespeople want the following:

To Be Understood.   As human beings, all people want to be understood by those whose opinions they value. Understanding is difficult because each person is a complex bundle of physical, psychological, and economic desires and drives. What salespeople want from their managers is the kind of sensitivity that can translate words into meaning.

To Be Valued.   If the salesperson is to cooperate to the fullest extent of his or her capacity, the manager-leader must value the person. The leader has two things to value: the person and the work the person does. Ideally, the sales manager should value both, but this is not always possible due to personality differences. If the supervisor does not at least value the salesperson's work, the individual should be dismissed, assuming that the manager's expectations of what the subordinate should be doing in the way of work are not unrealistic.

To Belong.   Maslow noted that people are social animals who crave companionship and satisfying social intercourse. At first it might seem that providing salespeople with satisfactory social relationships is not a particularly difficult task. The essence of selling is to work with people and to interact socially with customers. But this is not the case. The type of social intercourse required by the salesperson as an individual is not the salesperson-customer relationship.

If the salesperson is to cooperate fully, the manager must find ways to provide social satisfaction. Many companies use sales meetings as one means of achieving this end. Other companies encourage company salespeople in adjoining territories to meet regularly with each other to talk about mutual problems and to exchange ideas. When a supervisor visits salespeople in the field, calls on customers with them, and socializes with them after hours, the manager is adding to the salesperson's social satisfaction from the job. When a group of salespeople work out of a single office, there is the potential for various social activities. It is a prime responsibility of the leader-supervisor to see that follower-salespeople are able to relate themselves to some satisfying social group.

socialization
Process by which a person acquires the social knowledge and skills required to assume a role in the sales organization and participate as a contributing member of the sales force.

Of particular importance to salespeople is the need for *socialization*, the process by which a person acquires the social knowledge and skills required to assume a role in the sales organization and participate as a contributing member of the sales force. Sales managers must take an active role in helping salespeople assimilate themselves into the organization.[27] This process involves orienting recruits, defining job roles and clarifying them for all salespeople, training subordinates, and evaluating the progress of subordinates on an ongoing basis.

To Contribute.   To follow their supervisors to the fullest extent of their capacities, salespeople must know, or be shown, that they contribute to the work of their companies and the sales force. On the surface, this requirement for ardent followership appears too obvious to require special attention. A skeptical manager might say: "It should be no mystery to salespeople what they contribute. They contribute sales income to the company." Managers, however, must never assume that salespeople recognize that what they do contributes to the total sales effort. The contributions of salespeople must be explained clearly to them.

To Be Informed.   The sales supervisor is a major communications link between the salesperson and the higher echelons of the company, and there is a positive

SALES MANAGEMENT IN PRACTICE

AMERICAN EXPRESS

Salespeople want to be valued as employees and as individuals. American Express, like many companies, is showing its salespeople that they are valued by giving them flexibility and control over their family lives.

"Family friendliness" has become a watchword for progressive companies. Of the many programs and options that firms are offering employees, "job sharing" has been one of the most successful. Basically, job sharing involves two people sharing the wages, benefits, and responsibilities of one job so that they each have more time to devote to outside activities.

At American Express, the highest-ranking job sharers are two salespeople with young children. One salesperson works Monday, Tuesday, and Thursday; the other works Tuesday, Wednesday, and Friday. As with most job sharing arrangements, an overlap day is included to provide the opportunity for face-to-face interaction between sharers.

Employers reap many benefits from allowing their employees to share jobs. For one thing, there is the advantage of two employees' input on one job. Also, being family-friendly is a recruiting advantage, and allowing arrangements for new families keeps valuable employees in the work force when they might otherwise drop out. Finally, job sharing provides a way for employees to keep their skills up to date during the period that they also want to devote more time to their families.

In the future, sales managers will become increasingly less able to ignore their employees' family issues. This fact is to everyone's advantage—and the benefits to employers and to employees and their families are clear. American Express, for one, should need no convincing. In one year, its two job sharing salespeople were responsible for 20 percent of their division's new accounts. One of the sharers, who was responsible for direct marketing, beat her quota by 12 percent. The other sharer, who handled telemarketing, beat her quota by 8 percent.

relationship between motivation and performance feedback.[28] An informed salesperson is a better salesperson.

To Be Buffered and Protected.   The last requirement for the salesperson's full cooperation is to be protected from unnecessary pressures and diversions. At the very least, salespeople need their supervisors to pass these pressures on in the proper amounts and at the proper times.

All organizations generate pressures that distract people from the work they are doing. Some of these diversions, such as the special market intelligence reports required from field salespeople, are necessary, but many are not. If, for example, someone criticizes a salesperson to his or her supervisor, the salesperson will want the supervisor to place this criticism in its proper perspective and not magnify its importance; it is a distraction when one must defend oneself unnecessarily.

Salespeople also prefer that their supervisors not pass on diversions that they do not need to know about or participate in. They expect their supervisors to make them aware of these pressures only at the times when they need to know about them.

THE SALES MANAGER'S LEADERSHIP ROLES

Whether they recognize it or not, salespeople are always requesting some role response from their managers when the two parties interact. Managers, on their side, are always playing some role in their relations with salespeople.

Research has suggested that the functional area in which a manager performs has a major influence on the roles that the manager plays. For instance, production managers perform the decision roles of entrepreneur, disturbance-handler, resource allocator, and negotiator. In contrast, the leadership role, the training and rewarding of personnel, and the liaison role are more appropriate for sales managers.[29]

Figure 15-4 shows that the interaction between the role requested by the salesperson and the supervisor's role response will always produce a result: anger, satisfaction, frustration, pleasure, and so on. This makes role analysis a particularly critical leadership skill because of two conditions:

1. For the sales manager, the salesperson's role request is a given; the manager has to accept it as is and cannot say, "Don't give me that problem, give me another one."
2. The good manager has a specific result in mind that will come from the interaction between role request and response.

So, the manager's problem can be phrased as follows: "I want a specific result out of this interaction. I can't change the request. So then, what response to this request has the best chance of achieving the result I want?"

An event from the sports world illustrates this relationship. The coach of a professional football team was having difficulties with a star player. Although the player had the physical attributes and skills to be truly outstanding, the coach felt that he was not going all out. The given in the role situation was that the player was performing at less than full capacity. The result the coach wanted was all-out performance. The coach reasoned that the man was not playing to his full capacity because he believed he was so exceptionally skilled that his position on the first team was secure even without his full effort. The coach benched him at the start of several games in a row. After four games, the coach was well satisfied that the player was consistently performing to full capacity.

As noted, there is no such thing as "the" leadership role. Rather, leadership involves many roles. The supervisor must be capable of playing any one of several roles, depending on what the situation requires. When conditions require a particular role response, the leader must play that role and play it well. Sometimes the sales manager may be required to play more than one role with a salesperson in a given situation.

Superior Performer

The professional, superperformance, competence dimension of leadership is referred to as the "superior performer." Ideally, since the supervisor is a proven salesperson and knows a great deal about selling, salespeople respect the supervisor's orders and advice. When the supervisor suggests what salespeople should

FIGURE 15-4 Interaction of Role Request and Response.

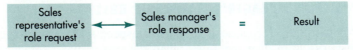

do, they cooperate fully because they know they are receiving direction from a professional: "Mel, your interview might have gone better if you had spent more time on our warranty program." "Betty Jo, the key to getting into that account is a fellow named Ralph Hawkins." When guidance and advice come from a superior performer, salespeople tend to cooperate fully and willingly.

Inspirational Leader

In the role of inspirational leader, the sales manager is the emotional catalyst for subordinates, the spark plug that gets things going. This role enables followers to attach themselves emotionally to a person and company. Visualize, for example, a large company—an organization of many thousand employees, perhaps a dozen plants, and as many warehouse and sales installations—sprawling, faceless, impersonal. How do salespeople become emotionally attached to such an organization so that they are motivated to give their last ounce of ability? The answer is through the supervisor in the role of inspirational leader.

Innovator

In the role of innovator, a leader is the source of problem-solving ideas for followers—how to win the big account, how to cover the territory more effectively, how to reduce expenses, how to make better use of promotional materials. When necessary, reps look to their supervisors to play this role. Sales managers must answer or at least help salespeople discover their own answers.

Guardian of the Status Quo

As a guardian of the status quo, the sales manager speaks for and represents the company. The manager is also the source of information about company history, policy, procedures, and its way of doing things. When necessary, the manager explains and enforces rules and procedures.

Parent Image

In the parent image role, the sales manager is the embodiment of what a parent should be: a kindly, loved, respected, and fair person who serves as arbiter, judge, and disciplinarian. In this role, the manager holds the world steady for followers so they can learn about it: what the rules are, how people are judged, how success is attained, and what constitutes failure.

INDIVIDUAL LEADERSHIP SKILLS

Before responding to the requirements for complete cooperation, a sales manager must first understand them. This involves developing and using individual leadership skills. The major skills required are perception, conceptual ability, and self-awareness.

Perception

A sales manager must be skilled at perceiving the meanings and causes of individual and group behavior. Without perceptiveness, the supervisor cannot understand and value salespeople, cannot show them how they contribute and belong to a social group, and cannot buffer them.

To the observant sales supervisor, many things have potential meaning that can explain individual and group behavior. Nothing that might possibly be useful is overlooked. The effective supervisor perceives meaning from those things that are not normally expected to contain messages. For instance, letters, reports, phone calls, and special studies are expected to help a supervisor understand individual and group behavior. Perceptive leaders look for meaning in rumors, mistakes, accidents, facial expressions, and tones of voice, noting what is not said or written and what is. They seek meaning in new or changed behavior patterns.

Conceptual Ability

Conceptual ability is the process by which one relates to and understands everything that happens. It is the way a person decodes and unscrambles experience. Conceptual ability is the means by which sales managers understand who they are, who their people are, what their companies are, what selling is, and why their companies are in business. There are two critical aspects of conceptual ability for sales leadership.

First, there must be mutual understanding between leader and follower of the conceptual scheme within which they are each working. For example, an important customer has drastically cut back a large order with only vague, evasive explanations. The salesperson believes the reason to be price. However, the supervisor sees it as a step in the customer's planned changeover to higher quality. Neither the salesperson nor the supervisor explains to the other his or her conceptualization of the problem, but they try to seek a solution together. Since they are working within two different conceptual schemes, they are wasting their time.

The second problem is the degree of reality of a person's conceptual scheme. Everyone must have a conceptual scheme by which to decode and arrange experience. Without such a scheme, one is helpless to understand anything or to take any action. The success of a person's actions is also the result of the realism of his or her conceptual scheme; that is, the accuracy with which that scheme reflects the real world.

Sometimes an unrealistic conceptual scheme occurs when a salesperson is promoted to a supervisory position and then fails to recognize that market conditions have changed. The new manager supervises salespeople, evaluates their activities, issues instructions, and interprets their actions against conditions that existed when the manager was a salesperson, not against current conditions.

Sales managers must question their concepts of themselves and their salespeople to ensure that they are as realistic and significant as possible. Questions might include the following:

- Why do I work? Why do my salespeople work?
- Are the quick and easy answers to those questions the right answers?
- What is the function of selling in my company?
- Why does my company exist? What do I really do? Should I be doing these things?

SALES MANAGEMENT IN PRACTICE

XEROX CORP.

Frank Pacetta, a district sales manager for Xerox Corp.,is an uncommon leader. In 1987, he took over an Independence, Ohio, office that was characterized by high turnover, low morale, angry customers, and bad performance. By the end of his first year, it was number one in its region.

Pacetta accomplished this turnaround by changing the entire atmosphere of the office. He arrived at seven every morning; his predecessor had arrived at eight. He increased the number of sales reps from thirty-six to forty-three so that they could give their customers more attention, and he spent huge amounts of money on promotional campaigns.

Pacetta's management style might be charac-terized as parental. For example, he always recognizes employees' birthdays and anniversaries. While he shows employees he cares about them, he also is a tough boss who inspires competitiveness by using money and prizes as motivational tools. Commissions, bonuses, and contests inspire high performance, and some of Pacetta's incentives are extremely motivational even though they do not involve money. Every month the eight sales managers in his district vote on who has done the best and the worst job. The person voted best gets a desirable parking place for the next month, and the person voted worst gets an ugly doll that hangs in his or her office. Weird, maybe. Motivating, certainly.

Frank Pacetta is making waves at Xerox, often fighting his company's bureaucracy in order to accomplish something for his customers. He expects a comparable degree of energy and drive from his salespeople, and he gets it.

- Do my people and I see (conceptualize) events in the same way? Could we improve our mutual concepts? How?
- What do our customers want from us? Are we providing these things? How?
- What are the real conditions in our market?

Sales managers can improve and enhance their perceptiveness regarding subordinates and their conceptual abilities by providing specific opportunities for salespeople to communicate their needs and ideas to management. Unfortunately, many companies fail to take advantage of the views and ideas of their employees because they lack efficient and effective upward communication networks. By using attitude surveys and other techniques to obtain input from salespeople, management can learn much about the needs and attitudes of the sales force.[30]

Self-Awareness

Self-awareness is a person's ability to recognize that a leader is an integral part of the management process. The traditional way of explaining and understanding the process is that it is the responsibility of managers to decide what must be done. Subordinates are expected to follow orders.

But this is a mechanistic concept, and not a realistic way to understand management. As the late U.S. Navy Admiral Grace Hopper—the inventor of COBOL, a computer language—once said, "You manage things, you lead people." Sales management is not an objective process like driving a car or doing a crossword puzzle. Sales managers are an integral part of their own leadership. Sales leadership is not simply a matter of turning the key in the ignition or filling in the correct words in the puzzle.

HUMAN RELATIONS SKILLS

human relations
Art of creating and
maintaining organiza-
tional cooperation for
maximum efficiency,
low cost, and high
personal job satis-
faction

A sales supervisor obtains a salesperson's cooperation by utilizing the human relations skills of executive leadership. *Human relations* is the art of creating and
maintaining organizational cooperation for maximum efficiency, low cost, and high
personal job satisfaction. Critical human relations skills for sales leadership and
supervision are delegation, communication, teamwork, participation, and discipline.

Delegation

Many people believe that if you want something done right, you must do it
yourself. This notion has no place in good supervisory leadership. People who sell
are evaluated on how well they sell. Sales managers are evaluated on how well their
people sell. Successful delegation is part of the sales manager's job.

Delegation is a hard skill for new managers to learn. This is especially so if the
new manager has been a successful salesperson. Often, such managers do not
delegate for the following reasons:

- It is risky. The manager is evaluated on salespeople's performance, and subordinates may foul up.
- Within the company's broad guidelines, delegation means that salespeople manage territories in their own way. The manager may feel a salesperson's way is
  not the best way.
- The manager does not understand or trust the information system that keeps
  him or her informed of market developments and sales performance. The
  manager believes that only personal observation and active participation in sales
  work will provide the necessary information.
- The manager has never learned to delegate, having been trained as a salesperson, not as a sales manager.

Sales managers must learn to delegate. There is simply not enough time for a
manager to take on all the problems of subordinates and also do a good job of
managing. There are at least two steps a manager should take to make delegation
more effective and less risky:

- Constantly coach, train, and counsel salespeople on sales techniques and territory management; help and encourage them to become effective problem solvers
  on their own.
- Study the company's sales information system carefully. Does it furnish the facts
  needed, in the necessary detail, at the proper time? Does the manager completely understand and trust the system? Is it being used effectively?

No one can deny that there is an element of personal risk in delegating responsibility. Salespeople make mistakes which make the manager look bad. However, the
essence of management is getting things done through people, and it demands the
development of delegation skills.

Communication

The communications skills of leadership involve the ability to recognize differences in people and in meanings and to use this understanding to transmit and

receive messages accurately. In short, without the ability to communicate, the manager cannot lead.

It is important to recognize two major aspects of leadership communication. First, communication takes place through several media, and the supervisor must be skilled in the use of them all. The manager communicates by written reports, letters, or memos and also verbally on a face-to-face basis and by telephone. Equally important, supervisors communicate by behavior, by smiles or frowns, by voice tones, by pats on the back, by firm handshakes, and by their conduct in the presence of others.

Second, effective communication is consistent. One message must not contradict another. For example, a manager sends a memo out to all his or her salespeople, directing them to reduce expenses. But then the manager takes a salesperson out to the most expensive restaurant in town. The communication between the sales manager and salespeople must reinforce, not contradict, itself.

Teamwork

The increased emphasis on seminar selling, national account management, and other group sales approaches has placed more attention on developing teamwork in the sales organization. Further, the need for greater coordination in dealing with the complex needs and purchasing requirements of large customers has important implications for sales supervision and leadership. In particular, sales managers must find ways to encourage and reward the kind of teamwork desired.[31]

To build and maintain a strong sales team, managers must take the following steps:

- Establish a clear-cut mission and appropriate goals for the team.
- Give team members an opportunity to get to know one another.
- Provide technical and emotional support to the team and its members.
- Recognize accomplishments and reward performance.

Some ways that sales managers have accomplished these tasks include the cross-training of team members, shared assignments, task forces, group problem-solving exercises, incentives based on team performance, participative meetings, and games, sports, and social activities. By providing opportunities for salespeople to learn teamwork, the manager enhances their cooperative skills.[32]

Participation

A means of providing salespeople with challenging jobs is to encourage them to take an active part in decision making. A manager should involve salespeople in decisions that affect them.[33] When salespeople are allowed to participate, they accept management decisions more willingly. They feel important when allowed to express their views. For example, salespeople should have a part in setting their quotas or other performance evaluation standards. The individual's performance relates to the particular conditions in his or her territory, and since salespeople are familiar with the conditions in their territories, they should be involved in setting the performance standards based on those conditions. Also, if they help set the goals, they will be more anxious to achieve them.

Active participation by salespeople has another major benefit. Solutions to problems will improve. The old adage "Two heads are better than one" is true. By encouraging participation, the sales manager brings the collective thinking of several people to bear on problems. There will be further discussion of participation by salespeople in the coverage of sales evaluation in Chap. 19.

Discipline

Orderly behavior is necessary in every organization, so the sales manager must establish certain standards of behavior for subordinates. These standards relate to conformance with company rules and procedures, behaving in a socially acceptable manner, and meeting ethical standards. In any organization, individual desires must generally conform to the wishes of the group. For example, a manager should discipline people when reports are turned in late, when instructions are ignored, when corporate taboos are violated, or when dishonest actions are committed.

Administering disciplinary actions provides sales managers with an uncomfortable leadership challenge, but appropriate punishment can have a positive impact on sales performance. For this to happen, disciplinary actions must be aimed at modifying specific undesirable behavior and must be consistent over time and across salespeople; the rationale for their application must also be clear to those being punished.[34]

Every sales manager must have an established disciplinary procedure to follow for specific violations. Negative incentives can take the form of a deferred promotion, demotion, transfer to a less desirable position, withdrawal of merit pay increases, and deprivation of regular or special assignments. The most dramatic form of discipline is discharge. The field manager usually has the authority to fire an unsatisfactory salesperson, but this action should be taken only after all other alternatives have been exhausted.

An established procedure for discipline helps a sales manager guard against overreacting when a problem occurs. The manager who becomes visibly upset with a problem subordinate will lose credibility with other members of the sales organization. For this reason, a sales manager must deal with disciplinary problems professionally and privately.[35]

Some of the most difficult disciplinary situations that sales managers face involve salespeople who abuse alcohol and drugs. Not all sales organizations have firm policies in place to deal with such abuse. Many sales managers also mistakenly believe that these problems are more serious for salespeople in general than they are for their own sales forces.[36] As a result, they are inclined to view a substance-abuse problem as an occasional occurrence and ignore it rather than confront the person who has the problem.[37]

Although it appears that the problems of alcohol and drug abuse are no more serious among salespeople than among workers in general, they are sufficiently pervasive and costly that sales managers must be prepared to deal with them. The following course of action is recommended:[38]

1. Assess the extent of the problem. Sales managers should be aware of the telltale signs of alcohol and drug abuse. They must be alert to the potential for substance abuse among their salespeople.
2. If there is no formal company or division-wide policy regarding substance abuse, sales managers should develop their own. They must ensure that all salespeople know what the policy is. They must be aware of the legal requirements, ethical concerns, and costs involved in dealing with substance abuse.
3. Sales managers must realize that they cannot ignore or tolerate substance abuse by salespeople. They must make sure that alcohol is used in moderation in conjunction with sales activities and that salespeople realize that drugs have no place in the business environment.
4. Sale managers must realize that informal counseling is not the way to deal with chronic substance abusers. This is no job for amateurs. Sales managers should be familiar with treatment resources available in the company or the community so they can refer problem salespeople to professionals for assistance.
5. Sales managers must lead by example. They must carefully watch their own drinking habits and must set a standard of drug-free behavior through their actions both on and off the job.

SUMMARY OF LEARNING GOALS

1. **Understand the elements of sales motivation.**

    What motivates salespeople depends on what their needs are, and needs vary from individual to individual. Sales managers must understand these needs if they are to determine the proper incentives to use for motivating their personnel.

2. **Describe the various needs that influence the behavior of sales personnel.**

    One distinction of types of needs is primary versus secondary. Primary needs are physical needs that must be satisfied immediately, while secondary needs can be satisfied at another time. Rational needs and emotional needs are another classification. Finally, there is Maslow's hierarchy of needs, which is based on the idea that needs of the lowest level must be satisfied before higher-level needs become important motivational forces. Maslow ranked needs in the following order: (1) physiological—bodily requirements to function normally; (2) safety—the desire for protection from threats, dangers, and deprivations; (3) social—the need to interact with others; (4) ego—the need to feel self-esteem; and (5) self-actualization—the desire for self-fulfillment.

3. **Describe the development of motivation theory in sales management.**

    Motivation theory in sales management has been influenced by expectancy theory, which is based on the idea that people decide how much effort to put into their work based on what they expect to get out of it. The effects of organizational commitment and the organizational climate for selling on the motivation of salespeople have also been studied. Organizational behavior modification is another framework for studying motivation; it is based on the principle that a behavior followed by a favorable consequence is likely to be repeated. Attribution theory states that people are motivated not only to maximize their rewards, but also to attain a mastery over the environment in which they work. Role clarity, or the extent to which a person understands what is expected from him or her on the job, also impacts motivation.

4. Outline the basic concepts of sales leadership.

No formula is applicable to all sales leadership situations, and sales managers must always be aware of the difficulties in dealing with different types of salespeople. The human relations skills required for effective sales leadership are substantial. Among other things, sales managers must understand what makes salespeople cooperate, they must understand role playing, and they must understand the leader-follower relationship.

5. Explain the leader-follower relationship.

The leader-follower relationship is an implicit or explicit contract under which the leader and follower each give something of value in return for receiving something of value. For example, the sales manager values time, energy, skills, attention, loyalty, interest, extra effort, imagination, knowledge, and devotion. By contrast, salespeople want to be understood, valued, belong, informed, buffered, and protected.

6. List the leadership roles sales managers are required to play.

Sales managers are required to play a variety of leadership roles. These include being superior performers, inspirational leaders, innovators, guardians of the status quo, and parental figures.

7. Identify the individual leadership and human relations skills important to sales management.

The individual leadership skills required for sales managers are perception, conceptual ability, and self-awareness. Human relations skills that sales managers must possess are the abilities to delegate responsibility, communicate well with subordinates, create a sense of teamwork, create an atmosphere of participation, and discipline subordinates effectively when necessary.

REVIEW QUESTIONS

1. Outline Maslow's hierarchy of needs. Cite examples of each level.
2. List factors that can affect sales force morale. How is morale related to motivation?

3. According to expectancy theory, under what circumstances will a salesperson be highly motivated? What implications for sales managers can be found in expectancy theory?

4. Differentiate between positive reinforcement, negative reinforcement, punishment, and extinction. Give examples of each.

5. Explain the cutoff point in salesperson cooperation. What happens if someone's cooperation level falls below that point? Who selects the degree of cooperation above the cutoff point? What costs are incurred through a low level of cooperation?

6. List the things that salespeople generally want in the leader-follower relationship. What happens if they do not receive these things?

7. Why is role analysis a particularly critical leadership skill? What roles are sales managers called upon to play?

8. Why are sales managers reluctant to delegate? What two steps can a sales manager take to make delegation more effective and less risky?

9. Why is effective communication so important for a sales manager? What are two major aspects of leadership communication?

10. Why is more attention being placed on developing teamwork in the organization today? How can a sales manager build and maintain a strong sales team?

DISCUSSION QUESTIONS

1. Many sales managers periodically go with their salespeople on calls. What are the benefits of this practice?

2. Sales contests can be an effective way to motivate the sales force. Jack Falvey, a well-known sales consultant, has suggested that sales contests should be set up so that it is possible for all salespeople to win.[39] Do you agree with Falvey? Why or why not?

3. Sales slumps can be a difficult challenge for sales managers. What signs could a perceptive sales manager look for in order to notice a salesperson entering into a slump? What could a sales manager do to help get a salesperson out of a slump?

4. Days Inn was experiencing a problem with high turnover; hoping to increase employee loyalty, it began hiring older workers. One person came out of retirement to work for Days Inn, and now he is supervising hundreds of reservation agents.[40] Do older people have advantages as sellers? What special leadership challenges might arise from hiring older salespeople?

5. Interview a salesperson. What type of leadership does this person appreciate in his or her job? What motivates this person the most effectively? Give a class report on your interview.

ETHICAL DILEMMA

Field sales manager Barbara Foley knows that one of her salespeople has a serious personal problem which has distracted the individual from selling. This poor sales performance may prevent the sales team from reaching its sales goal for the quarter. This, in turn, may result in the loss of the year-end bonus for the entire sales team. What should Barbara do?

The Car Seller's Lot

The careers of car salespeople are often characterized by job hopping from dealership to dealership in search of a better deal. This fact is partly due to circumstances in the economy and the automobile industry; for example, between 1986 and 1991, U.S. vehicle sales fell every year. Car salespeople are compensated almost entirely by commission, and they often do not receive even the most basic of benefits, such as insurance. These salespeople face a very harsh reality—when business is down, their incomes suffer.

The job hopping and lack of satisfaction with employers is hard on the salespeople and the dealers. By staying at one dealership, salespeople are able to build relationships with customers and generate repeat business. High turnover eliminates the possibility of realizing this potential. Also, desperate car salespeople are not effective sellers, becoming so obsessed with making a living that they get pushy and offensive with customers.

Some dealerships have solved these problems by simply eliminating the sales job and hiring hourly paid employees to assist self-serving customers. The automobiles are sold on a one-price-only basis, and haggling over prices is eliminated. Auto makers, not surprisingly, are not fond of this idea, and many are providing sales training programs and advocating the provision of benefits for salespeople.

The problems described above existed between Robert Williams, a 33-year-old car salesperson, and his employer. Williams had been in the car selling business for three years, during which he worked for six dealerships. He made $17,800 in his best year.

One day at work, Williams refused to stay after hours and help clean snow off the parking lot. The reason he would not stay late, he said, was that he could not afford a baby sitter for his 8-month-old child. Mr. Williams was fired for insubordination, and his job hunting efforts began again.

Questions

1. Where would you place Robert Williams on Maslow's hierarchy? Based on this placement, what would motivate him?

2. If you owned a car dealership, what would you do to improve your sales effort?

3. Discuss ways in which automobile manufacturers could accomplish their goals.

CHAPTER 16

SALES INCENTIVES

LEARNING GOALS

- Understand that sales incentives should be based on the individual needs and wants of sales personnel.
- Differentiate between nonfinancial and financial sales incentives.
- Emphasize the importance of sales force recognition and describe how it is best accomplished.
- Discuss the role of sales contests in motivating sales personnel.
- Describe how a sales contest should be developed.
- Identify the keys to conducting an effective sales meeting.
- Explain the factors that need to be considered in planning a sales meeting.

THE UNIQUE MOTIVATIONAL STYLE AT DATAFLEX

Talk about trophy value. When Rick Rose, president of Dataflex Corporation, was asked by one of his salespeople how much she had to sell to get a car like his, he bet her his car that she could not sell a certain amount for six months in a row. The salesperson won the bet, and Rose's car. This type of motivation, unusual anywhere else but Dataflex, is part of the reason that Rick Rose and his sales force manage to achieve the impossible as a matter of course.

Dataflex Corporation buys IBM, Hewlett-Packard, Compaq, and Apple computer equipment and resells it to large companies such as Exxon and Merck. In a recent year, Dataflex sales were $80 million, and incredibly, the company accomplished these high sales while incurring no bank debt. One factor in Dataflex's success is that it runs a lean sales effort. While some of its competitors support a hundred or more sales offices, Dataflex has only one. Also, Dataflex's salespeople are paid by commission only, which keeps the company's overhead low and is an important factor in the sales force's motivation to produce. Sales commission checks average $173,000 per year.

Dataflex's achievement of the elusive high-sales/low-costs combination is largely attributed to Rose, who is a former U.S. Naval Academy football player. Rose brings to his sales management duties a tough, inspirational atmosphere similar to that of the military or an athletic team. Rose has ten top-flight salespeople whom he calls "Navy Seals," and there is an early morning roll call each day. Rose personally hires all salespeople himself in an attempt to employ only those people who can work under his type of leadership.

In the very unique corporate environ-ment of Dataflex, it is hard to point to a single factor as the reason for the firm's successful sales management effort; how-ever, it does seem that Rose's less than orthodox sales management style works well in a competitive, commission-only sell-ing environment. And in an industry where many companies are losing money, selling is a little like doing battle.[1]

Chapter 16 discusses sales incentives. Richard Rose is exceptional in the way in which he motivates his sales force, and, al-though his approach would not work in every situation, it does work well for Dataflex. Rose is not necessarily a model to follow, but sales managers must, like Rose, come to understand their own corporate environ-ments and the needs of the individual mem-bers of their sales forces.

CHAPTER OVERVIEW

This chapter shifts our focus from leadership to incentives, the tools of sales motivation. As Chap. 15 emphasized, the field sales manager is perhaps the most effective motivator of sales personnel. Through day-to-day contacts, the manager sets the style and tone for the relationship with the company; however, personal supervision is limited by the time available to the manager, and sales incentives (including compensation) must also be used to motivate salespeople. A *sales incentive* can be defined as anything that is used to reward sales personnel for their accom-plishments.

sales incentive
Anything used to re-ward sales personnel for their accomplish-ments

In establishing incentives, the first task is to discover what each individual salesperson needs or wants. Motivational research has shown that people are usually much more diverse in their work values and motivation patterns than their managers suspect.[2] Therefore, a manager cannot motivate salespeople without understanding their desires. Although part of the supervisory task is to develop a general aware-ness of human behavior, this alone will not suffice. The sales manager must also identify the individual needs of sales personnel. Tom Stasizak—with four children and a mortgage—is concerned with security. Marge Clifton, who is single, is motivated by the potential for advancement. Obviously, Tom's needs and Marge's needs are different. The incentives used to motivate these two salespeople must also be different.

Sales trainees and older salespeople present special motivation problems. It is hard to motivate trainees, who must undergo long breaking-in periods before they are productive. It is difficult to give them a feeling of accomplishment. It is especially tough to generate enthusiasm for selling when trainees are technically trained but lack a sales orientation. For this reason it may be wise to reward beginners for their efforts to learn rather than for their ability to produce.[3] In contrast, older salespeople sometimes have limits on what they can earn, and occasionally feels their advancement and personal growth are restricted.[4]

A sales manager's challenge is first to determine the individual needs of sales personnel and then to provide the conditions for motivation—opportunities for growth, achievement, participation, responsibility, and recognition. The manager must also make sure that the basic conditions for good morale are provided— adequate pay, suitable physical surroundings, social opportunities, and the like. In part, these needs will be met through the various forms of sales incentives.[5]

TYPES OF INCENTIVES

In addition to the personal supervision aspects of motivation discussed in Chap. 15, there are two other major ways to motivate salespeople: financial and nonfinancial incentives. Like good leadership, well-chosen incentives will stimulate salespeople to use their existing energies and resources more effectively. In designing incentives, one can choose either special effort or continuing format approaches. A sales contest is an example of a special effort incentive, since a contest is designed to achieve a specific, short-term goal. On the other hand, compensation and promotion are related to the achievement of continuing, or long-term objectives.

Nonfinancial Incentives

nonfinancial incentives Incentive techniques used for specific, special effort situations

Nonfinancial incentives consist of a variety of incentive techniques used for specific, special effort situations. Recognition (honors and awards, special privileges, and communication), sales contests, and sales meetings and conventions are the major forms. These techniques will be covered in this chapter.

Nonfinancial incentives are usually designed to achieve one or two specific, short-range objectives. However, they must be coordinated with the company's long-range marketing goals and overall personnel program. For example, if a company has a long-range goal of balanced sales, it is unwise to introduce a sales contest that encourages salespeople to emphasize a specific product line at the expense of other product lines. Since sales contests have the power to redirect sal 's efforts, their use must be considered carefully.

Financial Incentives

financial incentives Direct monetary payments or indirect rewards with monetary value

fringe benefits Indirect monetary rewards including vacations, insurance plans, and pensions

Business organizations provide two forms of financial rewards. *Financial incentives* may be direct monetary payments, such as salaries and wages, or they may be indirect monetary rewards. These indirect rewards, commonly known as *fringe benefits*, include paid vacations, insurance plans, pensions, and the like.

Financial incentives have changed in recent years. More salespeople are now paid through a combination plan of salary and commissions or bonuses. Such plans provide stability of earnings and a direct incentive. Also, fringe benefits have become a more important part of the average salesperson's income. These and other trends will be discussed in Chap. 17.

AMWAY CORPORATION

If motivators are in the form of financial or nonfinancial incentives, then it can be said that Amway Corporation provides its distributors more of the latter than the former. Amway has over a million door-to-door distributors, who sell an average of $1700 worth of soap, cosmetics, vitamins, and thousands of other Amway products per year. Out of their profits, distributors are required to buy various self-help and inspirational materials from Amway. Also, distributors are expected to buy only Amway products for their personal use.

The average Amway distributor nets about $780 per year. While this is paltry financial incentive, Amway distributors are motivated strongly by abundant nonfinancial incentives. Rarely in

history have leaders been able to unite people under a single purpose as well as Amway founders Richard DeVos and Jay Van Andel. Amway holds motivational rallies, where attending distributors are inundated with talk of God, country, family, and rags-to-riches testimony. The rallies bring together distributors who share values and associate these values with the Amway affiliation. The message is, basically, that Amway is opportunity for those with pluck and moral fortitude. Even the name of the company is suggestive: "Amway" is perhaps only a shortened version of "American way."

There's no other business quite like Amway, where human relationships are as much a form of motivation as business relationships are. The incentive of shared values inspires a lot of individual enthusiasm and enough individual selling effort to add up to sales of $3.1 billion in a recent year.

Types of Nonfinancial Incentives

Recognition.   Salespeople, like most employees, respond well to recognition. In fact, one study indicated that nine out of ten employees feel that recognition is important or very important as a motivational factor.[6]

Sometimes a phone call or acknowledgment of an accomplishment at a sales meeting is appropriate. For best results, recognition should be given at a public meeting, be directed at objectively determined performance, and convey to recipients that the company clearly cares about them.[7] Other factors that will enhance the effects of recognition as a motivational technique include providing some form of recognition for approximately one-third to one-half of the sales force, involving top management in the recognition program, initiating the program with a special event, and communicating the program to employees in writing.[8] Some specific guidelines are presented in Table 16-1.

Honors and Awards.   These include trophies, plaques, certificates, blazers, membership in honorary organizations such as the Sales Advisory Council, and titles such as "Salesperson of the Year"; they are inexpensive and have considerable appeal to salespeople. For example, Prudential Insurance Company awards a "President's Citation" to agents in the top 3 percent of sales, and the life insurance industry's "Million Dollar Roundtable" is a widely publicized honor.

Just as important as the actual honor or award is the publicity that goes along with it. Awards to salespeople can be publicized through news releases to company

TABLE 16-1   **Recognition Program Guidelines**

Regardless of its size or cost, any recognition program should incorporate the following features, says consultant Dr. Richard Boyatiz of McBer and Co.:

- The program must be strictly performance-based with no room for subjective judgments. If people suspect that it is in any way a personality contest, the program will not work. Says Boyatiz: "It should be clear to anyone looking at the data that, yes, these people won."
- It should be balanced. The program should not be so difficult that only a few can hope to win, or so easy that just about everyone does. In the first case, people will not try; in the second, the program will be meaningless.
- A ceremony should be involved. If rings are casually passed out, or plaques sent through the mail, a lot of the glamour of the program will be lost.
- The program must be in good taste. If not, it will be subject to ridicule and, rather than motivate people, leave them uninspired. No one wants to be part of a recognition program that is condescending or tacky. Says Boyatiz: "The program should make people feel good about being part of the company."
- There must be adequate publicity. In some cases, sales managers do such a poor job of explaining a program or promoting it to their own salespeople that no one seems to understand or care about it. Prominent mention of the program in company publications is the first step in overcoming this handicap.

publications, local newspapers, and trade magazines. In discussing this form of recognition, sales management consultant Richard Boyatiz has written:

> People like to know that they are doing a good job . . . the thing that helps most, that makes people feel better about themselves and what they are doing is some kind of recognition. What's important is that it is done in some public way and treated with respect.[9]

Recognition programs can have a greater impact when they emphasize long-term performance. The recognition program can be used to communicate the firm's strategic goals and provide rewards for those sales personnel with track records of strong performance.[10] For instance, Pacific Northwest Bell has a recognition program, called "Club 20," that recognizes salespeople who are in the top 20 percent for two quarters in a row. They receive a ring especially designed with a place for eight diamonds, which are added to the ring each additional time they are ranked in the top 20 percent.[11]

Pentel of America, a manufacturer of office supplies, has developed a unique recognition program for its salespeople. Known as the "Samurai Award," it is given each year to two salespeople, one in commercial markets and one in mass markets. The award is based on both sales quotas and the achievement of quality sales expectations. Winners receive a cash award, a ring, and a week-long first-class trip for two to Japan.[12]

Another unique recognition program used by some companies is the preparation of a book that includes insights about selling techniques and accounts of experiences of the firm's top salespeople. AT&T Network Systems and Monsanto are two businesses that have used this approach to recognize their leading salespeople. These books also have training value since they are distributed to other members of the sales force. According to Claire Wherley, marketing operations director of AT&T Network Systems, "the feeling our winners got from seeing their names in print in that book wasn't something they could've gotten from any plaque or trophy."[13]

These types of recognition programs work because they enhance salespeople's prestige with their peers. Recognition is most effective when it is specific to the needs of the participants. Salespeople, in particular, are stimulated by the affirmation by peers that they are special. As one salesperson expressed it: "What a lot of people don't realize is that the prestige comes from the people you work with. They lift you up a little higher than themselves. It's like a temporary promotion."[14]

Special Privileges.   One manufacturer of consumer durables has its top sales reps arrive a day before the national sales meeting. They meet with market researchers and with research and development personnel to discuss new product lines. These top salespeople are recognized for their achievements by being asked to express their opinions. The company also gets the added benefits of receiving ideas that are based on the sales reps' extensive contacts with customers.

Training is another special privilege which can be used to recognize sales achievements. Koppers Company, a building products manufacturer, paid most of the costs for selected distributors' salespeople to attend a two-day selling skills course. In addition to helping the salespeople increase their selling effectiveness, the training program helped Koppers directly by emphasizing the company and its products.[15]

Special privileges can also be given at the local level. For instance, an insurance sales manager took an agent and the agent's spouse out to dinner as a special reward for a sale that the agent had been working on for three years. This reward had the added benefit of recognizing the support provided by the salesperson's spouse. Other relatively inexpensive special privileges and rewards that can be given at the local level include gift certificates, a special office parking space, and a gift of flowers for the salesperson or the spouse.

Communication.   It is also important to emphasize the role of communication as a motivating force. Salespeople may be based hundreds of miles from their home offices, so they need frequent recognition and reinforcement. Continuous communication can be maintained through written documents, phone calls, meetings, and visits to salespeople in the field.

As discussed in Chap. 15, personal contacts are the most effective form of motivation; however, continuous personal contacts are not always possible. A field sales manager cannot be working one on one with each salesperson at the same time. Planned phone calls are an acceptable substitute. One sales manager keeps in touch with salespeople by calling at least once a week. The manager carefully plans each call and writes down the main points to be covered. The calls usually include praise for some worthwhile acomplishment.

Another sales manager makes a special effort to recognize achievements of salespeople by keeping a record of noteworthy accomplishments and then responding in an appropriate manner. For example, one salesperson did an exceptional job of writing letters to customers. The manager sent this salesperson a note commending his efforts and put a copy in the individual's personnel file. The manager also makes a point of providing information on special achievements of subordinates to superiors so they will themselves commend the salespeople at the appropriate times.

Bulletins, announcements, letters, and other forms of written communication are also useful in motivating salespeople. A congratulatory letter from the boss may be remembered longer and valued more highly than a routine monetary reward. The sales bulletin is an ideal place to praise a salesperson. Contest winners should be spotlighted in sales bulletins and company publications. The salesperson then knows that colleagues and the home office are aware of accomplishments. It is also a good idea to mail sales bulletins to a salesperson's home as well as to the office. Spouses should be included in communication plans and efforts.

Many companies also cite individual sales achievements in monthly or quarterly sales reports. These reports can have a double impact: They recognize those people who are performing well, and may also stimulate poor performers to improve.

SALES CONTESTS

sales contests
Incentive techniques that award prizes for reaching specific sales goals

Sales contests are an established incentive technique used in specific, special effort sales situations. They are most popular with firms specializing in consumer goods although many industrial firms and distributors also run them. The types of sales contest used depends on the job to be done. In addition, sales contests can vary according to prizes awarded, methods of determining winners, and themes.

Sales contests help to achieve company goals by satisfying some of the salesperson's personal goals—recognition from peers, rewards for performance, personal esteem, and respect of one's family. The recognition involved with winning a sales contest helps the person gain self-confidence. As a result, salespeople are stimulated to improve their performance.[16]

Recent studies of sales contests and their impact on sales performance support this view. Contests can be effective in achieving short-term sales goals and enhancing overall job satisfaction for sales personnel.[17] However, they often do more than "increase sales." Some of the other reasons for conducting contests include opening new accounts, selling cooperative advertising, emphasizing high-profit items, reducing expenses, and recruiting new salespeople.

One especially interesting application of sales contests is to reward salespeople for acquiring product knowledge. This form involves salespeople at all levels of experience and expertise. A product knowledge contest carried out by SmithKline Bio-Science Laboratories generated responses from over 80 percent of the sales force. In addition to motivating salespeople to learn, this type of contest can also help the company gain a better understanding of its training program's effectiveness.[18]

Planning a Sales Contest

The key to a successful sales contest is planning. One writer has suggested that planning should be based upon the following premise: Imagine your salespeople as customers. Identify their needs and what segment of the source offers the most promise. Of course, do not forget to figure in a profit for the company.[19]

Planning sales contests requires expertise, and it is wise to seek outside help when developing one. Sources of help are the company's sales promotion manager and advertising manager, advertising agencies, sales premium representatives, major companies that have a premium organization, and trade associations in the premium field. Also, specialized sales incentive firms, such as E. F. MacDonald and Maritz, are now widely used. An incentive house will help the sales manager develop a contest program that coincides with the company's sales goals.

Sales force input is also essential when planning a sales contest. One writer suggested the selection of a "committee of sales superstars" to help select incentives and develop guidelines for the contest.[20] She noted that salespeople set tougher standards for themselves than their managers do; however, the rest of the sales force will respect these standards because they have been set by their own peers.

Sales force input is also helpful in selecting prizes and awards. Balfour, a producer of recognition products, asked its star performers what they wanted as sales incentives. They responded by saying that they wanted the same things they sell—rings, trophies, and other personalized, tangible awards. This and other changes implemented on the basis of suggestions from salespeople resulted in doubled sales for Balfour's Recognition Products Group over a four-year period.[21]

Like all important management tasks, planning a sales contest begins with establishing objectives. Challenging goals will stimulate salespeople to greater effort and higher levels of performance.[22] Some of the specific objectives for sales contests and incentives are shown in Table 16-2.

The other major factors to consider when planning a sales contest are theme, prizes, length, and promotion.

Theme.   A good sales contest theme is necessary to provide the play element, to sharpen competition, and to enhance promotion of the contest. Sports themes are often used since they provide the contest with a competitive atmosphere. Themes with an element of chance, such as poker or roulette, are also effective. Another approach is to use a theme that builds on a popular trend. For example, one company developed a "Shape Up" program that featured physical fitness equipment as prizes for sales personnel and managers.

Another company, software publisher Ashton-Tate, used a boxing theme for its technical knockout (TKO) sales incentive program. Winners received tickets to a championship prizefight in Las Vegas.[23]

TABLE 16-2 **Sales Incentive Objectives**

1. **Increase overall volume**
2. **Introduce new products**
3. **Sell new accounts**
4. **Improve morale and goodwill**
5. **Move full line or slow items**
6. **Bolster slow season**
7. **Offset competition**
8. **Support consumer promotion**
9. **Prepare for strong season**
10. **Build dealer traffic**

One of the most interesting and unusual themes of a sales contest was that of a "murder mystery" once used by E. F. Hutton Life Insurance Company. Called "Murder in Montreaux," this sales contest built on the interest in mystery novels. To win a grand prize trip to Montreaux, Switzerland, and other prizes, sales personnel not only had to meet sales goals but had to solve a murder mystery.[24]

Prizes. The incentives, or prizes, themselves are often the key to a successful contest. Money is still used extensively, but there is a growing trend toward noncash incentives.[25] For instance, merchandise catalogs offer the winners a choice of prizes and appeal to all members of a salesperson's family. Travel is also a good prize because it may have a strong appeal to the spouse. It is easy to dramatize and promote travel prizes by themes that tie into destinations.[26] For example, an incentive trip to Hawaii might have a theme of "Run for the Sun."

When travel is used as a contest prize, the contest may have added impact. Top producers who win an incentive trip one year are highly motivated to do what is necessary to win it again in subsequent years. This creates healthy peer pressure and spousal support for winning the contest. Further, the camaraderie of the group of salespeople who win these trips often transcends the experience of the travel. It is the "bonding," or feeling of closeness with other contest "winners," that motivates sales representatives to produce in order to take another trip.

Also gaining popularity are prizes that offer more practical rewards. For major contests, a company might offer scholarships for college to the children of the winning sales representatives. It is crucial to know in advance, however, that all sales representatives have children who are at or are approaching college age. A contest prize like this could demotivate a childless or single employee who is otherwise highly productive.

The reason many sales executives prefer these and other forms of nonmonetary incentives to cash is that the awards can be more easily dramatized and promoted. Executives also feel that salespeople respond better to noncash incentives.[27] Such incentives satisfy a salesperson's need for recognition. The acknowledgment of the person's achievement by supervisors, peers, family, and friends provides a powerful motivation to succeed again.[28] A summary of the strengths and weaknesses of incentive awards is presented in Table 16-3.

Length. The best length for a contest, in general, is the time required for all sales representatives to make a complete cycle of their territories. The duration will vary depending on the goals of the company and the level of award for the contest. Peak enthusiasm in a contest can only last for so long. After a few months, it is likely to diminish, unless regular promotion and tracking of each salesperson's progress is reported back to them to show them where they stand.

Promotion. A sales contest should be launched with fanfare to generate excitement and enthusiasm. For this reason, contests are often introduced during a national sales convention or at regional sales meetings. Followup promotion is also necessary; the excitement cannot be allowed to taper off. The sales force should be sold continuously on the prizes, winners should be recognized, and losers should be reminded that they are behind.

TABLE 16-3   Strengths and Weaknesses of Incentive Awards

Type of incentive	Advantages	Disadvantages
Travel	Extremely desirable and promotable Provides an exclusive venue for fostering team spirit and/or education "Bragging value" Provides good imagery for tie-ins during the qualification period	Too costly for many applications Travelers are out of the office during the trip Extensive efforts and experience required for high-quality delivery of the travel program
Merchandise	Extremely desirable and promotable since a good selection can appeal to every taste Immense variety allows its use for rewarding achievement at various levels and times in a program Has "trophy value" in that it is a concrete reminder of past performance and a constant reminder that future performance will be rewarded Items valued up to $400 for safety and length-of-service awards are tax-deductible to the company and excluded from employees' taxable income Can be obtained at wholesale prices and can be drop-shipped Redemptions occur at the end of a program, so major costs are incurred after results are in	Requires detailed administration Inappropriate for participants who are making a low wage
Cash	Desirable to everyone Easy to administer and simple to handle A medium understood by everyone Can provide an extra boost to a long-term program	Not promotable as exotic No trophy value Cannot be enhanced Tends to become an "expected" reward

Companies also should recognize the value of promoting a contest to a salesperson's spouse. This will involve another person in encouraging the salesperson to put forth extra effort.[29] Enthusiasm will be maintained if salespeople and their families are exposed to an initial and follow-through promotional program. As one authority has said, "The contest should be merchandised, promoted, and sold the same way one's products are."[30]

Do Sales Contests Motivate?

Although sales contests are used extensively, there are doubts about their effectiveness.[31] A frequent complaint is that they distort the normal sales pattern. It is argued that a contest does not really raise sales over the long run, but that it merely provides a short-term sales expansion.

A related criticism is that contests distract salespeople from their main job of selling. They encourage salespeople to concentrate on winning prizes. For example, one company ran a contest aimed at encouraging the sales force to set up dealer displays. The contest was successful; displays were placed in stores. Nevertheless, sales did not increase accordingly because many salespeople were so busy setting up the displays that they neglected to sell the products.

Sales contests sometimes fail because sales managers have not carefully planned for them. The timing may be off, the wrong prizes may be offered, or the goals may be unrealistic. Too often sales contests offer only a few prizes attainable by only the top salespeople. Sales contests should allow every participant who reaches established goals to earn prizes. All salespeople must have a chance to win or low morale will result. When salespeople compete for a limited number of top prizes, there are only a few happy winners and many unhappy or apathetic losers. For this reason, point systems tied to merchandise catalogs are sometimes used as prizes since they allow every participant to obtain some form of reward.

Another reason for contest failure is inadequate promotion. Poor internal communications results in salespeople not knowing enough about the contest. A contest must be well publicized to get everyone involved.

Despite the qualms of the critics, contests are widely used, and they work for most companies. Various studies have shown that executives generally consider special sales contests and incentives to be effective motivating forces. Contests work because they provide recognition, excitement, and rewards. Consider the following:

- *Recognition:* Everyone wants recognition. Salespeople want to feel important; they want status. A sales contest provides salespeople with an opportunity to earn recognition.
- *Excitement:* A sales contest puts a game element into what may otherwise be "just a job." The contest is a challenge to which a salesperson usually responds. It provides excitement, and helps to spice up the daily routine.
- *Rewards:* The prize is an effective motivator by itself. If all salespeople feel (as they should) that they have a chance of winning, the prize is usually a reward worth seeking. This is particularly true if the prize is something a salesperson would not normally buy.

To use contests effectively, sales managers must understand how they work. Every contest or incentive has at least one goal—either to improve some behavior or to sell more of a good or service. Behavior that is rewarded becomes behavior that is learned and repeated. If a sales contest is to motivate, salespeople must be aware of what management is trying to accomplish. Before committing to the contest, they will scrutinize the program thoroughly.[32] In particular, salespeople will ask themselves:

1. Is the contest simple? Is it understandable or is it so complicated that it is impossible to participate in?
2. Are the terms of the contest specific? How much needs to be sold and by what date? Are goals measurable, and will participants know where they stand at all times?
3. Are the contest's goals attainable, or is management expecting the impossible?
4. Is the contest well-timed? Can the goal be accomplished within the time frame? Is the contest scheduled at a conflicting or inconvenient time?

SALES MEETINGS AND CONVENTIONS

Most sales incentives are presented at gatherings of the sales force. This timing allows management to maximize their value. As a result, there is a close link between sales meetings and conventions and the use of sales incentives.

Sales managers are involved in planning and conducting sales meetings and conventions. *Sales meetings* are attended by salespeople from one sales office or district and usually held monthly or quarterly. *Sales conventions*, held once or twice a year, are national or regional gatherings of salespeople.

sales meetings
Monthly or quarterly gatherings of sales-personnel from one office or district

sales conventions
Annual or semiannual gatherings of regional or national sales forces

Sales meetings and conventions should be designed for specific purposes. For example, a meeting can emphasize training, such as explaining the firm's advertising campaign, assisting salespeople in improving their sales techniques, and providing new product information. A meeting can also be used to communicate changes in company policies or information on current market trends. Whatever the purpose, it must be specific and should be informational in nature; a meeting designed or promoted strictly for motivation will often be rejected by salespeople as a glorified pep talk.

Maryland Cup, which has a sales force of over 300 people, provides an example of the types of sales meetings held by a large national company.[33] The company holds a national sales meeting every five years. It is attended by the entire sales force and is designed to inspire salespeople and boost morale. The national meetings are supplemented by approximately two regional and two interregional meetings per year. These smaller gatherings deal with specific topics and have a training orientation. They allow for much greater involvement of the participants.

A poorly planned or executed sales meeting or convention is one of the biggest mistakes a field sales manager can make. Effective conventions and meetings are strong motivators, but poor ones are simply wastes of everyone's time and the company's money.[34] The keys to a good meeting are planning, participation, and evaluation.

Planning

A sales meeting is valuable only when it is worth more than the work in the office or field that will be interrupted. To make sure that this is the case, managers must plan the meeting carefully. In large part, a meeting's productivity depends on what happens prior to its occurrence, especially in its preparation stages.[35]

Objectives. The first critical step in planning a sales meeting is to formulate objectives. Unfortunately, failure to establish clear objectives is a critical mistake many leaders of sales meetings make. Objectives are needed to provide the basic thrust of the meeting and to indicate to participants how it will help them. Of course, the meeting's objectives must also be set in conjunction with a company's overall marketing and sales objectives. Major automobile manufacturers, for instance, orient their annual dealer meetings toward the goal of introducing the new models to their dealers and the press.

Once the objectives have been established, the sales manager must consider the meeting's theme, time and location, agenda and timetable, and the administrative arrangements for carrying it out.

Theme.   Each sales convention needs a theme to serve as a guide in planning the agenda and to stimulate enthusiasm. For participants, the theme indicates the basic purpose of the meeting. It is not necessary that each weekly or monthly sales meeting have a distinct theme. However, a general theme for the month or quarter may provide an effective orientation for regular sales meetings.

Themes for sales conventions are almost unlimited. Frequently, the conventions are run in conjunction with sales contests, so a joint theme is used for both. Sports, current events, and exotic places are common themes.

Time and Location.   It is essential that meetings be arranged far in advance and scheduled at times that will not interfere with selling activities. Monday mornings or Friday afternoons are good times for weekly or monthly sales meetings. Annual conventions should be held when business is slack, perhaps during the summer or during the Easter or Christmas seasons. Another advantage of scheduling sales meetings at "off-season" times and locations (e.g., Florida in the summer) is cost savings.[36]

Selecting a meeting place involves many considerations. The location suggests whether the purpose of the meeting is work or a reward.[37] For example, a meeting in Las Vegas or Hawaii will probably be viewed by the sales force as a reward-oriented meeting. By contrast, a hotel near Chicago's O'Hare Airport suggests a work-oriented meeting.

The size of the group will be a major factor in selecting the type of meeting site. It is also often important to get salespeople away from their normal surroundings, so company facilities may not be appropriate. Noncompany sites include hotels and conference centers. Airport hotels are popular because of their easy accessibility and their willingness to cater to business groups.

Meeting planners are most concerned about quality of service when they select a meeting site. Quality of food is the second most important concern, and rates are third.[38] Other considerations are convenience, type of accommodations, equipment, meeting room facilities, and reputation of the facility. Most planners agree it is wise to visit a site before a meeting is scheduled to check the facilities and services. Exact specifications and written confirmations will also help to ensure a successful meeting.[39]

Agenda and Timetable.   The agenda and timetable establish the basic structure and sequence of the meeting. It is essential that a written agenda and timetable be developed during the planning stages. As plans progress, these will be revised.

The agenda for a sales meeting is determined by the specific needs of a company and its sales force, but the meetings held by most companies cover similar subject matter. As Table 16-4 shows, sales progress reports and sales force feedback are two topics most likely to appear on a meeting's agenda.

Choosing the keynote speaker for a sales conference is an important decision when the agenda is developed. Business leaders, consultants, educators, and sports, entertainment, and media personalities are often used. They can be entertaining and can create a positive atmosphere for the meeting. In addition, many sports and entertainment figures can provide a motivational message. However, sales managers

TABLE 16-4   **Topics Included on Sales Meeting Agendas**

Topic	Always included, %	Sometimes included, %	Never included, %
Sales training	57	41	2
Product introductions	49	49	2
Information on competitors' efforts	56	43	1
Sales progress reports	76	23	1
Product promotions	54	41	5
Motivational talks	30	61	9
Recognition and awards for salespeople	37	55	8
Announcement of incentive programs	17	69	14
Sales force feedback	71	29	0

should be aware that talks by most motivational speakers will not have a long-term effect on salespeople.[40]

The customer should also be represented on the agenda. This may be accomplished by obtaining customer information through focus groups, surveys, interviews, and/or product evaluations prior to the meeting. Another option is to invite customers, former customers, and noncustomers to the meeting. By examining and analyzing customer input at sales meetings, the sales organization will find newer and better ways to become customer-driven.[41]

The final agenda and timetable serve as the program for the meeting. Topics, speakers and discussion leaders, times and places of sessions, and recreational activities are included. A printed program should be given to participants ahead of time so they will know exactly what they will be doing.

Administrative Arrangements.   There are many details associated with planning and conducting a conference or meeting. Space arrangements, food, speakers, recreational facilities, and the like must all be considered in advance. Establishing effective communications with the staff of the facility where the meeting will be held is critical. Staff members need to be informed of any specific requirements. It is especially important to inform the convention site's sales and catering staff of any special services, personnel, or facilities that will be needed. During the meeting the sales manager should continue to work closely with the staff.

When spouses and families are invited to a conference, special arrangements may be required. Plant tours and workshops will help these guests understand the salesperson's job better. Recreational activities, sightseeing trips, and similar activities will fill the time when the salespeople are in meetings. Finally, social activities should be family-oriented, so that spouses and family members will feel welcome at the conference.

Participation

The second key to a successful sales meeting is participation by the attendees. Active participation is essential. The exchange of ideas and experiences is vital. Unless the participants feel that they are free to express their ideas, they will not become actively involved in the meeting. As one writer has said: "If the information flows only one way, you might as well tape it and mail it out. No need to bring in an audience for token participation."[42]

There are many ways to effect participation from salespeople. One technique is to have them prepare special presentations in advance. One company has its top salespeople prepare and talk about how they closed the most difficult sale of the year, the most unusual sale of the year, or the most important sale of the year. The presentations are made to the entire sales force at the national sales meeting, and humorous gifts are awarded to the presenters. For this company, the opportunity to tell a personal success story is a potent motivator for the salesperson.

Other techniques for obtaining participation are skits, panel discussions, debates, case studies, and role playing. Each of them makes salespeople feel that they are part of the meeting. Each also provides a flow of ideas that may not be forthcoming from a formal presentation.

One of the authors vividly remembers a role-playing session with chain saw sales personnel. Afterward, many in the audience said that more was learned from the participation of an older salesperson than from anything else. This man was excellent at selling, but he was closed-mouthed about his sales techniques. When he was put in the role-playing situation, he willingly demonstrated why he was so outstanding.

When salespeople are given an opportunity to participate in a sales meeting, they also provide useful suggestions to management. A large office supplies manufacturer sets aside approximately one-third of most sales meetings to obtain feedback from its sales reps. After one national meeting, the company made changes in its cooperative advertising program and its bid policies for large customers as a result of these suggestions.

Evaluation

Sales conventions and meetings are expensive. Transportation, accommodations, entertainment, speakers, and the costs of planning for large numbers of salespeople involve major expenditures. Meetings also take the sales force away from selling. Unless a conference results in improved sales effort, the time spent at it may be a waste. For instance, if salespeople are at a convention solely because they see it as a company-paid vacation, the training time will be wasted.

One way to evaluate the results of a sales meeting is to measure some sort of sales activity, such as new accounts opened or increased sales of a particular product, afterward. Unfortunately, it may be weeks or months before sales results can be measured, and it may be too late to correct shortcomings of the meeting that caused salespeople to miss their objectives. For this reason, many sales meeting planners try to evaluate meetings at the time they are held or soon after they are over.

One approach is to ask participants for their evaluations during informal conversations at coffee breaks, meals, and other opportunities. Informal feedback can help the meeting planner identify problems and, if necessary, make adjustments while a meeting is going on.

Another approach involves formal questionnaires that ask specific questions. These can be completed at the end of the program, or attendees may be asked to complete them after they return home. For instance, a large insurance company

S A L E S   M A N A G E M E N T   I N   P R A C T I C E

SMITHKLINE BEECHAM

SmithKline Beecham really knows how to throw a sales meeting. At its meeting to introduce RespiSure, a swine vaccine, there was no less than a specially produced rap video featuring pigs as construction workers—highly appropriate for the meeting's theme, which was "Building for Our Future." The theme was used in the invitations, gifts, and all other parts of the meeting.

Rapping pigs are one thing, and cold cash is another. More recently, SmithKline introduced a feline vaccine. The product, which was highly technical, was the subject of a four-day sales meeting. At the end of the four days, each of the two hundred salespeople attending the meeting was given a round of questions to answer. High

scorers were then recruited to play on a "game show," complete with cash prizes.

The game show worked well on several levels. The cash aspect gave salespeople a direct incentive to learn about the new products. The format itself was exciting, expecially since "audience" members were encouraged to bet on which players would win. The questionnaires sent out to qualify participants let management know how much the sales force had learned without resorting to school-like tests and grading systems.

SmithKline has used the game show format for several of its sales meetings. The shows are produced by agencies, which charge about $8000 to $15,000 for one session. It is not possible to determine how many of these dollars result in extra sales. At highly technical companies like SmithKline, however, salesperson knowledge is a priceless asset.

sends out a survey two weeks after each meeting that includes questions on meals, hotel arrangements, services, the social program, and the business agenda. The responses are used to plan future sales meetings as well as to evaluate the meeting just completed. A sample meeting evaluation form is presented in Table 16-5.

TABLE 16-5 **Sales Meeting Evaluation Form**

Please give your honest comments on this questionnaire. Your personal evaluation is very important for the planning and administration of future meetings.

Scale 1 = Excellent   2 = Very good   3 = Fair   4 = Poor

1	2	3	4	Hotel overall
1	2	3	4	Meeting rooms
1	2	3	4	Sleeping rooms
1	2	3	4	Meals
1	2	3	4	Advance meeting promotional information
1	2	3	4	Meeting theme
1	2	3	4	Keynote speaker
1	2	3	4	Breakout sessions
1	2	3	4	Meeting overall

What did you like the most?

What did you like the least?

What do you want to see more of at future meetings?

What do you want to see less of at future meetings?

What was the most important thing you learned at this meeting?

What did you learn that will help you become a more effective sales representative?

What suggestions do you have for the content and programs of future meetings?

SUMMARY OF LEARNING GOALS

1. **Understand that sales incentives should be based on the individual needs and wants of sales personnel.**

   People are diverse in what they are motivated by; therefore, sales managers must identify the individual needs of the sales force.

2. **Differentiate between nonfinancial and financial sales incentives.**

   Nonfinancial incentives are nonmonetary techniques used for specific, special effort situations. Examples of special nonfinancial incentives include recognition, sales contests, and sales meetings and conventions. Financial incentives are direct monetary payments (such as salaries and commissions) or indirect rewards that have monetary value (such as paid vacations).

3. **Emphasize the importance of sales force recognition and describe how it is best accomplished.**

   Recognition is important to almost all employees. For best results, recognition should be given at a public meeting, be directed by objectively determined performance, and convey to recipients that the company clearly cares about them.

4. **Discuss the role of sales contests in motivating sales personnel.**

   Sales contests are most appropriately used in specific, special effort sales situations. They help achieve company goals by satisfying the personal goals of salespeople. Sales contests can be used not only to increase sales but also to achieve goals such as opening new accounts, selling cooperative advertising, emphasizing high-profit items, reducing expenses, and recruiting new salespeople.

5. **Describe how a sales contest should be developed.**

   The planning of sales contests should include input from various outside sources and also from the sales force. Challenging and stimulating goals should be established at the start of sales contest development. The other major factors to consider when planning a sales contest are theme, prizes, length, and promotion.

6. **Identify the keys to conducting an effective sales meeting.**

   Sales meetings should be designed for specific purposes. While they should be motivational, that should not be their only purpose.

7. **Explain the factors that need to be considered in planning a sales meeting.**

   When planning a sales meeting, a sales manager must be conscious of the meeting's objectives, which provide its basic thrust, and indicate to participants how the meeting will help them. Other elements that must be planned are the meeting's theme, time, place, agenda, timetable, and administrative arrangements.

REVIEW QUESTIONS

1. Why do sales trainees present a special problem when developing sales incentives? What can be done to help alleviate this problem? How does motivating older salespersons involve a management challenge?

2. Discuss the role of recognition in sales force incentives. Cite some examples of appropriate recognition.

3. How can a sales contest be inappropriate? Why must managers be very careful about introducing sales contests?

4. What are some sources of help to a sales manager who is planning a sales contest? What is the advantage of using sales force input to help plan a sales contest?

5. Why is an appropriate theme essential for an effective sales contest? Suggest some themes that might be used in a sales contest.

6. Why is catalog merchandise an effective sales contest prize? What are the advantages of travel prizes?

7. Why do so many executives prefer nonmonetary incentives to cash incentives? Explain.

8. What are two criticisms of sales contests? What are some of the reasons that sales contests sometimes fail?

9. Differentiate between a sales meeting and a sales convention. How often are each held?

10. What are some of the purposes for which a sales meeting or convention can be used? Should a meeting or convention be designed strictly for motivational purposes?

DISCUSSION QUESTIONS

1. Of the various incentives mentioned in this chapter, which do you think would be most motivating to you as a sales representative? Do you think your answer would be different if you were asked this same question ten years from now? If so, how and why? If not, why?

2. Several innovative sales contest ideas were described in this chapter. All sales contest themes—from boxing to murder mysteries—are successful in part because they provide an element of play and competition. Take any topic you know well, and develop a sales contest around that topic. Include a title for your contest, the general requirements for winning, and the prizes that will be awarded to winners.

3. The involvement of spouses in the sales incentive effort was advocated throughout this chapter. Discuss the potential roles that spouses can play in salesperson incentive. Do you see any problems with management's using spouses in efforts to provide sales force incentives?

4. In your own words, what is "trophy value"? What attributes do you think give a sales incentive trophy value? Think of the various nonfinancial incentives mentioned in this chapter. Which of these incentives have trophy value? Which do not? What advantages do these "trophies" have over cash rewards?

5. Spend a few hours at any convention or sales meeting happening in your town and evaluate the participation level of the attendants. Are you impressed with what you see at the meeting? What is your opinion of the agenda? Are participants taking the meeting seriously or do they seem to view it as a "company-paid vacation"? In your opinion, is this related to the participation level? (*Hint:* To find out where and when conventions or meetings are being held, call local hotels, read the business section of a newspaper, or call a local business and ask permission to sit in on a sales meeting.)

**E T H I C A L
D I L E M M A**

Sales contests can be an effective way to stimulate sales for a specific period of time. However, some salespeople may cheat in order to win. For instance, a salesperson may arrange to have a customer buy surplus merchandise which is later returned after the contest ends. How should sales managers deal with salespeople who cheat in contests?

SALES MANAGEMENT CASE

Re/Max—Giving Salespeople What They Want

In the early seventies, Dave Liniger was an extremely successful salesperson for a leading real estate company. Although he was making a respectable living, he had a problem with the system. The company took 50 percent of a salesperson's commission to pay for overhead. This meant that fixed costs such as advertising and office space were split unequally among the sales force—high-volume salespeople paid for more than their share of company fixed costs.

This situation was precisely the reason that many star real estate salespeople left their employers and struck out on their own. A fledgling, one-person real estate office could not, however, easily afford the advertising and other expenses needed to run a successful business.

Enter Dave Liniger and Re/Max. At Re/Max, real estate agents are given the advantages of a big company without the disadvantages. Re/Max agents keep 100 percent of their commissions and are supported by custom-designed office computer software, national advertising, and an awards program. In return, the agents pay Liniger an average of $1200 to $1500 per month in overhead and franchise fees. After subtracting fees from commissions, Re/Max agents take home on average over three times the amounts that they would if they paid half their commissions to their employer.

But the real genius of Re/Max lies in the type of salespeople it attracts. Only experienced agents with proven track records are tempted by join the company. Unless a salesperson's commissions are substantially larger than the monthly fee, the individual simply cannot afford to work at Re/Max. The company does not even provide sales training per se; all support is motivation-oriented or geared toward the selling sophisticate.

Questions

1. Describe the financial incentive that Re/Max provides its salespeople. What type of nonfinancial incentives are Re/Max salespeople gaining?

2. Name another type of business that could provide a franchise opportunity like Re/Max's.

3. Obviously, real estate companies do not want to provide a training ground for future Re/Max stars. What can they do to encourage their best people to stay with them?

CHAPTER *17* SALES COMPENSATION

LEARNING GOALS

- Discuss the role of money as a motivator.
- Identify the major trends impacting sales compensation.
- Outline the criteria for a good sales compensation plan.
- Explain the steps in developing a compensation plan.
- Describe the various compensation plans used in selling as well as the features of these plans.
- Discuss the role of fringe benefits in a sales compensation plan.
- Discuss how sales managers are paid.

COMPENSATION: EQUITABLE TREATMENT + COMPANY GOALS

Executive pay is under fire. With CEOs of many major companies making millions of dollars per year, critics are saying that no one can be worth so much money and that some of those dollars should be shared with employees, stockholders, and consumers. Current levels of executive pay certainly warrant a reevaluation. The discrepancy between the highest- and lowest-paid Americans is huge, with the average CEO of a major corporation making 85 times the pay of the average factory worker. In Japan, by contrast, that same figure is only 17 times.

The above statistics are so striking that they have received a great deal of media attention. The issue of executive compensation has become very volatile, especially for companies whose financial situation does not seem to justify big CEO paychecks. The repercussions of worldwide competition and a

tough U.S. economy are some factors that have added up to an outcry for more equitable compensation for all.

Pay based on performance is a goal for many companies and especially for companies' sales organizations. Oftentimes, however, situations outside salespeople's control can decrease sales volume, the traditional measure of salesperson performance. New bases for compensation are being developed by innovative companies seeking to establish equitable pay for performance standards. Methods of measuring profitability and customer service are being studied with keen interest; both issues have become crucial to companies as selling costs have risen and competition has intensified.[1]

Chapter 17 discusses sales force compensation. As you read on, keep in mind that the amount that salespeople make and the basis on which salespeople are paid should not only reflect equitable treatment but should also encourage salespeople to achieve company goals. In the development of compensation packages, sales managers must continually strive for effectiveness on both of these levels.

CHAPTER OVERVIEW

money-sensitive salespersons
Salespersons motivated to work harder by an increase in remuneration

leisure-sensitive salespersons
Salespersons not motivated to work harder by an increase in remuneration

income satisfiers
Salespersons who adjust the level of their activities and sales to maintain the same level of income

This chapter focuses on financial incentives. A sound compensation plan is essential to successful management of the sales force. There is confusion and disagreement, however, about the role of financial incentives as motivators. For instance, Professor Rene Darmon has suggested that the behavioral responses to financial incentives can fall into five categories. *Money-sensitive salespersons* will be motivated to work harder by an increase in remuneration. There are also salespersons for whom there is no (or no additional) motivation from a change in remuneration. *Leisure-sensitive salespersons* have been found to work less following increased remuneration, while *income satisfiers* adjust the level of their activities and sales to maintain the same level of income. Finally, it is conceivable that some salespersons are irrational and will react to a remuneration increase by decreasing sales and income.[2]

Sales practitioners are also uncertain about the impact of financial incentives. At one extreme is the sales manager who feels that sales personnel are motivated strictly by financial considerations. These managers rarely recognize other needs. At the other extreme are the proponents of internal growth needs. They argue that a salesperson is concerned with factors related to the job and that financial compensation is relatively unimportant as a true motivator of behavior.

An accurate view of money as a motivator lies somewhere between these two extremes. Financial compensation has several functions in motivating salespeople: It is the determinant of a salesperson's purchasing power, it is a symbol of status, and it is an indication of equitable treatment.

Most experienced sales managers agree that an effective sales compensation plan can be an important motivator. Increased sales are stimulated by a well-conceived compensation plan. It is especially significant that almost all salespeople view compensation as more than simply a payment for services rendered; it is related to recognition as well. A salary increase is a reward, but it is also a form of recognition for acceptable job performance.

Sales compensation consultant Thomas R. Mott has described the value of financial incentives in the following way:

> Ideally, a properly structured plan will send a loud and clear message about what salespeople should be doing and how well they're doing it. The plan will also provide that extra incentive to put the final touches on a sales presentation, drive to the next city late at night after a tough day, and so forth. Finally, it will keep salespeople focused on the most strategically desirable products or accounts, even though those may not be the easiest products to sell or the most likable customers. [3]

In contrast, an inadequate compensation plan can adversely affect all aspects of sales force operation. Depressed pay rates create dissatisfaction and lead to low morale. Turnover of salespeople is often directly related to low compensation. Other symptoms of a poor sales compensation plan include rising field sales expenses, declining sales, growing numbers of customer and salespeople complaints, product imbalance, and excessive loss of old accounts. [4]

Mott summed up the inadequacies of a poor sales compensation plan in the following way:

> An improperly structured plan . . . can distract, confuse, frustrate, and aggravate sales employees. At their worst, these plans can cause a sort of on-the-job semi-retirement that usually leads to resignations. [5]

Finally, sales managers must recognize that financial incentives are not the only way to stimulate salespeople. [6] Money decreases in importance as a motivator once a satisfactory level of earnings has been reached. Even those salespeople striving to reach a desired standard of living have other needs that must be met.

Chapter 17 discusses the development of a sound sales compensation plan. Compensation trends are reviewed, criteria for establishing a compensation plan are considered, and the steps for developing a plan are identified. Knowledge of sales compensation is important for all sales managers since adequate, equitable compensation is essential to sales force motivation. A diagram showing the relationship between motivation, evaluation, and compensation is presented in Fig. 17-1. The compensation plan is a key element in this linkage.

CRITERIA FOR A SOUND COMPENSATION PLAN

Designing a sound sales compensation plan is difficult. There is no one "best" compensation plan even for companies with similar product lines, markets, and size. A good compensation plan for a particular company must be developed from a careful analysis of that company's goals, capabilities, and requirements. [7]

A sound compensation plan for salespeople considers the needs of both the company and its sales force. From the company's standpoint, the basic consideration is to get salespeople to do what management wants done as efficiently as possible. Because sales compensation is a major sales expense, the dilemma for sales management is how to stimulate salespeople and maximize profitable sales, and still keep sales expenses at a minimum.

From the salesperson's point of view, the basic concern is to maximize earnings. Each salesperson wants a level of compensation that is felt to be fair in comparison to

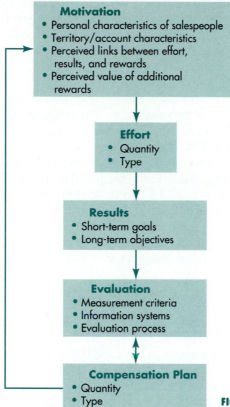

FIGURE 17-1 Links between Motivation, Evaluation, and Compensation.

the incomes of a peer group, other company employees, and the relevant labor market. The salesperson also wants a balance of security (a steady income) and payment for extra effort (incentive income). Achieving the proper balance presents another dilemma for sales management.

An effective compensation plan represents both points of view. The carefully developed sales compensation system attracts, motivates, and retains capable sales personnel while staying within the company's budget.[8] General characteristics of a good plan are described in more detail below.

Incentive

A sound compensation plan will stimulate salespeople to achieve the firm's goals. In particular, it must motivate salespeople to generate net profit rather than mere sales volume. A good plan will encourage salespeople to accomplish what management decides it wants done.[9]

Simplicity

An effective compensation plan is easily understood and relatively simple to operate. Salespeople should be able to calculate easily what their income will be. A plan that salespeople cannot understand loses its value as a motivator. Further, a plan should not attempt to motivate salespeople to achieve more than two or three important selling objectives. Incentive components must be based on measurable, clear factors. Complex sales compensation plans simply do not work.

Fairness

An essential element for any sales compensation plan is equity. The plan must be fair to both the company and its sales force. The company should be able to keep selling costs in line with volume. The compensation plan should also protect against windfall gains to salespeople in abnormal times.

Salespeople expect a plan to reward ability and productivity. This requires a constant scrutiny and willingness to revise the plan if necessary. Special care must be taken to even out inequities resulting from territorial differences.

Another aspect of fairness is what is known as "comparable worth." This has become an important social, legal, and political issue as more and more women have entered sales and other forms of employment.[10] In short, a sales compensation plan must not result in compensation inequities that reflect gender or other nonperformance differences.

Flexibility

A plan should be sufficiently flexible to take into account the rapidly changing needs of the firm and its salespeople. Changes in the supply of salespeople, products, and customers, as well as changes in the competitive situation, will require adjustments in sales compensation. For instance, a good plan will operate effectively through the ups and downs of the business cycle.

Companies are providing salespeople with flexibility in a number of creative ways. For example, a Canadian holding company offers its salespeople a choice of four different compensation mix options, ranging from 100 percent commission to 25 percent commission/75 percent base salary. Another company allows sales representatives to select dual "forecast" and "stretch" goals in each product category. A gas utility uses an adjustable compensation system that encourages superior performance by tying incentive compensation to quota achievement.[11]

Control

Salespeople should do what management pays them to do. The sales compensation plan should provide control and direction over sales force activities. A sound plan will strengthen the sales manager's supervision of sales personnel. However, no compensation plan can ever take the place of a good sales manager or act as a substitute for good leadership.

Competitiveness

The level of compensation must be competitive with the levels offered by other companies. Good pay is needed to attract, keep, and develop effective salespeople. Nothing leads to high sales turnover faster than a noncompetitive sales compensation plan.

SALES COMPENSATION TRENDS

Compensating field sales personnel is more difficult than paying most other employees. The conditions under which most salespeople work are less standardized and less easily controlled. Therefore, sales compensation plans are continuously undergoing change. To a large extent, the trends in sales force compensation reflect what has been happening in the marketplace.

Emphasis on Specific Goals

Many companies are now trying to relate sales compensation to specific management objectives. With the adoption of the marketing concept, special emphasis has been placed on tying sales compensation to some measure of profitability or other strategic marketing goal.[12]

As a result, many sales managers are starting to realize that their firms' strategic goals, such as increased market share, improved return on sales, and profitability growth, can be related to sales performance measures and compensation. For example, market share can often be increased through the introduction of a new product. However, the sales compensation plan must provide an incentive to salespeople for investing the extra time to sell the new product to a first-time buyer. Profitability can be increased by rewarding salespeople for selling at or close to list price. Likewise, compensation that offers rewards for focusing on account retention or the sale of strategically important products will help increase a firm's return on sales.[13] To achieve these goals, many sales organizations have turned to some form of combination sales compensation plan.

Shift to Combination Plans

For a number of years, companies have moved away from straight commission or straight salary plans toward combination plans. Most firms of all sizes now use combination compensation plans for their salespeople.[14] *Combination plans* use salaries plus commissions and/or bonuses to pay salespeople. Approximately 70 percent of American companies now use a form of salary plus incentive compensation to pay salespeople (see Table 17-1).

combination sales plans Sales compensation plans that include salary plus commissions and/or bonuses.

Combination plans are so popular because they provide great flexibility. The modern sales job is complicated. A salesperson must be a problem solver as well as a seller. Incentives can be related to the accomplishment of specific marketing objectives as well as to sales volume. It is especially important to relate sales compenstion

TABLE 17-1 Methods of Compensating Sales Representatives

	Sales reps	Senior sales reps	Account specialists	Government reps	Special market reps	Telephone sales reps
Salary only	17.6%	16.5%	26.3%	37.8%	27.4%	37.2%
Salary plus incentives	76.0%	79.6%	70.6%	59.5%	70.8%	60.8%
Commission only	6.4%	3.8%	3.1%	2.7%	1.9%	2.0%
No. of responses	551	442	160	74	106	148

DIAL CORPORATION

Regionalization has become a prevalent segmentation strategy for companies seeking to capitalize on the differences in tastes and preferences that exist among the markets across the United States. Procter & Gamble and Cargill are just two examples of companies that have "gone regional."

Dial Corporation, which produces soap, cleaning materials, and packaged foods, began regional efforts in 1989, when it divided the nation into eighteen segments and assigned a financial specialist, a marketing person, and a customer service representative to each.

For Dial, the move toward regionalization was not only an attempt at developing a more focused, and therefore more effective, basis for segmentation; the strategy was also a response to competition. The suc-

cess of the differentiation strategy, as both a proactive and a reactive effort, was extremely important to the Dial Corporation.

To instill Dial employees with a regional emphasis, a new compensation plan was developed. Within this new plan, team members' bonuses were based on sales volume, sales forecasting accuracy, and improved profitability for their region. Team members were also rewarded for their own individual performance.

By compensating its employees on both an individual and team basis, Dial succeeds in inspiring people to work hard, because the efforts of individuals pay off in the form of bonuses. Basing part of employee compensation on team factors, however, ensures that team members will work together and actually focus on their regions. Joining group incentives to individual incentives keeps employee drive intact while instilling the team loyalty that the corporation needs if its regionalization strategy is to work.

to the accomplishment of less quantitative objectives and tasks, such as customer service, marketing intelligence, and long-range developmental sales activities. In addition, combination plans satisfy the salesperson's desire for some stable base income. Specific forms of combination plans will be discussed later in this chapter.

Changing Sales Strategies and Tactics

Many companies have begun to revise their sales compensation plans to reflect changes in sales strategies and tactics. For instance, team selling requires a compensation program that rewards all members of the sales team appropriately.[15] Team compensation plans must offer incentives to nonsales members as well as to salespeople. This is especially important for high-tech firms that rely heavily on the contributions of technical people. The unique nature of high-tech firms requires that the sales compensation plan must take into consideration the complex organizational and motivational issues related to team selling.[16]

Xerox has developed a compensation program designed to enhance teamwork between sales and nonsales employees. The "Partnership Excellence" incentive program rewards districts that meet profitability and customer satisfaction goals through partnerships between sales managers, business operations managers, and service managers. During the first year, more than a quarter of the districts qualified for incentive awards.[17]

Companies are also structuring compensation programs for different types of sales specialists. For example, they may have separate plans for salespeople who concentrate on large accounts. It is recommended that national account managers (NAM) should always be paid significantly more than top field salespeople if a firm is to attract talented people to these challenging jobs. Further, incentive payouts should be based on performance measures in addition to simple territory sales volume, and a separate and distinct compensation plan should incorporate exceptional NAM performance measures.[18]

Compensation for people who sell services also reflects differences in sales strategies and approaches. Salespeople for business service firms are expected to be more entrepreneurial, and are often paid on a commission basis. Since they take more risks, they earn more money on average at all levels than their counterparts in consumer and industrial products sales. Further, top sales performers in business service firms earn a great deal more, while poor performers are severely penalized. Since companies in all industries are moving toward differentiating themselves on the basis of service, it is likely that compensation will reflect this trend.[19]

It is also interesting that businesses new to selling, such as banks and other financial institutions, have begun to include incentives as part of their compensation plans. These incentive plans are directly tied to sales performance results and have been effective in motivating bank employees to sell.[20]

A similar trend is taking place in retailing. In an effort to spur sales, traditional retailers are moving toward a greater emphasis on commissions. For instance, Nordstrom's sales personnel earn over half of their pay in commissions. It is felt that reliance on commissions is a key factor in Nordstrom's success.[21]

Fringe Benefits

The last major trend in sales compensation is the increased availability of fringe benefits, or indirect compensation payments. In most modern companies, even salespeople on straight commission are eligible for such benefits as pensions and insurance.

Changes in the nature of selling are largely responsible for this trend. Salespeople are no longer considered self-supporting free agents. They have closer ties with their companies. Companies must offer a range of health, welfare, and pension benefits to attract and retain good people.

Benefits that are available to nonsales personnel are now also available to the sales force. Most firms provide paid vacations, group life insurance, hospitalization, and major medical insurance. Pensions for salespeople are now accepted as normal, and most salespeople receive paid holidays. These and other forms of fringe benefits will be discussed in more detail later in the chapter.

DEVELOPING A COMPENSATION PLAN

Only rarely are field sales managers called upon to design sales compensation plans; but managers are usually responsible for administering the plans once they are formulated, and they may assist in revisions of plans. For these reasons, it is important that field sales managers understand the process by which a compensation plan for sales personnel is developed.[22] The basic steps in this process are as follows:

1. Review the sales job.
2. Determine specific objectives.
3. Establish the level of compensation.

4. Choose the method of compensation.
5. Implement the plan.

Job Review

The first step in designing or revising a compensation plan is to carefully review the sales job. The preparation of the job description was discussed in Chap. 12. It is sufficient at this point to reemphasize the value of the job description as a planning tool. Careful analysis of the job description will reveal what a company must pay to acquire and satisfy the sales personnel it wants.

Education and experience are the two prime qualities that require above-average compensation. If college education is a requisite for a sales job, compensation must be competitive with other college-level jobs. Likewise, if a company must hire only experienced salespeople because it lacks a sufficient training program, it must be prepared to pay more for that experience.

Some companies use compensation surveys to assist them in the evaluation of their sales compensation program.[23] An independent survey will help managers assess the effectiveness of their incentive and base pay rates. Statistical analysis can be used to supplement sales executives' judgments and guide them in making changes.

Establish Objectives

As discussed earlier, sales compensation objectives must be related to the company's sales and marketing goals. For example, manufacturers in mature markets will have different objectives than companies in high-growth industries. As a result, their compensation plans should be different.[24]

Compensation objectives must also be realistic. The compensation plan should be an aid to sales management.[25] One cannot expect it to overcome basic weaknesses in sales supervision. As management consultant Edwin Lewis has said: "Motivating the reps to penetrate key accounts, develop new markets and nurture relationships with clients is the job of the sales manager, not the compensation plan."[26]

Input from the sales force can be used to establish the plan's goals. These inputs and management's objectives are blended into a compensation plan that represents the best compromise between what are often conflicting compensation goals of management and sales pesonnel. Customers and their needs should also be considered when developing sales compensation objectives and plans. Customer sophistication determines the sales skills needed and the degree of influence the salesperson will have in the selling process.[27]

Level of Compensation

Sales compensation should be set at a level sufficient to attract, retain, and stimulate the type of salespeople desired. This usually involves paying about what other firms are paying for similar selling jobs. However, a smaller company may be forced to pay a premium to attract competent salespeople, particularly if it has a limited training program and is required to hire only experienced salespeople.

The level of sales compensation depends on several factors. Pay must be attractive enough to attract sales recruits. There must be a reasonable correlation between sales compensation and the pay of other employees. Competitors' pay plans must be examined, as must the company's own history of sales compensation. Finally, careful attention should be given to the relationship between sales compensation and profits. Management must estimate what sales compensation will cost the company. Overpaying or underpaying salespeople must be avoided.

Dangers of Overpaying

Although some companies overpay their salespeople, this is a bad practice.[28] Many factors influence sales volume, and higher sales compensation is not necessarily associated with greater productivity.[29] One possible result of overpaying salespeople is an adverse effect on company profits since sales compensation is usually the largest single element of selling costs. However, paying above the industry average is not a high-cost strategy if it reduces turnover and training costs.

Personnel problems are also created by overpaying salespeople. The morale of sales managers suffers if they resent the fact that some salespeople earn more than they do. It is also difficult to persuade top salespeople to take management positions if the latter involve cuts in pay.

Dangers of Underpaying

It is also important to guard against underpaying sales personnel. Two conditions may result if this is done: (1) The company may attract only poor salespeople, and poor performance will result, and (2) if good salespeople are hired at low pay, there will be excessive turnover. Good salespeople will be vulnerable to pirating by other firms.

compensation compression
Situation in which the range between the lowest- and best-paid salespeople is narrow

Another concern is *compensation compression*. This occurs when the difference in pay between below-average and above-average salespeople is narrow. When this takes place, higher-level performers become dissatisfied because their level of compensation does not reflect their superior performance. There is little incentive to achieve when even a subpar performer earns only slightly less than a top sales performer.[30]

Methods of Compensation

The traditional methods for paying salespeople are salaries, commissions, and bonuses.[31] As noted earlier, most firms now use some type of plan that combines these methods. The method of compensating salespeople is just as important as the level of compensation. In fact, many sales managers feel that it is the method of compensation, not the level, that influences the performance of the sales force. When choosing a method of compensation, three factors must be considered: motivation, control, and cost.

1. *Motivation.* Different methods of compensation will stimulate salespeople in different ways. Commissions and bonuses provide direct incentives to achieve, whereas salaries are less directly related to sales performance.
2. *Control.* Each method of compensation also provides a different form of control. When salespeople are on straight salary, they are directly responsible for their actions. A sales manager has direct control and can ask personnel to perform

various nonselling duties. The commission form of payment has the opposite effect: salespeople on commission consider themselves more independent than salaried salespeople and often perform only those activities that are immediately related to sales success. The bonus form of compensation provides control by inducing salespeople to point their efforts toward particular goals.

3. *Cost.* The various methods of compensating the sales force affect selling costs in different ways. Salaries are a fixed expense; commissions and bonuses are variable expenses. When business is good, a straight salary plan may provide higher profits. In a business slump, fixed selling expenses may cause losses. With commissions and bonuses, selling expenses vary with performance. They will be high when sales are good and low when sales are poor.

Figure 17-2 illustrates the relationship between sales and sales compensation expenses. Assume that a company has a choice between paying its fifty salespeople a salary of $50,000 a year or a commission of 5 percent of net sales. If sales are $50 million or less, the company will minimize selling expenses by paying its sales force on commission. If sales are more than $50 million, a salary form of compensation will minimize selling expenses.

Although cost is an important factor, it is not the only compensation consideration.[32] Sometimes the least expensive method of compensation may not be the best. Motivation and control are equally important. If projected sales in the above example are $60 million, it may be wise to still use a commission form of payment. The greater selling effort generated by a direct financial incentive may have important extra benefits.

Salary

salary Fixed sum of money paid at regular intervals

A *salary* is a fixed sum of money paid at regular intervals. A salesperson might be paid $800 a week, $3000 a month, or $35,000 a year. The amount paid is related to time rather than to the work achieved.

A straight salary is used when a salesperson's actual work function is not directly related to sales volume or to other quantitative measures of productivity. For example, when a salesperson is expected to perform many nonselling activities such as market research, customer problem analysis, servicing, and sales promotion, straight salary is a logical method. The salary compensates the salesperson for these nonselling duties. The salary level is based on many factors such as length of service, living requirements, general performance, and competitive salaries. Straight salary

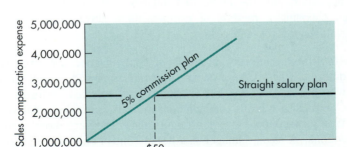

FIGURE 17-2
Relationship between Selling Expenses and Methods of Sales Compensation.

SALES MANAGEMENT IN PRACTICE

SOFTWARE 2000 INC.

The motivational strengths of commission-based pay can also be its greatest weaknesses. Understandably, quota-focused salespeople sometimes neglect company directives that do not have an immediate positive impact on commission checks.

Software 2000 Inc., a Massachusetts-based developer of IBM-compatible software, is one of the fastest growing companies in the United States. While the volume generated by the company's commission-based sales force certainly has been impressive, the timing of these sales was causing problems for the rest of the company. A disproportionate number of sales were being made in the last quarter, causing a hardship on production and customer service employees. At the end of every year, Software 2000 had a not-so-pitiable problem: It could not keep pace with its own sales volume.

Software 2000 management could have approached its inconsistent sales in many ways. The company determined, however, that its own commission structure was to blame. Individual quotas were set on an annual basis, and salespeople who made sales above and beyond their quota were paid higher commission rates for those sales. Once January 1 rolled around, the system started all over, so it was every salesperson's goal to sell as much as possible before year-end. When a new year began, commissions—and sales—were back to normal.

Software 2000 established a "rolling quota" for its sales force. Now the commission rate changes monthly, and it is based on the salesperson's performance over the previous six months. In this way, future pay is based on current performance, current pay is based on past performance, and the temptation for erratic selling behavior has been removed.

---

plans are also found in companies and industries in which an engineering orientation is needed for selling, such as the aerospace and industrial chemicals industries. A salary is needed because of the extended time required to close complex sales situations. A salary also encourages the salesperson to emphasize continued service after the sale.

Salaries are appropriate when a new product is introduced, when a new market is developed, or when a new salesperson is being trained. These situations are characterized by uncertainty for the salesperson. A salary provides sales trainees with a steady income while they adjust to their new positions.

The prime advantage of a straight salary is direct control. Salespeople can be required to perform activities that do not result in immediate sales. There is also more flexibility for management. It is easier to switch personnel to different customers and territories. The plan is also simple to operate and easy for the sales force to understand.

These advantages are often outweighed by the disadvantages associated with the lack of direct financial incentives.[33] Only routine motivation is provided by a salary, and this may lead to limited individual initiative and drive.

Commission

commission
Payment for the performance of a unit of work

A *commission* is a payment for the performance of a unit of work. A salesperson might be paid 3 percent of net sales, 5 percent of gross profits, or $1.25 for each 100 pounds sold. Straight commission plans are often used by firms in the leather products, furniture and fixtures, apparel, and real estate industries.

Straight commission plans are based on the principle that the earnings of salespeople should vary directly with performance. Salespeople are paid for results.

Commission payments have historically been based on dollar or unit sales volume; however, more and more companies are beginning to compute commission rates as a percentage of some measure of profitability.[34]

Direct motivation is the key advantage of the commission method of compensation. A strong incentive is provided to increase productivity. Salespeople are encouraged to think and conduct themselves as if they were in business for themselves. Strong performers are attracted and encouraged, whereas marginal performers are eliminated.

High earnings also provide salespeople on commission with recognition. In a study of real estate salespeople, researchers found the following:

> . . . pay and accomplishment were considered very important by both manager and salespeople. In commissioned selling the desire for a sense of accomplishment is rarely satisfied and salespeople constantly set higher monetary goals. Contrary to the idea that money ceases to be a motivator, commissioned salespeople appear to have a much higher need for recognition through pay than for individuals within other career fields.[35]

Loss of control over sales activities is the major limitation of straight commission. Its incentive to sell more may encourage overstocking, misrepresentation of goods, and other undesirable selling practices. Customer services and goodwill may also be neglected. Another weakness is the insecurity that salespeople may face because of irregular earnings.

Several modifications of the straight commission plan have been designed to overcome these disadvantages. Three of the most popular are commissions with drawing accounts, sliding commissions, and varied commissions.

drawing account
Money advanced against future commissions

Some companies provide their salespeople who work on commission with a *drawing account*, from which money is advanced against future commissions. Drawing accounts give salespeople some of the security of a salary, and allow management more control over sales activities. As a result, draws are most appropriate in sales situations that call for steady, short-term earnings and as a hiring tool.[36] However, a problem arises when a salesperson fails to earn enough commissions to repay the draw. When this happens, the person may quit or be fired, and the company must absorb the loss.

sliding commission plans
Commission plans in which the rate increases with increases in sales volume

Sliding commission plans use a changing commission rate. When a progressive commission plan is used, the commission rate increases proportionately with increases in sales volume. For instance, a salesperson may be paid 1 percent of net sales for sales up to $50,000, 1.5 percent of sales from $50,000 to $100,000, and 2 percent for all sales over $100,000. This type of commission plan provides a strong stimulus to increase sales.

regressive commission plans
Commission plans in which the rate decreases with increases in sales volume

Regressive commission plans work in reverse: The commission rate decreases proportionately with increases in sales volume. A salesperson may receive 1.5 percent of net sales up to $100,000, 1.0 percent for sales from $100,000 to $250,000, and 0.5 percent for all sales above $250,000. This plan gives a strong financial incentive to achieve initial sales and encourages goodwill activities. It may appear that a regressive plan goes against common sense, but it works well in those selling situations in which the major task is to make the initial sale. For example, a salesperson for heavy equipment should receive the greatest reward for closing the sale for the basic piece of equipment. Additional sales of supplies and maintenance items are routine and need not be rewarded as generously as the initial sale.

varied commission plans Commission plans that use variable rates to promote sales of the most profitable items

Varied commission plans are used to promote sales of the most profitable items. Higher commissions are given for selling products with high gross profitability and lower commissions for products with lower profitability. Although this plan is not as simple as a straight commission plan, it is more flexible. It also relates selling expenses to profitability.

Bonus

bonus Payment made at the discretion of management for a particular achievement

A *bonus* is a payment made at the discretion of management for a particular achievement. It is usually a reward for special effort and provides direct motivation. In contrast to commission payments, which relate directly to some measure of sales performance (usually sales volume), bonuses are less directly related to sales volume. They can be used to stimulate teamwork, improve communication, enhance productivity, and give firms a competitive edge in recruiting and retention of personnel.[37] In general, bonuses are considered additional incentives rather than part of the basic sales compensation plan.

Attainment of sales quotas is used frequently to determine eligibility for bonus payments. A division of a large Midwestern corporation developed an incentive plan based on quotas for four product categories. These were first set by negotiation between salespeople and their supervisors. Incentive payments were set up for sales in excess of quotas. The incentives emphasized sales of the most profitable products rather than sales volume alone. To encourage balanced selling, salespeople received a bonus only if they met quotas in three of the four product groups. If they met quotas in all four categories, their bonus was doubled.

Bonuses are also paid for extra effort related to the company's sales goals. These include bonuses based on the number of new accounts opened, on the performance of certain types of promotional work, and on reductions in expenses. For example, a salesperson might receive $100 for each new customer or $20 for setting up a floor display.

Some companies have also begun to use bonuses to encourage salespeople to assist in the sales forecasting process. There are mixed feelings on this issue. Proponents argue that sales forecasts will be more accurate because salespeople will strive to meet sales objectives that are based on forecasts they have projected. The more accurate a salesperson's forecast, the more the person will earn. Critics of these bonuses point to the complexity of sales forecasting and the salesperson's role in the forecasting process.[38] They suggest that paying a salesperson for the accuracy of the forecast will not necessarily result in a more accurate forecast. Some salespeople may project low forecasts to make sure they meet their sales estimates and earn a bonus.

Most bonus payments are in cash, but merchandise gifts and other rewards may be used. One pharmaceutical manufacturer has a plan that pays bonuses to salespeople in company stock. The goal is to create a common interest in profitability by making salespeople stockholders. Salespeople are offered shares of stock if district sales forecasts are met and if individual quotas are achieved. Regional sales managers, district sales managers, and retailers are also eligible for stock bonuses if their performances exceed expectations.

Combination Plans

In an earlier section it was observed that many salespeople and sales managers prefer a compensation plan that combines the security of a fixed base with incentive payments. The proportion of incentive pay depends on the company's objectives and on the nature of the selling task. When a salesperson's selling skill is the key to sales success, the incentive part of the salesperson's pay should be high.[39] When the product has been presold and the salesperson is primarily an order receiver, the incentive proportion of the salesperson's gross income should be smaller.

Combination plans often fail because they provide too little financial incentive for the salesperson to achieve the desired objectives. As a general rule, at least a quarter of the average salesperson's gross income should be in the form of incentive pay. If not, the sales incentive plan will not be truly effective.

Incentive earnings are paid annually, semiannually, quarterly, or monthly. In general, the shorter the time interval between performance and payment of the reward, the stronger the stimulus to the salesperson. However, in practice, payment of earned incentives may sometimes be deferred for several years. The standard life insurance plan, for example, involves paying the agent half of the commission when a policy is sold and the rest in regular payments over the next ten years.

point plan
Combination plan under which points, which are convertible to money, are given for selling various products, for performing certain duties, or for making certain intangible contributions

There are many forms of combination pay plans. One variation is the *point plan* under which points, or credits, are given for selling various products, for performing certain duties, or for making intangible contributions such as being cooperative, showing interest in the job, and showing initiative. At the end of the month, quarter, or year, the points are converted into monetary values and a bonus is paid to each salesperson who qualifies. Point plans complement a firm's basic compensation plan.

Another variation is to give seniority increases. One manufacturer provides a gradual increase in the incentive rate for each year a salesperson stays with the company. After twenty-five years of service a salesperson receives about 25 percent more incentive income for the same performance than what a person just joining the company earns. This type of plan provides incentive rewards for loyalty. One might argue, however, that this form of compensation encourages longevity, not productivity.

When a combination plan is used, it must be designed to reward performance. All too often differences in compensation for salespeople are based on such factors as length of service with the company and structure of the territory. Another problem occurs when salespeople receive both salary increases and bonuses that are rewards for the same performance. The sales manager who uses a combination plan must achieve a balance between salary increases for salespeople and changes in variable compensation. The chart in Fig. 17-3 suggests an approach for doing this.

Implementing the Plan

Implementation of a sales compensation plan involves pretesting the plan, selling it to the sales force, and evaluating it.

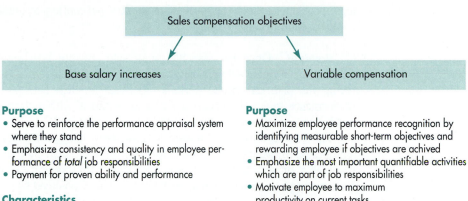

Sales compensation objectives

| Base salary increases | Variable compensation |

Purpose
- Serve to reinforce the performance appraisal system where they stand
- Emphasize consistency and quality in employee performance of *total* job responsibilities
- Payment for proven ability and performance

Characteristics
- Permanent compensation once earned
- Based primarily on *qualitative* assessment
- Measures continuous, on-going tasks
- Compensatory reward influenced by:
  — Labor market
  — Salary range position
  — Relationships to other employees
  — Performance relative to job responsibilities

Purpose
- Maximize employee performance recognition by identifying measurable short-term objectives and rewarding employee if objectives are achived
- Emphasize the most important quantifiable activities which are part of job responsibilities
- Motivate employee to maximum productivity on current tasks

Characteristics
- Variable compensation amounts; must be re-earned each year
- Based primarily on *quantitative* measures
- Compensatory reward influenced primarily by:
  — Group and/or individual performance
  — Sales
  — Sales growth
  — New accounts
  — Most saleable products
  — Competitive practice

FIGURE 17-3 **Deciding on Salary Increases or Changes in Variable Compensation.**

Pretest. Any new or revised compensation plan must be pretested. One method is to apply the new plan to the historical performance of selected individual salespeople and sales districts. If the results are satisfactory, the plan can then be tested further by introducing it in one or more sales districts. These results must be carefully reviewed to determine if any modifications are required before the plan is used in the other sales districts.

Sell. It is essential that the new or revised compensation plan be properly introduced to the salespeople affected. There is always resistance to change, especially change in methods of compensation. The success of the plan as a motivator will depend primarily on how well it is introduced.

Introducing the plan is a selling task. One must keep in mind the guidelines for good selling techniques. Most importantly, management must be "customer-oriented." The benefits to the sales force must be emphasized; however, it is better to go slowly and understate rather than overstate the benefits, in order to avoid possible future disappointment. A new or revised sales compensation plan must be carefully written and well-documented so that it can be communicated effectively to salespeople and sales managers. Such factors as quota determination, pay increases, sales evaluations, tax implications associated with noncash incentives, commission-splitting procedures, and payment terms must be clearly specified and communicated to the sales force. Written documentation will help avoid dissatisfaction and possible legal problems associated with salespeople's perception of unfair or discriminatory compensation practices.[40]

Evaluate.   Once the plan has been sold and put into operation, it should be evaluated. The field sales manager should have the major responsibility for administering the plan. A careful periodic appraisal of each salesperson's activities and performance under the plan is of major importance. Although drastic changes should not be necessary, minor adjustments may be required.

Three procedures can be used to test a new or revised sales compensation plan. The first is to compare earnings before and after the plan change. A second approach involves a survey of first-level sales managers to assess if the new or revised plan has impacted the sales management process in a positive way. The final test is an examination of turnover patterns, with particular emphasis on the quality of turnover. Although all three methods are essentially subjective in nature, they will provide management with a formal evaluation of the impact on the sales force of a change in the compensation plan.[41]

FRINGE BENEFITS

Indirect financial rewards, commonly known as fringe benefits, are now an important part of almost every salesperson's income. Fringe benefits were introduced in Chap. 16. This chapter will consider them in depth.

Company Benefits

Fringe benefits provided to salespeople tend to be the same as those given to other company employees. Even salespeople paid on straight commission are now receiving many company-paid benefits. It is estimated that fringe benefits can add from 25 to 40 percent to a salesperson's base pay.

Although the number and dollar value of fringe benefits vary from company to company, there are several benefits that are common to most employees, and thus to the sales force. These include insurance, paid vacations, paid leaves, retirement plans, and educational assistance.

Insurance.   Health, accident, disability, and life insurance coverage are now provided to most salespeople. Some companies require both sales and nonsales employees to pay a portion of the total costs of insurance. Dental- and vision-care insurance are popular benefit offerings at some companies.

Paid Vacations.   Most salespeople now receive a company-paid vacation. Usually, the length of the vacation time increases with the length of time a salesperson has worked for the company.

Paid Leaves.   Paid leaves include sick leave, maternity leave, paid jury time, and severance pay. Many companies require that a salesperson work for a certain length of time before being eligible for certain paid leaves.

Retirement Plans. Many salespeople now qualify for company retirement plans. In most cases a company contributes to a pension plan for its employees. Sometimes, however, employees must contribute a percentage of their income through payroll deductions. A recent option is the opportunity for salespeople and other employees to invest in individual retirement programs through payroll deductions.

Educational Assistance. With the increased desire for advanced education, many salespeople are taking advantage of company-sponsored educational programs. In general, companies with educational assistance programs pay for college courses and/or degrees that are relevant to the employee's job if the employee achieves a satisfactory grade. In some cases, employers also grant release time to permit employees to attend courses. Another form of educational assistance is sending salespeople to short continuing education programs.

Sales Force Benefits

Two fringe benefits that are more often made available to salespeople than to other employees are the personal use of a company car and club or association memberships.

Personal Use of Company Car. Since outside salespeople are on the road regularly, calling on prospects and customers, a company-owned or a leased car is usually a necessity. Many companies also allow their salespeople the personal use of company cars. Tax regulations may require salespeople to pay a portion of the car's operating costs.

Club or Association Memberships. To help salespeople meet prospects, companies often provide them with company-paid memberships in clubs or associations. As with company cars, salespeople often receive personal satisfaction from company-paid club or association memberships. Also, some companies use the memberships as rewards.

Other Benefits

In addition to the fringe benefits described above, there are many other types:

profit sharing Cash bonus based on profitability

stock purchase plan Award plan allowing employees to acquire a share in the business by purchasing stock at an attractive price

- *Profit sharing.* If a company's profits rise above a set level, employees receive a cash bonus.
- *Stock purchase plan.* Employees may acquire a share in the business by purchasing stock at a discount price, or the company may match purchases with additional shares.
- *Credit union.* A company-supported credit union allows its employee members to save regularly through payroll deductions or to borrow at low interest rates.
- *Employee services.* These include miscellaneous benefits like free parking, subsidized meals, recreational facilities, discounts on company products, and so forth.

cafeteria plan Tax-favored plan that allows employees to choose desired benefits

• *Cafeteria plan.* The trend toward providing salespeople and other employees with more fringe benefits has resulted in a new approach to providing such benefits through a cafeteria-style plan in which the employee chooses the desired benefits. The IRS also allows employees to pay for medical bills, child care, and health insurance in this manner with pretax dollars.

COMPENSATION FOR SALES MANAGERS

Like salespeople, sales managers receive direct and indirect financial rewards.[42] Top sales executives are rewarded generously for their efforts. Their compensation is usually comparable, or higher than, that of their contemporaries in other functional areas.[43]

A realistic estimate is that most field sales managers earn between $50,000 and $75,000 a year, whereas regional and national sales managers can earn well in excess of $100,000 a year.[44] The level of a sales manager's income varies according to the size of the company, the manager's level in the organization, the number of salespeople supervised, and the method of compensation.

As a person moves higher in the sales organization, indirect compensation in the form of fringe benefits becomes more important. These benefits include supplemental life insurance, company-paid medical examinations, social and country club memberships, first-class air travel, and similar perks. Higher-level sales executives are also likely to receive deferred compensation, such as stock options and supplemental pension plans.

A sales management issue of some concern is the level of pay for field sales managers. When a top salesperson who is earning high bonuses and/or commissions is asked to become a field sales manager, the individual must sometimes take a cut in pay. Some salespeople are willing to do this because they see the long-term career advancement and earnings potential of management. On the other hand, there are other qualified people who either refuse to take, or soon leave, a sales management position because of reduced compensation.

Senior management must find a way to deal with this problem. No salesperson should have to take a substantial cut in pay when promoted to management. One solution is to pay sales managers bonuses or commissions tied to the sales or earnings of their subordinates. This will help new sales managers retain their levels of compensation. Further, field sales managers will have an additional reason to stimulate salespeople to increase their productivity.

SUMMARY OF LEARNING GOALS

1. **Discuss the role of money as a motivator.**

   Money is one of several ways to motivate a sales force. It is the determinant of a salesperson's purchasing power, it is a symbol of status, and it is an indication of equitable treatment.

2. **Identify the major trends impacting sales compensation.**

   The current selling environment places an emphasis on specific goals that tie sales compensation to some measure of profitability or other strategic marketing goal. Combination plans are a way in which companies encourage their sales forces to focus not only on making sales but also on achieving less quantitative objectives, such as customer service. Team selling, national account management, service selling, and selling in new businesses, along with fringe benefits for salespeople, are just a few of the areas in which innovative approaches are being taken.

3. **Outline the criteria for a good sales compensation plan.**

   A good sales compensation plan is characterized by incentive, simplicity, fairness, flexibility, control, and competitiveness. All of these facets should be developed with the company's and the sales force's goals in mind, and those goals should, of course, be accomplished within budget.

4. **Explain the steps in developing a sales compensation plan.**

   Developing a sales compensation plan includes the following steps:

   - Reviewing the sales job
   - Determining specific objectives
   - Establishing the level of compensation
   - Choosing the method of compensation
   - Implementing the plan

5. **Describe the various compensation plans used in selling as well as the features of these plans.**

   Sales personnel are compensated through salaries, commissions, and bonuses. A salary is a fixed sum of money paid at regular intervals. It is often used when salespeople are expected to perform nonselling duties or when new markets, products, or salespeople are involved. The main advantage of salaries is that they provide management with control over the sales force. A commission is the payment for the performance of a unit of work. This method has the advantage of fostering an entrepreneurial sales force through direct motivation. A bonus is a payment made at the discretion of management for a particular achievement. Bonuses can be used to encourage many types of desired sales force behavior. Combination plans made up of two or more of the above types of compensation are often used as a way to meet the varying needs of the sales force.

6. **Discuss the role of fringe benefits in a sales compensation plan.**

   Fringe benefits are an excellent way to attract sales recruits and to retain existing sales personnel. Insurance, paid vacations, paid leaves, retirement plans, and educational assistance are the typical fringe benefits given to all employees, including sales personnel.

7. **Discuss how sales managers are paid.**

   Sales managers usually receive very generous compensation packages. As compared to field sales personnel, sales managers are more likely to receive fringe benefits and deferred compensation. Sometimes sales managers are granted bonuses and commissions based on the performance of their subordinates.

1. Discuss the behavioral responses to financial incentives suggested by Rene Darmon. Which responses do you consider most likely?
2. What effect does a properly structured sales compensation plan have on the sales force? What is the impact of an inadequate sales compensation plan?
3. What is management's goal for a sales compensation plan? What do salespeople like to see in their sales compensation plans?
4. Why is it important for sales managers to understand the process by which a compensation plan is developed? What two qualities require above-average compensation?
5. What problems arise from overpaying salespeople? Why should underpaying salespeople also be avoided?
6. Describe the basic methods for paying salespeople. Which of these methods provides the most motivation? Which provides the most control? How is cost affected by the method(s) chosen?
7. Explain the commission-based incentives of drawing accounts, sliding commissions, and varied commissions. Under what circumstances is each incentive appropriate?
8. What are the potential advantages of using bonuses to encourage salespeople to assist in the sales forecasting process? What are the potential disadvantages?
9. Under a combination plan, what type of sales jobs should depend on incentive compensation? Which should be based more on salary compensation?
10. Outline the steps in implementing a sales compensation plan. Briefly comment on each step.

**DISCUSSION
QUESTIONS**

1. Interview a sales manager about his or her firm's compensation system for sales personnel. Evaluate this plan and report your findings in class.
2. What type of compensation plan would you recommend for these selling situations?
   a. Oil company rep dealing with independent dealers
   b. Representative of a local "easy listening" station
   c. Medical equipment rep selling to urologists and hospitals
   d. Salesperson for a wine distributor
   Explain your reasoning in each situation.
3. In a recession economy, which compensation method would you prefer as a salesperson? Which method might be favored by management? Discuss a combination plan that would facilitate the goals of both parties.
4. Company stock is often awarded as a bonus to salespeople for good performance. Can you think of situations in which such a bonus would not be a substantial motivator? Under what circumstances would a stock award be especially attractive?
5. Should top salespeople earn more than their sales managers? Why or why not?

**E T H I C A L
D I L E M M A**

Many salespeople such as manufacturers' agents, real estate salespeople, and insurance agents are paid all or most of their compensation through commissions. This has led some salespeople to overload customers with unnecessary or excessive products, put added pressure on prospects to buy, and use other unfair practices. How should companies paying commissions deal with this issue?

SALES MANAGEMENT CASE

The Future of Child Care Benefits

Of all the topics related to employee work life, perhaps none is hotter than the child care issue. There are at least two reasons that child care has come to the forefront of sales management concerns. One is the relatively recent phenomenon of the two-career family. The second has to do with population changes, which have made some demographers predict a decreasing number of workers in the future. Because of the baby boom, workers have been plentiful in recent years, but employers in the future will have to compete harder for employees. The availability of child care benefits is an important factor in this type of labor market.

Like any form of compensation, good child care benefits can be used to recruit employees and reduce turnover. Also, child care has been emphasized by employers who recognize that parents at work, but distracted from their jobs because they are worried about their children or are trying to make arrangements for their children, are not optimally productive. A related issue is absenteeism; employees will miss work if their child is sick or they cannot make child care arrangements.

A less apparent motivation for developing child care programs is that good child care benefits are good public relations. Johnson & Johnson, which produces many products aimed at families, is at the forefront of child care programs, a fact that certainly does not hurt its reputation as a family-oriented company.

There are many ways in which companies can make their employees' child care burdens lighter. These methods take the form of flexible work arrangements, the provision of child care funds and facilities, and referral and counseling services. Du Pont, like Johnson & Johnson, is setting a good pace by building and renovating child care centers, setting up day care referral services, and giving employees with new babies or other special family needs six weeks paid time off and up to six months of unpaid time off with full benefits. Du Pont also offers the option of job sharing for new working mothers. Flextime and on-site day care are other new child care options, and paternity leave is also becoming more prevalent.

For salespeople, the child care issue can be especially hard to resolve. They often spend long days on the road or are out of town for extended periods. Adequate child care for such situations is difficult to find. Salespeople may therefore have a greater need for child care programs than employees with regular hours.

As more and more salespeople begin to ask for child care benefits, companies that lag behind are going to find it harder and harder to retain sales personnel. Providing good settings for children is a positive thing to do. With the enhanced recruiting, employee productivity, and public relations benefits that child care benefits bring to companies, this form of compensation makes good business sense.

Questions

1. Regardless of the future supply of workers, what factors might change the demand for workers in the future? How might the supply of and demand for child care benefits be affected by these factors?

2. Do you think child care benefits should be available as part of the entire sales force's compensation package or handled by a cafeteria plan? Explain.

3. Develop a creative program that a company could use to make employees' family responsibilities a little more manageable. Describe your idea in a paragraph or two.

INTERNATIONAL SALES MANAGEMENT

LEARNING GOALS

- Highlight the critical importance of international sales opportunities.
- Identify the major environmental challenges faced by international sales managers.
- Describe the key strategic issues involved in international sales and marketing management.
- List key differences between domestic and international sales techniques.
- Specify methods for organizing international sales activities.
- Examine the differences between domestic and international sales management practices.

A DIFFERENT WORLD

People from Kuwait end statements about the future with a phrase that means "God willing." Dennis Hall, a manufacturers's representative from Wisconsin, made a trip to Kuwait City after the Persian Gulf War, and he became very familiar with the Kuwaitis' dubious attitude about the future.

Hall was in Kuwait to sell peat moss (for soaking up oil) and face masks. He found it difficult to get the Kuwaitis to talk business at all, and when he could get an appointment, he often had to wait for hours after the scheduled time before he actually saw anyone.

Hall eventually achieved his selling goals in Kuwait, but not before many broken or rescheduled appointments. The treatment Hall received would be considered rude in the United States, but it's the way that business is done in Kuwait. Hall's experience

points to the dilemma faced by overseas marketers: Cultural differences between countries can be extreme. These differences do not only apply to the selling process. Managers who want to set up operations overseas often must deal with extensive red tape and bureaucracy before they can even get started. The management of salespeople native to another country can also involve learning a new set of rules. For example, the Japanese do not like individual performance-based compensation. Great Britain's tax structure has made many employees prefer objects to cash. In Hungary, overseas travel is a highly valued form of compensation.

Some of the most extreme cultural differences in the world exist between the two largest economic powers: Japan and the United States. Not only is Japan's overall business structure drastically different from that in the United States; Japanese salespeople are more humble (some would say "respectful") toward their customers than U.S. salespeople. The Japanese are also known for their reliance on facts and figures, their flexibility in solving customer problems, and their excellent customer service. In addition, business success in Japan is much more dependent on personal relationships than in the United States, where people tend to be more pragmatic.

"The Global Marketplace" has become a phrase with which almost everyone is familiar. More and more frequently, marketers will find themselves, like Dennis Hall, in another country playing a different game. In such situations, it is imperative that marketers understand how to deal with foreign businesspeople.[1]

Chapter 18 discusses the international sales force. As you read on, you will learn

that not only cultural differences but also economic and legal differences are factors in international selling. Though unique challenges are inherent in other countries, the rewards can be great. In today's marketplace, which is indeed global and becoming more so, an international perspective is a necessity.

CHAPTER OVERVIEW

The world has become a global marketplace made up of increasingly interdependent economies. The possibility of global reach opens up new vistas for resourceful, growth-oriented sales executives. John Naisbitt and Patricia Aburdene, authors of the bestseller *Megatrends 2000,* put it this way:

> We are in an unprecedented period of accelerated change, perhaps the most breathtaking of which is the swiftness of our rush to all the world's becoming a single economy.[2]

Sales managers responsible for international operations face a set of challenges quite different from those encountered in a domestic market. Although the selling process and the basic sales management tasks and tools remain the same, the markets and environmental conditions under which they are executed and applied differ from one country to the next. Labor laws or local business customs, for instance, may prevent the firing of salespeople, even in cases of incompetence. Religious rules may prohibit the charging of interest, such as in the case of Islam. Rules of proper sales conduct may not allow talking business unless and until the parties have become sufficiently acquainted to establish a bond of trust. Sometimes, all business dealings within a nation have to be channeled through a state agency.

Basically, international sales managers have to guide and coordinate the efforts of separate and distinct national sales organizations in the countries where the company does business. Their role is crucial to marketing success. Personal selling assumes an even greater role internationally than in the domestic market, since other elements of the promotion mix may be restricted either by law or other factors. For example, television commercials are highly regulated in many countries.

In this chapter, the dimensions of international selling and sales management are presented. After a brief discussion of international sales and marketing opportunities, environmental challenges that sales managers face in international markets are identified. Then, strategic issues for international sales and marketing are discussed.

The remainder of Chap. 18 focuses on the international selling process and its management. Cultural, economic, and other differences between nations require changes in selling approaches and methods. Structures for international sales organizations must be developed to meet company needs and market conditions. Finally, modifications of specific sales management practices are considered.

INTERNATIONAL SALES AND MARKETING OPPORTUNITIES

International markets are appealing because many domestic markets are mature or saturated. In contrast, many overseas markets are at an earlier development stage with substantial growth ahead. In New England, for example, markets are eroding in the face of increased foreign competition and declining demand. Many companies in the Northeast, however, are flourishing because they have added a global component to their corporate strategies.[3]

There are other important reasons for placing increased emphasis on international sales and marketing. Growth overseas can serve to substantially extend a product's life cycle, allowing the firm to benefit longer and more extensively from its investment. The desire to counteract the cyclicality of a company's domestic business by adding geographic markets whose business cycles differ from the U.S. pattern is an important reason for international sales and marketing. Excess capacity can be another motive for going aboard. All such reasons pertain to the pursuit of growth opportunities and the stability resulting from broadening a firm's sales bases.

It has been estimated that one-fourth of a typical U.S. industrial company's sales are generated overseas (compared with only 15 percent a decade ago). The most globally oriented firms generate between 35 and 50 percent of their total revenues from overseas sales, and many companies with world-renowned brands are reporting that international sales are increasing at least 50 percent faster than domestic sales. Companies with well-known brands that are prospering overseas include Johnson & Johnson, Tambrands, Tiffany, Procter & Gamble, and H. J. Heinz.[4]

Global marketing is not just for the *Fortune* 500 companies. Many small businesses are also pursuing international markets aggressively, as the following statistics demonstrate:

- Thirty-seven percent of companies with fewer than five hundred employees are exporting overseas.
- A quarter of all exporting companies—more than 160,000 firms—employ fewer than 100 people.
- Among the small companies currently exporting, 56 percent said their export sales had increased over the previous year, and 41 percent said their export sales had grown faster than domestic sales.[5]

These statistics suggest the importance of international business. The following examples are indicative of specific industry and company efforts:

- By the year 2000, about 65 percent of all helicopter sales will be outside North America. The American helicopter industry is expected to grow slowly, but helicopter operations in the Pacific Rim and Eastern Europe are projected to grow rapidly and should provide a large market for new and used aircraft. Specific sales opportunities include law enforcement, emergency medical service, and small-package and document delivery services.[6]

- International sales of software account for about 34 percent of software publishers' revenues. Annual market growth in the United States has slowed, while European and Japanese personal computer and software sales are booming. Software publishers believe that it is essential to have offices in many regions. For instance, Microsoft Corporation has over twenty subsidiaries.[7]

- Siemens is one of Europe's largest companies. The electronics giant has restructured its organization to streamline corporate decision making for international sales. One of the firm's biggest challenges is its effort to sell its public switching systems to the Bell operating companies in the United States.[8]

- Loctite Corporation, a New England manufacturer of a thousand different adhesives, sealants, and bonding agents, doubled its size during the second half of the 1980s. The majority of the firm's growth came from outside the United States, and about 60 percent of Loctite's sales come from international markets. The firm has over twenty-four subsidiaries, joint ventures in India, the People's Republic of China, France, and Norway, and distribution in more than eighty countries.[9]

- Amway Corporation is one of the world's largest person-to-person marketing companies. The firm has over one million independent distributors worldwide. Early successes in Canada and Australia proved the Amway approach could work outside the United States. In the early 1970s, the company began an ambitious expansion program that eventually included Western Europe, Central America, and the Western Pacific. Recent successes include Germany, Japan, and the Republic of Korea.[10]

- Audio Authority, a Kentucky manufacturer of switching equipment and displays for automobile audio retailers and home audio retailers, had only five international distributors in 1988. Attendance at international consumer electronic trade shows convinced company executives to make a stronger effort to get international business. Less than three years later, Audio Authority had twenty-three distributors in twenty-two countries.[11]

As these examples and the preceding discussion indicate, the trend toward global business is firmly established and growing. Firms throughout the world will have to adopt advanced sales and marketing strategies and techniques to prosper in international markets. Of particular importance to sales management is the need to develop partnerships with global customers to encourage teamwork with other functions within their company, and to employ the latest information and communications technologies throughout the sales organization.[12] To do this, sales managers must understand the environmental challenges they face.

INTERNATIONAL SALES MANAGEMENT CHALLENGES

Firms that have decided to pursue global markets encounter a number of risks, difficulties, and obstacles that surpass those present in domestic marketing. These challenges can and do occur in every sector of the environment, but tend to be concentrated in the economic, legal, and cultural environments.

Economic Factors

developed economies Economic systems, dominated by private enterprise, in which consumers have high levels of disposable income

developing economies Economic systems undergoing the shift from export-led growth to domestic development

underdeveloped economies Preindustrial economic systems with low growth rates

Each of the over two hundred countries in the world is at a slightly different stage in terms of economic development. As a result, economic differences have a major impact on global sales strategies.

One of the most important considerations is the level of purchasing power. This is usually expressed in the form of gross domestic product per inhabitant (GDP/capita), which in turn serves as a measure of a country's stage of economic development. The United States, Japan, Canada, and most of Western Europe are considered *developed economies*. Private enterprise dominates, and consumers have high levels of disposal income. Not surprisingly, these developed countries also have the most sophisticated sales and marketing systems and programs.

In contrast, there are many countries that are at a lesser stage of economic development. Some, such as Singapore, South Korea, Taiwan, Kuwait, and Venezuela, have largely made the transition to an industrial economy and are considered *developing economies*. The shift in these countries from export-led growth to domestic development will mean increased spending and greater sales opportunities. In fact, many advanced selling and marketing approaches have already become part of the business systems of these countries.

In other cases, countries are still mired in a primitive, preindustrial stage of economic development. Known as *underdeveloped economies,* these are countries where living standards are low and there is little promise of economic growth. Ethiopia, Pakistan, Chad, and Haiti are examples. Although potential demand for many products in these countries appears large, the true market potential is substantially reduced by the lack of purchasing power.

A somewhat different group of countries with a mixed economic history emerged during the late 1980s and early 1990s. These include the Eastern European countries (Poland and Hungary, for example) and the republics (Russia, Ukraine, Georgia, and so forth) of the former Soviet Union. On the one hand, these countries lack the purchasing power needed because of the past failures of the communist system; however, they are rich in natural and human resources and, with help from the developed economies, should soon present attractive sales opportunities.

economic infrastructure A nation's communications, transportation, and financial systems

Another key factor that is tied to a country's stage of economic development is the *economic infrastructure,* which consists of a country's communication, transportation, and financial systems. The lack of an adequate infrastructure can make it very difficult to obtain or fulfill an order. For instance, an inadequate telecommunications system impedes the information flow between customers, overseas field sales offices, and world headquarters. Likewise, an outdated transportation system makes trips to potential customers difficult and expensive.

Legal Constraints

A significant limitation to sales and marketing activities in many countries are trade barriers and legal constraints erected by host governments. Government officials under the influence of pressure groups can create hurdles ranging in severity from minor annoyances to total prohibition. Sometimes a prohibitive tariff is imposed. For example, 300 percent of the value of cars is charged when they are imported into Colombia. Other nations, such as Japan, have established many specific import restrictions on certain products like medical equipment, argicultural commodities, and telecommunications equipment. Sometimes political differences such as those between Cuba and the United States lead to bans on all exports and imports.

Host country governments tend to favor indigenous enterprises and discriminate against foreign-owned business. They can place restrictions on foreign firms in general, zero in on specific industries, or single out individual operations. Restrictions on ownership of businesses are widespread, particularly in the Third World. Most countries do not permit 100 percent foreign ownership of a firm. Rather, they insist on participation by local partners whose involvement may be graduated depending upon how essential the goverment judges an industry to be in its economy.

To regain control over their natural resources, various nations have expropriated foreign corporations, offering some compensation in return. This extreme act shows the vulnerability of overseas assets to changes in political priorities. As a matter of fact, it can safely be said that political stability is the single most important factor affecting international sales efforts. Whether communist or capitalist, absolutist or parliamentary, success is possible in any political environment provided it remains predictable. Political instability, so frequent in emerging nations, is the worst enemy of international business. When an agreement is reached legitimately with a country's legal government today and a substantial investment is made, it is discouraging to see a new government in power tomorrow that reverses prior commitments.

Fortunately, as the threat of widespread global conflict eases, trade restrictions are also easing. For instance, the South Korean government has begun to open Korea's tightly controlled market to outsiders. After a landslide victory in local elections in 1991, the government of Roh Tae-Woo gave foreigners permission to enter South Korea's retail markets. Restrictions are also being lifted on financial services marketing, data processing, and other business activities. [13]

Perhaps the most dramatic changes in legal constraints are taking place in what were formerly the communist countries of the world. Begun by Russian General Secretary Mikhail Gorbachev's perestroika policy of the late 1980s, the economic reforms in these countries have been quick and dramatic. They provide many opportunities for sales and marketing ventures.

United Nations Convention on Contracts for the International Sale of Goods (CISG) Agreement covering the sale of goods between commercial buyers and sellers located in different countries

Another significant legal development that will impact global sales and marketing activities is the ratification by the United Sates and other nations of the *United Nations Convention on Contracts for the International Sale of Goods (CISG)*. In general, the Convention applies to contracts for the sale of goods between commercial buyers and sellers located in different countries. It represents an effort at the unification of international trade laws across economic, legal, developmental, and political barriers. The adoption of this convention is expected to be a great benefit for international businesses. [14]

Cultural Differences

A final group of managerial challenges, and potentially the most pervasive, results from the cultural environment. Culture can be defined as the distinctive way of life of a people. As shown in Fig. 18-1, a nation's culture includes many factors that have an impact on personal selling and sales management.[15]

Most of the difficulties that American businesses encounter in foreign markets are the result of cultural ignorance and misunderstandings. Mistakes by salespeople and managers include the misuse of titles, being impatient with foreigners, and offending people by seemingly meaningless actions.[16] Even the friendly act of gift giving can cause serious problems if not done properly.[17]

One of the most serious hurdles that an international sales manager has to overcome is the language barrier. Sales managers who do not understand the local language are at a clear disadvantage. (See Table 18-1.) They suffer from a communication, the thus information, gap. Culturally diverse nations are characterized by a bewildering multiplicity of languages and dialects (India and Nigeria count about two hundred each) and may well borrow a nonnative (colonial) language as the official one (Nigeria is part of the anglophone zone in Africa). Widespread illiteracy (over half of the world's population is illiterate) can render communication with some buyers extremely difficult.

Hand gestures and body language are another form of communication that international salespeople and their managers must understand. Americans and Europeans shake hands when greeting customers and other business acquaintances. Japanese and other Asians are more comfortable with a traditional bow from the

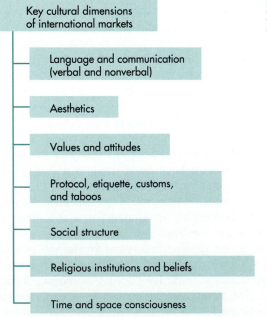

FIGURE 18-1 Impact of Cultural Dimensions on Personal Selling and Sales Management.

TABLE 18-1 **Do You Speak English?**

Even though they are supposed to speak the same language, the British humorously say that they speak English and that people from the United States speak American. Here are some of the differences.

If you are looking for an apartment, you look for a "flat" in England.

If you want to ride an elevator, look for a sign that says "lift."

If you want some candy, ask for "sweets," and if you want a cookie, ask for a "biscuit."

The restroom is unknown. "Do you want to rest?" they may ask. Ask for the toilet or the "loo."

If you hear the British refer to a "lorry," they are talking about a truck.

If you have a car and a "petrol" station attendant asks, "Do you want me to check under the 'bonnet'?"—fear not, he is referring to the hood. The trunk is called the "boot."

"Queue" is a word you need to learn. It is a long-standing British custom to wait in line for almost everything. It is a breach of etiquette to break into a "queue" (simply pronounced Q).

You go to the "chemist" for your drugstore needs; trash is called "rubbish"; and a mail box is often called a "pillar box."

"I am going to the theatre" means that you are actually going to see a live, stage performance and not a movie. In England, you go to the "cinema" to see a movie.

If you do something terribly naughty, the man who arrests you is the "bobby"—not the policeman. And if you are really in big trouble, you seek the services of a "solicitor" rather than a lawyer.

waist. Even seemingly meaningless gestures can be misinterpreted. A young American computer sales representative completed a successful sales presentation to his Brazilian customers with the classic American "OK" sign. This gesture—thumb and forefinger forming a circle, other fingers pointing up—is considered an obscene gesture in Brazil. Needless to say, the salesperson was quite embarrassed when he learned the meaning of his well-intended gesture.[18]

Religion is another factor of great relevance to international sales management. It can affect the motivational patterns of sales personnel, from the Protestant work ethic to the Nirvana (wantlessness) of Hinduism. It determines when people do not work: Holidays, prayer periods, and the Sabbath are just some examples. It governs dietary habits: Nonkosher food is taboo in Judaism, pork in Islam, and beef in Hinduism. And it influences business practices: The Koran prohibits the charging of interest.

Business and private customs, too, can vary from culture to culture. North Americans tend to approach a business deal straightforwardly and directly. Latin businesspeople prefer to get to know a person first before they start talking business. Their unhurried style requires a great deal of patience. Bargaining over price and terms is often a lengthy process. Decision-making styles also differ significantly between cultures.[19] American managers are trained to make decisions quickly on their own. In Japan, on the other hand, an elaborate procedure is in place that emphasizes joint decisions and group harmony. This practice slows down decision making considerably, but expedites implementation.

There are far too many cultural differences between peoples throughout the world to cover in this chapter. As noted earlier, some of the most significant differences are with Japan. Those salespeople and companies that have been suc-

---

AVON

Avon is taking advantage of both economic and social conditions in the Chinese city of Guangzhou to entrench a direct selling force there. In the United States, direct-sales companies like Avon are having trouble recruiting salespeople; one reason for this problem is the relatively recent phenomenon of large numbers of women in the full-time work force.

In Guangzhou, however, direct selling, and Avon, are perceived as new and different. Professionals, mostly women, have started selling Avon on the side, and many are actually making more money as part-time Avon representatives than they do at their full-time jobs. Guangzhou, located in a capitalistic-oriented province, is home to women who are progressive and ready to experiment with makeup, so the market is ripe.

The combination of people willing to sell Avon and people willing to buy Avon has made the Chinese venture a success. There were special obstacles to overcome in the beginning; Avon negotiated with government authorities for five years to get permission for a venture in northern China. All of this effort was in vain, but finally, a Japanese advisor suggested that Avon look into Guangzhou instead. Also, Avon avoids communication and transportation difficulties by having salespeople pick up orders in a central location. By contrast, in the United States, Avon delivers merchandise directly to salespeople.

The efforts in China are paying off. Avon hopes to expand into other provinces, and the company predicts sales of $50 million to $60 million in five years. Avon's products and its direct-selling methods, and Guangzhou's social and economic climate, have added up to an international selling success story.

---

cessful in Japan have learned that preparation and patience are essential. Selling in Japan is based on respect; a salesperson must concentrate on developing a rapport with buyers and building relationships. Japanese buyers will ask many probing questions to determine if a salesperson has the desired knowledge, sincerity, and conviction. Most importantly, the Japanese want to have some understanding of and feeling for the people involved before discussing business issues.[20] Some other insights for selling in other countries are presented in Table 18-2.

TABLE 18-2 **Insights for Selling Abroad**

- In *Italy*, allow plenty of time for appointments. Italians are known for warming up to a conversation, and a customer could very well spend several hours chatting with a salesperson.
- In *Switzerland*, one may wish to include degrees or a corporate title on a business card. The Swiss hold a great deal of respect for degrees and titles.
- In the *Middle East*, do not be too distant or aloof. People in the Arab world consider the sense of touch as a means of communication.
- In *Brazil*, do not attempt to speak Spanish to a Brazilian businessperson. The Brazilians take great pride in the fact that they are the only country in South America to speak Portuguese.
- In *France*, address a contact as Monsieur or Madame until invited to do otherwise. If the person has a title, use it as well.
- In *Japan*, high-pressure sales tactics seldom work. Allow a customer plenty of time to gain trust.
- In *Hong Kong*, avoid the classic navy blue suit with white shirt. This color combination denotes mourning in Hong Kong.
- In *Germany*, try to speak a few words of German such as "guten morgen" ("good morning") and "bitte" ("please"). Although most Germans speak English, a salesperson will score points by trying to speak German.

STRATEGIC ISSUES FOR INTERNATIONAL SALES AND MARKETING

Companies engage in international sales and marketing when they do business in more than one country. The relatively simple step of crossing the geopolitical boundaries of one's home country can add considerable complexity to sales and marketing tasks. The parameters change and uncertainty increases as marketing decision makers move onto unknown turf. The environmental influences are different, and the elements of the marketing mix are also subject to different constraints. A sales executive must obtain adequate information before entering overseas markets, and he or she must select the appropriate mode for international sales and marketing.

Adapting the Marketing Mix

global marketing strategy Use of the same marketing strategy in each nation in which a firm operates

A complex issue for international sales managers is the question of whether the marketing approach should remain identical from country to country or whether allowances should be made for differences in local conditions. Good arguments can be presented for either side. It is certainly more economical to use a standardized *global marketing strategy*—selling the same product at a uniform price through identical channels, supported by a worldwide promotional campaign. Theodore Levitt has called this the "globalization of markets." He has argued that technology has standardized global markets, so companies should produce globally similar products and market them in the same way to people throughout the world.[21] This approach is followed by Kodak, Sony, and the Coca-Cola Company.

The global approach will not work for all companies, however. Adaptation of product, price, distribution, or promotion may be necessary for a number of reasons. Government regulations in the host country can affect product design, the price that can be charged, the distribution channel that must be chosen, or what can be said or shown in advertising or other forms of promotion. What is legal and successful in the United States may not be permissible or may not work in another country. Sales strategies may have to be adapted as a result of legal constraints, competitive pressures, religious convictions, technical specifications, or simply the need to localize the approach.

To compete successfully in Japan, foreign companies must have a strong commitment to quality, a willingness to adjust to the market, and a long-term perspective. Apple Computer's sales faltered in Japan until it developed a Japanese-language operating system for its Macintosh computer and convinced several key software developers to convert their software to the new system.[22]

Obtaining International Information

Obtaining information about a country and its markets is a challenge for sales executives, especially when a company has no local contacts in the country. Sergey Frank, an international sales and marketing troubleshooter for General Tire Company, has suggested research and creative networking as the proper approach.[23] The first step is to go to the local Chamber of Commerce, an international trade fair, or one of a firm's own customers that does business in the country. Frank has pointed out that just about every country has an international Chamber of Commerce that deals with sales and marketing inquiries. In addition, most countries have trade development offices that provide commercial information and other forms of assistance.

One can also contact a major accounting firm that has an office in the country or a management consulting firm that has overseas facilities. In addition, Frank has suggested contacting magazine editors for information:

> Just contact a magazine's editor and ask him what's going on in his country or in other countries. Every industry is organized in a specific way and has its own sources of communication, like trade fairs, magazines, etc.[24]

With the growing importance of international sales, many of the professional sales publications identified in Chap. 4 are featuring articles on international sales management issues and opportunities in specific regions and countries. These will also be helpful to the sales executive who is considering entering a foreign market or expanding international sales activities.[25] Some of these publications, many professional organizations, trade associations, universities, and government agencies also sponsor trade shows, seminars, and conferences that deal with international sales opportunities and challenges. In addition to providing information for overseas selling, seminars, conferences, and trade shows also provide sales leads and opportunities to contact potential distributors.[26]

An excellent source of information for U.S. firms considering export possibilities is the United States Commerce Department's National Trade Data Bank (NTDB). Containing over 100,000 different documents, the NTDB is an extensive source of up-to-date information on overseas markets. Combined with an international sales executive's own experience and expertise, marketing information from the NTDB can help a firm decide which markets are best for its products. The information is available for use in most Commerce Department's district offices, at nearly seven hundred libraries, and for direct sale to the public.[27]

A company's international sales force and its distributors' sales forces can be valuable sources of information. Data gathered by salespeople are used to prepare forecasts and make company or product image decisions. In addition, multinational firms can use information to aid in product design decisions.[28]

Information from international salespeople is especially valuable in the market entry phase. Sales personnel can become a specialized research team and collect information about market potential and entry logistics (price, distribution, import regulations, and so forth). They can be very helpful in overcoming cultural and marketing barriers associated with entering foreign markets. After establishing itself in an overseas market, a company may wish to use international salespeople to gather information on competitors and any new market requirements.[29] Some specific reasons that multinational companies must rely more on international sales forces than domestic sales forces for market data are presented in Table 18-3.

Entering Overseas Markets

Various entry modes exist for international markets; these are identified in Fig. 18-2. International marketing often begins in a passive fashion—so-called *passive exporting*. A company's sales organization receives an unsolicited inquiry from abroad based on its listing in a directory or a referral. It responds by forwarding a catalog and

passive exporting
Unsolicited orders from overseas

TABLE 18-3 **Reasons for Involving International Sales Forces in Marketing Research**

- Foreign published data is often unreliable, necessitating primary information gathering for cross checking.
- U.S. management does not understand foreign customers or foreign sales techniques to make effective, educated decisions on marketing strategy.
- International sales in many countries rely more on relations so that more information areas need monitoring and more people in the marketing and sales process need the information.
- In a volatile market, close monitoring of the market may only be possible through use of the sales force, since by the time information was released, it would be obsolete.
- The increased complexity and competition in foreign marketing result in more information being needed to formulate successful marketing strategies.
- Too often, domestic strategy is copied, but increased competition in international markets necessitates the need for more information and marketing research by the sales force to design "aggressive" marketing strategies.

a hastily computed price list. More or less to its surprise, the company receives an initial order. Additional orders follow and sales management begins to wonder what would happen if it actively solicited overseas business.

active exporting
Invested export efforts either through indirect or direct approaches

Moving from passive to *active exporting,* sales management can choose between an indirect and a direct route. It can use independent intermediaries (sales agents and distributors), or it can use a company sales force and distribution system. Research suggests that U.S. firms are more likely to integrate the sales and distribution channels in highly similar industrialized countries (Western Europe) than in Japan and Southeast Asia, which are culturally dissimilar.[30]

indirect exporting
Selling overseas through domestic intermediaries

export management company
Foreign manufacturers' representative

Indirect exporting involves selling overseas through domestic intermediaries. A low-investment approach for many small firms is to use an *export management company,* which is a manufacturers' representative for overseas sales. Most export management companies specialize in a few noncompeting lines within broad product categories and offer a broad range of sales and marketing services.[31] Although this approach is less expensive than direct exporting, it has some disadvantages: little market information filtering back from the sales organization to corporate decision

FIGURE 18-2 Entry Modes for International Marketing.

makers, no in-house exporting expertise being developed, and no control over sales efforts and thus sales and profits.

Direct exporting, on the other hand, although it requires a substantially higher commitment of corporate resources, affords sales management the multiple rewards of greater control, greater sales, and greater profits. *Direct exporting* means a producer deals directly with overseas buyers who may be either intermediaries or ultimate users. Sales management plays a very active role in soliciting and servicing overseas accounts. Since all merchandise is manufactured at home and then shipped abroad, risks are limited and managerial decision-making flexibility is high.

direct exporting Dealing directly with overseas buyers who may be either intermediaries or ultimate users

An alternative path to capitalizing on international markets is licensing. Like exporting, it often happens passively, in that a firm is contacted by a potential licensee with the request for a license. *Licensing* refers to granting the contractual permission to use industrial property rights such as patents, trademarks, or know-how during a specified time period in a given geographic area. The fees and royalties involved in such an arrangement look attractive, since no effort is required and payoffs appear to be forthcoming from money risked by others. Although this perspective is correct in many cases, sales management often grants rights for too large an area (an entire continent) or too long (thirty years). Belatedly, sales managers discover that the company could have benefited considerably more from cultivating the market itself.

licensing Granting the contractual permission to use industrial property rights such as patents, trademarks, or know-how during a specified time period in a given geographic area

Countertrade represents another option. *Countertrade* refers to foreign sales that are at least partially concluded through bartering arrangements. In other words, the U.S. firm would sell its products overseas, and the foreign buyer would pay at least partially with its own products. The U.S. sales managers would then have to find a market for the foreign products they took in this exchange. Countertrade is now a significant part of many overseas sales efforts. Perhaps the best known foreign countertrade arrangement is Pepsi's receipt of vodka in exchange for its own sales in Russia.

countertrade Foreign sales that are at least partially conducted through bartering arrangements

A fourth frequently used approach is represented by joint ventures. Although equity shares and the degree of actual participation vary, all *joint ventures* involve a separate legal entity in which local partners participate. Whether mandated by law or not, joint ventures reduce a firm's alien status and its vulnerability to political problems. The foreign partner's business connections or distribution system is often vital to the success of the international marketing effort. Many successful American products and firms in Japan, such as KFC (formerly Kentucky Fried Chicken), Nike, Nabisco, Caterpillar Tractor, and Hewlett-Packard, are joint ventures.

joint ventures Legal entities in which foreign and local partners participate

Wholly owned subsidiaries—overseas units owned by the parent company—are permissible in developed countries such as the United States, Japan, and Germany. These units give management control, but require substantial investment and severely restrict flexibility. They will only be chosen in countries that are politically stable. It also helps if a country is economically promising, in that it presents a ready-made market, but it is often sufficient for a location to have a low-cost or high-skill local labor pool available or to provide duty-free access to related markets such as the member nations of the European Community.

wholly owned subsidiaries Overseas units owned by a parent company

management contracts Home-country firm's managing an operation for an overseas owner.

The final entry mode utilizes *management contracts*. Instead of owning assets, the home country firm simply manages an operation for an overseas owner. This procedure is common in the hotel business, where chain hotels are often owned by local investors but managed for a fee by the international chain—Hilton, Sheraton, and so on—whose name they bear. Such projects frequently involve training of owner-employed personnel.

INTERNATIONAL SALES TECHNIQUES

As the earlier discussions and examples in this chapter have shown, selling and sales management are no longer restricted by political and geographic boundaries. One writer has commented:

> The act of selling is becoming more and more global and transcultural. In the past, those in international sales were a special breed; most of us spent our worklives talking to clients who we totally understood and who shared our feelings, pastimes and culture. No more! In today's business environment, the next man or woman on your list of "leads" may reside half-way around the world and possess an entirely different cultural heritage.[32]

Basic selling skills transcend some cultural differences, but the style, pace, and setting of sales interviews and negotiations vary greatly from country to country.[33] A salesperson cannot assume that a customer conducts business as the salesperson does, even though the customer may speak English and dress like the salesperson. To conduct business in foreign countries, salespeople must learn about each country's customs and cultures.

Preliminary Steps in the Selling Process

In an earlier section of this chapter, the importance of gathering information on international markets was discussed. A major use of this information is to identify sales leads and qualify prospects. A salesperson must have access to this information and must know how to use it to identify and qualify potential overseas customers.

Most of the prospecting methods discussed in Chap. 4 are used by salespeople in foreign markets; however, because the company and its products may not be well known, more emphasis should be placed on publicity and trade shows to stimulate interest and generate sales leads.[34] For instance, product publicity in foreign business and trade publications will stimulate inquiries from potential buyers. These sales leads can then be sent to foreign salespeople or distributors for followup.

Trade shows also offer an excellent opportunity to stimulate product interest and generate sales leads for a company that wishes to increase sales overseas. However, trade show exhibitors must be sensitive to the different ways of doing business in foreign countries. Foreign trade show visitors are accustomed to more formality than Americans. They are looking for thoughtful answers to their questions and an opportunity to examine products thoroughly. When dealing with foreign buyers at a trade show, salespeople should try to build goodwill, not close sales.[35]

Perhaps the best way to establish contacts with prospects in other countries is through referrals. A mutual acquaintance will have the effect of transforming a complete stranger into a potential trustworthy associate. Buyers in many countries outside the United States prefer to do business with people they consider friends.[36]

Early in the selling process salespeople must learn to slow down when dealing with foreign buyers. American buyers typically make purchases based on product features or company reputations. In many foreign countries, however, personal relationships are more important. Prospects want to discuss their company, its needs, and its philosophy. They also want to learn more about the salesperson, especially the person's values. As a result, the process of building personal rapport may take weeks, months, or even years. U.S. salespeople must learn to live with a slower sales cycle.[37]

In Germany, this lengthy approach to selling has been called "reflective selling." According to leading German sales expert Erich Norbert Detroy, "In reflective selling, the salesperson provides the customer with an emotional and logical experience that is a true reflection of the customer's situation, not of the salesperson's."[38] Salespeople must take more time to listen to customers' needs and to identify buying motives. The key is to focus on establishing trust.

During the early stages of the selling process, salespeople must also recognize the importance of waiting to meet the decision maker. Decision making tends to be more centralized in countries outside the United States. As a result, salespeople will be introduced to the decision maker only after several meetings. For example, in Japan, additional executives, increasing in rank, attend meetings as the selling process advances. U.S. salespeople are expected to follow the Japanese lead by including a senior salesperson, then sales managers and executives, in sales meetings as they progress.[39]

Advanced Steps in the Selling Process

Language and other cultural differences affect sales presentations in many ways. As noted, more time must be spent during the approach, or warmup, phase of the sales presentation to establish rapport with overseas buyers. Salespeople must be especially concerned with the difficulties of communication, even if the sales negotiations are in English.

Many prospects and customers outside the United States are likely to speak English as a second or third language. However, they probably have different lifestyles and often work under completely different business systems. Therefore, it is unwise to assume that if foreign buyers speak English well, communication is simple. Sales presentations must be adapted to cross-cultural settings.[40]

The first important point to remember is that a salesperson must speak clearly and take time to warm up the buyer. The listener not only has to absorb what a salesperson is saying, but also has to become used to how it is being said. Voice quality, accent, and speed of delivery all affect the listener's comprehension.

To further help the listener, a salesperson should use as many visual aids as possible. This way, the listener will be using two of the five senses rather than only one. A salesperson must choose examples and illustrations carefully and must be especially careful when using humor to make a point. Jokes in an international setting are risky because of the many cultural and social differences involved.

Asking questions, an important part of most sales presentations, must be done with care. International buyers may be reluctant to respond to a question, not because they do not know the answer, but because they are afraid of making an error in a language with which they are not totally comfortable.

To help buyers "save face" in situations where they are unable to respond correctly to a question due to a language difficulty, a salesperson can ask, "Would you like me to state the question in another way?" rather than saying, "Did you understand the question?" This approach allows the buyer to gracefully accept that he or she may not have understood the language used in the question.

Japanese customers pose special communications challenges. They are more reserved than Americans. A salesperson will find less facial expression, more pauses, silence, and softer speech. Japanese customers will not provide as much positive feedback to open-ended questions, nor will they show much enthusiasm for the sales presentation. As a result, salespeople must also be more reserved. Further, they must be modest about themselves and extra polite to their Japanese customers. [41]

Cultural differences in other countries also impact sales presentations in many ways. For instance, as a rule, French people do not like to talk about money. When French salespeople get to the point of discussing price, they begin to feel uncomfortable because they have not been trained to talk about money. In contrast, most American salespeople are better prepared to talk about prices. [42]

Another important difference between U.S. and French salespeople is that U.S. salespeople are more direct. When Americans want something, they ask. In contrast, French salespeople do not want to risk offending someone. They tend to approach issues indirectly and take much longer to make a request. According to France's top sales trainer, Jean-Pierre Tricard, French salespeople are often afraid of leading a prospect to the close. Tricard also feels that French salespeople do not handle objections well. He has pointed out that they blame lost sales on the product, price, competition, and so forth—never recognizing that they themselves might be at fault. [43]

Time and Territory Management

Like their domestic counterparts, international sales managers are also concerned about improving sales productivity and customer service. Because salespeople and their managers may be located great distances from one another, time and territory management become crucial in international selling. Customer service over great distances is another concern.

Symbol Technologies, which sells its patented bar code and data collection devices worldwide, has turned to sales automation to increase productivity and enhance customer service. Each of Symbol's approximately fifty overseas sales representatives in Europe, the Far East, and South America was provided a lap-top

SALES MANAGEMENT IN PRACTICE

LESTER TELEMARKETING INC.

Companies wanting to tap into international markets can choose from a multitude of selling options. At one extreme, companies set up separate sales forces in the foreign countries. At the other extreme is Lester Telemarketing Inc., which offers international telemarketing services to its clients.

What is unusual about Lester's service is that it is performed by bilingual telemarketers who speak the languages of the countries they call. Bob Lester, president of the company, started the international program in 1990. To find his uniquely qualified employees, he recruited from the foreign language department of a nearby university. Also, he contacted Chinese and Japanese restaurants in the area to ask them for help.

Lester also had to find ways to get the telephone numbers of foreign businesses. In most countries, there is not an availability of specialized mail and phone lists as there is in the United States. To overcome this problem, Lester developed a second aspect of the service, called "Telefind," in which the bilingual telemarketers develop lists from scratch by spending large amounts of time on the phone to other countries' directory assistance operators.

Not surprisingly, a telemarketing position at Lester is not a nine-to-five job. Callers to Europe arrive for work at two a.m., when European business hours are just beginning. Callers to Asia and South American have their own appropriate times as well.

Lester's international telemarketing services are unusual and innovative. In the future, however, the number of companies with an international approach to business may be the rule rather than the exception.

---

computer and an off-the-shelf sales automation package. The reps transmit customer orders and reports to regional, division, and head offices on a weekly basis using regular telephone lines.[44]

STRUCTURES FOR INTERNATIONAL SALES ORGANIZATIONS

In developing a sales program for overseas markets, sales management has to develop an appropriate organizational structure. Depending upon the level of commitment and control desired, a number of alternative choices are available to the resourceful sales executive. The alternatives are shown in Fig. 18-3. They range from a complete lack of an overseas presence to presence by proxy and ultimately to one's own sales organization overseas. The avenue chosen depends on the project's sales potential, the intensity of coverage desired, and environmental constraints.

Long-Distance Selling

Sometimes an international marketing firm does not require a sustained selling effort overseas. This may be the case in the selling of engineering or construction projects or of management contracts. In-depth expertise and high-level contacts are often essential in such situations. This typically requires the personal involvement of senior executives. They have to build trust in the capabilities and commitment of the firm and win the confidence of the officials awarding the contract.

long-distance selling One-time sale effort to a foreign customer

In such cases, personal *long-distance selling* is a one-time, not a continuous, activity, and followup account servicing is not required after the bid is awarded. This lack of an ongoing selling presence in the host country represents one extreme of the international sales organization continuum.

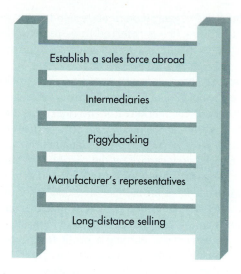

FIGURE 18-3 Structures for International Sales Organizations.

Manufacturers' Representatives

Companies desiring year-round sales representatives abroad without the cost of maintaining a full-time sales force often choose to retain manufacturers' representatives. Like their domestic counterparts, manufacturers' representatives are independent sales agents who work on a commission basis. They typically represent several foreign manufacturers of complementary, noncompeting lines. Ideally, they are well established and respected in their respective fields and geographic areas.

Manufacturers' representatives provide low-cost coverage for their principals because they can spread their expenses among the different lines; however, since they rely on commissions, they tend to emphasize easy-to-sell products and lines and neglect more difficult, but possibly more profitable, merchandise. They likely exert less effort on behalf of items novel to their country. The manufacturers' representatives may also prove difficult to control and motivate.[45] Unlike domestic representatives, they are often protected by law or contracts to such an extent that they are almost impossible to dismiss. Besides, they may be so well established and well connected (particularly in the Middle East) that it is inadvisable to terminate or bypass them.

Firms must choose their foreign representatives carefully, provide positive sales support and training programs, and continually monitor the representatives' sales efforts.[46] Inquiries for references at currently represented firms are an absolute must in picking overseas representatives. The U.S. Department of Commerce can also be helpful in both locating and evaluating potential representatives abroad.

Piggybacking

There is another alternative available for low cost market entry overseas. Sales executives can work out a deal with a foreign manufacturer to be represented in the host country. This arrangement requires that the other manufacturer have a suc-

piggybacking
Practice of a foreign
seller representing
complementary, non-
competing lines
carrier Firm (in pig-
gybacking) selling its
services and exper-
tise
rider Buyer (in pig-
gybacking) of the
carrier's services

cessful, well-functioning sales organization in place and be active in complementary, noncompeting lines. Such a practice is referred to as *piggybacking.* The firm selling its services and expertise is called the *carrier,* and the company seeking entry and availing itself of these services is termed the *rider.*

One company alone may have difficulty justifying the expense of employing its own sales force in a specific host country, but two firms can share the cost and risk of penetrating an attractive overseas market. For the rider, this kind of agreement also eliminates the need to identify and communicate with representatives abroad, and frequently the problem of having to overcome a language or even broader cultural barrier. These problems are taken care of by the carrier who already has experience in setting up its own sales organization in the foreign country.

For the rider, piggybacking is an inexpensive and quick way to enter a host country. The carrier may act in either of two capacities and be compensated accordingly. It can serve as an agent, receiving a commission on sales, or it can function as a merchant intermediary, earning a profit from the resale of the goods carried. Although piggybacking cuts the risks for the rider, it is likely to create dependency. The rider must also be sure that the quality of representation is at the desired level. Finally, sales managers must recognize that piggybacking is not as readily available as the other entry options, since nonmarketing, but compatible, producers with effective overseas sales organizations are often difficult to find.

Japan is a country in which U.S. businesses have found piggybacking effective. Matsushita Electric formed AMAC Corporation as a part of its Panasonic subsidiary that sells U.S. products to Japanese customers. Since its creation in 1981, AMAC has signed agreements with one hundred U.S. firms to sell their products through the five-hundred-member Panasonic sales force. Sequent Computer Systems of Beaverton, Oregon, and WYCO of Boston, a manufacturer of high-tech optical instruments, are two of AMAC's satisfied clients. Sequent's president, Casey Powell, notes, "Panasonic has been effective at providing the contacts we need. Business in Japan is a contact business."[47]

Intermediaries

A firm that wants to retain a reasonable amount of control over its sales in a host country may choose to set up its own distributor or dealer network and attempt to generate orders through the intermediaries' sales forces. In this case, the burden of the sales effort falls on the intermediaries. In turn, they are given territorial protection. Sole distributorships are common for imported liquor. Authorized dealerships are typical for earth-moving and farm equipment.

Needless to say, it is crucial to choose intermediaries—often called "middlemen" —carefully. A poorly performing intermediary can ruin a market, whereas a hard-working intermediary can build sizable volume. The firms gain in reputation and market access by teaming up with leading wholesalers and retailers. However, for firms other than well-known manufacturers, intermediaries may require constant attention. It may become necessary to make intermittent visits and contacts from headquarters in order to generate buyer awareness and enthusiasm. Usually, a substantive training program for the overseas sales personnel has to be put into place.

To meet long delays resulting from Japan's extremely complex distribution system, many multinational companies are turning to intermediaries. For small businesses, especially, the role of Japanese distributors and export management companies can be critical to doing business.[48]

A success story is Coleman Company, a producer of tents, sleeping bags, coolers, stoves, and other camping supplies. It took almost twelve years from the time Coleman opened an office in Tokyo until the firm mastered the Japanese distribution system and became a strong competitor. Coleman did this by staffing its operation with Japanese nationals in order to learn about the idiosyncracies of Japan's distribution system. The firm's patience paid off; Nippon Coleman Company's sales rose fourfold in a three-year period.[49]

Establish a Sales Force Abroad

The ultimate level of both commitment and control occurs when a company establishes its own sales force abroad. This step requires a great deal of confidence in the stability and potential of a market, so it is rarely chosen as an initial approach. Creating a foreign sales force simultaneously increases fixed costs and decreases a company's flexibility. This avenue should be selected only if the sales and profit potential in a specific nation warrants it.

Industry habits account for major differences in subsidiary sales structures abroad. In large part, U.S. multinational corporations take proven sales structures into overseas markets. They make adjustments to structures when subsidiary sales increase. Most multinational firms use traditional territorial designs or feature territory with either product or customer designations. High-technology firms are likely to be organized by product to allow their subsidiaries to compete on the basis of technology.[50]

Environmental factors have only limited effects on sales organizations. In some cases, independent sales organizations will be used to supplement the firm's own sales force in geographically large markets, such as Australia, Brazil, Canada, and culturally diverse markets like the Philippines and Indonesia. In other locations, multinational firms may be able to take advantage of cultural similarities and a common language to consolidate sales organizations (for example, Central America and France or Holland with Belgium).[51]

global account managers Global version of national account managers

A recent trend in international sales organization is global account management. Xerox, for example, uses this approach. *Global account managers* carry out a wide range of sales functions and duties. They must obtain as much customer information as possible to prepare a business plan that accurately addresses an international customer's business strategy and objectives. They must develop, communicate, and oversee the implementation of this business plan worldwide. Local account managers from foreign locations should be brought into this process also. An effective communications network must be developed and maintained to assure that customer satisfaction is achieved in all customer locations worldwide. Finally, the global account manager must focus and coordinate the worldwide resources of the firm in support of the customer, in all places where both parties operate.[52]

INTERNATIONAL SALES MANAGEMENT PRACTICES

Because sales strategies and personal selling approaches are affected by cultural, economic, and other differences between countries, sales management practices must also be adjusted. As in the United States, sales management activities must be interrelated. For instance, sales organization and selection practices must be connected with the sales training practices used.[53] Unfortunately, there is evidence that, even in developed countries, sales managers are not prepared to carry out key sales management tasks. A survey of one thousand British companies revealed that a large number of them lacked a system for evaluating sales performance. Many firms also did not accept the important role of training and development as a part of sales management.[54]

The outcome of these global sales management differences is that selling will fluctuate in quality, effectiveness, and results throughout the world. It is essential that multinational corporations have adequate procedures to hire qualified sales personnel, to provide them with the needed training and development, and to offer appropriate sales incentives and compensation.[55]

Recruitment and Selection

As in domestic sales management, hiring the correct personnel for sales and sales management positions is a critical sales management task. If an inappropriate person is placed in an international sales position, the results could be disastrous. For example, a company introducing a technical product in Europe did not choose its European sales manager carefully. The manager disliked the French and made no effort to ingratiate himself or to learn the French language and culture. He even treated the sales force abruptly. A competitor was able to take over much of the market and most of the manager's sales force.[56]

In a similar situation, one of Sunbeam Corporation's general managers in Italy was Swiss and unfamiliar with the Italian culture and market. Another Sunbeam unit had an experienced local manager. This unit prospered, while Sunbeam Italiana, hampered by ineffective leadership, went out of business.[57]

Foreign sales forces can be composed of three different types of salespersons, or some combination thereof. First, there is the salesperson who is a citizen of the home country, but works abroad. These people are chosen because of their product and technical knowledge as well as for their selling skills. They face a variety of problems, not the least of which are cultural assimilation and acceptance. They also face visa restrictions, especially in Third World nations that limit working permits for foreigners. These salespeople tend to be used in a given country for limited time periods, typically during the startup and building period. Ideally, they serve as trainers. In the long term, it is advantageous to utilize a sales force made up largely or exclusively of nationals of the host country. This second type of salesperson possesses the tremendous advantage of cultural identity.

The third type of salesperson is neither a citizen of the home country nor of the host country, but rather of a third nation. This cosmopolitan individual is exemplified by an Indian working for a U.S. firm in a black African country. The same prejudices and restrictions that hamper expatriates may also apply in this case.

Foreign sales managers often stay in an assigned country for lengthy periods. Providing a vital link to world headquarters and training and employment to nationals, they are generally welcomed by host country governments. They become fluent in the country's language, adapt to its customs, and associate with local leaders.

Recruiting and hiring sales personnel overseas is difficult because of cultural and economic obstacles.[58] Personal selling is not viewed as a desirable occupation in many countries, and it is often taught in vocational and trade schools rather than in colleges. This is true in Saudi Arabia, for example.

In Japan, the "job for life" attitude of employers and employees affects the hiring process. Job hopping is not at all common, and college graduates are expected to join companies for life. Japanese employers use a number of tactics to keep employees, and there is a stigma associated with switching jobs. As a result, college recruiting practices in Japan are extremely intense. Many more resources are spent to recruit college graduates for sales and other management trainee positions. This also has important implications for sales training. Since few experienced people are hired, Japanese firms must invest more in training their sales representatives.[59]

According to a study of salesperson selection overseas, four major factors complicate sales recruiting and selection. These are education differences, ethnic composition, religious orientation, and social class environment. These factors were identified by examining the selection process and hiring criteria in a number of multinational corporations (including IBM, Honeywell, Kimberly-Clark, and Hewlett-Packard).[60]

Specific differences in sales recruitment and selection abroad included:

1. Educational qualifications are more highly prized abroad than in the United States. This is due to major differences in educational systems throughout the world. The United States has a collegiate system that educates 45 percent of the 18- to 21-year-old age group. Many of these students study business and related practical disciplines. In contrast, the European educational system tends to be more elitist and emphasizes liberal arts and sciences. Systems in developing countries are able to satisfy only a small portion of the demands for educated personnel. As a result, recruiting educated personnel, which is not a problem in the United States, is a challenge overseas.

2. Less-orthodox hiring criteria, such as social class and religious or ethnic back-grounds, influence perhaps a fourth of the sales selection decisions made abroad. In India, for example, the social caste system makes it difficult for a sales representative to sell outside his/her own social level. In the United States, these factors are less likely to be considered and, if they are taken into account, the hiring firm may be subject to legal sanctions for violating equal employment opportunity guidelines.

3. Religious, ethnic, and social class factors are evident in both developed and developing countries. Some examples: Latin American cultures (Costa Rica, El

Salvador, Mexico, and Peru) are greatly influenced by the Catholic religion, and employers look for religious standing as an indicator of character and responsibility. There are ethnic biases in Germany that favor hiring native Germans over legally sanctioned guest workers from other countries. Belgium is ethnically split between its Flemish and French cultures, and sales recruiters should be aware that not all Belgians are bilingual. In Malaysia, there are tensions between the native Malays (55 percent of the population), who are Muslims, and the Chinese (33 percent), who are Buddhists. These and other differences make the use of standardized hiring criteria overseas dangerous.[61]

When choosing sales managers, multinational companies are very careful to select people who can adapt to cultural differences. AT&T formed an international human resources council to set policies and deal with the key human resources needs of its growing international business activities. The starting point for AT&T's international assignment program is candidate recruiting and selection. A cultural screening process is used to make sure that candidates and their families possess the needed skills, interests, values, and cultural adaptability to have a positive and productive experience in a foreign land.[62]

Compaq is another multinational company that places special emphasis on hiring. The firm hires internationally with many different cultures and languages represented. Han Gutsch, director of human resources for international operations, has been quoted as saying that his firm looks for people with initiative, talent, and especially potential. To make sure that a local focus is obtained, Compaq's personnel strategy is based on autonomous teams, and local teams each include a human resources director. One of the human resources director's major responsibilities is to ensure that Compaq is attractive to potential recruits.[63]

Sales Training and Development

Although basic selling skills transcend national boundaries, multinational sales training must be adapted to the nationality of salespeople and the cultures in which they will be selling. For example, rapport between customers and salespeople is often more important in Europe than a supplier's reputation and size. Since Europeans conduct business much differently than their U.S. counterparts, sales training programs developed for U.S. trainees must be modified for European sales personnel. For one thing, experienced international sales trainers have found that Europeans will not respond to training unless ample time is provided for extensive group discussion and review.[64]

For many multinational companies, global sales training has become a reality. In 1991, Nippon Wilson Learning delivered $67 million worth of management, sales, and service training programs in twenty-five countries throughout the world. Its customers included IBM, Du Pont, Toyota, Dow Chemical, BMW, Bank of Tokyo, and Sony.[65]

According to Shozo Mori, president of the Tokyo-based training organization: "Five years from now, there will be no more geographic boundaries in this business. We are all world citizens depending on each other."[66]

Mori believes that global sales training will grow because of rapid advances in communications. As he has pointed out, the technology already exists to deliver information and training programs to every country in the world in English, together with subtitles in the local language. He sees his firm growing through expanded global training services and the development of a global satellite communications services network. According to Mori:

> We all have the same basic qualities. These don't depend on race or color. To be successful in selling globally, we need to stress our common base. Once we've agreed on that common base, it will become easy to identify the differences and then we can be successful in working on these differences.[67]

Preparing sales managers for international assignments also poses unique challenges for companies and their management development programs.[68] Gary Wederspahn, director of program design and development for the consulting firm Moran, Stahl and Boyer, has observed:

> Very few companies are responding to the need of international managers to learn how to deal with people using intercultural skills.[69]

He went on to explain:

> The globalization of the world's economy means that business risks and opportunities transcend cultural and national boundaries. Therefore, the middle and upper managers who deal with the global economy need to be able to maximize the opportunities and manage the risks. In order to do that, they need to understand foreign customers, colleagues, business partners, officials, and so on.

Wederspahn's firm has developed a four-phase training program to prepare managers for international assignments. The first phase is designed to make participants aware of the existence of cultural differences and their impact on business outcomes. Next, managers learn attitudes and how they are shaped. The third phase provides factual knowledge and practical information about the foreign country. Finally, participants are given instruction in such skill building areas as language, nonverbal communication, cultural stress management, and adjustment and adaptation skills.[70]

Forum Corporation is another firm that helps companies prepare their managers for international operations. Senior vice president Gerald Jones feels that managers who are closest to the country's customers are the people who need training the most. He has noted: "People in direct contact with the customer must be able to change quickly. They need training not in traditional topics, but in innovation, agility, and adaptability.[71]

Forum's approach is to make international management training more market-specific. It teaches international managers critical skills in gathering customer data. Forum's training programs also emphasize the strategic needs of the organization. According to Jones, an understanding of customers' needs is essential to strategic planning and international operations. He has commented: "When [managers] learn about their customers' strategies, they can create their own customer-based strategies."[72]

IBM and Xerox have similar sophisticated international management training and development programs, which are costly to develop and carry out. In addition, language and cultural differences will slow down sales and management training and add further to its cost. Training is essential, however. Salespeople and their managers must understand the cultural dynamics of the countries in which they sell.[73]

Sales Incentives and Compensation

As discussed in Chaps. 16 and 17, key elements in any sales strategy are sales incentives and compensation. Multinational companies must recognize that they will be confronted with a range of circumstances that require adjustments to U.S. sales compensation and incentive policies and methods. For instance, many Asian insurance companies pay a substantial portion of their agent's compensation in salary rather than commissions, as is the case in the United States. Bonuses are also an integral part of sales compensation in the Far East.[74] In other countries, such as Brazil, sales force compensation must be modified to contend with high levels of inflation.

In cultures similar to the United States, sales incentives also tend to be similar. A study of industrial firms in South Africa revealed that self-satisfaction in doing a good job and the desire for more money are the main factors that motivate sales personnel.[75] A study of the use of travel incentives as motivators for a life insurance sales force in the United Kingdom reported that incentive travel is a strong motivator and valued more highly than other types of incentives.[76]

One of the major strengths of modern Japanese corporations is that employees are deeply dedicated to the survival and prosperity of the company that employs them. They are confident that if they serve the company well, their own interests will also be served. This feeling results from the concept of *marugakae*, or "total embrace"—the management philosophy that impels major companies to provide employees with everything from company commissaries and athletic facilities to company vacation homes.[77]

marugakae
Japanese management philosophy; literally, "total embrace"

The concept of individual rewards and recognition, so important to sales management in the United States, is at odds with the Japanese team approach to business. As a Japanese executive has explained:

> Something that might work in an American company would be giving out an award for the most outstanding worker. In Japan, everybody else would get jealous and the guy chosen for the award would feel very uneasy, too. The person you are trying to give the incentive to may be ostracized by his own group.[78]

As a result of these cultural differences, Japanese salespeople are normally paid a straight salary. If bonuses are given, they are based on company rather than individual performance. Sales representatives of a Japanese firm all receive an identical percentage bonus. This is the same percentage bonus received by other employees of the firm.[79]

SUMMARY OF LEARNING GOALS

1. Highlight the critical importance of international sales opportunities.

When domestic markets are mature and saturated, international markets often represent an opportunity for growth. International markets can also substantially increase a product's life cycle, counteract the cyclic nature of a domestic business, and use up excess capacity. These advantages of international markets are evidenced by many companies reporting that international sales are increasing at least 50 percent faster than domestic sales.

2. Identify the major environmental challenges faced by international sales managers.

The major environmental challenges facing international sales managers are economic factors, legal constraints, and cultural differences.

3. Describe the key strategic issues involved in international sales and marketing management.

Companies must decide whether the marketing approach should remain identical from country to country or whether allowances should be made for local conditions. While a standardized global marketing strategy is economical, it will not work in situations where adaptation of product, price, distribution, or promotion is necessary because of government regulations, competitive pressures, religious convictions, or technical specifications in the host country.

Companies must also determine ways to obtain information about foreign markets. Sources of information include chambers of commerce, international trade fairs, customers that do business in other countries, accounting or consulting firms, magazine editors, the U.S. National Trade Data Bank, and international sales forces.

Finally, companies must decide how they will enter international markets. Possible modes of entry are exporting, licensing, countertrade, joint ventures, management contracts, and wholly owned subsidiaries.

4. List key differences between domestic and international sales techniques.

Differences in domestic and international sales techniques may involve style, pace, and setting of sales interviews and negotiations. In general, publicity and trade shows take on added importance in foreign markets, and the sales process often takes longer and requires more patience. Visual aids are a way to break language barriers, and international salespeople must develop a sensitivity to uncertainty on the part of foreign businesspeople.

5. Specify methods for organizing international sales activities.

Organizational formats available to international sales managers include long-distance selling, manufacturers' representatives, piggybacking, intermediaries, and a sales force abroad.

6. Examine the differences between domestic and international sales management practices.

Sales managers have to deal with different types of salespeople for international sales management. Salespeople may be citizens of the home country, natives of the host country, or citizens of a third country. Recruiting and hiring sales personnel overseas is difficult because of economic obstacles, and personal selling is not a desirable occupation in many countries. Educational qualifications, "unorthodox" hiring criteria, and religious, ethnic, and social class factors are other issues that can affect sales management practices. Sales training and development and sales incentives and compensation are other areas in which international sales managers face unique challenges.

REVIEW QUESTIONS

1. What shift is being made within developing economies? What does this shift imply for sales and marketing?
2. Describe what is meant by an underdeveloped economy. What can you say about such an economy's demand? Its purchasing power?
3. What is the most important factor affecting international sales and marketing? What is CISG? How does it affect international sales managers?
4. List some of the cultural dimensions of international markets. How do these factors impact personal selling and sales management?
5. What is the advantage of indirect exporting? What are its disadvantages?
6. Why is licensing an attractive option? What is a common mistake made by sales managers using this approach?
7. List the organizational structures that an international selling effort can employ. On what factors should a decision about organizational structure be based?
8. What is the advantage of using manufacturers' representatives in foreign markets? What limitations exist with this form of selling?
9. How is piggybacking beneficial for the carrier? For the rider?
10. Why is a sales force abroad rarely used as an initial entry mode in a foreign market? What is an overseas sales force's effect on fixed costs? On flexibility?

DISCUSSION QUESTIONS

1. Interview a student from a foreign country to find out what that student finds surprising about American culture. Does the student know of U.S. sales activities that would be unacceptable in his or her country? How are similar activities handled in the student's country?
2. The Nomura Securities Company is a Japanese brokerage firm that employs a group of salespeople called "middies," middle-aged women who peddle investments door to door.[80] Do you think such an approach would work in the United States? Why or why not? Why are middies effective salespeople in Japan?
3. Russia's ruble is not considered valuable by most marketers, and even Russians sometimes will not accept their country's currency. Which mode of entry might be appropriate for a U.S. sales manager who wants to sell in Russia but is concerned about accepting rubles?
4. Systems Center, Inc., is a producer of computer software employing thirty-nine sales agents who are natives of the country in which they sell. Systems Center treats its commission-based foreign agents exactly as it would treat a sales agent in the United States.[81] Would you be surprised to find out that Systems Center had an agent in Japan? Why or why not?
5. Pick a foreign country. Then devise sales strategies for entering this market for the following firms:
   a. Microsoft
   b. Procter & Gamble
   c. Tyson Foods
   d. Dresser Industries

E T H I C A L
D I L E M M A

Gifts of cash and expensive products are frequently an expected part of doing business in countries outside the United States and Canada. How should salespeople and sales managers deal with gifts when doing business with international customers?

SALES MANAGEMENT CASE

A New Europe

Europe's efforts at unification have stimulated many American firms to work harder at establishing a European presence. The strategy of most of these businesses is to have themselves entrenched in Europe by the time market integration occurs. In this way, companies will be positioned to take advantage of new opportunities in Europe.

Viewlogic Systems Inc., a company that has had an international presence for years, is one of many organizations that have stepped up efforts abroad. In 1990, Viewlogic replaced its foreign distributors with direct sales forces supported by the venture capital of foreign investors. In this way, Viewlogic was able to transfer risk overseas and keep the multimillion dollar expense off its balance sheet and income statement. In short, Viewlogic gained the benefits of a direct sales force while incurring little risk.

Any investment in international business is riskier than domestic enterprise. European investment based on confidence in the European Community (EC) is made riskier by the potential for protectionism. The European Common Market was designed for the removal of internal restrictions to business, but it is not necessarily an invitation for foreign businesses to establish themselves in Europe. Also, with the monumental task that has been undertaken, it is naive to think that all Common Market efforts will be completed on schedule; difficult tax, worker rights,

and border control issues will demand attention for a long time to come.

Questions

1. Which mode of entry did Viewlogic use originally? Which mode does the company use now?

2. There are currently twelve nations in the EC, but others are applying for membership. Do you predict that an expanded EC would increase or decrease protectionism? Justify your answer.

3. In your opinion, would a U.S. business expanding into Europe face its greatest challenge in the form of economic factors, legal constraints, or cultural differences? Explain.

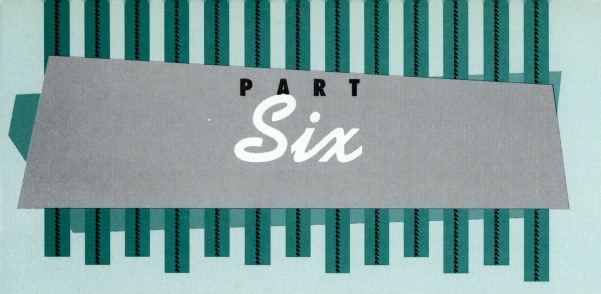

PART
Six

EVALUATING SALES FORCE PERFORMANCE

CHAPTER *19*

SALES EVALUATION

LEARNING GOALS

- Specify the steps in the development and management of a sales evaluation program.
- Explain the reasons for and difficulties associated with sales force evaluation.
- Describe sales quotas and performance measures and how they should be established.
- List information sources used in evaluation.
- Understand that sales performance should be evaluated at the lowest possible level of supervision.
- Explain the factors that determine the best frequency for formal sales evaluation programs.
- Outline the various methods of evaluation.
- Discuss the alternative policies for involving salespeople in evaluation programs.

EVALUATING THE SALES FORCE

The salesperson evaluation system should reflect first and foremost the needs of the company. Good sales incentive and compensation programs, discussed in Chaps. 16 and 17, are designed to motivate desirable behaviors. Evaluation, in turn, should be consistent with a company's reward systems and its stated goals.

Symantec Corporation, a California-based software-database company, is a niche player among giants. The company is growing through the acquisition of small companies that are not expected to produce giant revenues right away but hold promise for the future.

The inherent riskiness of Symantec's new products makes accurate sales figures crucial. Symantec evaluates, and rewards, its sales representatives not for how much they sell to distributors, but for how much the distributors sell to retailers. As a result, Symantec's sales reps are anxious to help solve store problems, and they are discouraged from pushing inappropriate products on distributors in order to make quota.

United States Surgical is another company that evaluates its salespeople according to how well they help achieve organizational goals. The company is on the cutting edge of surgical laparoscopy instruments, which use a tiny television camera inside the body to avoid the need for open surgery. U.S. Surgical also offers absorbable orthopedic products. These items, like the sutures and surgical staples the company already makes, dissolve in the body and eliminate the need for stitch removal.

Since U.S. Surgical desires to come out with new products continually, it is imperative that the firm's sales force be able to interact professionally with physicians and understand their needs. The sales force actually goes into operating rooms to help surgeons use new products and to obtain information about what the surgeons like or do not like. U.S. Surgical sales trainees go through a six-week course in anatomy, scrub technique, and company products. The course involves daily exams, and around 20 percent of the trainees fail.[1]

Sales force evaluation greatly affects a company's ability to compete. Chapter 19 will discuss the development and management of a sales evaluation program. The pro-

cess is full of challenges and difficulties, but for innovative and successful companies like Symantec and U.S. Surgical, a well-designed evaluation program's benefits certainly justify the efforts involved in its development.

CHAPTER OVERVIEW

"How am I doing?" Everybody, including salespeople, needs and wants this feedback. Chapter 19 will examine the critical tasks of designing a sales evaluation program and of managing it effectively. Each individual sales manager must decide which procedures are applicable to the company's situation and how complex and sophisticated the sales evaluation program should be.

Sales evaluation systems, which provide needed feedback, vary on the basis of whether the firm is large or small; whether it is in consumer, industrial, government, or export sales; whether it sells goods or services; whether it employs few or many salespeople. The evaluation may be formal or informal, its form may be simple or complex, and its conclusions may be based on objective criteria or on executive opinion. Whatever the scope, sales evaluation takes place in all companies, because without it the supervision of salespeople is impossible.

There are five distinct steps in the development and management of a systematic evaluation program for sales performance. These are shown in Fig. 19-1. The first two steps were discussed in earlier chapters; the last three are considered here.

Sales management's evaluation of its personnel should lead to corrective action if deficiencies are spotted. The goal of evaluation programs is to improve future sales force productivity. Too often evaluation is thought of as a negative attempt to find out which salespeople are not doing their jobs. To be sure, this is one aspect of evaluation, but the more realistic view of performance evaluation is that it is a positive activity for the personal development of sales representatives.

Proper development and management of the evaluation program is essential to the success of a sales organization. Yet, despite the critical importance of evaluation, it is still a sales management activity that is difficult and inexact. It is an art striving to

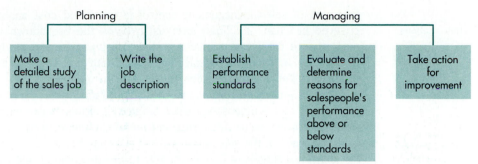

FIGURE 19-1 Steps in the Development of a Sales Evaluation Program.

become a science. As uncertain as it is, experience has proven that if sales evaluation is used with a full recognition of its problems and limitations, it pays real dividends.

SALES EVALUATION PRINCIPLES

Evaluation of performance is a very sensitive issue. Consequently, a sales evaluation program must be tailored to the individual company in which it is used. For one company, calls per day may be an important criterion of sales performance, while for another firm new accounts opened may be a far more critical standard. One company may evaluate its people annually, another quarterly. Each firm must design its own evaluation program based on its sales goals and strategies and the needs of its sales personnel. However, there are some generally accepted principles in all good sales evaluation programs.[2] A sales evaluation program must be the following:

1. *Realistic*. It must reflect territories, competition, experience, sales potential, and so forth as they truly are.
2. *Continuous, known, expected*. It must show a salesperson when and how work is evaluated.
3. *Constructive, not destructive*. It must show a salesperson what needs improvement and how to improve sales performance.
4. *Motivating*. It must stimulate a salesperson to improve.
5. *Informative*. It must provide useful information about a salesperson and the territory for management.
6. *Participatory*. It must involve salespersons in their own evaluations.
7. *Objective, not subjective*. It must be based on standards, not on opinions or prejudices.
8. *Flexible*. It must be adaptable to changing market conditions.
9. *Specific*. It must fit the company and the sales force involved.
10. *Economical*. It must be worthwhile in terms of money and time.

EVALUATION AND CONTROL

The evaluation of sales performance is part of the management control process. Evaluation involves comparing planned and actual results, identifying reasons for deviations, and making appropriate changes in sales goals and strategies. Another

sales analysis
Breakdown and study of sales performance data

cost analysis
Breakdown and study of sales expense data

sales force control system Procedures for monitoring, directing, and compensating sales personnel

outcome-based control systems
Control systems that monitor the final outcomes of the sales process

behavior-based control systems
Control systems that monitor the individual stages, or behaviors, in the sales process

key part of sales management control is sales and cost analysis, which will be covered in Chap. 20. *Sales analysis* involves the breakdown and study of sales performance data, whereas *cost analysis* involves a similar study of sales expense data. These activities help a sales manager identify areas of high and low productivity in order to better allocate sales efforts and resources.

A *sales force control system* provides a set of procedures for monitoring, directing, evaluating, and compensating sales personnel. Sales force control systems can be divided into two major categories: *outcome-based control systems*, which monitor the final outcomes of the sales process, and *behavior-based control systems*, which monitor individual stages, or behaviors, in the sales process.[3] Table 19-1 presents a summary of the differences between these two forms of sales force control systems.

The outcome-based control system is more appropriate for those types of selling situations that involve entrepreneurship. Salespeople are held accountable for their results, but they are left alone to achieve the results in their own way. In contrast, behavior-based control systems require a direct, "hands-on" management control approach. Sales managers are expected to vigorously monitor and direct the activities of their salespeople. Performance evaluation is based on more complex, subjective assessments involving what salespeople know and do (inputs), rather than what they achieve (outputs).[4]

In practice, most sales organizations and managers use a mix of these two approaches. Sales evaluation programs include performance standards that attempt to measure salespeople's activities, attitudes, knowledge, personal traits, and other inputs as well as sales volume, share of market, and other results and outputs. Also, sales managers differ greatly in their personal evaluation philosophy. Some managers practice laissez-faire management whereby the salesperson has almost total responsibility for performance. On the other hand, some managers will be very specific in defining their expectations for salespeople and will keep a tight rein on sales activities.

In addition to the general benefits of effective management control, there are a number of specific reasons for sales evaluation. These can be summarized in terms of the following management objectives:

- Discover how and where each person needs improvement. Individualized development is then possible.

TABLE 19-1   **Sales Force Control Systems**

Outcome-based control system	Behavior-based control system
Relatively little monitoring of salespeople by management	Considerable monitoring of salespeople's activities and results
Relatively little managerial direction or effort to direct salespeople	High levels of management direction or the intervention in the activities of salespeople
Straightforward objective measures of results (outcome), rather than measures of the methods salespeople use to achieve results, used to evaluate and compensate the sales force	Subjective and more complex methods based largely on what salespeople bring to the selling task, rather than sales outcomes, used to evaluate and compensate the sales force.

CAREERS USA

Marilyn Ounjian, owner and chief executive officer of Careers USA, takes a behavior-based approach to evaluation and management control. Ounjian monitors her sales force's activities through sales force reports faxed to her daily. A salesperson herself, Ounjian is able to read between the lines of the reports in order to spot potential problems or opportunities. Of the sections in the report, "orders in" is the very last in priority—according to Ounjian, if everything else is going well, the orders will follow.

The need for control measures became apparent as Careers USA grew to twenty-one offices in nine states. Accustomed to having close contact with her salespeople and their clients, Ounjian was concerned about losing touch with her business. The reports are simple, she says, and they do not ask for any information that is not absolutely necessary. Ounjian encourages salespeople to fill out the reports immediately after visiting clients, while their ideas are fresh. After she sees the reports, the information is entered into a computerized data bank.

Though simple, Ounjian's daily sales report provides a great deal of information. In the "comments" section of the report, Ounjian looks for statements indicating an active or a passive sales approach. A "time in, time out" section shows how salespeople are spending their time, and the report tells Ounjian whether or not they are reaching their weekly quota of fifty cold calls, twenty appointments, two lunches, and four presentations. These efforts, according to Ounjian, should produce a weekly 10 percent sales increase.

Other, less obvious information is apparent to the experienced eyes of Ounjian; for example, one salesperson was turning in positive reports, but her sales were declining. Ounjian called the salesperson's clients to uncover the problem, and she discovered that the salesperson hadn't been making calls for six months. Another employee trailed the salesperson for a day and discovered that she came to the office from 8:30 to 9:00 in the morning, went home, and then returned at 4:00 in the afternoon with sales reports completed. A behavior-based control system, while unnecessary for some selling situations, certainly has its advantages.

- Check and evaluate the performance standards for salespeople. Poor performance may indicate inadequate standards.
- Spot individuals who are ready for promotion, salary increases, or assignment to new territories and responsibilities.
- Keep sales job descriptions current and on target with changing market conditions.
- Obtain evidence about salespeople who should be terminated.
- Verify the sales compensation plan, training, supervision, recruitment, territory assignments, and operating procedures.

Sales managers also realize that an effective sales evaluation program provides feedback to sales personnel. Performance feedback allows representatives to know whether or not they are doing a good job. It also allows them to take corrective action when needed.

THE DIFFICULTIES OF EVALUATION

Problems in evaluating sales performance are so common and difficult that they discourage some companies from employing a formal sales evaluation program at all. Other firms use only very simple plans. When sales management creates and operates an evaluation plan, it knows that these obstacles will always make any plan something less than perfect.

The measurement and evaluation of sales performance, like all aspects of sales management, will be affected by situational, environmental, and personal factors. For instance, territorial and product differences must be considered. Differences in the backgrounds of salespeople also make evaluation more difficult. Further, many sales supervisors feel that they do not have enough information or adequate appraisal methods to evaluate subordinates, or they lack the needed "people skills."[5] These factors suggest several major obstacles to sales personnel evaluation.

Isolation of Salespeople

Most salespeople do their work outside the personal observation of their supervisors. In consumer goods industries—such as food, drug, hardware, liquor, and cosmetics—sales supervisors consider themselves fortunate if they can spend one selling day a month in the field with each of their salespeople. The isolation of salespeople creates two problems in evaluating their work.

Evaluation by Inference.   Since a field sales manager can only occasionally observe salespeople's performance, the sales supervisor must infer conclusions from indirect evidence. For example, records for the last quarter show that Sandra Marshall's calls per day, new accounts opened, dollar volume sold, and gross margin earned are well below her quotas. The supervisor must infer that Sandra is neglecting her job. This may actually be true, but conditions might have existed under which these same facts would lead to a very different conclusion—for example, strikes against Sandra's three biggest customers.

Evaluation by inference can lead to incorrect conclusions. Just as the courts are extremely careful when they deal with circumstantial evidence, the sales supervisor should handle inferential evaluations with great care. Inference should be checked against personal information and observation.

Bias of Direct Observation.   When the supervisor evaluates salespeople by traveling with them, two potential forces of bias are present. First, the salesperson may try to look good by calling only on easy, friendly customers. Jim Beeker, a sales supervisor of a toy manufacturer, became curious about the kinds of customers he was visiting when he traveled with his field salespeople. Analysis showed that 80 percent of his calls with salespeople were made on customers who represented 75 percent of the salespeople's volume. A second bias in field observation is that the presence of the salesperson's superior may change a customer's normal behavior. Observing salespeople at work is a useful and important evaluation tool, but it should be used carefully.

Finding and Relating Performance Factors

One cannot evaluate a salesperson's performance until the functions the person should be performing are known. In even simple selling jobs, it may be difficult to identify the specific performance factors that are critical to sales success and then to rate these factors in relation to one another.

Regarding salesperson evaluation, some might ask, "What's the problem?" Salespeople are hired to sell goods and services at a profit. Why is it so hard to evaluate their performance? The problem stems from the difficulty of determining what creates profit for a specific company, territory, or unit: Is it service? Advertising and promotion? Technical assistance? Advice on inventory control? Further, traditional nonselling evaluation measures may be inadequate because of salesperson activities that do not result in actual sales output until months or even years after they are performed.

Lack of Control over Some Performance Conditions

Another difficulty in evaluation is that salespeople's performance is always influenced—for better or worse—by external conditions over which they and/or their company have little control (for example, a competitor cuts its price, there is a business slowdown, or a government agency issues a report that is critical of the product). It is difficult to design an evaluation program that takes such external forces into account.

Fact versus Judgment

A persistent problem in evaluation is that the information used is of two sorts: fact and judgment. Fact is usually quantifiable, judgment is nonquantifiable. While fact can be stated and used in the form of figures or other fairly exact measures, judgment cannot. An example of quantifiable fact is number of calls per day. An example of nonquantifiable judgment is the extent of the salesperson's product knowledge.

It may seem difficult to use both fact and judgment in evaluation. However, this perceived difficulty will diminish if it is remembered that the purpose of evaluating sales performance is to facilitate personnel development. The key issues are to determine why the performance is below expectations and to help the person improve.

ESTABLISHING PERFORMANCE STANDARDS

The third step in the design and management of a sales evaluation program is the selection of performance standards that will indicate how people are doing with regard to the tasks established by the sales job description. These performance standards are often called "quotas." As defined in Chap. 9, a sales quota is a sales goal assigned to a salesperson, region, or other marketing unit for use in managing sales efforts.

It is the manager's responsibility to make sure that sales performance goals and quotas are well developed and clearly stated. These goals and quotas also must be consistent with the company's overall goals and strategies.[6] This is accomplished by basing quotas on the sales objectives that are formulated during the sales planning process. The establishment of sales goals and quotas is a natural extension of the sales manager's planning function.

Since sales performance goals and quotas also impact sales motivation, they must be fair and equitable. Sales goals and quotas must motivate people while being neither too easy nor too difficult to reach. This will involve adapting performance standards to industry conditions, regional economies, the company's marketing objectives, and the salesperson's individual record. Salespeople should be consulted and permitted to provide input in setting performance measures.[7]

Salespeople should also be consulted regarding the difficulty of the sales tasks involved. There is a tendency for sales managers' evaluation of salespeople to be influenced by the effort expended by salespeople, not by the difficulty of the sales task involved. By including salespeople in the evaluation process, managers will be able to incorporate task difficulty information into the development of standards and other aspects of performance appraisal.[8]

General Guidelines

A great many indexes and combinations of performance measures are available to sales management. The growth of information sciences, the explosion of knowledge, and the availability of computers have made it possible to know, at great speed and in great detail, virtually anything one might wish to know about sales performance. The limiting factors are the time and expense of generating, collecting, analyzing, and appraising such information. Management must spend time designing an evaluation reporting and analysis system. The salesperson must spend time filling out reports on sales activities. And management must spend still more time collecting, analyzing, and appraising the results.

The more measurements that are used in the evaluation of sales performance, the more time is required. Consequently, a company must study carefully what is needed to evaluate sales performance and to employ only those items that will give the necessary information.

Since no two selling jobs are the same, performance in each kind of selling job must be measured by its own standards. The two basic criteria for the selection of performance measures are discussed below.

What Is Needed?   Managers are evaluated on how well they make decisions under conditions of constant uncertainty, so every executive wants all the information available before making any evaluation or decision. For example, a sales manager might like to know the exact details of a sales slippage for a particular group of customers. However, the reality of the situation is that the manager might have to take corrective action on the basis of what he or she currently knows. Information costs money, and the more information and detail required, the greater the cost. Consequently, there are several critical questions that must be answered regarding which performance measurements should be used: What information is essential to evaluation? What information is not essential to evaluation? What information can the firm afford to obtain? What information can the firm not afford to obtain?

How Efficient Is the Information Source?   Having decided which measures to use, critical questions arise concerning the efficiency of the information source. Does it provide only the information desired, or does the source charge for unneeded data? Is the information sufficiently accurate? If not, what degree of inaccuracy is present? Will the source provide timely information?

Dangers of Using a Single Standard

The use of a single standard, such as a quota, for the evaluation of sales performance has the tempting advantages of being easy for salespeople and their supervisors to understand and of being economical to plan and administer. It is likely, however, to cause more problems than it solves. The consensus of most sales managers and researchers is that there is no single, foolproof method of measuring a salesperson's performance.

Consider the kinds of undesirable side effects that can develop from the use of any single standard of evaluation. Imagine a salesperson whose performance is evaluated solely on a gross-dollar sales volume quota. The salesperson is expected to bring in a certain number of dollars in sales in the next quarter to meet or exceed the quota. It would be only natural for a person to react to a single standard by ignoring other important aspects of the job. For example, to achieve a certain gross-dollar sales volume level, the person might let sales expenses get out of control, refuse to open new accounts, resist spending the time to introduce and promote new products, neglect the lower-priced items in the line, minimize customer service, or skip small or less active accounts. It is conceivable that this is just what the company wants the salesperson to do, but this would be a rare instance. In today's dynamic marketplace, a company does not want a salesperson to overlook any or all of these important tasks.

Single standards of evaluation—most often sales volume—are used in some companies, but they are always dangerous because they have a strong tendency to create harmful side effects in sales performance. A more likely case is that several standards are applied for sensible evaluation and supervision of salespeople and for the avoidance of undesirable behavior.

The insurance industry has recognized that the proper evaluation of sales agents involves many standards in addition to sales volume. Performance appraisals of insurance sales personnel also consider whether or not a salesperson seeks new business, tries to improve selling skills and product knowledge, handles customers' complaints properly, assists other sales personnel, works cooperatively with inside people, and responds positively to constructive criticism.[9]

Specific Measures of Performance

Specific sales performance goals and quotas are frequently derived from a company's sales forecast. They can be established for virtually any result and time period that are relevant to a particular selling job. Some examples are new accounts opened, sales expenses, number of units sold, calls made per day, and number of product demonstrations made. Virtually all firms include a measure of sales volume in their sales evaluation programs.

Specific measures of sales performance include two types: (1) the salesperson's effort, or input, and (2) the salesperson's results, or output. Measuring salespeoples' input will show what they did. Measuring output will tell how they did. The two types of measurements can also be combined, so that by evaluating a salesperson's input, a sales manager can determine the reasons behind the individual's output.

Tables 19-2 and 19-3 show the most frequently used standards of performance, along with indications of which activities or results can be used to measure the

TABLE 19-2 Input Measures of Sales Activities

Standard	Activity measured	% of sales managers who use
Calls per day	Time utilization, application	57
Nonselling activities (public relations, etc.)	Attitude toward job, etc.	90
Hours worked per day	Application to job, planning ability	. . .
Correspondence, phone calls made	Attitude toward job, selling ability	25
Problem-solving ideas generated	Creativity in managing oneself and the territory	69
Management of time	Business ability, efficiency, attitude toward job	73
Product, policy, and procedure knowledge	Attitude toward company and job, selling ability	59–89
Ability as market "intelligence agent"	Value as information source, assistance to company	72
Personal appearance	Value as company representative, selling ability	82
Personality traits: judgment, honesty, emotional stability, self-discipline, responsibility	Selling skills, value to company	. . .

relative usage of each standard. In evaluating sales performance some of the standards can be quantitatively measured; others require the sales manager's judgment and experience. A survey of industrial companies revealed that most firms use a combination of quantitative (sales volume in dollars, net profit dollars, and sales volume compared to the previous year) and qualitative (product knowledge, initiative, and ethical behavior) measures of performance.[10]

Territorial Adjustments

Territory differences must be taken into account when developing performance measures for specific salespersons. Even though initial territory design procedures attempt to minimize differences between sales territories, territories will never be completely equal. As a result, territory situation factors should be included in the sales evaluation process. Specifically, sales goals and quotas must be adjusted for differences in territory characteristics.[11]

Sales performance measures that will be affected by territory differences must be identified. Then territory-adjusted quotas or goals should be established. This task is best accomplished through a process of statistical analysis combined with discussions between the sales manager and salespersons.[12]

For example, a district sales manager for a pharmaceutical firm has ten salespeople reporting to her. In general, each salesperson is expected to make twelve calls per day. However, one salesperson has an urban territory in which all prospects and customers are within a five-mile radius. In contrast, another salesperson covers a large rural territory which includes several small towns. It is clear that the twelve-

TABLE 19-3 Output Measures of Sales Results

Standard	Results measured	% of sales managers who use
Dollar or unit sales volume	Dollar or unit "score"	81
Customer service sales calls or assignments	Service provided, amount of customer service work done	24
Share of market attained	Competitive standing in the territory	18
Number of orders written	Volume of business, frequency of orders taken	. . .
Number of reorders	Frequency of repeat business, customer loyalty, selling skill	17
Expenses	Selling cost one represents, one's interest in expense control	22–41
Gross margin on orders	Contribution to overhead, price lines sold	14
Number of active accounts	Territory coverage, potential	43
Calls made	Activity rate, aggressiveness	57
Promotion work done	Number of nonselling, sales supporting activities	12–28
Sales against quota or sales budget	Relative sales results against bogey, standing relative to other salespeople	54
Sales versus territory potential	Territory coverage, sales record	34
Average order size	Nature of business written, size of customer, territory conditions, sales skills	15
Ratio of orders to calls	Time allocation, sales success, territory coverage, sales skill, planning ability	26
Average of canceled orders	Sales skill, nature of business written	14
Number of new accounts opened	Aggressiveness, kind of customers called on, planning activity	71

calls-per-day measure must be adjusted to deal with the geographical difference between these two territories.

Profitability Focus

Historically, sales evaluation measures have emphasized volume. But today, profitability has become the yardstick for measuring sales performance. For example, Professor Rene Darmon stresses the need to focus on profitability, not sales volume, when assessing sales performance:

. . . salespersons may sell different product mixes with very different profit outlooks as the result of quite different selling abilities. A company should prefer the performance of the salespeople whose product mixes yield higher profits, but not necessarily the performance of salespersons who develop the largest sales volume.[13]

Darmon has proposed a procedure that takes into consideration a salesperson's entire expected career path and expected value to the company. The approach, which involves a quantitative procedure based on a long-range forecasting model, uses probability estimates to predict a salesperson's expected long-range contribution to profits.[14]

Another way to focus on profitability is to establish sales goals and quotas that have a connection to profits. Unfortunately, there are many companies and thousands of salespeople whose performance measures do not encourage them to attain the best product mix, customer mix, or gross margins.[15] Sales managers must make sure that profitability expectations are a key factor in the development of sales performance standards.

The ROI (return on investment) model described in Chap. 10 is another profit-oriented approach that has come to be regarded as an integrating tool for measuring sales performance.[16] Chapter 10 also notes that, for sales evaluation purposes, ROI is usually adapted to ROAM (return on assets managed). ROAM uses items like accounts receivable and inventories as the relevant investment figures.

The following formula is used for determining ROAM:

$$\text{ROAM} = \frac{\text{net profit}}{\text{sales}} \times \frac{\text{sales}}{\text{assets managed}}$$

A sales territory with sales of $400,000, net profits of $20,000, and assets managed of $100,000 would have a ROAM of 20 percent. In other words, this sales territory has earned the company 20 percent on the dollars it has invested. Whether or not 20 percent is an acceptable return on assets managed would depend on the ROAM in other sales territories and on corporate objectives and alternative uses of the company's resources.

INFORMATION SOURCES FOR EVALUATION

Once the measures for evaluating sales performance have been chosen, questions arise concerning the sources of such information. Where does a sales manager find the information needed to develop the performance standards selected? Where can information for evaluating sales performance be obtained? What are the advantages and weaknesses associated with each information source? The major sources of evaluative information are considered in the sections that follow.

Company Records

A company's own history is often a useful source of data from which performance norms can be built. Invoices, historical volume experience by territory or by customer class, customer complaints, bills of sale, volume-cost-profit experience with various kinds of promotions and lines, the history of individual salespeople, and other aspects of company experience are useful in establishing performance standards for salespeople.

A tire manufacturer wished to expand from regional distribution in the Midwest into the New England market. The firm sought to establish dollar sales volume quotas as performance measurements for salespeople in New England. Investigation showed that the social, economic, and competitive characteristics of the proposed

New England sales territories were similar to those of selected Midwestern territories in which the company had sold for years. So the company's historical sales volume in these comparable Midwestern territories was used to establish sales quotas for the new territories.

Customers

Customers themselves are often fruitful sources of data on sales performance because they are in close and frequent contact with salespeople. For instance, an effective marketing planning and control tool is supplier evaluation. A rating system for suppliers can be developed that is based on a survey of customers' criteria for suppliers. Sales managers can use this system to provide better service to their customers.

Potential advantages of customer evaluations include the following:

1. Customers can provide fresh, vital, up-to-the-minute evaluation information.
2. Customers' information is firsthand and not, therefore, subject to distortion by being transmitted through several senders before reaching the supplier's management.
3. Customers are reminded that the supplier company is concerned with them, their operations, and their problems.
4. Customers can provide new ideas on how to improve service.
5. Customers can provide useful comparisons of a firm's salespeople with competitors' representatives.

The potential weaknesses and risks of this approach include the following:

1. Information from customers on salespeople's performance is random and unweighted. One never can be exactly sure how to appraise it. Customers are likely to evaluate the performance in ways too vague to be useful: "Your rep certainly got us out of a bad spot on that one" or "Your rep goofed on that shipment."
2. Seeking evaluation information on salespeople from customers can boomerang on the sales manager. Unless it is done carefully and with the salesperson's complete knowledge and support, collecting this information from customers will appear to the salesperson as an unfair intrusion into his or her relationships with customers. Under such conditions, morale and effectiveness can suffer.

Reports from Salespeople

Perhaps the most widely used source of evaluation evidence is the information that salespeople themselves furnish through reports, both written and oral. These **call reports** Oral or written sales performance summaries provided by salespeople to managers reports from salespeople are known as *call reports*. Since salespeople have intimate, current knowledge of their territories and of their own operations, they can furnish territory coverage information for supervision purposes along with evaluation data in the same report. Thus, a carefully designed reporting system will save the expense of double reporting for the two purposes.

A sales manager must handle this information with care since, like most people, sales personnel will do what they can to protect themselves from criticism, to make themselves look good, to make the job as easy as possible, and to maximize their

SALES MANAGEMENT IN PRACTICE

AU BON PAIN COMPANY

■ Au Bon Pain Company (ABP) is a restaurant franchise that keeps up with its sixteen hundred employees by monitoring them with specially trained mystery shoppers, who visit restaurants and then fill out ABP-designed questionnaires that ask about the quality of food and service. Employee scores on the questionnaire have much to do with how the employees are evaluated and eventually compensated; servers receive gift prizes for good mystery shopper scores, and managers' profit sharing is tied in part to how well their stores do.

ABP started its mystery shopper program in 1987 and has seen substantial increases in scores since the program's beginnings. Shoppers are hired through newspaper ads and word of mouth. Once hired, the shoppers go through a training session, where they are informed about company goals and philosophies and where they try different foods to see how ABP meals should taste. After training, the shoppers hit the restaurants, where they are expected to stay for at least twenty minutes. Restaurants are visited three times over four-week periods.

The benefits of the mystery shopper evaluation method are twofold. First, the evaluation provides information to management and acts as a basis for compensation. Second, and more important, is the effect that the program has on employee customer-service performance; employees are always on their toes because they never know when a mystery shopper will arrive.

There are many applications of a mystery-shopper-like program to sales forces. For example, "mystery callers" could contact inbound telemarketers to evaluate customer service and selling skills, or the phone numbers of mystery callees could be inserted into the lists of outbound telemarketers. The use of mystery shoppers of all kinds is on the rise. In New Hampshire there is a business called "Customer Perspectives" that employs 35 mystery shoppers and sends them out to client businesses. Started in the early 1980s, the company has experienced a 48 percent average yearly growth in gross revenues. The success of Customer Perspectives may be an indication of the future prevalence of the mystery shopper in sales management situations.

---

incomes. Salespeople as a group are no more or less honest or self-seeking than any other group of employees. However, if a manager does discover a salesperson cheating on reports, strong disciplinary action or dismissal should follow quickly.

More important and prevalent than out-and-out dishonesty is the tendency for salespeople to subtly favor themselves in all instances when they have a legitimate choice on what to report. For instance, in one company, calls per day is an important performance evaluation factor. A salesman, Bob Carson, has made ten bona fide calls on customers and has run into another customer in a restaurant; they have lunch and discuss baseball the whole time. How many calls does Bob report for the day? He is likely to report eleven. This tendency suggests why many companies try to collect evaluative evidence on all important job performance factors from more than one source.

Prevention is the easiest way to avoid false or "fudged" call reports.[17] If salespeople are aware that the information from their reports will be used to help them make sales, they are less likely to submit untruthful reports. Involving salespeople in the design of call reports and their use is also helpful. Finally, sales managers must use call reports properly. They are meant to monitor sales activities and to compile market information, not to hinder or restrict the salesperson.

Another issue is the negativism that most salespeople have toward call reports and other paperwork. Too often sales reporting forms ask for too much detail, for relatively unimportant information, or for information that is difficult and time-consuming for a salesperson to compile. Salespeople should be asked to provide only relevant information that is needed for sales planning, management control, and performance evaluation. Further, sales activity reports should be designed carefully to minimize sales force resistance and to reduce the time required to complete the reports.

Sales call reports are being used in a number of new ways. Companies like American Airlines, 3M, and Wilson Learning use call reports to evaluate new salespeople. By monitoring the call reports of new hires closely, sales managers can learn much about their selling activities and patterns and their suitability for their jobs. Other companies use the information from call reports to assess sales training and schedule refresher training courses. In some companies, sales managers spend almost as much time analyzing call reports as their salespeople do completing them.[18]

Managers' Field Visits

As the earlier discussion of field coaching indicated, visits to the field can be an important source of evaluation information. An experienced field sales manager describes the benefits of field visits in this way:

> I want to be sure that salespeople are highlighting the product lines we want them to, that they're dropping off literature to the appropriate people, and that they know the people behind the scenes at the plants—maintenance superintendents, tool crib super-intendents, plant engineering people, quality control people, etc.
>
> I want to see whether they can solve problems that may come up and can answer impromptu questions to the customer's and my satisfaction. When a salesperson tries to fake it, he or she doesn't come across well. Any smart customer can see right through that. And it leaves a bad impression—both of the salesperson and the company.[19]

A Manager's Personal Insights

Although managers usually cannot state it in figures, symbols, charts, or graphs, an experienced sales manager has an intuitive sense in evaluating the performance of salespeople. The manager has usually been a salesperson and is experienced in the industry and company. Good sales managers know their salespeople well—as professionals and as individuals. From this knowledge comes a valuable insight to be used in the evaluation of subordinate salespeople's work.

Some sales management experts disagree with this contention and advocate that the evaluation of sales performance can and should be completely objective and scientific, with no room for subjective judgment by the manager. The great majority of salespeople and sales managers, however, support the view that instinct can be as useful in evaluation as any of the other scientific measures. Instinct and science are seen as complementary.

External Sources

External forces also influence salespeople's performance. Shifts in buying power in a territory, in population, in economic activities, and in number of potential customers all can affect sales performance and influence a salesperson's evaluation.

The effective evaluation program includes performance measures based on the information coming from outside the company. For instance, if it appears that the sales expense ratio is high, a manager compares it with industry statistics on selling expenses.

Many sources of such information are available at little or no cost. These sources are of two general types: governmental and private. The governmental sources consist of federal and state agencies and bureaus. The private sources are trade, industry, and professional associations and groups.

There are also a number of selling and sales management publications that provide useful information for sales evaluation. *Sales & Marketing Management* publishes many articles and reports plus several special issues including its *Sales Manager's Budget Planner*. This publication provides annual cost-per-call data for consumer, industrial, and service salespeople. It also compiles statistics from a number of other organizations. Dartnell Corporation publishes newsletters, bulletins, and other information, including an annual *Survey of Sales Compensation*. Information on sales incentives is published by *Incentive Magazine*. Other secondary sources of information include *Training, American Salesman, Journal of Personal Selling & Sales Management, Industrial Marketing Management,* and other periodicals, many of which are cited in this book.

WHO SHOULD EVALUATE SALES PERFORMANCE?

An important distinction exists between who should design a sales evaluation program and who should operate it. The evaluation plan should be designed by those in the company who have the most sales experience, who know the company, its products, and markets in the greatest detail, and who are experienced in developing evaluation programs. In most companies, these requirements necessitate that the evaluation program be originally designed and periodically reviewed by top sales executives. But who in the company should actually make evaluations and work with them once the plans have been designed? Should it be top sales executives? Regional sales managers? Field sales managers? Corporate staff evaluation specialists? Sales or personnel consultants?

Industry practice varies in the level at which sales evaluation takes place. However, the weight of the evidence supports the conclusion that it should be done at the lowest possible level of supervision, preferably by the salesperson's immediate supervisor—the field sales manager.

There are a number of reasons to support this conclusion:

1. The salesperson-supervisor relationship is strengthened. Research has shown that the sales supervisor is an important determinant of a salesperson's job satisfaction.[20] Evaluation of performance by the salesperson's immediate supervisor facilitates a closer working relationship between the two. They must work together on the individual's problems, and they share the satisfaction of improving the person and the work. If well managed by the supervisor, participative evaluation brings the supervisor closer to the sales force, thereby making other supervisor responsibilities easier and more effective. The sales force's morale is bolstered because salespeople appreciate the interest their supervisor has in their work.

2. Mutual commitment is enhanced. When the salesperson and the supervisor share in sales evaluation, they are both personally and publicly committed to improving the salesperson's performance and solving problems. This greatly improves the effectiveness of evaluation and its followup.

3. Supervisor responsibility is established. The supervisor is responsible for the performance results of the sales force. The field sales manager is judged by and evaluated on how well or poorly salespeople perform; through their work the manager succeeds or fails. Consequently, it is only reasonable that the supervisor play a major role in evaluating sales performance and in working out remedial action with salespeople based on the evaluations. When a supervisor does not have an important part in the evaluation of sales performance, a classic administrative mistake is likely to occur—that of assigning the supervisor responsibility for sales performance without assigning the necessary authority to remedy mistakes.

4. Communication of goals and remedies is clear and direct. Perhaps the most important reason that a salesperson's immediate supervisor should play a major role in the evaluation is so that both parties can clearly understand what is right and wrong with the salesperson's performance and what remedial actions should be taken. If someone other than the salesperson's immediate supervisor evaluates performance, a third party is introduced and communication is immediately made more difficult. Resentment can quickly appear. Both the salesperson and supervisor begin to wonder about the third party, asking themselves questions that could have been avoided: "What standards are being used?" "What does the evaluator mean?" "Why did the evaluator decide that?" "What information is being used?" "Why did the evaluator recommend that I do that to solve my problems rather than something else?" "What right does this person have to evaluate my work?"

FREQUENCY OF EVALUATION

The frequency of evaluation refers to the frequency of formal evaluation, exclusive of the routine evaluations made almost daily in normal sales operations. Clearly, when a salesperson is judged (evaluated) to have made a mistake of some significance, it should be brought to the person's attention as soon as possible and not stored for some future formal evaluation. Apart from individual, routine corrections, how often should salespeople be evaluated under a formal evaluation program? The following critical issues must be considered to decide what frequency of evaluation is optimum for any individual sales group.

Time Required to Evaluate

evaluation time cycle Amount of time necessary to complete the steps in an evaluation plan

Each formal evaluation plan operates on its own *evaluation time cycle*—the sum of the amount of time necessary, with any given evaluation plan, to complete all the steps of the evaluation. With simple plans, the evaluation time cycle is short— perhaps a matter of only a week or so. With more elaborate plans the time cycle may run to months.

Consider the example of a time cycle analysis made by an office equipment manufacturer. With the evaluation standards that have been selected, data collection requires ninety days, information processing takes ten days, and supervisors work with salespeople five days. The total evaluation time cycle thus includes one hundred five days. Of course, this does not mean that this company spends one hundred five full-time days on each evaluation cycle, but rather it takes that period to complete an evaluation cycle. Another company might require a month or two weeks.

A survey of sales evaluation practices revealed that the frequency of evaluation varied from a weekly to an annual interval. Most companies, however, formally evaluate sales personnel quarterly, semiannually, or annually.[21]

Sales managers cannot formally evaluate their personnel any more frequently than the evaluation time cycle will allow. If the cycle requires one hundred five days, management cannot formally evaluate any more frequently. The evaluation time cycle sets a limit on the frequency of formal evaluation possible under any given evaluation program.

Intrusion of Evaluation

The salesperson's and the supervisor's jobs are made up of current and future activities. Current activities are those that are performed in the present to achieve immediate results. Future activities are those that are performed in the present to achieve future results. For the salesperson, selling, calling on customers, opening new accounts, providing service, and filling out reports are current activities. These are functions that must be performed now. For the supervisor, traveling with salespeople and calling on customers are current activities. They are current responsibilities with immediate payoffs.

By contrast, evaluation is a future activity for both the salesperson and the manager. Like training, evaluation is performed not to gain immediate benefits, but to achieve desired future goals. All future activities are based on the concept of delayed gratification: the giving up of something presently of value in the expectation of receiving something of greater value in the future. The college student gives up present income in the expectation that a degree will produce greater returns (personal, social, and economic) in the future. In short, future activities intrude on current activities, draining time, money, energy, and attention. When evaluating past performance in order to improve future performance, the sales manager cannot be selling, calling on customers, or performing any other current activity.

One criterion of evaluation frequency becomes the amount of intrusion on current activities that can be tolerated. How much time can salespeople and managers spend away from their present activities in order to evaluate? There is no all-inclusive answer. This is a judgmental decision to be made by each company in light of its own needs and conditions. One company may decide that for the sake of future performance their salespeople and supervisors must forego a considerable amount of current activity in the expectation of more substantial future gain. Others may severely limit evaluation, preferring to emphasize present gain over potential future payoffs.

Time Required for Remedial Action

The last issue that should be considered in determining the appropriate frequency of evaluation is the length of time it takes for salespeople to solve problems that

SALES MANAGEMENT IN PRACTICE

GRANITE ROCK COMPANY

Granite Rock Company is a construction materials company that, unlike its competitors, does not treat its products like commodities. While most of the industry sees price as the sole basis for competition, Granite Rock charges a premium for its products, which, it claims, are better than the rest. Obviously, this pricing strategy requires not only high-quality products but also excellent customer service.

Granite Rock uses customer survey forms to determine whether or not it is giving customers what they want. Customers are asked to answer questions regarding not only how Granite Rock is serving their needs but also how the firm measures up against its competitors. The data from the forms are used to create charts and graphs that show managers and employees how Granite Rock is doing and point to areas for improvement. Most salespeople monitor the charts themselves.

Customer-provided data can make up an important part of a company's evaluation program. For companies like Granite Rock, where customer service is the difference between success and failure, "How're we doing" information is every bit as relevant as market share, sales volume, or managerial evaluations of performance.

---

are indicated by the evaluation and to perform the functions on which they are evaluated. It is pointless to evaluate salespeople before they are able to react to the last evaluation. If, for example, an important performance criterion is the number of new accounts opened, and if it usually takes six months to open a new account, it makes little sense to formally evaluate this activity more than twice a year, since only at the end of that interval can any realistic results be observed.

In summary, the best frequency of formal evaluation is the frequency that is established in relation to the evaluation time cycle; that is no more intrusive on present selling and management activities than is acceptable; and that takes into account the time required to remedy mistakes, solve problems, and perform the activities being evaluated.

METHODS OF SALES FORCE EVALUATION

Sales organizations have developed a wide variety of methods for evaluating sales personnel. These methods have been developed to provide salespeople with feedback on their sales performance, to identify areas of performance that should be modified or improved, and to provide information to management for specific actions such as promotions, transfers, and compensation adjustments. The most widely used methods are ranking, rating scales, and essays. After reviewing these procedures, this section will also consider new methods for sales performance evaluation.

Ranking

Ranking requires the evaluator to list all salespeople in order of their performance, beginning with the top performer. This appears to be a simple task, but in practice ranking is difficult. One problem is deciding how people are to be ranked. When a sales supervisor ranks subordinates, the manager may be using factors that are so vague and broadly defined that their application to the salesperson and the job

ranking Evaluation method in which all salespeople are listed in order of their performance

is questionable. Another concern is that the sales manager may put too much emphasis on personality traits when ranking subordinates. Finally, it has been pointed out that ranking fails to provide subordinates with the feedback needed for self-improvement.

Despite these weaknesses, ranking is still a popular performance evaluation method. A frequently used form of ranking is the *20-60-20 approach*. As employed by Goodyear and other companies, this ranking method involves listing subordinates from top to bottom, with the best performer at the top and the least satisfactory performer at the bottom. Then the list is divided into three groups. The top group includes the top 20 percent of performers, the bottom group are the lowest 20 percent of the performers, and the remainder are in the middle 60 percent.

20-60-20 approach Ranking method that divides salespeople into three groups made up of the top 20%, the middle 60%, and the lowest 20%

To illustrate this procedure, suppose that a field sales manager has ten subordinates. The manager begins by identifying the top performing salesperson, Jim Marshall. Then the poorest performing salesperson, Mike Reilly, is identified and placed at the bottom of the list. The process continues in this manner until all ten salespeople have been ranked. After reviewing the list, the manager divides it into the three groups. Marshall and Sardi are in the top 20 percent, Tolson and Reilly are in the bottom 20 percent, and the remainder are in the middle 60 percent. The entire list is shown below:

1.	Jim Marshall	20%
2.	Beth Sardi	
3.	Jim Greene	
4.	Bob Russo	
5.	Sue Jensen	
6.	Larry Ruggeri	60%
7.	Walter Alton	
8.	Tom Carson	
9.	Carol Tolson	
10.	Mike Reilly	20%

Many companies use this procedure to identify people for special rewards and recognition (top 20 percent) or special corrective action (bottom 20 percent). Sometimes salary increases are tied to the ranking. For example, the average performers (middle 60 percent) may receive a 6 percent salary increase, the top 20 percent performers may receive a 9 percent increase, and the lowest 20 percent performers may receive a 3 percent increase

Although this procedure has the advantage of simplicity, it may not be the best method for evaluating salespeople. In addition to the ranking difficulties cited earlier, the procedure also has the weakness of being too structured. It may be impossible to rank everyone or to place them in the 20-60-20 groupings. For example, suppose four of the ten salespeople listed above are truly outstanding. Is it fair that Green and Russo receive a 6 percent increase when they are really not that much different from Marshall and Sardi, who have received a 9 percent increase? Similarly, Tolson and Reilly may be new salespeople who are performing satisfactorily given their levels of experience and knowledge. In fact, they may even be performing better than other salespeople higher on the list when their inexperience is taken into consideration.

Rating Scales

rating scales
Evaluation method in which behavior factors and performance criteria are established and salespeople are evaluated on the extent to which they meet the criteria

Rating scales, another widely used sales evaluation method, identify specific desired traits, behavior factors, or performance criteria. Subordinate salespeople are rated on a scale based on the extent to which they exhibit the desired behavior, or the extent to which they meet the desired performance criteria.

To illustrate this approach, a few examples of criteria and a typical rating scale are shown below.

Criteria	Outstanding	Good	Satisfactory	Poor	Very poor
Manages time well				X	
Demonstrates leadership skills		X			
Shows maturity and judgment when dealing with others			X		
Enthusiastic about the job	X				
Motivated to perform well	X				

This brief example illustrates the advantage of a rating scale over rankings. Specific ways that a salesperson may improve or maintain desired performance levels are identified. In this illustration the salesperson needs help in managing time more effectively, and although judged satisfactory, this person could show improvement in dealings with others.

Unfortunately, rating scales also have a major weakness: the uneven interpretation of performance criteria and ratings. Unless each evaluator clearly understands what each criterion means and what the ratings mean, confusion and dissatisfaction can result. For instance, how does one define leadership skills? Problems also occur when sales performance evaluators interpret the ratings differently. For instance, one field sales manager may feel that "outstanding" is to be used only in a very few exceptional situations, whereas another may rate people "outstanding" more often. Differences between evaluators make it difficult to compare people rated by more than one sales manager.

Essays

essays Evaluation method in which sales managers write brief narratives that describe the performance of salespeople

A third approach is *essays*, or brief narratives by the sales manager that describe the performance of a salesperson. Although essays allow more flexibility and appear to be simple, they are not consistent and tend to be subjective. Each supervisor has a different writing style and emphasis.

Even when asked to respond to a specific question, the essay writer is likely to interpret the question in a unique way. Suppose that a company asked its sales supervisors to respond briefly to the following: "Please assess this salesperson's potential for advancement." One sales manager writes the following: "Jeff has excellent potential for advancement. He works hard, makes at least eight calls per day, gets his reports in on time, and is liked by his customers." Although these comments are relevant, they are related more to the person's performance of the present job than to the person's potential for advancement. The manager's interpretation of this question did not allow a response with information that would help assess the salesperson's promotion potential.

New Methods for Evaluating Salespeople

Because of the limitations of traditional sales evaluation methods, sales researchers and managers have been searching for better ways to evaluate sales performance. Several of the new approaches to sales performance appraisal use quantitative techniques. As noted earlier, some authorities suggest a long-run approach for evaluating a salesperson's profit potential. One method combines historical personnel and accounting data.[22] In a similar approach, a management consultant has suggested that multivariate statistical analysis can be used to assess the effect of a salesperson on volume, profit, and other pertinent measures.[23]

Still another sales expert has suggested that a sales manager should compare sales performance data over several years using trend line analysis.[24] He has pointed out that fitting a straight line to several years' sales data provides the sales manager with a more accurate picture of a salesperson's growth rate than does a year-by-year comparison. This mathematical procedure, which employs the statistical technique known as the "least-squares analysis," is relatively simple to use.

Several analytical approaches to the evaluation of field salespeople were compared in a recent study. The purpose was to determine if an improved analytical framework could be created. The researchers found that career cycles and multiple-regression models provided some insights into sales performance. Territory sales were found to increase with a salesperson's experience and with the number of calls.[25]

The most valuable findings on sales force performance were provided by a performance matrix. This format allows a sales manager to review and compare the accomplishments of salespeople along several dimensions at the same time. The researchers combined the key measures of sales revenue, contribution margin percentage, calls, and age in a single diagram. The inclusion of age in the matrix allows management to track career paths of salespeople. The matrix approach also highlights key differences in calls and growth rates across performance levels.[26]

BARS Behaviorally anchored rating scale; a five-step process used to evaluate sales personnel

A performance appraisal system that has been recommended for evaluation of sales performance is called a *behaviorally anchored rating scale (BARS)*.[27] Advocates of this approach have suggested that management can identify which behaviors are associated with achieving desired results. They contend that the BARS system will minimize the weaknesses of traditional sales performance methods.[28]

The BARS system follows a five-step development procedure that involves both supervisors who use BARS (raters) and their subordinates (ratees). The process begins with the description of specific critical incidents of effective and ineffective sales performance behavior. These critical incidents are then reviewed and refined into a smaller set of performance dimensions. The third step is to have another group of sales personnel review the performance dimensions. Then they are asked to rate

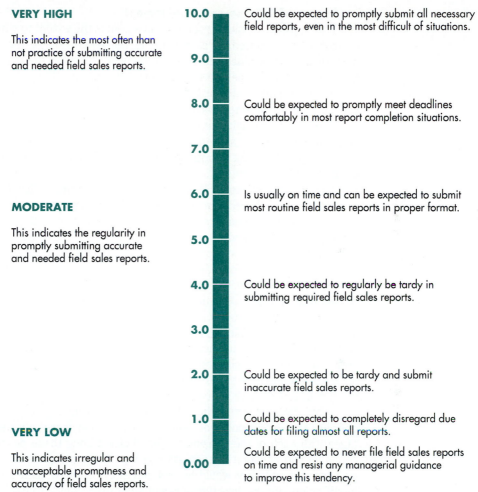

VERY HIGH

This indicates the most often than not practice of submitting accurate and needed field sales reports.

10.0 — Could be expected to promptly submit all necessary field reports, even in the most difficult of situations.

9.0

8.0 — Could be expected to promptly meet deadlines comfortably in most report completion situations.

7.0

MODERATE

This indicates the regularity in promptly submitting accurate and needed field sales reports.

6.0 — Is usually on time and can be expected to submit most routine field sales reports in proper format.

5.0

4.0 — Could be expected to regularly be tardy in submitting required field sales reports.

3.0

2.0 — Could be expected to be tardy and submit inaccurate field sales reports.

1.0 — Could be expected to completely disregard due dates for filing almost all reports.

VERY LOW

This indicates irregular and unacceptable promptness and accuracy of field sales reports.

0.00 — Could be expected to never file field sales reports on time and resist any managerial guidance to improve this tendency.

FIGURE 19-2 Sales Position Performance Dimension and Behavioral Anchors.

the critical incidents on a l-to-10-point scale. The final step is the emergence of the behaviorally anchored rating scales for the set of dimensions that remain. An example of a performance dimension and behavioral anchors is shown in Fig. 19-2.

Although the BARS approach has received only limited application to sales organizations, results have been promising. It has been observed that the BARS approach "offers potential means of reducing role conflict and role ambiguity in sales positions. Such a reduction could create greater job satisfaction, higher motivation, and lower salesforce turnover than is experienced with more traditional evaluation formats."[29]

INVOLVING THE SALESPERSON

As earlier chapters have noted, the current trend is toward greater involvement of salespeople in sales management activities. But how does this trend relate to sales force evaluation?

Degree of Salesperson Involvement

The degree of a salesperson's involvement is the extent to which the salesperson is allowed or required to participate in the evaluation of the salesperson's own performance: how much the salesperson is consulted in the evaluation process and how much detail the person is given about the results. Firms have typically adopted one of three policies toward salesperson involvement: complete participation, no participation, or selected participation.

The complete participation policy is based on the propositions that the salesperson and the company share a common interest in performance evaluation, that the salesperson has useful information to contribute, and that the evaluation is for the guidance of all concerned.

The no-participation policy is based on the premise that management is best qualified to set standards and evaluate results and that the results of sales evaluation are the property of management to be used in any way it sees fit. The selective participation policy seeks a middle ground between these two extremes.

The best policy for a particular company is the one that best suits its needs. These policies cannot be judged on ideal, social, or ethical grounds. One policy is not better or worse than the others because it is more democratic, or humane, or considerate. Rather, selection must be made based on the characteristics of the particular market, products, competition, customers, and sales force. In some companies, for example, a restricted budget for evaluation, a need for constant and speedy evaluation, or the necessity for the performance of current activities will not only justify a no-participation policy, but will make it the only policy possible. Each approach is applicable to particular sets of conditions and is a good or bad policy only in relation to how well it fits the conditions in which the policy operates.

Table 19-4 analyzes the advantages and disadvantages of the two extreme policies. The middle policy of selective participation shares advantages and disadvantages with each of the extremes. The choice among these policies depends on the condition and situation of each sales group. Many companies now operating with a no-participation policy would be well advised to review their approach to see if its modification—in the direction of selective or even complete participation—might not deliver substantial advantages. Both the selective participation policy and the complete participation policy have the following advantages:

1. They avoid the negative effect on the salesperson's morale that can occur when the person sees evaluation as secret, unilateral, and high-handed.
2. They provide the evaluation with an extra ingredient: the salesperson's intimate knowledge of the territory, customers, and of the person's own operations and habits.
3. They do not reward or punish a salesperson according to standards that the person does not fully understand or with which the person does not fully agree.
4. They make it easier for the salesperson to see specifically how performance can be improved because the person knows precisely how and by whom he or she will be evaluated.
5. They improve the communication of job requirements between the salesperson and the supervisor.
6. They communicate a genuine interest on the part of management in what the salesperson is doing.

TABLE 19-4 Advantages and Disadvantages of Complete and No-Participation Policies

Feature or condition	Complete participation policy		No-participation policy	
	Advantages	Disadvantages	Advantages	Disadvantages
Completeness of information	More complete, because of salesperson's data			Less complete, no salesperson's data
Accuracy of data	More complete, so data are usually more accurate			Less complete, so data are usually less accurate
Usefulness of evaluation for salesperson's development purposes	Can be used to a large extent			Can be used to a limited extent only
Probable attitude of salesperson toward evaluation system	Open, cooperative, and helpful in self-development			Secret, high-handed, unilateral, and difficult to use in self-development
Impact on salesperson's time		Taken from present activities by evaluation	Not taken from present activities by participation in evaluation	
Salesperson's relation with supervisor		Salesperson can challenge, debate standards and results	Salesperson cannot debate evaluation because the person knows nothing about it	
Cost of evaluation		Higher costs of collecting, processing, and analyzing salesperson's data	Cheaper because there are no data from salesperson to process and evaluate	
Time of evaluation cycle		More time because more data	Less time because less data	

MBO Management by objectives; a process of joint goal setting by salespeople and their managers

Participation by personnel in goal setting and performance evaluation can help reduce job-related ambiguity.[30] *Management by objectives (MBO)*—joint goal setting by salespeople and their managers—and similar participative programs can be used to encourage participation and communication between sales supervisors and subordinates during the evaluation process. When this happens, salespeople will perform better and be more satisfied with their jobs because they better understand the expectations for their jobs.

Some sales managers have learned that simply asking salespeople for their opinions and then following up on their suggestions where appropriate are at least as good at motivating salespeople as elaborate sales contests, expensive recognition rewards, and exotic meeting locations. However, surveys of salespeople and their first-line managers reveal that the views and opinions of salespeople often go largely ignored. When asked "How do you rate your company at listening to field concerns?" almost half of the sales reps responded "below average" or "one of the worst."[31]

Thus, sales managers must both involve their salespeople in sales evaluation and follow up on their input and suggestions.

Methods of Involving Salespeople

Companies that involve their salespeople in their own evaluations use several techniques to accomplish this purpose. Those used most often are participation in setting standards, evaluation interviews, self-evaluation by salespeople, appraisal of the evaluation program itself by salespeople, and having salespeople appraise their managers.

Setting Standards. Sales quotas and other performance standards can be achieved only if a company's salespeople accept them. This is the major reason why salespeople should be involved in the process of establishing sales performance standards. Although asking salespeople to assist in setting their quotas requires caution, participation is a means of increasing a salesperson's commitment to the quotas. Furthermore, research has shown that salespeople are reasonably accurate when they provide quota estimates.[32]

Another argument for involving salespeople in setting quotas is that each territory is different, and nobody is better qualified to assess the unique characteristics of a sales territory than the salesperson who covers it. A sales representative knows about the plans and problems of individual prospects and customers and can use this information in the establishment of realistic quotas. Further, because of direct contact with customers, salespeople can also provide valuable information about competitors.[33]

Evaluation Interviews. Most companies require their sales supervisors to review each person's evaluation in a personal interview after each evaluation cycle. This evaluation interview is intended to transmit evaluation results to the salesperson; to allow the person to clarify any necessary points, to object, or to raise questions; and to allow the supervisor and the salesperson to agree on the action that must be taken. Companies using this technique report that it is a very important management activity. They point out that it translates the evaluation into meaningful action by the salesperson and reemphasizes the company's performance standards. The evaluation interview is a strong motivator for the salesperson and a source of detailed market information for the supervisor. The supervisor has an additional chance to evaluate the salesperson and is given an opportunity to provide refresher training.

A sales manager must be thoroughly trained and prepared to conduct evaluation interviews. When a manager is not properly prepared, the evaluation interview can turn into a negative rather than a positive force. Careful preparation and the right frame of mind will increase the probability that the sales evaluation interview will aid the self-development of a salesperson. Suggested guidelines for conducting a sales evaluation interview are presented in Table 19-5.

Self-Evaluation by a Salesperson. Another technique that is used to increase a salesperson's participation in formal evaluation programs is to request the salesper-

TABLE 19-5 Guidelines for Sales Evaluation Interviews

1. **Do your homework! Prepare for the interview by thoroughly reviewing the sales rep's records and performance history.**
2. **Select the right place, where you will be alone, and the right time, when you are relaxed and feel helpful toward the subordinate.**
3. **Open the interview by establishing a relaxed atmosphere. Reassure the rep that the interview is to help him or her do a better job and that you are ready to help in any way you can.**
4. **Encourage the rep to talk. Listen carefully to what the rep has to say. Show your interest and check your own understanding by asking questions.**
5. **Present a balanced review of the person's work performance, citing positive factors as well as those needing improvement. It is usually best to begin with a positive factor. Some interviews use the "sandwich technique" where strong and weak points are alternated.**
6. **Establish and maintain throughout the interview a logical, helping orientation. To the greatest extent possible, deal with facts, not hunches or opinions. Remind the rep that the purpose is to help the rep do a better job. A "shape up or ship out" interview is not an evaluation development interview. It is a disciplinary interview. Remind the rep that you are there to help solve problems.**
7. **Do not end the interview until you and the rep have agreed to a remedial action plan, including what both of you will do to help improve specific weaknesses brought out in the evaluation.**
8. **Be careful not to make, or even imply, promises, such as a salary raise or promotion, that you are not sure you can keep.**

son to perform the same evaluation with the same standards as the evaluator. The evaluations are compared and form the basis for a salesperson-supervisor conference and planning session. Interestingly enough, when this technique is employed, the salesperson is usually more critical than the supervisor is.

Self-evaluation draws a salesperson's attention to specific aspects of sales performance and highlights clearly what changes must be made. In particular, an honest, penetrating assessment of an individual's own performance may help put an end to a sales slump. For example, one salesperson found that he was too much of a "nice guy" to his customers. He was quick to accept prospects' objections. As a result of his self-evaluation, he resolved to be more assertive in selling situations.

When properly managed, this technique also makes it easier for a supervisor to work with salespeople on their evaluations and to attain their enthusiastic, constructive cooperation for improving their performance.

Appraisal of the Evaluation Program by Salespeople. Involvement is also achieved when a manager solicits salespeople's appraisal of the evaluation system itself, either informally or formally. Informally, when traveling with sales personnel, the supervisor might seek their reactions to, and comments about, the evaluation program. Is it measuring the right activities? In the right terms? Over the proper time period? Is there something the salesperson wants to report about performance that the plan does not allow? Sometimes companies also provide their salespeople with the opportunity to review the sales evaluation system in writing.

For example, one sales authority has developed an extensive questionnaire designed to provide insights from salespeople about various sales management activities and programs that are related to sales effectiveness. Included are salespeople's perceptions of marketing strategy, goods and services, sales jobs and activities, goals, organization, support systems, compensation, and time allocation. The sales authority who developed this assessment tool feels that results will be valid because salespeople are knowledgeable and will be encouraged to provide truthful responses since they have a vested interest in the outcome.[34]

Appraisal of Sales Managers by Salespeople.

An interesting trend in recent years has been to have salespeople appraise their sales managers. IBM, RCA, Syntex, and Libbey-Owens-Ford are some of the companies that are incorporating a subordinate appraisal process into the overall sales evaluation system. They feel that subordinate appraisals can be used to improve managerial effectiveness, to evaluate and promote personnel, to alter corporate culture, to reduce costs of promotion decisions, and to reassign workloads.[35]

Evaluation of sales managers by their salespeople is also being used to develop training programs for sales managers. It is suggested that sales managers seek out and make use of regular feedback on their performance from the people they supervise. At GE, for instance, a manager's peers and subordinates are asked to fill out an evaluation questionnaire whenever a sales manager is scheduled to attend a training program. The results are used to show managers how they compare to other sales managers and to structure training activities.[36]

Behavioral Self-Management

BSM Behavioral self-management; a process whereby a person actively implements specific procedures to control his or her own behavior

Because sales force evaluation systems are costly and time-consuming, and may result in subjective appraisals, it has been suggested that *behavioral self-management (BSM)* be used to control the methods salespeople use to achieve results.[37] The focus of this approach is on promoting autonomy and self-control so that salespeople manage their own behavior. It is believed that this approach would be less expensive to sales organizations than outcome-based or behavior-based control systems that require external monitoring and direction.

Behavioral self-management has been described as "a process whereby a person actively implements specific procedures to control his or her own behavior."[38] Selling is a complex activity, so encouraging self-management in a selling environment is likely to be particularly effective. Salespeople have more detailed information about their customers than their managers do. Allowing them to decide what sales approach to take with a customer and how to manage the selling process is likely to improve their sales effectiveness.

One of the critical tools for behavioral self-management is self-monitoring. This requires that a person observe his or her own actions and record their occurrence. Diaries, tally sheets, graphs, and charts can be used to measure behavior. For example, a salesperson will learn much about time allocation by recording the amount of time spent traveling, making sales calls, preparing reports, and so forth. The simple act of observing one's own behavior may result in meaningful changes in the behavior being monitored.

Self-monitoring, goal setting which focuses on specific behavior changes, and other behavioral self-management techniques should be encouraged by sales manag-

SALES MANAGEMENT IN PRACTICE

WAL-MART STORES INC.

Wal-Mart, America's biggest retailer, has grown from a small store in Arkansas in 1963 to 1880 stores with annual sales around $55 billion. Wal-Mart's sheer economic power has allowed the company to exercise channel control not available to others. For example, Johnson & Johnson, NCR Corporation, IBM, and other suppliers have set up nearby offices to serve the retail giant.

Traditionally, Wal-Mart has bought from independent salespeople representing several manufacturers. These intermediaries received commissions that ranged from 2 to 3 percent of a transaction's value. In 1991, however, Wal-Mart announced that it was going to change its policy and only work directly with its suppliers. The stated incentive for the policy change was to enable the company to react quickly to changes in the marketplace and to ensure steady streams of merchandise. The new policy is a major shakeup for some manufacturers, but requests from an account like Wal-Mart simply cannot be refused.

While increased flexibility and speed in acquiring merchandise are the stated goals of Wal-Mart's new buying policy, lower prices may also result when saved commission expenses are passed on to customers. Although the new policy may seem like a win-win situation, there is at least one group of "losers"—the manufacturers' representatives. Groups of representatives have threatened Wal-Mart with lawsuits, citing unfair trade practices. Whether or not Wal-Mart ends up in court remains to be seen, but in similar cases, awards against companies have been large. WD-40, for example, was ordered by a California court to pay $10.3 million for replacing eight outside sales agencies with an in-house sales force. Although there was a termination clause in WD-40's contracts with the agencies, the jury held that WD-40 had given the agencies verbal assurances that their services would continue to be used. Clearly, the termination side of evaluation must be handled carefully.

---

ers. Managers can help their salespeople learn how to control their own behavior through setting specific goals, monitoring their progress, and identifying strategies and actions to achieve goals. Self-management by salespeople can be a key contributing factor in achieving sales organizational goals.

EVALUATION FOLLOWUP

If the formal sales evaluation program is a good one, it will show the specific selling activities each person did well or poorly, and will suggest the reasons behind these results. A good evaluation program indicates where changes are and are not required to improve each person's selling performance. Therefore, unless something is done about the evaluation, unless it results in worthwhile change, it will have been a waste of money, time, and effort. The evaluation process must include followup, which is the identification of the remedial actions to be taken and the check by the supervisor that the remedial plan is being followed.

Followup is necessary because remedial activities frequently involve a change in work habits or make the job more difficult or less pleasant. When left to one's own devices, everyone tends to resist change by returning to old habits. Without followup, the salesperson will often revert to past practices and repeat the same mistakes.

When reviewing sales performance and discussing sales behavior changes with salespeople, a manager must be both assertive and responsive.[39] Assertiveness provides an approach for giving negative feedback, a task many sales managers resist. The sales manager must be direct and tell the subordinate what is deficient, what needs to be done, and why.

At the same time, the sales manager must also be responsive to the subordinate. The manager must provide the salesperson with an opportunity to explain how he or she sees the situation. Then, the two can reach an agreement on the problem.

The desired result of the discussion between the salesperson and the manager is the development of an improvement plan. This is an action plan that identifies who is to do what and when. Also included is a date for review.

A procedure many companies use to ensure evaluation followup is a postevaluation report from the sales supervisor to a superior. The report should present a balanced view of the salesperson's performance. If the report is too critical, a salesperson may become discouraged. In contrast, a report that is too positive might give a salesperson a false sense of security. A balanced report notes positive achievements and summarizes the steps needed to improve specific aspects of performance. Then, subsequent progress reports are prepared and submitted.

A similar followup procedure involves making special entries on a salesperson's regular activity report. These entries state the problems the last evaluation showed, the plan for correction, steps taken to solve the problems, and results to date. When traveling with a salesperson, the supervisor may take advantage of the opportunity to review carefully the progress and current status of problems that appeared in the evaluation. Finally, the salesperson submits special reports to the supervisor concerning the specific problems uncovered by the evaluation.

TRAINING THE EVALUATORS

Evaluation is such a complex process that supervisors and other executives who undertake it must be trained and guided in its use. A person who is skilled at doing something is not always the best person to appraise another person's performance of that task. A top-flight sales executive is not necessarily a great evaluator of other people's sales performance. A manager must be trained, counseled, and guided on how to evaluate the performance of others effectively.

Alcoa developed a performance evaluation program that involves salespeople in determining their own sales goals and setting individual performance objectives. This system was designed to involve the salesperson and to open up the lines of communication between sales supervisors and subordinates. Before the system could be implemented, however, Alcoa's sales supervisors had to be trained. In fact, "thorough training in conducting performance appraisals was seen as the most important element of success in the program."[40]

Required Evaluation Skills

Good evaluators must possess certain skills, experience, and insights. Abilities include the following:

1. How to assess the significance of each performance measure being used (for example, that the number of promotions secured with customers is in part a measure of the person's aggressiveness)

2. How to spot meaningful patterns of results (for example, whether a salesperson's calls per day have been trending steadily up or down)
3. How to identify the significance of interrelationships between several performance indexes (for example, the number of new accounts opened and the person's expenses)
4. How to use performance measures to infer conclusions about the person and his or her selling skills (for example, that most accounts and orders are small may at least imply that one is not skillful in handling large accounts)
5. How to cross-check evaluation evidence by placing one set of observations against another (for example, the comparison of a salesperson's activity reports to field visits with salespeople)
6. How to explain problems and deficiencies to salespeople and work out remedial actions with them (for example, the preparation of a revised call schedule so that the salesperson allocates selling time properly)
7. How to be as objective and unbiased as possible, by evaluating a salesperson against established performance standards; how to avoid judging a salesperson on the basis of one's own record or according to personal likes and dislikes (for example, not expecting an inexperienced salesperson to handle price objections as effectively as the sales manager can after many years of selling experience)
8. How to cope with the different personalities and behavior patterns of salespeople (for example, remaining calm and under control when a "hothead" becomes angry when a performance weakness is pointed out)[41]

Training Methods

The skills and insights of sales performance evaluation must be transmitted to evaluators by some form of training. Methods used to impart the necessary knowledge and skills to evaluators are seminars, evaluation manuals, and personal observation and critique.

Seminars. Supervisors who are about to assume evaluation responsibility are gathered in a group for a seminar. Under the direction of skilled evaluators, they study cases, problems, and exercises in sales evaluation. They hear lectures and instructions and exchange their views and insights with experienced evaluators and their peers.

Evaluation Manuals. Manuals provide sales evaluators with new information and with a reference source during the evaluation process. Collective company experience is assembled in a "how-to" instruction manual that new evaluators must master and experienced evaluators are expected to review periodically. Someone, usually the sales training manager, is responsible for revising the manual as procedures and conditions change.

Observation and Critique. In this procedure, an experienced evaluator is assigned to a new evaluator, and together they work through a number of individual evaluations. The experienced evaluator advises the novice on the appropriate evaluations to be made.

SUMMARY OF LEARNING GOALS

1. **Specify the steps in the development and management of a sales evaluation program.**

   The steps in the development of a sales evaluation program include: (1) making a detailed description of the sales job; (2) writing the job description; (3) establishing performance standards; (4) evaluating and determining reasons for salesperson performance above or below standards; (5) taking action for improvement.

2. **Explain the reasons for and difficulties associated with sales force evaluation.**

   Sales force evaluation is performed in order to discover which salespeople need to improve, to evaluate salesperson standards, to spot those who are ready for job changes, to keep job descriptions current, to supply evidence about salespeople who should be terminated, and to cross-check sales policies. Sales force evaluation is limited by the isolated nature of the salesperson's job, the difficulty of finding and relating performance factors, the lack of control over some performance conditions, and the use of fact and judgment.

3. **Describe sales quotas and performance measures and how they should be established.**

   Sales quotas and performance measures are standards by which managers evaluate salesperson performance. They are frequently derived from a company's sales forecast, and are based on salesperson input (What did the salesperson do?) or salesperson output (How did the salesperson do?).

4. **List information sources used in evaluation.**

   There are a number of sources of evaluative information. Major sources are company records, customers, reports from salespeople, sales managers' field visits, a manager's personal insights, and external sources.

5. **Understand why sales performance should be evaluated at the lowest possible level of supervision.**

   The benefits of sales performance evaluations being conducted at the lowest level possible are the following: (1) The salesperson-supervisor relationship is strengthened, (2) mutual commitment is enhanced, (3) supervisor responsibility is established, and (4) communication of goals and remedies is clear and direct.

6. **Explain the factors that determine the best frequency for formal sales evaluation programs.**

   Three factors determine the best frequency for formal sales evaluation programs. These factors are (1) the time required to evaluate, (2) the intrusion of evaluation that can be tolerated, and (3) the time required for remedial action.

7. **Outline the various methods of evaluation.**

   The most commonly used evaluation methods are ranking, rating scales, and essays. Other, newer evaluation methods include multivariate statistical analysis, trend line analysis, career cycles and multiple-regression models, performance matrices, and behaviorally anchored rating scales.

8. **Discuss the alternative policies for involving salespeople in evaluation programs.**

    The alternatives for involving salespeople in the evaluation process are complete participation, no participation, and selected participation. Complete participation is based on the propositions that the salesperson and the company share a common interest in performance evaluation, that the salesperson has useful information to contribute, and that the evaluation is for the guidance of all concerned. The no-participation policy is based on the premise that management is best qualified to set standards and evaluate results and that results of sales evaluation should be used by management in any way they see fit. Selected participation is on a middle ground between these two extremes.

REVIEW QUESTIONS

1. Outline the steps in the development of a sales evaluation program. Group these steps into planning and managing stages.
2. What is the purpose of a sales force control system? For what types of selling situations is an outcome-based control system appropriate? For what types of selling situations is a behavior-based control system appropriate?
3. Identify the major input standards of sales evaluation. How is each activity measured?
4. Identify the major output standards of sales evaluation. How is each activity measured?
5. At what level should sales evaluations be conducted? Justify your opinion.
6. What is meant by an evaluation time cycle? How is this concept used by sales management?
7. What are some of the potential disadvantages of using a ranking system to evaluate salespeople? What special problems does the 20-60-20 version of the ranking system present?
8. What advantage does a rating scale have over a ranking system? What are the major weaknesses of rating scales?
9. What are the advantages of an essay-writing approach to salesperson evaluation? What are the disadvantages?
10. What skills and information are important for an evaluator to possess? How should evaluators be trained?

DISCUSSION QUESTIONS

1. Interview a sales manager. Inquire about the input and output measures used by the manager's firm. Report your findings to the class.
2. Suppose a company routinely boosts sales quotas assigned to its representatives by more than the rate of inflation. What is the likely effect on the sales force? How can related problems be overcome?
3. Field visits are a popular source of information in the sales evaluation process. How can a sales manager improve the quality of information that results from these visits? What rules should be set for field visits? Discuss.
4. Suppose a company has a policy of putting on probation sales personnel ranked in the lowest 10 percent of its sales force. If the representatives do not move out of this group following the evaluation time cycle, they are terminated. Relate this evaluation system to the material in Chap. 19. What is your opinion of this approach? Discuss.
5. If an A-B-C-D-F grading system is thought of as a rating scale, what are the standard "performance criteria" in most of your classes? What general disadvantages of rating

scales apply to the typical grading system? Have you been evaluated in any unique ways by teachers striving to eliminate these disadvantages? Explain.

**E T H I C A L
D I L E M M A**

There is a human tendency to like some people more than others. As this chapter suggested, sales evaluation must be based on objective standards, not subjective opinions or prejudices. How can a sales manager overcome personal feelings when evaluating sales personnel?

SALES MANAGEMENT CASE

IBM—Responding to Its Environment

IBM is making changes in order to better compete in its rapidly growing industry, and these changes have placed evaluation in the limelight. The computer industry has been invaded by many small, "lean and mean" companies that can respond quickly to customer needs and run efficiently enough to provide products at prices lower than IBM's. The early 1990s also forced IBM to operate in a tough economy in which consumers tended to delay purchases of durable goods.

The situations described above have been blamed for a lower market value for IBM stock, sluggish revenues (and a sales deficit for the first time ever), and decreasing worldwide market share and return on stockholders' equity. IBM has responded by doing what so many companies are forced to do in hard times: reduce the number of employees. Resorting to cutbacks was very uncomfortable for IBM because of the company's no-layoffs policy.

IBM has used voluntary buyout and early retirement incentives and attrition to cut its work force by over 50,000 employees. The company has fired marginal employees, but it has not violated its no-layoff policy. IBM developed a numerical ranking system used to evaluate performance, and 70 percent of the employees leaving in 1992 scored in the bottom half of the scale.

The job cutbacks are a temporary solution to IBM's problems. Looking into the future, IBM is restructuring itself into a confederation of small companies. This structure is aimed at enhancing competitiveness and enabling the firm to respond quickly to market threats and opportunities.

Cutbacks and decentralization have implications for all employees, but the IBM sales force is especially affected. In the mid-1980s, IBM's U.S. sales force of 20,000 delivered $26 billion in revenues; in 1990 25,000 salespeople produced only $27 billion. Disappointed CEO John Akers is purported to have said that he did not get a good return on the 5000 extra salespeople. It must be recognized, however, that the situation might have been much worse if the extra salespeople had not been hired.

IBM watchers blame the corporation's troubles on both internal and external factors. Some observers are pessimistic about the future of the company. Many wonder, too, what the implications of IBM's activities are for other firms; because the company has been known for its paternalism, its layoff-like behavior might lead other companies to reduce employee security. The actions of IBM will not go unnoticed. Rather, events at this American giant will have a ripple effect on the business environment across the country.

Questions

1. What factors could explain the failure of IBM's increased sales force to turn around the company?

2. Who should perform the numerical ranking of IBM sales employees? On what criteria should the evaluations be based?

3. If you were currently applying for a sales job at IBM, what features would you find attractive about the company? What would be potential drawbacks to working there? Could IBM's recent situation hurt its future recruiting efforts? Explain.

CHAPTER *20*

SALES AND COST ANALYSIS

LEARNING GOALS

- Understand the nature, objectives, and difficulties of sales control.
- Outline the sales control process.
- Explain how sales analysis assists sales managers.
- Understand the nature of cost analysis and the steps involved.
- Explain the concepts related to profitability analysis.
- Identify the principles of sales and cost analysis.
- Describe sales audits.

THE COST-EFFECTIVE SALES FORCE

When Hewlett-Packard (HP) automated its sales force, it had in mind the goals of improved customer service and productivity. By equipping every salesperson with a portable computer, HP achieved both its goals.

Before the automation, HP had experimented for awhile with measuring the activities of its sales force with watches that went off every 43 minutes, at which time the salespeople were to record what they were doing. From this data, the company determined that salespeople were spending only 26 percent of their time with customers; the remaining time was spent in meetings, travel, and administrative tasks. Aware of its own increasing cost per order dollar, HP wanted to improve both the quality and the quantity of salesperson time with customers.

Currently, all HP salespeople are equipped with portable computers and modems, and they can use any phone to access office data. By decreasing travel time to and from the office, salespeople increased their selling time by 27 percent. There has also been a 10 percent increase in order performance, which may have been caused by the sales force's enhanced ability to meet customer needs.

HP's centralized data base includes information from field sales, order management, direct marketing, field service, and central marketing. The data are easily accessible and interconnected, and salespeople not only obtain information but can also submit orders through their portable computers.

HP telemarketers receive as many as

30,000 inquiries per month. With the new system, telemarketers classify the inquiries and enter that information into the data base. A promising lead is sent to a salesperson's portable computer, where it stays until the salesperson takes action on it. When the salesperson does follow up on the lead, this too is recorded in the data base, and a "closed loop" of information is formed. All known data on customers are kept in one place in a complete profile.

As a result of the automation, inquiry fulfillment takes only one week, whereas it previously took six weeks. Cost per order has been cut by 10 percent. Less measurable, but no less important, is the extent to which customers are being better served.

Chapter 20 is about sales and cost analysis. The topic is a timely one—in a recent five-year period, the median cost per sales call for the consumer, industrial, and service industries went up by 77, 40, and 35 percent, respectively. With these rising costs, the sales force must become more efficient. Like Hewlett-Packard, companies must find ways to make their sales forces cost-effective. This involves integrating sales force

activities with inventory control, database management, and other company systems. In the increasingly complex field of selling, this effort is becoming more and more challenging.[1]

CHAPTER OVERVIEW

sales control
Comprehensive effort encompassing sales and cost analysis and including such periodic projects as sales audits

The *sales control* function at any company includes sales and cost analyses. Some companies also do more advanced projects such as sales audits. These activities attempt to measure past performance to achieve better resource utilization in the future. The results of cost or profitability analysis form the basis of sales management decision making about product, account, and/or territorial emphasis, and may even result in elimination decisions.

Sales analysis involves the examination of a company's sales results to improve sales forecasting accuracy and help direct future sales efforts. The second component of sales control, cost analysis, has as its thrust the investigation of the costs of selling. Cost and contribution factors are analyzed on a unit-by-unit basis to estimate the contributions of various sales units to a company's overall profitability. Both sales and cost analysis are aimed at identifying problems and opportunities so that sales operations can be streamlined and resources redirected.

A particular concern of sales management is that, as more and more sales data become available, decision makers must learn to use information effectively. Sales managers must not lose sight of the fact that data analysis is a tool, not an end in itself. It should be used not as a substitute for, but as an aid in, decision making. As computers make more and more detailed sales data printouts possible, sales managers must learn how to integrate the newly available data into traditional sales management functions.

To help provide this integration, companies have begun to carry out sales audits. This procedures involves an in-depth scrutiny of the entire sales operation. In contrast to ongoing sales analysis, which tends to emphasize tactical considerations, a sales audit questions organizational issues and strategic directions.

THE NATURE OF SALES CONTROL

Sales control is a key responsibility of sales management. Far from being an after-the-fact investigation to determine when, where, how, and why things went wrong, sales control aims to effect midcourse corrections where appropriate. It is the task of sales management to shape the controllable elements of the sales effort in such a way as to realize the sales objectives of the firm.

The nature and focus of sales control has changed in recent years. In the past, the job of the sales manager was to achieve the sales organization's volume goals and to accomplish this at a reasonable cost. The sales control challenge is more complex today. Reaching sales volume targets and controlling sales expenses are still important, but sales managers and their selling organizations are also expected to contribute to the company's bottom line by improving the profitability of sales.[2] Further, they are expected to integrate sales activities with research and development, finance, and other business functions.

Objectives of Sales Control

Sales control is designed to keep a firm's sales efforts on the prescribed course. It makes sales planning a meaningful endeavor. To accomplish this, marketing and sales intelligence are needed. Data about markets and sales activities must be gathered, assessed, and transmitted from the field sales force to management. To obtain the best results salespeople and their managers must be aware of the intelligence-gathering process and the objectives of sales control.[3]

The measurement of sales performance is an important objective of sales control. Effective control requires feedback that enables an evaluation of the sales results achieved in the marketplace. This task has to be done at a level of detail appropriate for remedial action, but even the measurement process itself may produce results. In fact, anything that is measured is better-performed. Accurate measurements also form the basis for any reward system. This encourages the sales force to supply timely feedback.

A second objective of sales control is to spot problems early. The feedback system must operate smoothly, and timely reports must be generated on a frequent basis. The tighter the control system, the less impact a threatening event such as a competitive price drop will have before it is discovered and counteracted. Continuous feedback also helps detect a deterioration of a salesperson's performance, which may enable the supervisor to engage in corrective counseling.

A third objective of a well-functioning sales control system is to identify emerging opportunities quickly, before they become evident to competitors. The company can then enter the market with an appropriate offering before an industry-wide onrush sets in. This third objective of the sales control system requires an entrepreneurial spirit and a highly sensitive ability to read the market; sales managers are uniquely qualified to undertake this dynamic aspect of sales control.

Sales control asks, "Why did it happen?" Ideally it also answers the question. This analysis leads to the logical questioning of what the company can do to optimize results under the current circumstances. Sales control goes beyond mere diagnosis to both initiate and guide strategic and tactical decisions.

The Sales Control Process

As shown in Fig. 20-1, the activities involved in sales control take place in a three-step sequence:

1. Goals are set.
2. Results are compared with goals and investigated.
3. Corrective action is taken.

The establishment of goals is part of the sales planning and sales budgeting processes. Sales planning sets sales volume targets, or sales quotas, that act as standards against which actual performance is evaluated.

Sales budgeting also sets target cost levels and provides budgetary allowances for the various types of sales-related activities. The budgeted amounts permit comparison of actual spending levels with anticipated expenditures.

In the second step of the sales control process, actual sales and costs are compared with the goals. Significant sustained differences indicate that something is amiss. Consistent substantial sales above quota and/or spending levels that are significantly below the budgeted allocations might bring into question the accuracy of the planning and budgeting process. On the other hand, continuous underachievement of sales volume or excessive spending suggests that the process is out of control.

The causes for the divergences have to be identified so that action may be taken. The data have to be broken down to reveal their true composition. If action is taken without first investigating the reasons for the deviations, more harm than good may result. If a region's performance is disappointing, the blame may be laid on the regional sales manager and could lead to dismissal. However, this action would only worsen the situation if the true problem were caused by underpricing by the competition.

FIGURE 20-1 Sales Control Process.

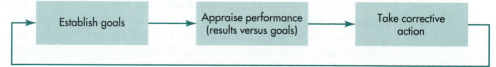

Once sales management is satisfied that the causes of the over- or underachievement have been correctly documented, it should take action. Two options exist: Modify the goals or alter the performance. Goal modification entails revision of the sales plan or sales budget. This should be done if events have rendered the original plan inadequate. Environmental scanning reveals such shifts in external factors. By contrast, alteration of performance should be done if the goals remain unchallenged but results are not up to par.

Difficulties of Sales Control

Sales control is not easy, and even those companies that have extensive sales control procedures realize that the difficulties involved will make the control process less than ideal. One problem is the lack of control over external factors. Sales results are almost always affected, for better or for worse, by external conditions over which salespeople and their managers have little or no control. The country is in economic recession. The Federal Trade Commission begins an investigation of industry sales practices. A major competitor lowers prices. It is impossible to design sales control systems that are flexible enough to handle all of the possible external factors.

A second issue is the difficulty of identifying performance variables. There are many components of the marketing mix, and it is very difficult to identify and isolate specific performance variables that contribute to sales success or failure. It is often not possible to pinpoint exactly what creates sales and profits for a specific customer, product, or market. Is it a product feature, aggressive sales tactics, or a very competitive price? Sometimes even the most experienced sales manager does not know for sure.

A third difficulty is that the information needed to measure and control sales activities may be unavailable or difficult and costly to obtain. Even the best marketing information system has limits, especially when one tries to acquire hard-to-get information such as buyers' purchasing plans and motives. Further, sales information gathering is complicated by the time lag between sales planning and marketplace responses. While difficult, the information can—and must—be obtained.

SALES ANALYSIS

A comprehensive sales analysis program is crucial to the development, implementation, and control of a company's sales policies and activities. Sales managers need timely reports that highlight challenges and opportunities in a condensed fashion. These reports provide them with a critical edge in spotting trends, directing sales resources, and integrating sales force activities with other company functions.

Sales analysis supplies management with background information for sales planning. As the sales plan is being implemented, sales analysis continually compares actual with planned results. An evaluation program reviews both the nature and extent of sales force efforts and the influence of external variables. Once the degree to which controllable and uncontrollable factors are affecting the results has been determined, sales management can decide whether to take corrective action or to revise the sales plan, or both.

SALES MANAGEMENT IN PRACTICE

T & K ROOFING COMPANY

In 1988, Iowa-based T & K Roofing Company had a problem. Profit margins had gone down, and rejected bids had gone up. To determine the reasons behind these disturbing trends, T & K management devised a Lost-Job Survey that was sent out to prospects who had rejected the company's bids.

T & K's Lost-Job Survey serves several purposes. It is a sales force evaluation tool, asking question about the quality of salespeople's presentations, relationship-building efforts, competence, and appearance. It also provides marketing intelligence, and it helps future sales efforts in that it is one more contact with the prospect.

T & K has mailed out around fifteen hundred surveys over the past few years, and the thousand that were returned have proven very informative. One is-

sue that came out of the surveys was that some customers desired a different product than what T & K offered, and in response to this, T & K began offering additional types of roofs. Also, it was determined that T & K salespeople were only selling part of the company's product line; products providing high commissions were being pushed harder. To alleviate this problem T & K changed sales force compensation from commission to salary, hoping that salespeople would focus on customer needs rather than commission checks.

Since 1988, the competition T & K faces has intensified, but even so, the company has managed to double its sales. Effective sales control measures such as T & K's Lost-Job Survey are invaluable resources for companies who want to find out what is going on in the field, and why.

Sales analysis must provide a sufficiently detailed picture of sales activity so that the manager can take the appropriate action. A data gathering and reporting system that will include selective sales information in the categories of products, markets, customers, and personnel must be developed. After information has been collected, sales managers can pursue analyses in such specific areas as net sales, sales territories, goods and services, market segments, and specific accounts.[4]

Components of Sales Analysis

Sales analysis concentrates on the revenue component of the sales equation. It involves the gathering, classifying, comparing, and studying of company sales data.

Sales analysis begins with data gathering. Strictly speaking, this is not part of the analytical effort, but the quantity and quality of data vitally affect the quality of sales analysis. Without proper data gathering, sales analysis would suffer from the well-known "garbage in garbage out" phenomenon.

Many sources of information for sales analysis exist. Sources include data from the marketing information system (see Chap. 8), other sources of sales information such as those described in Chap. 19, and internal sales information derived from the company's accounting and financial systems.

Data are sometimes specifically collected for sales analysis. With the growing availability of specialized software, many sales managers are able to compile their own sales data and analysis systems. They are able to perform a wide variety of analytical procedures that add to their monitoring, analytical, and management control capabilities.[5]

In fact, the breadth and depth of modern sales analysis depends on the availability and use of an effective "sales tracking" software package. To illustrate what can be accomplished, consider the features of Sales Analysis, a software package developed and marketed by Computer Associates International.[6] Sales Analysis helps sales managers to do the following:

- Automatically retrieve and combine sales data from a firm's data base
- Quickly determine how sales compare from period to period by displaying a report, which provides cumulative periodic totals for key sales indicators such as quantity sold, invoice amount, average invoice amount, and so forth
- Find out exactly what was sold, to whom it was sold, and how much was charged for each transaction
- Store information and produce summary reports based on weekly, biweekly, monthly, bimonthly, quarterly, semiannual, or annual results
- Isolate specific trends or problem areas in a company's sales performance by creating, defining, and printing summary reports that combine and organize selected sales details
- Produce summary reports which compile item sales by customer, customer sales by item, items sales by salesperson, and so forth
- Compare actual sales to forecasts by storing and printing budget information within a firm's summary reports
- Create and print graphs and charts and perform additional analysis

As the above discussion shows, the primary task of sales analysis is to convert raw sales data into actionable information for sales managers. This process involves editing and structuring the data, as well as tabulating and cross-tabulating them. It also involves breaking them down in various ways. A number of comparisons are possible: Current data can be compared with past data to measure their change over time; current results of different territories, accounts, or products can be compared with each other; and/or internal performance data can be compared with external measures. The final step in sales analysis is interpretation, or drawing conclusions from the data.

Ratios and Performance Indexes

Many sales managers use ratios or performance indexes to analyze sales performance.[7] To calculate a ratio one divides one number (numerator) by another (denominator) to express a relationship. For instance, a student's grade point average is a ratio determined by dividing the number of quality points earned in courses taken by the number of credit hours. Ratios can then be used to compare performance of different units. Susan Marston had a semester 3.40 grade point average and made the Dean's list; Bob Bates had a 2.72 grade point average; Mark Parker had a 1.45 grade point average (2.00 is a "C") and was placed on academic probation for the coming semester. As this example illustrates, ratios can be used not only to make comparisons, but also to suggest specific actions whether they be rewards (Dean's list) or discipline (academic probation).

In Chap. 19 many of the performance measures used in sales management were listed. Some of these take the form of ratios. For example, one measure of a salesperson's effective use of time is calls per day. Other examples are average order size, ratio of orders to calls, and sales against quota or sales budgets.

Sometimes ratios are converted to indexes to establish a common numeric reference. This involves multiplying the ratio by a number, usually 100 or 1000. For instance, the Consumer Price Index is perhaps the best known index used in business and economic analysis. Some of the performance indexes that have been developed for sales analysis include the following:

$$\frac{\text{Sales this period}}{\text{Sales in prior period}} \times 100$$

$$\frac{\text{Sales}}{\text{Quota}} \times 100$$

$$\frac{\text{Sales}}{\text{Budget}} \times 100$$

$$\frac{\text{Closes}}{\text{Calls}} \times 1000$$

sales batting average Sales analysis index formed by dividing a salesperson's closes by the salesperson's calls and multiplying this result by 1000

For example, the closes/calls × 1000 index, which is often called the *sales batting average,* is used to compare salespersons' effectiveness in closing sales. Salesperson Joe Adams made 170 calls during a given month from which 35 sales resulted. His sales batting average was 210 [(35/170) × 1000] for the month. In contrast, Linda Clark's sales batting average from the same month was 340 [(62 sales/185 calls) × 1000]. Assuming territory conditions and market potentials of the two territories are roughly the same, this analysis reveals that the sales closing performance of Linda Clark was stronger than that of Joe Adams.

Ratios and performance indexes are used in sales analysis to compare the performance of one company to another, to compare performance between sales units, and to identify trends. However, to obtain an accurate performance comparison, it may be necessary to remove seasonal and irregular elements from the data. Sales researcher Dick Berry has developed a technique that involves the calculation of sales performance ratio values after irregularities and seasonal factors have been removed from a time series of sales data.[8] The values are then converted to an index base referenced to 100. The index series that results can then be used to show how each period's sales relate to all others. Thus, specific sales and market changes can be identified.

COST ANALYSIS

The sales and accounting functions are brought together in the process of cost analysis. This process is carried out to measure and consequently improve both the efficiency and effectiveness of sales operations. Costs have to be classified and categorized to reveal points for improvements. The natural account data supplied by the accounting function has to be transformed into functional cost data.

What Is Cost Analysis?

Cost analysis can be described as the gathering, classifying, comparing, and study of company cost data as they relate to the profit contribution of the sales function. Gathering cost data is the responsibility of the accounting function. Sales managers typically do not get involved in collecting this information. External data are used for comparative purposes only. These external cost data are usually not sold commercially by specialized agencies (as are sales data) but are made available to members or subscribers of a regular service program by trade associations and trade publications.

Internal cost accounting records also constitute secondary data because they are generated for accounting purposes and sales management has no control over their compilation. Raw accounting data need to be translated from natural (accounting) to functional (sales) accounts. Once the data have been reworked to suit the needs of sales control, they can be compared to (a) past data for the same segment, (b) current data for other comparable internal segments, and (c) recent industry averages. Cost trends can be spotted over time.

Cost analysis serves a number of specific sales management purposes and objectives:

1. To measure the efficiency of sales operations in disaggregated form
2. To heighten cost consciousness and encourage profit rather than volume orientation in sales and territory managers
3. To identify direct-sales-related expenditures and contributions to fixed costs and profitability on a segment-by-segment basis.
4. To allocate indirect operating expenses to determine net profit (before income taxes) for individual segments
5. To enhance the effectiveness of sales-related expenditures and improve resource utilization
6. To spot and correct unusual expense patterns
7. To support a company's defense against charges of illegal price discrimination
8. To facilitate sales control by helping to hold sales managers accountable for optimum results.

To proceed with this challenging task, an understanding has to be gained of the different types of costs as they relate to cost analysis. Depending on the perspective, they can be categorized in several ways.

Cost Classifications

One approach to cost classification is based on the criterion of timing relative to the obtaining of orders. Order-getting costs are somewhat speculative in nature, since they are incurred before an order is received. They include direct-selling expenses such as salesperson compensation, travel, entertainment, training, sales meetings, and sales offices; advertising and sales promotion expenditures; and marketing research and sales administration costs. Order-filling costs (also called "logistics costs"), on the other hand, are triggered by sales orders. They are related to the fulfillment portion of the sales function and encompass warehousing, packing, materials handling, shipping, servicing, billing, credit, collection, bad debts, and clerical expenses.

The second distinction refers to how expenses are traced to specific sales units. Direct costs can be determined precisely on a case-by-case basis and attributed directly to the sales unit that caused them. They relate either to manufacturing (primarily in the form of direct materials and direct labor, the prime ingredients in cost of goods sold) or to selling, where they may include any number of the above expense items. Indirect costs cannot be traced to individual sales units and must be distributed on some reasonable basis among all entities of the sales function. In the contribution margin approach, these overhead costs are treated as common costs and remain undistributed.

A third breakdown, which was described in Chap. 10, is based on the volume sensitivity of the cost behavior. Fixed costs do not vary with the sales volume and are often mistakenly considered permanently set. An example is the depreciation of an office building. Although the acquisition cost is normally distributed over the expected life of the structure, this depreciation could be accelerated or replaced by a sale-and-leaseback arrangement. In the long run, no cost element is fixed. Every cost figure can be altered by managerial decisions. Variable costs fluctuate with volume variations: the higher the sales volume, the higher the total variable costs; the lower the sales volume, the lower the total variable costs. If no orders are received, total variable costs shrink to zero. On a per unit level, however, variable costs tend to remain essentially constant over the relevant volume range, whereas fixed costs per unit decline with increasing volume, and vice versa.

This leads to the fourth categorization. Controllable costs are those that can be influenced by a sales manager's decision-making authority. In other words, the manager can determine the actual expenditure level and should be held responsible for it. Uncontrollable costs, on the other hand, are outside the sales manager's influence.

A fifth classification relates to the function that generates and uses the cost data. Natural costs are the expense classifications found in accounting records, such as salaries. By contrast, functional costs are related to specific business activities.

These distinctions will make understanding the steps involved in the cost analysis process easier. The process is designed to examine the profitability of individual sales segments by allocating functional costs to them.

Cost Analysis Procedure

The cost analysis procedure usually proceeds in four steps:

1. Converting natural costs into functional costs
2. Allocating functional costs to sales units
3. Determining efficiency and profitability of each unit
4. Deciding on appropriate action

Step 1.   The figures obtained from the natural accounts are broken down and distributed back to their points of origin within the sales function. Salaries, for instance, are split among selling, promotion, sales research, and the like. Time sheets or logs can be used to reclassify such natural accounts. For space-related costs, the relative amount of space occupied by a function provides a reasonable basis.

Step 2.   The second step allocates functional costs to the individual sales units. The allocation basis will tend to differ depending upon the type of functional account in question and the type of unit (product, customer, or territory).

Step 3.   Conclusions are drawn about each unit's efficiency and profitability. As introduced in Chap. 10, return on investment (ROI) is the measure most often used. As a reminder, ROI can be computed by using a simple equation.

$$\text{ROI} = \frac{\text{net profit}}{\text{sales}} \times \frac{\text{sales}}{\text{assets employed}}$$

Sales management often restates this equation for the purpose of territorial analysis. The return on assets managed (ROAM) of an individual sales territory can be determined by employing the formula noted in Chap. 19. Note that, in the formula below, the concept of "contribution margin" has been substituted for "net profit" that appeared in Chap. 19. (See the following section on profitability analysis.) In other words, ROAM can be used in both incremental and full cost approaches.

$$\text{ROAM} = \frac{\text{contribution margin}}{\text{sales}} \times \frac{\text{sales}}{\text{assets managed}}$$

The assets managed consists of the average accounts receivable and inventory that are needed to adequately serve the territory under consideration. This formula offers a useful measure for profitability analysis on a territory-by-territory level.

To determine a sales unit's efficiency, an analysis of variances has to be conducted. The purpose of such an undertaking is to identify variances from norms and the causes of the variances. This approach, known as "variance analysis," will be covered in the next section.

Step 4.   Many managers view the role of cost analysis as exhausted at this point, but the process is useless unless it leads to action. So the fourth and final step is to decide on and take appropriate action. Two basic avenues are available for dealing with weak products, customers, or territories: (a) eliminate them, or (b) improve their performance. This, after all, is the objective of the entire cost analysis exercise.

To improve profitability, sales managers must understand their firms' financial systems and be prepared to change the way their salespeople do business.[9] Managers must learn to shift from their traditional focus on volume to an emphasis on profitability. Sales quotas must be linked to profits, and salespeople must learn how to negotiate prices that provide the company with reasonable profits. Improving sales performance may also require a new compensation plan linked to profitability, which may mean redefining the sales job and redirecting selling efforts.

Profitability Analysis

It is difficult to judge whether a particular sales unit is doing well or poorly simply by looking only at its cost or sales records. Declining cost levels might be related to deteriorating sales. Conversely, rising costs may be related to a substantial sales expansion. Astute sales managers insist on relating cost data to appropriate sales figures to compute contribution margins. This computation is outlined in Fig. 20-2. *Cost of goods sold*—essentially, direct materials and direct labor employed in the manufacture of goods—is deducted from new sales receipts to arrive at the gross margin (or profit). Direct-sales-related expenditures, such as commissions and

cost of goods sold
Direct materials and direct labor employed in the manufacture of goods

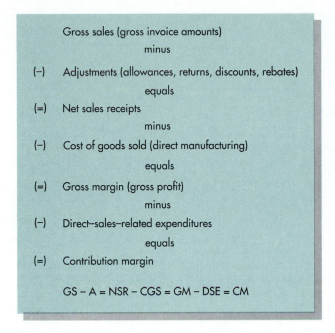

Gross sales (gross invoice amounts)

minus

(–)   Adjustments (allowances, returns, discounts, rebates)

equals

(=)   Net sales receipts

minus

(–)   Cost of goods sold (direct manufacturing)

equals

(=)   Gross margin (gross profit)

minus

(–)   Direct–sales–related expenditures

equals

(=)   Contribution margin

GS – A = NSR – CGS = GM – DSE = CM

FIGURE 20-2 Computation of Contribution Margin.

contribution margin Sales unit's contribution to fixed cost and profit found by deducting cost of goods sold and direct-sales-related expenditures from gross margin

travel, are then subtracted. The result is called the *contribution margin* of a sales unit. It represents the amount that this unit contributes to the firm's fixed cost and profit.

Advocates of the contribution margin approach point out that attempting to allocate indirect operating expenses to individual sales units serves no useful purpose. Direct sales expenditures are at least in part under control of sales or territory managers, so they are the only ones that are considered. However, some analysts feel that cost analysis should determine net profitability for each sales unit being studied. Proponents of the full-cost approach go a step further than the contribution margin approach by deducting from this amount allocated shares of overhead expenses to arrive at net profit.

A specific technique sales managers can use for profitability analysis is known as "profit variance analysis." This procedure helps managers identify why profits have changed.

Figure 20-3 shows selected data from a company's income statement for a specific product. For purposes of this analysis, the focus will be on gross profit, which is determined by subtracting cost of sales from net sales. Changes in gross profit from one period to the next may result from any one of a combination of variances:

1. *Price variance.* If the selling price per unit goes up or down, it will affect gross profit. Thus, the price variance indicates the change in sales dollars due to changes in the selling price from one period to another. To compute price variance, the current units are kept constant:

	Last year	This year	Change
Number of units sold	120,000	125,000	5,000
Price per unit	$ 60	$ 70	$ 10
Cost per unit	$ 45	$ 60	$ 15
Condensed Income Statement			
Net sales	$7,200,000	$8,750,000	$1,550,000
Cost of sales	$5,400,000	$7,500,000	$2,100,000
Gross profit	$1,800,000	$1,250,000	(–$550,000)

FIGURE 20-3 Selected Statistics for Profit Variance Analysis.

Current year's units at current year's price	$8,750,000
Current year's units at last year's price	7,500,000
Favorable price variance	$1,250,000

The increased selling price contributed $1,250,000 to sales revenue and therefore to gross profit. This reflects a favorable price variance.

2. *Volume variance.* If the quantity sold changes, gross profit will change. To compute volume variance, last year's selling price is kept constant and units sold are varied:

Current year's units sold at last year's price	$7,500,000
Last year's units sold at last year's price	7,200,000
Favorable volume variance	$ 300,000

With no change in selling price, sales revenue would have increased $300,000 because of the increase in volume. This increase in revenue would have a favorable effect on gross profit.

3. *Cost-price variance.* Changes in overall cost of sales caused by rising or falling costs going up or down will affect gross profit. To compute this variance, current units are kept constant and costs are varied:

Current year's units sold at current year's cost	$7,500,000
Current year's units sold at last year's cost	5,625,000
Unfavorable cost-price variance	$1,875,000

The increase in the unit cost for goods sold caused a $1,875,000 increase in the cost of sales. This has a very unfavorable impact on gross profit.

4. *Cost volume variance.* This will occur when changes in total costs are caused by

changes in the number of units sold. Last year's cost is kept constant and the units sold are variable in this computation:

Current year's units sold at last year's cost	$5,625,000
Last year's units sold at last year's cost	5,400,000
Unfavorable cost-volume variance	$ 225,000

Because of the 5000 increase in units sold this year, the cost of goods sold would have been $225,000 more in the current period. This has an unfavorable impact on gross profit.

The $550,000 decrease in gross profit for this product between the current year and last year is explained by the computed variances. Figure 20-4 summarizes these computations. Hindsight suggests that the manager responsible for sales of this product did not increase the price enough to cover the higher costs, or that the company did not take appropriate steps to contain costs. Although volume increased and total sales revenue grew, gross profit decreased as a result of much higher cost of sales.

This procedure can be used to compute variances for each good or service a company offers. It will allow a sales manager to analyze the contribution that each item makes toward gross profit and the reasons for variations in gross profit of each good or service from period to period.

This technique and other forms of profitability analysis reveal essentially two ways a sales organization can increase its sales profitability: sell more high-margin products or reduce the discounts, allowances, and other price concessions made to customers.[10] To determine whether or not profits can be improved and how involves further profitability analysis:

FIGURE 20-4 Summary of Profit Variance Analysis.

	Sales	Cost of sales	Gross profit
Current year	$ 8,750,000	$ 7,500,000	$ 1,250,000
Last year	$ 7,200,000	$ 5,400,000	$ 1,800,000
Difference	$ 1,550,000	$ 2,100,000	($ −550,000)
Changes due to:			
Price variance	$1,250,000		$ 1,250,000
Volume variance	$ 300,000		$ 300,000
Cost-price variance		($−1,875,000)	($−1,875,000)
Cost-volume variance		($− 225,000)	($− 225,000)
Total	$ 1,550,000	($−2,100,000)	($− 550,000)

1. Product line financial analysis asks, "Are there significant differences in the gross margins of the products or product lines that the sales force sells?" If differences exist, profitability may be increased by selling more of the products with higher gross margins. For instance, better quality "premium" products are usually more profitable than "economy" products.

2. Sales process analysis involves close scrutiny of the types of discounts, allowances, and other types of pricing concessions that salespeople give to customers. Other factors to consider include special packaging, shipping or financial terms, customer services provided with the sale, and free samples. Each of these concessions will reduce a company's margin. By reducing the size of the concessions, a salesperson can improve profitability.

3. Customer analysis reveals that doing business with certain customers produces more profit than doing business with other customers. It usually requires careful analysis to identify which customers provide the best margins. Specific factors to consider include the customer's size, the size of the average order, and the customer's industry. By concentrating on customers with high margins, a sales organization can increase profits. For instance, customers located close to a firm's production facility may be more profitable because shipping costs are lower.

4. Sales territory analysis looks closely at the profitability of each sales territory in an attempt to determine which territories are more profitable, how salespeople in these territories produce higher profits, and how this information might be used to increase profits in other sales territories. For example, the most profitable territories are sometimes those that concentrate on a particular industry. This suggests that focusing on industry niches may be an effective sales strategy. Another territory strategy might be to concentrate on selling to customers who do not demand extensive price concessions.

After profitability analysis has identified the best way to increase sales profitability, sales management must direct the sales force toward ways to increase profits. Sales supervision, communications, and monthly territory reports can be used to point out to salespeople that sales profitability as well as volume is important. Other management tools include compensation and incentive programs that are designed to improve profits, performance reviews that emphasize profits, and training programs that develop value-added selling skills to help salespeople reduce their dependence on discounts and other forms of price concessions.

PRINCIPLES OF ANALYSIS

Effective sales and cost analysis is based on a number of principles and techniques that describe the characteristics or behavior of data. These concepts include management by exception, the iceberg principle, and the 80–20 rule.[11]

Management by Exception

Management by exception involves using an analytical approach known as exception reporting. Rather than reporting everything that has happened, an exception

SALES MANAGEMENT IN PRACTICE

SCOTT PAPER

Recent economic conditions have worked to change the balance of power between retailers and manufacturers. Retailers, facing slim profit margins and a weakened economy, have started calling the shots for manufacturers, making them work harder than ever to earn shelf space for their products. Scott Paper, a consumer paper goods producer competing with giants like Procter & Gamble, has been affected by these trends, and the company has changed its sales control measures in response.

For Scott, satisfying retailers meant switching from a volume-based control measure to profitability measures. Not only Scott's profitability, but also the retailers' profitability, are emphasized.

Scott began its change to profitability in the mideighties by changing sales force compensation in order to reward a profitability rather than volume focus. A new discipline had to be instilled among salespeople as they underwent training in data processing and financial analysis.

Scott Paper's sales philosophy of helping customers maximize their return on Scott products is highly appropriate in today's relationship-oriented selling effort. By having a long-term interest in its customers' welfare, Scott is securing its own future success.

---

report identifies only those instances in which actual performance differs from standard performance by a significant amount. A sales manager can then skip over performance that is expected and concentrate on exceptions. For instance, a sales exception report might show those salespeople who have sold less than 85 percent of their sales quota and those who have sold more than 115 percent of quota. Similarly, a sales expense report might identify those sales territories in which expenses are 20 percent or more above budget.

Managing by exception can save a sales manager considerable time and effort. However, the effectiveness of this approach depends on the setting of realistic, measurable performance standards. As discussed in Chap. 19, this is not always easy to do. Also, sales managers must learn how to go beyond exception reports to determine the real causes for differences between actual and expected levels of performance.

Iceberg Principle

iceberg principle
Concept that managers should view not only aggregate data when evaluating sales performance; data should be broken down to permit insight into the performance of individual sales segments

The *iceberg principle* suggests that it is a fallacy to review only aggregate data and compare them with past company performance. Total sales revenue may suggest an acceptable growth pattern; however, a closer look may signal future trouble. This may be due to different growth curves in the various segments of the company's business; a significant portion of its revenue base could actually be declining, but this fall could be hidden by new sales. The data must be broken down to permit insight into the performance of individual sales segments.

Sales data can be organized according to products, customer categories, or geographic criteria (or all three bases). Product sales analysis reveals strong and weak products; analysis by account types results in a breakdown of the customer base into account sizes, which translates into improved call frequencies; and geographic sales analysis identifies performance levels. Multiple measures are desirable to properly judge performance at any of these levels. Although absolute sales revenues per product, account, or territory are meaningful and important and should be compared to results achieved in past periods, comparison of relative performance measures are equally essential. Actual sales are commonly related to sales quotas, resulting in quota attainment ratios. Many firms separately compare actual sales with sales potential to obtain the degree of potential realization. Finally, a firm's sales in a given segment should be related to total industry sales in that area to indicate share trends.

Similar thinking should be part of the sales manager's assessment of cost data. Total costs may reveal only a small portion of the information and insights needed for effective cost control. For example, a financial consultant analyzing sales administration costs concluded through detailed analysis that products generating 20 percent of the company sales created about 80 percent of the company's paperwork, as measured by number of purchase orders, credit memos, and other written materials. After completing the cost analysis, the company took a number of measures to reduce costs, including dropping some products, raising prices on others, and setting a minimum dollar amount for certain customer orders.[12]

80-20 Rule

The example above illustrates another analytical principle. Whichever criteria are used for sales and cost analysis, a limited number of units account for a large portion of sales, or a limited number of cost items account for a large portion of costs. This rule was first identified by Vilfredo Pareto, a Swiss professor of political economics, who observed that a minority of a country's working population earns the majority of its personal income. As a result, this principle, which explains the inequality of cause and effect, is also know as "Pareto analysis."

80-20 rule Principle that roughly 80 percent of a company's results come from 20 percent of its customers

As applied to sales analysis, the *80-20 rule* states that roughly 80 percent of the results—good and bad—will come from 20 percent of the customers. Although the percentages may vary, the basic pattern holds true in most circumstances. This concept suggests that there is a great deal of inefficiency and wasted effort in selling that could be redirected toward higher-volume opportunities. A chart that illustrates this principle is presented in Fig. 20-5.

When used as a sales analytical tool, the 80-20 rule will help a sales manager focus on specific details and identify sales opportunities and problems. For example, a company was faced with a projected negative cash flow for a coming year. Using a computer spreadsheet, management listed the yearly forecast for sales, cost of sales, and gross profit for each product. It then sorted products according to their gross profit, going from the largest to the smallest. This analysis revealed that about 25 percent of the company's products contributed 80 percent of its gross profits. Further analysis suggested two specific courses of action. First, it identified several products that the company needed to discontinue to save administrative expenses, inventory costs, and factory space. Second, analysis pointed out many products that required price adjustments.[13]

The 80-20 rule also has direct applicability to cost and expense control. For instance, spreadsheet analysis of a firm's expenses showed that roughly 15 percent of all expense categories accounted for about 80 percent of all expenses. It was clear that cost cutting had to focus on this limited list of expenses.

A word of caution about the 80-20 rule is in order, however. Management must not go overboard when taking action based on this analytical approach since drastic

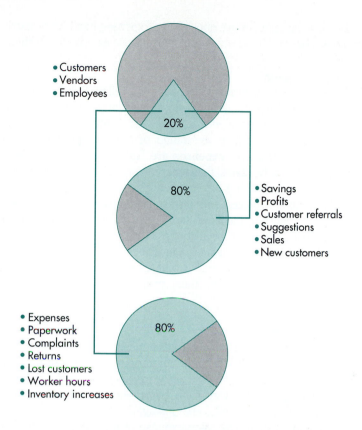

- Customers
- Vendors
- Employees

20%

80%

- Savings
- Profits
- Customer referrals
- Suggestions
- Sales
- New customers

- Expenses
- Paperwork
- Complaints
- Returns
- Lost customers
- Worker hours
- Inventory increases

80%

In most companies 80% of the results — good and bad — come from 20% of your customers

FIGURE 20-5 The 80-20 Rule.

action may hinder a company's sales efforts. A company that relies on a few high-volume accounts is susceptible to personnel changes, competitive overtures, and the like, and can become a vulnerable, or even captive, source. A healthy account mix includes both medium-sized and small accounts. They provide stability and may represent future growth opportunities.

Low sales volume in a territory may also be due to inadequate effort by the territory manager, competition, or sheer lack of potential. Complete abandonment of the territory is one option, but there are other choices. Switching to manufacturer's representatives could reduce costs but still maintain coverage, or business can be conducted by direct mail (catalog) or through telemarketing. If key accounts with headquarters elsewhere have plants in the territory, it may be impractical to discontinue service.

SALES EXPENSES

Sales expenses are a major cost of doing business. As a result, management sometimes regards them as a necessary evil. This is unfortunate, because sales expenses are an investment; their purpose is to generate sales in the same way that any promotional expenditure does. Sales expenses must be properly supervised, but they must also be liberal enough to permit salespeople to do their jobs effectively.

T & E Expenses

Travel and entertainment expenses—so-called T & E—represent a major portion of the operating budgets of most sales organizations. A *Sales & Marketing Management* survey revealed that travel and entertainment expenses as a percentage of sales volume fall in the range of 6 to 10 percent for most companies. Automobile and air travel expenses are half of the overall sales budget for most companies.[16] Clearly, sales managers must take an active role in managing and controlling these and other sales expenses.

Another sales management concern is compliance with federal income tax laws. Tax legislation and Internal Revenue Service rulings have set strict limits on business expenses. Although these regulations are concerned primarily with limiting excessive entertainment and business gift expenses, they also require more detailed recording of all sales expenses.[15] Companies require receipts for transportation and lodging, and each salesperson must maintain a daily record of all other business expenses.

Current Practices

Most companies have a liberal sales expense policy. A majority pay all reasonable expenses rather than set allowances for various expenses or for certain time periods. Expense items that companies usually pay include travel, automobile mileage and upkeep, lodging, meals away from home, job-related entertainment, promotional expenditures, telephone calls, and postage.

Like compensation, the sales expense plan must be fair to salespeople and the company. There should be no net gain or loss to either party. The expense plan must not hamper selling activities in any way. It should be simple and economical to operate and should provide an effective means of controlling expense accounts.

limited-payment plans Expense policy that sets maximum reimbursements

There are many methods used to reimburse salespeople for expenses. *Limited-payment plans* establish a maximum amount that the company will pay. For example, a salesperson might receive 22 cents a mile for automobile transportation, $45 a day for meals, and $80 a day for lodging when on the road. Limits are appropriate when a salesperson's expenses are predictable and repetitive. However, companies that use this procedure must recognize geographical differences in sales costs. An excellent source of information on cost differences is *Sales & Marketing Management*'s annual "Sales Manager's Budget Planner," formerly called the "Survey of Selling Costs."

A number of companies have adopted closer monitoring procedures to maintain control over sales expenses. For instance, travel and entertainment budget/expense reviews are being pushed from every quarter to every month, or from every month to every week. Companies have also established much tighter caps on per diem expenses for lodging and meals, and many require prior approval for expenses that are considered "extraordinary."[16]

For those companies that pay all reasonable expenses, an effective procedure is to have salespeople use credit cards. Along with avoiding the necessity for carrying large sums of cash, credit cards provide the company with accurate records of sales expenses. Another popular method is to provide sales people with a supply of predated blank checks. These are written to cover expenses and are cashed periodically (usually at the end of every week). Assuming proper safeguards have been established to protect the company and its salespeople, this method has the advantage of providing almost immediate reimbursement for expenses.

SALES AUDITS

Sales managers are also involved in an important trend—integrative management. Fundamental question about environment, organization, strategies, and systems need to be asked. These studies take the form of sales audits.

sales audit In-depth scrutiny of the entire sales organization

A *sales audit* is a cross-functional exercise that scrutinizes the entire sales operation. Figure 20-6 illustrates the encompassing scope of this review. It covers the environment of sales management and extends to an evaluation of the sales management organization. The sales management planning system is the third area addressed by a typical sales audit. Finally, sales management functions are evaluated.

Sales audits have to conducted in an objective, detached manner. Sales managers cannot be expected to bring the necessary level of objectivity to this task due to their personal involvement. For this reason, outside consultants are often brought in.

A comprehensive sales audit can benefit a sales organization in many ways. In a general sense, it will provide a clear picture of the sales "health" of the company. The information provided by the audit will form the basis for sales strategy and resource allocation decisions. Also, periodic sales audits can help a sales manager anticipate and avoid problems.

For example, a producer of women's apparel learned through an audit that sales of its new line of brassieres were being hurt by a high and increasing backlog of orders. After discussing the problem with retailers, the audit team concluded that the firm's salespeople had not communicated the backlog to their managers, and nobody had told the plant manager in charge of producing this product line to increase production. What was needed to resolve the backlog and avoid the problem in the future was better communication and coordination between sales and production.[17]

The sales audit process typically follows a five-step sequence that proceeds from fact finding to evaluation and report presentation:

1. Examination of sales objectives with regard to precision, appropriateness, realism, and challenge
2. Review of the plans and policies formulated in pursuit of these objectives as well as the allocation of resources to individual segments as compared with the company's philosophy and priorities
3. Evaluation of the methods, programs, and procedures utilized in plan implementation as measured against the stated objectives
4. Study of organization structure and staffing to determine adequacy of structure, delegation, human relations, and individual qualifications
5. Development of recommendations for improvement based on the appraisal of objectives, plans, methods, and organization

Given the general framework outlined above, there are specific questions that should be addressed in a sales audit. Table 20-1 presents a detailed list of questions concerning all aspects of the sales function that a sales audit should try to cover. The

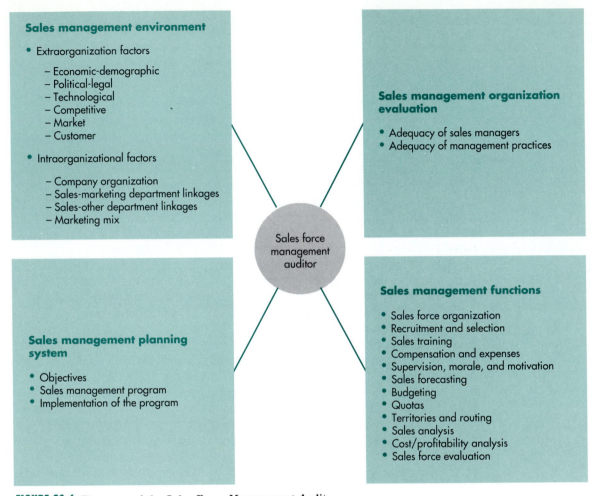

Sales management environment

• Extraorganization factors

  – Economic-demographic
  – Political-legal
  – Technological
  – Competitive
  – Market
  – Customer

• Intraorganizational factors

  – Company organization
  – Sales-marketing department linkages
  – Sales-other department linkages
  – Marketing mix

Sales management organization evaluation

• Adequacy of sales managers
• Adequacy of management practices

Sales force management auditor

Sales management planning system

• Objectives
• Sales management program
• Implementation of the program

Sales management functions

• Sales force organization
• Recruitment and selection
• Sales training
• Compensation and expenses
• Supervision, morale, and motivation
• Sales forecasting
• Budgeting
• Quotas
• Territories and routing
• Sales analysis
• Cost/profitability analysis
• Sales force evaluation

FIGURE 20-6 Elements of the Sales Force Management Audit.

answers to these questions provide a thorough analysis of a company's sales efforts. However, one should recognize that a great number of questions listed in the outline involve qualitative judgments. As a result, detachment and impartiality are essential in sales auditing.

A CONCLUDING THOUGHT

Chapter 20 concludes your study of sales management. The authors hope that our text has given you the background you will need for a successful career in selling. Perhaps you will want to keep your text as a reference source as you climb the career ladder.

Remember . . . only the best make it in selling. As a result, there is no faster way to the top. We hope *Sales Management* has given you the inspiration to set out on this exciting journey. Good luck . . . and good selling!

TABLE 20-1   **Sales Audit Questions**

I. Sales management environment
   A. Extraorganizational factors
      1. *Economic-demographic.* What does the company expect in the way of economic and demographic trends among different markets?
      2. *Political-legal.* What existing and prospective political-legal forces affect sales management?
      3. *Technology.* What technological developments are likely to affect the management of the sales force?
      4. *Competitors.* Determine the following:
         a. Who are the company's competitors?
         b. What are their strengths and weaknesses?
         c. What are the competitive practices in the industry?
      5. *Markets.* What are the differences across markets with respect to the following:
         a. Opportunities?
         b. Company sales practices?
      6. *Customers.* Answer the following:
         a. What do customers expect from salespeople in the way of service?
         b. What do customers think about the company's sales force?
         c. How do customers make their buying decisions?
   B. Intraorganizational factors
      1. *Company organization.* Determine the following:
         a. What are the firm's and marketing department's objectives?
         b. What is the organizational structure of the firm (who reports to whom)?
      2. *Sales-marketing department linkages.* Are there good communications and relations between the sales department and the following divisions:
         a. Advertising?
         b. Sales promotion?
         c. Public relations?
         d. Product managers?
         e. Market research?
         f. Service?
      3. *Sales-other department linkages.* Are there good communications and relations between the sales department and the following divisions:
         a. Research?
         b. Production?
         c. Traffic/shipping?
         d. Accounting/finance
         e. Data processing?
         f. Personnel?
         g. Legal?
      4. *Marketing mix.* What is the role of personal selling in our marketing mix?
II. Sales management planning system
   A. Objectives
      1. What are the sales department's objectives?
      2. Are the objectives measurable?
      3. Are the objectives realistic and appropriate?
   B. Sales management programs
      1. What is the company's sales strategy?
      2. Is the organization allocating sufficient resources to accomplish the sales department objectives?
      3. Are the resources being allocated efficiently among the various market opportunities?
   C. Implementation of the program
      1. Does the company have an adequate sales management information system for planning and control purposes?
III. Sales management organization evaluation
   A. *Adequacy of sales managers.* Does the company have a high-level sales executive to direct the sales management effort in an adequate fashion?

TABLE 20-1 (Continued)

   B. *Adequacy of management practices.* Concerning the sales management group:
1. Is the organizational structure (span of control) effective?
2. Are the managers capable?
3. How effective are management recruitment and selection efforts?
4. Do the managers need additional training?
5. Is the company's incentive system for the managers appropriate?
6. Is the evaluation process used to assess the managers adequate?

IV. Sales management functions
  A. Sales force organization
1. How is our sales force organized (by product, by customer, by territory)?
2. Is the type of organization appropriate given the current intraorganizational and extraorganizational conditions?
3. Does this type of organization adequately service the needs of customers?
  B. Recruitment and selection
1. How many salespeople does the company have?
2. Is the number adequate in light of company objectives and resources?
3. Does the company serve customers adequately with this number of salespeople?
4. How is sales force size determined?
5. What is the turnover rate? What has been done to try to change it?
6. Does the company have adequate sources from which to obtain recruits? Has it overlooked some possible sources?
7. Is there a job description for each sales job? Is each job description current?
8. Do the descriptions enumerate the necessary sales job qualifications? Have they been recently updated? Are they predictive of sales success?
9. Are the selection and screening procedures financially feasible and appropriate?
10. Does the company use a battery of psychological tests in its selection process? Are the tests valid and reliable?
11. Do recruitment and selection procedures satisfy the equal employment opportunity guidelines?
  C. Sales training
1. How is the sales training program developed? Does it meet the needs of management and sales personnel?
2. Does the company establish training objectives before developing and implementing the training program?
3. Is the training program adequate in light of the company's objectives and resources?
4. What kinds of training is currently provided to salespeople?
5. Does the training program need revising? What areas of the training program should be improved or deemphasized?
6. What methods are used to evaluate the effectiveness of the training program?
7. Can the company afford to train internally or should it use external sources?
8. Is there an ongoing training program for senior salespeople? Is it adequate?
  D. Compensation and expenses
1. Does the sales compensation plan meet company objectives in light of its financial resources?
2. Is the compensation plan fair, flexible, economical, and easy to understand and administer?
3. What is the level of compensation, the type of plan, and the frequency of payment?
4. Are the salespeople and management satisfied with the compensation plan?
5. Does the compensation plan ensure that the salespeople perform the necessary sales job activities?
6. Does the compensation plan attract and retain enough quality sales performers?
7. Does the sales expense plan meet the company's objectives in light of its financial resources?
8. Is the expense plan fair, flexible, and easy to administer? Does it allow for geographical, customer, and/or product differences?
9. Does the expense plan ensure that the necessary sales job activities are performed?
10. Can the expenses incurred by sales personnel be easily audited?

TABLE 20-1   (Continued)

E. Supervision, morale, and motivation
   1. What kinds of supervisory tools are used? How adequate are they given the company's supervisory needs?
   2. How does the company try to motivate the salespeople? How successful is it at motivating them?
   3. Is the sales force highly motivated?
   4. Is sales force morale high?
   5. Has the company made conscious attempts to improve morale and motivation in the sales force? How successful were the efforts?
   6. Does the company use individual or group motivational tools?
   7. Does it use both tangible and intangible incentives to motivate salespeople? Which incentives should be emphasized, which deemphasized?

F. Sales forecasting
   1. Is there a formal sales forecasting process?
   2. Who is involved in the forecasting process?
   3. How efficient and effective is the forecasting process in terms of its timeliness and accuracy?
   4. What forecasting methods are used? Are these methods appropriate for the company's particular requirements?

G. Budgeting
   1. Does the company use budgeting procedures? If not, why not? If it does, how is the budgeting process implemented?
   2. What budgets does the company prepare? How accurate are they? Are the budgets flexible? Are they used in sales force evaluations?
   3. Does the company try to adhere to our budgets?
   4. Do the budgets help the company attain its goals?

H. Quotas
   1. Does the company set quotas? If so, how are they set? Who participates in quota setting?
   2. What kinds of quotas are used? Are they adequate in light of company objectives?
   3. Is the company profit- or sales-volume-oriented in terms of quotas?
   4. Are the quotas realistic, flexible, fair, and attainable?
   5. Do the quotas account for an individual salesperson's experience and background as well as territorial, product, and customer differences?
   6. Do the quotas ensure that the necessary sales job activities are performed?

I. Sales territories and routing
   1. How does the company set territories? Does it consider product, customer, salesperson, competitive, and topographical differences when establishing territories?
   2. Do present territorial definitions permit the company to meet our objectives?
   3. Are territories allocated fairly?
   4. Does the company use routing schedules? Is routing necessary?
   5. How are the routes determined? What are the necessary inputs used to determine the routes?
   6. Is the routing schedule efficient in terms of the company's financial and temporal resources?
   7. What routing plan (for example, cloverleaf) is used?

J. Sales analysis
   1. What kinds of sales analysis (such as total sales volume, by product/product line, by customer, by territory) are performed?
   2. How is the sales analysis done? How frequently is it performed? Who performs the analysis?
   3. Is the sales analysis perfunctory or is it periodic and systematic?
   4. Does the company use the results of the sales analysis? How are they used? How successful is the company at using the results?

K. Cost/profitability analysis
   1. What kinds of cost analyses are performed?
   2. How is the cost analysis done? How frequently is it performed? Who performs the analysis?
   3. Is the cost analysis perfunctory or is it periodic and systematic?

TABLE 20-1 (Concluded)

    4. Does the company use the results of the cost analysis? How are they used? How successful is the company at using the results?

L. Sales force evaluation

    1. Does the company have a systematic approach to evaluating sales personnel? Who does the evaluation?

    2. Is the present evaluation system adequate in light of company objectives?

    3. What are the key performance dimensions evaluated? Are these adequate?

    4. Who sets the performance standards?

    5. Are the performance standards fair, flexible, and attainable?

    6. Is evaluation used to set future goals for sales personnel?

    7. Is the evaluation used to punish, reward, or develop the salespeople? How?

    8. Do the salespeople have redress after the evaluation?

    9. Are there periodic performance appraisals of salespeople? Are these frequent enough?

SUMMARY OF LEARNING GOALS

1. Understand the nature, objectives, and difficulties of sales control.

Sales control is a comprehensive effort encompassing sales and cost analysis and including such periodic projects as sales audits. The objectives of sales control are (1) to keep a firm's sales activity on the prescribed course, (2) to spot detrimental developments early, and (3) to identify emerging opportunities. Difficulties of sales control involve the lack of control over external factors, the identification of performance variables, unavailable or costly data, and the time lag between sales planning and marketplace response.

2. Outline the sales control process.

Sales control includes three steps: (1) setting performance standards, (2) comparing results to standards and investigating reasons for results, and (3) taking corrective action.

3. Explain how sales analysis assists sales managers.

Sales analysis assists sales managers by providing them with a sufficiently detailed picture of sales activities upon which to identify trends and develop comparisons. Based on the conclusions drawn from this information, sales managers may take specific action.

4. Understand the nature of cost analysis and the steps involved.

Cost analysis is the gathering, classifying, comparing, and study of company cost data as they relate to the profit contribution of the sales function. The cost analysis process is made up of four steps: (1) converting natural costs into functional costs, (2) allocating functional costs to sales units, (3) determining efficiency and profitability of each unit, and (4) deciding on appropriate action.

5. Explain the concepts related to profitability analysis.

Profitability analysis helps sales managers determine why profits change from one period to another. Changes in price, volume, cost-price, or cost-volume will all lead to a change in profitability. One type of profitability analysis, profit variance analysis, looks at changes in gross profit from one period to the next that result from a combination of variances.

6. **Identify the principles of sales and cost analysis.**

In sales and cost analysis, management by exception suggests that a sales manager concentrate on performance that differs from standard performance by a significant amount. The iceberg principle states that it is a mistake to look only at aggregate sales data; rather, a manager should study data in detail to spot trends and trouble spots. The 80-20 principle says that 20 percent of a firm's products, customers, and territories generate 80 percent of the firm's sales volume. An area of special concern and to which these principles are often applied is the assessment of sales expenses.

7. **Describe sales audits.**

Sales audits are comprehensive examinations used to help sales management study the firm's environment, organization, strategies, and systems. Both the nature and extent of sales force efforts and the influence of external variables are evaluated.

REVIEW QUESTIONS

1. What is the difference in focus between sales control and a sales audit? How has sales control changed in recent years?

2. Generally speaking, how is a ratio converted to an index? What are some of the indexes used in sales analysis?

3. Janet Pawicki made 137 sales calls last month. She also closed 43 sales during this period. What is her sales batting average?

4. What two sources usually provide cost data? What is the difference between a natural and a functional account? To what three things are cost data compared?

5. What is the purpose behind a profit variance analysis? What factors can cause a variance in gross profit? How do each of these factors affect sales? Cost of sales? Gross profit?

6. In what two ways can a sales organization increase profitability? What types of analyses are used to determine which of these two approaches is appropriate?

7. Assume a territory had $1.5 million in sales; allowances of $50,000; cost of goods sold of $600,000; and direct-sales-related expense of $100,000. Further assume that the territory was charged with inventory of $2.0 million, and carried accounts receivable of $1.0 million. What is the territory's ROAM?

8. What is the advantage of management by exception? What are its limitations?

9. How is the iceberg principle related to the 80-20 rule? What is suggested by the 80-20 phenomenon? Should a firm eliminate all sales accounts that fare poorly in a comparison of volume to expenses? Why or why not?

10. How do sales audits benefit sales organizations? What four sales management issues are audited?

DISCUSSION QUESTIONS

1. Think of a product that failed. Did the lack of sales control contribute to its demise? What could sales management have done differently?

2. Describe in your own words what a ratio is. Think of any ratio that you hear about on a frequent basis or that you have used. What constitutes the numerator and denominator of this ratio? How difficult is the gathering of the data needed to calculate the ratio? How is the ratio used to determine specific action? (*Hint:* Sports statistics are a good source.)

3. In Germany, there is a group of small and midsize companies, known as the "Mittelstand," which produces two-thirds of Germany's impressive gross domestic product. These companies pour huge amounts of money into research and development, exhibiting less concern for earnings growth than for producing a quality product. Some experts have

suggested that the Mittelstand is an appropriate model for U.S. companies to follow.[18] If such a focus were more prevalent in the United States, what different activities would be expected from the sales force? What measurements described in this chapter would be less important? Describe some relevant ratios or performance indexes that might be developed to evaluate a salesperson's contribution to research and development and quality efforts.

4. Is it fair for a company to evaluate a sales executive solely in terms of a sales/quota ratio and return on assets managed? Is such a policy in the company's best interest? Why or why not?

5. Using published sources, prepare a cursory sales audit of a company of your choosing. What did you learn from this exercise?

ETHICAL DILEMMA

While analyzing last year's sales records to prepare the coming year's budget, district sales manager Mary Shao discovers that a large sale was incorrectly credited to her district. Mary's district had been recognized as the most improved district in the region, but correction of this error would place her district second. Should Mary report the error?

SALES MANAGEMENT CASE

Reps versus Sales Force

The question of using independent distributor representatives or an in-house sales force is much debated. There is of course no one best answer, but in the final analysis, the best decision is the one that involves the most sales for the least cost.

The dollar size of a company's average sale is one factor that can be used in judging the profitability of reps or a sales force. This number is used to compute the cost per sales call for a sales force and for sales reps.

Whether a company should use reps or a sales force may be determined as follows:

Step one: salesperson cost per year / number of sales calls per salesperson per year = cost of average sales call

The percentage of sales represented by the cost of sales calls is then calculated:

Step two: average number of calls per client per year × cost of average sales call = average cost per client per year

Step three: average cost per client per year / average sales per client per year = cost as a percentage of sales

If the number computed in step three is larger than the rep commission percentage, then the reps should

be used. If the reps' commission is larger, a sales force should be used.

Questions

1. Use the following data to determine whether to use a sales force or reps:

- Average salesperson cost per year = $100,000
- Number of selling days per year = 160
- Average number of calls per salesperson per day = 3
- Average number of calls per client per year = 8
- Average sales per client per year = $10,000
- Sales rep commission = 10 percent

2. In its "1991 Sales Manager's Budget Planner," *Sales & Marketing Management* estimated the cost of the average sales call in a metro area to be the following:

    - Industrial industry—172.11
    - Consumer industry—143.49
    - Service industry—115.71

    Using an average sales per client per year of $10,000, 8 calls per client per year, and a 10 percent sales rep commission, determine whether reps or a sales force should be used for each of the three industries above.

3. What other factors should be considered in the rep versus sales force decision?

NOTES

CHAPTER 1

1. David Woodruff, "Life after Lee at Chrysler," *Business Week,* March 30, 1992, pp. 24–25; Ronald Grover and David Woodruff, "Chrysler Knocks, and Kerkorian Answers—Again," *Business Week,* October 21, 1991, p. 38; William F. Crittenden and Kathleen Kelly, "Leaders in Selling and Sales Management: Lee A. Iacocca," *Journal of Personal Selling & Sales Management,* vol. 11, Summer 1991, pp. 67–70; Alex Taylor III, "Can Iacocca Fix Chrysler—Again?" *Fortune,* April 8, 1991, pp. 50–54; James B. Treece and David Woodruff, "Crunch Time Again for Chrysler," *Business Week,* March 25, 1991, pp. 92–94.

2. See, for example, David J. Good, "Sales in the 1990s: A Decade of Development," *Review of Business,* vol. 12, Summer 1990, pp. 3–6.

3. William A. O'Connell and William Keenan, Jr., "The Shape of Things to Come," *Sales & Marketing Management,* vol. 142, January 1990, p. 36.

4. Quoted in Thayer C. Taylor, "Sales Management: How the Game Will Change in the 1990s," *Sales & Marketing Management,* vol. 141, June 1989, p. 52.

5. O'Connell and Keenan, "The Shape of Things to Come," p. 38.

6. Michael H. Morris, Ramon Avila, and Eugene Teeple, "Sales Management as an Entrepreneurial Activity," *Journal of Personal Selling & Sales Management,* vol. 10, Spring 1990, p. 5.

7. *Ibid.,* p. 9.

8. Oren Harari and Linda Mukai, "A New Decade Demands a New Breed of Manager," *Management Review,* vol. 79, August 1990, pp. 20–21.

9. *Ibid.,* pp. 21–24.

10. An interesting discussion of the qualifications for sales management appears in Alan J. Dubinsky and Thomas N. Ingram, "Important First-Line Sales Management Qualifications: What Sales Executives Think," *Journal of Personal Selling & Sales Management,* May 1983, pp. 18–25; see also Steve Zurier, "What Makes a Good Sales Manager?" *Industrial Distribution,* vol. 79, April 1990, p. 43.

11. Jack Falvey, "Sales Managers Belong in the Field," *Sales & Marketing Management,* vol. 140, February 1988, p. 75.

12. Kenneth Friedenreich and Howard Stevens, "Which Salesperson Will Make the Best Manager?" *Sales & Marketing Management,* vol. 140, March 1988, pp. 69–71; see also Jack Falvey, "Don't Teach Salespeople to Manage," *Sales & Marketing Management,* vol. 140, April 1988, pp. 17–18.

13. Jack Falvey, "The Making of a Manager," *Sales & Marketing Management,* vol. 141, March 1989, p. 42.

14. For some other clues about why some sales managers fail, see Nick Nykodyn and Katie George, "Stress on the Job," *Personnel,* vol. 66, July 1989, pp. 56–59; Ayala Pines and Elliot Aronson, "Why Managers Burn Out," *Sales & Marketing Management,* vol. 141, February 1989, pp. 34–38.

15. Bernard L. Rosenbaum and Nick Ward, "Why Sales Managers Need More and Better Management Training—And How Can You Give It," *Training,* April 1982, pp. 44–49.

16. Kathryn Scovel, "What's Topping the Charts in Management Training?" *Human Resource Executive,* April 1990, p. 37; see also McRae C. Banks and Allen L. Bures, "Management Training: What Companies Want and How They Get It," *SAM Advanced Management Journal,* vol. 52, Winter 1987, pp. 26–31.

17. Scovel, "What's Topping the Charts in Management Training?" p. 38.

18. "Study Reveals Sales-Training Needs of Business Marketers," *Marketing News,* vol. 23, March 13, 1989, p. 6.

19. Nancy Shepherdson, "Sales Management Training," *Bank Administration,* vol. 65, September 1989, pp. 32–35; see also Susan A. Smith, "How to Turn Line Managers into Sales Managers," *Bank Marketing,* vol. 21, January 1989, pp. 35–37.

20. John I. Coppett and William A. Staples, "An Exploratory Study of Training Programs for First Level Sales Managers," *Akron Business and Economic Review,* Fall 1980, pp. 36–41.

21. Alan J. Dubinsky and Thomas N. Ingram, "From Selling to Sales Management: A Development Model," *Journal of Business and Industrial Marketing,* vol. 2, Spring 1987, pp. 27–36.

22. Bob Filipczak, Beverly Geber, and Brad Lee Thompson, "Training Today: Six Signs of the Future; Get in Line, Soldier! Focus Shifts to 'Core Skills,'" *Training,* vol. 28, January 1991, pp. 95–96.

CHAPTER 2

1. Arthur Bragg, "Shell-Shocked on the Battlefield of Selling," *Sales & Marketing Management,* vol. 142, July 1990, pp. 52–58.

2. "Consulting the Recruiting Consultant," *Sales & Marketing Management,* vol. 135, December 9, 1985, p. 51.

3. For an excellent overview of career opportunities in marketing, see Barbara A. Pletcher, *On the Right Track: A Guide to a Successful Sales Career,* Sacramento, CA: National Association for Professional Saleswomen, 1984; *Careers in Marketing,* Chicago, IL: American Marketing Association, 1983.

4. "1991 Sales Manager's Budget Planner," *Sales & Marketing Management,* vol. 144, June 22, 1992, p. 68.

5. *Ibid.*, p. 68.

6. *Ibid.*, p. 68.

7. William Keenan, Jr., "Executive Pay: A Bitter Pill," *Sales & Marketing Management*, vol. 143, November 1991, p. 48.

8. Bill Kelley, "Are You Getting the Most from Your Company Cars?" *Sales & Marketing Management*, vol. 141, October 1989, pp. 73–74.

9. The relationship between personal and professional growth is discussed in John Hafer and M. Joseph Sirgy, "Professional Growth versus Personal Growth of Salespeople: A General Systems Model," *Journal of Personal Selling & Sales Management*, vol. 3, November 1983, pp. 22–30.

10. Bill Kelley, "Ideal Selling Jobs," *Sales & Marketing Management*, vol. 140, December 1988, p. 31.

11. *Ibid.*, p. 26.

12. "Marketing Newsletter," *Sales & Marketing Management*, vol. 138, February 1987, p. 74.

13. Louis E. Boone and John C. Milewicz, "Is Professional Selling the Route to the Top of the Corporate Hierarchy?" *Journal of Personal Selling & Sales Management*, vol. 9, Spring 1989, p. 43.

14. Milan Moravec, Marshall Collins, and Clinton Tripodi, "Don't Want to Manage? Here's Another Path," *Sales & Marketing Management*, vol. 142, April 1990, p. 70.

15. *Ibid.*, pp. 75–76.

16. Myron Gable and B. J. Reed, "The Current Status of Women in Professional Selling," *Journal of Personal Selling & Sales Management*, vol. 7, May 1987, p. 36; see also Carol Vipperman and Barbara Mueller, *Solutions to Sales Problems: A Guide for Professional Saleswomen*, Englewood Cliffs, NJ: Prentice-Hall, 1983, pp. 2–6.

17. Michael P. Wynne, *Sci-Tech Selling: Selling Scientific and Technical Products and Services*, Englewood Cliffs, NJ: Prentice-Hall, 1987; William L. Shanklin and John K. Ryans, Jr., *Essentials of Marketing High Technology*, Lexington, MA: Lexington Books, 1987, pp. 92–101; Jeanne Greenberg, "High Tech, Not High Pressure," *Nation's Business*, vol. 74, May 1986, pp. 54R–55R.

18. For more information and examples of these and similar sales career opportunities, see Howard Schneider, "Training in the Trenches: Building a Bank Sales Force," *Banker's Monthly*, vol. 108, January 1991, pp. 28, 30; Delia A. Sumrall and Nermin Eyuboglu, "Policies for Hospital Sales Programs: Investigating Differences in Implementation," *Journal of Health Care Marketing*, vol. 9, December 1989, p. 41–47; Kamran Kasharin and John A. Murray, "Managing a Bank's Salesforce," *International Journal of Marketing*, vol. 7, June 1989, pp. 9–6; David J. Lefkowith, "The Dangerous Challenge of Utility Marketing," *Public Utilities Fortnightly*, vol. 122, August 18, 1988, pp. 9–14; Kari E. Super, "More Hospitals Turn to Sales Forces, but Monetary Incentives Lag," *Modern Healthcare*, vol. 17, March 13, 1987, pp. 116ff; Al Urbanski, "Wells Fargo's Sales Force Tames the Wild West," *Sales & Marketing Management*, vol. 138, January 1987, pp. 38–41.

19. Bert J. Kellerman and Firooz Hekmat, "Personal Selling

and Sales Management in the Marketing Curriculum: A Status Report," *Journal of Personal Selling & Sales Management*, vol. 9, Fall 1989, pp. 35–45; Arthur Bragg, "Personal Selling Goes to College," *Sales & Marketing Management*, vol. 140, March 1988, pp. 35–37.

20. Eugene M. Johnson, "How Do Sales Managers View College Preparation for Sales?" *Journal of Personal Selling & Sales Management*, vol. 10, Summer 1990, pp. 69–72; Ralph M. Gaedeke and Dennis H. Tootelian, "Employers Rate Enthusiasm and Communication as Top Job Skills," *Marketing News*, March 27, 1989, p. 14.

21. Johnson, "How Do Sales Managers View College Preparation for Sales?" p. 71.

22. Boone and Milewicz, "Is Professional Selling the Route to the Top of the Corporate Hierarchy?" p. 43. The original source for these data was David L. Kurtz, Louis E. Boone, and C. Patrick Fleenor, *CEO: Who Gets to the Top in America*, East Lansing, MI: Michigan State University Press, 1989, pp. 125, 130.

23. Arthur Bragg, "Is a Mentor Program in Your Future?" *Sales & Marketing Management*, vol. 141, September 1989, p. 54.

24. For additional insights on interviewing from the sales candidate's perspective, see Alice Shane, "Facing Up to a Recruiter," *Sales & Marketing Management*, vol. 141, May 1989, pp. 38–45.

25. Frederick I. Trawick, Jr., John E. Swan, and David R. Rink, "Back-Door Selling: Violation of Cultural versus Professional Ethics by Salespeople and Purchaser Choicc of the Supplier," *Journal of Business Research*, vol. 17, November 1988, pp. 229–309.

26. For an interesting discussion of the ethical dimension of various sales practices, see, Frederick I. Trawick, Jr., and John E. Swan, "How Salespeople Err with Purchasers: Overstepping Ethical Bounds," *Journal of Business and Industrial Marketing*, vol. 3, Summer 1988, pp. 5–11.

27. Raymond Dreyfack, "The Selling Edge," *American Salesman*, vol. 35, February 1990, pp. 25–28.

28. Robin Derry, "Ethics: Standards We Must Not Stretch," *Best's Review*, vol. 91, September 1990, pp. 38–40.

29. Joseph A. Bellizzi and Robert E. Hite, "Supervising Unethical Salesforce Behavior," *Journal of Marketing*, vol. 53, April 1989, pp. 36–47.

30. Thomas R. Wotruba, "A Comprehensive Framework for the Analysis of Ethical Behavior, with a Focus on Sales Organization," *Journal of Personal Selling & Sales Management*, vol. 10, Spring 1990, pp. 29–42.

31. Another model is presented in Alan J. Dubinsky and Barbara Loken, "Analyzing Ethical Decision Making in Marketing," *Journal of Business Research*, vol. 19, September 1989, pp. 83–107.

32. "Honesty Is Now Top Attribute for Sales Reps," *Marketing News*, vol. 21, July 17, 1987, p. 8.

33. David J. Burns and John M. Lanasa, "Sharing the Burden of Ethical Conduct: The Educational System and the Corporation," *Review of Business*, vol. 12, Summer 1990, pp. 33–38;

Arthur Bragg, "Ethics in Selling, Honest!" *Sales & Marketing Management,* vol. 138, May 1987, pp. 42–44.

CHAPTER 3

1. William C. Brisick, "The Last of the College Travelers," *Publishers Weekly,* January 19, 1990, pp. 62–64.

2. Thomas L. Powers, Warren S. Martin, Hugh Rushing, and Scott Daniels, "Selling Before 1900: A Historical Perspective," *Journal of Personal Selling & Sales Management,* vol. 7, November 1987, pp. 1–7. Much of the discussion that follows is from David L. Kurtz, "The Historical Development of Professional Selling," *Business and Economic Dimensions,* August 1970, pp. 12–18.

3. Powers et al., "Selling Before 1900: A Historical Perspective," p. 6.

4. See Alfred Gross, *Salesmanship,* 2nd ed., New York: The Ronald Press Company, 1959, p. 554.

5. Jack Falvey, "Selling in the Nineties," *Sales & Marketing Management,* vol. 143, October 1991, p. 10.

6. For a thorough review of the development of selling during this period, see Thomas L. Powers, William F. Koehler, and Warren S. Martin, "Selling From 1900 to 1949: A Historical Perspective," *Journal of Personal Selling & Sales Management,* vol. 8, November 1988, pp. 11–21.

7. Joseph A. Bellizzi, A. Frank Thompson, and Lynn J. Loudenback, "Cyclical Variations of Advertising and Personal Selling," *Journal of the Academy of Marketing Science,* Spring 1983, pp. 142–155; Donald Robinson, "The Salesman: Ambassador of Progress," New York: *Sales and Marketing Executives-International,* 1967, p. 10.

8. Powers et al., "Selling From 1900 to 1949: A Historical Perspective," p. 18.

9. For a modern view of standardized sales presentations, see Marvin A. Jolson, "Canned Adaptiveness: A New Direction for Modern Salesmanship," *Business Horizons,* January-February 1989, pp. 7–12.

10. A. R. Hahn, "Selling's Path-Finder," *Sales Management,* December 15, 1952, pp. 96–97.

11. *Ibid.,* p. 97.

12. *Ibid.,* p. 96.

13. Robert A. Reeves and Hiram C. Barksdale, "A Framework for Classifying Concepts and Research in the Personal Selling Process," *Journal of Personal Selling & Sales Management,* November 1984, pp. 7–16; and, William J. E. Crissy, Isabella C. M. Cunningham, and William H. Cunningham, *Effective Selling: A Short Course for Professionals,* New York: John Wiley and Sons, 1977, pp. 5–16.

14. Carl Rieser, "The Salesman Isn't Dead–He's Different," *Fortune,* November 1962, p. 124. Copyright © 1962 Time Inc. All rights reserved.

15. "The New Supersalesman: Wired for Success," *Business Week,* January 6, 1973, p. 44. Copyright © 1973. Used by permission.

16. F. G. (Buck) Rodgers, *The IBM Way: Insights into the World's Most Successful Marketing Organization,* New York: Harper & Row, 1985.

17. James Lorenzen, "Needs Analysis Replacing Product Presentation," *Marketing News,* vol. 20, April 25, 1986, p. 8.

18. Marc Hequet, "No More Willy Loman," *Training: Sales Training Supplement,* May 1989, pp. 11–13.

19. Frank V. Cespedes, Stephen X. Doyle, and Robert J. Freedman, "Teamwork for Today's Selling," *Harvard Business Review,* vol. 67, March-April 1989, p. 44.

20. For an approach to implement a systems selling strategy, see Dan T. Dunn, Jr., and Claude A. Thomas, "Strategy for Systems Sellers: A Grid Approach," *Journal of Personal Selling & Sales Management,* vol. 6, August 1986, pp. 1–10.

21. Jim Rapp, "Team Selling Is Changing the Sales Trainer's Role," *Training: Sales Training Supplement,* May 1989, pp. 6–10.

22. Moncrief has developed a similar classification which includes five types of industrial sales jobs: missionary, trade services, trade seller, order taker, and institutional seller. William C. Moncrief, III, "Five Types of Industrial Sales Jobs," *Industrial Marketing Management,* vol. 17, May 1988, pp. 161–167; William C. Moncrief, III, "Selling Activity and Sales Positions Taxonomies for Industrial Salesforces," *Journal of Marketing Research,* vol. 23, August 1986, pp. 261–270.

23. Bill Stack, "Truck Driving Sales Force Hauls in Extra Customers," *Marketing News,* vol. 10, May 8, 1989, p. 2.

24. Thomas R. Wotruba, "The Evolution of Personal Selling," *Journal of Personal Selling & Sales Management,* vol. 11, Summer 1991, pp. 1–12. Copyright © 1991. Used by permission of Journal of Personal Selling & Sales Management.

25. Lynda Lawrence, "Phase Change: Larry Wilson on Selling in a Brave New World," *Training: Sales Training Supplement,* February 1988, pp. 11–17.

26. See also Thomas P. Reilly, "Sales Force Plays Critical Role in Value-Added Marketing," *Marketing News,* vol. 12, June 5, 1989, p. 8.

27. Leslie M. Fine and David W. Schumann, "Researching the Buyer/Seller Dyad: A Model of the Relationship Development Process," in *1990 AMA Winter Educators' Conference: Marketing Theory and Applications,* David Lichtenthal, Robert E. Spekman, and David T. Wilson, eds., Chicago, IL: American Marketing Association, 1990, pp. 109–114.

28. For research leading to a framework for buyer-seller relationships, see F. Robert Dwyer, Paul H. Schurr, and Sejo Oh, "Developing Buyer-Seller Relationships," *Journal of Marketing,* vol. 51, April 1987, pp. 11–27; see also Kaylene C. Williams and Rosann L. Spiro, "Communication Style in the Salesperson-Customer Dyad," *Journal of Marketing Research,* vol. 22, November 1985, pp. 434–442.

29. Barton A. Weitz, "Effectiveness in Sales Interactions: A Contingency Framework," *Journal of Marketing,* vol. 45, Winter 1981, pp. 85–102.

30. Kaylene C. Williams, Rosann L. Spiro, and Leslie M. Fine, "The Customer-Salesperson Dyad: An Interaction/Communication Model and Review," *Journal of Personal Selling & Sales Management,* vol. 10, Summer 1990, pp. 29–43.

31. F. B. Evans, "Selling as a Dyadic Relationship," *The American Behavioral Scientist,* May 1963, pp. 76–79.

32. Robert E. Hite and Joseph A. Bellizzi, "Differences in the Importance of Selling Techniques between Consumer and Industrial Salespeople," *Journal of Personal Selling & Sales Management,* vol. 5, November 1985, pp. 19–30.

33. Edith Cohen, "A View from the Other Side," *Sales & Marketing Management,* vol. 142, June 1990, pp. 108–110; "PAs Examine the People Who Sell to Them," *Sales & Marketing Management,* vol. 135, November 11, 1985, pp. 38–41; Kate Bertrand, "Rep Quality Top Buyer Value," *Business Marketing,* September 1989, p. 40; H. Michael Hayes and Steven W. Hartley, "How Buyers View Industrial Salespeople," *Industrial Marketing Management,* vol. 18, May 1989, pp. 73–80; "Good Salespeople Make the Difference," *Purchasing,* vol. 106, February 23, 1989, pp. 19–21.

34. Martin Everett, "This Is the Ultimate in Selling," *Sales & Marketing Management,* vol. 141, August 1989, pp. 28–38.

35. Steve Fishman, "The Longest Sale," *Success,* May 1989, p. 49–52.

36. Michael D. Hutt, Wesley J. Johnston, and John R. Ronchetto, Jr., "Selling Centers and Buying Centers: Formulating Strategic Exchange Patterns," *Journal of Personal Selling & Sales Management,* vol. 5, May 1985, pp. 33–40.

37. *Ibid.,* p. 38; see also William Atkinson, "A New Approach to Sales Training," *Training,* vol. 26, March 1989, pp. 57–60; Richard Cardozo and Shannon Shipp, "New Selling Methods Are Changing Industrial Sales Management," *Business Horizons,* September-October 1987, pp. 23–28.

38. Michael Selz, "Vendor in the Street Faces Tougher Curbs," *The Wall Street Journal,* February 11, 1992, p. B1.

CHAPTER 4

1. Tom Murray, "Seminar Selling," *Sales & Marketing Management,* September 1990, vol. 142, pp. 54–58, 85–86.

2. Harvey B. Mackay, "The CEO Hits the Road (and Other Sales Tales)," *Harvard Business Review,* vol. 68, March-April 1990, pp. 32–44.

3. James Koch, "Portrait of the CEO As Salesman," *Inc.,* March 1988, p. 45. Copyright 1988 by Goldhirsh Group, Inc., 38 Commercial Wharf, Boston, MA 02110.

4. Saul W. Gellerman, "The Tests of a Good Salesperson," *Harvard Business Review,* vol. 68, May-June 1990, p. 69.

5. For specific examples of successful salespeople and how they sell, see Leslie Brennan, "Sales Secrets of the Incentive Stars: Some Perennial Winners Talk About What It Takes to Stay on Top Year after Year," *Sales & Marketing Management,* vol. 142, April 1990, pp. 88–100; Martin Everett, "Selling's New Breed: Smart and Feisty," Sales & Marketing Management, vol. 141, October 1989, pp. 52–64.

6. David M. Szymanski and Gilbert A. Churchill, Jr., "Client Evaluation Cues: A Comparison of Successful and Unsuccessful Salespeople," *Journal of Marketing Research,* vol. 27, May 1990, pp. 163–174.

7. Gerald Michaelson, "It's a Small World If You've Got a Big Network," *Sales & Marketing Management,* vol. 140, August 1988, p. 74.

8. William L. Willard, "Target Marketing in the Real World," *Life Association News,* vol. 83, June 1988, pp. 121–127.

9. Dorothy Leeds, "To Find Golden Opportunities . . . Pan for Prospects," *Personal Selling Power,* vol. 10, November-December 1990, pp. 26–27.

10. Len D'Innocenzo, "How to Discover New Prospects from within Your Established Accounts," *Personal Selling Power,* vol. 10, April 1990, p. 60.

11. Kate Bertrand, "Survey Finds Trade Shows Influence Buying Decisions," *Business Marketing,* March 1990, p. 34.

12. Richard Kriesman, "Getting Ready For Show Time," *Inc.,* August 1986, pp. 87–88.

13. Betsy Wiesendanger, "Are Your Salespeople Trade Show Duds?" *Sales & Marketing Management,* vol. 142, August 1990, pp. 40–46; see also Lawrence B. Chonko and John F. Tanner, Jr., "Relationship Selling at Trade Shows: Avoid the Seven Deadly Salespeople," *Review of Business,* vol. 12, Summer 1990, pp. 13–18.

14. "Clearly Defined Objectives Result in Successful Trade Shows," *Sales & Marketing Management in Canada,* vol. 28, January-February 1987, pp. 22–23.

15. Tom Eisenhart, "Going the Integrated Route," *Business Marketing,* December 1990, pp. 24–32; see also K. Dean Black, "Supporting Your Sales Force with Direct Marketing," *Sales & Marketing Management in Canada,* vol. 27, September 1986, pp. 12–14.

16. Kate Bertrand, "Lead Management Fuels Sales" *Business Marketing,* November 1989, p. 36.

17. Bill Kelley, "Picking the Best From the Rest," *Sales & Marketing Management,* vol. 141, July 1989, p. 28.

18. Marvin A. Jolson, "Prospecting by Telephone Prenotification: An Application of the Foot-in-Door Technique," *Journal of Personal Selling & Sales Management,* vol. 6, August 1986, pp. 39–42.

19. *Ibid.,* p. 41.

20. William E. Gregory, Jr., "Time to Ask Hard-Nosed Questions," *Sales & Marketing Management,* vol. 141, October 1989, pp. 88–93.

21. Daniel L. Lional, "Empathy—Your Best Sales Tool," *American Salesman,* vol. 35, June 1990, pp. 26–27.

22. Daniel Caust, "A Plan for Every Customer," *Sales & Marketing Management,* vol. 125, July 7, 1980, p. 36.

23. Martin Everett, "Selling to the CEO," *Sales & Marketing Management,* vol. 140, November 1988, p. 61.

24. For a thorough discussion of the buying center and the various forms of buying influences, see Robert B. Miller and Stephen E. Heiman with Tad Tuleja, *Strategic Selling,* New York: Warner Books, 1985, pp. 72–87.

25. Harvey B. Mackay, "Humanize Your Selling Strategy," *Harvard Business Review,* vol. 66, March-April 1988, pp. 36–47.

26. *Ibid.,* p. 37.

27. Jack Falvey, "Without a Goal for Every Call, a Salesperson is Just a Well-Paid Tourist," *Sales & Marketing Management,* vol. 141, June 1989, p. 92.

28. *Ibid.,* p. 96.

29. Stephen Schiffman, "Real Sales Pros Know How to Handle Humiliation," *Marketing News,* March 19, 1990, p. 7.

CHAPTER 5

1. Tom Richman, "Send in the Clowns," *Inc.*, September 1991, pp. 119–121; Virginia Randall, "How He Turned the Magic of Business into the Business of Magic," *Nation's Business*, June 1991, p. 11.

2. Barton Weitz, Harish Sujan, and Mita Sujan, "Knowledge, Motivation, and Adaptive Behavior: A Framework for Improving Selling Effectiveness," *Journal of Marketing*, vol. 50, October 1980, pp. 174–191.

3. An instrument for measuring the degree to which salespeople practice adaptive selling is presented in Rosann L. Spiro and Barton A. Weitz, "Adaptive Selling: Conceptualization, Measurement, and Nomological Validity," *Journal of Marketing Research*, vol. 27, February 1990, pp. 61–69.

4. John T. Molloy, "Clothes: Your First and Last Sales Tool," *Marketing Times*, March/April 1981, p. 28.

5. Much has been written about the importance of clothing in business. For overall guidance, see Ron Kolgraf, "Salesman in the Gray Flannel Suit," *Industrial Distributor*, April 1981, p. 103; see also, Mortimer Levitt, "Clothes: The Executive Look and How to Get It," *Marketing Times*, September/October 1980, pp. 18–22; John T. Molloy, *The Woman's Dress for Success*, Chicago: Follett, 1977; John T. Molloy, *Dress for Success*, New York: Peter H. Wayden, 1975.

6. Norman D. Chilton, "First Impressions That Last," *Journal of Forms Management*, vol. 12, November 1987/January 1988, pp. 21–22.

7. David M. Szymanski, "Determinants of Selling Effectiveness: The Importance of Declarative Knowledge to the Personal Selling Concept," *Journal of Marketing*, vol. 52, January 1988, p. 67.

8. For some additional techniques, see Homer B. Smith, "The First Three Minutes of a Successful Sales Approach," *Personal Selling Power*, vol. 10, April 1990, pp. 38–39.

9. Leslie Brennan, "Sales Secrets of the Incentive Stars," *Sales & Marketing Management*, vol. 142, April 1990, p. 94.

10. Monroe Murphy Bird, "Gift-Giving and Gift-Taking in Industrial Companies," *Industrial Marketing Management*, vol. 18, May 1989, pp. 91–94.

11. Nido R. Qubein, "The Power of the Right Question at the Right Time," *Personal Selling Power*, vol. 10, October 1990, p. 48.

12. Neil Rackham, *SPIN Selling*, New York: McGraw-Hill, 1988.

13. Gerhard Gschwandter, "How Sales Achievers Solve Problems," *Personal Selling Power*, vol. 10, November-December 1990, p. 10.

14. Abner Littel, "Sales Consultants Solve Prospects' Problems," *Personal Selling Power*, vol. 10, May-June 1990, p. 48.

15. For some specific listening styles and techniques, see Ruth T. Bennett and Rosemary V. Wood, "Effective Listening Via Listening Styles," *Business*, vol. 39, April-June 1989, pp. 45–48.

16. Helen Berman, "To Close Sales Ask Questions," *Personal Selling Power*, vol. 11, March 1991, pp. 48–49.

17. Camille P. Schuster and Jeffrey E. Danes, "Asking Questions: Some Characteristics of Successful Sales Encounters," *Journal of Personal Selling & Sales Management*, vol. 6, May 1986, pp. 17–27.

18. For specific tips, see James E. Lukaszewski and Paul Ridgeway, "To Put Your Best Foot Forward, Start by Taking These 21 Simple Steps," *Sales & Marketing Management*, vol. 142, June 1990, pp. 84–86.

19. Marvin A. Jolson, "Canned Adaptiveness: A New Direction for Modern Salesmanship," *Business Horizons*, January-February 1988, pp. 7–12.

20. The concept of persuasion is discussed in G. Ray Funkhouser, "A Practical Theory of Persuasion Based on Behavioral Science Approaches," *Journal of Personal Selling & Sales Management*, vol. 4, November 1984, pp. 17–25.

21. For guidelines on sales negotiation, see Robert E. Kellar, "How Good Are You at Negotiating?" *Sales & Marketing Management*, vol. 141, February 1989, pp. 29–32; Homer B. Smith, "How to Concede—Strategically," *Sales & Marketing Management*, vol. 140, May 1988, pp. 79–80.

22. Richard Kern, "Making Visual Aids Work For You," *Sales & Marketing Management*, vol. 141, February 1989, p. 45.

23. Robert B. Settle and Pamela L. Alreck, "Risky Business," *Sales & Marketing Management*, vol. 141, January 1989, p. 48.

24. Daniel K. Weadcock, "Your Troops Can Keep Control and Close the Sale—by Anticipating Objections," *Sales & Marketing Management*, vol. 124, March 17, 1980, p. 104.

25. Andrea J. Moses, "How to Overcome Objections," *Personal Selling Power*, vol. 11, July-August 1991, pp. 38–39.

26. Paul H. Schurr, Louis H. Stone, and Lee Ann Beller, "Effective Selling Approaches to Buyers' Objections," *Industrial Marketing Management*, vol. 14, August 1985, pp. 195–202.

27. Robin T. Peterson, "Sales Representative Utilization of Various Widely-Used Means of Answering Objections," in *AMA Educator Proceedings*, Susan P. Douglas and Michael R. Solomon, eds., Chicago, IL: American Marketing Association, 1987, pp. 119–124.

28. Homer Smith, "The Right Time to Close," *Personal Selling Power*, vol. 11, September 1991, p. 37.

29. Jack Falvey, "For the Best Close, Keep an Open Mind," *Sales & Marketing Management*, vol. 142, April 1990, p. 12; see also Tim Conner, "The New Psychology of Closing Sales," *American Salesman*, vol. 32, September 1987, p. 25.

30. An early, popular book was Julius Fast, *Body Language*, New York: Evans, 1970.

31. A related article of interest is William G. Nickels, Robert F. Everett, and Ronald Klein, "Rapport Building By Salespeople: A Neuro-Linguistic Approach," *Journal of Personal Selling & Sales Management*, vol. 3, November 1983, pp. 1–7. For additional insights into body language and selling, see Gerhard Gschwandtner, "How to Read Your Prospect's Body Language," *Industrial Marketing*, July 1981, pp. 55–59; Gerhard Gschwandtner, "Nonverbal Selling Power," *Training and Development Journal*, November 1980, pp. 64–66ff.

32. John E. Swan, I. Frederick Trawick, and David W. Silva, "How Industrial Salespeople Gain Customer Trust," *Industrial Marketing Management*, vol. 14, August 1985, pp. 203–211.

33. Brennan, "Sales Secrets of the Incentive Stars," p. 100.

34. Frank K. Sonnenberg, "The Power of Cross-Selling," *Journal of Business Strategy*, vol. 9, January-February 1988, pp. 56–59.

35. Cynthia R. Cauthern, "Moving Technical Support into the Sales Loop," *Sales & Marketing Management*, vol. 142, August 1990, pp. 58–61.

36. Lynda Schuster, "Houston's Car Buyers Keep Coming Back to Jim Dailey's Down-Home Salesmanship," *The Wall Street Journal*, August 17, 1980, p. 17.

37. Techniques and strategies for handling complaints are presented in Cathy Goodwin and Ivan Ross, "Consumer Evaluations of Responses to Complaints," *The Journal of Consumer Marketing*, vol. 7, Spring 1990, pp. 39–47; see also Jerry Plymire, "What We Need Are More Complaints," *Business Marketing*, vol. 75, March 1990, p. 74.

38. Betsy Weisendanger, "A Conversation On Conversation with Deborah Tannen," *Sales & Marketing Management*, vol. 143, April 1991, pp. 38–42.

39. "Doctors Say Drug Companies Offer Gifts, Some Valuable," *Arkansas Democrat-Gazette*, April 3, 1992, p. 3A.

CHAPTER 6

1. Bob Attanasio, "How PC-based Sales Quotas Boost Productivity, Morale," *Sales & Marketing Management*, vol. 143, September 1991, pp. 148–150.

2. Several experts favor territorial crossovers to maintain account service continuity. See Ron Kolgraf, "Strategies of Territory Management," *Industrial Distribution*, November 1978, p. 36. In contrast, Litton Microwave Cooking Products has a policy against crossovers. See Rayna Skolnick, "Thou Shalt Not Cross Territory Lines at Litton Microwave," in *Time and Territory Management*, special report by *Sales & Marketing Management*, May 24, 1976, p. 34.

3. See Kolgraf, "Strategies of Territory Management," p. 35.

4. Robert F. Vizza and Thomas E. Chambers, *Time and Territorial Management for the Salesman*, New York: Sales Executives Club, 1971, p. 6.

5. *Ibid.*, p. 9.

6. For an excellent review of these activities and procedures, see John D. Louth, "Establishing Sales Territories," in *Handbook of Modern Marketing*, 2nd ed., Victor P. Buell, ed., New York: McGraw-Hill, 1986, pp. 69.1–69.11.

7. For example, see Tom Eisenhart, "Drawing a Map to Better Sales," *Business Marketing*, vol. 75, January 1990, pp. 59–63.

8. See A. Parasuraman, "Assigning Salesmen to Sales Territories: Some Practical Guidelines," *Industrial Marketing Management*, 1975, p. 336.

9. An excellent discussion of call allocation appears in Raymond W. LaForge, Clifford E. Young, and B. Curtis Hamm, "Increasing Sales Productivity through Improved Sales Call Allocation Strategies," *Journal of Personal Selling & Sales Management*, vol. 3, November 1983, pp. 52–59.

10. A model for analyzing sales territory potential and performance is presented in Adrian B. Ryan and Charles B. Weinberg, "Territory Sales Response Models," *Journal of Marketing Research*, vol. 24, May 1987, pp. 229–233.

11. Bill Kelley, "How Much Help Does a Salesperson Need?" *Sales & Marketing Management*, vol. 141, May 1989, pp. 32–35.

12. Richard T. Hise, "Salesmen's Routing," in *Beacham's Marketing Reference*, Walton Beacham, Richard T. Hise, and Hale N. Tongren, eds., Washington, DC: Research Publishing, 1986, pp. 839–840

13. "When It Hits the Fan, So Do Most Time Management Strategies," *Personal Selling Power*, vol. 11, May–June 1991, p. 49.

14. A recent study found that at least a partial association exists between time spent contacting customers and sales performance. See William A. Weeks and Lynn R. Kahle, "Salespeople's Time Use and Performance," *Journal of Personal Selling & Sales Management*, vol. 10, Winter 1990, pp. 29–37.

15. See, for example, Jack Falvey, "Get Salespeople to Face Up to Making More Calls," *Sales & Marketing Management*, vol. 140, June 1988, pp. 86, 88.

16. See Robert F. Vizza, "ROTI: Profitable Selling's New Math," in *Time and Territory Management*, special report by *Sales & Marketing Management*, May 24, 1976, pp. 17ff; see also Vizza and Chambers, *Time and Territorial Management for the Salesman*, pp. 16ff.

17. See also "How Do Managers Effectively Manage Their Time?" *Sales & Marketing Management*, vol. 142, July 1990, pp. 24, 26; Erik Colonius, "How Top Managers Manage Their Time," *Fortune*, June 4, 1990, pp. 250–262; Carl K. Clayton, "How To Manage Your Time and Territory For Better Sales Results," *Personal Selling Power*, vol. 10, March 1990, p. 46.

18. See Anne Oakley, "Stop Time Wasters without Wasting Your Time," *Personal Selling Power*, vol. 10, May-June 1990, p. 18.

19. Thomas N. Ingram, "Improving Sales Force Productivity: A Critical Examination of the Personal Selling Process," *Review of Business*, vol. 12, Summer 1990, pp. 7–12, 40; see also Jerry Colletti, "Are You Tough Enough to Raise Sales Productivity?" *Sales & Marketing Management*, vol. 140, October 1988, pp. 50–54.

20. William A. O'Connell, "A 10-Year Report on Sales Force Productivity," *Sales & Marketing Management*, vol. 140, December 1988, p. 33.

21. *Ibid.*

22. See, for example, Richard N. Cardozo, Shannon H. Shipp, and Kenneth J. Roering, "Implementing New Business-to-Business Selling Methods," *Journal of Personal Selling & Sales Management*, vol. 7, August 1987, pp. 17–26.

23. William A. O'Connell and William Keenan, Jr., "The Shape

of Things to Come," *Sales & Marketing Management*, vol. 142, January 1990, p. 39.

24. L. Brent Manssen, "Using PCs to Automate and Innovate Marketing Activities," *Industrial Marketing Management*, vol. 19, August 1990, pp. 209–213; Brian Dillon and Cory Statton-Smith, "Why Automate? An Analysis of Sales Automation Benefits," *Sales & Marketing Management in Canada*, vol. 31, June 1990, pp. 12–15; Phil Corse and Marc Martinez, "Benefits Outweigh Pitfalls of Sales Force Automation," *American Salesman*, vol. 34, March 1989, pp. 9–15; Thayer C. Taylor, "How the Best Sales Forces Use PCs and Laptops," *Sales & Marketing Management*, vol. 140, April 1988, pp. 64–74; see also Al Wendell and Dale Hempeck, "Sales Force Automation—Here and Now," *Journal of Personal Selling & Sales Management*, vol. 7, August 1987, pp. 11–16.

25. Rowland T. Moriarty and Gordon S. Schwartz, "Automation to Boost Sales and Marketing," *Harvard Business Review*, vol. 67, January-February 1989, p. 100.

26. Louis A. Wallis, *Computer-Based Sales Force Support*, New York: The Conference Board, 1990; Harry S. Dent, Jr., "Automating Your Sales Force," *Small Business Report*, vol. 15, December 1990, pp. 29–39; Sam Licciardi, "Paper-Pushing Sales Reps Are Less Productive," *Marketing News*, vol. 24, November 12, 1990, p. 15; Thayer C. Taylor, "Laptop and the Sales Force: New Stars in the Sky," *Sales & Marketing Management*, vol. 138, April 1987, pp. 50–55; Tom Badgett, "Making Your Sales Force More Productive," *Personal Computing*, vol. 10, July 1986.

27. "Computer-Based Sales Support: Shell Chemical's System," *Marketing: The Conference Board's Management Briefing*, vol. 4, April-May 1989, pp. 4–5.

28. "Marketer Uses His Computer to Become a Sales Champion," *Marketing News*, May 11, 1984.

29. Wendell and Hempeck, "Sales Force Automation—Here and Now," *Journal of Personal Selling & Sales Management*, pp. 11–12. Reprinted by permission.

30. Jerome A. Colletti, "Integrating Computers into the Selling Process," *Small Business Report*, vol. 13, February 1988, p. 56.

31. Timothy D. Schellhardt, "Moving Up May Not Mean Moving Around as Much," *The Wall Street Journal*, October 4, 1991, p. B1.

32. Dana Bottorff, "At Nestor, Silence Ceased Being a Virtue When Revenues Began Fading Away," *New England Business*, May 2, 1988, pp. 41, 43.

33. Susan Horey, "Speeding Up List Fulfillment," *Folio: The Magazine for Magazine Management*, April 1991, pp. 51–52.

CHAPTER 7

1. Zachary Schiller and John Carey, "Procter & Gamble: On a Short Leash," *Business Week*, July 22, 1991, pp. 76–78; Sandra D. Atchison and Kevin Kelly, "The FDA Is Growling at Drugmakers, Too," *Business Week*, July 1, 1991, pp. 34–35; Lois Therrien, John Carey, and Joseph Weber, "The Cholesterol Is in the Fire Now," *Business Week*, June 10, 1991, pp. 34–35; John Carey and Zachary Schiller, "The FDA Is Swinging 'a Sufficiently Large Two-by-Four,'" *Business Week*, May 27, 1991, p. 44.

2. Allan J. Magrath, "Eight Ways to Avoid Marketing Shock," *Sales & Marketing Management*, vol. 141, April 1989, pp. 55–56.

3. Diane Crispell, "Workers in 2000," *American Demographics*, March 1990, pp. 38–39.

4. *Ibid.*, p. 36.

5. Denise M. Topolnicki, "Avon's Corporate Makeover," *Working Women*, vol. 13, February 1988, pp. 57–61; see also Christine A. Rossell, "Avon Calling . . . Nobody's Home," *ZIP/Target Marketing*, vol. 9, April 1986, pp. 19–20.

6. Crispell, "Workers in 2000," p. 38.

7. Alice Cuneo, "Diverse by Design," *Business Week/Reinventing America 1992*, October 23, 1992, p. 72.

8. John Naisbitt and Patricia Aburdene, *Megatrends 2000*, New York: Avon Books, 1991, pp. 5–6.

9. *Ibid.*, p. 6.

10. "Is the Electronic Age a Boon to the Sales Force?" *American Salesman*, vol. 35, May 1990, p. 4.

11. Jack Falvey, "As Selling Goes Hi-Tech, Make Sure It Computes for You," *Sales & Marketing Management*, vol. 140, December 1988, p. 15.

12. Sam Licciardi, "Paper-Pushing Sales Reps Are Less Productive," *Marketing News*, vol. 23, November 12, 1990, p. 15; see also William J. Young, "Have Computers Revolutionized Sales Management?" *Management Review*, vol. 76, April 1987, pp. 54–55.

13. Louis A. Wallis, *Computer-Based Sales Force Support*, New York: The Conference Board, 1990, p. 7.

14. An interesting framework for preparing a competitive analysis and using the information for making sales force decisions is presented in Daniel C. Smith and John E. Prescott, "Couple Competitive Analysis to Sales Force Decisions," *Industrial Marketing Management*, vol. 16, February 1987, pp. 55–61.

15. "The Future of Banking: Special Report," *Business Week*, April 22, 1991, pp. 72–76.

16. Kathleen Hawk, "Non-Traditional Products Instill True Sales Culture," *Bank Marketing*, vol. 22, November 1990, pp. 25–27; Michael N. Trigg, "State of the Industry—1987: Sales and Service Cultures Are Interchangeable—Not Mutually Exclusive," *Bank Marketing*, vol. 19, September 1987, p. 30.

17. Judith A. Pennington, "Okay, Our People Are Selling, Now What Do We Do?" *Bottomline*, vol. 5, October 1988, pp. 25–26; see also "Trust Marketing: Cultivating a Sales Culture," *Trusts & Estates*, vol. 126, November 1987, pp. 10, 12; Jack Eastman, "Banking and Sales Are Not Mutually Exclusive," *Bank Marketing*, vol. 19, February 1987, pp. 6, 8; M. R. Grubbs and R. Eric Reidenbach, "Managing the Change to a Sales Organization," *Magazine of Bank Administration*, vol. 62, June 1986. pp. 40–44.

18. Karl A. Boedecker, Fred W. Morgan, and Jeffrey J. Stoltman, "Legal Dimensions of Salespersons' Statements: A Review and Managerial Suggestion," *Journal of Marketing*, vol. 55, January 1991, p. 70.

19. *Ibid.*, pp. 76–78.

20. Walecia Konrad and Harris Collingwood, "200,000 Foam Tomahawks: That's Not Chopped Liver," *Business Week*, November 11, 1991, p. 48.

CHAPTER 8

1. Walecia Konrad, "Cheerleading, and Clerks Who Know Awls from Augers," *Business Week*, August 3, 1992, p. 51.

2. Edward F. Walsh, "A Primer for Planning," *Sales & Marketing Management*, vol. 142, November 1990, p. 75.

3. Kenneth R. Evans and John L. Schlacter, "The Role of Sales Managers and Salespeople in a Marketing Information System," *Journal of Personal Selling & Sales Management*, vol. 5, November 1985, p. 49.

4. Craig Mellow, "The Best Source of Competitive Intelligence," *Sales & Marketing Management*, vol. 141, December 1989, pp. 24–26.

5. Jay E. Klompmaker, "Incorporating Information from Salespeople into the Marketing Planning Process," *Journal of Personal Selling & Sales Management*, vol. 1, Fall/Winter 1981, pp. 76–82.

6. Ellen Neuborne, "Dillard's Muscle-Flexing Wins Praise," *USA Today*, April 23, 1992, p. 38.

7. *PIMSLETTER*, No. 1, Cambridge, MA: Strategic Planning Institute, 1977.

8. Michael E. Porter, *Competitive Strategy: Techniques for Analyzing Industries and Competitors*, New York: Free Press, 1980, Chap. 2.

9. Orville C. Walker, Jr., and Robert W. Ruekert, "Marketing's Role in the Implementation of Business Strategies: A Critical Review and Conceptual Framework," *Journal of Marketing*, vol. 51, July 1987, p. 17.

10. William Strahle and Rosann L. Spiro, "Linking Market Share Strategies to Salesforce Objectives, Activities, and Compensation Policies," *Journal of Personal Selling & Sales Management*, vol. 6, August 1986, pp. 11–18.

11. Leon A. Wortmen, "Flying by His 'Seat of the Pants,'" *Business Marketing*, vol. 74, December 1989, pp. 44–48.

CHAPTER 9

1. David Thurber, "Japan Retires 7 Catfish after 16 Years, Ends Study of Quake Sensing Ability," *Arkansas Democrat-Gazette*, April 3, 1992, p. 2A; Peter Coy, "Not Just a Yuppie Toy," *Business Week*, February 24, 1992, pp. 36–38; Rob Norton, "Why Economists Miss the Mark," *Fortune*, January 27, 1992, p. 24; Gary Slutsker, "Country Cousin," *Forbes*, September 30, 1991, pp. 42–43; Amy Bernstein, "Pie on the '90s," *U.S. News & World Report*, September 23, 1991, p. 18; Robert D. Hof, Julie Amparano Lopez, and Chuck Hawkins, "For Cellular, a Sudden Hang-up," *Business Week*, May 6, 1991, pp. 127–129; "Skepticism for the Numbers," *Marketing News*, January 7, 1991, p. 20.

2. The authors are indebted to James P. Jennings of St. Louis University for his numerous contributions to Chap. 9.

3. Steward A. Washburn, "Don't Let Sales Forecasting Spook You," *Sales & Marketing Management*, vol. 140, September 1988, pp. 118, 121.

4. Essam Mahmond, Gilliam Rice, and Naresh Malhotra, "Emerging Issues in Sales Forecasting and Decision Support Systems," *Journal of the Academy of Marketing Science*, vol. 16, Fall 1988, pp. 47–61.

5. Mark J. Lawless, "Effective Sales Forecasting—A Management Tool," *Journal of Business Forecasting*, vol. 9, Spring 1990, p. 2.

6. For specific information on the application of marketing research techniques to sales forecasting see Thomas C. Kinnear and James R. Taylor, "Demand Measurement and Forecasting," Chap. 22 in *Marketing Research: An Applied Approach*, 4th ed., New York: McGraw-Hill, 1991, pp. 715–723; Donald S. Tull and Del I. Hawkins, "Sales Forecasting," Chap. 21 in *Marketing Research: Measurement and Method*, 5th ed., New York: Macmillan, 1990, pp. 637–675; Harper W. Boyd, Jr., Ralph Westfall, and Stanley F. Stasch, "Market and Sales Analysis Research," Chap. 22 in *Marketing Research: Text and Cases*, 7th ed., Homewood, IL: Richard D. Irwin, 1989, pp. 759–786.

7. For more information on test marketing, see Pat Seelig, "All Over The Map," *Sales & Marketing Management*, vol. 141, March 1989, pp. 58–64; "Special Report on Test Marketing," *Advertising Age*, August 24, 1987, pp. S1–S12.

8. William S. Sachs, "Forecasting New Product Outcomes in Packaged Goods," *Journal of Business Forecasting*, vol. 6, Winter 1987/1988, pp. 20–23; see also Barry L. Bayus, "Forecasting Sales of New Continent Products: An Application of the Compact Disc Market," *Journal of Product Innovation Management*, vol. 4, December 1987, pp. 243–255.

9. For a detailed study which shows how these surveys can be used by sales managers see Richard Kern, "The Four Surveys: Putting Them to Work, Survey of Buying Power," *Sales & Marketing Management*, vol. 139, July 27, 1987, pp. A8–A30.

10. Dennis F. Ellis, "How To Use Macroforecasts in Sales Forecasting," *Journal of Business Forecasting*, vol. 6, Fall 1987, pp. 19–21.

11. John D. Walter, Jr., "The Business Economist at Work: Dow Corning Corporation," *Business Economics*, vol. 21, July 1986, pp. 46–48.

12. Bernard Lashinsky, "The Business Economist at Work: Inland Steel Industries," *Business Economics*, vol. 25, July 1990, pp. 49–52.

13. For a review of sales forecasting techniques and practices see David M. Georgoff and Robert G. Murdick, "Manager's Guide to Forecasting," *Harvard Business Review*, vol. 64, January-February 1986, pp. 110–120; Geoffrey Lancaster and Robert Lomas, "A Managerial Guide to Forecasting," *International Journal of Physical Distribution and Materials Management*, vol. 16, June 1986, pp. 1–38.

14. Robin T. Peterson, "The Role of Experts' Judgement in Sales Forecasting," *Journal of Business Forecasting*, vol. 9, Summer 1990, pp. 16–21.

15. Robin T. Peterson, "Sales Force Composite Forecasting—An Exploratory Analysis," *Journal of Business Forecasting*, vol. 8, Spring 1989, pp. 23–27.

16. Jacob Gonek, "Tie Salesmen's Bonuses to Their Forecasts," *Harvard Business Review*, vol. 56, May-June 1978, pp. 116–123.

17. Rob Van Rycke, "Over-Confidence Leads to Unrealistic Sales Forecasts," *Sales & Marketing Management in Canada*, vol. 27, May 1986, pp. 16–17.

18. James E. Cox, Jr., "Approaches for Improving Salespersons' Forecasts," *Industrial Marketing Management*, vol. 18, November 1989, pp. 51–55.

19. J. Harold Ranck, Jr., "Avoiding the Pitfalls in Sales Forecasting," *Management Accounting*, vol. 68, September 1986, pp. 51–55.

20. Joachin Laner and Terrence O'Brien, "Sales Forecasting Using Cyclical Analysis," *Journal of Business and Industrial Marketing*, vol. 3, Winter 1988, pp. 25–35.

21. Edward B. Fischler and Robert F. Nelson, "Integrating Time-Series and End-Use Methods to Forecast Electricity Sales," *Journal of Forecasting*, vol. 5, January-March 1986, pp. 15–30.

22. N. Carroll Mohn, "Forecasting Sales With Trend Models—Coca-Cola's Experience," *Journal of Business Forecasting*, vol. 8, Fall 1989, pp. 6–8.

23. George Kress and John Snyder, "ABC of Box-Jenkins Models," *Journal of Business Forecasting*, vol. 7, Summer 1988, pp. 2–8.

24. Charles W. Gross and Jeffrey E. Sohl, "Improving Smoothing Models with An Enhanced Industrial Scheme," *Journal of Business Forecasting*, vol. 8, Spring 1989, pp. 13–18.

25. Ambar G. Rao and Masataka Yamada, "Forecasting with a Repeat Purchase Diffusion Model," *Management Science*, vol. 6, June 1988, pp. 734–752.

26. J. Scott Armstrong, Roderick J. Brodie, and Shelby H. McIntyre, "Forecasting Methods for Marketing: Review of Empirical Research," *International Journal of Forecasting*, vol. 3, 1987, pp. 355–376.

27. Timothy A. Davidson, "Forecasters: Who Are They? Survey Findings," *Journal of Business Forecasting*, vol. 6, Spring 1987, pp. 17–19.

28. Douglas J. Dalrymple, "Sales Forecasting Practices: Results from a United States Survey," *International Journal of Forecasting*, vol. 3, 1987, pp. 379–391.

29. Benito E. Flores and Edna M. White, "A Framework for the Combination of Forecasts," *Journal of the Academy of Marketing Science*, vol. 16, Fall 1988, pp. 95–103.

30. These criteria were first suggested in John L. Clark and Peter T. Elgers, "Evaluating the Sales Forecast," Michigan Business Review, May 1968, pp. 14–18.

31. Charles W. Gross, "Bridging the Communications Gap between Managers and Forecasters," *Journal of Business Forecasting*, vol. 6, Winter 1987/1988, pp. 6–9.

CHAPTER 10

1. Brent Bowers, "Small Firms Get Help from Advisory Boards," *The Wall Street Journal*, September 23, 1991, p. B1; and Jane Applegate, "Winning Advice That Isn't Costly," *Los Angeles Times*, May 31, 1991, p. D3.

2. "Sales Budgeting: The Sales Manager's Role," *Small Business Report*, vol. 11, June 1986, p. 22.

3. A. J. Magrath, "Financial Literacy for Marketers," *Sales & Marketing Management*, vol. 140, August 1988, p. 38.

4. Approximately two out of three firms engage in sales forecasting first, followed by budget development. See Larry S. Lowe, C. Richard Roberts, and James W. Cagley, "Your Sales Forecast-Marketing Budget Relationship: Is It Consistent?" *Management Accounting*, January 1980, p. 31.

5. Bill Kelley, "Recession-Proofing Your Sales Force," *Sales & Marketing Management*, vol. 143, February 1991, pp. 36–38.

6. *Ibid.*, p. 41.

7. "How to Budget for Sales," *Agency Sales Magazine*, vol. 17, May 1987, pp. 13–14.

8. For those sales managers who wish to use comparative data, the "Survey of Selling Costs" compiled annually by *Sales & Marketing Management* is an excellent source of information.

9. Terry Lloyd, "Winning the Budget Battle," *Sales & Marketing Management*, vol. 141, April 1989, p. 32.

10. The application of return on investment criteria to sales management was first described in J. S. Schiff and Michael Schiff, "New Sales Management Tool: ROAM," *Harvard Business Review*, vol. 55, July/August 1977, pp. 59–66.

11. This example and discussion are adapted from Donald J. Plumley, "All Right, How Much Will It Cost?" *Sales & Marketing Management*, vol. 141, pp. 50–55. Copyright: December 1989. Used by permission of Sales & Marketing Mangement.

12. For another view of the steps involved in the budgeting process see Mark J. Lawless, "A Forecasting Approach to Operating Profit," *Journal of Business Perspective*, vol. 9, Summer 1990, pp. 6–10.

13. See Donald J. Walt, "Productivity Measurement: A Management Accounting Challenge," *Management Accounting*, May 1980, p. 25.

CHAPTER 11

1. Tom Murray, "Starting a Salesforce from Scratch," *Sales & Marketing Management*, vol. 143, April 1991, pp. 51–58.

2. David Calfee, "Organize Sales Force to Meet Changing Marketplace Needs," *Marketing News*, vol. 24, March 5, 1990, p. 30; see also Edward B. Flanagan, "Reshaping the Sales Structure," *Marketing Communications*, vol. 11, January 1986, pp. 19–22, 63.

3. For a review of marketing organization approaches and suggestions for improving the structure and performance of marketing activities, see Robert W. Ruekert, Orville C. Walker, Jr., and Kenneth J. Roering, "The Organization of Marketing Activities: A Contingency Theory of Structure and Performance," *Journal of Marketing*, vol. 49, Winter 1985, pp. 13–25.

4. Peter F. Drucker, "The Coming of the New Organization," *Harvard Business Review*, vol. 66, January-February 1988, p. 45. Copyright © 1988 by The President and Fellows of Harvard College, all rights reserved.

5. *Ibid.*, pp. 45–53.

6. Martin Everett, "America's Best Salesforce: Metal Products—Gillette Hones Salespower to a Fine Edge," *Sales & Marketing Management,* vol. 138, June 1987, p. 59.

7. An interesting discussion appears in Ram C. Rao and Ronald E. Turner, "Organization and Effectiveness of the Multiple-Product Salesforce," *Journal of Personal Selling & Sales Management,* vol. 4, May 1984, pp. 24–30; see also Jayashree Mahajan and Asoo J. Vakharia, "A Multiobjective Approach and Empirical Application of Sales-Organization Design," *Decision Sciences,* vol. 21, Summer 1990, pp. 608–625.

8. Rayna Skolnik, "Campbell Stirs Up Its Salesforce," *Sales & Marketing Management,* vol. 136, April 1986, p. 56.

9. Rod Kopp and John Faier, "Sizing Up Your Salesforce," *Business Marketing,* vol. 75, May 1990, pp. 42–45.

10. Harold J. Novick, "Target Your Sales Channels, Too," *Industry Week,* vol. 238, March 6, 1989, pp. 11–12.

11. Kathy Murray, "Thanks for the Advice," *Forbes,* vol. 141, May 2, 1988, pp. 62, 64.

12. Allan J. Magrath, "To Specialize or Not to Specialize," *Sales & Marketing Management,* vol. 141, June 1989, pp. 66–67.

13. *Ibid.*, p. 64.

14. Dan T. Dunn, Jr., and Claude A. Thomas, "High Tech Organizes for the Future," *Journal of Personal Selling & Sales Management,* vol. 10, Spring 1990, p. 43. Copyright © 1990. Used by permission.

15. *Ibid.*, pp. 53–54.

16. *Ibid.*, p. 45.

17. *Ibid.*, p. 52.

18. John R. Dougherty and Christopher Gray, "The Role of Sales and Marketing in Planning and Scheduling," *Industrial Management & Data Systems,* July-August 1987, pp. 20–24.

19. John E. Merchant, "Teamwork for Profit," *Credit & Financial Management,* vol. 89, May 1987, p. 33.

20. Kevin F. Sullivan, Richard A. Bobbe, and Martin R. Strasmore, "Transforming the Salesforce in a Maturing Industry," *Management Review,* vol. 77, June 1988, p. 46.

21. Kevin E. Carey, "Merging Two Salesforces into One," *Sales & Marketing Management,* vol. 138, March 1987, pp. 102–104.

22. David Perry, "How You'll Manage Your 1990s Distribution Portfolio," *Business Marketing,* vol. 74, June 1989, p. 56.

23. Benson P. Shapiro and John Wyman, "New Ways to Reach Your Customers," *Harvard Business Review,* vol. 59, July-August 1981, pp. 103-110; see also Shannon Shipp, Kenneth J. Roering, and Richard N. Cardozo, "Implementing a New Selling Mix," *Journal of Business & Industrial Marketing,* vol. 3, Summer 1988, pp. 55–63; Richard Cardozo and Shannon Shipp, "New Selling Methods are Changing Industrial Sales Management," *Business Horizons,* vol. 30, September-October 1987, pp. 23–28; Richard N. Cardozo, Shannon H. Shipp, and Kenneth J. Roering, "Implementing New Business-to-Business Selling Strategies," *Journal of Personal Selling & Sales Management,* vol. 7, August 1987, pp. 17–26; and Howard Sutton, *Rethinking the Company's Selling and Distribution Channels,* New York: The Conference Board, 1986.

24. Shapiro and Wyman, "New Ways to Reach Your Customers," p. 103.

25. Portions of this section are based on Eugene M. Johnson and William J. Meiners, "Telemarketing: Trends, Issues, and Opportunities," *Journal of Personal Selling & Sales Management,* vol. 7, November 1987, pp. 65–68.

26. Donald M. Cloud, "The Evolving Face of the Telemarketing Industry," *Telemarketing,* July 1980, p. 54.

27. Bob Stone and John Wyman, *Successful Telemarketing,* Englewood Cliffs, NJ: Prentice-Hall, 1985, p. 6.

28. Eugene M. Johnson and William J. Meiners, "A Study of Selected Telemarketing Organizational Issues," *Journal of the American Telemarketing Association,* vol. 6, June 1990, p. 17.

29. William C. Moncreif, Shannon H. Shipp, Charles W. Lamb, Jr., and David W. Cravens, "Examining the Roles of Telemarketing in Selling Strategy," *Journal of Personal Selling & Sales Management,* vol. 9, Fall 1989, pp. 1–12; Judith J. Marshall and Harrie Vredenburg, "Successfully Using Telemarketing in Industrial Sales," *Industrial Marketing Management,* vol. 17, February 1988, pp. 15–22; see also John C. Coppett and Roy Dale Voorhees, "Telemarketing: Supplement to Field Sales," *Industrial Marketing Management,* vol. 41, August 1985, pp. 213–216.

30. Marshall and Vredenburg, "Successfully Using Telemarketing in Industrial Sales," p. 15.

31. William C. Moncreif, Charles W. Lamb, Jr., and Terry Dielman, "Developing Telemarketing Support Systems," *Journal of Personal Selling & Sales Management,* vol. 6, August 1986, pp. 48–49.

32. Richard L. Bencin and Donald J. Janovic, eds., *Encyclopedia of Telemarketing,* Englewood Cliffs, NJ: Prentice-Hall, 1989; Stone and Wyman, *Successful Telemarketing* (see Ref. 27); Bill Kelley, "Is There Anything That Can't Be Sold By Phone?" *Sales & Marketing Management,* vol. 141, April 1989, pp. 60–64. For a number of specific examples and case studies, see Earl L. Bailey, *A Growing Role for Business-to-Business Telemarketing,* New York: The Conference Board, 1988; Murray Romen, *Telemarketing Campaigns That Work!,* New York: McGraw Hill, 1983.

33. Elaine Santoro, "Beyond the Gas Pump," *Direct Marketing,* vol. 53, March 1991, pp. 28–29.

34. Jerome A. Colletti and Gary S. Tubridy, "Effective Major Account Sales Management," *Journal of Personal Selling & Sales Management,* vol. 7, August 1987, p. 1.

35. Kate Bertrand, "Sales Management: The Special Touch," *Business Marketing,* vol. 72, March 1987, p. 50; see also, Philip Maher, "Focus on Sales Management—NAM: Hard Work, but Profitable," *High-Tech Marketing,* vol. 3, February 1986, p. 54.

36. Colletti and Tubridy, "Effective Major Account Sales Management," p. 1.

37. Shapiro and Wyman, "New Ways to Reach Your Customers," pp. 104–105.

38. Richard P. Aschman, "Eastment Kodak Company," *NAMA Journal,* vol. 31, Fall 1989, pp. 10–11.

39. Sutton, *Rethinking the Company's Selling and Distribution Channels,* pp. 10–11.

40. Robert McCarthy, "IBM Meets the Real World," *High-Tech Marketing,* September 1985, pp. 56–64.

41. Edwin E. Bobrow, "Suddenly, an Urge to Boost Their Potential," *Sales & Marketing Management,* vol. 128, June 7, 1982, p. 37.

42. Wilson Harrell, "Selling: Going for Brokers," *Inc.,* vol. 8, May 1986, pp. 167–170; see also Carol Rose Carey, "A Low-Cost Way to Find Top Salespeople," *Inc.,* March 1982, pp. 119–120.

43. Lois C. DuBois and Roger H. Grace, "The Care and Feeding of Manufacturers' Reps," *Business Marketing,* December 1987, p. 52.

44. Robert C. Lindsley, "A Searcher's Guide to Finding the 'Right' Rep," *Sales & Marketing Management,* vol. 128, June 7, 1982, p. 52.

45. DuBois and Grace, "The Care and Feeding of Manufacturers' Reps," p. 62.

CHAPTER 12

1. Richard Poe, "The Executive Sell," *Success,* May 1991, pp. 61–69.

2. Richard Kern, "IQ Tests for Salesmen Make a Comeback," *Sales & Marketing Management,* vol. 140, April 1988, p. 45.

3. Raymond LaForge and David W. Cravens, "Steps in Selling Effort Deployment," *Industrial Marketing Management,* July 1982, p. 184.

4. Walter J. Semlow, "How Many Salesmen Do You Need?" *Harvard Business Review,* vol. 37, May-June 1959, pp. 126-132.

5. Arthur Meiden, "Optimizing the Number of Industrial Salespersons," *Industrial Marketing Management,* February 1982, pp. 63–74.

6. R. S. Howick and M. Pidd, "Salesforce Deployment Models," *European Journal of Operational Research,* vol. 48, October 16, 1990, pp. 295–310.

7. Leonard M. Lodish, "A User-Oriented Model for Salesforce Size, Product, and Market Allocation Decisions," *Journal of Marketing,* Summer 1980, pp. 70–78.

8. For a similar method which uses the statistical approach of trend analysis, see "The Optimum Number of Salespeople—Maximize Salesforce Effectiveness," *Small Business Report,* vol. 11, March 1986, pp. 85–89.

9. Gregory B. Salsbury, "Properly Recruit Salespeople to Reduce Training Cost," *Industrial Marketing Management,* April 1982, p. 144.

10. Timothy J. Trow, "The Secret to a Good Hire: Profiling," *Sales & Marketing Management,* vol. 142, May 1990, pp. 44-46ff.

11. Jeffrey J. Sager and Gerald R. Ferris, "Personality and Salesforce Selection in the Pharmaceutical Industry," *Industrial Marketing Management,* vol. 15, November 1986, pp. 319–324.

12. Dan C. Weilbaker, "The Identification of Selling Abilities Needed for Missionary Type Sales," *Journal of Personal Selling & Sales Management,* vol. 10, Summer 1990, pp. 45–58.

13. Thomas Rollins, "How to Tell Competent Salespeople from the Other Kind," *Sales & Marketing Management,* vol. 142, September 1990, p. 118.

14. Thomas R. Wotruba, Edwin K. Simpson, and Jennifer L. Reed-Draznik, "The Recruiting Interview as Perceived by College Student Applicants for Sales Positions," *Journal of Personal Selling & Sales Management,* vol. 9, Fall 1989, p. 22.

15. Arthur Bragg, "Grads Give Recruiters Low Grades," *Sales & Marketing Management,* vol. 140, May 1988, pp. 48–49.

16. For an interesting review of recruiting sources and approaches, see Liz Amante, "Help Wanted: Creative Recruitment Tactics," *Personnel,* vol. 66, October 1989, pp. 32–36; Morton E. Grossmen and Margaret Magnus, "Hire Spending," *Personnel Journal,* February 1989, pp. 73–76.

17. Jack Falvey, "The Old College Try," *Sales & Marketing Management,* vol. 140, May 1988, pp. 46–47.

18. Jon M. Hawes, "How to Improve Your College Recruiting Program," *Journal of Personal Selling & Sales Management,* vol. 9, Summer 1989, p. 48.

19. Falvey, "The Old College Try," p. 47.

20. From Northwestern Mutual Life Insurance Company's internship program booklet for college students. Used by permisison.

21. Allan Halcrow, "Employees Are Your Best Recruiters," *Personnel Journal,* vol. 67, November 1988, pp. 42–49.

22. Marianne Matthews, "If Your Ads Aren't Pulling Top Sales Talent," *Sales & Marketing Management,* vol. 142, February 1990, pp. 75–79.

23. For more on executive recruiters, see "Executive Search: Management Headache or Opportunity for Creative Change," *Management Review,* April 1982, pp. 27–28; "Executive Recruiters Start Raising Fees, Prompting Some Companies to Go It Alone," *The Wall Street Journal,* August 4, 1981, p. 33; "Where Headhunters Hunt," *Industry Week,* February 9, 1981, pp. 42–47.

24. James B. Weitzul, "EEOC's 'Bottom Line' Approach and Sales Personnel Selection," *Best's Review—Life and Health Insurance Edition,* July 1980, p. 82.

25. *Ibid.,* pp. 82–83.

26. Richard Nelson, "Maybe It's Time to Take Another Look at Tests as a Sales Selection Tool," *Journal of Personal Selling & Sales Management,* vol. 7, August 1987, p. 37.

27. Diane Crispell, "Workers in 2000," *American Demographics,* March 1990, pp. 37–38.

28. Herbert M. Greenberg and Ronald L. Bern, *The Successful Salesman: Man and His Sales Manager,* Philadelphia, PA: Auerbach Publishers, 1972, p. 80.

29. "Job Matching Leads to Better Sales Performance," *Personnel,* January-February 1981, pp. 45–47; Herbert M. Greenberg and Jeanne Greenberg, "Job Matching for Better Sales Performance," *Harvard Business Review,* vol. 58, September-October 1980, pp. 128–133.

CHAPTER 13

1. Teri Lammers, "The Foolproof Interviewer's Guide," *Inc.,* December 1991, pp. 127–132; Martin Everett and Betsy

Wiesendanger, "What Price Employee Loyalty?" *Sales & Marketing Management*, vol. 143, October 1991, p. 32; "For Merrill Lynch Trainees, It's Pay Me Now and Pay Me Later," *Sales & Marketing Management*, vol. 143, July 1991, p. 24; Charles Waller, "Rx for Dealer Turnover: Pay Them To Stay," *Sales & Marketing Management*, vol. 142, September 1990, p. 33.

2. For an interesting discussion of this issue, see Arthur Bragg, "Are Good Salespeople Born or Made?" *Sales & Marketing Management*, vol. 140, September 1988, pp. 74–78.

3. Frank F. Stahlschmidt, "On Recruiting and Selection," *Life Association News*, vol. 81, November 1986, pp. 152–153.

4. Lynn G. Coleman, "Salesforce Turnover Has Managers Wondering Why," *Marketing News*, vol. 23, December 4, 1989, p. 6.

5. For some interesting comparative data, see Bragg, "Are Good Salespeople Born or Made?" p. 76.

6. Coleman, "Salesforce Turnover Has Managers Wondering Why," p. 21.

7. Thomas N. Ingram and Keun S. Lee, "Salesforce Commitment and Turnover," *Industrial Marketing Management*, vol. 19, May 1990, pp. 149–154; Rene Y. Darmon, "Identifying Sources of Turnover Costs: A Segmental Approach," *Journal of Marketing*, vol. 54, April 1990, pp. 46–56; Marvin A. Jolson, Alan J. Dubinsky, and Rolph E. Anderson, "Correlates and Determinants of the Salesforce Turnover: An Exploratory Study," *Journal of Personal Selling & Sales Management*, vol. 7, November 1987, pp. 9–27.

8. George H. Lucas, Jr., A. Parasuraman, Robert A. Davis, and Ben M. Enis, "An Empirical Study of Salesforce Turnover," *Journal of Marketing*, vol. 51, July 1987, pp. 53–55.

9. James W. Obermayer, "Don't Risk Sales Leakage!" *Business Marketing*, vol. 75, February 1990, pp. 44–48.

10. Wesley J. Johnston and Martha C. Cooper, "Industrial Salesforce Selection: Current Knowledge and Needed Research," *Journal of Personal Selling & Sales Management*, vol. 1, Spring-Summer 1981, p. 49.

11. "How Not To Hire a Salesforce," *Sales Manager's Bulletin*, September 30, 1982, p. 4.

12. Johnston and Cooper, "Industrial Salesforce Selection: Current Knowledge and Needed Research," p. 50.

13. "New England Life Takes Steps to Insure Its Future," *Sales & Marketing Management*, vol. 135, August 12, 1985, p. 74. Copyright: August 1985. Reprinted by permission of Sales & Marketing Management.

14. E. James Randall, "Selecting the Successful Salesperson," *Review of Business*, vol. 12, Summer 1990, pp. 19–24.

15. Alan J. Dubinsky and Thomas E. Barry, "A Survey of Sales Management Practices," *Industrial Marketing Management*, April 1982, p. 136.

16. Dubinsky and Barry, "A Survey of Sales Management Practices," p. 136.

17. Randall, "Selecting the Successful Salesperson," p. 19.

18. Michael W. Mercer and John J. Sears, "Using Scorable Interview Tests in Hiring," *Personnel*, June 1987, pp. 57–60.

19. Thomas F. Casey, "Making the Most of a Sales Selection Interview," *Personnel*, vol. 7, September 1990, pp. 41–43; and Phil Faris, "No More Winging It," *Sales & Marketing Management*, vol. 137, August 1986, p. 90.

20. Arthur Bragg, "Checking References," *Sales & Marketing Management*, vol. 142, November 1990, p. 68.

21. *Ibid.*, p. 73.

22. "Looking for a Job? You May Be Out before You Go In," *Business Week*, September 24, 1990, pp. 128–130.

23. Richard Nelson, quoted in Richard Kern, "IQ Tests for Salesmen Make a Comeback," *Sales & Marketing Management*, vol. 140, April 1988, p. 44.

24. Richard Nelson, "Maybe It's Time To Take Another Look at Tests as a Sales Selection Tool," *Journal of Personal Selling & Sales Management*, vol. 7, August 1987, pp. 34-35.

25. For a review of the advantages and disadvantages of psychological tests see Kate Bertrand, "Hiring Tests: Sales Managers' Dream or Nightmare?" *Business Marketing*, July 1990, pp. 34–42.

26. C. Patrick Fleenor, "Assessment Center Selection of Sales Representatives," *Journal of Personal Selling & Sales Management*, vol. 7, May 1987, p. 57.

27. E. James Randall, Earnest F. Cooke, and Lois Smith, "A Successful Application of the Assessment Center Concept to the Salesperson Selection Process," *Journal of Personal Selling & Sales Management*, vol. 5, May 1985, p. 54.

28. Fleenor, "Assessment Center Selection of Sales Representatives," pp. 57–59.

29. Randall, Cooke, and Smith, "A Successful Application of the Assessment Center Concept to the Salesperson Selection Process," pp. 53–61.

30. Richard Nelson, quoted in Richard Kern, "IQ Tests for Salesmen Make a Comeback," pp. 45–46.

31. W. E. Patton, III, "Drug Abuse in the Salesforce," *Journal of Personal Selling & Sales Management*, vol. 8, August 1988, p. 22.

32. Arthur Bragg, "A New Twist: 'Auditioning' for a Job," *Sales & Marketing Management*, vol. 140, July 1988, p. 30.

33. *Ibid.*, p. 32.

34. Bob Woods, "Recruiting the Best and the Brightest," *Sales & Marketing Management*, vol. 129, August 16, 1982, p. 51.

35. Robert Goddard, Jeremy Fox, and W. E. Patton, "The Job-Hire Sale," *Personnel Administrator*, vol. 34, June 1989, pp. 120–125.

CHAPTER 14

1. Fleming Meeks and Jean Sherman Chatzky, "Hear, Watch, and Sell the Customer," *Forbes*, November 11, 1991, pp. 218–224; Tom Richman, "An In-House Sales School," *Inc.*, May 1991, pp. 85–86; Michael Barrier, "The Power of a Good Idea," *Nation's Business*, November 1990, pp. 34, 36; Harlan S. Byrne, "Paychex Inc.: Newer Services Promise Sharp Gains in Growth," *Barron's*, March 12, 1990, pp. 52–53.

2. This concept was first introduced in Marvin A. Jolson, "The Salesperson's Career Cycle," *Journal of Marketing*, vol. 38, Fall 1974, pp. 39–46. For more recent studies of the salesper-

son's career cycle, see William L. Cron, Alan J. Dubinsky, and Ronald E. Michaels, "The Influence of Career Stages on Components of Salesperson Motivation," *Journal of Marketing,* vol. 52, January 1988, pp. 78–92; John C. Hafer, "An Empirical Investigation of the Salesperson's Career Stage Perspective," *Journal of Personal Selling & Sales Management,* vol. 6, November 1986, pp. 1–7; William L. Cron, "Industrial Salesperson Development: A Career Stage Perspective," *Journal of Marketing,* vol. 48, Fall 1984, pp. 41–52.

3. William Keenan, Jr., "The Nagging Problem of the Plateaued Salesperson," *Sales & Marketing Management,* vol. 141, pp. 36–37. Copyright: March 1989. Reprinted by permission of Sales & Marketing Management.

4. Daniel C. Feldman and Barton A. Weitz, "Career Plateaus in the Salesforce: Understanding and Removing Blockages to Employee Growth," *Journal of Personal Selling & Sales Management,* vol. 8, November 1988, p. 26.

5. Alan J. Dubinsky and Thomas E. Barry, "A Survey of Sales Management Practices," *Industrial Marketing Management,* April 1982, pp. 136–137.

6. Andrew W. Brogowicz and Joseph L. Belonax, Jr., "Why Teaching Johnny to Sell is Easier Said than Done," *Sales & Marketing Management,* vol. 127, December 7, 1981, p. 67; and Eugene M. Johnson, "Why Johnny Can't Sell," *Sales & Marketing Management,* vol. 127, August 17, 1981, pp. 62–63.

7. For an example see Bobbi Linkemer, "Women in Sales: What Do They Really Want?" *Sales & Marketing Management,* vol. 141, January 1989, pp. 61–65.

8. Arthur Bragg, "Shell-Shocked on the Battlefield of Selling," *Sales & Marketing Management,* vol. 142, July 1990, pp. 52–58.

9. Robin T. Peterson, "What Makes Sales Training Programs Successful?" *Training and Development Journal,* vol. 44, August 1990, pp. 59–64.

10. Phil Anderson, "Refresher Sales Training," *Training—Sales Training Supplement,* May 1989, pp. 19–22.

11. Marc Hequet, "No More Willy Loman," *Training—Sales Training Supplement,* May 1989, p. 12.

12. R. W. Free and T. W. Peay, "Building a Total Sales Management System," *Training and Development Journal,* November 1981, p. 52.

13. David Morris, "Sales Training Should Change with the Times," *Marketing News,* vol. 21, July 3, 1987, p. 13.

14. "Study Reveals Sales-Training Needs of Business Marketers," *Marketing News,* vol. 23, March 13, 1989, p. 6.

15. See, for example, Neil Rackham and John Wilson, "Sales Training in the 1990s," *Training and Development Journal,* vol. 44, August 1990, pp. 48–52; Meg Kerr and Bill Burzynski, "Missing the Target: Sales Training in America," *Training and Development Journal,* vol. 42, July 1988, pp. 68–70; Dick Schoaf and Tom Cothran, "Sales Training in the Era of the Customer," *Training—Sales Training Supplement,* February 1988, pp. 3–4; Edward R. Del Gaizo, "Sales Training: Changing Roles, Changing Needs," *Training and Development Journal,* vol. 41, May 1987, pp. 46–47.

16. Efram G. Mallach, "The Truth about Training for Com-

puter Sales," *Training and Development Journal,* vol. 40, November 1986, pp. 54–56.

17. Michael J. Major, "Sales Training Emphasizes Service and Quality," *Marketing News,* vol. 24, March 5, 1990, p. 5.

18. Thomas W. Leigh, "Cognitive Selling Scripts and Sales Training," *Journal of Personal Selling & Sales Management,* vol. 7, August 1987, pp. 39–48.

19. Malcolm E. Shaw, "Sales Training in Transition," *Training and Development Journal,* February 1981, pp. 74–83.

20. Clyde E. Harris and Rosann L. Spiro, "Training Implications of Salesperson Influence Strategy," *Journal of Personal Selling & Sales Management,* vol. 1, Spring-Summer 1981, pp. 10–17.

21. Ronald H. King and Martha B. Booze, "Sales Training and Impression Management," *Journal of Personal Selling & Sales Management,* vol. 6, August 1986, pp. 51–60.

22. Earl D. Honeycutt, Jr., Clyde E. Harris, ad Stephen B. Castleberry, "Sales Training: A Status Report," *Training and Development Journal,* vol. 41, May 1987, p. 43.

23. For specific suggestions, see Pat Burke Guild, "How to Involve Learners in Your Lectures," *Training,* April 1983, pp. 43–45.

24. Betsy Niesyn, "Diary of a Sales Training Class," *High-Tech Marketing,* vol. 3, August 1986, pp. 17–20.

25. Larry J.B. Robinson, "Role Playing as a Sales Training Tool," *Harvard Business Review,* vol. 65, May-June 1987, pp. 34–35.

26. For a review of the use of video in business, see Steven S. King, "It's Show Time for Business," *Nation's Business,* vol. 77, April 1989, pp. 54–56.

27. Russell H. Granger, "Use of Video Camera Can Improve Your Sales Results," *Rough Notes,* vol. 129, December 1986, pp. 32–33.

28. Robinson, "Role Playing as a Sales Training Tool," p. 35.

29. "Humor as a Sales Training Tool," *D & B Reports,* vol. 33, November-December 1985, pp. 52–53.

30. Bristol Voss, "John Cleese Gets Serious about Training," *Sales & Marketing Management,* vol. 143, March 1991, p. 69.

31. Paul Kleyman and Mia Amato, "Video: Gaining the Marketing Edge," *Marketing Communications,* vol. 13, July 1988, pp. 34–39.

32. Jack Falvey, "The Most Neglected Training Tool," *Sales & Marketing Management,* vol. 142, January 1990, pp. 51–52.

33. *Ibid.,* p. 53.

34. K. Randall Russ, Joseph F. Hair, Robert C. Erffmeyer, and Debbie Easterling, "Usage and Perceived Effectiveness of High-Tech Approaches to Sales Training," *Journal of Personal Selling & Sales Management,* vol. 9, Spring 1989, p. 46; see also Randy Ross, "Technology Tackles the Training Dilemma," *High Technology Business,* vol. 8, September 1988, pp. 18–23.

35. Russ, Hair, Erffmeyer, and Easterling, "Usage and Perceived Effectiveness of High-Tech Approaches to Sales Training," *Journal of Personal Selling & Sales Management,* vol. 8, September 1988, pp. 47–48. Copyright © 1988. Used by permission.

36. *Ibid.,* p. 52.

37. Robert H. Collins, "Sales Training: A Microcomputer-Based Approach," *Journal of Personal Selling & Sales Management,* vol. 6, May 1986, pp. 71–76; see also Arthur Bragg, "Electronic Training Comes of Age," *Sales & Marketing Management,* vol. 143, March 1991, pp. 76–78.

38. Collins, "Sales Training: A Microcomputer-Based Approach," p. 71.

39. Bragg, "Electronic Training Comes of Age," p. 76.

40. Collins, "Sales Training: A Microcomputer-Based Approach," pp. 71–74.

41. Arlyn R. Rubash, Rawlie R. Sullivan, and Paul H. Herzog, "The Use of an 'Expert' to Train Salespeople," *Journal of Personal Selling & Sales Management,* vol. 7, August 1987, pp. 49–55.

42. Kate Bertrand, "Lights, Camera, Training!" *Business Marketing,* vol. 75, December 1990, pp. 16–18; see also Al Urbanski, "Electronic Training May Be in Your Future," *Sales & Marketing Management,* vol. 140, March 1988, pp. 46–48.

43. Judith Steele, "Sales Training, Up Close and Personal," *Business Marketing,* vol. 75, June 1990, pp. 70, 72.

44. Patricia Sellers, "How IBM Teaches to Sell," *Fortune,* vol. 117, June 6, 1988, pp. 141–146.

45. Kerry J. Rottenberger, "Sales Training Enters the Space Age," *Sales & Marketing Management,* vol. 142, October 1990, pp. 46–50.

46. Diane Lynn Kastiel, "Putting Videoconferences to Work for Sales and Marketing," *Business Marketing,* vol. 71, June 1986, pp. 100–104; see also "Tapping into Corporate Communications," *Marketing Communications,* vol. 11, May 1986, pp. 49–54.

47. Rottenberger, "Sales Training Enters the Space Age," p. 46.

48. *Ibid.,* p. 50.

49. Beverly Geber, "Who Should Do the Sales Training?" *Training,* vol. 24, May 1987, pp. 69–76.

50. Dennis A. Miller, "Ten Ways to Improve Sales Training Programs," *Marketing News,* August 22, 1980, p. 4.

51. W. Wossen Kassaye, "Improving Our Performance in Sales Training," *Journal of Professional Services Marketing,* vol. 5, February 1990, pp. 143–152.

52. Robert E. Lefton and V. R. Buzzotta, "Trainers, Learners and Training Results," *Training and Development Journal,* November 1980, pp. 12–18.

53. "How to Build Sales Training Symmetry," *Training,* June 1981, p. 13.

54. For an interesting discussion of the experience of attending the most famous self-help seminar, the Dale Carnegie Course, see Bill Kelley, "How To Make Friends and Sell To People," *Sales & Marketing Management,* vol. 141, August 1989, pp. 40–42.

55. Homer Kempfer, "Getting Your Money's Worth from Outside Training," *Training and Development Journal,* May 1980, pp. 116–118.

56. William Kennan, Jr., "Are You Overspending on Training?" *Sales & Marketing Management,* vol. 142, January 1990, pp. 56–60; see also Arthur Bragg, "Prove That You Produce Sales," *Sales & Marketing Management,* vol. 141, January 1989, pp. 55–59.

57. Joanne Levine, "Smith Kline: Testing Knowledge," *Incentive,* vol. 162, October 1988, pp. 62–63.

58. Earl D. Honeycutt and Thomas H. Stevenson, "Evaluating Sales Training Programs," *Industrial Marketing Management,* vol. 18, August 1989, pp. 215–222.

59. Ruth D. Salinger and Basil S. Deming, "Practical Strategies for Evaluating Training," *Training and Development Journal,* August 1982, p. 20.

60. Robert C. Erffmeyer, K. Randall Russ, and Joseph F. Hair, Jr., "Needs Assessment and Evaluation in Sales Training Programs," *Journal of Personal Selling & Sales Management,* vol. 11, Winter 1991, pp. 27–28.

61. Gerry Marx, "Let Customers Write Your Training Program," *Training and Development Journal,* November 1982, pp. 40–43.

62. For a discussion of this and other sales training fallacies, see Jack Falvey, "The Top Ten Sales Training Myths," *Small Business Reports,* vol. 15, March 1990, pp. 68–70.

63. William H. Cover, "Curbstone Coaching," *Training and Development Journal,* November 1980, p. 33.

64. *Ibid.,* p. 33.

65. Arnold L. Schwartz, "For Success in Coaching: Know When to Hold Back," *Personal Selling Power,* April 1991, pp. 58–59.

66. Jack Falvey, "Let Customers Teach the Troops about Products," *Sales & Marketing Management,* vol. 141, September 1989, pp. 94–95.

CHAPTER 15

1. Bill Kelley, "From Salesperson to Manager: Transition and Travail," *Sales & Marketing Management,* vol. 144, February 1992, pp. 32–36; Kathy Rebello and Evan I. Schwartz, "Microsoft: Bill Gates's Baby Is on Top of the World. Can It Stay There?" *Business Week,* February 24, 1992, pp. 60–64; Andrea Rothman, "Can Wayne Calloway Handle the Pepsi Challenge?" *Business Week,* January 27, 1992, pp. 90–98; Teri Lammers, "Sales Suggestions Anyone?" *Inc.,* October 1991, p. 156; "The Superstars of Selling," *Sales & Marketing Management,* vol. 143, March 1991, p. 47–48.

2. Stewart A. Washburn, "Fire Up Your Salesforce," *Business Marketing,* vol. 75, July 1990, p. 54.

3. William L. Cron and John L. Slocum, "The Influence of Career Stages on Salespeople's Job Attitudes, Work Perceptions, and Performance," *Journal of Marketing Research,* vol. 23, May 1986, pp. 119–129.

4. Abraham H. Maslow, *Motivation and Personality,* 2nd ed., New York: Harper & Row, 1970.

5. A contrary viewpoint is expressed in an article that questions the usefulness of Maslow's work on sales management. See Robert L. Berl, Nicholas C. Williamson, and Terry Powell, "Industrial Sales Force Motivation: A Critique and Test of Maslow's Hierarchy of Needs," *Journal of Personal Selling & Sales Management,* vol. 4, May 1984, pp. 32–39.

6. Bernard L. Rosenbaum and Nick Ward, "Why Sales Managers Need More and Better Management Training—and How You Can Give It," *Training,* April 1982, p. 45.

7. Stephen X. Doyle and Benson P. Shapiro, "What Counts in Motivating Your Sales Force?" *Harvard Business Review,* vol. 58, May-June 1980, p. 136.

8. Dick Berry and Ken Abrahamsen, "Three Types of Salesmen to Understand and Motivate," *Industrial Marketing Management,* July 1981, p. 212.

9. Jack Falvey, "It's Loyalty That Binds the Salesforce Together," *Sales & Marketing Management,* vol. 141, July 1989, pp. 24–25.

10. R. Kenneth Teas and James C. McElroy, "Casual Attributions and Expectancy Estimates: A Framework for Understanding the Dynamics of Salesforce Motivation," *Journal of Marketing,* vol. 50, January 1986, pp. 75–86; see also Pradeep K. Tyagi, "Perceived Organizational Climate and the Process of Salesperson Motivation," *Journal of Marketing Research,* vol. 19, May 1982, pp. 240–254; R. Kenneth Teas, "An Empirical Test of Models of Salespersons' Job Expectancy and Instrumentality Perceptions," *Journal of Marketing Research,* vol. 18, May 1981, pp. 209–226.

11. Thomas L. Quick, "The Best Kept Secret for Increasing Productivity," *Sales & Marketing Management,* vol. 141, July 1989, pp. 34–38.

12. Ronald E. Michaels, William L. Cron, Alan J. Dubinsky, and Eric A. Joachimsthaler, "Influence of Formalization on the Organizational Commitment and Work Alienation of Salespeople and Industrial Buyers," *Journal of Marketing Research,* vol. 25, November 1988, pp. 376–383; see also Lawrence B. Chonko, "Organizational Commitment in the Salesforce," *Journal of Personal Selling & Sales Management,* vol. 6, November 1986, pp. 19–27.

13. Thomas N. Ingram, Kuen S. Lee, and Steven J. Skinner, "An Empirical Assessment of Salesperson Motivation, Commitment, and Job Outcomes," *Journal of Personal Selling & Sales Management,* vol. 9, Fall 1989, pp. 25–33.

14. Pradeep K. Tyagi, "Organizational Climate, Inequities, and Attractiveness of Salesperson Rewards, *Journal of Personal Selling and Sales Management,* vol. V, November 1985, pp. 31–32.

15. *Ibid.,* p. 35.

16. Robert A. Scott, John E. Swan, M. Elizabeth Wilson, and Jenny J. Roberts, "Organizational Behavior Modification: A General Motivational Tool for Sales Management," *Journal of Personal Selling Sales Management,* vol. 6, August 1986, pp. 61–70.

17. *Ibid.,* pp. 68–69.

18. Harish Sujan, "Smarter versus Harder: An Exploratory Attributional Analysis of Salespeople's Motivation," *Journal of Marketing Research,* vol. 23, February 1986, pp. 41–49.

19. Louis W. Fry, Charles M. Futtrell, A. Parasuraman, and Margaret A. Chmielewski, "An Analysis of Alternative Causal Models of Salesperson Role Perceptions and Work-Related Attitudes," *Journal of Marketing Research,* vol. 23, May 1986, pp. 153–163; see also Ronald F. Bush and Paul Busch, "The Relationship of Tenure and Age to Role Clarity and Its Consequences in the Industrial Salesforce," *Journal of Personal*

Selling & Sales Management, vol. 1, Fall/Winter 1981-1982, pp. 17–23; Douglas N. Behrman, William J. Bigoness, and William D. Perreault, Jr., "Sources of Job Related Ambiguity and Their Consequences Upon Salesperson's Job Satisfaction and Performance," *Management Science,* November 1981, pp. 1246–1260.

20. Fry et al., p. 154.

21. For some different views of sales leadership and the various styles of leadership, see John K. Butler, Jr., and Richard M. Reese, "Leadership Style and Sales Performance: A Test of the Situational Leadership Model," *Journal of Personal Selling & Sales Management,* vol. 11, Summer 1991, pp. 37–46; Robert E. Hite and Joseph A. Bellizzi, "A Preferred Style of Sales Management," *Industrial Marketing Management,* vol. 15, August 1986, pp. 215–223; Frank E. Moriya and John C. Gockley, "Grid Analysis for Sales Supervision," *Industrial Marketing Management,* vol. 14, November 1985, pp. 235–238.

22. Larry Wilson, *Selling in the '90s,* Chicago, IL: Nightingale-Conant, 1988, p. 35.

23. Gary Couture, "Fast Track to Leadership?" *Manage,* vol. 38, Third Quarter 1986, p. 26. Copyright © 1986. Used by permission.

24. Ajay K. Kohli, "Effects of Supervisory Behavior: The Role of Individual Differences among Salespeople," *Journal of Marketing,* vol. 53, October 1989, p. 47.

25. Jack Falvey, "Managing the Maverick Salesperson," *Sales & Marketing Management,* vol. 142, September 1990, pp. 8, 12; see also Bill Kelley, "How to Manage a Superstar," *Sales & Marketing Management,* vol. 140, November 1988, pp. 32–34.

26. Myron Glassman and R. Bruce McAfee, "How to Turn Problem Salespeople into Winners," *Personal Selling Power,* vol. 11, March 1991, pp. 58–61; see also Thomas L. Quick, "Salvaging the Problem Salesperson," *Sales & Marketing Management,* vol. 141, April 1989, pp. 41–44; Victor M. Johnson, "Sales Slipping? Try Changing Your Culture," *Sales & Marketing Management,* vol. 140, May 1988, pp. 82–83; Jack Falvey, "How to Keep That Slump from Turning into a Disaster," *Sales & Marketing Management,* vol. 140, August 1988, pp. 21–22.

27. Alan J. Dubinsky, Roy D. Howell, Thomas N. Ingram, and Danny N. Bellinger, "Salesforce Socialization," *Journal of Marketing,* vol. 50, October 1986, pp. 192–193.

28. Kenneth Teas and James F. Howell, "Salespeople Satisfaction and Performance Feedback," *Industrial Marketing Management,* October 1981, pp. 49–57.

29. Joseph G. P. Paolillo, "Role Profiles for Managers in Different Functional Areas," *Group and Organization Studies,* vol. 12, March 1987, pp. 109–118.

30. Alan Zaremba, "The Upward Network," *Personal Journal,* vol. 68, March 1989, pp. 34–39; see also Gary A. Schroeder, "Using an Attitude Survey to Increase Sales Effectiveness," *Personnel,* vol. 66, February 1989, pp. 51–55.

31. Frank S. Cespedes, Stephen X. Doyle, and Robert J. Freedman, "Teamwork for Today's Selling," *Harvard Business Review,* vol. 67, March-April, 1989, pp. 44–48.

32. The vertical-dyad linkage model has been suggested as a

model for studying the infrastructure of a sales team and the implications for sales managers. See Stephen B. Castleberry and John F. Tanner, Jr., "The Manager-Salesperson Relationship: An Exploratory Examination of the Vertical-Dyad Linkage Model," *Journal of Personal Selling & Sales Management*, vol. 6, November 1986, pp. 29–37.

33. For a different view of this leadership approach, see Jan P. Muczyk and Bernard C. Reimann, "Has Participative Management Been Oversold?" *Personnel*, vol. 64, May 1987, pp. 52–56.

34. Ajay K. Kohli, "Some Unexplored Supervisory Behaviors and Their Influence on Salespeople's Role Clarity, Specific Self-Esteem, Job Satisfaction, and Motivation," *Journal of Marketing Research*, vol. 22, November 1985, p. 431.

35. "What's the Problem with Problem Employees?" *Sales Manager's Bulletin*, January 30, 1982, p. 4.

36. W. E. Patton, III, "Drug Abuse in the Salesforce," *Journal of Personal Selling & Sales Management*, vol. 8, August 1988, pp. 21–33; Martin Everett, "Drugs Can Bust Your Salesforce," *Sales & Marketing Management*, vol. 138, March 1987, pp. 44–50; W. E. Patton, III, and Michael Questell, "Alcohol Abuse in the Salesforce," *Journal of Personal Selling & Sales Management*, vol. 6, November 1986, pp. 39–50.

37. Everett, "Drugs Can Bust Your Salesforce," p. 45.

38. These guidelines are adapted from W. E. Patton, III, and Michael Questell, "Alcohol Abuse in the Salesforce," *Journal of Personal Selling & Sales Management*, vol. 6, November 1986, pp. 47–48; and from W. E. Patton, III, "Drug Abuse in the Salesforce," *Journal of Personal Selling & Sales Management*, vol. 8, August 1988, pp. 31–32. Copyright © 1986 and 1988. Used by permission.

39. Jack Falvey, "Make 'Em All Winners," *Sales & Marketing Management*, vol. 143, June 1991, pp. 8–11.

40. Kathleen Teltsch, "New Study of Older Workers Finds They Can Become Good Investments," *The New York Times*, May 21, 1991, p. 16.

CHAPTER 16

1. "Wanted: Salespeople with Drive," *Inc.*, June 1991, p. 14; Echo Montgomery Garrett, "In Search of the Sales Mind," *Success*, May 1991, pp. 32–34; Matthew Schifrin, "The Magician, the Dry Cleaner and the Secretary," *Forbes*, December 10, 1990, pp. 152–156.

2. For further discussion, see also Jerry McAdams, "Rewarding Sales and Marketing Performance," *Personnel*, vol. 64, October 1987, pp. 8–16; Yao Apasu, "The Importance of Value Structures in the Perception of Rewards by Industrial Salespersons," *Journal of the Academy of Marketing Science*, vol. 15, Spring 1987, pp. 1–10.

3. Kenneth Friendenreich, Donald J. Moine, and Sally C. Stevens, "How to Motivate Your Salesforce," *Working Woman*, vol. 11, June 1986, p. 22.

4. For a detailed discussion of the relationship between career stage and salespeople's motivation, see William L. Cron, Alan J. Dubinsky, and Ronald E. Michaels, "The Influence of Career Stages on Components of Salesperson Motivation," *Journal of Marketing*, vol. 52, January 1988, pp. 78–92.

5. Matthew Shank and Cynthia Lunnemann, "Proper Pay and Rewards Help Retain Sales Force," *Marketing News*, vol. 24, March 5, 1990, p. 7.

6. Holly Rawlinson, "Make Awards Count," *Personnel Journal*, October 1988, p. 140.

7. *Ibid.*, p. 141.

8. Thomas R. Wotruba, John S. MacAfie, and Jerome A. Colletti, "Effective Salesforce Recognition Programs," *Industrial Marketing Management*, vol. 20, February 1991, pp. 9–15.

9. Richard Boyatiz, as quoted in Bill Kelley, "Recognition Reaps Rewards," *Sales & Marketing Management*, vol. 136, June 1986, p. 101.

10. Maureen Meisner, "Long-Term Sales Recognition," *Incentive*, vol. 165, January 1991, pp. 31–32.

11. Bill Kelley, "Recognition Reaps Rewards," p. 104.

12. Erika Penzer, "Pentel of America: The Pen and the Sword," *Incentive*, vol. 163, December 1989, pp. 56–57.

13. Al Urbanski, "Motivational Masterpieces," *Sales & Marketing Management*, vol. 139, September 1987, p. 60.

14. Jane Templeton, "Peer Prestige Puts POW in Salespower," *Sales & Marketing Management*, vol. 138, June 1987, p. 70.

15. Al Urbanski, "Motivational Masterpieces," p. 62.

16. Albert R. Wildt, James D. Parker, and Clyde E. Harris, Jr., "Sales Contests: What We Know and What We Need To Know," *Journal of Personal Selling & Sales Management*, vol. 1, Fall/Winter 1980-1981, p. 59.

17. Richard F. Beltramini and Kenneth R. Evans, "Salesperson Motivation to Perform and Job Satisfaction: A Sales Contest Participant Perspective," *Journal of Personal Selling & Sales Management*, vol. 8, August 1988, pp. 35–42; and Albert R. Wildt, James D. Parker, and Clyde E. Harris, Jr., "Assessing the Impact of Salesforce Contests: An Application," *Journal of Business Research*, vol. 15, April 1987, pp. 145–155.

18. Joanne Levine, "Smith Kline: Testing Knowledge," *Incentive*, vol. 162, October 1988, pp. 62–63; see also "Product Knowledge and Sales Skills," *Incentive Marketing*, vol. 161, August 1987, pp. 50, 52.

19. Sally Stevens, "10 Incentive Mistakes to Avoid at All Costs," *Sales & Marketing Management*, vol. 130, April 4, 1983, p. 86.

20. *Ibid.*, p. 84.

21. "Balfour Practices What It Preaches," *Sales & Marketing Management*, vol. 126, April 6, 1981, p. 84.

22. Sandra Hile Hart, William C. Moncrief, and A. Parasuramen, "An Empirical Investigation of Salespeople's Performance, Effort and Selling Method During a Sales Contest," *Journal of the Academy of Marketing Science*, vol. 17, Winter 1989, pp. 29–39.

23. Kate Bertrand, "Incentive Program Punches Up Sales," *Business Marketing*, vol. 75, March 1990, p. 40.

24. Joe Agnew, "Marketing's Murder: Sleuthing Adds Life to Sales-Incentive Contest," *Marketing News*, vol. 21, April 24, 1987, pp. 1, 3.

25. Marjorie J. Caballero, "Stepping Up Performance: Incentives in a Salesforce Contest," *Baylor Business Review*, vol. 6, Fall 1988, pp. 16–20.

26. For further insights about travel as an incentive, see Joseph Conlin, "What Fortune 500 Execs Think of Incentive Travel," *Successful Meetings*, vol. 38, November 1989, pp. 100–106; Steve Weinstein, "Oh, the Romance of Travel: Nothing Motivates the Sales Staff like an Exotic Trip," *Marketing News*, vol. 23, March 13, 1989, pp. 1, 2; Bill Hastings, Julia Kiely, and Trevor Watkins, "Salesforce Motivation Using Travel Incentives: Some Empirical Evidence," *Journal of Personal Selling & Sales Management*, vol. 8, August 1988, pp. 43–51.

27. "Facts Survey: Sales Incentives," *Incentive*, vol. 164, September 1990, pp. 55–56.

28. Marjorie J. Caballero, "Selling and Sales Management in Action: A Comparative Study of Incentives in a Salesforce Contest," *Journal of Personal Selling & Sales Management*, vol. 8, May 1988, pp. 55–58; see also Andre J. San Augustine and Joel N. Greene, "The Psychology of Noncash Incentives," *Sales & Marketing Management*, vol. 128, April 5, 1982, pp. 112, 114.

29. G. A. Marken, "A Well-Run Incentive Program is Best Sales Staff Motivator," *Marketing News*, October 15, 1982, p. 5.

30. *Ibid.*, p. 5.

31. The dangers involved in sales contests are pointed out in Thomas R. Wotruba and Donald J. Schoel, "Evaluation of Salesforce Contest Performance," *Journal of Personal Selling & Sales Management*, vol. 3, May 1983, pp. 1–10; also see Roy W. Walters, "Incentives: Carrot-on-a-Stick That Prevents Future Growth," *Marketing Times*, March/April 1982, pp. 18–19.

32. Additional insights about salespeople's views of contests are presented in Beltramini and Evans, "Salesperson Motivation to Perform and Job Satisfaction: A Sales Contest Participant Perspective," pp. 35–42.

33. Rayna Skolnik, "Sales Meetings: Everyone's into the Act," *Sales & Marketing Management*, vol. 129, July 5, 1982, p. 56.

34. Jack Falvey, "Sales Meetings Usually Do More Harm than Good," *Sales & Marketing Management*, vol. 140, September 1988, pp. 107–108; Bill Voelkel, "Ten Ways to Screw Up a Sales Meeting," *Sales & Marketing Management*, vol. 140, June 1988, p. 46.

35. Joseph Conlin, "Management Strategy: Get Control!" *Successful Meetings*, vol. 38, June 1989, pp. 37–38.

36. Homer Smith, "Balance the Budget for Better Meetings," *Sales & Marketing Management*, vol. 136, March 10, 1986, p. 76.

37. Julie Swor, "Site Design: Meeting of the Minds," *Training*, vol. 24, December 1987, p. 89.

38. Rayna Skolnik, "Keeping Costs Low and Quality High," *Sales & Marketing Management*, vol. 129, November 15, 1982, pp. 98–99.

39. Bill Voelkel, "Ten Ways to Screw Up a Sales Meeting," p. 46.

40. Bill Kelley, "Can Sports Stars Really Motivate Your Salesforce?" *Sales & Marketing Management*, vol. 139, December 1987, pp. 36–40; see also Kevin T. Higgins, "Motivating the Salesforce: Does 'Rah-Rah' Talk Still Translate into Action?" *Marketing News*, vol. 20, July 14, 1986, p. 10.

41. Christine S. Filip, "Invite Your Customer to the Next Sales Meeting," *Sales & Marketing Management*, vol. 142, November 1990, pp. 105–107.

42. Jack Falvey, "Sales Meetings Usually Do More Harm than Good," p. 107.

CHAPTER 17

1. William Keenan, Jr., "Executive Pay: A Bitter Pill," *Sales & Marketing Management*, vol. 143, November 1991, pp. 48–56; John A. Byrne, "The Flap over Executive Pay," *Business Week*, May 6, 1991, pp. 90–96.

2. Rene Y. Darmon, "The Impact of Incentive Compensation on the Salesperson's Work Habits: An Economic Model," *Journal of Personal Selling & Sales Management*, vol. 7, May 1987, pp. 21–32.

3. Thomas R. Mott, "Is Your Sales Compensation Plan a Demotivator?" *Sales & Marketing Management*, vol. 141, p. 61. Copyright: February 1989. Reprinted by permission of Sales & Marketing Management.

4. For some of the reasons behind these difficulties, see Kate Bertrand, "The 12 Cardinal Sins of Compensation," *Business Marketing*, vol. 74, September 1989, p. 51.

5. Mott, "Is Your Sales Compensation Plan a Demotivator?" p. 61.

6. Stewart A. Washburn, "Fire Up Your Sales Force," *Business Marketing*, vol. 75, July 1990, pp. 52–54; see also Stephen X. Doyle and Benson P. Shapiro, "What Counts Most in Motivating Your Salesforce," *Harvard Business Review*, vol. 58, May-June 1980, pp. 133–140.

7. Jay R. Schuster and Patricia K. Zingheim, "Sales Compensation Strategies at the Most Successful Companies," *Personnel Journal*, vol. 65, June 1986, pp. 112–116.

8. Leon Winer, "A Sales Compensation System That Maximizes Motivation and Economy," *Advanced Management Journal*, Spring 1982, p. 46.

9. Rene Y. Darmon, "Compensation Plans That Link Management and Salesman's Objectives," *Industrial Marketing Management*, April 1982, pp. 151–163.

10. Sami M. Abbasi, Joe H. Murrey, Jr., and Kenneth W. Hollman, "Comparable Worth: Should You Reexamine Your Compensation Program?" *SAM Advanced Management Journal*, vol. 51, Spring 1986, pp. 26–35.

11. Dean Walsh and Joanne Dahm, "Going Flex-Four Adjustable Comp Plans That Work," *Sales & Marketing Management*, vol. 141, September 1989, pp. 16–21.

12. Robert J. Freedmen, "For More Profitable Sales, Look beyond Volume," *Sales & Marketing Management*, vol. 141, August 1989, pp. 50–53.

13. William T. Gauthier, "Meeting Business Objectives through Innovative Sales Compensation Design," *Compensation and Benefits Management*, vol. 7, Autumn 1990, pp. 40–45.

14. Alan J. Dubinsky and Thomas E. Barry, "A Survey of Sales Management Practices," *Industrial Marketing Management*, April 1982, p. 137; see also Charles A. Peck, *Compensating Field Sales Representatives*, New York: The Conference Board, 1982.

15. Tom Murray, "Team Selling: What's the Incentive?" *Sales & Marketing Management*, vol. 143, June 1991, p. 89.

16. Craig A. Tumwall and Michael K. Mount, "Sales Compensation in High-Tech Firms: The Motivational Issues," *Compensation and Benefits Review*, vol. 21, January-February 1989, pp. 43–47.

17. Kate Bertrand, "Incentives Reward Teamwork," *Business Marketing*, vol. 74, December 1989, p. 29.

18. Gary Turbridy, "How to Pay National Account Managers," *Sales & Marketing Management*, vol. 136, January 13, 1986, p. 50.

19. William Keenan, Jr., "The Difference in Selling Services," *Sales & Marketing Management*, vol. 142, March 1990, pp. 48–52.

20. Brian Dunn and Susan Kurzrock, "Effective Tests for Sales Compensation Plans," *Banker's Magazine*, vol. 172, September-October 1989, pp. 65–68; John J. Storck, "Winning With Money," *Bank Systems and Equipment*, vol. 24, December 1987, pp. 64–65; James J. Hubbard, "Sales Management Update: A Little Incentive Can Go a Long Way," *Bank Marketing*, vol. 19, June 1987, pp. 8, 10.

21. Stephanie Della Cagna, "The Invasion of the Nordies," *New England Business*, vol. 12, January 1990, pp. 24–25; see also Amy Dunkin, "Now Salespeople Really Must Sell for Their Supper," *Business Week*, July 31, 1989, pp. 50, 52.

22. For a review of the development of a sales compensation plan, see Frank V. Cespedes, "A Preface to Payment: Designing a Sales Compensation Plan," *Sloan Management*, Fall 1990, pp. 59–69; "Salesforce Compensation Part 2: Balancing Company and Salesforce Needs," *Small Business Report*, vol. 12, April 1987, pp. 69–74; "Salesforce Compensation Part 1: The Dual Challenge: Effective and Realistic Motivation," *Small Business Report*, vol. 12, March 1987, pp. 68–74; Robert J. Freedman, "How to Develop a Sales Compensation Plan," *Compensation and Benefits Journal*, vol. 18, March-April 1986, pp. 41–48.

23. James P. Hanley, "Conducting a Sales Compensation Survey," *Compensation and Benefits Management*, vol. 6, Autumn 1989, pp. 65–70.

24. Kate Bertrand, "Sales Strategies Drive Pay Plans," *Business Marketing*, vol. 73, December 1988, p. 30.

25. Mott, "Is Your Sales Compensation Plan a Demotivator?" p. 63.

26. As quoted in Bertrand, "The 12 Cardinal Sins of Compensation," p. 51.

27. John K. Moynahan and Gary M. Locke, "Designing an Effective Sales Compensation System," *Compensation and Benefits Management*, vol. 4, Autumn 1987, pp. 61–62.

28. John K. Moynahan, "When the Sky's the Limit, It Pays To Take Along Your Parachute," *Sales & Marketing Management*, vol. 129, September 15, 1982, p. 116.

29. Douglas J. Dalrymple, P. Ronald Stephenson, and William Cron, "Wage Levels and Sales Productivity," *Business Horizons*, December 1980, pp. 57–60.

30. William Keenan, Jr., "Is Your Sales Pay Plan Putting the Squeeze on Top Performers?" *Sales & Marketing Management*, vol. 142, January 1990, pp. 74–75.

31. For a review of industry practices, see Lesley Barnes, "Finding the Best Sales Compensation Plan," *Sales & Marketing Management*, vol. 137, August 1986, pp. 46–49.

32. For another perspective on this issue, see George John and Barton Weitz, "Salesforce Compensation: An Empirical Investigation of Factors Related to Use of Salary Versus Incentive Compensation," *Journal of Marketing Research*, vol. 26, February 1989, pp. 1–14.

33. John K. Moynahan, "Straight Salary Has Many Angles," *Sales & Marketing Management*, vol. 136, March 10, 1986, pp. 76, 78.

34. Paul S. Bradley, "Linking Incentive Pay for Salespeople to Their Profit Contributions," *Journal of Compensation and Benefits*, vol. 5, May-June 1990, pp. 350–354.

35. L. Joseph Rosenberg, C. Kendrick Gibson, and Donald B. Epley, "How to Retain Real Estate Salespeople: What Things Work," *Journal of Personal Selling & Sales Management*, vol. 1, Spring-Summer 1981, p. 41. Copyright © 1981. Used by permission.

36. Joanne Dahm, "Using Draws Wisely in Your Compensation Plan," *Sales & Marketing Management*, vol. 142, August 1990, p. 93; see also Rick Dogen, "Don't Be Too Quick on the Draw," *Sales & Marketing Management*, vol. 140, September 1988, pp. 58–65.

37. Fred K. Foulkes, "Why Bonus Plans Are Good for Business," *Personnel*, vol. 62, August 1985, pp. 72–73.

38. John K. Moynahan, "Using Bonuses to Inspire Sharper Sales Forecasts Is a Risky Assignment," *Sales & Marketing Management*, vol. 127, December 7, 1981, p. 90.

39. Stewart A. Washburn, "Sales Incentives: Follow the Money," *Business Marketing*, vol. 75, September 1990, p. 68.

40. Matt S. Walton, III, "How to Draft a Sales Compensation Plan," *Personnel*, vol. 62, June 1985, pp. 71–74.

41. John K. Moynahan, "Three Ways to Test Your New Pay Plan," *Sales & Marketing Management*, vol. 138, January 1987, pp. 84–85.

42. An interesting discussion appears in Danny N. Bellenger, James B. Wilcox, and Thomas N. Ingram, "An Examination of Reward Preferences for Sales Managers," *Journal of Personal Selling & Sales Management*, vol. 4, November 1984, pp. 1–6.

43. William Keenan, Jr., "Executive Pay: The Good News (and the Bad)," *Sales & Marketing Management*, vol. 142, November 1990, pp. 38–48.

44. The average compensation (base salary plus commissions, bonuses, and other cash incentives) for sales supervisors was $66,085 in 1990; "1991 Sales Manager's Budget Planner," *Sales & Marketing Management*, vol. 143, June 17, 1991, p. 73. The median compensation level for top sales executives in 1990 was $155,600; Keenan, "Executive Pay: The Good News (and the Bad)," p. 38.

CHAPTER 18

1. Michael P. Cronin, "A Globetrotting Guide to Managing People," *Inc.*, April 1992, p. 122; Tony Horwitz, "Peat Moss, Anyone? Selling It in Kuwait Can Bog You Down," *The Wall Street Journal*, May 30, 1991, pp. A1, A11; George Leslie, "U.S. Reps Should Learn To Sell 'Japanese Style,'" *Marketing News*, October 29, 1990, p. 6.

2. John Naisbitt and Patricia Aburdene, *Megatrends 2000*, New York: Avon Books, 1990, p. 1.

3. Gregory Sandler, "The Search for New Markets," *New England Business*, vol. 12, December 1990, p. 46.

4. Jordan E. Goodman, "Go For Global Profits with America's Best-Known Brands," *Money*, vol. 20, August 1991, pp. 43–49.

5. M. Daniel Rosen, "EC '92: A Guide For the Small Company," *Sales & Marketing Management*, vol. 142, September 1990, p. 96.

6. Nicholas C. Kernstock, "International Sales to Lead Helicopter Market Growth," *Aviation Week & Space Technology*, vol. 134, March 18, 1991, pp. 161–162.

7. Rachel Parker, "Software Spoken Here," *InfoWorld*, vol. 12, June 25, 1990, pp. 47–49.

8. Barbara N. Berkman, "Rebuilding the House of Siemens on a Worldwide Foundation," *Electronic Business*, vol. 16, August 6, 1990, pp. 28–32.

9. Gregory Sandler, "Sticky Business," *World Trade*, vol. 4, August-September 1991, pp. 60–66.

10. "Amway: Distributing International Passports to Success," *Business Korea*, vol. 8, April 1991, pp. 79–80.

11. "Exporting Pays Off," *Business America*, vol. 112, March 25, 1991, p. 24.

12. Kate Bertrand, "Get Ready for Global Capitalism," *Business Marketing*, January 1990, pp. 52–53.

13. Laxmi Nakarmi, "Korea Throws Open Its Doors," *Business Week*, July 29, 1991, p. 46.

14. Noel J. Para, "New Taboos on the International Sale of Goods," *Management Review*, vol. 80, July 1991, pp. 33–36; see also Mark A. Goldstein, "U.N. Convention Demystifies International Sales Contracts," *Business Credit*, vol. 92, November-December 1990, pp. 20–21; Virginia G. Maurer, "The United Nations Convention on Contracts for the International Sale of Goods," *Syracuse Journal of International Law & Commerce*, vol. 15, Spring 1989, pp. 361–389; John E. Murray, Jr., "CISG Governs International Sales," *Purchasing World*, vol. 31, December 1987, pp. 32, 34.

15. For an excellent overview of cultural factors and their impact on international business, see Philip R. Harris and Robert T. Moran, *Managing Cultural Differences*, 2nd. ed., Houston, TX: Gulf Publishing Company, 1987.

16. Charles F. Valentine, "Blunders Abroad," *Nation's Business*, vol. 77, March 1989, p. 54; see also "Culture Clashes Cause Most Global Failures," *Marketing News*, July 31, 1987, pp. 21–22, 24; William W. Locke, "The Fatal Flaw: Hidden Cultural Differences," *Business Marketing*, April 1986, pp. 65ff; and, David A. Ricks, *Big Business Blunders*, Homewood, IL: Dow Jones-Irwin, 1983.

17. For a practical guide to this and other international business practices and behavior, see Robert E. Axtell, *Do's and Taboo's Around the World*, Elmsford, NY: The Benjamin Company, 1985. This book is distributed by The Parker Pen Company.

18. *Ibid.*, p. 39.

19. David K. Tse, Kam-hon Lee, Ilan Vertinsky, and Donald A. Wehrung, "Does Culture Matter? A Cross-Cultural Study of Executives' Choice, Decisiveness, and Risk Adjustment in International Marketing," *Journal of Marketing*, vol. 52, October 1988, pp. 81–95.

20. George Leslie, "U.S. Reps Should Learn to Sell Japanese Style," *Marketing News*, vol. 24, October 29, 1990, p. 6; "The Delicate Art of Doing Business in Japan," *Business Week*, October 2, 1989, p. 120; Edward T. Hall and Mildred Reed Hall, "Selling to a Japanese," *Sales & Marketing Management*, July 1987, pp. 58ff; John McClenahan, "Yes, You Can Sell in Japan," *Industry Week*, March 23, 1987, pp. 88–89, 92.

21. Theodore Levitt, "The Globalization of Markets," *Harvard Business Review*, vol. 61, May-June 1983, pp. 92–102.

22. Joel Dreyfuss, "How to Beat the Japanese at Home," *Fortune*, August 1987, pp. 80, 82.

23. "Gaining a Global Outlook," *Sales & Marketing Management*, vol. 144, January 1992, p. 55.

24. *Ibid.*

25. For example, see Gerard Gschwandtner, "Selling and Marketing in Japan," *Personal Selling Power*, vol. 12, January-February 1992, pp. 42–52; George Schenk, "Sales Management in Poland," *Personal Selling Power*, vol. 11, October 1991, pp. 60–63; David A. Rochlin, "Economic Conditions in Europe Require Centralized Marketing," *Marketing News*, December 24, 1990, p. 5; M. Daniel Rosen, "EC '92: A Guide for the Small Company," *Sales & Marketing Management*, vol. 142, September 1990, pp. 96–106.

26. Steven Golob, "Sell Overseas at Trade Fairs," *Nation's Business*, vol. 76, March 1987, pp. 57–59.

27. "How to Use the National Trade Data Bank to Sell in Foreign Markets," *Personal Selling Power*, vol. 11, November-December 1991, p. 38.

28. Lawrence B. Chonko, John F. Tanner, Jr., and Ellen Reid Smith, "Selling and Sales Management in Action: The Salesforce's Role in International Marketing Research and Marketing Information Systems," *Journal of Personal Selling & Sales Management*, vol. 11, Winter 1991, pp. 69–79.

29. *Ibid.*, p. 73.

30. Erin Anderson and Anne T. Coughlan, "International Market Entry and Expansion via Independent or Integrated Channels of Distribution," *Journal of Marketing*, vol. 51, January 1987, p. 79.

31. "A Low-Investment Way to Break into Exporting," *Profit-Building Strategies for Business Owners*, vol. 18, May 1988, pp. 12–13.

32. Alf H. Walle, "Conceptualizing Personal Selling for International Business: A Continuum of Exchange Perspective," *Journal of Personal Selling & Sales Management*, vol. 6, November 1986, p. 9. Copyright © 1986. Used by permission.

33. Brian H. Flynn, "Homing In on Foreign Sales Customs," *Business Marketing*, June 1987, p. 91.

34. Hank Walshak, "Publicity's a 'Must' for International Marketers," *Marketing News*, July 9, 1990, p. 14.

35. Allen Konopacki, "Trade-Show Diplomacy Reaps More Sales," *Successful Meetings*, vol. 3, January 1988, pp. 56–58.

36. Flynn, "Homing In on Foreign Sales Customs," p. 92.

37. *Ibid.*

38. Gerhard Gschwandtner, "How To Sell In Germany," *Personal Selling Power*, vol. 11, September 1991, p. 57.

39. Flynn, "Homing In On Foreign Sales Customs," p. 92.

40. This discussion is taken from Norman Oches, "Cross-Cultural Presentations—How to Make Them More Effective," *Sales & Marketing Management*, vol. 141, September 1989, pp. 82, 84.

41. Martin J. Seldman, "How to Land Lucrative Japanese Accounts: Learn the Lingo," *Personal Selling Power*, vol. 10, July-August 1990, pp. 22–23.

42. Gerhard Gschwandtner, "How to Sell in France," *Personal Selling Power*, vol. 11, July-August 1991, p. 56.

43. *Ibid.*, pp. 56–57.

44. Eric J. Adams, "Stalking the Global Sale," *World Trade*, vol. 4, June-July 1991, pp. 34–36.

45. John K. Keitt, Jr., "Pitfalls and Promises of Foreign Distributors," *Management Review*, vol. 79, May 1990, pp. 16–19.

46. G. A. Marken, "Finding Global Sales Partners," *Industry Week*, June 1, 1987, p. 52.

47. "It Helps to Have a Friend," *Sales & Marketing Management*, vol. 139, December 1987, pp. 25–26.

48. Karen Berney, "Competing in Japan," *Nation's Business*, vol. 74, October 1986, p. 28.

49. "Exports Lighting the Way For Coleman's Future," *Providence Sunday Journal*, December 15, 1991, pp. F-1, F-2.

50. John S. Hall and Richard R. Still, "Organizing the Overseas Salesforce: How Multinationals Do It," *Journal of Personal Selling & Sales Management*, vol. 10, Spring 1990, pp. 63–65.

51. *Ibid.*, p. 65.

52. O. E. McDaniel, "The New Name of the Game: Global Account Marketing," *NAMA Journal*, vol. 32, Fall 1990, pp. 1, 5.

53. George J. Avlonitis and Kevin A. Boyle, "Linkages between Sales Management Tools and Practices: Some Evidence from British Companies," *Journal of the Academy of Marketing Science*, vol. 17, Spring 1989, pp. 137–145.

54. John Lidstone, "Sales Management: Death of a Salesman," *Marketing*, vol. 27, October 2, 1986, pp. 36–37.

55. For an early look at the challenges of developing global sales management techniques, see Richard R. Still, "Sales Management: Some Cross-Cultural Aspects," *Journal of Personal Selling & Sales Management*, vol. 1, Spring-Summer 1981, pp. 6–9.

56. David A. Ricks, *Big Business Blunders*, Homewood, IL: Dow Jones-Irwin, 1983, p. 57. This book contains many examples of marketing mistakes made by multinational businesses.

57. Myron M. Miller, "Sunbeam in Italy: One Success and One Failure," *International Marketing Review*, vol. 7, January 1991, pp. 68–73.

58. "Native Sales Staffs Pose Problems for U.S. Firms," *Marketing News*, May 8, 1989, p. 7.

59. Yao Apasu, Shigeru Ichikawa, and John L. Graham, "Corporate Culture and Salesforce Management in Japan and America," *Journal of Personal Selling & Sales Management*, vol. 7, November 1987, p. 60.

60. John S. Hill and Meg Birdseye, "Salesperson Selection in Multinational Corporations: An Empirical Study," *Journal of Personal Selling & Sales Management*, vol. 9, Summer 1989, p. 39. Copyright © 1989. Used by permission.

61. *Ibid.*, pp. 39–47.

62. Don Ferenci, "It's Not Just an Overseas Job, It's an Adventure," *Focus*, May 23, 1989, p. 9.

63. Anne Ferguson, "Compaq's Personnel Solution," *Management Today*, May 1989, pp. 127–128.

64. Brian H. Flynn, "The Challenge of Multinational Sales Training," *Training & Development Journal*, vol. 41, November 1987, pp. 54–55; see also Melvin W. Kellett, "Conducting International Sales Training," *Training & Development Journal*, vol. 35, November 1981, pp. 30–33.

65. Gerhard Gschwandtner, "Global Sales Training—the Future Is Now," *Personal Selling Power*, vol. 12, January-February 1992, p. 66.

66. *Ibid.*

67. *Ibid.*, p. 67.

68. Madelyn R. Callahan, "Preparing the New Global Manager," *Training & Development Journal*, vol. 43, pp. 29–32. Copyright March 1989, the American Society for Training and Development. Reprinted with permission. All rights reserved. See also Jim de Wilde, "How to Train Managers for Going Global," *Business Quarterly*, vol. 55, Winter 1991, p. 41ff.

69. *Ibid.*, p. 30.

70. *Ibid.*

71. *Ibid.*, p. 32.

72. *Ibid.*

73. For an overview of cultural training issues and approaches, see J. Stewart Black and Mark Mendenhall, "Cross-Cultural Training Effectiveness: A Review and Theoretical Framework for Future Research," *Academy of Management Review*, vol. 15, January 1990, pp. 113–136.

74. Frank Zaret, "Adapting Distribution and Compensation to Cultural Needs," *Market Facts*, vol. 8, September-October 1989, pp. 26–27, 45–47.

75. Russell Abratt and Michael R. Smythe, "A Survey of Sales Incentive Programs," *Industrial Marketing Management*, vol. 18, August 1989, pp. 209–214.

76. Bill Hastings, Julia Kiely, and Trevor Watkins, "Salesforce Motivation Using Travel Incentives: Some Empirical Evidence," *Journal of Personal Selling & Sales Management*, vol. 8, August 1988, pp. 43–51.

77. Robert C. Christopher, *Second to None: American Companies in Japan*, New York: Fawcett Columbine, 1986, p. 99.

78. *Ibid.*, p. 110.

79. Apasu, Ichikawa, and Graham, "Corporate Culture and Sales Force Management in Japan and America," p. 61.

80. "Homey Side of the Hard Sell," *New York Times*, March 10, 1991, p. F6.

81. "Exporting Pays Off," *Business America*, December 2, 1991, p. 23.

CHAPTER 19

1. Michael P. Cronin, "Sales Rewards for 'Real' Revenues," *Inc.*, May 1992, p. 141; Jennifer Reese, "United States Surgical: Getting Hot Ideas from Customers," *Fortune*, May 18, 1992, pp. 86–87; Richard A. Shaffer, "Symantec's Little Hits," *Forbes*, November 25, 1991, p. 196; "U.S. Surgical, Biomet to Make Absorbable Orthopedic Products," *The Wall Street Journal*, July 11, 1991, p. C15.

2. For an overview of management performance appraisal programs, see Lloyd Baird, *Managing Performance*, New York: John Wiley and Sons, 1986; John H. Bernardine and Richard Beatty, *Performance Appraisal: Assessing Human Behavior at Work*, Boston, MA: Kent Publishing Company, 1984; Richard I. Henderson, *Performance Appraisal*, 2nd ed., Reston, VA: Reston Publishing Company, 1984; Steven J. Carroll and Craig E. Schneider, *Performance Appraisal and Review Systems*, Glenville, IL: Scott Foresman and Company, 1982.

3. Erin Anderson and Richard L. Oliver, "Perspectives on Behavior-Based versus Outcome-Based Salesforce Control Systems," *Journal of Marketing*, vol. 51, October 1987, p. 76.

4. *Ibid.*, pp. 76–77.

5. Walter O. Einstein and June LeMere-La Bonte, "Performance Appraisal: Dilemma or Design?" *SAM Advanced Management Journal*, Spring 1989, pp. 26–30.

6. Bruce D. Buskirk, "Make Sure Salesforce Tactics, Firm's Goals Don't Conflict," *Marketing News*, March 18, 1983, p. 20.

7. Regina Eisman, "Setting Fair Sales Quotas," *Incentive*, vol. 163, September 1989, pp. 192–196.

8. John C. Mowen, Janet C. Keith, Stephen W. Brown, and Donald W. Jackson, "Utilizing Effort and Task Difficulty Information in Evaluating Salespeople," *Journal of Marketing Research*, vol. 22, May 1985, pp. 185–191.

9. Bill Stiles, "Agents: How to Evaluate Your Sales Personnel," *Agency Sales Magazine*, vol. 20, October 1990, pp. 15–19.

10. Michael H. Morris and Sean R. Aten, "Salesforce Performance Appraisal: Contemporary Issues and Practices," in *Progress in Marketing Thought*, Louis M. Capella, Henry W. Nash, Jack M. Starling, and Ronald D. Taylor, eds., Mississippi State, MS: Southern Marketing Association, 1990, pp. 413–418.

11. John C. Mowen, Keith J. Fabes, and Raymond W. LaForge, "Effects of Effort, Territory Situation, and Rates on Salesperson Evaluation," *Journal of Personal Selling & Sales Management*, vol. 6, May 1986, pp. 1–2.

12. *Ibid.*, p. 7.

13. Rene Y. Darmon, "Identifying Profit-Producing Salesforce Members," *Journal of Personal Selling & Sales Management*, vol. 2, November 1982, p. 15.

14. *Ibid.*, pp. 14–23.

15. Jerry Colletti, "Are You Tough Enough to Raise Sales Productivity?" *Sales & Marketing Management*, vol. 140, October 1988, p. 50.

16. The application of ROI to sales evaluation was first suggested by Michael Schiff, "The Use of ROI in Sales Management," *Journal of Marketing*, July 1963, pp. 70–73; see also Michael Schiff, "The Sales Territory as a Fixed Asset," *Journal of Marketing*, October 1960, pp. 51–53.

17. "To Tell the Truth," *Sales & Marketing Management*, vol. 139, November 1987, p. 81.

18. Arthur Bragg, "Is the Call Report on the Way Out?" *Sales & Marketing Management*, vol. 139, November 1987, pp. 79–83.

19. "Monitoring Sales Calls to Increase Productivity," *Sales Manager's Bulletin*, August 15, 1983, p. 2. Copyright © 1983. Copyrighted material reprinted with permission of *Sales Manager's Bulletin* and the Bureau of Business Practice, 24 Rope Ferry Road, Waterford, CT 06386.

20. P. Kenneth Teas and James F. Horrell, "Salespeople Satisfaction and Performance Feedback," *Industrial Marketing Management*, June 1981, p. 55.

21. Donald W. Jackson, Janet E. Keith, and John L. Schlacter, "Evaluation of Selling Performance: A Study of Current Practices," *Journal of Personal Selling & Sales Management*, vol. 3, November 1983, p. 48.

22. Darmon, "Identifying Profit-Producing Salesforce Members," pp. 14–23.

23. Robert C. Ferber, "Sales Execs Should Use Multivariate Analysis Techniques to Measure Field Force Operations," *Marketing News*, November 27, 1981, p. 20.

24. Robert F. Soergel, "Forget the Figures, Track the Trend," *Sales & Marketing Management*, vol. 128, April 5, 1982, p. 58.

25. Douglas J. Dalrymple and William M. Strahle, "Career Path Charting: Framework for Salesforce Evaluation," *Journal of Personal Selling & Sales Management*, vol. 10, Summer 1990, pp. 59–62.

26. *Ibid.*, pp. 63–67.

27. A. Benton Cocanougher and John M. Ivancevich, "BARS Performance Rating for Salesforce Personnel," *Journal of Marketing*, July 1978, pp. 87–95.

28. *Ibid.*, p. 87.

29. *Ibid.*, p. 94.

30. Douglas N. Behrman, William J. Bigoness, and William D. Perreault, Jr., "Sources of Job Related Ambiguity and Their Consequences Upon Salespersons' Job Satisfaction and Performance," *Management Science*, November 1981, pp. 1257–1258.

31. Don Waite, "When Salespeople Talk, Does Management Listen?" *Sales & Marketing Management*, vol. 135, October 7, 1985, pp. 43–45.

32. Thomas R. Wotruba and Michael L. Thurlow, "Salesforce Participation in Quota Setting and Sales Forecasting," *Journal of Marketing*, April 1976, pp. 11–16.

33. "Salesforce Feedback: The Inside Source of Marketing Information," *Small Business Report*, January 1987, pp. 22–25.

34. Gary A. Schroeder, "Using an Attitude Survey to Increase Sales Effectiveness," *Personnel*, vol. 66, February 1989, pp. 51–55.

35. John H. Bernardin and Richard W. Beatty, "Can Subordinate Appraisals Enhance Managerial Productivity?" *Sloan Management Review*, vol. 28, Summer 1987, pp. 63–73.

36. Jack Carew, "When Salespeople Evaluate Their Managers," *Sales & Marketing Management*, vol. 141, March 1989, pp. 24–27.

37. This discussion is based on Daniel A. Sauers, James B. Hunt, and Ken Bass, "Behavioral Self-Management as a Supplement to External Salesforce Controls," *Journal of Personal Selling & Sales Management*, vol. 10, Summer 1990, pp. 17–28.

38. *Ibid.*, p. 18.

39. Thomas L. Quick, "Salvaging the Problem Salesperson," *Sales & Marketing Management*, vol. 141, April 1989, pp. 41–44.

40. "A Modern Approach to Sales Personnel Evaluations," *Sales Manager's Bulletin*, May 15, 1981, pp. 5–6.

41. "Performance Evaluation by Personality," *Sales Manager's Bulletin*, March 30, 1983, pp. 5–6.

CHAPTER 20

1. "Hey, Where's My Survey of Selling Costs?" *Sales & Marketing Management*, vol. 143, March 1991, pp. 42–45; William J. Murphy, "Automated Service that Generates Sales," *Information Strategy: The Executive's Journal*, Summer 1990, pp. 45–49; Jef Graham, "At Hewlett-Packard: Information Support Systems Catapult Sales to New Levels," *Marketing Communications*, February 1988, pp. 19–23.

2. Gary S. Turbridy, "Stay on Top of the Bottom Line!" *Sales & Marketing Management*, vol. 142, May 1990, p. 56.

3. Troy A. Festervand, Stephen J. Grove, and R. Eric Reidenbach, "The Salesforce as a Marketing Intelligence System," *Journal of Business and Industrial Marketing*, vol. 3, Winter 1988, pp. 53–59.

4. "Sales Analysis: A Revealing Look at Company Performance," *Small Business Report*, vol. 13, March 1988, pp. 52–57.

5. James W. Busbin, Ernest P. Gross, and Thomas Dillon, "Improving Spreadsheet Control for Sales Managers through the Use of the Systems Development Life Cycle," *Journal of Personal Selling & Sales Management*, vol. 10, Summer 1990, p. 101.

6. This review is based on Leon A. Wortmen, "A Marketing Management System—Strictly for Professionals," *Business Marketing*, vol. 72, July 1987, pp. 17–18. Copyright © 1987. Used by permission.

7. Dick Berry, "Sales Performance: Fact or Fiction?" *Journal of Personal Selling & Sales Management*, vol. 6, August 1986, pp. 71–72.

8. *Ibid.*, pp. 71–79; see also Dick Berry, "A Method to Portray and Analyze Sales Performance," *Industrial Marketing Management*, vol. 16, May 1987, pp. 131–144; Dick Berry, "Sales Analysis without the Guesswork," *Sales & Marketing Management*, vol. 138, January 1987, pp. 90–92.

9. Jerry Colletti, "Are You Tough Enough to Raise Sales Productivity?" *Sales & Marketing Management*, vol. 140, October 1988, pp. 50–54.

10. This discussion is based on Gary S. Turbridy, "Stay on Top of the Bottom Line!" *Sales & Marketing Management*, pp. 56–60. Copyright: May 1990. Reprinted by permission of Sales & Marketing Management.

11. For an interesting review of the analytical tools presented in this section, see Charles W. Kyd, "No More Trivial Pursuits," *Inc.*, vol. 11, January 1989, pp. 121–122.

12. *Ibid.*, p. 122.

13. *Ibid.*

14. William Keenan, Jr., "Are You Getting Your Money's Worth?" *Sales & Marketing Management*, vol. 141, May 1989, pp. 46–47.

15. For guidance on tax regulations for business entertainment, see Bill Chastain, "Entertaining a Tax Deduction," *Nation's Business*, vol. 76, March 1988, pp. 55–56.

16. Keenan, "Are You Getting Your Money's Worth?" pp. 50–51.

17. Eugene M. Johnson and Bernard A. Rausch, *Strategic Marketing Planning*, 2nd ed., Boston, MA: American Management Association, 1989, p. 40.

18. Gail E. Schares, John Templeman, Robert Neff, William J. Holstein, and Stanley Reed, "Think Small: The Export Lessons to Be Learned From Germany's Midsize Companies," *Business Week*, November 4, 1991, pp. 58–65.

PHOTO CREDITS

p. 4, Eric Gay/AP/Wide World Photos; p. 24, Photo Works; p. 26, Guy Gillette/Photo Researchers; p. 44, AP/Wide World Photos; p. 47, Charlie Westerman/Gamma Liaison; p. 65, John Garaventa/Gamma Liaison; p. 67, Rhoda Sidney/Monkmeyer; p. 85, Photo Works/Monkmeyer; p. 86, Arnold Adler; p. 107, Donald L. Miller/Monkmeyer; p. 109, Courtesy TTG Inc.; p. 137, Stella Johnson; p. 142, Barry Thumma/AP/Wide World Photos; p. 164, United States Virgin Islands; p. 166, Ann States/SABA; p. 188, Douglas Fowley/Gamma Liaison; p. 191, CTIA; p. 212, AP/Wide World Photos; p. 213, Courtesy Service Corps of Retired Executives; p. 233, Courtesy Dwight Cendrowski/Chrysler Corp.; p. 236, Courtesy Pilot Corp. of America; p. 263, Courtesy DEPTCOR; p. 266, Courtesy Advantage Refreshment Systems; p. 290, Courtesy Dow Chemical Co.; p. 292, Grant LeDuc/Monkmeyer; p. 325; Jacques Chenet/Woodfin Camp & Associates; p. 327, Courtesy Paychex; p. 355, Center for Creative Leadership in Greensboro, North Carolina; p. 360, Courtesy PepsiCo.; p. 382, AP/Wide World Photos; p. 384, Tom Iannuzzi; p. 401, T. Michael Keza; p. 402, Eric Ben/SIPA; p. 423, Cindy Charles/Gamma Liaison; p. 425, Robert Isaacs/Photo Researchers; p. 451, Toby Talbot; p. 456, Mark Zemnick; p. 488, Dan Chidester/Image Works; p. 491, Courtesy Hewlett-Packard; p. 516, Gary Rothstein/Redstone Agency.

ACKNOWLEDGMENTS

CHAPTER 1

"Reebok International, Ltd." (page 7): Keith H. Hammonds, "The 'Blacktop' Is Paving Reebok's Road to Recovery," *Business Week*, August 12, 1991, p. 27; "1991 Marketing Achievement Awards," Sales & Marketing Management, vol. 143, August 1991, p. 36.

Table 1-1 (page 12): William A. O'Connell and William Keenan, Jr., "The Shape of Things to Come," *Sales & Marketing Management*, vol. 142, January 1990, p. 38.

"Assured Enterprises" (page 13): From Larry Light, "No-Load Life Insurance: A Bigger Bang for Your Buck," *Business Week*, May 25, 1992, p. 134; Susan Greco, Nancy Lyons, Robert A. Mamis, Martha E. Mangelsdorf, Anne Murphy, and Edward O. Welles, "Do-It-Yourself Marketing," *Inc.*, November 1991, pp. 52-68.

Figure 1-2 (page 15): Adapted from Steven J. Lyonski and Eugene M. Johnson, "The Sales Manager as a Boundary Spanner: A Role Theory Analysis," *Journal of Personal Selling & Sales Management*, November 1983, p. 9. Copyright © 1983. Used by permission.

Table 1-3 (page 17): Reprinted from Donald B. Buest and Havva J. Meric, "The Fortune 500 Companies' Selection Criteria for Promotion to First Level Sales Management: An Empirical Study," *Journal of Personal Selling & Sales Management*, Fall 1989, pp. 47-52. Copyright © 1989. Used by permission.

Table 1-4 (page 18): G. David Hughes and Charles H. Singler, *Strategic Sales Management*, Reading, MA: Addison-Wesley, © 1983. Used by permission of the authors.

"Death of a (Type of) Salesman" (page 24): Steve Emmons, "Hard Times on the Used Car Lot, or How to Sell the Sizzle," *Los Angeles Times*, December 1, 1991, pp. E1, E15; Neal Templin, "Auto Pitchmen Duel for Dubious Award as Slickest Salesman," *The Wall Street Journal*, October 24, 1991, pp. A1, A4; Larry Armstrong, "Who's the Most Pampered Motorist of All?" *Business Week*, June 10, 1991, pp. 90-92.

CHAPTER 2

Figure 2-2 (page 29): Adapted from David L. Kurtz and H. Robert Dodge, "Multiple Career-Path Options for Salespeople," *Professional Selling*, 6th ed., p. 53. Copyright © 1991. Used by permission of Richard D. Irwin, Inc.

Table 2-1 (page 31): *Sales & Marketing Management*, vol. 144, September 1992, pp. 46-64.

Table 2-2 (page 31): William Keenan, Jr., "America's Best Sales Force: Six at the Summit," *Sales & Marketing Management*, vol. 142, June 1990, p. 66.

"Loctite Corporation" (page 32): Bill Kelley, "Making It Different!" *Sales & Marketing Management*, vol. 143, May 1991, pp. 52-60; Susan Caminiti, "America's Fastest-Growing Companies," *Fortune*, April 22, 1991, pp. 67-76.

"AT&T" (page 33): Paul Cone, "How To Sell in Writing," *Sales & Marketing Management*, vol. 143, November 1991, pp. 71-76; Timothy D. Schellhardt, "How to Boost Sales: Pen a Better Letter," *The Wall Street Journal*, October 4, 1991, p. B1; David Topus, "Put It in Writing—But Write It Right," *Marketing News*, April 29, 1991, p. 7; Bob Garfield, "Corporate Character Assassination," *Advertising Age*, October 22, 1990, p. 35.

Figure 2-3 (page 41): Reprinted from Thomas R. Wotruba, "A Comprehensive Framework for the Analysis of Ethical Behavior, With a Focus on Sales Organizations," *Journal of Personal Selling & Sales Management*, vol. X, Spring 1990, p. 31. Copyright © 1990. Used by permission.

"The Job Search" (page 44): Rick Tetzeli, "A Blitz of Resumes," *Fortune*, June 15, 1992, p. 12; Rick Tetzeli, "Finding Work via Trading Cards," *Fortune*, June 15, 1992, pp. 12-13; Ripley Hotch, "This Is Not Your Father's MBA," *Nation's Business*, February 1992, pp. 51-52; Arthur P. Gould, "Tailor the Job Search to the Job," *The New York Times*, February 16, 1992, p. F13; Dana Wechsler Linden, Jody Brennan, and Randall Lane, "Another Boom Ends," *Forbes*, January 20, 1992, pp. 76-80; Penny Singer, "Grimly, Graduates Are Finding Few Jobs," *The New York Times*, June 23, 1991, p. WC10; Elizabeth M. Fowler, "Students Find Job Search Much Harder," *The New York Times*, March 19, 1991, p. D18.

CHAPTER 3

"John H. Patterson" (page 50): "Taking a Closer Look," *AT&T Focus*, June, 1991, pp. 12-14; Jon M. Hawes, "Leaders in Selling and Sales Management: John H. Patterson," *Journal of Personal Selling & Sales Management*, vol. 5, November 1985, pp. 59-61; Samuel Growther, *John H. Patterson: Pioneer in Industrial Welfare*, Garden City, NY: Garden City Publishing Company, 1926, pp. 128-129.

Table 3-1 (page 51): Samuel Growther, *John H. Patterson: Pioneer in Industrial Welfare*, Garden City, NY: Garden City Publishing Company, 1926, pp. 128-129.

"F. G. (Buck) Rodgers" (page 56): Gerhard Gschwandtner, "An Interview with Buck Rodgers: Selling Solutions at IBM," *Management Review*, vol. 76, July 1987, pp. 48-51; Peter Spooner, "Buck Rodgers' Way to the Stars," *Chief Executive*, September 1986, pp. 35-36; Michael D. Hutt, "Leaders in Sales and Sales Management: F. G. (Buck) Rodgers," *Journal of Personal Selling & Sales Management*, vol. 3, November 1983, pp. 60-61.

Table 3-2 (page 58): Reprinted by permission of the publisher from "Ten Key Activities of Industrial Salespeople" by William C. Moncrief III in *Industrial Marketing Management*, vol. 15, November, pp. 309–317. Copyright 1982 by Elsevier Science Publishing Co., Inc.

"Everybody's World" (page 65): Dorothy J. Gaiter, "Fair Trade: A Black Entrepreneur Vaults Racial Barriers in a Southern Town," *The Wall Street Journal*, April 29, 1992, pp. A1, A10; Jenny C. McCune, "The Best Revenge: Your Own Business," *Success*, May 1991, p. 19; Bill Kelley, "Selling in a Man's World," *Sales & Marketing Management*, vol. 143, January 1991, pp. 28–35.

CHAPTER 4

"Sanford Corporation" (page 70): Don Wallace, "Home Is Where the Sales Are," *Success*, May 1991, pp. 46–47.

"Andrew Corporation" (page 75): Jack Falvey, "Making the Most of Booth Duty," *Sales & Marketing Management*, vol. 143, February 1991, pp. 86–87; Sandra Pesmen, "Shifting from Show & Tell to Sell, Sell, Sell," *Business Marketing*, February 1991, pp. T6–T7; Richard Szathmary, "Losing the Trade Show Battle? Call a Meeting in the 'War Room,' " *Sales & Marketing Management*, vol. 142, September 1990, pp. 162, 165.

Table 4-3 (page 76): Reprinted from Robert M. Goss, Jr., "How Valuable Are Your Prospects?" *Personal Selling Power*, vol. 11, November-December, p. 32. © 1991 by *Personal Selling Power*. Reprinted by permission of the publisher.

Figure 4-3 (page 80): Reprinted from "Planning the Sales Call," *Sales Manager's Bulletin*, Issue 985, January 30, 1980. Copyright © 1980. Copyrighted material reprinted with permission of *Sales Manager's Bulletin* and the Bureau of Business Practice, 24 Rope Ferry Road, Waterford, CT 06386.

Figure 4-4: Reprinted by permission.
Figure 4-4 (page 8): Reprinted by permission. "Any Prospects" (page 85): "Bush Signs Junk Fax Bill," *Marketing News*, January 20, 1992, p. 1; Carol J. Loomis, "Have You Been Cold-Called?" *Fortune*, December 16, 1991, pp. 109–115; Bruce Ingersoll, "Congress Closer to Restricting Auto-Dialing," *The Wall Street Journal*, November 27, 1991, pp. B1, B2; Jeffrey H. Birnbaum, "House Says 'Sorry, Wrong Number' to Telephone Sales," *The Wall Street Journal*, November 19, 1991, p. B1; Jay Finegan, "48 Hours with the King of the Cold Calls," *Inc.*, June 1991, pp. 101–107.

CHAPTER 5

Table 5-1 (page 91): Reprinted from Gerhard Gschwandtner, "The Art of Asking Better Questions," *Personal Selling Power*, vol. 11, January-February, p. 31. © 1991 by *Personal Selling Power*. Reprinted by permission of the publisher.

"*Farah, Inc.*" (page 94): Claire Poole, "We Did What We Had To Do," *Forbes*, December 9, 1991, pp. 148–153; Gabriella Stern, "Chief Executives Are Increasingly Chief Salesmen," *The Wall Street Journal*, August 6, 1991, pp. B1, B7.

"Town & Country" (page 99): Jean Guarino, "Silent Partner," *The Chicago Tribune*, April 6, 1991, pp. 4C, 5C.

"Selling to Businesses" (page 107): Marian B. Wood and Evelyn Ehrlich, "Segmentation: Five Steps to More Effective Business-to-Business Marketing," *Sales & Marketing Management*, vol. 143, April 1991, pp. 59–62; Jim Cusimano, "Selling Approach Streamlines Complex Biz-to-Biz Sales," *Marketing News*, March 4, 1991, pp. 12–13.

CHAPTER 6

Table 6-1 (pages 112–113): Originally developed by Dick Lopata for the National Association of Wholesale-Distributors. Used with permission from *Industrial Distribution*, November, 1978, pp. 36ff.

"Hyatt Hotels" (page 121): Patricia Sellers, "How To Remake Your Sales Force," *Fortune*, May 4, 1992, pp. 96–103; Martin Everett, "Hyatt Has No Reservations about Sales Excellence," *Sales & Marketing Management*, vol. 143, September 1991, p. 55.

Figure 6-1 (page 123): Adapted from Robert F. Vizza and Thomas E. Chambers, "Model of Time and Territorial Management for Salesmen," *Time and Territorial Management for the Salesman*, p. 8. Copyright © 1971 by Sales Executive Club, New York. Used by permission of Sales & Marketing Executives of Greater New York.

Figure 6-3 (page 127): Reprinted from William A. O'Connell and William Keenan, Jr., "The Shape of Things to Come," *Sales & Marketing Management*, p. 39. Copyright: January 1990. Reprinted by permission of Sales & Marketing Management.

Figure 6-4 (page 127): Reprinted from William A. O'Connell and William Keenan, Jr., "The Shape of Things to Come," *Sales & Marketing Management*, p. 39. Copyright: January 1990. Reprinted by permission of Sales & Marketing Management.

"*Electronic Liquid Fillers, Inc.*" (page 131): John Case, "The Time Machine," *Inc.*, June 1990, pp. 48–56; John Case, "Touch of Glass," *Inc.*, December 1989, p. 131.

Table 6-4 (page 134): From "Computer-based Sales Support: Shell Chemical's System," *Marketing: The Conference Board's Management Briefing* (4) April-May 1989, p. 5. Reprinted with permission of The Conference Board, NYC.

"For Automated Sales Forces, There Is No Time To Waste" (page 137): Jagannath Dubashi, "On the Ball," *Financial World*, June 11, 1991, pp. 50–51; Alan Radding, "Spalding Sports Moves Cautiously in Pitching Laptops to Sales Reps," *ComputerWorld*, April 10, 1989, pp. SR9-SR10.

CHAPTER 7

Table 7-1 (page 145): Adapted from Allan J. Magrath, "Eight Ways to Avoid Marketing Shock," *Sales & Marketing Management*, pp. 56–57. Copyright: April 1989. Used by permission of Sales & Marketing Management.

"Coachmen Industries" (page 151): Antony J. Michels, "An Office with a Steering Wheel," *Fortune*, December 16, 1991, pp. 12–13; "Offices on the Go," *Inc.*, November 1991, p. 206; Bristol Voss, "Making Your Mobile Office More Efficient," *Sales & Marketing Management*, vol. 143, March 1991, pp. 85–86.

"Schweppe & Company" (page 155): From Kathleen Madigan and Christina Del Valle, "What's Haunting the Housing Industry," *Business Week*, February 3, 1992, pp. 58–60. Copyright © 1992. Used by permission. Cynthia Crossen, "A Realtor Stays Hot in a Cold Market by Going for Blood," *The Wall Street Journal*, January 29, 1992, pp. A1, A8.

Table 7-3 (page 161): Adapted from Karl A. Boedecker, Fred W. Morgan, and Jeffrey J. Stoltman, "Legal Dimensions of Salespersons' Statements: A Review and Managerial Suggestion," *Journal of Marketing*, vol. 55, January 1991, p. 72.

"*Threats, Opportunities, Response*" (page 164): Carolyn T. Geer, "The Joys of Blending," *Forbes*, December 23, 1991, pp. 61–63; Paul B. Carroll, "Salespeople on Road Use Laptops to Keep in Touch," *The Wall Street Journal*, April 25, 1991, p. B1; Timothy D. Schellhardt, "Sales Squads Receive High-Tech Help," *The Wall Street Journal*, March 6, 1991, p. B1; Alan Rosenthal, "Using Incentives: Tough Times Give Incentives New Muscle," *Business Marketing*, March 1991, pp. T1, T6.

CHAPTER 8

Table 8-1 (page 169): Adapted from E. M. Johnson and B. A. Rausch, *Strategic Marketing Planning*, 2nd ed., © 1989. Used by permission of American Management Association.

"Progressive Insurance" (page 171): Melissa Campanelli, "The Secrets of America's Best Sales Forces," *Sales & Marketing Management*, vol. 144, pp. 92–93. Reprinted by permission of Sales & Marketing Management. Copyright January 1992. Betsy Wiesendanger, "Progressive's Success Is No Accident," *Sales & Marketing Management*, vol. 143, September 1991, p. 57; Rick Friedman, "Progressive Targets 24-Hour Claims Settlement," *Insurance & Technology*, October/November 1990, pp. 6, 8.

Figure 8-4 (page 173): Used with permission from Louis A. Wallis, *Decision-Support Systems for Marketing*, New York: The Conference Board, Inc., 1982, p. 2.

Table 8-2 (page 174): Adapted from E. M. Johnson and B. A. Rausch, *Strategic Marketing Planning*, 2nd ed., p. 26. © 1989. Used by permission of American Management Association.

Figure 8-7 (page 180): Orville C. Walker, Jr., and Robert W. Ruekert, "Marketing's Role in the Implementation of Business Strategies: A Critical Review and Conceptual Framework," *Journal of Marketing*, vol. 51, July 1987, p. 17.

"Campbell Soup Company" (page 181): Adapted from Barbara Hetzer, "Pushing Decisions Down the Line at Campbell Soup." Used with permission, *Business Month*, July 1989. Copyright © 1989 by Goldhirsh Group, Inc., 38 Commercial Wharf, Boston, MA 02110. Tom Peters, "Letting Go of Controls," *Across the Board*, June 1991, pp. 14–18; Dana Wechsler Linden and Vicki Contavespi, "Incentivize Me, Please," *Forbes*, May 27, 1991, pp. 208–212.

Table 8-3 (page 183): Adapted from Edward F. Walsh, "A Primer for Planning," *Sales & Marketing Management*, p. 78. Copyright: November 1990. Used by permission of Sales & Marketing Management.

"Curad—Converting a Marketing Strategy into a Sales Gain" (page 188): Reprinted from Betsy Weisendanger, "Profiles in Marketing: Paul Amatangelo," *Sales & Marketing Management*, p. 12. Copyright: January 1993. Reprinted by permission of Sales & Marketing Management.

CHAPTER 9

"Waste Energy, Inc." (page 195): Adapted from Jay Finegan, "Burning Ambition." Used with permission, *Inc.*, August 1991. Copyright 1991 by Goldhirsh Group, Inc., 38 Commercial Wharf, Boston, MA 02110.

"American Greetings" (page 202): Adapted from "Street Smart Selling." First appeared in *Success*, May 1991. Used with permission of *Success* magazine. Copyright © 1991 by *Success*, Inc. Mark Landler and Seth Payne, "Publicity? Why, It Never Even Occurred to Us," *Business Week*, September 24, 1990, p. 46; "PR Offensive Hits Persian Gulf," *Advertising Age*, September 3, 1990, p. 53.

"Where's the Camera When You Need It. . . ." (page 212): From Joan E. Rigdon, "For Cardboard Cameras, Sales Picture Enlarges and Seems Brighter Than Ever," February 11, 1992, pp. B1, B2. Reprinted by permission of *The Wall Street Journal*, © 1992 Dow Jones & Company, Inc. All Rights Reserved Worldwide. Mark Maremont and Robert Neff, "The Hottest Thing since the Flashbulb," *Business Week*, September 7, 1992, p. 72.

CHAPTER 10

"Elan Frozen Yogurt" (page 217): Adapted from Tom Richman, "Product Sampling." Used with permission, *Inc.*, October 1991. Copyright 1991 by Goldhirsh Group, Inc., 38 Commercial Wharf, Boston, MA 02110.

"Mid-States Technical Staffing Services" (page 224): Adapted from Jill Andresky Fraser, "Making Salespeople Collect." Used with permission, *Inc.*, April 1992. Copyright 1992 by Goldhirsh Group, Inc., 38 Commercial Wharf, Boston, MA 02110; "Should Salespeople Be Involved in Collections?" *Sales & Marketing Management*, vol. 143, June 1991, pp. 16, 20.

Figure 10-3 (page 228): Adapted from Eugene M. Johnson and Bernard A. Rausch, *Strategic Marketing Planning*, 2nd ed. (Boston: American Marketing Association, 1989), p. 12. © 1989. Used by permission of American Management Association.

"Weathering a Recession—And Coming Out of One" (page 232): David Woodruff, "Chrysler Yells 'Look at Me' to an Upscale Audience," *Business Week*, May 25, 1992, p. 30; Jack Falvey, "The Battle of the Budget," *Sales & Marketing Management*, vol. 143, November 1991, pp. 10, 12; "Archive Corp.: Company Says It Has Plans to Consolidate Sales Forces," *The Wall Street Journal*, September 10, 1991, p. C6; Ron Suskind, "Model American Cuts Back Staff amid Cash Crunch," *The Wall Street Journal*, July 26, 1991, p. B3; Stuart Elliott, "Time Inc. Official Explains Magazine Reorganization," *The New York Times*, July 3, 1991, p. D15; "Bell Atlantic Corp.: Improved Customer Service Is Aim of Sales

Force Mix," *The Wall Street Journal*, January 15, 1991, p. C11.

CHAPTER 11

"Procter & Gamble" (page 251): Zachary Schiller, "Not Everyone Loves a Supermarket Special," *Business Week*, February 17, 1992, pp. 64–68; Zachary Schiller, "No More Mr. Nice Guy at P&G—Not by a Long Shot," *Business Week*, February 3, 1992, pp. 54–56.

"Lotus Development Corporation" (page 255): From Tom Murray, "Team Selling: What's the Incentive?" *Sales & Marketing Management*, vol. 143, pp. 88–92. Copyright June 1991. Reprinted by permission of Sales & Marketing Management.

Table 11-1 (page 258): Adapted from William C. Moncrief, Shannon H. Shipp, Charles W. Lamb, Jr., and David W. Cravens, "Examining the Roles of Telemarketing in Selling Strategy," *Journal of Personal Selling & Sales Management*, vol. IX, Fall 1989, p. 5. Copyright © 1989. Used by permission.

"Telemarketing—Better Than License Plates?" (page 263): Aaron Bernstein, Dori Jones Yang, Zachary Schiller, and Russell Mitchell, "There's Prison Labor in America, Too," *Business Week*, February 17, 1992, pp. 42–44; Michael W. Miller, "That Sales Pitch Interrupting Dinner Is by a Real Con Man," *The Wall Street Journal*, January 2, 1992, pp. 1, 34; Norm Bendell, "Dial 800-Prison," *Sales & Marketing Management*, vol. 143, February 1991, p. 34.

CHAPTER 12

"Shopsmith Inc." (page 277): "Need Help? Try Asking Your Customers," *Sales & Marketing Management*, vol. 143, April 1991, p. 25; Richard J. Maturi, "Knotty Problems," *Industry Week*, September 17, 1990, pp. 31–32; Thomas W. Kopp, "Making Trainees Want to Learn," *Training and Development Journal*, June 1988, pp. 43–47.

Figure 12-4 (page 283): Adapted and reprinted from Arthur R. Pell, "Writing Help-Wanted Ads for Salespeople," *Marketing Times*, May-June 1983, p. 22.

"Valuing Diversity at Monsanto" (page 285): James E. Ellis, "Monsanto's New Challenge: Keeping Minority Workers," *Business Week*, July 8, 1991, pp. 60–61; Shari Caudron, "Monsanto Responds to Diversity," *Personnel Journal*, November 1990, pp. 72–80.

"Dow Chemical Company—Walking the Walk" (page 290): Melissa Campanelli, "The Secrets of America's Best Salesforces," *Sales & Marketing Management*, vol. 144, January 1992, pp. 92–93; Bristol Voss, "Dow Makes It Big by Thinking Small," *Sales & Marketing Management*, vol. 143, September 1991, p. 46; William Brandel, "Dow Shakes Up Customer Service with Worldwide Integration Strategy," *Computerworld*, September 11, 1989, pp. 62, 64.

CHAPTER 13

Table 13-1 (page 294): Reprinted from Arthur J. Bragg, "Recruiting and Hiring Without Surprises," *Sales & Marketing*

Management, p. 52. Copyright: August 1980. Reprinted by permission of Sales & Marketing Management.

Figure 13-1 (page 298): Reprinted from Wesley J. Johnston and Martha C. Cooper, "Industrial Sales Force Selection: Current Knowledge and Needed Research," *Journal of Personal Selling & Sales Management*, Spring-Summer 1981, p. 50. Copyright © 1981. Used by permission.

"Body Shop" (page 299): Rahul Jacob, "Body Shop International: What Selling Will Be Like in the '90s," *Fortune*, January 13, 1992, pp. 63–64; Laura Zinn, "Whales, Human Rights, Rain Forests—and the Heady Smell of Profits," *Business Week*, July 15, 1991, pp. 114–115; John Elkington, Julia Hailes, and Joel Makower, *The Green Consumer*, New York: Tilden Press, 1990, p. 233.

Table 13-2 (page 300): Reprinted by permission of the publisher from "A Survey of Sales Management Practices" by Alan J. Dubinsky and Thomas E. Berry, *Industrial Marketing Management*, April, p. 136. Copyright 1982 by Elsevier Science Publishing Co., Inc.

Table 13-4 (pages 311–312): Inspired by "The Job Interview: Making It Work for You," Sales Consultants International, Cleveland, Ohio.

Table 13-5 (page 312): From "Finding the Best: Job Interviewing Skills." Used by permission of Sales Consultants International, Cleveland Ohio.

Figure 13-5 (page 318): Adapted from Sales Aptitude Corporation, a division of Personnel Sciences Center.

"Performance Factors, Inc." (page 320): From Joan O'C. Hamilton, "A Video Game that Tells if Employees Are Fit for Work," *Business Week*, June 3, 1991, p. 36. Copyright © 1991. Used by permission.

"Finding Salespeople Who Write Right" (page 325): Larry Reibstein and Karen Springen, "Spotting the Write Stuff," *Newsweek*, February 17, 1992, p. 44; Arthur Bragg, "Checking References," *Sales & Marketing Management*, vol. 142, November 1990, pp. 68–73; "Graphology: The Power of the Written Word," *The Economist*, June 16, 1990, pp. 97–98; M. Susan Taylor and Kathryn K. Sackheim, "Graphology," *Personnel Administrator*, May 1988, pp. 71–76.

CHAPTER 14

Figure 14-1 (page 328): Reprinted from Marvin A. Jolson, "The Salesman's Career Cycle," *Journal of Marketing*, July 1974, p. 39.

"Kraft USA" (page 332): From Suzy Barrett, Richard L. Ranges, and Stuart M. Lasky, "How Kraft Builds Business Managers from Sales Trainees," *Sales & Marketing Management*, pp. 110–111. Copyright: May 1991. Reprinted by permission of Sales & Marketing Management.

"Aetna Life and Casualty" (page 345): Kerry J. Rottenberger, "Sales Training Enters the Space Age," *Sales & Marketing Management*, vol. 142, October 1990, pp. 46–50; Kathryn W. Porter, "Tuning in to TV Training," *Training and Development Journal*, April 1990, pp. 73–77; Joseph Oberle, "What's on BTV? A Teleconference Update," *Training*, August 1989, pp. 52–57.

Table 14-4 (page 349): Reprinted from Robert C. Erffmeyer, K. Randall Russ, and Joseph F. Hair, Jr., "Needs Assessment and Evaluation in Sales Training Programs," *Journal of Personal Selling & Sales Management*, vol. 11, Winter 1991, p. 25. Copyright © 1991. Used by permission.

"*Developing Creativity*" (page 355): "Prairie-Dog Vacuum Sucks Pests from Holes," *Arkansas Democrat-Gazette*, January 24, 1992, p. 5A; Bristol Voss, "What's the Big Idea?" *Sales & Marketing Management*, vol. 143, pp. 36–41. Copyright: May 1991. Reprinted by permission of Sales & Marketing Management. Ray Wise, "The Boom in Creativity Training," *Across the Board*, June 1991, pp. 38–42.

CHAPTER 15

Figure 15-1 (page 362): Adapted from *Motivation and Personality*, 2nd ed., by Abraham H. Maslow. Copyright 1954 by Harper & Row, Publishers, Inc. Copyright © 1970 by Abraham H. Maslow. Reprinted by permission of HarperCollins Publishers Inc.

Figure 15-2 (page 364): Reprinted from Thomas L. Quick, "The Best Kept Secret for Increasing Productivity," *Sales & Marketing Management*, pp. 34–38. Copyright: July 1989. Reprinted by permission of Sales & Marketing Management.

Table 15-1 (page 365): Reprinted from Pradeep K. Tyagi, "Organizational Climate, Inequities and Attractiveness of Salesperson Rewards," *Journal of Personal Selling & Sales Management*, vol. 5, November 1985, p. 32. Copyright © 1985. Used by permission.

"American Express" (page 371): Alan Deutschman, "Pioneers of the New Balance," *Fortune*, May 20, 1991, pp. 60–68. © 1991 Time Inc. All rights reserved.

"Xerox Corp." (page 375): Adapted from J. S. Hirsch, "Salesforce: To One Xerox Man, Selling Photocopiers Is a Gambler's Game," September 23, 1991, pp. A1, A8. Reprinted by permission of *The Wall Street Journal*, © 1991 Dow Jones & Company, Inc. All Rights Reserved Worldwide.

"The Car Seller's Lot" (page 382): David Woodruff, "What's This—Car Dealers with Souls?" *Business Week*, April 6, 1992, pp. 66–67; Gregory A. Patterson, "Tough Business: A Car Salesman Finds It's Also Hard for Him to Get a Good Deal," *The Wall Street Journal*, March 10, 1992, pp. A1, A7.

CHAPTER 16

"Amway Corporation" (page 386): Adapted from Paul Klebnikov, "The Power of Positive Inspiration," *Forbes*, December 9, 1991, pp. 243–249. Reprinted by permission of FORBES magazine. © Forbes Inc., 1991.

Table 16-1 (page 387): Reprinted from Bill Kelley, "Recognition Reaps Rewards," *Sales & Marketing Management*, vol. 136, p. 104. Copyright: June 1986. Reprinted by permission of Sales & Marketing Management.

Table 16-2 (page 390): Reprinted from "Facts Survey: "Sales Incentives," *Incentive*, vol. 164, September 1990, p. 56. Copyright © 1990. Reprinted by permission.

Table 16-3 (page 392): Reprinted from Todd Englander and Bruce Bolger, "How to Run an Incentive Program," *Incentive*, vol. 164, July 1990, p. 20. Copyright © 1990. Reprinted by permission.

Table 16-4 (page 396): Reprinted from Rayna Skolnik, "Planning a Meeting That's Worth the Effort," *Sales & Marketing Management*, p. 99. Copyright: November 1982. Reprinted by permission of Sales & Marketing Management.

"SmithKline Beecham" (page 398): Cyndee Miller, "Training Pays Off—in Cash," *Marketing News*, July 22, 1991, p. 23; Mary Ann Hanson, "Rappin' Pigs Provide the Punch," *Agri Marketing*, May 1991, pp. 36–37; Joanne Levine, "SmithKline: Testing Knowledge," *Incentive*, October 1988, pp. 62–63.

Table 16-5 (page 398): Adapted from E. M. Johnson and B. A. Rausch, *Strategic Marketing Planning*, 2nd ed., p. 12. © 1989. Used by permission of American Management Association.

"Re/Max—Giving Salespeople What They Want" (page 401): Richard Poe, "The Will to Win," *Success*, March 1991, pp. 50–55; Roger Thompson, "The Rise of Re/Max," *Nation's Business*, April 1990, pp. 29–31. Adapted by permission, Nation's Business, April 1990. Copyright 1990, U.S. Chamber of Commerce; Tom Richman, "The 'Ownership' Factor," *Inc.*, August 1987, pp. 74–78.

CHAPTER 17

Figure 17-1 (page 405): Reprinted from "A Preface to Payment: Designing a Sales Compensation Plan" by Frank V. Cespedes, *Sloan Management Review*, vol. 32, Fall 1990, p. 60, by permission of publisher. Copyright 1990 by the Sloan Management Review Association. All rights reserved.

Table 17-1 (page 407): Reprinted with permission of Wyatt Data Services, *Sales & Marketing Compensation Report*, 35th ed., 1990/1991, p. 35.

"Dial Corporation" (page 408): From Tom Murray, "Team Selling: What's the Incentive?" *Sales and Marketing Management*, pp. 88–92. Copyright: June 1991. Reprinted by permission of Sales and Marketing Management.

"Software 2000 Inc." (page 413): Partly adapted from Tom Richman, "Commissions that Smooth Out Sales." Used with permission, *Inc.* magazine, July 1991. Copyright 1991 by Goldhirsh Group, Inc., 38 Commercial Wharf, Boston, MA 02110. Mark McLaughlin, "Following Success on the Road to 2000," *New England Business*, October 1989, pp. 27–29.

Figure 17-3 (page 417): Reprinted from John A. Fischer, "Fighting Inflation for Every Dollar," *Sales & Marketing Management*, p. 62. Copyright: June 1980. Reprinted by permission of Sales & Marketing Management.

"The Future of Child Care Benefits" (page 423): Aaron Bernstein, Joseph Weber, Lisa Driscoll, and Alice Cuneo, "Corporate America Is Still No Place for Kids," *Business Week*, November 25, 1991, pp. 234–238; Joseph Weber, "Meet DuPont's 'In-House Conscience,'" *Business Week*, June 24, 1991, pp. 62–65; Keith H. Hammonds and William C. Symonds, "Taking Baby Steps toward a Daddy Track," *Business Week*, April 15, 1991, pp. 90–92; Betsy Wiesendanger, "Child Care Grows Up," *Sales & Marketing Management*, vol. 142, July 1990, pp. 92–96.

CHAPTER 18

"Avon" (page 432): Adapted from Andrew Tanzer, "Ding-dong, Capitalism Calling," *Forbes*, October 14, 1991, pp. 184, 186. Reprinted by permission of FORBES magazine. © Forbes Inc., 1991.

Table 18-3 (page 435): Reprinted from Lawrence B. Chonko, John F. Tanner, Jr., and Ellen Reid Smith, "Selling and Sales Management in Action: The Sales Force's Role in International Marketing Research and Marketing Information Systems," *Journal of Personal Selling & Sales Management*, vol. 11, Winter 1991, p. 77. Copyright © 1991. Reprinted by permission.

"*Lester Telemarketing Inc.*" (page 440): "Connecticut Telemarketing Company Takes on the World," *Marketing News*, June 10, 1991, pp. 16, 17.

"A New Europe" (page 451): Albert G. Holzinger, "Selling in the New Europe," *Nation's Business*, December 1991, pp. 18–24; Thomas J. Duesterberg, "Prepare Now for the 1992 Export Market," *Business America*, February 25, 1991, pp. 8–9; Joshua Hyatt, "Exporting the Risk," *Inc.*, November 1990, pp. 163–164.

CHAPTER 19

"Careers USA" (page 459): Adapted from Elizabeth Conlin, "The Daily Sales Report." Used with permission, *Inc.* magazine (January 1991). Copyright 1991 by Goldhirsh Group, Inc., 38 Commercial Wharf, Boston, MA 02110.

Table 19-2 (page 464): The last column of the table is adapted from a survey of 213 sales executives; see Donald W. Jackson, Jr., Janet E. Keith, and John L. Schlacter, "Evaluation of Selling Performance: A Study of Current Practices," *Journal of Personal Selling & Sales Management*, vol. 3, November 1983, pp. 46–47.

Table 19-3 (page 465): Adapted from Donald W. Jackson, Jr., Janet E. Keith, and John L. Schlacter, "Evaluation of Selling Performance: A Study of Current Practices," *Journal of Personal Selling & Sales Management*, November 1983, vol. 3, pp. 46–47. Copyright © 1983. Used by permission.

"Au Bon Pain Company" (page 468): Partly adapted from Leslie Brokaw, "The Mystery-Shopper Questionnaire." Used with permission, *Inc.* magazine, June 1991. Copyright 1991 by Goldhirsh Group, Inc., 38 Commercial Wharf, Boston, MA 02110. Beth Wolfensberger, "The Rise of the Mystery Shopper," *New England Business*, December 1990, pp. 78–79. Used by permission of Oxbow.

"Granite Rock Company" (page 473): Adapted from Edward O. Welles, "How're We Doing?" Used with permission, *Inc.* magazine, May 1991. Copyright 1991 by Goldhirsh Group, Inc., 38 Commercial Wharf, Boston, MA 02110.

Figure 19-2 (page 477): A. Benton Cocanougher and John M.

Ivancevich, "BARS Performance Rating for Salesforce Personnel," *Journal of Marketing*, July 1978, p. 92.

"Wal-Mart Stores Inc." (page 483): "Cutting Out the Middlemen," *The New York Times*, February 2, 1992, p. F5; "WD-40 Co.," *The Wall Street Journal*, January 24, 1992, p. B4; "Wal-Mart Stores Inc.: Group Charges Retailer with Unfair Trade Practices," *The Wall Street Journal*, January 17, 1992, p. A5; Michael Selz, "Independent Sales Reps Are Squeezed by the Recession," *The Wall Street Journal*, December 27, 1991, p. B2; Andrea Harter, "Factory-Direct Dealing to Save Wal-Mart Money," *Arkansas Democrat-Gazette*, December 4, 1991, pp. 1D, 3D; John Huey, "America's Most Successful Merchant," *Fortune*, September 23, 1991, pp. 46–59; Andrea Harter, "Personnel Posted to Service Wal-Mart Fuel Area Growth," *Arkansas Democrat*, April 15, 1991, pp. 1D, 2D.

"IBM—Responding to Its Environment" (pages 488–489): David Kirkpatrick, "Breaking up IBM," *Fortune*, July 27, 1992, pp. 44–58; John Schwartz, "The Blues at Big Blue," *Newsweek*, December 16, 1991, pp. 44–46; John W. Verity, Thane Peterson, Deidre Depke, and Evan I. Schwartz, "The New IBM," *Business Week*, December 16, 1991, pp. 112–118; Carol J. Loomis, "Can John Akers Save IBM?" *Fortune*, July 15, 1991, pp. 40–56; Paul B. Carroll, "Akers to IBM Employees: Wake Up!" *The Wall Street Journal*, May 29, 1991, pp. B1, B2; Paul B. Carroll, "IBM Wants Its Managers to Encourage Certain Workers to Leave the Company," *The Wall Street Journal*, May 23, 1991, p. A4; Thomas McCarroll, "The Humbling of a Computer Colossus," *Time*, May 20, 1991, pp. 42–44.

CHAPTER 20

"T & K Roofing Company" (page 495): Adapted from Terri Lammers, "The Lost-Job Survey." Used with permission, *Inc.* magazine, April 1992. Copyright 1992 by Goldhirsh Group, Inc., 38 Commercial Wharf, Boston, MA 02110.

"Scott Paper" (page 505): Betsey Weisendanger, "Scott Paper Is on a Roll," *Sales & Marketing Management*, vol. 143, September 1991, p. 50. Reprinted by permission of Sales & Marketing Management. Copyright Sept. 1991; Thomas L. Brown, "The New Salesperson," *Industry Week*, May 7, 1990, p. 14.

Figure 20-5 (page 507): From Charles W. Kyd, "No More Trivial Pursuits." Used with permission, *Inc.* magazine, January 1989. Copyright 1989 by Goldhirsh Group, Inc., 38 Commercial Wharf, Boston, MA 02110.

Figure 20-6 (page 510): From Alan J. Dubinsky and Richard W. Hansen, "The Salesforce Management Audit," *California Management Review*, Winter 1981, p. 87. Copyright 1981 by The Regents of the University of California. Reprinted from the *California Management Review*, vol. 24, no. 2. By permission of The Regents.

"Reps versus Sales Force" (pages 516–517): Partly adapted from Tom Richman, "Reps or Salesforce." Used with permission, *Inc.* magazine, December 1991. Copyright 1991 by Goldhirsh Group, Inc., 38 Commercial Wharf, Boston, MA 02110. "A User's Guide to the Sales Manager's Budget Planner," *Sales & Marketing Management*, vol. 143, June 17, 1991, pp. 4–10.

NAME INDEX

SUBJECT INDEX